RACE and RACIALIZATION

RACE and RACIALIZATION
essential readings

Editors:
Tania Das Gupta
Carl E. James
Roger C.A. Maaka
Grace-Edward Galabuzi
Chris Andersen

Canadian Scholars' Press Inc.

Toronto

Race and Racialization: Essential Readings
edited by Tania Das Gupta, Carl E. James, Roger C.A. Maaka, Grace-Edward Galabuzi, and Chris Andersen

First published in 2007 by
Canadian Scholars' Press Inc.
425 Adelaide Street West, Suite 200
Toronto, Ontario
M5V 3C1

www.cspi.org

Canadian Scholars' Press Inc. gratefully acknowledges financial support for our publishing activities from the Government of Canada through the Book Publishing Industry Development Program (BPIDP).

Library and Archives Canada Cataloguing in Publication
Race and racialization : essential readings / [edited by] Tania Das Gupta ... [et al.].
Includes bibliographical references.
ISBN 978-1-55130-335-2
1. Race. 2. Racism. 3. Race relations. 4. Race awareness.
I. Das Gupta, Tania, 1957-
HT1521.R239 2007 305.8 C2007-905070-0

Interior design and composition: Aldo Fierro
Cover design: John Kicksee / KIX BY DESIGN
Cover art by Patricia Marroquin, "Circle of Life 435173," from iStockphoto.

Printed and bound in Canada

Canadä

MIX
Paper from responsible sources
FSC® C004071

TABLE OF CONTENTS

PREFACE • vii

PART 1: RACE THROUGH TIME

Part 1A: Early Theories of Race

Chapter 1: Race and Progress, Franz Boas • 4
Chapter 2: The Concept of Race, Ashley Montagu • 10
Chapter 3: The Classification of Races in Europe and North America: 1700–1850, Michael Banton • 15

Part 1B: Colonialism and the Construction of Race

Chapter 4: Towards Scientific Racism, Gustav Jahoda • 24
Chapter 5: Antecedents of the Racial Worldview, Audrey Smedley • 31
Chapter 6: Latent and Manifest Orientalism, Edward W. Said • 45
Chapter 7: The West and the Rest: Discourse and Power, Stuart Hall • 56

Part 1C: Thinking Through Race in the 21st Century

Chapter 8: Does "Race" Matter? Transatlantic Perspectives on Racism after "Race Relations," Robert Miles and Rudy Torres • 65
Chapter 9: When Place Becomes Race, Sherene H. Razack • 74
Chapter 10: Is There a "Neo-Racism"?, Etienne Balibar • 83
Chapter 11: The Relationship between Racism and Antisemitism, Michael Banton • 89
Chapter 12: Global Apartheid? Race and Religion in the New World Order, Ali A. Mazrui • 95
Chapter 13: The Lore of the Homeland: Hindu Nationalism and Indigenist "Neoracism," Chetan Bhatt • 101

PART 2: EXPERIENCES OF COLONIALISM AND RACISM

Part 2A: Indigeneity and Colonialism

Chapter 14: Settling In: Epidemics and Conquest to the End of the First Century, Noble David Cook • 116
Chapter 15: The Guaraní: The Economics of Ethnocide, Richard H. Robbins • 121
Chapter 16: The Indians Are Coming to an End: The Myth of Native Desolation, Matthew Restall • 125
Chapter 17: Saami and Norwegians: Symbols of Peoplehood and Nationhood, Trond Thuen • 132

Part 2B: Colonialism, Slavery, and Indentured Labour

Chapter 18: Of Our Spiritual Strivings, W.E.B. Du Bois • 144
Chapter 19: Capitalism and Slavery, Eric Williams • 149
Chapter 20: Prelude to Settlement: Indians as Indentured Labourers, Verene Shepherd • 155

PART 3: RACE, RACISM, AND INSTITUTIONS

Part 3A: Racism in the Education System

Chapter 21: Resistance and Renewal: First Nations and Aboriginal Education in Canada, Celia Haig-Brown • 168

Chapter 22: Toward an Antiracist Agenda in Education: The Case of Malta, Carmel Borg and Peter Mayo • 179

Chapter 23: The Denial of Difference: Reframing Anti-racist Praxis, George J. Sefa Dei • 188

Part 3B: Racism and Employment

Chapter 24: Working Precariously: The Impact of Race and Immigrant Status on Employment Opportunities and Outcomes in Canada, Cheryl Teelucksingh and Grace-Edward Galabuzi • 202

Chapter 25: The Integration of Racism into Everyday Life: The Story of Rosa N., Philomena Essed • 209

Chapter 26: "They Can Be Hired in Masses; They Can Be Managed and Controlled like Unthinking Slaves," Tomás Almaguer • 217

Part 3C: Racism, the Media, and Popular Culture

Chapter 27: The Imaginary Indian: The Image of the Indian in Canadian Culture, Daniel Francis • 234

Chapter 28: "Our Enemies among Us!"—The Portrayal of Arab and Muslim Americans in Post–9/11 American Media, Robert Morlino • 240

Chapter 29: Races, Racism and Popular Culture, John Solomos and Les Back • 247

Part 3D: Racism in the Justice System and Police Force

Chapter 30: Inflammatory Rhetoric? Baseless Accusations? A Response to Gabor's Critique of Racial Profiling Research in Canada, Scot Wortley and Julian Tanner • 260

Chapter 31: The Criminalization of Indigenous People, Chris Cunneen • 266

PART 4: RACE: LIMITATIONS AND PRIVILEGE

Part 4A: Race, Privilege, and Identity

Chapter 32: Identity, Belonging, and the Critique of Pure Sameness, Paul Gilroy • 280

Chapter 33: How Jews Became White Folks and What That Says about Race in America, Karen Brodkin • 293

Chapter 34: Between Black and White: Exploring the "Biracial" Experience, Kerry A. Rockquemore • 301

Chapter 35: Color and the Changing Racial Landscape, Margaret Hunter • 309

Chapter 36: Language Matters, Vijay Agnew • 316

Part 4B: Working against Racism

Chapter 37: Imperialism, History, Writing and Theory, Linda Tuhiwai Smith • 328

Chapter 38: Anti-racism, Social Movements and Civil Society, Cathie Lloyd • 339

Chapter 39: Racism/Anti-racism, Precarious Employment, and Unions, Tania Das Gupta • 350

Chapter 40: "Reverse Racism"? Students' Responses to Equity Programs, Carl E. James • 356

Chapter 41: How Gay Stays White and What Kind of White It Stays, Allan Bérubé • 363

Copyright Acknowledgements • 373

PREFACE

In fall of 2004, Megan Mueller, editorial director at Canadian Scholars' Press Inc., called about a book titled *Race and Racialization: Essential Readings*. Over lunch, she described how she had brought together numerous works by authors from all over the world on these topics. She had already consulted with eight leading race and ethnicity academics in Canada and five international scholars on the idea of such a book. Reviewers were overwhelmingly positive and urged her to publish such a book. They pointed out that a book pulling together Canadian and non-Canadian scholarship, bringing together indigenous scholars and scholars of colour, had not been done before and it was badly needed.

The work of editing would entail cutting down the number of chapters; editing down each of the chapters to a manageable length; writing openers and closers for each section, including pedagogical tools, such as questions for critical thought, additional annotated readings, and so forth. In the beginning, the work of editing appeared simple enough, but it became more challenging as it progressed further.

Megan mentioned that Dr. Roger Maaka, head of Native Studies at the University of Saskatchewan, and Chris Andersen from the University of Alberta were editing a separate collection on *The Indigenous Experience* and that they would contribute one full section in the proposed new reader on *Race and Racialization*. This was an intriguing collaboration in the making. Soon after, Carl James and Grace-Edward Galabuzi joined the editorial group.

A lunch meeting between Carl and Tania Das Gupta (Grace was unable to join us) was facilitated by Megan, and that was the first crack at going through the table of contents. It was at this meeting that a lot of the foundational principles of this book were delineated. One of the first principles established was that we did not want the indigenous section to stand separate from the rest of the book as it had been originally conceptualized. Neither did we want the names of Roger and Chris to be listed in such a way that they appeared to be separate from the rest of us. We wanted the indigenous contributions to be well integrated; we did not want them to be segregated from the non-indigenous experiences, as has so often been the case in anti-racism scholarship and, of course, in colonial and settler state practices and policy-making. We did not want a "reservation" mentality to permeate the book. At the same time, we wanted to make sure that the indigenous experience was not equated with non-indigenous experiences or diluted in the general discussion of those experiences.

The balancing of these two concerns is a fundamental objective in this book. What we aspired to do was to draw links between the colonization of indigenous peoples in various regions and the colonization of Asians, Africans, the inhabitants of the Americas, Caribbeans, and various "others," and their linked experiences with "race" and racism under colonial and neo-colonial relationships. In established texts, these experiences in different parts of the globe are examined separately and aimed at different audiences, so that there is no opportunity to draw linkages between our experiences, which may be separated by time and space, but which are connected to the dynamics of capitalist expansion and the search for new lands, resources, markets, and, of course, cheaper labour. In connection with these imperatives, we wanted to draw a linkage between, on the one hand, colonization, racism, and "race" discourse, and, on the other, various labour formations in the Americas and the Caribbean, including slavery of Africans and indentureship of Asians. We were also mindful of the basis of colonialism and racism in capitalist expansion and globalization and their intersections with class, gender, sexuality, religion, and other oppressive discourses as they became articulated in concrete ways in people's lives.

Several meetings between Carl and Tania further developed the conception of the book, specifically through refining the table of contents. Apart from the issues mentioned above, we wanted to have sections on identities and resistance to "race" and racism so that the many nuances of the topics were covered in the book. An additional concern was that we wanted the chapters to reflect a wide diversity of experiences, rather than the usual white/black binary so prevalent in the literature to date, to offer readers a more complicated understanding of the process of racialization and more comparative perspectives of how racism has worked in different settings. Section and sub-section titles were also re-conceptualized at these meetings so that there was consolidation of topics and a more logical flow to them. We also wanted to make sure that chapters on indigeneity were integrated throughout the book in addition to one section being devoted to it alone. Throughout, our understanding of "racialization" follows on Robert Miles's (1989) conceptualization of the term. That is, "a process of categorization, a representational process of defining an Other (usually, but not exclusively) somatically" (75). This process of categorization attributes meaning to a "real or alleged biological characteristic."

In order to capture and present a paradigm such as the one we shared, additional chapters had to be pulled in over and above what Megan had pulled together. So, rather than cut back on chapters, we ended up with a much larger book. Inclusiveness was more important to us than length at this point, although Megan reminded us that the latter was important in terms of keeping the book accessible and affordable. At this point, Grace, Roger, and Chris stepped in. Grace gave us his input about our collection of chapters and made several significant additions and deletions from his perspective. Roger and Chris took on the section on indigeneity and pared it down to the essential chapters. They also provided perspectives on other sections of the book. The process of developing the table of contents was laborious, requiring us to read and consider each potential chapter individually and in relation to the rest of the chapters.

REFERENCE

Miles, Robert. 1989. *Racism*. London: Routledge.

THE ORGANIZATION OF THE BOOK

The editors brought their respective interests and expertise to the more specific editing done in each section of the book. Part 1 deals with theoretical discussions of "race," presenting the major debates in the literature. Here, Tania took on section 1A (Early Theories of Race), Chris and Roger worked on section 1B (Colonialism and the Construction of Race), and Grace completed it with section 1C (Thinking Through Race in the 21st Century). Part 2 deals with the experiences of colonialism and racism. Roger and Chris handled the first section, 2A (Indigeneity and Colonialism), while Tania looked at 2B (Colonialism, Slavery, and Indentured Labour). Part 3 deals with institutional racism. The first section, 3A (Racism in the Education System), was handled by Carl; the second, 3B (Racism and Employment), by Grace; the third, 3C (Racism, the Media, and Popular Culture), by Tania; and the fourth, 3D (Racism in the Justice System and Police Force), by Chris. Finally, part 4 deals with questions of disadvantages and privileges due to "race," and also questions of identity and resistance. Carl worked on this entire part, which was made up of two sections: 4A (Race, Privilege, and Identity) and 4B (Working against Racism). The critical questions and additional annotated readings are intended to provide a means for examining, interrogating, and further discussing the issues raised in various chapters, and to point to further work that could be done.

Despite our effort to be inclusive, some gaps may exist. Nonetheless, we hope that readers will find this collection provocative and useful in furthering their understanding of "race," racism, racialization, and other intersecting topics.

A NOTE FROM THE PUBLISHER

Thank you for selecting *Race and Racialization: Essential Readings*, edited by Tania Das Gupta, Carl E. James, Roger C.A. Maaka, Grace-Edward Galabuzi, and Chris Andersen. The editors and publisher have devoted considerable time and careful development (including meticulous peer reviews) to this book. We appreciate your recognition of this effort and accomplishment.

This volume distinguishes itself on the market in many ways. One key feature is the book's well-written and comprehensive part openers, which help to make the readings all the more accessible to both general readers and undergraduate students. The part openers add cohesion to the section and to the whole book. The themes of the book are very clearly presented in these section openers. Further adding value to the book, the editors have composed annotated further readings for each section.

For the university and college market, critical thinking questions pertaining to each section of this reader can be found on the CSPI web site at www.cspi.org.

ACKNOWLEDGEMENT

A very special thanks is owed to Dr. Althea Prince who planted the seed for this book. Her idea for this book sparked the initial research phase and fuelled the manuscript during its lengthy developmental phase. Many thought-provoking conversations in Althea's office served to strengthen this book beyond measure.

PART 1

RACE THROUGH TIME

PART 1A

EARLY THEORIES OF RACE

Few words have generated as much debate and controversy as the word "race." Those of us who think about, study, and write about racism are aware that even today this is an area of tension and division. There are those who employ the word "race" in their work and insist on it, others use it in a critical manner, while some prefer to use other words, such as "racialization." The contemporary debate will be reflected in a later section. This opening section gives us a sense of this long debate with roots in the 17th century and possibly earlier. Admittedly, this debate was taking place among European men, including biologists, geneticists, physicians, philosophers, and clergymen, and some of dubious disciplinary origins.

Franz Boas's chapter is actually an address by him as the president of the American Association for the Advancement of Science in 1931. Readers are alerted to the fact that given the time in which he made this presentation, some of the terminology used by him is highly problematic. While we must critique his use of the term "race" to refer to different groups of people, such as blacks, whites, Asians, and Northern and Southern Europeans, his arguments against anti-miscegenation hysteria, sometimes referred to as "race mixing" or even "race degeneration" by eugenic stalwarts, reflect an important debate in the scientific community at that time. Referring to studies of populations from a biological perspective, he argues that wherever there have been populations, there has been mingling among groups and that there is no evidence to suggest that this results in degeneration. He further argues that intense inbreeding sometimes results in health problems and that certain changes in human anatomy can result from environmental, cultural, and social conditions as opposed to human selection. Moreover, there is no biological evidence to connect bodily form and its physical and mental functions. In this connection, he discusses briefly the IQ controversy in the USA. He insists that racial hostility has no biological or natural basis, but rather is socially based.

The chapter by Ashley Montagu, an address on genetics, makes a case for abandoning the use of the term "race" and suggests using other terms to refer to different groups of people, terms such as "ethnic groups" or "genogroups." Readers can explore whether these words suggested by him are acceptable or not in light of some current writings that assert that even seemingly neutral concepts such as "ethnicity" are subject to social construction and power relations. Nevertheless, Montagu's main argument in favour of throwing out problematic terms used to build "the master's house" and searching for new ones is worth considering. Further, he critiques the "scientific" approach of making conclusions about human species on the basis of what other animal species do or don't do, because, as he argues, one cannot equate all animal groupings with human groupings, as the latter, unlike the former, are subject to "culture, that is to say, the man-made [sic] part of the environment" in addition to nature. His opposition to the use of "race" in studying populations is based on the fact that the word has a very problematic set of associations and assumptions underlying it, such as those based in race typology; he insists that it is impossible to use the word in any other way.

The final chapter, by Michael Banton, provides a genealogy of the term "race" in Europe. He argues that early writings based in biblical thinking reveal a deep-seated assumption of monogenesis (single origin) and the importance of environmental effects on phenotypical differences, as well as a lack of interest in the classification of "races." Referring to many writers, he demonstrates that although slavery and colonialism were well entrenched by the 17th century, and although racial feelings and structures were the norm, these did not develop into an intellectual ("scientific") tradition of "race typology" until the early to mid-19th century. While earlier the word "race" had been associated with lineage, it later became associated with "variety," "type," or "class" and thus with the theory of polygenesis (separate origins). The latter evolved in some writings to an association with phenotypical, cultural, and even national differences. Banton suggests that although there was no agreement on the meaning of "race" among biologists and anthropologists, and although race typologists were opposed to imperialism on grounds that "inferior races" could not adapt to Western European ways, the word "race" gained popularity due to political and scientific developments in the mid- to late 19th century.

CHAPTER 1

RACE AND PROGRESS[1]

Franz Boas

Permit me to call your attention to the scientific aspects of a problem that has been for a long time agitating our country and which, on account of its social and economic implications, has given rise to strong emotional reactions and has led to varied types of legislation. I refer to the problems due to the intermingling of racial types.

If we wish to reach a reasonable attitude, it is necessary to separate clearly the biological and psychological aspects from the social and economic implications of this problem. Furthermore, the social motivation of what is happening must be looked at not from the narrow point of view of our present conditions but from a wider angle.

The facts with which we are dealing are diverse. The plantation system of the South brought to our shores a large Negro population. Considerable mixture between White masters and slave women occurred during the period of slavery, so that the number of pure Negroes was dwindling continually and the colored population gradually became lighter. A certain amount of intermingling between White and Indian took place, but in the United States and Canada this has never occurred to such a degree that it became an important social phenomenon. In Mexico and many parts of Central and South America it is the most typical case of race contact and race mixture. With the development of immigration the people of eastern and southern Europe were attracted to our country and form now an important part of our population. They differ in type somewhat among themselves, although the racial contrasts are much less than those between Indians or Negroes and Whites. Through Mexican and West Indian immigration another group has come into our country, partly of South European, partly of mixed Negro and mixed Indian descent. To all these must be added the East Asiatic groups, Chinese, Japanese and Filipinos, who play a particularly important rôle on the Pacific Coast.

The first point in regard to which we need clarification refers to the significance of the term race. In common parlance when we speak of a race we mean a group of people that have certain bodily and perhaps also mental characteristics in common. The Whites, with their light skin, straight or wavy hair and high nose, are a race set off clearly from the Negroes with their dark skin, frizzly hair and flat nose. In regard to these traits the two races are fundamentally distinct. Not quite so definite is the distinction between East Asiatics and European types, because transitional forms do occur among normal White individuals, such as flat faces, straight black hair and eye forms resembling the East Asiatic types; and conversely European-like traits are found among East Asiatics. For Negro and White we may speak of hereditary racial traits so far as these radically distinct features are concerned. For Whites and East Asiatics the difference is not quite so absolute, because a few individuals may be found in each race for whom the racial traits do not hold good, so that in a strict sense we cannot speak of absolutely valid hereditary racial traits.

This condition prevails to a much more marked extent among the different, so-called races of Europe. We are accustomed to speak of a Scandinavian as tall, blond and blue-eyed, of a South Italian as short, swarthy and dark-eyed; of a Bohemian as middle-sized, with brown or gray eyes and wide face and straight hair. We are apt to construct ideal local types which are based on our everyday experience, abstracted from a combination of forms that are most frequently seen in a given locality, and we forget that there are numerous individuals for whom this description does not hold true. It would be a rash undertaking to determine the locality in which a person is born solely from his bodily characteristics. In many cases we may be helped in such a determination by manners of wearing the hair, peculiar mannerisms of motion, and by dress, but these are not to be mistaken for essential hereditary traits. In populations of various parts of Europe many individuals may be found that may as well belong to one part of the continent as to another. There is no truth in the contention so often made that two Englishmen are more alike in bodily form than, let us say, an Englishman and a German. A greater number of forms may be duplicated in the narrower area, but similar forms may be found in all parts of the continent. There is an overlapping of bodily form between the local groups. It is not justifiable to assume that the individuals that do not fit into the ideal local type which we construct from general impressions are foreign elements in the population, that their presence is always due to intermixture with alien types. It is a fundamental characteristic of all local populations that the individuals differ among themselves, and a closer study shows that this is true of animals as well as of men. It is, therefore, not quite proper to speak in these cases of traits that are hereditary in the racial type as a whole, because too many of them occur also in other racial types. Hereditary racial traits should be shared by the whole population so that it is set off against others.

The matter is quite different when individuals are studied as members of their own family lines. Racial heredity implies that there must be a unity of descent, that there must have existed at one time a small number of ancestors of definite bodily form, from whom the present population has descended. It is quite impossible to reconstruct this ancestry through the study of a modern population, but the study of families extending over several generations is often possible. Whenever this study has been undertaken we find that the family lines represented in a single population differ very much among themselves. In isolated communities where the same families have intermarried for generations the differences are less than in larger communities. We may say that every racial group consists of a great many family lines which are distinct in bodily form. Some of these family lines are duplicated in neighboring territories and the more duplication exists the less is it possible to speak of fundamental racial characteristics. These conditions are so manifest in Europe that all we can do is to study the frequency of occurrence of various family lines all over the continent. The differences between the family lines belonging to each larger area are much greater than the differences between the populations as a whole.

Although it is not necessary to consider the great differences in type that occur in a population as due to mixture of different types, it is easy to see that intermingling has played an important part in the history of modern populations. Let us recall to our minds the migrations that occurred in early times in Europe, when the Kelts of Western Europe swept over Italy and eastward to Asia Minor; when the Teutonic tribes migrated from the Black Sea westward into Italy, Spain and even into North Africa; when the Slav expanded northeastward over Russia, and southward into the Balkan Peninsula; when the Moors held a large part of Spain, when Roman and Greek slaves disappeared in the general population, and when Roman colonization affected a large part of the Mediterranean area. It is interesting to note that Spain's greatness followed the period of greatest race mixture, that its decline set in when the population became stable and immigration stopped. This might give us pause when we speak about the dangers of the intermingling of European types. What is happening in America now is the repetition on a larger scale and in a shorter time of what happened in Europe during the centuries when the people of northern Europe were not yet firmly attached to the soil.

The actual occurrence of intermingling leads us to consider what the biological effect of intermixture of different types may be. Much light has been shed on this question through the intensive study of the phenomena of heredity. It is true we are hampered in the study of heredity in man by the impossibility of experimentation, but much can be learned from observation and through the application of studies of heredity in animals and plants. One fact stands out clearly. When two individuals are mated and there is a very large number of offspring and when furthermore there is no disturbing environmental factor, then the distribution of different forms in the offspring is determined by the genetic characteristics of the parents. What may happen after thousands of generations have passed does not concern us here.

Our previous remarks regarding the characteristics of local types show that matings between individuals essentially different in genetic type must occur in even the most homogeneous population. If it could be shown, as is sometimes claimed, that the progeny of individuals of decidedly distinct proportions of the body would be what has been called disharmonic in character, this would occur with considerable frequency in every population, for we do find individuals, let us say, with large jaws and large teeth and those with small jaws and small teeth. If it is assumed that in the later offspring these conditions might result in a combination of small jaws and large teeth a disharmony would develop. We do not know that this actually occurs. It merely illustrates the line of reasoning. In matings between various European groups these conditions would not be materially changed, although greater differences between parents would be more frequent than in a homogeneous population.

The essential question to be answered is whether we have any evidence that would indicate that matings between individuals of different descent and different type would result in a progeny less vigorous than that of their ancestors. We have not had any opportunity to observe any degeneracy in man as clearly due to this cause. The high nobility of all parts of Europe can be shown to be of very mixed origin. French, German and Italian urban populations are derived from all the distinct European types. It would be difficult to show that any degeneracy that may exist among them is due to an evil effect of intermating. Biological degeneracy is found rather in small districts of intense inbreeding. Here again it is not so much a question of type, but of the presence of pathological conditions in the family strains, for we know of many perfectly healthy and vigorous intensely inbred communities. We find these among the Eskimos and also among many primitive tribes among whom cousin marriages are prescribed by custom.

These remarks do not touch upon the problem of the effect of intermarriages upon bodily form, health and vigor of crosses between races that are biologically more distinct than the types of Europe. It is not quite easy to give absolutely conclusive evidence in regard to this question. Judging merely on the basics of anatomical features and health conditions of mixed populations there does not seem to be any reason to assume unfavorable results, either in the first or in later generations of offspring. The mixed descendants of Europeans and American Indians are taller and more fertile than the pureblood Indians. They are even taller than either parental race. The mixed blood Dutch and Hottentot of South Africa and the Malay mixed bloods of the Island of Kisar are in type intermediate between the two races, and do not exhibit any traits of degeneracy. The populations of the Sudan, mixtures of Mediterranean and Negro types, have always been characterized by great vigor. There is also little doubt that in eastern Russia a considerable infusion of Asiatic blood has occurred. The biological observations on our North American mulattoes do not convince us that there is any deleterious effect of race mixture so far as it is evident in anatomical form and function.

It is also necessary to remember that in varying environment human forms are not absolutely stable, and many of the anatomical traits of the body are subject to a limited amount of change according to climate and conditions of life. We have definite evidence showing changes of bodily size. The stature in European populations has increased materially since the middle of the nineteenth century. War and starvation have left their effects upon the children growing up in the second decade of our century. Proportions of the body change with occupation. The forms of the hand of the laborer and that of the musician reflect their occupations. The changes in head form that have been observed are analogous to those observed in animals under varying conditions of life, among lions born in captivity or among rats fed with different types of diet. The extent to which geographical and social environment may change bodily form is not known, but the influences of outer conditions have to be taken into consideration when comparing different human types.

Selective processes are also at work in changing the character of a population. Differential birth-rate, mortality and migration may bring about changes in the hereditary composition of a group. The range of such changes is limited by the range of variation within the original population. The importance of selection upon the character of a population is easily overestimated. It is true enough that certain defects are transmitted by heredity, but it cannot be proved that a whole population degenerates physically by the numerical increase of degenerates. These always include the physically unfit, and others, the victims of circumstances. The economic depression of our days shows clearly how easily perfectly competent individuals may be brought into conditions of abject poverty and under stresses that only the most vigorous minds can withstand successfully. Equally unjustified is the opinion that war, the struggle between national groups, is a selective process which is necessary to keep mankind on the onward march. Sir Arthur Keith, only a week ago, in his rectoral address at the University of Aberdeen is reported to have said that "Nature keeps her human orchard healthy by pruning and war is her pruning hook." I do not see how such a statement can be justified in any way. War eliminates the physically strong, war increases all the devastating scourges of mankind such as tuberculosis and genital diseases, war weakens the growing generation. History shows that energetic action of masses may be released not only by war but also by other forces. We may not share the fervor or believe in the stimulating ideals; the important point is to observe that they may arouse the same kind of energy that is released in war. Such a stimulus was the abandonment to religion in the middle ages, such is the abandonment of modern Russian youths to their ideal.

So far we have discussed the effects of heredity, environment and selection upon bodily form. We are not so much concerned with the form of the body as with its functions, for in the life of a nation the activities of the individual count rather than his appearance. There is no doubt in my mind that there is a very definite association between the biological make-up of the individual and the physiological and psychological functioning of his body. The claim that only social and other environmental conditions determine the reactions of the individual disregards the most elementary observations, like differences in heart beat, basal metabolism or gland development; and mental differences in their relation to extreme anatomical disturbances of the nervous system. There are organic reasons why individuals differ in their mental behavior.

But to acknowledge this fact does not mean that all differences of behavior can be adequately explained on a purely anatomical basis. When the human body has reached maturity, its form remains fairly stable until the changes due to increasing age set in. Under normal conditions the form and the chemical constitution of the adult body remain almost stable for a number of years. Not so with bodily functions. The conditions of life vary considerably. Our heart beat is different in sleep and in waking. It depends upon the work we are doing, the altitude in which we live, and upon many other factors. It may, therefore, well be that the same individual under different conditions will show quite different reactions. It is the same with other bodily functions. The action of our digestive tract depends upon the quality and quantity of the food we consume. In short, the physiological reactions of the body are markedly adjusted to conditions of life. Owing to this many individuals of different organic structure when exposed to the same environmental conditions will assume a certain degree of similarity of reaction.

On the whole it is much easier to find decided differences between races in bodily form than in function. It cannot be claimed that the body in all races functions in an identical way, but that kind of overlapping which we observed in form is even more pronounced in function. It is quite impossible to say that, because some physical function, let us say the heart beat, has a certain measure, the individual must be White or Negro—for the same rates are found in both races. A certain basal metabolism does not show that a person is a Japanese or a White, although the averages of all the individuals in the races compared may exhibit differences. Furthermore, the particular function is so markedly modified by the demands made upon the organism that these will make the reactions of the racial groups living under the same conditions markedly alike. Every organ is capable of adjustment to a fairly wide range of conditions, and thus the conditions will determine to a great extent the kind of reaction.

What is true of physiological function is equally true of mental function. There exists an enormous amount of literature dealing with mental characteristics of races. The blond North-Europeans, South Italians, Jews, Negroes, Indians, Chinese have been described as though their mental characteristics were biologically determined. It is true, each population has a certain character that is expressed in its behavior, so that there is a geographical distribution of types of behavior. At the same time we have a geographical distribution of anatomical types, and as a result we find that a selected population can be described as having a certain anatomical type and a certain kind of behavior. This, however, does not justify us in claiming that the anatomical type determines behavior. A great error is committed when we allow ourselves to draw this inference. First of all it would be necessary to prove that the correlation between bodily form and behavior is absolute, that it is valid not only for the selected spot, but for the whole population of the given type, and, conversely, that the same behavior does not occur when the types of bodily build differ. Secondly, it would have to be shown that there is an inner relation between the two phenomena.

I might illustrate this by an example taken from an entirely different field. A particular country has a specific climate and particular geological formation. In the same country is found a certain flora. Nevertheless, the character of soil and climate does not explain the composition of the flora, except in so far as it depends upon these two factors. Its composition depends upon the whole historical evolution of plant forms all over the world. The single fact of an agreement of distribution does not prove a genetic relation between the two sets of observations. Negroes in Africa have long limbs and a certain kind of mental behavior. It does not follow that the long limbs are in any way the cause of their mental behavior. The very point to be proved is assumed as proved in this kind of argumentation.

A scientific solution of this problem requires a different line of approach. Mental activities are functions of the organism. We have seen that physiological functions of the same organism may vary greatly under varying conditions. Is the case of mental reactions different? While the study of cretins and of men of genius shows that biological differences exist which limit the type of individual behavior, this has little bearing upon the masses constituting a population in which great varieties of bodily structure prevail. We have seen that the same physiological functions occur in different races with varying frequency, but that no essential qualitative differences can be established. The question must be asked whether the same conditions prevail in mental life.

If it were possible to subject two populations of different type to the same outer conditions the answer would not be difficult. The obstacle in our way lies in the impossibility of establishing sameness of conditions. Investigators differ fundamentally in their opinion in regard to the question of what constitutes sameness of conditions, and our attention must be directed, therefore, to this question.

If we could show how people of exactly the same biological composition react in different types of environment, much might be gained. It seems to me that the data of history create a strong presumption in favor of material changes of mental behavior among peoples of the same genetic composition. The free and easy English of Elizabethan times contrast forcibly with the prudish Mid-Victorian; the Norse Viking and the modern Norwegian do not impress us as the same; the stern Roman republican and his dissolute descendant of imperial times present striking contrasts.

But we need more tangible evidence. At least in so far as intelligent reaction to simple problems of everyday life is concerned, we may bring forward a considerable amount of experimental evidence that deals with this problem. We do not need to assume that our modern intelligence tests give us a clue to absolutely biologically determined intelligence—whatever that may mean—they certainly do tell us how individuals react to simple, more of less unfamiliar, situations. At a first glance it would seem that very important racial differences are found. I refer to the many comparative tests of the intelligence of individuals of various European types and of Europeans and Negroes. North Europeans tested in our country were found as a whole decidedly superior to South Europeans, Europeans as a whole to Negroes. The question arises, what does this mean? If there is a real difference determined by race, we should find the same kind of difference between these racial types wherever they live. Professor Garth has recently collected the available evidence and reaches the conclusion that it is not possible to prove a difference due to genetic factors, that rather all the available observations may be easily explained as due to differences in social environment. It seems to me the most convincing proof of the correctness of this view has been given by Dr. Klineberg, who examined the various outstanding European types in urban and rural communities in Europe. He found that there is everywhere a marked contrast between rural and urban populations, the city giving considerably better results than the country and that furthermore the various groups do not follow by any means the same order in city and country; that the order rather depends upon social conditions, such as the excellence of the school systems and conflicts between home and school. Still more convincing are his observations on Negroes. He examined a considerable number of Negroes in southern cities who had moved to the city from rural districts. He found that the longer they lived in the city the better the results of the tests came to be, so that Negroes who had lived in the city for six years were far superior to those who had just moved to the city. He found the same result when studying Negroes who had moved from the South to New York, an improvement with the time of residence in New York. This result agrees with Brigham's findings for Italians who had lived for varying periods in the United States. It has often been claimed, as was done in the beginning by Brigham, that such changes are due to a process of selection, that more poorly endowed individuals have migrated to the country in late years and represent the group that has just come to the city. It would be difficult to maintain this in view of the regularity with which this phenomenon reappears in every test. Still, Dr. Klineberg has also given definite evidence that selection does not account for these differences. He compared the records of the migrating groups with those who remained behind. The records collected in Nashville and Birmingham showed that there is no appreciable difference between the two groups. The migrants were even a little below those who stayed at home. He also found that the migrants who came to New York were slightly inferior to those who remained in the South.

I have given these data in some detail, because they show definitely that cultural environment is a most important factor in determining the results of the so-called intelligence tests. In fact, a careful examination of the tests shows clearly that in none of them has our cultural experience been eliminated. City life and country life, the South and the North present different types of cultural background to which we learn to adapt ourselves, and our reactions are determined by these adaptations, which are often so obscure that they can be detected only by a most intimate knowledge of the conditions of life. We have indications of such adaptations in other cases. It would seem that among the Plains Indians the experience of girls with bead work gives to them a superiority in handling tests based on form. It is highly desirable that the tests should be examined with greatest care in regard to the indirect influence of experience upon the results. I suspect strongly that such influences can always be discovered and that it will be found impossible to construct any test in which this element is so completely eliminated that we could consider the results as an expression of purely biologically determined factors.

It is much more difficult to obtain convincing results in regard to emotional reactions in different races. No satisfactory experimental method has been devised that would answer the crucial question, in how far cultural background and in how far the biological basis of personality is responsible for observed differences. There is no doubt that individuals do differ in this respect on account of their biological constitution. It is very questionable whether the same may be said of races, for in all races we find a wide range of different types of personality. All that we can say with certainty is that the cultural factor is of greatest importance and might well account for all the observed differences, although this does not preclude the possibility of biologically determined differences. The variety of response of groups of the same race but culturally different is so great that it seems likely that any existing biological differences are of minor importance. I can give only a few instances. The North American Indians are reputed as stoic, as ready to endure pain and torture without a murmur. This is true in all those cases in which culture demands repression of emotion. The same Indians, when ill, give in to hopeless depression. Among closely related Indian tribes certain ones are given to ecstatic orgies, while others enjoy a life running in smooth conventional channels. The buffalo hunter was an entirely different personality from the poor Indian who has to rely on government help, or who lives on the proceeds of land rented by his White neighbors. Social workers are familiar with the subtle influence of personal relations that will differentiate the character of members of the same family. Ethnological evidence is all in favor of the assumption that hereditary racial traits are unimportant as compared to cultural conditions. As a matter of fact, ethnological studies do not concern themselves with race as a factor in cultural form. From Waitz on, through Spencer, Tylor, Bastian, to our times, ethnologists have not given serious attention to race, because they find cultural forms distributed regardless of race.

I believe the present state of our knowledge justifies us in saying that, while individuals differ, biological differences between races are small. There is no reason to believe that one race is by nature so much more intelligent, endowed with great will power, or emotionally more stable than another, that the difference would materially influence its culture. Nor is there any good reason to believe that the differences between races are so great that the descendants of mixed marriages would be inferior to their parents. Biologically there is no good reason to object to fairly close inbreeding in healthy groups, nor to intermingling of the principal races.

I have considered so far only the biological side of the problem. In actual life we have to reckon with social settings which have a very real existence, no matter how erroneous the opinions on which they are founded. Among us race antagonism is a fact, and we should try to understand its psychological significance. For this purpose we have to consider the behavior not only of man, but also of animals. Many animals live in societies. It may be a shoal of fish which any individuals of the same species may join, or a swarm of mosquitoes. No social tie is apparent in these groups, but there are others which we may call close societies that do not permit any outsider to join their group. Packs of dogs and well-organized herds of higher mammals, ants and bees are examples of this kind. In all these groups there is a considerable degree of social solidarity which is expressed particularly by antagonism against any outside group. The troops of monkeys that live in a given territory will not allow another troop to come and join them. The members of a closed animal society are mutually tolerant or even helpful. They repel all outside intruders.

Conditions in primitive society are quite similar. Strict social obligations exist between the members of a tribe, but all outsiders are enemies. Primitive ethics demand self-sacrifice in the group to which the individual belongs, deadly enmity against every outsider. A closed society does not exist without antagonisms against others. Although the degree of antagonism against outsiders has decreased, closed societies continue to exist in our own civilization. The nobility formed a closed society until very recent times. Patricians and plebeians in Rome, Greeks and barbarians, the gangs of our streets, Mohammedan and infidel, and our modern nations are in this sense closed societies that cannot exist without antagonisms. The principles that hold societies together vary enormously, but common to all of them are social obligations within the group, antagonisms against other parallel groups.

Race consciousness and race antipathy differ in one respect from the social groups here enumerated. While in all other human societies there is no external characteristic that helps to assign an individual to his group, here his very appearance singles him out. If the belief should prevail, as it once did, that all red-haired individuals have an undesirable character, they would at once be segregated and no red-haired individual could escape from his class no matter what his personal characteristics might be. The Negro, the East Asiatic or Malay who may at once be recognized by his bodily build is automatically placed in his class and not one of them can escape being excluded from a foreign closed group. The same happens when a group is characterized by dress imposed by circumstances, by choice, or because a dominant group prescribe for them a distinguishing symbol—like the garb of the medieval Jews or the stripes of the convict—so that each individual no matter what his own character may be, is at once assigned to his group and treated accordingly. If racial antipathy were based on innate human traits this would be expressed in interracial sexual aversion. The free intermingling of slave owners with their female slaves and the resulting striking decrease in the number of full-blood Negroes, the progressive development of a half-blood Indian population and the readiness of intermarriage with Indians when economic advantages may be gained by such means, show clearly that there is no biological foundation for race feeling. There is no doubt that the strangeness of an alien racial type does play an important role, for the ideal of beauty of the White who grows up in a purely White society is different from that of a Negro. This again is analogous to the feeling of aloofness among groups that are characterized by different dress, different mannerisms of expression of emotion, or by the ideal of bodily strength as against that of refinement of form. The student of race relations must answer the question whether in societies in which different racial types form a socially homogeneous group, a marked race consciousness develops. This question cannot be answered categorically, although interracial conditions in Brazil and the disregard of racial affiliation in the relation between Mohammedans and infidels show that race consciousness may be quite insignificant.

When social divisions follow racial lines, as they do among ourselves, the degree of difference between racial forms is an important element in establishing racial groupings and in creating racial conflicts.

The actual relation is not different from that developing in other cases in which social cleavage develops. In times of intense religious feeling denominational conflicts, in times of war national conflicts take the same course. The individual is merged in his group and not rated according to his personal value.

However, nature is such that constantly new groups are formed in which each individual subordinates himself to the group. He expresses his feeling of solidarity by an idealization of his group and by an emotional desire for its perpetuation. When the groups are denominational, there is strong antagonism against marriages outside of the group. The group must be kept pure, although denomination and descent are in no way related. If the social groups are racial groups we encounter in the same way the desire for racial endogamy in order to maintain racial purity.

On this subject I take issue with Sir Arthur Keith, who in the address already referred to is reported to have said that "race antipathy and race prejudice nature has implanted in you for her own end—the improvement of mankind through racial differentiation." I challenge him to prove that race antipathy is "implanted by nature" and not the effect of social causes which are active in every closed social group, no matter whether it is racially heterogeneous or homogeneous. The complete lack of sexual antipathy, the weakening of race consciousness in communities in which children grow up as an almost homogeneous group; the occurrence of equally strong antipathies between denominational groups, or between social strata—as witnessed by the Roman patricians and plebeians, the Spartan Lacedaemonians and Helots, the Egyptian castes and some of the Indian castes—all these show that antipathies are social phenomena. If you will, you may call them "implanted by nature," but only in so far as man is a being living in closed social groups, leaving it entirely indetermined what these social groups may be.

No matter how weak the case for racial purity may be, we understand its social appeal in our society. While the biological reasons that are adduced may not be relevant, a stratification of society in social groups that are racial in character will always lead to racial discrimination. As in all other sharp social groupings the individual is not judged as an individual but as a member of his class. We may be reasonably certain that whenever members of different races form a single social group with strong bonds, racial prejudice and racial antagonisms will come to lose their importance. They may even disappear entirely. As long as we insist on a stratification in racial layers, we shall pay the penalty in the form of interracial struggle. Will it be better for us to continue as we have been doing, or shall we try to recognize the conditions that lead to the fundamental antagonisms that trouble us?

NOTE

1. Address of the president of the American Association for the Advancement of Science, Pasadena, June 15. *Science*, N.S., vol. 74. (1931) pp. 1–8.

CHAPTER 2

THE CONCEPT OF RACE[1]

Ashley Montagu

In this paper I desire to examine the concepts of race as they are used with reference to man. I shall first deal with the use of this term by biologists and anthropologists, and then with its use by the man-on-the-street, the so-called layman—so-called, no doubt, from the lines in Sir Philip Sidney's sonnet:

I never drank of Aganippe well
  Nor ever did in shade of Tempe sit,
And Muses scorn with vulgar brains to dwell;
  Poor layman I, for sacred rites unfit.

I shall endeavor to show that all those who continue to use the term "race" with reference to man, whether they be laymen or scientists, are "for sacred rites unfit." Once more, I shall, as irritatingly as the sound of a clanging door heard in the distance in a wind that will not be shut out, raise the question as to whether, with reference to man, it would not be better if the term "race" were altogether abandoned.

At the outset it should, perhaps, be made clear that I believe, with most biologists, that evolutionary factors, similar to those that have been operative in producing raciation in other animal species, have also been operative in the human species—but with a significant added difference, namely, the consequences which have resulted from man's entry into that unique zone of adaptation in which he excels beyond all other creatures, namely culture, that is to say, the man-made part of the environment.

On the evidence it would seem clear that man's cultural activities have introduced elements into the processes of human raciation which have so substantially modified the end-products that one can no longer equate the processes of raciation in lower animals with those which have occurred in the evolution of man. The factors of mutation, natural selection, drift, isolation, have all been operative in the evolution of man. But so have such factors as ever-increasing degrees of mobility, hybridization, and social selection, and it is the effects of these and similar factors which, at least so it has always seemed to me, makes the employment of the term "race" inapplicable to most human populations as we find them today.

Of course there exist differences, but we want a term by which to describe the existence of these differences. We do not want a prejudiced term which injects meanings which are not there into the differences. We want a term which as nearly mirrors the conditions as a term can, not one which falsifies and obfuscates the issue.

Terminology is extremely important, and I think it will be generally agreed that it is rather more desirable to allow the conditions or facts to determine the meaning of the terms by which we shall refer to them, than to have pre-existing terms determine the manner in which they shall be perceived and ordered, for pre-existing terms constitute pre-existing meanings, and such meanings have a way of conditioning the manner in which what we look at shall be perceived. Each time the term "race" is used with reference to man, this is what, I think, is done.

The term "race" has a long and tortured history. We cannot enter upon that here. The present-day usage of the term in biological circles is pretty much the sense in which it was used in similar circles in the 19th century, namely, as a subdivision of a species the members of which resemble each other and differ from other members of the species in certain traits. In our own time valiant attempts have been made to pour new wine into the old bottles. The shape of the bottle, however, remains the same. The man-on-the-street uses the term in much the same way as it was used by his 19th century compeer. Here physical type, heredity, blood, culture, nation, personality, intelligence, and achievement are all stirred together to make the omelet which is the popular conception of "race." This is a particularly virulent term, the epidemiology of which is far better understood by the social scientist than by the biologist—who should, therefore, exercise a little more caution than he usually does when he delivers himself on the subject.

The difficulty with taking over old terms in working with problems to which they are thought to apply is that when this is done we may also take over some of the old limitations of the term, and this may affect our approach to the solution of those problems. For what the investigator calls "the problem of human races" is immediately circumscribed and delimited the moment he uses the word "races." For "race" implies something very definite to him, something which in itself constitutes a solution, and the point I would like to make is that far from the problem meaning something like a solution to him, it should, on the contrary, constitute itself in his mind as something more closely resembling what it is, namely, a problem requiring investigation.

Instead of saying to himself, as the true believer in "race" does, "Here is a population, let me see how it fits my criteria of 'race,'" I think it would be much more fruitful of results if he said to himself, instead, "Here is a population, let me go ahead and find out what it is like. What its internal likenesses and differences are, and how it resembles and how it differs from other populations. And then let me operationally describe what I have found," that is, in terms of the data themselves, and not with reference to the conditions demanded by any pre-existing term.

The chief objection to the term "race" with reference to man is that it takes for granted as solved problems which are far from being so and tends to close the mind to problems to which it should always remain open. If, with ritual fidelity, one goes on repeating long enough that "the Nordics" are a race, or that "the Armenoids" are, or that "the Jews" are, or that races may be determined by their blood group gene frequencies, we have already determined what a "race" is, and it is not going to make the slightest difference whether one uses the old or the new wine, for we are back at the same old stand pouring it into the old bottles covered with the same patina of moss-like green.

It is the avoidance of this difficulty that T.H. Huxley had in mind when in 1865, he wrote, "I speak of 'persistent modifications' or 'stocks' rather than of 'varieties,' or 'races,' or 'species,' because each of these last well-known terms implies, on the part of its employer, a preconceived opinion touching one of those problems, the solution of which is the ultimate object of the science; and in regard to which, therefore, ethnologists are especially bound to keep their minds open and their judgments freely balanced" (1865, 209–10).

It is something to reflect upon that, a century later, this point of view has still to be urged.

In the year 1900, the French anthropologist Joseph Deniker published his great book, simultaneously in French and in English, *The Races of Man*. But though the title has the word in it, he objected to the term "race" on much the same grounds as Huxley. The whole of his introduction is devoted to showing the difficulties involved in applying to man the terms of zoological nomenclature. He writes, "We have presented to us Arabs, Swiss, Australians, Bushmen, English, Siouan Indians, Negroes, etc., without knowing if each of these groups is on an equal footing from the point of view of classification."

"Do these real and palpable groupings represent unions of individuals which, in spite of some slight dissimilarities, are capable of forming what zoologists call 'species,' 'subspecies,' 'varieties,' in the case of wild animals, or 'races' in the case of domestic animals? One need not be a professional anthropologist to reply negatively to this question. They are *ethnic groups* formed by virtue of community of language, religion, social institutions, etc., which have the power of uniting human beings of one or several species, races, or varieties, and are by no means zoological species; they may include human beings of one or of many species, races, or varieties." "They are," he goes on to say, "theoretic types" (1900, 2–3).

When, in 1936, Julian Huxley and A.C. Haddon published their valuable book on "race," *We Europeans*, they took pains to underscore the fact that "the existence of ... human subspecies is purely hypothetical. Nowhere does a human group now exist which corresponds closely to a systematic sub-species in animals, since various original sub-species have crossed repeatedly and constantly. For the existing populations, the non-committal term *ethnic group* should be used.... All that exists today is a number of arbitrary ethnic groups, intergrading into each other" (1936, 106). And finally, "The essential reality of the existing situation ... is not the hypothetical sub-species or races, but the *mixed ethnic groups*, which can never be genetically purified into their original components, or purged of the variability which they owe to past crossing. Most anthropological writings of the past, and many of the present fail to take account of this fundamental fact" (1936, 108). "If *race* is a scientific term," these authors point out, "it must have a genetic meaning" (1936, 114).

Haddon, as an anthropologist, was familiar with Deniker's book, and it is possible that the noncommittal term "ethnic group" was remembered by him as one more appropriately meeting the requirements of the situation and thus came to be adopted by both authors in their book. It was from this source, that is from Huxley and Haddon, that I, in turn, adopted the term "ethnic group" in 1936 and have consistently continued to use it since that time. The claim is that the noncommittal general term "ethnic group" meets the realities of the situation head on, whereas the term "race" does not. Furthermore, it is claimed that "ethnic group" is a term of heuristic value. It raises questions, and doubts, leading to clarification and discovery. The term "race," since it takes for granted what requires to be demonstrated within its own limits, closes the mind on all that.

It is of interest to find that quite a number of biologists have, in recent years, independently raised objections to the continuing use of the term "race," even, in some cases, when it is applied to populations of lower animals. Thus, for example, W.T. Calman writes, "Terms such as 'geographical race,' 'form,' 'phase,' and so forth, may be useful in particular instances but are better not used until some measure of agreement is reached as to their precise meaning" (1949, 14). Hans Kalmus writes, "A very important term which was originally used in systematics is 'race.' Nowadays, however, its use is avoided as far as possible in genetics" (1948, 45). In a later work Kalmus writes, "It is customary to discuss the local varieties of humanity in terms of 'race.' However, it is unnecessary to use this greatly debased word, since it is easy to describe populations without it" (1958, 30). G.S. Carter writes that the terms "'race,' 'variety,' and 'form' are used so loosely and in so many senses that it is advisable to avoid using them as infraspecific categories" (1951, 163). Ernst Hanhart objects to the use of the term "race" with reference to man since he holds that there are no "true races" among men (1953, 545). Abercrombie, Hickman, and Johnson, in their *A Dictionary of Biology* (1951), while defining species and subspecies consistently, decline even a mention of the word "race" anywhere in their book. L.S. Penrose in an otherwise highly favorable review of Dunn and Dobzhansky's excellent *Heredity, Race and Society*, writes that he is unable "to see the necessity for the rather apologetic retention of the obsolete term 'race,' when what is meant is simply a given population differentiated by some social, geographical or genetical character, or ... merely by a gene frequency peculiarity. The use of the almost mystical concept of race makes the presentation of the facts about the geographical and linguistic groups ... unnecessarily complicated" (1952, 252).

To see what Penrose means, and at the same time to make

our criticism of their conception of "race," let us turn to Dunn and Dobzhansky's definition of race. They write, in the aforementioned work, "Races can be defined as populations which differ in the frequencies of some gene or genes" (1952, 118). This definition at once leads to the question: Why use the word "race" here when what is being done is precisely what should be done, namely, to describe populations in terms of their gene frequency differences? What, in point of fact, has the antiquated, mystical conception of "race" to do with this? The answer is: Nothing. Indeed, the very notion of "race" is antithetical to the study of population genetics, for the former traditionally deals with fixed clear-cut differences, and the latter with fluid or fluctuating differences. It seems to me an unrealistic procedure to maintain that this late in the day we can re-adapt the term "race" to mean something utterly different from what it has always most obfuscatingly and ambiguously meant.

We may congratulate ourselves, and in fact often do, that the chemists of the late 18th and early 19th centuries had the good sense to throw out the term "phlogiston" when they discovered that it corresponded to nothing in reality, instead of attempting to adapt it to fit the facts which it was not designed to describe, and of which, indeed, it impeded the discovery for several centuries. The psychologists of the second decade of this century had the good sense to do likewise with the term "instinct" when they discovered how, like a bunion upon the foot, it impeded the pilgrim's progress toward a sounder understanding of human drives (Bernard 1924).

It is simply not possible to redefine words with so long-standing a history of misuse as "race," and for this, among other cogent reasons, it is ill-advised. As Simpson has said, "There ... is a sort of Gresham's Law for words; redefine them as we will, their worst or most extreme meaning is almost certain to remain current and to tend to drive out the meaning we prefer" (1953, 268).

For this reason alone it would appear to me unwise to afford scientific sanction to a term which is so embarrassed by false meanings as is the term "race." There is the added objection that it is wholly redundant, and confusingly so, to distinguish as a "race" a population which happens to differ from other populations in the frequency of one or more genes. Why call such populations "races" when the operational definition of what they are is sharply and clearly stated in the words used to convey what we mean, namely, populations which differ from one another in particular frequencies of certain specified genes? Surely, to continue the use of the word "race" under such circumstances is to exemplify what A.E. Housman so aptly described as "calling in ambiguity of language to promote confusion of thought" (1933, 31).

When populations differ from each other in the frequency of the sickle-cell gene or any other gene or genes, all that is necessary is to state the facts with reference to those populations. That is what those populations are in terms of gene frequencies. And those are the operative criteria which we can use as tools or concepts in giving an account of the realities of the situation—the actual operations.

I have thus far said nothing about the anthropological conception of "race" because this is to some extent yielding to genetic pressure, and because the future of what used to be called the study of "race" lies, in my view, largely in the direction of population genetics. The older anthropological conception of "race" still occasionally lingers on, suggesting that it is perhaps beyond the reach both of scientific judgment and mortal malice. Insofar as the genetic approach to the subject is concerned, many anthropologists are, as it were, self-made men and only too obviously represent cases of unskilled labor. However, my feeling is that they should be praised for trying rather than blamed for failing. The new anthropology is on the right track.

Recently Garn and Coon (1955) have attempted to adapt the terms "geographic race," "local race," and "microgeographical race," for use in the human species. They define, for example, "A geographical race" as, "in its simplest terms, a collection of (race) populations having features in common, such as a high gene frequency for blood group B, and extending over a geographically definable area" (1955, 997).

In this definition I think we can see, in high relief as it were, what is wrong with the continuing use of the term "race." The term "geographical race" immediately delimits the group of populations embraced by it from others, as if the so-called "geographical race" were a biological entity "racially" distinct from others. Such a group of populations is not "racially" distinct, but differs from others in the frequencies of certain of its genes. It was suggested by the UNESCO group of geneticists and physical anthropologists that such a group of populations be called a "major group" (Montagu 1951, 173–82). This suggestion was made precisely in order to avoid such difficulties as are inherent in the term "geographical race." Since Garn and Coon themselves admit that "geographical races are to a large extent collections of convenience, useful more for pedagogic purposes than as units for empirical investigation" (1955, 1000), it seems to me difficult to understand why they should have preferred this term to the one more closely fitting the situation, namely, "major groups." It is a real question whether spurious precision, even for pedagogical purposes, or as an "as if" fiction, is to be preferred to a frank acknowledgment, in the terms we use, of the difficulties involved. Garn and Coon are quite alive to the problem, but it may be questioned whether it contributes to the student's clearer understanding of that problem to use terms which not only do not fit the conditions, but which serve to contribute to making the student's mind a dependable instrument of imprecision, especially in view of the fact that a more appropriate term is available.

The principle of "squatter's rights" apparently applies to words as well as to property. When men make a heavy investment in words they are inclined to treat them as property, and even to become enslaved by them, the prisoners of their own vocabularies. High walls may not a prison make, but technical terms sometimes do. This, I would suggest, is another good reason for self-examination with regard to the use of the term "race."

Commenting on Garn's views on race, Dr. J.P. Garlick has remarked, "The use of 'race' as a taxonomic unit for man seems out of date, if not irrational. A hierarchy of geographical, local and micro-races is proposed, with acknowledgements to Rensch and Dobzhansky. But the criteria for their definition are nowhere made clear, and in any case such a scheme could not do justice to the many independent fluctuations and frequency gradients shown by human polymorphic characters. Surely physical anthropology has outgrown such abstractions as 'Large Local Race.... Alpine: the rounder-bodied, rounder-headed, predominantly darker peoples of the French mountains, across Switzerland, Austria, and to the shores of the Black Sea'" (1961, 169–70).

Garn and Coon do not define "local races" but say of them that they "can be identified, not so much by average differences, but by their nearly complete isolation" (1955, 997). In that case, as Dahlberg (1942) long ago suggested, why not call such populations "isolates"?

"Microgeographical races" also fail to receive definition, but are described as differing "only qualitatively from local races." In that case, why not use some term which suggests the difference?

In short, it is our opinion that taxonomies and terms should be designed to fit the facts, and not the facts forced into the procrustean rack of pre-determined categories. If we are to have references, whether terminological or taxonomical, to existing or extinct populations of man, let the conditions as we find them determine the character of our terms or taxonomies, and not the other way round.

Since what we are actually dealing with in human breeding populations are differences in the frequencies of certain genes, why not use a term which states just this, such as *genogroup*, and the various appropriate variants of this?[2] If necessary, we could then speak of "geographic genogroups," "local genogroups," and "microgenogroups." A genogroup being defined as a breeding population which differs from other breeding populations of the species in the frequency of one or more genes. The term "genogroup" gets as near to a statement of the facts as a term can. The term "race" goes far beyond the facts and only serves to obscure them. A *geographic genogroup* would then be defined as a group of breeding populations characterized by a marked similarity of the frequencies of one or more genes.

A *local genogroup* would be one of the member populations of a geographic genogroup, and a *microgenogroup* a partially isolated population with one or more gene frequency differences serving to distinguish it from adjacent or nonadjacent local genogroups.

It is to be noted that nothing is said of a common heredity for similarity in gene frequencies in a geographic genogroup. The common heredity is usually implied, but I do not think it should be taken for granted, except within the local genogroups and the microgenogroups. One or more of the genogroups in a geographic genogroup may have acquired their frequencies for a given gene quite independently of the other local populations comprising the geographic genogroup. This is a possibility which is, perhaps, too often overlooked when comparisons are being made on the basis of gene frequencies between populations, whether geographic or not.

But this must suffice for my criticism of the usage of the term "race" by biologists and anthropologists. I wish now to discuss, briefly, the disadvantages of the use of this term in popular usage, and the advantages of the general term "ethnic group."

The layman's conception of "race" is so confused and emotionally muddled that any attempt to modify it would seem to be met by the greatest obstacle of all, the term "race" itself. It is a trigger word. Utter it, and a whole series of emotionally conditioned responses follow. If we are to succeed in clarifying the minds of those who think in terms of "race" we must cease using the word, because by continuing to use it we sanction whatever meaning anyone chooses to bestow upon it, and because in the layman's mind the term refers to conditions which do not apply. There is no such thing as the kind of "race" in which the layman believes, namely, that there exists an indissoluble association between mental and physical characters which make individual members of certain "races" either inferior or superior to the members of certain other "races." The layman requires to have his thinking challenged on this subject. The term "ethnic group" serves as such a challenge to thought and as a stimulus to rethink the foundations of one's beliefs. The term "race" takes for granted what should be a matter for inquiry. And this is precisely the point that is raised when one uses the noncommittal "ethnic group." It encourages the passage from ignorant or confused certainty to thoughtful uncertainty. For the layman, as for others, the term "race" closes the door on understanding. The phrase "ethnic group" opens it, or at the very least, leaves it ajar.

In opposition to these views a number of objections have been expressed. Here are some of them. One does not change anything by changing names. It is an artful dodge. Why not meet the problem head-on? If the term has been badly defined in the past, why not redefine it? Re-education should be attempted by establishing the true meaning of "race," not by denying its existence. It suggests a certain blindness to the facts to deny that "races" exist in man. One cannot combat racism by enclosing the word in quotes. It is not the word that requires changing but people's ideas about it. It is a common failing to argue from the abuse of an idea to its total exclusion. It is quite as possible to feel "ethnic group prejudice" as it is to feel "race prejudice." One is not going to solve the race problem this way.

Such objections indicate that there has been a failure of communication, that the main point has been missed. The term "ethnic group" is not offered as a substitute for "race." On the contrary, the term "ethnic group" implies a fundamental difference in viewpoint from that which is implied in the term "race." It is not a question of changing names or of substitution, or an artful dodge, or the abandonment of a good term which has been abused. It is first and foremost an attempt to clarify the fact that the old term is unsound when applied to man, and should therefore not be used with reference to him. At the same time "ethnic group," being an intentionally vague and general term, is designed to make it clear that there is a problem to be solved, rather than to maintain the fiction that the problem has been solved. As a general term it leaves all question of definition open, referring specifically to human breeding populations, the members of which are believed to exhibit certain physical or genetic likenesses. For all general purposes, an "ethnic group" may be defined as one of a number of breeding populations, which populations together comprise the species *Homo sapiens*, and which individually maintain their differences, physical or genetic and cultural, by means of isolating mechanisms such as geographic and social barriers.

The re-education of the layman should be taken seriously. For this reason I would suggest that those who advocate the redefinition of the term "race," rather than its replacement by a general term which more properly asks questions before it attempts definitions, would do well to acquaint themselves with the nature of the laymen as well as with the meaning of the phenomena to which they would apply a term which cannot possibly be redefined. If one desires to remove a prevailing erroneous conception and introduce a more correct one, one is more likely to be successful by introducing the new conception with a distinctively new term rather than by attempting redefinition of a term embarrassed by longstanding unsound usage. Professor Henry Sigerist has well said that "it is never sound to continue the use of terminology with which the minds of millions of people have been poisoned even when the old terms are given new meanings" (1951, 101).

There is, apparently, a failure on the part of some students to understand that one of the greatest obstacles to the process of re-education would be the retention of the old term "race," a term which enshrines the errors it is designed to remove. The deep implicit meanings this term possesses for the majority of its users are such that they require immediate challenge whenever and by whomsoever the term "race" is used.

Whenever the term "race" is used, most people believe that something like an eternal verity has been uttered when, in fact, nothing more than evidence has been given that there are many echoes, but few voices. "Race" is a word so familiar that in using it the uncritical thinker is likely to take his own private meaning for it completely for granted, never thinking at any time to question so basic an instrument of the language as the word "race." On the other hand, when one uses the term "ethnic group," the question is immediately raised, "What does it mean? What does the user have in mind?" And this at once affords an opportunity to discuss the facts and explore the meaning and the falsities enshrined in the word "race," and to explain the problems involved and the facts of the genetic situation as we know them.

The term "ethnic group" is concerned with questions; the term "race" is concerned with answers, unsound answers, where for the most part there are only problems that require to be solved before any sound answers can be given.

It may be difficult for those who believe in what I.A. Richards has called "The Divine Right of Words" to accept the suggestion that a word such as "race," which has exercised so evil a tyranny over the minds of men, should be permanently dethroned from the vocabulary, but that constitutes all the more reason for trying, remembering that the meaning of a word is the action it produces.

NOTES

1. Presented at the University Seminar on Genetics and the Evolution of Man, Columbia University, December 6, 1959.
2. The term "genogroup" was suggested to me by Sir Julian Huxley during a conversation on September 29, 1959.

REFERENCES

Abercrombie, M., C.J. Hickman, and M.L. Johnson. 1951. *A dictionary of biology*. Harmondsworth: Penguin Books.

Bernard, L.L. 1924. *Instinct*. New York: Henry Holt and Co.

Calman, W.T. 1949. *The classification of animals*. New York: John Wiley and Sons.

Carter, G.S. 1951. *Animal evolution*. New York: Macmillan Co.

Dahlberg, G. 1942. *Race, reason and rubbish*. New York: Columbia University Press.

Deniker, J. 1900. *The races of man*. London: The Walter Scott Publishing Co. Ltd.

Dunn, L.C., and Th. Dobzhansky. 1952. *Heredity, race and society*. Rev. ed. New York: The New American Library of World Literature.

Garlick, J.P. 1961. Review of *Human races and Readings on race*, by S.M. Garn. *Annals of Human Genetics* 25:169–70.

Garn, S.M., and C.S. Coon. 1955. On the number of races of mankind. *American Anthropologist* 57:996–1001.

Hanhart, E. 1953. Infectious diseases. In *Clinical genetics*, ed. Arnold Sorsby. St. Louis: Mosby.

Housman, A.E. 1933. *The name and nature of poetry*. New York: Cambridge University Press.

Huxley, J.S., and A.C. Haddon. 1936. *We Europeans: a survey of "racial" problems*. New York: Harper and Bros.

Huxley, T.H. 1865. On the methods and results of ethnology. *Fortnightly Review*. Reprinted in *Man's place in nature and other anthropological essays*. London: Macmillan Co., 1894.

Kalmus, H. 1948. *Genetics*. Harmondsworth: Pelican Books.

———. 1958. *Heredity and variation*. London: Routledge and K. Paul.

Montagu, M.F. Ashley. 1951. *Statement on race*. Rev. ed. New York: Henry Schuman.

Penrose, L.S. 1952. Review of *Heredity, race and society*, by Dunn and Dobzhansky. *Annals of Human Eugenics* 17:252.

Sigerist, H. 1951. *A history of medicine*. Vol. 1. New York: Oxford University Press.

Simpson, G.G. 1953. *The major features of evolution*. New York: Columbia University Press.

CHAPTER 3

THE CLASSIFICATION OF RACES IN EUROPE AND NORTH AMERICA: 1700–1850

Michael Banton

The classification of *homo sapiens* into varieties was a feature of eighteenth-century natural history, and must be seen in that context. That classifactory enterprise appears, at least to start with, to have been independent of the increased use of the word "race" or its equivalent in several West European languages.

*****

The dominant view at that time was that everything in the world was the work of the Creator. It was expressed in John Milton's *Paradise Lost* (1677) as he described the creation of each of the most familiar animals. As the naturalist John Ray declared in 1688, "the number of true species in nature is fixed and limited and, as we may reasonably believe, constant and unchangeable from the first creation to the present day." Differences between living things were to be traced back to the intentions of the Creator and explanations took the form of genealogies. Any discussion of differences between humans had to assume that they were all descended from a single original pair (the doctrine of monogenesis).

LINEAGE AND VARIETY IN PARALLEL

The naturalists who devised the first classifications were primarily interested in plants, but believed, reasonably enough, that the principles underlying the classification of plants must apply to all living things, for all were the works of the same Creator. The modern pioneer in the study of natural history was an English clergyman, John Ray (1627–1705), author of *The Wisdom of God Manifested in the Works of the Creation.* John P. Greene, in his very useful study of the rise of evolutionary biology, *The Death of Adam* (1957, p. 15), testifies that in Ray's mind there was no scientific problem in the natural order; it was God's work. Yet in his praise of the Creator there was a lurking anxiety that indicated the direction from which his static view of the universe was to be challenged. Even a believer had difficulty discerning God's design. There were the species created by God, but there were also "accidents" of variation in the size and colour of specimens, in the number of leaves, and so on. Just as Ray would not accept that a black cow and a white cow, or two similar fruits with a different taste, were necessarily separate species, so he would make no such distinction between a Negro and a European.

*****

Immanuel Kant (1724–1804), the great philosopher, concluded from his study of human variation that the only character invariably transmitted from one generation to another was that of skin colour. [...] Both he and Buffon amplified some of the stereotypes of their age but rejected the polygenist claim that the different varieties of *homo* derived from separate creations.

The most careful eighteenth-century classification of humans was that by the German anatomist J.F. Blumenbach (1752–1840), the author (in Latin) of *On the Natural Variety of Mankind*. [...] In 1770 he divided *homo* into four divisions, but in the second (1781) edition of his book, he introduced the five-fold classification that was to become famous. These five varieties he called Caucasian, American, Mongolian, Malay and Ethiopian, the second and fourth being seen as intermediates between the other varieties. Blumenbach collected evidence of Negro accomplishments to bolster his belief in the unity of the human species. The variations within that species were, he thought, differences of degree arising from the general biological process of degeneration (by which he seems to have meant not deterioration but the modification that arises as one generation succeeds another). Changes of climate and the domestication of a species could accelerate this process.

*****

As Greene (1957, pp. 221–2) remarks, most of the eighteenth-century writers on race were more concerned to explain the origins of races than to classify them. Samuel Stanhope Smith, indeed, dismissed attempts at classification as "a useless labour" since it was so difficult to draw the necessary distinctions. [...] Only when the general processes responsible for variation were understood would it be possible to explain particular kinds of variation, like the differences between Caucasians and Ethiopians. To this problem there were three main kinds of response. The popular answer was to regard variation as the result of divine intervention, blackness being a curse or punishment upon the descendants of Ham. The second answer was that environmental influences, in some as yet unexplained manner, gave rise to variations which were then inherited. The third kind of answer was that the variations had been there all along, having been part of the Creator's intention.

*****

To discover the relations between the internal and external history of racial thought in this period, it is necessary to examine the work of particular authors in relation to the movements of their time. In producing theoretical explanations of physical and cultural variation, the authors may have been influenced by the assumptions about human variation which they shared with other members of their societies who were not engaged in scientific enquiries. [...] The theories of the scientists may in turn have contributed to the assumptions of the age. There would appear to have been an interaction between racial theories on the one hand and racial consciousness on the other. The problematical nature of that interaction has often been overlooked, sometimes through a superficial reading of a passage in Eric Williams' *Capitalism and Slavery*. Williams wrote:

> Slavery in the Caribbean has been too narrowly identified with the Negro. A racial twist has therefore been given to what is basically an economic phenomenon. Slavery was not born of racism; rather, racism was the consequence of slavery. Unfree labor in the New World was brown, white, black and yellow; Catholic, Protestant and Pagan (1944, p. 7).

The thrust of this argument lies in the first sentence. There was no reason for Williams to deny that there were white prejudices against blacks before New World slavery. There is now no reason for anyone else to deny that such prejudices were increased by slavery. To take the matter further, however, it is essential to separate the various strands that constitute the complex now known as racism.

As is so often the case, the historical record offers less evidence than might be desired, but there is little that cannot be harmonized with the thesis that men and women have used differences of physique and culture to draw boundaries and exclude competitors whenever it has suited them to do so. In the early conflicts with the Spaniards Sir Francis Drake was ready to enter alliances with the Negro refugees from Spanish settlements who were called Cimarrons. There was little evidence of white prejudice then. But when the whites in seventeenth-century Virginia perceived the native Americans as a threat, or wanted their land, then the prejudice appeared. Edmund S. Morgan (1975, pp. 327, 331, 386) concluded that, to start with, English servants seem not to have resented the substitution of African servants for more of their own kind, but from the late 1660s the Virginia assembly deliberately set out to raise the status of lower-class whites by fostering contempt for blacks and native Americans. "Racism thus absorbed in Virginia the fear and contempt that men in England, whether Whig or Tory, monarchist or republican, felt for the inarticulate lower classes. Racism made it possible for white Virginians to develop a devotion to the equality that English republicans had declared to be the soul of liberty...." This was the era in which the institution of permanent black slavery was becoming established in the United States. The readiness of the English to use differences of physique and culture to this end may also have been influenced by the assumptions which they brought with them to the New World.

By the standards of the twentieth century, scarcely any Englishmen of the eighteenth century were racially conscious. A few who had returned to England after living in the West Indies might be so described, but their influence was limited. At that time the word race was rarely used either to describe peoples or in accounts of differences between them. Anthony J. Barker (1978) has studied the literature of this period more thoroughly than any other author. He reports that there was a theory of African inferiority at this time, but that it is not to be found in the works of the intellectuals. [...] When, after about 1787, the debate about the abolition of the slave trade started, it was conducted within a framework of existing knowledge. For the abolitionists the central issues were the doubtful morality and necessity of the trade. Only a handful of pro-slavery writers asserted that blacks were inferior; most pointedly rejected such views except in so far as they contended that only Negroes could work in extreme heat.

*****

One of the major eighteenth-century changes in the external conditions likely to influence racial thought was the Declaration of Independence of the United States in 1776. A majority of the whites chose to break away from the country with which they had previously identified themselves. They had to create a new sense of national identity. They decided that what should distinguish their nation would be political institutions designed to create a more perfect union, to establish a higher standard of justice and to insure domestic tranquility. Forgetting the Afro-Americans, some of them looked to the seventeenth-century radical belief that Anglo-Saxon institutions were the source of political liberty. This belief had been used to counter the claim of kings to rule by divine right and it was paralleled by a similar belief in France that freedom had been brought to the country from the Germany described by Tacitus. In France, in England, and in the United States, the first political use of a concept of race was in the context of struggles between whites, and it used race in the sense of lineage rather than type (Horsman, 1982; Poliakov, 1974).

New World slave owners had been aware from an early period that blacks did not suffer much from yellow fever and malaria, though these diseases devastated European populations (on the slave ships about 20 per cent of the crew died on each voyage). There were other diseases from which blacks suffered more severely, like cholera, tuberculosis, whooping cough, tetanus and some with a dietary origin (Kiple and King, 1981). These differences, together with the obvious tensions and conflicts of interest inherent in so unequal a relationship as that of slavery, might be expected to have encouraged theories of racial inequality. Therefore the judgement of a leading historian, George M. Fredrickson (1971, p. 43), is of particular interest. He has found that prior to the 1830s, although black subordination was widespread in the United States, and whites commonly assumed that Negroes were inferior "open assertions of *permanent* inferiority were exceedingly rare."

LINEAGE AND VARIETY CONFUSED

The academic study of racial relations has been dominated by scholars from the English-speaking world, and particularly by social scientists who have either grown up in the United States or have unconsciously taken over assumptions originating there. Scientific reasoning requires precise definitions, yet much research in this field has been based on the conceptions of race which are current among ordinary members of the North American public, relatively untouched by the studies which have exposed the cultural bias. Because of the economic power of the United States and the highly developed nature of its mass communications media, that country's folk definitions of race have been transmitted to other regions as if they represented universal categories within social science instead of reflecting the very special way in which relations between reds, whites and blacks developed in United States history. To start with, other languages lacked any words corresponding to the meaning of race in American English; they have had to find or devise translations, but the correspondence is not always very close. It is important, therefore, to examine the manner in which the word has acquired its present meanings.

Changes in the West European languages were closely linked. Colette Guillaumin (1972, p. 19), who has studied French usage, found that at the beginning of the nineteenth century there was an important change. She wrote "the term 'race' itself acquired the sense of human group as it lost its narrower sense of lineage." While race continued to mean lineage for many people (and indeed continues to the present day to retain that sense), it acquired the *additional* significance of designating a class or type of animal or human.

The change can be seen in Cuvier's great work *The Animal Kingdom* first published in Paris in 1817. Near the beginning is a section entitled "Variétés de l'espèce humaine" which starts:

> Quoique l'espèce humaine paraisse unique, puisque tous les individus peuvent se mêler indistinctement, et produire des individus féconds, on y remarque de certaines conformations héréditaires qui constituent ce qu'on nomme des *races*.

This usage, which made race and variety synonymous, seems to have worried Cuvier's first English translator, for in the 1827 London translation the last sentence appears as "... which constitute what are called *varieties*." In several of the passages where Cuvier wrote race, this translator put variety. Yet in the next English translation (published in New York in 1831) the sentence runs "... which constitute what are termed races" and "race" is used thereafter.

It is easy to understand how race and variety came to appear synonymous. To start with, in English and French writing, race was used to designate a lineage or a line of descent. Then, in natural history, people began to classify plants and animals, and named the least general classes genera, species and varieties. Similar specimens were classed together. They were similar because they were of common descent. So membership in a historically constituted unit (race) and membership in a classification made at a moment in time with little information about antecedents (genus, species or variety) seemed two ways of saying the same thing. That they were not may be clarified by a simple example. According to the Old Testament, Moses was a Levite who married a Midionite woman, Zipporah, who bore him two sons, Gershon and Eliezer. Later he married an Ethiopian woman (his brother and sister "spoke against him" for doing so). Imagine that this wife also bore him a son. That son would be just as much of the race of Levi as Gershon and Eliezer. But if some contemporary anthropologist had set out to classify the individuals, Moses, Gershon and Eliezer would have been accounted Semites and Moses' third son a hybrid; he would not have been assigned to the same "race" as Gershon, Eliezer and Moses, using race in the sense of variety.

*****

In 1784 Johann Gottfried von Herder in *Ideen zur Philosophic der Geschichte der Menschheit* had protested about those who

> have thought fit to employ the term races for four or five divisions, according to regions or origin or complexion. I see no reason for employing this term. Race refers to a difference of origin, which in this case either does not exist or which comprises in each of these regions or complexions the most diverse "races" (Herder, 1969, p. 284).

Kant criticized Herder for his "inadequate and unsympathetic treatment of race." Some (e.g. Dover, 1952) have argued that Herder's conception of the nation implied a distinctive variety of humanity with permanent and inherited characters of its own, and that this was more dangerous than the classifications he opposed. Whatever view be taken of this, the observations of Kant and Herder should have suggested to their contemporaries that an equation of "race" with "variety" was not to be taken for granted. After Cuvier's book had been translated, the English physician James Cowles Prichard noticed what was happening, and in 1836 he protested, "races are properly successions of individuals propagated from any given stock." He objected to the tendency to use the word "as if it implied a distinction in the physical character of a whole series of individuals" (quoted at greater length in Banton, 1977, p. 30). Prichard was respected as an authority on matters of race but his warning passed unheeded.

Thus it came about that race in English and French confused descent with phenotypical classification, though in both these languages the word continued to be used to denote commonality of descent and so was sometimes equated with nation as well. In Italian, the use of *razza* seems very similar, having on occasion the sense either of lineage or variety. German usage is not very different, with the addition that the same word covers what in English would be "breed"—as in *Hunderasse* (French also fails to differentiate breed from race). In Russian, the equivalent word is a nineteenth-century addition to the vocabulary, having the sense of variety and with less of the ambiguities of the West European languages. In the many languages which derive from Sanskrit, however, the possibilities for misunderstanding European usage seem greater. In Sanskrit the two words closest to "race" are *j tá* and *vaṉsá*, the former translated as "race, kind, sort, class, species," the latter as "pedigree or genealogy"; both are close to the sense of race as lineage and lack the taxonomic connotations of variety or sub-species. In Arabic, the word *unsur* seems close to race as lineage and would be used in a translation of a reference to "the ethnic minority problem," but there is in addition the word *jins*, corresponding to the Greek *genos* and translating race as variety. In Japanese, *jinshu* was probably introduced in the nineteenth century to translate race as variety, so that the language has three words: *shu* for species, *henshu* for variety and *jinshu* for a human race constituted by people sharing common physical characteristics; in the written form all these words share the character for seed. In Chinese, race can be translated by *renzhong* which, when written, combines two characters, one for "human" and the other for "species" or "type." Another possible translation is *zhongzu*, which combines the second character of renzhong with one representing class, or group with common characteristics, or, on its own, race or nationality. It would therefore seem possible that the confusion Cuvier failed to discourage has been spread to other languages.

The specialists consulted about the problem of finding equivalents for the different senses of race in English refer to the associations that words have because of the other connections in which they are used in the lives of the peoples who speak these languages.[1] Translation often causes difficulty, but it would appear that the possibilities of misunderstanding with respect to ideas of race and racial relations are greater than usual. Readers from outside West Europe and North America might bear this in mind when considering the loose way in which the word was used in some languages during the nineteenth and early twentieth centuries.

THE DOCTRINE OF RACIAL TYPES

*****

Faced with the evidence of human diversity, eighteenth-century scholars such as Buffon and Blumenbach, and their succesors like Samuel Stanhope Smith and Prichard, had inclined to the theory that all humans had a common origin (monogenesis), but hidden agencies associated with either their environments or their habits had caused them to diversify; some varieties had made greater progress because of their opportunities and social institutions; relations between varieties were seen in moral terms. By contrast, Cuvier had maintained that the differences had been the result of a great catastrophe, since which these had remained without change; ability to progress, and the character of inter-racial relations were determined by the inherent capacities of races.

The man who, in the United States, did most to develop the thesis that the different varieties of *homo* represented permanent types was the Philadelphian physician Samuel George Morton, but it is difficult to tell how far he was directly influenced by Cuvier. In 1830 Morton chose to deliver a lecture on the skulls of the five varieties identified by Blumenbach. Being unable to obtain sufficient skulls for his purpose, he started his own collection. To start with Morton was very cautious in the conclusions he drew, but he became bolder as his views gained support, and he lived in an environment in which many white Americans were ready to welcome a theory that both stated blacks to be inferior and advanced an explanation for it. Morton became the leader of a school which denied that blacks and whites were varieties of the species *homo*. They argued that *homo sapiens* was the genus and that it was divided into several species. Blacks and whites were separate species. [...] The question was whether these differences had a physical origin, implying permanent inferiority, or whether they had an environmental origin, in which case the backward peoples could be expected to catch up.

*****

The perspective which sees the efforts of Morton and his successors as the working out of one from a limited number of possible solutions to a problem within the field of natural history (though not only within that field), is strengthened by the evidence which shows very similar arguments to have been developed, almost independently and virtually simultaneously, in several other countries. Chronologically the first of the books to set out the typological view systematically was *The Natural History of the Human Species* (1848) by Charles Hamilton Smith, a retired English army officer who counted himself a disciple and friend of Cuvier's. Next came the Scottish anatomist, Robert Knox, another pupil of Cuvier's, who published a set of lectures, *The Races of Men*, in London in 1850. Then, in 1853–55, the four volumes of Count Arthur de Gobineau's *Essai sur l'inégalité des races humaines* was published in Paris; the first volume is the only one to have been translated into English and it is this which has attracted all the attention. Gobineau was apparently unacquainted with the work of the other typologists, though he had noticed Morton's table of the cranial capacity of skulls of different races when it was reprinted in a German book, and gave it a prominent place in his own argument. Next there appeared in Philadelphia in 1854 a very substantial work edited by J.C. Nott and G.R. Gliddon entitled *Types of Mankind*. Nott and Gliddon were much more aware of the work of like-minded contemporary scholars and they pulled the available arguments together.

It has been customary to refer to the writing of Smith, Knox, Gobineau, Nott and Gliddon as "scientific racism," yet their key concept was not race but type. One source of dispute about the definition of racism can therefore be avoided by referring to their school as that of racial typology. It should be noted that while these five authors agreed on some major propositions, there were differences between them, particularly with respect to the questions of hybridity and acclimatization.

*****

The line of argument developed by Morton, Knox and Nott is the true polygenesis, denying the religious belief that all humans were descended from Adam and Eve. Yet the differences among the typologists were small by comparison with the principles on which they agreed. They shared a belief that variations in the constitution and behaviour of individuals were the expression of differences between underlying types of a relatively permanent kind. In classifying these variations, they treated physical and cultural differences as equally characteristic of types. How people behaved was as relevant to classification as their size and shape. Obviously, descriptions and classifications of ways of behaving were far more subjective and liable to distortion than those based upon physical measurements, but the typologists were usually quite unconcerned about this.

*****

The typologists also agreed in seeing human groupings, including nations, as the expression of biological types and in interpreting racial antagonism in the same way. Some have seen their arguments as little more than the rationalization of personal prejudice, but this is a very superficial view. There were other writers in the middle years of the century, especially in the United States, who compiled volumes about the superiority of whites over blacks. The typological theory was more persuasive than such works because it was less particular. It claimed to account for the characters of all the races of the world by reference to principles which also explained the distribution of particular kinds of plants and animal life. It was a theory with considerable intellectual pretension, and, in a pre-Darwinian world, of some plausibility.

The typologists were passionately concerned with the affairs of their generation. For most it was important to resist the representatives of organized religion who claimed to determine the proper scope of scientific research. The European typologists were impressed by the revolutions of 1848. Knox saw them as the struggle of races and thought they demonstrated the truth of what he had been preaching. De Gobineau presented his *Essay* as a commentary upon the causes underlying the events of that year. Though there were upheavals overseas which would be seen in racial terms (like the American Civil War), the focus was upon problems nearer home (such as the conflict in Ireland). The whole thrust of typological reasoning was that the colonization of overseas territories was doomed to failure; Knox, for example, scorned "that den of all abuses, the office of the Colonial Secretary." The 1850s and 1860s were not a time when the British wished to expand their overseas possessions; indeed Gladstone's cabinet of 1868 is sometimes taken to mark the high point of *anti*-imperial sentiment. Not until later in the century is it worthwhile hunting for links between racial consciousness and imperialism.

In the United States, white Southerners were divided along class lines, but both classes defended slavery on Biblical grounds, leading Stanton (1960, p. 194) to conclude that "the South turned its back on the only respectable defence of slavery it could have taken up." This requires some qualification. For decades there had been a Southern Bourbon tradition which defended slavery as an institution independently of any question of racial difference. Non-slave holding whites disliked it. Some aspired to become slave holders themselves and many were anxious to protect and increase their privileges at the expense of black workers. With the extension of the suffrage in the 1830s to white males by the weakening of property-owning qualifications, the white workers' influence grew and the planter class had to adjust to their beliefs, demands and phobias (Fredrickson, 1971, pp. 69–70). In a changed political atmosphere what had earlier seemed an irreligious mode of reasoning got a more sympathetic welcome.

A FURTHER CONFUSION

By the late 1850s, therefore, discussion of racial issues displayed what to a later generation might appear a contradiction. On the one hand the word "race" had come into greatly increased use in English, French and other West European languages to refer to social units which would nowadays be designated peoples or perhaps nations. On the other hand, firstly, there was no agreement amongst natural historians or anthropologists about the definition of race, and, in particular, whether it was to be equated with species or variety. Secondly, those who had done most to draw attention to racial explanations within anthropology, the typologists who took the position of Knox and Nott, had argued that racial types were suited to their historical environments and could not acclimatize to new ones. Their doctrine contended that imperialism was folly. Thirdly, those within the typological school who most deviated from the "no acclimatization" principle, and were most inclined to argue for white superiority, were C.H. Smith and Gobineau. Smith was the least well-known of these authors and de Gobineau's four volumes made little initial impact. As Poliakov (1974, p. 206) writes, de Gobineau's views on race were resolutely ignored by all his French contemporaries except Ernest Renan and Taine, and they did not start to attract attention until they were taken up in Germany in the 1880s (but cf. Barzun 1965, pp. 61–77).

Why, then, was the idea of race so popular, and why did it become even more influential? Two considerations seem important. Firstly, the idea of race became associated with that of nation and it proved useful to nineteenth-century nationalist movements, perhaps because of the very confusion as to its meaning in natural history. Secondly, throughout the nineteenth century evolutionary thought was gathering strength, receiving a major boost from Darwin in 1859, though strongly associated in many people's minds with the works of Herbert Spencer. Throughout this period there were major problems concerning the means by which evolution might operate. Some of these could not be solved before the rediscovery in 1900 of the principles earlier formulated by Mendel, but important as that was, it was by no means the end of the story. The early Mendelians thought that the new experimental evidence had dealt a death blow to selection theory since a particulate theory of inheritance implied to them a discontinuity in evolution (Mayr, 1982, p. 547). Thus the confusion in the biological understanding of human variation in the latter part of the nineteenth century cannot be understood apart from the history of science. Biologists were confused because they were ignorant of principles which later generations regard as the true explanations, and such confusion is unavoidable.

NOTE

1. Colleagues at the University of Bristol have been most helpful in assisting me with this question. I would like to thank Rohit Barot, David Chambers, Michael Costello, D.H. Higgins, Richard Peace, Rodney Sampson and Frank Shaw. Professor J. Derek Latham wrote to me about usage in Arabic and Mrs Hiroko Minamikata about Japanese. I fear that I have been unable to integrate all that they kindly told me.

REFERENCES

Banton, M. 1977. *The Idea of Race.* London: Tavistock.

Barker, A.J. 1978. *The African Link: British Attitudes to the Negro in the Era of the Atlantic Slave Trade, 1550–1807.* London: Frank Cass.

Barzun, J. 1937. *Race: A Study in Modern Superstition.* New York: Harcourt Brace Revised ed. New York: Harper, 1965.

Bendyshe, T. 1865. The History of Anthropology. *Memoirs read before the Anthropological Society of London,* Vol. 1, pp. 335–458.

Blumenbach, J.F. 1865. *The Anthropological Treatises of Johann Friedrich Blumenbach....* London: Anthropological Society of London.

Buffon, G.L. 1971. *De l'homme.* Présentation et notes de Michèle Duchet. Paris: Maspero.

Dover, C. 1952. The Racial Philosophy of Johann Herder. *British Journal of Sociology,* Vol. 3, pp. 124–33.

Fredrickson, G.M. 1971. *The Black Image in the White Mind: The Debate on Afro-American Character and Destiny, 1817–1914.* New York: Harper and Row.

Fryer, P. 1984. *Staying Power: The History of Black People in Britain.* London: Pluto.

Gobineau, Comte de. 1853–55. *Essai sur l'inégalité des races humaines.* Paris: Firmin-Didot.

Greene, J.P. 1957. *The Death of Adam: Evolution and its Impact on Western Thought.* New York: Mentor Books.

Guillaumin, C. 1972. *L'idéologie raciste: genèse et langage actuelle.* Paris: Mouton.

Herder, J.G. von. 1969. *On Social and Political Culture* (selections). Cambridge: Cambridge University Press.

Horsman, R. 1982. *Race and Manifest Destiny: The Origins of American Racial Anglo-Saxonism.* Cambridge, Mass.: Harvard University Press.

Kiple, K.F., and King, V.H. 1981. *Another Dimension to the Black Diaspora: Diet, Disease, and Racism.* Cambridge: Cambridge University Press.

Knox, R., 1850. *The Races of Men: A Fragment.* 2nd ed. 1862, subtitled *A Philosophical Enquiry into the Influence of Race over the Destinites of Nations.* London: Renshaw.

Mayr, E. 1982. *The Growth of Biological Thought: Diversity, Evolution, Inheritance.* Cambridge, Mass.: Harvard University Press.

Morgan, E.S. 1975. *American Slavery, American Freedom: The Ordeal of Colonial Virginia.* New York: Norton.

Morton, S.G. 1839. *Crania Americana; or, a Comparative View of the Skulls of Various Aboriginal Nations of North and South America, to which is prefixed an Essay on the Varieties of the Human Species.* Philadelphia and London.

Morton, S. G. 1844. *Crania Aegyptica; or, Observations on Egyptian Ethnography, Derived from Anatomy, History, and the Monuments.* Philadelphia and London.

Nott, J.C., and Gliddon, S.G. 1854. *Types of Mankind; or, Ethnological Researches.* Philadelphia: Lippincott.

Poliakov, L. 1974. *The Aryan Myth: A History of Racist and Nationalist Ideas in Europe.* London: Chatto, Heinemann.

Smith, C.H. 1848. *The Natural History of the Human Species.* Edinburgh: Lizars.

Smith, S.S. 1810. *An Essay on the Causes of the Variety of Complexion in the Human Species.* 2nd ed., reprinted Cambridge, Mass.: Harvard University Press, 1965.

Stanton, W. 1960. *The Leopard's Spots: Scientific Attitudes towards Race in America, 1815–59.* Chicago: University of Chicago Press.

Williams, E.E., 1944. *Capitalism and Slavery.* Chapel Hill: University of North Carolina Press.

FURTHER READING

Banton, Michael. 1977. *The Idea of Race.* Cambridge: Tavistock Publications.

This book explores the intellectual context within which particular relationships between racial groups emerged. Further, it posits that one cannot separate the sociology of race relations from the history of the idea of "race." In order to understand a certain set of racial relations, one has to understand the knowledge base on which these are based, including how "race" is understood. Moreover, since the understanding of "race" has changed over history, one has to have a historical perspective in order to understand both the current knowledge base and the social relationships based on that knowledge. Chapters 3 and 5 in the book are particularly relevant, the former looking at race typology from 1850 onwards, and the latter at social Darwinism.

Graham, Richard, ed. 1990. *The Idea of Race in Latin America.* Austin: University of Texas Press.

This book is a collection of three chapters on Brazil, Argentina, Cuba, and Mexico, focusing on these societies between 1870 and 1940. The authors point out that following independence from Spain and Portugal, the people in these countries faced a contradiction of having highly mixed societies (ethnically speaking) and yet being dominated by European ideas around racism. The idea that "whitening" the nation through racial mixing would redeem them was dominant, thus demonstrating that racial thinking was hegemonic. This was often reflected in public policies.

Montagu, Ashley. 1965. *The Idea of Race.* Lincoln: University of Nebraska Press.

This short book is a collection of three chapters, two of which were lectures that the author had given in 1964. The book differentiates between the "social" and "biological" ideas of "race," touching on a variety of writers, including Englishman John Foxe who wrote in 1570, Aristotle in Greece, and the Arab scholar Ibn Khaldun who wrote in 1300. It talks about how the ideology of racism was developed with the combination of both aspects of "race," and he systematically argues against it from both social and biological perspectives.

Montagu, Ashley. 1951. *Statement on Race.* New York: Henry Schuman.

In the author's own words, this book is "an extended discussion in plain language of the UNESCO statement by experts on race problems." On July 18, 1950, following World War II and the Nazis' extermination of millions of Jews on the basis of alleged racial inferiority, a group of academics issued a statement establishing in writing that "race" is a myth, as are the notions that "race" determines mental aptitude, temperament, or social habits. In this book, the author amplifies each section of the statement and discusses the facts and findings on which it is based.

Robb, Peter. 1995. *The Concept of Race in South Asia.* Delhi: Oxford University Press.

This collection of essays, largely coming out of a workshop held in the School of Oriental and African Studies in London, explores whether there were homegrown varieties of racial discourses in pre-colonial South Asian texts and to what extent these interacted, co-mingled with, or resisted European race ideology in colonial times. Several chapters deal with British colonial writings applying racial classifications on Indian subjects. Other chapters explore to what extent racial perspectives may have influenced oppositional identities as articulated in pan-Islamic and nationalist texts in colonial India.

PART 1B

COLONIALISM AND THE CONSTRUCTION OF RACE

Although contemporary scholars from a wide range of disciplines have reached a general (if unstable) consensus that no solid scientific evidence exists explaining the validity of race, historically science played a crucial role in upholding and explaining the validity not only of the classification of different races, but also the notion that the white or Caucasian race was superior to all others; that is to say, contemporaneous science and philosophy defended the existing racial hierarchies of both Europe and North America. The four readings in this section examine some of the reasons why, as well as the different ways in which, Western nation-states attempted to colonize non-Western, largely non-Christian societies.

In his chapter entitled "Towards Scientific Racism," Gustav Jahoda traces the ways in which respected German and French thinkers of the late 17th and early 18th centuries grappled intellectually with the issue of whether the different races could reasonably be said to belong to different species, and if so, where the "black race" fell between Caucasians and apes. This debate gave rise to nascent theories about how to differentiate between races, including examining the shape of the skull and making determinations about the beauty, ugliness, or adaptability of different races (e.g., those who could tolerate pain or wide swings in temperature, or heal more quickly, or eat a wider range of less refined food were considered "backward," while those who suffered in physical situations were more likely to be seen as part of advanced or superior civilizations). In particular, Jahoda explains the ways in which the craniology developed by a French scientist (i.e., taking measurements of skulls and their facial angles) not only became the scientific standard for differentiating between the races, but also was positioned as support for the racial theories about the similarities between the black race and apes.

In "Antecedents of the Racial Worldview," Audrey Smedley argues that if various Western European nations (e.g., England, Spain, France, the Netherlands, etc.) were primarily responsible for the majority of global colonization projects, this was not necessarily a random occurrence. Rather, she argues that these countries (she focuses on England and Spain in particular) possessed several distinctive societal features and prior experiences that made them more likely to attempt to colonize indigenous peoples both economically and culturally. For example, Smedley demonstrates how England's early incorporation of capitalism with its associated ideologies of individualism and property, the racial ideologies formed in England's interactions with the Irish, England's burgeoning nationalism, and its particular brand of Christianity all conspired to form the economic and social bases for their imperial policies. Likewise, Smedley traces the ways in which features of the Inquisition era in Spain—a belief in the hereditary character of social status, a hardening of ethnic difference, and the growing intolerance of religious (but also cultural) diversity by the Spanish Catholic Church—served as a moral basis for Spain's colonial policies.

Spawning a distinctive field of literature after him, Edward Said argued that far from representing a true or accurate depiction of a particular region, "the Orient" instead constituted a systematic regime of representation within which Westerners thought about, came to "know," and ultimately attempted to colonize the diversity of indigenous nations in specific geographic spaces. Importantly, Said argues that Westerners' sense of the geographical regions they came to perceive as "the Orient" did not reflect any reality, but instead represented the prejudices and stereotypes that Westerners held about "Orientals." Said argues that over time certain sets of observations about the Orient solidified into natural or taken-for-granted truths (usually depicting the Orient as backward or deficient and Western society as dominant and superior). Said refers to this bedrock of truth that shaped the opinions of the vast majority of Orientalists (i.e., those who studied the Orient) as "latent Orientalism." Thus, despite the apparently diverse sets of views and knowledges produced with respect to the Orient (what Said refers to as "manifest Orientalism"), all writers relied in one way or another on a construction of the Orient as fundamentally different from—and inferior to—"the West."

Building on the theoretical insights of Said's *Orientalism*, Stuart Hall examines perhaps one of the most hallowed social constructs in the Western world, the very idea of "the West": its character, its boundaries, and its coherence as a subject of study and as a valid differentiating principle of societies. Specifically, Hall examines how a discourse of "the West" established itself in a seemingly natural differentiation against "the other" (for example, Said's "the Orient"). Hall underlines the importance of discourse as a crucial medium between the production of knowledge and the subsequent representation of reality. In other words, the very act of talking about and creating knowledge about something shapes the ways we understand and act upon it. For example, notions of beauty may differ drastically from region to region, differences that result from how they are embedded in different discourses. According to Hall, powerful discourses (like that of "the West") successfully reproduce themselves by borrowing from and folding within themselves earlier discourses.

Like Said, Hall makes the point that "the West" as a regime of knowledge relied heavily on archival documents, myth and folklore, travellers' tales, fictional writings, and government reports; each of these forms of knowledge played a role in how "the West" became constructed in government, intellectual circles, and the popular imagination. Also like Said, Hall emphasizes that with sufficient time and effort, certain ways of understanding and talking about the world can become so natural or taken for granted that they come to be seen as "true" and, in doing so, make it difficult for alternative understandings of the world to take root (in our society, for example, think about the difficulties for discourses that position beauty as "inner" to do battle with externalized, physical images of beauty).

CHAPTER 4

TOWARDS SCIENTIFIC RACISM

Gustav Jahoda

The debate in Germany reflected the changing climate of opinion, progressively tilting against the Enlightenment view of savagery as a stage in the evolution of humanity. The debate was wide-ranging, including Herder and Kant, but I shall concentrate on a small group of key figures in close contact, the most outstanding of whom was Blumenbach, whose views were diametrically opposed to those of Meiners, his colleague at the University of Gottingen. Meiners was a polygenist who wrote in defence of slavery, Blumenbach a monogenist who stressed the unity of the human species. Their personal styles were equally contrasting: Meiners a speculative philosopher with a heavy ideological commitment, Blumenbach a sober scientist concerned with empirical evidence.

There was also Soemmering, who had been a close friend of Blumenbach while they were undergraduates. Another friend of Soemmering's was Johann Georg Forster (1754–94), who while still in his teens had accompanied his father on Cook's second voyage. Blumenbach, it will be recalled, had been critical of Soemmering's book; but Soemmering's other friend, Forster, was much more ambiguous in his response, seemingly not wishing to offend. He declared that, not being an anatomist himself, he was not qualified to judge, but he suggested to Soemmering that he should mention the decisive argument for the humanity of the Negroes, namely their capacity for speech. Forster's views are set out most clearly in his critique of two essays by Kant on the subject of race. Accusing Kant of applying philosophical categories without reference to empirical reality, he warmly recommended Soemmering's book. Forster's adherence to the Great Chain is indicated by his reference to "the fruitful thought, that everything in creation is linked by small steps [Nuancen]" (Forster [1786] 1969, Vol. 2, p. 85). In a lengthy and rather convoluted passage he discussed the relationship between whites, blacks and apes in the series of animals on earth. It boils down to the statement that, though among the various human types blacks most closely resemble the apes, there remains a critical gap: "Thus an ape-like human is no ape" (p. 86). Forster was unable to make up his mind as regards monogeny or polygeny, but while uncertain about some issues he clearly abhorred slavery, making an emotional appeal against the animalization entailed by its practice.

As will already have become apparent, the major figure who stressed the full humanity of blacks was Johann Friedrich Blumenbach (1752–1840), professor of medicine and natural history, who is generally regarded as the founder of physical anthropology. He had become inspired by his teacher Buttner, who possessed a fine collection of naturalia and frequenty displayed at his lectures travel books with illustrations of exotic peoples. Blumenbach later assembled a famous collection of skulls, and throughout his life remained an avid reader of travel reports; but unlike many others, notably his colleague Meiners, Blumenbach was a critical reader. He went so far as to arrange the reports about particular peoples in chronological order, and compared them. He found quite striking contradictions and inconsistencies, noting also that if a work was regarded as a *locus classicus*, the tendency was merely to copy it (cf. Plischke 1937). Blumenbach had scant regard for the doctrine of the Great Chain, certainly treating it as inapplicable within the human species. Moreover, he was rather sceptical about a number of then current beliefs, such as the supposed "fact" that savage women give birth as easily as animals.

Blumenbach's major work was his *De generis humani varietate nativa* ([1795] 1865), which pioneered an empirical approach to the classification of races by the shape of the skull. He refuted some of Linnaeus' more extravagant notions, showing, for instance, that albinos are not a separate species but people who suffer from an infirmity that affects both skin and eyes. He also went to great trouble to investigate and disprove some of the stories used by Linnaeus to support his contentions.[1] Blumenbach did not devise any system of measurement but proposed a method of comparison whereby skulls, with the lower jaws removed, are placed on a surface and viewed from above, the so-called *norma verticalis*. In practice he made little use of his method and did not base his classification on it. The reason why it is important is that it led in the 19th century to the elaboration of the "cephalic index" (i.e. the ratio of the breadth of the skull to its length expressed as a percentage) by Anders Retzius (1796–1860), which subsequently became one of the main tools of craniology.

Of chief concern here are Blumenbach's views about racial differences, based on the study of both his extensive collection of skulls and of the contemporary travel literature. In his view, skull shapes suggest a division into five major races, namely Caucasian, Mongolian, Ethiopian, American and Malaysian. He enthused about the beauty and symmetry of a young female Georgian skull, which probably accounts for his view that the Caucasian is the highest type and also the original race from which others were subsequently derived by a process he called "degeneration." For him this term had no negative connotations, and he meant by it a diversification resulting from the influence of climatic and other factors that came to be transmitted by heredity. At the same time Blumenbach rejected any sharp dividing lines between such races, emphasizing the unity of humankind as a species:

> No variety of mankind exists, whether of colour, countenance, or stature, etc., so singular as not to be

> connected with others of the same kind by such an imperceptible transition, that it is very clear that all are related and only differ from each other in degree. ([1795] 1865, pp. 98–9)

It must be admitted that in his earlier writings Blumenbach had painted a rather unflattering portrait of the physical characteristics of "Ethiopians," as he had initially termed Africans; he described them variously as having a "knotty forehead," "puffy lips" and being often "bandy-legged." Later he radically shifted his position, possibly as a result of a personal encounter.[2] Certainly in his later years he made a point of getting to know Africans, reading the literature about them, and collecting and measuring African skulls. As a result, he criticized others who depicted blacks as inferior or even as a separate species, stressing that Africans have the same mental abilities and potential as the rest of humanity. He referred to "the good disposition and faculties of our black brethren" and devoted several pages to citing examples of black ability, concluding as follows:

> there is no so-called savage nation known under the sun which has so much distinguished itself by such examples of perfectibility and original capacity for scientific culture, and thereby attached itself so closely to the most civilized nations of the earth, *as the Negro*. (Blumenbach [1795] 1865, p. 312; emphasis in original)

Blumenbach was later extensively cited by writers such as the anatomist Tiedemann (1837), who were concerned to show that blacks are full members of the human family rather than intermediate between humans and apes. Blumenbach was strongly opposed to the teachings of Meiners, a defender of slavery, whom Soemmering had called "the beloved philosopher of our fatherland" (1784, p. xiii). The views propagated by Meiners were distasteful to Blumenbach, though as a colleague in Gottingen he attacked him only obliquely.

Christoph Meiners (1747–1816) described himself as "a teacher of wordly wisdom [Weltweisheit]", in other words a philosopher. He was a man of immense erudition who exerted considerable influence in his time. Like Vico, the ambitious Meiners wanted to found a "new science" dealing with the nature of man, his past and his future. Unlike Vico's, his teachings were fundamentally based on ideas of racial and sexual inequality and did not endure, though they were temporarily resurrected by Nazi race theorists. The wide range of his writings, and their reception, have been surveyed by Rupp-Eisenreich (1983), and I shall merely present some selected aspects relevant to my theme.

Nowadays Meiners usually rates only a cursory mention in histories of anthropology, focused on his idiosyncratic criteria for the classification of races. In his *Sketch of the history of mankind* (Meiners 1785) he proposed that "One of the most important characteristics of tribes and peoples is beauty or ugliness" (p. 43), claiming that only people of Caucasian stock (but excepting Slavs) deserve the epithet of beauty. While in this early work it was only one, albeit an important criterion for the classification of peoples, it later became for him *the* major one. In a subsequent lengthy article Meiners (1788) sought to document in detail the characteristics of the "ugly peoples." Those of mongoloid descent, he alleged, resemble "the feeble-minded or lunatics of our continent inasmuch as they have much thicker skulls and much larger heads" (p. 280). In American savages the hair grows almost down to their eyebrows; in China women are preferred whose eyes are as piggish [schweinsartig] as possible; the faces of Negroes have an apish appearance; and so on.

In other writings Meiners (1787) put forward a theory concerning what may be roughly translated as the "adaptability" of different peoples, with a strong accent on the animality of the "ugly races." Meiners started with the observation that humans have settled in the most diverse climatic conditions and utilize a wide range of foodstuffs, unlike animals confined to a narrow ecological range and limited to certain kinds of nourishment. Yet paradoxically humans are more sensitive to pain and adverse weather, suffer more illnesses and recover more slowly from injuries, and cannot cope with raw or indigestible foods.

While this is true of humans in general, there are substantial variations in adaptability among the different races of man:

> The more intelligent and noble people are by nature, the more adaptable, sensitive, delicate and soft is their body; on the other hand, the less they possess the capacity and disposition towards virtue, the more they lack adaptability; and not only that, but the less sensitive are their bodies, the more can they tolerate extreme pain or the rapid alteration of heat and cold; the less they are exposed to illnesses, the more rapidly their recovery from wounds that would be fatal for more sensitive peoples, and the more they can partake of the worst and most indigestible foods ... without noticeable ill effects. (Meiners 1787, pp. 211–2)

Belief in such hardiness of the backward races formed at that time part of the conventional wisdom, pushed by Meiners to greater extremes. For him the noblest race were the Celts, and he points out that they were able to conquer various parts of the world. Yet they are more sensitive to heat and cold, fall more easily prey to sickness, and their delicacy is shown by the fact that they are fussy about what they eat.

The Slavs are clearly an inferior race, less sensitive and more resistant to disease. This is illustrated by a series of anecdotes: for instance, Russians are content with rough food and can eat poisonous fungi without coming to any harm; other Slavs bake sick people in an oven and then make them roll in the snow—saunas were not fashionable in Meiners' Germany. Below the Slavs are the peoples of the Middle East and Asia, all limited in intelligence and of an evil disposition, which goes together with lack of adaptability and insensitivity.

Meiners went on to discuss the Negroes and Americans who "approach animals most closely." With regard to the

Negroes, he referred to the anatomical studies of Soemmering, expressing his conviction that it is not only their colour but their whole bodily structure that governs their capacities, dispositions and temperament. Thus in the Negroes the parts of the head concerned with the mastication of food, i.e. jaw muscles and bones, and teeth, are much bigger and stronger than those of Europeans. Their heads are larger, but the brain is smaller and the nerves coarser. They can eat practically anything, such as raw and stinking rotten meat. Their females give birth as easily as wild beasts. They are seldom ill, even in the West Indies where they are maltreated, and can endure any amount of pain "as if they had no human, barely animal, feeling." Meiners tells the story of a Negro, condemned to death by slow-burning fire; when his back was already half cooked, he asked for a pipe and smoked it placidly. Lest this evoke some admiration in the reader, Meiners added: "If one wanted to attribute this quiet endurance of [suffering] not to the lack of feeling of the thick-skinned and coarse-nerved Negro, but to his steadfastness, then one would have to rate [the lowest kinds of animals] more highly than the greatest heroes of antiquity and modern times" (1787, p. 230).

If the Negroes are bad, according to Meiners, the Americans are even worse. [...] Other confabulations abound: American skulls are so thick that, as the Spanish conquerors found, the best blades shatter on them. Their skin is thicker than that of an ox. They can walk naked in the hottest sun as well as the coldest winter. The Americas harbour the most gluttonous monsters—they can feed on all kinds of foul offal, drink the most polluted water and consume without ill effect vast quantities of alcohol that would kill the strongest beast. They live to a ripe old age, without diminution of their strength: one can see 100-year-old men jumping on to their horses as easily as the fittest youngsters. They seldom suffer illness, and make miraculous recoveries from the severest wounds. There is a lengthy account of the self-inflicted wounds of their endurance tests and their unbelievable cruelty to their enemies, described in lovingly grisly detail over several pages.

At the same time, the Americans are not only the most unfeeling of peoples, they are also the least adaptable: they cannot get used to other climates, food or modes of life. When the Jesuits brought Indians to their mission, they began to die in large numbers. They were, Meiners argued, quite unable to adapt to their changed circumstances, lapsing into a deadly melancholy. Examples of this kind abound, without any suggestion that European diseases might have been the cause. Here again Meiners seemed anxious lest the reader be led to draw the wrong conclusion, namely that the Americans are so happy in their way of life that depriving them of it kills them:

> one can only conclude from this that the unfeeling Americans are ... so lacking in adaptability that they are almost as little able as wild beasts to get used to another climate, and even more so to other kinds of food and modes of life. (Meiners 1787, p. 246)

Meiners greatly expanded on these and other themes in a large work entitled *Researches on the variations in human nature* (1815). It contains more alleged anatomical details of various races, and their supposed sexual peculiarities are examined in prurient detail. For instance, men in north-east Asia are said to have very small genitals and their women, by contrast, very large ones; owing to this misfit, the women disdain their own men, preferring Russians and Cossacks. In addition, American (Indian) women and Negresses are said to have always shown a decided preference for Europeans; this was a stereotypical theme in the (male-authored) literature on blacks. Meiners failed to explain why black women should be so keen on white men, given the fact that he dwelt in some detail on the extraordinarily large and "animal-like" penis of Negro males. Generally he maintained that unduly weak (as among American Indians) and unduly strong sexual drives (as among Africans, Chinese, Japanese and peoples of the South Sea Islands) were equally bad—only Europeans have it just right.

I should make it clear once again that the above is certainly not a balanced account of Meiners' approach. His writings contain many sensible and perceptive passages; for instance, some of his comments on the abilities and shortcomings of various peoples foreshadow topics of study by 20th-century cross-cultural psychologists.[3] Nonetheless, the notion of the permanent inferiority and animal-likeness of the "ugly races" runs as a constant thread through most of his writings. His reading was wide but quite uncritical; furthermore, he was apt to select from the mass of material which he perused those aspects that fitted in with his thesis.

I have dealt with Meiners at some length, since his ideas were the subject of lively, often critical discussions. He was read by the young Hegel, and probably contributed to Hegel's demonic image of Africa, which he described as a place where one can find the most terrible manifestations of human nature (Hegel [1832] 1992, Vol. 12, pp. 120–9).

REACTION IN FRANCE: VIREY AND THE HUMAN-LIKENESS OF APES

The writings of Meiners, with their strident ideological message, were widely understood as applying the lessons of history to the contemporary situation. In a French translation of one of his works the preface refers to the decadence of Rome with its "multitudes of slaves and foreigners ... in such a corrupting atmosphere they degraded by their admixture the entire mass of the people" (cited in Rupp-Eisenreich 1983, p. 135). A similar line was taken by the Nazi historian von Eickstedt who wrote in praise of Meiners, coupling his name with that of Virey and others like him. There is in fact evidence that Virey was familiar with the writings of Meiners (Rupp-Eisenreich 1985). However, apart from the denigration of savages, their approaches to the issue did not have much in common. Unlike Meiners, Virey was a believer in the Great Chain and argued most vigorously in the style of Long and White. Moreover, in order to render his often bizarre arguments of the close relation between blacks and apes more plausible, he took over some old notions about the supposedly remarkable accomplishments of apes.

Jules Virey (1775–1847) was a naturalist and professor of pharmacy, a follower of Rousseau and a fervent admirer of Buffon.[4] Nonetheless he was, unlike Buffon, a polygenist who believed that humans consist of separate species. His *Histoire naturelle du genre humain* was essentially a work of popularization that achieved a wide circulation. In the first edition, published in 1801, he, rather like Meiners, dichotomized humans into fair and dark; in later ones he used Camper's "facial angle" to categorize races, a notion to which I shall return. In the earlier editions there are passages indicating that his imagination ran along much the same lines as Long's, as, for instance, in the passage [...] about the sexual congress in darkest Africa between Negresses and satyrs. That passage was left out in later editions, which abandoned the poetry of dark passions and assumed a somewhat more detached tone. Nonetheless, Virey voiced some quaint ideas, such as his belief that colours influence the character of everything in organic nature. Thus he said that white animals are mostly innocent and guileless, while black ones are violent and nasty; this, he suggested, applied even to flowers: white ones are harmless, and dark ones are often poisonous. This comes oddly from someone who practised pharmacy!

According to Virey, Negroes are deficient in "morality," a term used by him in a very broad sense to include thought and knowledge, political and religious ideas. While lacking in moral relationships with each other, they have relatively more physical ones:

> negresses abandon themselves to love with transports unknown anywhere else: they have large sexual organs, and those of the negroes are proportionately voluminous; for generally, as the organs of generation acquire great activity among humans, so the intellectual faculties suffer a loss of energy. (Virey 1824, Vol. II. pp. 45–6)

This "energy theory," as I will show in due course, gained further prominence later in the 19th century. Elsewhere Virey contended that Negro intelligence is less active because of "the narrowness of the cerebral organs." For the same reason the heads of their infants are smaller, which accounts for the ease with which savage women give birth.

Virey constantly harped on the "animality" of blacks:

> Moreover, the negro brutally abandons himself to the most villainous excesses; his soul is, so to say, more steeped in the material, more encrusted in animality, more driven by purely physical appetites....
>
> If man consists mainly of his spiritual faculties, it is incontestable that the negro is less human in this respect; he is closer to the life of brutes, because we see him obeying his stomach, his sexual parts, in sum his senses, rather than reason. (Virey 1834, Vol. 2, p. 117)

The most extreme degradation, according to Virey, is to be found among the Hottentots, whose physique he characterized as being similar to that of the great apes. Their rudimentary speech, almost like the clucking of guinea-fowl, is close to the muffled cluckings of orang-utans. They, together with Papuans, display "extreme resemblances" to apes. Actually the Negroes themselves, averred Virey, recognize their parentage with the apes, whom they regard as savage and lazy Negroes.

The counterpoint to this tirade is a chapter on orang-utans, spelling out in detail their human-like behaviour as supposedly noted by observers. They easily learn things like eating at table using cutlery and a tooth-pick, making their beds, and even playing the flute. They can be taught to dress themselves, tie their shoe-laces, and the females have a well-developed sense of modesty. As regards modesty, if this were true, then by Virey's own logic female apes would be closer to white women than black ones! At any rate, for him all this proved the family resemblance between the higher apes and what for him was the lowest form of humanity. Virey conceded at one point that he did not pretend blacks and apes were of the same species, but on the very same page also commented:

> when one notes how much the orang-outan shows the signs of intelligence, how much his morals [moeurs], his actions, his habits are analogous to those of negroes, how much he is susceptible to education, it seems to me that one cannot disagree that the least perfect of blacks is very close to the first of the apes. (Virey 1834, Vol. 2, p. 118)

Virey's strategy was to humanize the anthropoid apes and dehumanize the blacks (see figure 4.1). As might have been expected, Virey's views, like those of Long,[5] were well received and extensively borrowed across the Atlantic, since they provided ammunition for defenders of slavery. For example, Gwenebault (1837), who acknowledged his debt to Virey, referred to the "extreme lasciviousnes of negro women ... their simple and animal mode of living" (p. 94). He conveyed the impression that practically everything they do is animal-like, including even their manner of resting: "Europeans sit on chairs, Asiatics cross-legged on earth or carpets, but the Negro either in Africa or New Guinea ... remains squatting on his haunches, like the monkey" (p. 106). Apart from his success in America, Virey was also for a time widely read in France, and his work went through several editions. But many of his views were so patently absurd that it was difficult to take him seriously, and his writings later fell into well-deserved oblivion.

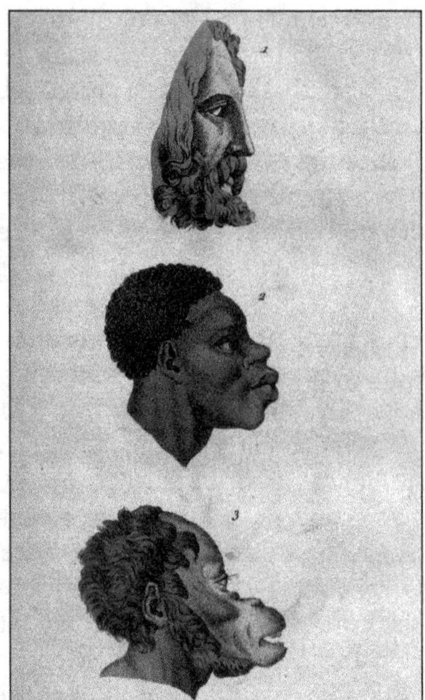

Figure 4.1 A classical Greek profile juxtaposed with those of a "Negro" and an ape. Note the incipient "muzzle" of the "Negro," approximating to that of the ape (i.e. progressively lower "facial angle").
Source: Virey (1824).

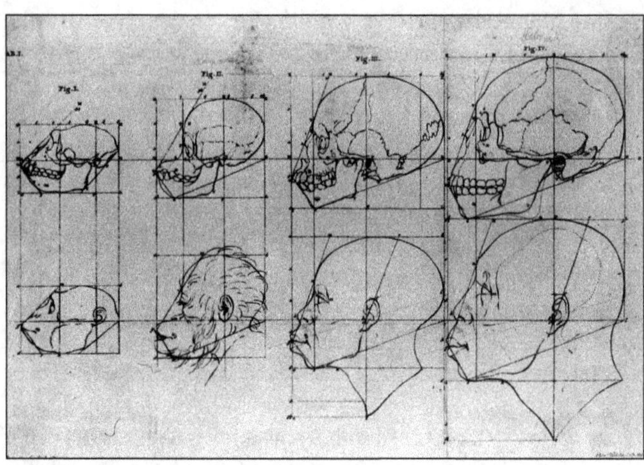

Figure 4.2 Camper's illustration of "facial angles"
Source: Camper (1794).

CAMPER'S "FACIAL ANGLE"

The mode of classification that came to be adopted by Virey, and subsequently many others, had been devised by Camper. Previous classifications of human types had been based on criteria that were largely arbitrary, and there had been no clear way of deciding between them. The work of Camper from the 1760s onwards seemed to offer the promise of an objective criterion which involved measurement, the hallmark of science. Camper is often still only remembered as the man who first introduced quantification[6] thereby paving the way for the craniological measures (see figure 4.2) that became ever more elaborate as the 19th century progressed (e.g. Baker 1974; Curtin 1965).

While the "facial angle" as such has often been mentioned and explained, and will therefore be only summarily described in a footnote,[7] an important aspect of the story is less well known, namely the fact that the method introduced by Camper came to be interpreted in a manner he had never intended, and that was quite contrary to his own views (Visser 1990). In effect, it was hijacked by those who believed in, and wished to prove, the existence of a racial hierarchy from the noble European to the lowest savage.

Petrus Camper (1722–89), a versatile Dutchman, was not only an outstanding comparative anatomist but also an artist and sculptor of great skill. A staunch monogenist, he emphasized in his lectures the unity of mankind, and the relative superficiality of differences he attributed to environmental causes. This did not mean a lack of interest in the varieties of forms encountered in nature. On the contrary, in his posthumously published *Works* (1794) he recounted his fascination, from an early age, with differences between animals and human races. He also studied theories of art from the Greeks onwards, noting that most European artists painted Negroes with the faces of Europeans.

Camper looked for some principle according to which the appearances of various human groups could be captured, which would also serve as a guide for their correct artistic representation. At the same time he was concerned with the concept of beauty, whose most perfect expression he saw in classical Greek sculpture. Convinced that the artists of antiquity must have worked to some abstract rules which enabled them to achieve the perfect harmony of their creations, he wanted to rediscover them. Concentrating on heads, he collected skulls of people of different ages, sexes and races. Comparing their various features, he arrived at a structural characteristic that seemed to provide the key. Accordingly, he devised a method for the quantitative assessment of the structure of the skull, whose rationale was both aesthetic and scientific.[8]

Camper identified "facial angle" as a major source of error in the representation of different races, an idea he presented to the Academy of Drawing in 1770. He also noted that facial angles displayed a regular decline from Greek and Roman busts (90–95°) to European (80°), Negro (70°), and orangutan (58°) heads. Thus the angle could be said to correspond to a scale from ape via savage to civilized, and Camper was of course well aware of that. In discussing some of his comparative illustrations he commented:

> The assemblage of cranium, and profiles of two apes, a negro and a Calmuck, in the first place, may perhaps excite some surprise: the striking resemblance between

> the race of Monkies and of Blacks, particularly upon a superficial view, has induced some philosophers to conjecture that a race of blacks originated from the commerce of the whites with ourangs and pongos; or that these monsters, by gradual improvements, finally became man. (Camper 1794, p. 32)

In writing this, Camper was merely mentioning speculations that were widespread in his time, and went on to refute them forcefully. He denied that the range of facial angles corresponds to a scale of superiority–inferiority, and never linked it to the Great Chain. Camper specifically stated that the resemblance between Negro and ape as regards a projecting jaw is merely superficial, and that there is an unbridgeable gulf between them, while there is no significant difference between whites and blacks. He also stated that everybody was descended from a single pair, it being immaterial whether that pair was black or fair. Subsequent changes, he suggested, were brought about by environmental factors such as climate, nutrition, manners, customs and education. Camper's work, originally published in 1792, received much acclaim and was soon translated into French, German and English. The only critical voice was that of Blumenbach who had two reservations: first, he objected to the facial angle being treated as the only criterion for racial classification, which Camper in fact had never claimed; second, he questioned the validity of the method because of the arbitrariness of the baseline, a critique that was justified.

The subsequent fate of Camper's ideas was an unfortunate one, since in spite of his explicit disclaimers, the regular gradient from Greek perfection to apes was later taken by many of his successors to reflect a fundamental biological feature. Visser (1990) suggests a number of reasons why this occurred. Well before publication, Camper's work had become known through informal channels, and he himself described it personally to Blumenbach and Soemmering among others. One important source of distortion was a summary of his 1770 address prepared by the then director of the Academy of Drawing. In this summary facial angles were directly linked to the doctrine of the Great Chain, and as the summary was widely circulated, also in translation, its misrepresentation gained broad currency. Moreover, it appealed to those who believed in the affinity between blacks and apes. This was true for Soemmering, White and Virey, who used this distorted version to bolster their own views. Opponents of the ape-connection theory, such as James Cowles Prichard (1786–1848), mistakenly criticized Camper on the same basis. But it was the adoption and elaboration of that version by the great Cuvier that had the most fateful consequences. The importance of Camper's "facial angle" is evident from the fact that it was applied by craniologists for most of the 19th century, and Broca (1874) devised a so-called "goniometer" for its more accurate measurement. It was not until a Congress of the German Anthropological Society in 1882 that a revised eye–ear plane came to be substituted for Camper's "facial angle" (Hoyme 1953).

Hence, paradoxically, a measure devised by a convinced monogenist for the purpose of analysing aesthetic principles became a prime tool in the hands of 19th-century race theorists for demonstrating the proximity between blacks and apes. The manner in which this occurred will be the topic of the next chapter. [...]

NOTES

1. He was able to establish that the famous "Wild Peter" had been the mute mental defective child of a widower, turned out of his home by a new stepmother. Or again, he rebuked with gentle wit some of Linnaeus' categorizations: The custom of making women thin by a particular diet is very ancient, and has prevailed amongst the most refined nations, so politeness and respect forbid us to class it, with Linnaeus, amongst deformities. (Blumenbach [1795] 1865, p. 128)
2. During a visit to Switzerland, he saw from behind a female form which struck him by its harmonious and beautiful shape. He spoke to the girl, who turned her face on Blumenbach, and he saw to his stupefaction the features of an African lady.... Blumenbach was enchanted ... [and his] delight reached its height when he realised that the girl was not only beautiful, but also witty and sensible. (Debrunner 1979, pp. 142–3)
   Blumenbach seems to have had quite a flirtation with her, and the experience clearly made a great impression on him.
3. Such topics include what Meiners described as their lack of visual judgement, which his examples indicate relate to what would now be called visual space perception (1815, Vol. 3, p. 222). On the other hand, he mentioned their good visual memory (pp. 224–5), and certain manual skills. Yet overall he asserted their complete unfitness for arts and sciences (p. 223).
4. For a detailed account of Virey's life and teachings cf. Benichou and Blanckaert (1988).
5. It is not clear whether Virey had actually read Long; although he referred to some publications in English, I have not come across any direct reference to Long. Nonetheless, in view of the prevalence of scholarly exchanges at that period it is virtually certain that Virey was familiar with Long's work.
6. At about the same time Daubenton (1764) proposed a measure of the angle of the head in both animals and men, relating to the position of the hole at the base of the skull ("Le grand trou occipital") through which the nerves pass into the brain. According to Barzun (1938), "Daubenton was measuring in degrees the position of the head on top of the spinal column and correlating the measure of that angle with the amount of will-power in the several races" (p. 52). This was not in the *Mémoire* I consulted, nor was I able to trace any other one where it appeared.

7. The method which Camper devised may be briefly outlined as follows. He placed a skull in a position where the orifices of the ears and the lowest part of the nasal aperture were level, and this he somewhat arbitrarily designated as the horizontal. He then drew a line between the forehead and the foremost part of the front teeth, ignoring any intersection with the nasal bones. The angle between those two lines came to be known as the "facial angle." A high angle is one where the forehead is more or less on a vertical line with the chin, while a low value indicates a forward projection of the jaw in relation to the cranium, a characteristic that came to be known as "prognathism" (cf. Baker 1974; Cowling 1989; Curtin 1965).
8. For more detail cf. Blanckaert (1987) or Gould (1991).

REFERENCES

Baker, J.R. 1974. *Race*. London: Oxford University Press.

Barzun, J. 1938. *Race: A study in modern superstition*. London: Methuen.

Benichou, C., and C. Blanckaert. *Julien-Joseph Virey*. Paris: Vrin.

Blanckaert, C. 1988. Les "vissitudes de l'angle facial" et les débuts de la craniométrie. *Revue de Synthèse* 4e série, No. 3–4, p. 417.

Blumenbach, Johann Friedrich. [1795] 1865. *The anthropological treatises of Johann Friedrich Blumenbach*, trans. and ed. Thomas Bendyshe. London: The Anthropological Society.

Campers, Petrus. 1794. *The works of the later Professor Camper*, trans. T. Cogan. London: Dilly.

Cowling, M. 1989. *The artist as anthropologist*. Cambridge: Cambridge University Press.

Curtin, P.D. 1965. *The image of Africa*. London: Macmillan.

Daubenton, M. 1764. Mémoire sur les différences de la situation de grand trou occipital dans l'homme et dans les animaux. *Mémoires de l'Académie des Sciences* 1 (September).

Debrunner, H.W. 1979. *Presence and prestige: Africans in Europe*. Basel: Basler Afrika Bibliographien.

Forster, Georg. [1786] 1969. Noch etwas über die Menschenrassen. In *Wekre* (4 vols.). Frankfurt: Insel.

Gould, S.J. 1991. Petrus Camper's angle. In *Bully for Brontosaurus*. London: Hutchinson Radius.

Gwenebault, J.H. 1837. *The natural history of the Negro Race*. Dowling: South Carolina.

Hegel, Georg Wilhelm Friedrich. [1832] 1992. *Vorlesungen über die Philosophie der Gerschichte*. In *Werke*, Vol 12. Frankfurt-arn-Main: Suhrkamp.

Hoyme, L.E. 1953. Physical anthropology and its instruments: an historical study. *Southwestern Journal of Anthropology* 9: 408–30.

Long, Edward [under pseudonym "A Planter"]. 1772. *Candid Reflection upon a judgement ... on what is commonly called the Negroe-Cause*. London.

———. 1774. *History of Jamaica*. 3 vols. London.

Meiners, Christoph. 1785. *Grundriss der Geschichte der Menschheit*. Lerngo: Meyer.

———. 1787. Ueber die grosse Verschiedenheit der Biegsamkeit und Unbiegsamkeit, der Härte und Weichheit der verschiedenen Stämme, und Racen der Menschen. *Göttingisches Magazin* 1: 210–46.

———. 1788. Einige Betrachtungen über die Schönheit der menschlichen Bildung un über den Hang aller hässlichen Völker, sich noch mehr zu verhässlichen. *Göttingisches Magazine* 2: 270–92.

———. 1815. Unter Suchungen über die Verschied enheiten der Mrnschennaturen. 3 vols. Tübingen: Cotta.

Plischke, H. 1937. *Johann Friedrich Blumenbach's Einfluss auf die Entdeskungreisenden seiner Zeit*. Hörtingen: Vandenhoeck & Ruprecht.

Rupp-Eisenreich, B. 1983. Des choses occultes en histoire des sciences humanines: Le destin de la "science nouvelle" de Christoph Meiners. *L'Ethnographie* LXXIX: 131–83.

———. 1985. Christoph Meiners et Joseph-Marie de Gérando: Un chapitre du comparatisme anthropologique. In D. Droixhe and P.-P. Jossiaux (eds.), *L'homme des Lumières et la découverle de l'autre*. Brussels: Université Libre de Bruxelles.

Soemmering, Samuel Thomas. 1784. *Ueber die körpliche Verschiedenheit de Negers vom Europaer*. Frankfurt.

Tiedermann, F. 1837. *Das Hirn des Negers mit dem des Europäers und Orang-Outans nerglichen*. Heidelberg: Winter.

Virey, Jules J. 1801. *Histoire naturelle du genre humain*. 2 vols. Paris.

———. 1824. *Histoire naturelle du genre humain*. 3 vols. Brussels: Wahlen.

———. 1834, *Histoire naturelle du genre humain*. 3 vols. Brussels: Hauman.

Visser, R. 1990. Die Rezeption der Anthropologie Petrus Campers. In G. Mann and F. Dumont (eds), *Die Natur des Menschen*. Stuttgart: Fischer.

White, Charles. 1799. *An account of the Regular Gradation in Man*. London: Dilly.

CHAPTER 5

ANTECEDENTS OF THE RACIAL WORLDVIEW

Audrey Smedley

Certain features of European societies and their experiences during the explorations of the fifteenth through the seventeenth centuries help us to understand the source of their varying attitudes toward human differences. Some of the major influences on the development of European ideas and values were their previous historical contacts (or lack thereof) with non-European peoples; the attitudes derived from strongly held religious beliefs; a growing national ethnocentrism, particularly in England and Spain; and a generalized image of the natural and social world in terms of hierarchy. This seminal stage in the evolution of a racial worldview is reflected in the emergence of certain cultural predispositions and elements of thought in Europe during the several centuries before the late eighteenth-century revolutionary era.

For the English, some of the seeds of a racial worldview were in place long before they encountered peoples in the New World and in Africa who were dramatically different from themselves. In this chapter, after a discussion of some general characteristics of this period, we will look at several specific events and circumstances of English life and sociopolitical experiences that affected their views of other peoples. Because the English drew some of their cultural cues in the New World from the Spanish, we will also briefly consider aspects of Spanish culture that influenced certain practices toward non-Europeans in the New World.

THE AGE OF EUROPEAN EXPLORATION

In the fifteenth century the northern Europeans, and the peoples of the British Isles in particular, had a very limited direct knowledge of the world. Few of them had traveled even to the southernmost regions of the Eurasian continent, although political and commercial intercourse had increased since the Crusades. Although many influences had percolated into southern Europe from the East and especially from North Africa, virtually everything that European savants knew about these regions was encompassed within the stock of scripturally based knowledge, was draped in fairy tales and myths, or came from bits and pieces of theories derived from the newly discovered writings of the ancients. As Margaret Hodgen (1964) has emphasized, "The Renaissance and Reformation were only in part periods of dazzling enlightenment. They were streaked and furrowed with inherited ignorance, confusion, and traditionalism" (359).

During the Crusades, roughly the eleventh through the thirteenth centuries, thousands of Europeans, mostly men, had converged on the islands of the eastern Mediterranean and had attacked towns in the Near East. Those who survived the many battles and returned home brought new tastes and knowledge of Eastern cultures to Europe. Their experiences contributed to the profound social and economic changes that were already beginning to take place in Europe. Beyond the Crusaders, there were very few individuals, men such as the Polos (Marco Polo and his father and uncle), Daniel of Kiev, Benjamin of Tudela, John de Piano Carpini, and Lancelot Mallocello, who for various reasons ventured far beyond the then known boundaries of Europe.

The details of the adventures and travels of such men did not become widely known. With the general level of literacy low, communication between intellectuals, religious and political leaders, commercial travelers, geographers, merchants, and adventurers was quite random and slow, especially before the invention and widespread use of the printing press. Still, many Europeans, especially in the cities and port towns, through rumors and hearsay, heard about bizarre and extraordinary peoples and customs. The often exaggerated tales revealed to them news about the "heathen Mohammedans" and "Turks," and even stories of a fabled black king named Prester John from some strange land beyond the Mediterranean, who some historians later thought might have been the king of Ethiopia.

Southern Europeans, however, were less isolated and more sophisticated about the diversity of peoples and cultures of the Old World. The Mediterranean world itself from time immemorial had seen an intermingling of peoples from Europe, Asia, and Africa. In what are now Spain and Portugal, congeries of Islamic peoples (which included Arabs, Egyptians, Berbers, Carthaginians, Libyans, and others) had invaded from North Africa and settled as early as the beginning of the eighth century. The various waves of invaders, immigrants, soldiers, sailors, merchants, slaves, scholars, and religious leaders helped to keep viable a huge intercommunication zone. Complex networks of trade and travel not only existed among the peoples of the lands bordering the Mediterranean but also connected some of the peoples of western Africa and the Sudan zone, the eastern Mediterranean, the Saudi Arabian peninsula, East African trading cities, the Iranian plateau, and parts of India and China. Indeed, although northern Europeans tended to languish in relative isolation during the Middle Ages, this was a period of advanced development for many of the peoples of the Islamic world.

Famous Muslim travelers of this period covered even more territory than did their European counterparts. Al-Masudi traveled in India, Sri Lanka, China, Russia, Persia, and Egypt as early as the tenth century. Al-Idrisi, a geographer and cartographer of great repute, traversed throughout North Africa and Asia Minor. In the process he compiled a description of the known world and created a map that was still used in eighteenth-century Europe. He was the first of the great geographers to show that the world was round, and this in the early twelfth century. Al-Idrisi's renown was such that he was commissioned by the Norman king of Sicily to prepare a comprehensive geography of the world.

Perhaps the best known of the Islamic travelers was Ibn Battuta, a fourteenth-century Moroccan who traveled from West Africa to what is now Sumatra and the Indonesian islands, leaving excellent descriptions of great states, from the empire of Mali in West Africa to those of India and China. What he had to say about the world was of vital importance to some Europeans, both for scholars and commercial travelers. Yet his works lapsed into obscurity with the change in the focus of attention toward Atlantic exploration. Interest in them did not revive until the mid-twentieth century when scholars experienced a reinvigorated concern for Africa and for the precolonial history of its people. Battuta's understanding and tolerance of other cultures, as well as his relatively objective approach toward the reconstruction of human history, had to lie in abeyance until the era of modern anthropological and historical inquiry.

Some Europeans, nevertheless, benefited from the knowledge that Islamic scholars had about the world, from the translations that made Greek and Roman scholarship again available, as well as from the numerous elements of technology originated and/or transmitted by the Islamic world. The great scholar Ptolemy's *Geography*, with its principles of calculation by latitude and longitude, was rediscovered and translated early in the fourteenth century and generated great excitement in some circles. Even so, the knowledge of peoples and cultures outside Western Europe, for the vast majority of educated people, was acquired second and third hand and, as we shall see, was always filtered through the prism of European religious beliefs, myths, legends, and social values.[1]

Those Europeans with the most direct knowledge of the cultural and physical diversity of humankind—the peoples of Spain, Portugal, southern Italy, and the islands of the Mediterranean—had experienced a heterogeneity of peoples and cultures long before the Age of Discovery. Spaniards, particularly in the urban centers, had interacted with Africans and Middle Easterners of many ethnic backgrounds. Among their conquerors, the Moors (a term taken from the Almoravid invasion of the eleventh century) consisted of many people from North and West Africa, where the religiously inspired movement had congealed. From as far south as the Senegal River, the leaders of the Islamic jihads, or Holy Wars, had conscripted followers who were eager to spread the words of Muhammad. Swarthy sailors of Arab dhows from the coastal areas of southern Arabia and eastern Africa were seen as far north as the western coasts of France.

Columbus's epic voyage to the New World was part of an ongoing push westward for new routes to the East. Although historians have identified his voyages as among the first and most famous, there were numerous others that took advantage of new sailing techniques to venture into unknown regions. In 1494 the pope divided all of the newly discovered, yet unexplored, "heathen" lands of the world between Spain and Portugal, which provided great impetus to Spanish and Portuguese adventurers as well as to those of other nationalities. Pedro Alvares Cabral claimed what is now Brazil for Portugal in 1500. For Spain, Amerigo Vespucci explored much of Central America and Mexico beginning in 1497, and Alonso de Ojeda established a Spanish settlement in Panama in 1508. Ponce de Léon, Balboa, Gomés, Magellan, Cortés, de Soto, and Pizarro are merely the more well known of what was to become a vast army of "conquistadors" who explored the New World and gathered much of its riches during the first half of the sixteenth century.

Within the first century of the discoveries, Europeans had established themselves permanently in new colonies. Each group brought with them their different experiences with strangers and their different perceptions of and beliefs about the nature of humanity. It was the Roman Catholic church with its focus on the papacy, its heritage from ancient Rome, and its stress on the salvation of souls that dominated the Spanish and Portuguese settlements. But, as we shall see later, northern Europeans, especially the English, brought unique historical experiences and quite different cognitive values that governed their views of the native peoples they encountered.

THE RISE OF CAPITALISM AND THE TRANSFORMATION OF ENGLISH SOCIETY

English society in the sixteenth and seventeenth centuries experienced much turmoil connected with massive social, economic, religious, and political changes. The Protestant revolution and subsequent political developments of the sixteenth century enhanced the power of the monarchy and created divisions and conflict among the nobles, gentry, and aristocracy. In the seventeenth century two major revolutions transformed the monarchy and led to the concentration of power at the highest levels in the hands of Parliament, representing the triumph of republican ideology over the values of divine kings and absolute monarchy.

The greatest changes were economic. Historians have widely held that the sixteenth century also marked the gradual demise of feudal society and the rise of early capitalism. Capitalism evolved as a new economic system both in England and in western Europe, particularly in the Netherlands. It was complex, often drastic, and multifaceted in that it had implications for all aspects of culture and society. Dramatic and irreversible changes in social organization and values, in politics, and in attitudes toward wealth and property took place. According to many scholars, the major elements of this process were the rise of free wage labor, the separation of this labor from the land and from the means and instruments of economic production, and the transformation of both labor and land into commodities exchanged on a widening world market.[2]

It was the emergence of a "bourgeois" class whose increasing wealth was based on commerce, trade, and finance that was to leave the greatest legacy. A largely urban middle class composed of merchants in the growing overseas trade, financiers, bankers, shopkeepers, artisans, manufacturers, and industrialists who serviced them took form, eventually creating a life-style of vast material consumption and challenging the gentry and the nobility for influence in government. Some wealthy merchants obtained large estates, purchased royal titles (such as knighthoods and baronetcies), and even married some of their offspring into the aristocratic class. An entrepreneurial spirit characterized town life, and even the younger sons of the gentry, prevented by the rule of primogeniture from inheriting their fathers' estates, often turned to commerce and trade and helped to provide a veneer of polish and refinement to the rough-and-tumble competitiveness of town life.

Merchant capitalism fostered other values—of individualism, absolute private property, and the unrestrained accumulation of wealth. It was a concomitant, and a cause, of the breakdown of kinship and community ties, a process that had begun in an earlier feudal period. Feudalism had tended to associate men with particular areas of land, the fiefs granted by the king or a noble lord to a wealthy individual for his services. Lords, villeins, tenants, and serfs were bound to landed estates and to one another through personal ties and through obligations to the land and to one another. In this way generations of kinspeople had remained settled together, with tenants and serfs working the same lands.

Profound changes in the nature of kinship ties began early in England. Marc Bloch (1961) noted that, from the thirteenth century on, there was a contraction in the social recognition of kinship. Kindreds that had existed under feudalism had begun to atrophy and were slowly being replaced by much smaller families. Because of the frequency of voluntary refusal or withdrawal from the obligations of kinship, the cluster of kinsmen bound by obligations of vengeance, for example, had diminished to include only first or second cousins.[3]

Increases in trade and the development of free wage labor in the wake of the decline of feudal estates and serfdom were major factors in the attenuation of kinship ties, as individual men were forced to become mobile in order to sell their labor. Also, increasingly, protection from wealthy and politically powerful men became more important than the support of a circle of kinspeople. As the towns and cities grew and as various episodes of warfare dislocated people, some men found their only options for making a living away from their native villages and families. They then had opportunities to engage in adventures abroad (on the Continent, or in Ireland), to participate in the many wars that abounded in England and on the Continent, and for a few men, to occupy themselves in the private accumulation of wealth. Throughout the period of the Hundred Years' War, part of which was during the reign of Edward III (1327–1377), for example, English soldiers returned from France with massive amounts of plunder and loot, injecting a new sense of acquired personal wealth and inspiring in others the desire for more.

Another trend, the enclosure movement; beginning in the fifteenth century, resulted in the transformation of what were once communal lands, forests, and meadows in English villages to private property, enclosed by hedges and held in absolute possession by landowners whose objectives were the production of commodities for growing towns and greater profits. When the English learned to fence in parcels of land and the use of titles became widespread, the sense of exclusive private use of natural resources expanded and matured. Some became very wealthy as the value of these lands increased, while others, those dispersed or dislocated by the privatization of land, were reduced to abject poverty (see below).

Of great significance was the development of the use of money "in the relations of life to such an extent that it was possible to buy for money goods of any kind and to secure any variety of services" (Dietz 1932, 119). Although the English church denounced the sins of usury, hoarding, and profiteering, Dietz tells us that "worldly pursuits acquired an importance of their own, and the unity of all activity envisaged in the Christian view of life was broken, never to be achieved again" (122). Gold and silver, which could buy virtually anything, totally transformed English life.

Opportunities for acquiring wealth not only became greater from the onset of the sixteenth century, but new forms of social inequality based on acquired wealth also came into play, particularly in urban areas. Many historians distinguish this newly created property, linked with the rise of the middle class and the values associated with it, as "bourgeois property," those forms of wealth privately held to the exclusion of all others. The accumulation of private wealth became a dominant cultural value, one that was underscored by the increasingly atomistic nature of society and one that linked individuals to a new sense of social identity. As the Genoveses (1983) note, "Material possessions ... became the sine qua non of respectable and responsible selfhood" (275).

The power of the church to establish and maintain ethical and moral standards had already atrophied and begun to decline before the rise of capitalism as a way of life. Thus the pursuit of wealth by individuals was unencumbered by the demands either of kinship or of any other moral order.

For several centuries merchant capitalists involved in trading and financial institutions had been developing a collective power based on their wealth and investments in overseas enterprises. The constellation of cultural features that emerged with and surrounded the life-styles of the merchant capitalists provided some of the ideological ingredients of the continuing bourgeois revolution that brought about industrial capitalism. But some Marxists, like the Genoveses, have argued persuasively that merchant capital hindered rather than advanced economic development toward industrial capitalism. They insist that it was a conservative force that "played handmaiden to feudalism in the early overseas expansion," led to the reinstitution of serfdom in parts of Europe, and was responsible for colonial conquests in the New World and the subsequent exploitation of slave labor (1983, 6–8). Merchant capital was transformed during the crises of the seventeenth century when the feudal system was finally abolished.

C.B. MacPherson (1962) characterized the unifying political thought of English society beginning in the seventeenth century as based on a central theme that he calls "possessive individualism." He says, "The basic assumptions of possessive individualism—that man is free and human by virtue of his sole proprietorship of his own person, and that human society is essentially a series of market relations—were deeply embedded in the seventeenth-century foundations" (270). It was more than just a political theme. Its features impacted on economic, religious, and social institutions, on values, laws, customs, and beliefs about individual, natural, and civil rights, and the whole range of cultural phenomena. It was intricately linked to the English conception of property, the sense of proprietorship that extended beyond mere material matter, and its connection to the English concepts of individual autonomy and freedom.

Looking at some of the dominant political philosopher-theorists of the century who reflected and articulated the values of merchant capitalists and industrialists, MacPherson (1962) shows that freedom was equated with rights in property, with property defined in an unusual way. The basic right that any man had was the right to property in his own person, his body, labor, and capacities. A man may only alienate his labor property by "selling" it to another man, an indicator of the market or contractual nature of the relationships among men. Exercising proprietary rights in his own selfhood, independently of the will of others, gives a man freedom, and such freedom makes him fully human (264).

Among other implications of the theory of possessive individualism, MacPherson shows that it justified the appropriation and accumulation of property in land and in other resources and goods. A man is fully free when he can accumulate and retain the property of his own labor, holding it exclusively against the demands of others. MacPherson notes that John Locke's philosophy called for the right to unlimited acquisitions of property, which he defined as "Life, Liberty and Estate" (1962, 198). Government exists to protect men in the exercise of their property rights. Thus Locke made a positive value out of the unequal appropriation of most of the wealth (capital) by a few individuals, reasoning that such accumulation was a "natural right" (MacPherson 1962, 208–221). These ideas and ideals, as well as Locke's general vision of civil rights and human liberties, were transported to the American colonies in varying forms and modifications and ultimately became part of the worldviews and rhetoric of most Americans.

Capitalist ideology, then, had taken shape and form before the English turned fully to African slavery as a way of producing commodities for a world market that would make them rich. Many historians tend to agree that English culture, as manifest in its early development of a capitalist ethos, differed from most of the cultures of western Europe, which lagged behind in their development toward industrial capitalism. Most striking and emphatic about the uniqueness of the English economy and culture is the work of Alan Macfarlane (1978). In arguing that the English had ceased being a rural peasant society by as early as the thirteenth century, Macfarlane points to the atomistic quality of life already expressed in that century, manifest in its individualism and privatization of wealth. Wage labor, land commoditization, absolute and exclusive ownership of property, extensive geographic and social mobility, a decline in kinship ties and arranged marriages—all predate the sixteenth century. Primogeniture, which signifies private property in real estate, was "apparently firmly established in England by the thirteenth century" and was "widespread" even "among those at the lower levels of society" (87–88).

Macfarlane (1978) quotes from a number of medieval sources authored by foreign travelers in England that described the extreme individualism of the English, sometimes seen as arrogance, their preoccupation with their own private interests, their overbearing pride, and their suspiciousness not only of strangers but also of one another. "Combined with their self-confidence and arrogance went a mutual suspiciousness: each individual was out for himself and trusted no one else," Macfarlane paraphrases (174). Writers spoke of English wealth, their abundance of food and fine clothes, their love of freedom and independence, their pursuit of money and trade, and their lack of affection toward their children.[4] "All these writers," he notes, "clearly felt that there was something different not only about the economy, but also the personality of the English" (173).

Thus a market mentality, social interactions based on contract rather than status, and transactions governed by the laws of supply and demand had already characterized the English socioeconomic system, Macfarlane argues, even before the Protestant revolution and the emergence of capitalism. If the English were perceived as so culturally distinct by their European contemporaries long before the age of exploration and conquest, surely these cultural traits impacted uniquely on the nature and quality of their colonial experiences. Their ideologies about individualism and property guided their assault on native lands. They also helped to determine the kind of slavery that grew in North America. Possessive individualism and the near sacredness of property and property rights in seventeenth-century English culture facilitated the transformation of Africans into slave property and their concomitant demotion to nonhuman forms of being.

SOCIAL ORGANIZATION AND VALUES OF EARLY CAPITALISM

At the apex of the hierarchical English social order was the monarch and his/her relatives, a genealogical reticulum of births and marriages that cut across polities and that constituted the royalty. Aristocrats and nobles were in the next tier, and these families provided the ruling class. Below this ruling elite were the gentry: large landowners, farmers, merchants, commercial agents, and wealthy craftsmen, artisans, and financiers in the towns and ports. Next came the yeomen landowners, the proper and respectable farmers. The working class constituted the bulk of the people, and they were mostly small farmers, laborers, small craftsmen, or petty traders. Near the bottom were the working poor, the unemployed or irregularly employed unskilled laborers, and finally the vagabonds, paupers, and masterless, homeless men, women, and children who tended to cluster in the poorhouses and byways of towns and villages.

Although the hierarchical system appeared rigid, there was some flexibility and movement both vertically and horizontally across social barriers. This was particularly true of the bourgeoisie in the urban centers. Wealthy merchants, for example, flourished with the expansion of overseas trade. Their political power increased along with their wealth as they competed for the attentions of royalty. They educated their offspring well and sometimes married them to royalty. But Macfarlane (1978) has also found considerable geographical and social mobility in some rural parishes as well, with a "growing cleavage between rich and poor" that often split entire families (70). Individuals left their natal homes in their teens and often never returned to their hometowns or villages.

Businesses, government, and the church had imposed on the English public the values of hard work and sobriety; and free labor, it was assumed, would work toward these goals. Such labor had been attracted to the towns and cities for burgeoning commercial, banking, and shipping enterprises. But in the sixteenth and seventeenth centuries, England experienced large population movements exacerbated by the migrations of peasants displaced as a result of the enclosure movement. There were not enough jobs for the poor. Now, through no fault of their own, the poor were without work. These conditions produced a large class of idle, "rootless" men (and women) who roamed the streets and byways of the cities and towns, scratching, stealing, and begging for food.

English propertied classes saw these people, often called "vagabonds," as a threat to their sense of proper social order. Their communities had long been structured in hierarchies of what some saw as clear and seemingly unambiguous statuses. Men of substance and civility were men who owned property and thus were also men who had power, or at least could wield some influence in the governance of the society. But a man without property was essentially a social nonentity, unable to undertake civil responsibilities and with no basis for exercising civil rights. Laboring men worked for those who owned property, and they were bound together by civil laws, contracts, and statutes. Thus the identity of a man in terms of his lands, stock, money, or other resources, or his attachment as a subordinate to a man with property, was a fixed part of the hierarchical system.

We have seen associated with this concept certain ideas about personal freedom. For a man to acquire property during these times of vigorous change, he had to be free to sell his labor, to acquire some semblance of education or training, to make his fortune as best he could without social constraints. A man lacking such ambitions was suspect or was considered part of the rabble that constituted the underclasses. Most men saw personal freedom as the normal status for the English, an ideology that, as Henri Pirenne tells us, had deep roots in medieval cities among the middle classes ([1925] 1952, 193). Indentured servitude became one of the main ways of linking an impoverished person to a master in order that the former might work a few years, acquire sufficient funds to establish himself, or seek his fortune elsewhere.

The greatest concern that Englishmen had was with those "masterless" men who went about robbing, raping, and looting. To the proper English they lacked some of the major qualities of Protestantism, self-control, responsibility, ambition, and thrift. Bourgeois English rigidity about personal behavior, the containment of the emotions, a sense of dignity and good taste, and submission to the rules of social propriety no doubt has a much longer history. But suffice it to say that with the development of the Protestant ethic, the autonomy of the individual was greatly elevated, and certain ideals and standards of personal behavior came to be established. Conformity to the formal rules of one's social class position was heavily monitored by one's peers, or would-be peers, and by one's betters. This contrasted sharply with the behavior of the vagabonds, looters, and "mischievous" men, some of whom were swept up off the streets of such cities as London and Liverpool and shipped off to the New World to work as bonded laborers.

Thus it was that English values about the holding and ownership of property and its linkage to a proper social and civil identity became firmly established. English beliefs about or obsession with property became so transfigured that ultimately they were conjoined with religious values. Success in the acquisition of material goods was equated with, and in some important sense confused with, rewards for the pious. The aggrandizement of material wealth seemed to confer moral virtues on individuals. It was these values that Anglican, Puritan, and other Englishmen brought with them to the New World, values that would have a long-term effect on the ways by which they viewed and dealt with other non-English and non-European groups. In the New World they elevated individual property rights to a position sanctioned by divine authority and superior to all other rights, including the human rights of indigenous peoples and those whom they bought as slaves.

ENGLISH ETHNOCENTRISM AND THE IDEA OF THE SAVAGE

Leonard Liggio (1976), in exploring the race idea and raising a more general question about the comparative differences between the English colonization practices and those of other Europeans, asks, "How is it possible to explain the fact that the English developed the most racist attitudes toward the natives wherever they expanded or established overseas colonies?" He proposes an unexpected hypothesis, that it was the English experience with the Irish "which was the root of English racial attitudes" (1976, 1). Perhaps because of the intractable and seemingly irreconcilable contemporary conflict between these two peoples, other historians have turned their attention to this long-standing belligerence for insights into the general English attitudes toward indigenous peoples and the nature of English colonial and imperial policies.[5]

Throughout the sixteenth and seventeenth centuries, and especially during the reign of Elizabeth I, Englishmen focused their attention, and a great deal of hostility, toward Ireland and the Irish people. The era was punctuated by periodic attempts to finally conquer the Irish, on the one hand, and by several major Irish rebellions, on the other. The last of the sixteenth-century rebellions (1597), which brought forth the wrath of Queen Elizabeth and the final triumph of her forces over the native chieftain Hugh O'Neill, was the climax of four centuries of repeated invasions, implacable Irish resistance, and failed attempts to consolidate English power over the western island. A brief review of this history is very instructive.

The first invasion and attempt to settle Ireland occurred under Henry II in 1169 and 1171, as part of the expansion of Anglo-Norman civilization following the Norman invasion of England. By the end of the century, most of Ireland was under some semblance of English control in the form of Anglo-Norman barons who had been given titles to Irish lands, which they ruled as personal fiefdoms. But the scattered Irish clans, lacking a centralized government, proved impossible to vanquish and control. Within a short time they had regained most of their lands and had begun the first of several great revivals of Gaelic culture that flourished from time to time throughout the thirteenth through the fifteenth centuries.

One development, however, was particularly upsetting and threatening to the nominal rulers of Ireland. Those Englishmen who had settled in Irish lands (called Old English), especially in remote areas away from the pale, intermingled with the Irish and increasingly "went native," that is, they assimilated Irish culture and language. To halt what the English saw as the erosion of civilized culture and the degeneracy of Englishmen in Ireland, the English Crown established legal restrictions forbidding Englishmen to wear Irish dress or hairstyles, to speak the Irish language, or to intermarry or trade with the Irish. These restrictions, the Statutes of Kilkenny, also outlawed Irish games, poetry, and music, apparently under the assumption that these cultural features were too seductive for young Englishmen to resist. Such prohibitions, and others, stayed in effect until the seventeenth century. But they had little consequence for the preservation of English culture, even though increasingly more Englishmen were encouraged to settle in Ireland throughout this period and to promote English culture.

The English were frustrated by their inability to establish complete suzerainty over Irish lands (some of which were in the control of Irish brigands) or to transform the natives and absorb them into English culture. Throughout the period of English attempts to subdue these lands and peoples, one ostensible objective was to spread English civilization. But the underlying reality and primary aim was the confiscation of Irish lands, the establishment of an agrarian economy, and the exploitation of native labor.

The English attitude toward the Irish, almost from the beginning of penetration into the western island, was one of contempt for Irish culture or life-styles. This was matched by intense Irish hatred of all that was English. Thus extreme ethnocentrism ensued between these two peoples early in the contact period, which is a common result of situations in which one people attempt to conquer another. But the conflict was not only based on the ethnic chauvinism of two peoples competing for political supremacy, as in the case of the many other confrontations between the emerging nation-states of Europe. The hostility between the Irish and English went much deeper. It exemplified an age-old struggle, symbolized in biblical times in the conflict between Cain and Abel, and one that has resurged many times in many places throughout human history. It was the clash between a people who were nomadic or seminomadic pastoralists and those who settled on the land as farmers and cultivated a sedentary way of life. It was a fundamental conflict between two very different life-styles, two different views of the world, two different value systems, and two different sets of problems and solutions for them.

We should understand how the incompatibility between these major subsistence patterns has led to extreme hatred and conflict in many areas of the world and perhaps early in the history of settled living. Pastoralism, an economy based on the herding of animals, is a way of life that has proved highly adaptive in many areas of the world. The basic needs of pastoral societies are herds of domestic or semidomestic animals that are amenable to human manipulation and control, grazing land sufficient to maintain the herds and provide for increases in their numbers, accessible water and salt, and strategies for protecting this highly mobile form of wealth and the requisite resources. It is a life-style that requires the human community to adjust itself to the needs of the herds. This means that cultural ways are oriented around and circumscribed by territorial mobility and the placement of highest value on and intense interaction with the animal herds.

In recent millennia, pastoralism has been sustained as a specialized way of life in areas marginal to agriculture. Yet, in many places, pastoralists seeking expansion of grazing land for their herds and farmers attempting to increase their crop production have come into conflict over land, a situation not unlike that of the American farmers and cattle ranchers of the Old West.

Although many recent studies have shown that there is a great deal of variation in the cultures of nomadic pastoral people so that it is impossible to speak of a "typical" nomadic way of life (Dyson-Hudson and Dyson-Hudson 1980), certain features have appeared both in history and in the comparative ethnographic literature that reflect common themes in such cultures.[6] Herding peoples do not recognize land or territory as having specific boundaries, nor have they evolved the concept of property associated with bounded pieces of land. The territory over which they roam belongs to all in the community. Because of their need for mobility and for often rapid movements, they usually have very little of what sedentary peoples would identify as private property. Most material goods must be portable and often disposable. Their dwellings are generally not permanent, nor do they seem to be very solid to those people who value proper houses and all the accoutrements that accompany them. Tents or other types of dwellings that can be taken apart and packed for moving are the common living quarters, but, depending on the environment, most activities take place outside. Some groups who live in relatively harsh environments and engage in seasonal migrations, like the Kazakhs of northern China, may have permanent houses of sod and/or logs for their winter dwellings.

Among many pastoralists, human dependence on animal herds is virtually complete. The basic diet of milk, such substances as butter and yogurt processed from milk, meat from older animals or surplus bulls, and blood extracted from adult animals generally suffices, but may be supplemented with occasional vegetables. Skins of animals are used for a wide variety of utensils, clothing, storage containers, bedding, and so forth. Even the hoofs, horns, bones, tails, and entrails have their uses, so that little is wasted. Such usage contrasts sharply with the diet and materials utilized or exploited by farmers.

Camping units (or some other form of community unit) where face-to-face contact is possible from time to time are usually autonomous both politically and economically, operating well beyond the sphere of control of centralized authorities. When there are quarrels between units, one mechanism of resolving them is for one group to move away. More typical, however, is the institutionalization of feuding relationships, continuous and insistent conflict that separates herding units. But constant preparedness for fighting, even wholesale combat, means that nomadic herders are perceived by sedentary peoples as being militaristic and aggressive.[7] An argument has been made that this type of behavior is necessary and children are so conditioned to it because of the need to protect a form of wealth that is volatile and easily stolen (Goldschmidt 1965). It is indeed a characteristic of many nomadic pastoralists that they engage in a high level of feuding with others and that the raiding of the animals of other groups, usually to replenish their own losses, is commonplace (Sweet 1965).

One of the more striking cultural themes among virtually all nomadic pastoralists is their love for their animals, which are often accorded priority in their ideologies over love of kinspeople or wives. Some of the best known and most cherished poetry among the Arabs is that which honors or praises their animals or a particular animal. Among East African pastoralists, songs are composed to cattle, and women and cattle are expressed in folk sayings as literally substitutes for one another in men's hearts. Concomitant with this life-style is an extraordinary love of freedom of movement and a disdain for farmers who are bound to the land and who scratch in the earth for a living.

The Gaelic peoples of Ireland shared many of the habits and customs known from studies of nomadic peoples in the Old World. Because they were a herding people, cattle were their greatest form of wealth and most strategic resource. But techniques of growing crops were not unknown, and many Irish families grew some barley and oats, primarily to feed their animals during the long winter months. Farming, however, was not considered fitting for a man's major occupation. It was generally left to women. For a man, his herd was the source of his prestige and pride, and each family spent a lifetime trying to increase its herds. Like all pastoralists, they believed that their way of life was far superior to the wretched lives of farmers, valuing above all the freedom that it gave them.

English culture by contrast was ordered, structured, and controlled. Men were bound in permanent relationships of stratified ranks to one another and to property in land, houses, and commercial enterprises. The centralized governance of a strong civil state was mirrored in the hierarchical structure of the church, the parish, and the town. It was a system that provided for the preeminent values of order, stability, and security. Until the Reformation, it also imposed restraints on the freedom of individuals. What made the English culture most distinct from that of the Irish was the advanced elaboration of the jural concept of rights in property in land and the social identity and status that derived therefrom.

From the standpoint of English cultural values, Irish utilization of the land was a monstrous waste; the rich soil that their animals trampled could be put to better use cultivating grains, vegetables, and other goods to be marketed abroad and in expanding urban centers. Moreover, the younger sons of English gentlemen who had no hopes of inheriting paternal lands could earn their fortunes from great estates that would be planted in Ireland with the aid of Irish labor. Yet all attempts to force Irishmen to settle on the land were rebuffed. When the English met their intransigence by confiscating and destroying their cattle, they fled into the forests and let it be known that they preferred starvation to life as forced laborers on English farms.

Each people thus expressed the different orientations of their cultures, their different values, interests, and beliefs, and their differing ways of viewing the world. Extreme ethnic chauvinism bred of such contrasting understandings of different worlds was exacerbated by the enduring conflicts, fundamentally over land. Neither side displayed the moderating force of Christian benevolence, although both groups claimed to be on the side of God.

The contempt and hatred that the English had for Irish culture were expressed by Giraldus Cambrensis as early as 1187. "They are a wild and inhospitable people," he claimed. "They live on beasts only, and live like beasts.... This people despises agriculture, has little use for the money-making of towns."[8] He described their un-cleanliness, their flowing hair and beards infested with lice, their barbarous dress and their laziness. "They think that the greatest pleasure is not to work and the greatest wealth is to enjoy liberty." James Myers (1983) asserts that it was this inordinate love of liberty to which Giraldus Cambrensis and his successors objected, and this critique of the Irish continued throughout succeeding centuries.

At the time that Columbus was exploring the New World, the English under Henry VII in 1494 began a new policy designed to settle the Irish problem once and for all through forced colonization. Henry VIII, however, was more benign in his approach, preferring to provide mechanisms by which the Irish would voluntarily submit to his rule. But it was he who built defensive forts and established the first standing army in Ireland with the intention of ridding the fertile areas of all those who refused to submit to English rule. The colonization policy was continued by Henry VIII's successors.

Irish resistance throughout the sixteenth century enraged many of the English, who persisted in viewing the Irish as "rude, beastly, ignorant, cruel and unruly infidels" (Liggio 1976, 8). According to William Thomas, writing in 1552, the "wild" Irish were unreasonable beasts who knew neither God nor good manners and who lived with their wives and children in filth along with their animals (Liggio 1976, 8). Some Englishmen argued what was to become a familiar strain in European attitudes toward Indians and Africans in the New World during the coming centuries: that the Irish were better off as slaves of the English than they were retaining the brutish customs of their traditional culture. While confiscating Irish lands, many English military leaders, some of whom were later to be involved in the colonization of New England and the Virginia colonies, regularly killed women and children, which has prompted some historians to accuse the English of genocide.[9] Humphrey Gilbert, whom David B. Quinn (1966) called a "bloodthirsty sadist," justified this barbaric treatment by arguing that the men who fought the war could not be maintained without the women who milked the cattle and provided them with food "and other necessaries" (127). During the final years of the Nine Years' War, many of the Irish were driven off to western Ireland and their chief form of wealth, their cattle, was destroyed. Lands were taken over by the younger sons of English gentry, who subsequently set about to create an agricultural and commercial society. The Irish who remained were reduced to involuntary laborers. Under English law they were not allowed to own land, hold office, be apprenticed to any skill or craft, or serve on juries. Their principal identity was that of cheap labor.

Toward the middle of the seventeenth century, another more widespread rebellion by the Irish and by some of the Old English took place. This was followed by extremely repressive measures on the part of the English under Oliver Cromwell. According to Liggio:

> Cromwell's army in Ireland, often New England Puritan led or inspired, carried out the most complete devastation that Ireland experienced until that time. Extermination became a policy. Massacres were carried out. Prisoners of war were transported to servitude in the new English colonies in the West Indies. Ireland like New England was taken with the Bible in one hand, the sword in the other. Lord Clarendon observed that the Cromwellian policy was to act without "any humanity to the Irish nation, and more especially to those of the old native extraction, the whole *race* whereof they had upon the matter sworn an utter extirpation" (1976, 28).

The significance of this brutal treatment and the transportation of large numbers of captive peoples of both sexes to the sugar plantations in the West Indies rested upon the growing image of the Irish as something less than human, as a people whose capacity for civilization was stunted. This view took form slowly but was perhaps common among some English elite by the early seventeenth century.

Unremitting disdain for the customs and habits of the "wild" Irish is found throughout the literature of the sixteenth and seventeenth centuries. Edmund Campion, himself a Catholic, excoriated the Irish for their supposed cannibalism, their lewd marriage customs (they had trial marriages, and sometimes engaged in polygamy and free sexual behavior), their "whores" and "strumpets ... too vile and abominable to write of" (quoted in Myers 1983, 26–30). And Barnabe Rich in his 1610 description of Irish peoples, manners, and customs claimed that the Irish were educated in "treason, in rebellion, in theft, in robbery, in superstition, in idolatry" (quoted in Myers 1983, 130). In their resistance to British civilization, Rich noted that "the Irish had rather still retain themselves in their sluttishness, in their uncleanliness, in their rudeness, and in their inhuman loathsomeness, than they would take any example from the English, either of civility, humanity, or any manner of decency" (Myers 1983, 131).

The habits and customs of the Irish reminded some learned men of the descriptions of primitive peoples found in the recently recovered literature of the ancient Greeks and Romans. Doubts about the capacity of such barbaric people to accommodate themselves to civilized behavior hardened. Many men may well have come to believe a notion, first expressed in the early fourteenth century, that it was "no more a sin to kill an Irishman than a dog or any other brute." Thus there crystallized in the English mind, out of this long saga of tension and hostility, a very real image of barbarism that had concrete referents in the Irish but that could be abstracted to apply to others.

Perhaps worst of all was the heathenism of the Irish. Despite the fact of their nominal Catholicism, Englishmen could see nothing in Irish behavior that was suggestive of morality and virtue. In fact, like Campion, many tended to blame Irish heathenism on their adherence to the papal religion, albeit it was a tenuous linkage. Their alleged wildness, lack of self-control, and tendency to drunkenness and violence were all evidence of the insufficiency of Catholicism to uplift people.

This antagonism to Catholicism had its origins in the tumultuous breakaway of diverse groups from the older Roman

Catholic establishment that began during the early part of the sixteenth century. Although we know of this historical transformation as the Protestant revolution, it was not a single episode in European history, but multiple defections from the Roman Catholic church for various reasons. Henry VIII was a critical figure in this revolt, and his support of hostilities against the Irish had as much to do with his anger against the pope for the latter's failure to sanction his divorce as it did with hatred for the Irish. Still, the antagonism against the Irish was compounded by an intensity of opposition to the powers of the church and by growing competition with Spain, another Catholic country, some leaders of which sided with fellow churchmen in Ireland.

At the same time, Englishmen were beginning to receive reports about the indigenous peoples encountered by the Portuguese and Spanish in their New World ventures. Interaction between the Spanish and English was intensified during this century. For a while there were close diplomatic, commercial, and political contacts between the two countries, punctuated by the marriage of Henry VIII to a Spanish princess, Catherine of Aragon, and the brief ascendancy of Phillip II of Spain to the joint possession of the English Crown by virtue of his marriage to Henry's daughter, Mary I, from 1553 to 1558. English merchants and sea captains visited Spain frequently, and English politicians and adventurers studied closely the developing colonial policies of the Spanish. Quinn points out that, for the first time, Englishmen began to regard their problems with the Irish as similar to those presented by the natives of the New World to the Spanish. They found that some of the same qualities of a barbarous and uncivilized people were attributed to the New World natives by the Spanish. Moreover, Spanish settlers were demanding laws enforcing perpetual servitude on the indigenous peoples of the Spanish colonies, a situation the English found most congenial to their own goals.

Following the successful and brutal squashing of the Desmond rebellion in Munster (1579–1583), the English consciously attempted to establish plantations in that region based on Spanish models and the principles that they perceived to be operant in both Spanish colonial settings and in the Italian Mediterranean island plantations. Again, after the final victory over "the O'Neill" in 1603, which "marked the passing of Gaelic civilization and the beginning of England's first meticulously planned effort to effect the cultural subjugation of an alien people" (Myers 1983, 8), England planned to create a colonial outpost along plantation lines. At the heart of the plantation model was the coercive exploitation of Irish labor, with the objective of "maintaining the labor force in a permanent state of inferiority to and dependence on the English settlers" (Quinn 1958, 27).

It is not surprising that the English view of the Irish was solidified by the seventeenth century into an image summed up in the term "savage." It was the invention in the English mind of the savage that made possible the development of policies and practices that could be perpetuated for gain, unencumbered by reflections on any ethical or moral considerations. The savage was first of all a "heathen," a godless and immoral creature, "wicked, barbarous and uncivil." He was lazy, filthy, evil, superstitious, and an idol worshipper, and was given to lying, stealing, treachery, murder, and double-dealing. His nomadic tendencies and presumed lack of social order or laws were the antithesis of the habits of civilized man who was sedentary and bound not only to land but also to other men by laws. The savage was a cannibal whose lust and licentiousness never yielded to the strictures of self-control, of which he was totally lacking.[10] Granted, some of the Irish had been transformed into civilized men, but for late seventeenth-century Englishmen this goal, which was an early rationalization for settlement in Ireland, became more and more remote. What did increase in the ideology and images about the Irish were the beliefs that (1) the Irish were incapable of being civilized, that the "wild" Irish, those who most vigorously resisted English hegemony, would remain untamed; and (2) the only way to bring them under some form of civilized control was to enslave them. Indeed, Irish people formed the bulk of the servile peoples who were eventually transferred to the New World English plantations during the seventeenth century.

To document and confirm the growing beliefs about the unsuitability of Irishmen for civilization, many of the Englishmen pointed to the experiences of the Spanish with New World natives. They cited Spanish practices of exterminating Indians not only as justification for policies of killing Irish men, women, and children but as an appropriate solution for those who refused to be enslaved.

In the English collective consciousness, "the savage" was thus a kind of composite of these streams of negative ideas and images that flourished during a period of much social disorder, change, and unrest. The savage came to embody all of those repulsive characteristics that were contrary and opposed to English beliefs, habits, laws, and values. The imagery induced hatred for all things Irish, which has persisted among many English people right up to the twentieth century. But it also had a feedback effect: It was of enormous convenience for those who hoped to profit from the plantations created in Irish lands.[11]

The English were not unique in their attitudes. As Hodgen (1964) has pointed out, for this period of ethnological reflection European opinion in general was "anti-savage, and strongly so" (362), an attitude that was not challenged until well into the period of the Enlightenment, which began toward the end of the seventeenth century. But such attitudes were more strongly felt by Englishmen and were instrumental in molding the English's cognitive perceptions of other conquered peoples in the New World as well as later in the Middle East, India, Burma, South Asia, and Africa. They became important subthemes to the ideology of race and in the characterization of racial differences.

ENGLISH NATIONALISM AND SOCIAL VALUES IN THE SIXTEENTH AND SEVENTEENTH CENTURIES

The consolidation of an image of the savage was a major factor in the evolution of English attitudes toward aliens. It fed into an expanding cultural chauvinism as Englishmen began to view themselves as not only distinctive from others but superior. Events seemed to propel them toward increasing nationalism and an arrogant pride in being English, a trend that had been nourished during the Hundred Years' War. The break with the Roman Catholic church in the sixteenth century was both a political and a religious underscoring of the separateness of the English polity from the rest of Europe. Consciousness of being English, not yet perceived in biological terms, flowered during Elizabethan times (1559–1603). A sense of growing competition with other Europeans, particularly the Spanish, made them turn inward, where for some a sense of unity and purpose was found by harkening back to an ancient mythical time of greatness and glory.

Reginald Horsman (1976, 1981) points out that the myth of Anglo-Saxonism originated during this period. Depicted as a branch of a heroic and freedom-loving Germanic peoples, Anglo-Saxons were described not only as great lovers of liberty but also as originators of civilization's free institutions and equitable laws. It is worth noting, and Horsman specifically points out, that this early form of Anglo-Saxonism was not racial. It was rooted in the attempt to rationalize the existence of a pure pre-Norman church, and thus to justify Henry VIII's break with the Roman Catholic church. It was also consonant with developing ethnocentrism in other emerging states of Europe. The focus on biologically inherited "racial" features as a way of explaining Anglo-Saxon cultural institutions did not take place until the mid to late eighteenth century, a timing that [...] was not fortuitous.

The unexpected English defeat of the Spanish Armada in 1588 was a major event in the eclipse of Spanish domination of the seas. It spelled the rise of this once isolated island culture, which eventually not only assumed supremacy of the seas, but became the most vigorous and successful of the competing, empire-building states of Europe. England's citizenry became increasingly united around a peculiar sense of their own English identity and superiority, which ultimately precluded the acceptance of others as equals.

A basic element in that identity was religion. The English were Christian first and, even though they were becoming highly secular and materialistic in their cultural orientation, were conditioned to that sense of religiosity that pervaded much of Europe during this time. Most important, from the time of Henry VIII on, they were predominantly Protestant, and their consciousness of an identity dramatically wrenched from the stale traditionalism of an archaic Catholicism was at its peak. Among Protestants themselves, various sects (Anglicans, Puritans, Presbyterians, and such splinter groups as the Dissenters and Arminians) vied with one another in and out of Parliament for ascendancy in political, economic, and religious matters.

The priority given to religion as a major diacritic of a person's or a people's identity in Europe is explicable in the wider framework of European history and culture. It was a time when all of Europe was undergoing tremendous social and political turmoil. One factor in this was the decline of feudalism, as we have seen. These older forms of labor bound to landed estates gradually gave way to a very different contract laborer who was for hire and, most importantly, was mobile, a fact that promoted social instability. Social dislocations also resulted from periodic pestilence and disease, going back at least to the Black Death of 1348–1350, which disrupted all lives and institutions. In the absence of scientific understanding of epidemic disease and of methods to combat it, such crises called forth supernatural explanations and supernatural supplications. No institution was more suitable to deal with this than was the church.

Then there was the sudden discovery of a whole new world drawing people into contact not only with an unanticipated paganism, but also to its lure of great wealth apparently there for the grasping by anyone with sufficient ambition, motivation, and greed. In this context, precedents for how people were to relate to one another were absent or elusive. The possibility of adventure and profit attracted men and women away from familiar forms of social control, from family, kinsmen, employers, patrons, friends, and clients, and into interaction with alien merchants, adventurers, pirates, sailors, and other strangers. The frequent anonymity of these new interactions underscored the need for a familiar identity—to which others could relate. With growing competition and protonationalistic conflicts among the various nations of Europe, Englishmen, like other Europeans, often found it critical to establish political and/or commercial alliances predicated on religious affiliation. Thus, Catholicism, Protestantism, or one of its variants was often the key to not only another person's identity, but also to how the person was to be treated.

Another factor underscoring the importance of some religious attachment was the existence of an atmosphere thick with the belief in and fear of witchcraft. Anthropologists have long observed that in times of enormous social, political, and economic disorder, of devastating warfare or of massive inexplicable natural disasters, human beings commonly turn to some form of witchcraft beliefs to help explain disaster, restore order, and regain control of their lives and of natural phenomena.

From about the twelfth century on, much more intense attention to and concern with witches and their activities took place. This seemed to reach a crescendo in the fifteenth century, as various sects began to break from the Roman church and to devise their own theologies and measures of the faith. Although all of the Protestant groups were opposed to the alleged oppressive nature of the Roman Catholic church, and especially to the Inquisition, they retained much of the underlying theological, historical, and scriptural beliefs. One of these beliefs had to do with the nature of the devil and how he manifests himself.

Christian tradition has it that the devil is the anti-Christ, the incarnation of all evil, who was in mortal combat with the forces of good in order to win men's souls. The devil had the ability to enter men's (and women's) bodies, or to make a compact with individuals to carry out malevolent aims. Thus one knew the existence of this evil force by the behavior and actions of those individuals in league with the devil. If Christianity created the devil, it also prescribed means of reckoning with this evil—through obedience and living an exemplary life, through prayer and the intervention of the Holy Mother, and, more directly, through the sign of the cross or the use of holy water. A good Christian theoretically could not be harmed by the courtship of the devil.

Reputation as a good Christian was a major protection against being accused of witchcraft. Those who were not Christian often became identified with the devil, evil, and sinfulness. This sense of identity was solidified in most of Europe and helps to explain why relationships between Europeans and the indigenous peoples whom they colonized often became so harsh and cruel. As we shall see later, when heathens were perceived to be as wicked as, or agents of, the devil, then there need be no moral restraints against brutalizing or killing them.

Coinciding with the rise of witchcraft, and a factor in the drastic social changes occurring, was the breakup of the Muslim empire in Spain and the subsequent expulsion of Jews and Moors. While the Moors made their way back to North Africa and other parts of the Mediterranean world, the Jews began a series of migrations that led some of them to other parts of Europe and to England (and some to America). The growing presence of these Jews was perceived as a threat in Europe and made Christians even more conscious and protective of their own religious identities.

Thus, in the context of a multiplicity of forces that swirled around them and often threatened their sense of security, Christians in Europe magnified the importance of religion not only as a criterion of identity but also as a source of protection, security, and comfort. For many who traveled abroad, in whatever direction, a strong religious faith had greater force even than allegiance to king, patron, or community.

HEREDITARY SOCIAL IDENTITY: THE LESSON OF CATHOLIC SPAIN

Because of the mutual influences that the Spanish and English had on one another during the early centuries of exploration and colonization, it is useful to consider those features of Spanish life and thought that may have influenced English ideologies about human differences. As already suggested, the Spanish had quite a different history and experience with human diversity from the English. Since the eighth century, the peninsula had been dominated by a civilization that was among the world's most tolerant, at least for a while. Under Muslim hegemony, Spain had experienced the formation of a heterogeneous, multicultural, multi-"racial" society. For a while, Muslims, Christians, and Jews led culturally productive lives together and had remarkably benign relationships among themselves, with some exceptions, even to the point of considerable intermarriage (Castro 1971, 499). However, with the rise to political power of some of the Christian kingdoms and with the thrust to regain Spanish territory for the Catholic church ("the Reconquest"), beginning as early as the ninth century, Jews and Muslims came under pressure to convert. Conflict ensued, and the entire social system gradually became rigidified into three ethnic-religious "castes" whose relationships in the fifteenth and sixteenth centuries were often characterized by fear, mistrust, envy, and hatred.

Some 300,000 Jews became Christian by the end of the fifteenth century, a time when the marriage of Ferdinand and Isabella had become the political fulcrum symbolizing the rise of modern Catholic Spain. Known as "conversos," these former Jewish families were rich and urban; they also constituted the largest proportion of the educated. The Moors, who tended to be concentrated in the southern regions of Spain, in Valencia, Granada, and Castile, underwent forced baptisms early in the sixteenth century, but their customs, traditions, and language (Arabic) continued intact for a while. The Moors came to constitute an underclass of laboring people who remained somewhat culturally distinct from the Spanish. Eventually, the state expelled all of the Moriscos, as they were called; some 275,000 were shipped off to North Africa between 1609 and 1614.

Jealous of the wealth, power, and influence of the Jewish families who had converted, many of whom were using their new Christian identity to advance themselves in the civil or church hierarchies, some of the Christian leaders began to question the theological probity of some conversos. Many Christians in the countryside, of peasant backgrounds, emerged as antagonists, not only to the already declining Muslim influence but also to what they believed to be the Jewish domination of trade, commerce, banking, scholarship, and the arts. In a drama characterized by intrigues, petty jealousies, and varied political machinations, opponents began to charge that some of the conversos and their descendants (the New Christians) were secretly practicing Judaism. An inquisition directed at heretics was established in 1478, sanctioned by the Catholic kings and the church. It was designed to weed out recalcitrant converts or "secret" Jews by investigating personal behavior and genealogies for the taint of Jewishness. Some of the ideas that became basic ingredients of a racial worldview were set in motion during this period of rising Christian intolerance and rampant persecution of Jews and Moors.

A major contribution to Western thought was the belief engendered by the Inquisition in the hereditary nature of social status, a theme often carried through in the extreme. Family ties were closely scrutinized to discover the "hidden Jew," and a social stigma was attached to anyone or any family that had even a remote association with someone prosecuted by the Inquisition. Although lineal descent seemed to be the avenue of heritability of social standing (vis-à-vis the church) this was not consistently observed. The result was that many

Spaniards, including some non-Jews, sought a certificate of "purity" that, for a fee, would be issued by the church. It constituted a guarantee of one's genealogical purity from "any admixture of Jew or Moor" or from condemnation by the Holy Office (Roth 1964, 197–207). These "certificates of Limpieza de Sangre" (purity of blood) were not only a major source of revenue for the church, but were also vital requirements for social mobility, as certain occupations and activities were closed by law to the families of converts.

The idea that social standing is inheritable is an ancient one associated with societies in which there are class divisions, occupational specializations, and private or lineage property. Spanish folk ideology and the practices of the Spanish church and state seemed to define Jewishness and Moorishness as something almost biological, using the idiom of "blood" ties. Elaborate tests for finding social genealogical connections were incipient mechanisms for establishing social placement. And the Spanish use of the term "race," along with "castas," for both Jews and Moors bespeaks a potentially new kind of image of what were essentially ethnic (religious) differences.[12]

Americo Castro (1971) agrees that what was occurring in Spain under the Inquisition was a hardening of ethnic differences, rather than an appeal to some biogenetic reality. He says, "From the fifteenth century on, 'purity of blood' has meant consciousness of caste" (68). It has nothing to do with physical traits or "racial physical type." Yet to equate sections of the society with breeding lines of animals, even symbolically, is to suggest a kind of permanency and immutability to their social qualities that are found only in biological transmission. This attests to the great degree to which Catholic political powers, both papal and secular, were anxious and willing to separate out these populations and to eliminate the Jewish and Moorish cultural influences among them. In this way, the Catholic leaders of Spain could extend and consolidate their power over a population that was essentially homogeneous in religion and culture and uniformly responsive to imposed laws and sanctions.

But any idea of biologically hereditary social positions was contradicted by the more massive uses of conversion, essentially baptism, to eliminate the presence of Jews and Moors in Spanish society. The vast majority of those converted remained Christian, and the acceptance of these former Jews and former Muslims and their descendants as legitimate members of the Catholic community and the state is in opposition to the tenets of modern race ideology, which precludes forever the possibility of such a transformation. The apparent contradiction between the reality of the alteration of social identity, under pressure, and the notion that social identity is a concomitant of unique biological features that are exclusive and unalterable was never resolved and probably never even recognized by the thinkers and philosophers of the Inquisition.

One of the reasons for this may be that, though some of the attitudes and beliefs about the Moors and Jews were expressed in a seemingly biological idiom, at the deepest layer of reality was the more archaic sense of interconnectedness between generations, which stemmed from a peasant context. In the anthropological study of kinship, scholars have argued that kinship is a cultural creation, unrelated to actual biological realities. Human populations take the basic facts of our animal biology, sex differences and the bisexual mode of reproduction, and configure genealogical connections in a variety of patterns. We then imbue certain of these connections with moral and jural qualities. The result is what anthropologists study as kinship. The fact that kinship patterns, processes, obligations, and connections differ from one population to another is the clearest indication of their arbitrary and culturally created nature. Thus anthropologists have come to recognize that kinship relationships are best analyzed as social, sometimes sociopolitical, constructions.

Throughout most of human history and in all human societies, an emphasis on a true biological connection has been absent or irrelevant, in large part because the male role in parturition was little understood. Nor could the biological father (genitor) of a child be precisely known. It was not until the use of modern technology, beginning with the invention of the microscope, the discovery of genetic material, and the invention of electron microscopes in the twentieth century, that it has been possible to ascertain with certainty the actual biological father of any child. Yet every human society has created the role of the "pater," or social father, and has surrounded it with certain moral and jural prescriptions. In many societies, the pater is the husband of the mother, regardless of who the "genitor" is or was, and it is irrelevant that the two may not be the same. In some societies a man whose wife does not become pregnant within a reasonable time may, in fact, call upon another man to beget children for him. His (legal) fatherhood of those children is never questioned.

Adoption and the purchase of children to create kinsmen (and women) in the next generation have been widespread throughout human history, long before the industrial world order emerged. Thus genealogical descent is a jural concept that links men and women together over generations. It is only in the modern world that we have confused biological and social fatherhood, assuming the necessity of both to be the same.

This sense of kinship as an elemental social device for structuring human relations has been perpetuated, especially among peasants and poor people who have little or no property to transmit but who maintain customs of mutual obligations and responsibilities that are deemed essential for the preservation of the society. That human beings structure their kinship systems on biological models stemming from the facts of bisexual reproduction should not obscure the fundamental social nature of kinship. That we culturally create such relationships and imbue the ideologies that we build up around them and attach to them with biological parallelisms in symbols, terms, and expressions conveys a need to make them natural and indissoluble.

Although I have not seen a study of the Spanish Inquisition that expresses this, I suspect that any statute under which, for example, a man would have to prove that his grandmother was not a Jew was more a reflection of the real fact that social behavior, identity, and wealth are transmitted within the genealogical context of families than it was a belief that Jewishness actually resides in the blood. It reflected the jural dimensions of structured kinship rather than the fact of biological connection, the significance of "pater" rather than "genitor." The cognitive connection linking biology and social status did not seem to appear until the crystallization of the idea of "race" in the eighteenth century.

A clearly related aspect of the Spanish experience is the restructuring of the Spanish state as a Catholic society. The thrust for homogeneity in society by religion, certainly not by "bloodline," was one of the many ramifications of nation-state building in Europe in general.[13] Obviously, such homogeneity is best facilitated by eliminating those sects that vary from desired theology, belief, and ritual. The easiest way to make Spain exclusively Catholic was by conversion, a process totally unrelated to biology, and this is what was done.

Exclusiveness, however, is fundamental to the ideology of race, and it can only be maintained by the erection of social-cultural boundaries between populations that (1) become broad barriers against interaction between "races," (2) preclude any possibility of egalitarian relationships, and (3) do not recognize or provide for intermediate realities. Such boundaries are most effective when they can be transmuted into a biological axiom. The experience of the Spanish is suggestive in that they came very close to infusing a "racial" element into the criteria of social identity; but more important was their elevation of *religious/cultural* homogeneity to a high social value.

The Spanish brought with them to the New World many of the cultural features of the Inquisition era and infused them onto the societies created in the colonial setting. Among these were the idea of "castas," the belief that "purity" of one's Hispanic genealogy entitled one to higher social status; the fear of mixture or taint in the lineage; judicial codes, customs, and proceedings of the Inquisition; religious fervor and intolerance; and most of all the customs, practices, and traditions of medieval slavery. Many of the Spanish customs and habits of thought were no doubt picked up by the English.

Thus some of the major ingredients for the ideology and worldview of "race" were present in the thought patterns and understandings of both Spanish and English peoples during the critical period when European colonial settlements in the New World began. All of the European conquerers and colonizers turned to the use of the term "race" (raza, race, reazza). They all shared a common belief that their victims were some form of "savages," despite recognized diversity among the cultures of indigenous peoples and different conceptions of savagery in the European minds. And all of the Europeans initiated the practice of slavery, both with Indians and with imported Africans. Yet the degree to which they conceptualized and institutionalized the perceived differences varied [...] for reasons that relate to their histories, experiences, and demographic realities. The English took the term "race" and molded it into a phenomenon unlike that of their competitors, structuring closed and exclusive groups out of the melange of peoples of the Americas. It is to the history of the English in America that we must now turn in order to examine those facets of culture and experience that led them to this point.

NOTES

1. See Boies Penrose (1955) for a description of early travels by Europeans and the fables, myths, and tales concocted by them about peoples and places unknown at that time.
2. Karl Marx and Max Weber were major writers of the nineteenth century who provided theoretical paradigms for the transition from peasant feudal society to industrial capitalism. For more than a century, many historians of England have documented, interpreted, and reinterpreted the development of modern capitalism and its attendant features. The theory simplified here is fairly conventional. See, for example, Bober ([1927] 1965), Genovese and Fox-Genovese (1983), and Macfarlane (1978).
3. Most of Europe had developed a dual or bilateral system of kinship in which connections on both sides, maternal and paternal, were given almost equal recognition. A corollary and perhaps consequence of this was the absence of corporate kinship groups with stable, permanent, and exclusive membership. Instead, each generation of siblings had a circle of relatives unique to it, known as kindreds, radiating outward on both sides. Obligations of kinsmen were based loosely on genealogical closeness, with the greatest sense of solidarity between brothers, then first cousins, second cousins, and so forth. In some cases, this could be extended to sixth or seventh cousins, but at that distance (which no doubt also frequently corresponded to geographic distance) the sense of responsibility was muted.
4. See especially Chapter 7 in which Macfarlane (1978) observes that these traits of the English, described by a writer of the late fifteenth century, most certainly evolved long before that time.
5. For examples, see Canny (1973) and Quinn (1966).
6. See the section on pastoralism in Cohen (1974) and the papers in Goldschmidt (1965). Although I concur with the perspective that views cultures as open, dynamic systems, it is also true that there are persisting themes manifest over broad ranges of time in many areas of the world. My concerns here are the frequent examples of seemingly irreconcilable differences and overt hostilities that have recurred between mobile herding societies and sedentary cultivators.
7. Because of their militarism and aggression and the facility for rapid mobility, some nomadic herders have from time to time throughout history come to dominate their sedentary neighbors. In some cases, vast movements of large pastoral groups have led to conquests and to the consolidation of large new empires, as for example the migrations of

Turkish peoples in Russia, the Middle East, northern India, and Persia, the Fulani in West Africa, and the Mongols in Asia.

8. Quoted in Myers (1983, 15),
9. See brief descriptions of the brutal Munster and Ulster uprisings and the eventual conquests by the British forces in Liggio (1976) and in Quinn (1966).
10. After some of their campaigns, the English pursued a scorched-earth policy, destroying livestock and vegetation so that the Irish would be reduced to famine. It was reported that some turned to eating human flesh (Quinn 1966, 132), which confirmed the imagery of cannibalism to the English.
11. For various reasons the plantations established in Ireland were, by and large, failures, which prompted even greater interest in the New World and in the creation of plantation societies there, especially in the Caribbean Islands (see Quinn 1966 and Jones 1942).
12. Ronald Sanders (1978) makes an important point about the Spanish attitude toward and treatment of Jews. "In this notion that a certain group within society is unclean and should be quarantined we can perceive an incipient racism—still only incipient, however, since the idea remains that the uncleanness resides in doctrine, not in blood" (25).
13. Robert Berkhofer, Jr., has recognized the political significance of such homogeneity. "One king, one faith, one law," he notes, protects the political stability of new regimes in a time of religious (and secular) conflicts. (Personal communication.)

REFERENCES

Bloch, Marc. 1961. *Feudal Society*. London: Routledge & Kegan Paul.

Bober, M.M. [1927] 1965. *Karl Marx's Interpretation of History*. Reprint. New York: W.W. Norton.

Canny, Nicholas P. 1973. "The Ideology of English Colonialization: From Ireland to America." *William and Mary Quarterly*, 3d Ser. 30: 575–598.

Castro, Americo. 1971. *The Spaniards*. Berkeley: University of California Press.

Cohen, Yehudi, ed. 1974. *Man in Adaptation*. Chicago: Aldine.

Dietz, F.C. 1932. *A Political and Social History of England*. New York: Macmillan.

Dyson-Hudson, R., and N. Dyson-Hudson. 1980. "Nomadic Pastoralism." *Annual Review of Anthropology*, vol. 9. Palo Alto, Calif.: Annual Reviews.

Genovese, E., and E. Fox-Genovese. 1983. *Fruits of Merchant Capital*. New York: Oxford University Press.

Goldschmidt, W. 1965. "Theory and Strategy in the Study of Cultural Adaptability." *American Anthropologist* 67, no. 2: 402–434.

Hodgen, Margaret. 1964. *Early Anthropology in the Sixteenth and Seventeenth Centuries*. Philadelphia: University of Pennsylvania Press.

Horsman, Reginald. 1976. "Origins of Racial Anglo-Saxonism in Great Britain Before 1850." *Journal of the History of Ideas* 37, no. 3: 239–262.

———. 1981. *Race and Manifest Destiny*. Cambridge: Harvard University Press.

Jones, Howard M. 1942. "Origins of the Colonial Idea in England." *American Philosophical Society* 85, no. 5: 448–465.

Liggio, Leonard P. 1976. "English Origins of Early American Racism." *Radical History Review* 3, no. 1: 1–36.

Macfarlane, Alan. 1978. *The Origins of English Individualism*. Oxford: Basil Blackwell.

MacPherson, C.B. 1962. *The Political Theory of Possessive Individualism*. Oxford: Clarendon Press.

Myers, James P., ed. 1983. *Elizabethan Ireland*. Hamden, Conn.: Archon Books.

Penrose, Boies. 1955. *Travel and Discovery in the Renaissance, 1420–1620*. Cambridge: Harvard University Press.

Pirenne, Henri. [1925] 1952. *Medieval Cities*. Reprint. Princeton, NJ: Princeton University Press.

Quinn, D.B. 1958. "Ireland and Sixteenth-Century European Expansion." *Historical Studies*. New York: Hilary House.

———. 1966. *Elizabethans and the Irish*. Ithaca, NY: Cornell University Press.

Roth, Cecil. 1964. *The Spanish Inquisition*. New York: W.W. Norton.

Sanders, Ronald. 1978. *Lost Tribes and Promised Lands: The Origins of American Racism*. Boston: Little, Brown & Co.

Sweet, Louise. 1965. "Camel Raiding of North Arabian Bedouin: A Mechanism of Ecological Adaptation." *American Anthropologist* 67, no. 4: 1,132–1,150.

CHAPTER 6

LATENT AND MANIFEST ORIENTALISM

Edward W. Said

In Chapter One, I tried to indicate the scope of thought and action covered by the word *Orientalism*, using as privileged types the British and French experiences of and with the Near Orient, Islam, and the Arabs. In those experiences I discerned an intimate, perhaps even the most intimate, and rich relationship between Occident and Orient. Those experiences were part of a much wider European or Western relationship with the Orient, but what seems to have influenced Orientalism most was a fairly constant sense of confrontation felt by Westerners dealing with the East. The boundary notion of East and West, the varying degrees of projected inferiority and strength, the range of work done, the kinds of characteristic features ascribed to the Orient: all these testify to a willed imaginative and geographic division made between East and West, and lived through during many centuries. In Chapter Two my focus narrowed a good deal. I was interested in the earliest phases of what I call modern Orientalism, which began during the latter part of the eighteenth century and the early years of the nineteenth. Since I did not intend my study to become a narrative chronicle of the development of Oriental studies in the modern West, I proposed instead an account of the rise, development, and institutions of Orientalism as they were formed against a background of intellectual, cultural, and political history until about 1870 or 1880. Although my interest in Orientalism there included a decently ample variety of scholars and imaginative writers, I cannot claim by any means to have presented more than a portrait of the typical structures (and their ideological tendencies) constituting the field, its associations with other fields, and the work of some of its most influential scholars. My principal operating assumptions were—and continue to be—that fields of learning, as much as the works of even the most eccentric artist, are constrained and acted upon by society, by cultural traditions, by worldly circumstance, and by stabilizing influences like schools, libraries, and governments; moreover, that both learned and imaginative writing are never free, but are limited in their imagery, assumptions, and intentions; and finally, that the advances made by a "science" like Orientalism in its academic form are less objectively true than we often like to think. In short, my study hitherto has tried to describe the *economy* that makes Orientalism a coherent subject matter, even while allowing that as an idea, concept, or image the word *Orient* has a considerable and interesting cultural resonance in the West.

I realize that such assumptions are not without their controversial side. Most of us assume in a general way that learning and scholarship move forward; they get better, we feel, as time passes and as more information is accumulated, methods are refined, and later generations of scholars improve upon earlier ones. In addition, we entertain a mythology of creation, in which it is believed that artistic genius, an original talent, or a powerful intellect can leap beyond the confines of its own time and place in order to put before the world a new work. It would be pointless to deny that such ideas as these carry some truth. Nevertheless the possibilities for work present in the culture to a great and original mind are never unlimited, just as it is also true that a great talent has a very healthy respect for what others have done before it and for what the field already contains. The work of predecessors, the institutional life of a scholarly field, the collective nature of any learned enterprise: these, to say nothing of economic and social circumstances, tend to diminish the effects of the individual scholar's production. A field like Orientalism has a cumulative and corporate identity, one that is particularly strong given its associations with traditional learning (the classics, the Bible, philology), public institutions (governments, trading companies, geographical societies, universities), and generically determined writing (travel books, books of exploration, fantasy, exotic description). The result for Orientalism has been a sort of consensus: certain things, certain types of statement, certain types of work have seemed for the Orientalist correct. He has built his work and research upon them, and they in turn have pressed hard upon new writers and scholars. Orientalism can thus be regarded as a manner of regularized (or Orientalized) writing, vision, and study, dominated by imperatives, perspectives, and ideological biases ostensibly suited to the Orient. The Orient is taught, researched, administered, and pronounced upon in certain discrete ways.

The Orient that appears in Orientalism, then, is a system of representations framed by a whole set of forces that brought the Orient into Western learning, Western consciousness, and later, Western empire. If this definition of Orientalism seems more political than not, that is simply because I think Orientalism was itself a product of certain political forces and activities. Orientalism is a school of interpretation whose material happens to be the Orient, its civilizations, peoples, and localities. Its objective discoveries—the work of innumerable devoted scholars who edited texts and translated them, codified grammars, wrote dictionaries, reconstructed dead epochs, produced positivistically verifiable learning—are and always have been conditioned by the fact that its truths, like any truths delivered by language, are embodied in language, and what is the truth of language, Nietzsche once said, but

> a mobile army of metaphors, metonyms, and anthropomorphisms—in short, a sum of human relations, which have been enhanced, transposed, and embel-

> lished poetically and rhetorically, and which after long use seem firm, canonical, and obligatory to a people: truths are illusions about which one has forgotten that this is what they are.[1]

Perhaps such a view as Nietzsche's will strike us as too nihilistic, but at least it will draw attention to the fact that so far as it existed in the West's awareness, the Orient was a word which later accrued to it a wide field of meanings, associations, and connotations, and that these did not necessarily refer to the real Orient but to the field surrounding the word.

Thus Orientalism is not only a positive doctrine about the Orient that exists at any one time in the West; it is also an influential academic tradition (when one refers to an academic specialist who is called an Orientalist), as well as an area of concern defined by travelers, commercial enterprises, governments, military expeditions, readers of novels and accounts of exotic adventure, natural historians, and pilgrims to whom the Orient is a specific kind of knowledge about specific places, peoples, and civilizations. For the Orient idioms became frequent, and these idioms took firm hold in European discourse. Beneath the idioms there was a layer of doctrine about the Orient; this doctrine was fashioned out of the experiences of many Europeans, all of them converging upon such essential aspects of the Orient as the Oriental character, Oriental despotism, Oriental sensuality, and the like. For any European during the nineteenth century—and I think one can say this almost without qualification—Orientalism was such a system of truths, truths in Nietzsche's sense of the word. It is therefore correct that every European, in what he could say about the Orient, was consequently a racist, an imperialist, and almost totally ethnocentric. Some of the immediate sting will be taken out of these labels if we recall additionally that human societies, at least the more advanced cultures, have rarely offered the individual anything but imperialism, racism, and ethnocentrism for dealing with "other" cultures. So Orientalism aided and was aided by general cultural pressures that tended to make more rigid the sense of difference between the European and Asiatic parts of the world. My contention is that Orientalism is fundamentally a political doctrine willed over the Orient because the Orient was weaker than the West, which elided the Orient's difference with its weakness.

This proposition was introduced early in Chapter One, and nearly everything in the pages that followed was intended in part as a corroboration of it. The very presence of a "field" such as Orientalism, with no corresponding equivalent in the Orient itself, suggests the relative strength of Orient and Occident. A vast number of pages on the Orient exist, and they of course signify a degree and quantity of interaction with the Orient that are quite formidable; but the crucial index of Western strength is that there is no possibility of comparing the movement of Westerners eastwards (since the end of the eighteenth century) with the movement of Easterners westwards. Leaving aside the fact that Western armies, consular corps, merchants, and scientific and archaeological expeditions were always going East, the number of travelers from the Islamic East to Europe between 1800 and 1900 is minuscule when compared with the number in the other direction.[2] Moreover, the Eastern travelers in the West were there to learn from and to gape at an advanced culture; the purposes of the Western travelers in the Orient were, as we have seen, of quite a different order. In addition, it has been estimated that around 60,000 books dealing with the Near Orient were written between 1800 and 1950; there is no remotely comparable figure for Oriental books about the West. As a cultural apparatus Orientalism is all aggression, activity, judgment, will-to-truth, and knowledge. The Orient existed for the West, or so it seemed to countless Orientalists, whose attitude to what they worked on was either paternalistic or candidly condescending—unless, of course, they were antiquarians, in which case the "classical" Orient was a credit to *them* and not to the lamentable modern Orient. And then, beefing up the Western scholars' work, there were numerous agencies and institutions with no parallels in Oriental society.

Such an imbalance between East and West is obviously a function of changing historical patterns. During its political and military heyday from the eighth century to the sixteenth, Islam dominated both East and West. Then the center of power shifted westwards, and now in the late twentieth century it seems to be directing itself back towards the East again. My account of nineteenth-century Orientalism in Chapter Two stopped at a particularly charged period in the latter part of the century, when the often dilatory, abstract, and projective aspects of Orientalism were about to take on a new sense of worldly mission in the service of formal colonialism. It is this project and this moment that I want now to describe, especially since it will furnish us with some important background for the twentieth-century crises of Orientalism and the resurgence of political and cultural strength in the East.

On several occasions I have alluded to the connections between Orientalism as a body of ideas, beliefs, clichés, or learning about the East, and other schools of thought at large in the culture. Now one of the important developments in nineteenth-century Orientalism was the distillation of essential ideas about the Orient—its sensuality, its tendency to despotism, its aberrant mentality, its habits of inaccuracy, its backwardness—into a separate and unchallenged coherence; thus for a writer to use the word *Oriental* was a reference for the reader sufficient to identify a specific body of information about the Orient. This information seemed to be morally neutral and objectively valid; it seemed to have an epistemological status equal to that of historical chronology or geographical location. In its most basic form, then, Oriental material could not really be violated by anyone's discoveries, nor did it seem ever to be revaluated completely. Instead, the work of various nineteenth-century scholars and of imaginative writers made this essential body of knowledge more clear, more detailed, more substantial—and more distinct from "Occidentalism." Yet Orientalist ideas could enter into alliance with general philosophical theories (such as those about the history of mankind and civilization) and diffuse world-hypotheses, as philosophers sometimes call them; and in many ways the professional contributors to Oriental knowledge were anxious to couch their formulations and ideas, their scholarly work, their considered contemporary observations, in language and terminology whose cultural validity derived from other sciences and systems of thought.

The distinction I am making is really between an almost unconscious (and certainly an untouchable) positivity, which I shall call *latent* Orientalism, and the various stated views about Oriental society, languages, literatures, history, sociology, and so forth, which I shall call *manifest* Orientalism. Whatever change occurs in knowledge of the Orient is found almost exclusively in manifest Orientalism; the unanimity, stability, and durability of latent Orientalism are more or less constant. In the nineteenth-century writers I analyzed in Chapter Two, the differences in their ideas about the Orient can be characterized as exclusively manifest differences, differences in form and personal style, rarely in basic content. Every one of them kept intact the separateness of the Orient, its eccentricity, its backwardness, its silent indifference, its feminine penetrability, its supine malleability; this is why every writer on the Orient, from Renan to Marx (ideologically speaking), or from the most rigorous scholars (Lane and Sacy) to the most powerful imaginations (Flaubert and Nerval), saw the Orient as a locale requiring Western attention, reconstruction, even redemption. The Orient existed as a place isolated from the mainstream of European progress in the sciences, arts, and commerce. Thus whatever good or bad values were imputed to the Orient appeared to be functions of some highly specialized Western interest in the Orient. This was the situation from about the 1870s on through the early part of the twentieth century—but let me give some examples that illustrate what I mean.

Theses of Oriental backwardness, degeneracy, and inequality with the West most easily associated themselves early in the nineteenth century with ideas about the biological bases of racial inequality. Thus the racial classifications found in Cuvier's *Le Règne animal*, Gobineau's *Essai sur l'inégalité des races humaines*, and Robert Knox's *The Races of Man* found a willing partner in latent Orientalism. To these ideas was added second-order Darwinism, which seemed to accentuate the "scientific" validity of the division of races into advanced and backward, or European-Aryan and Oriental-African. Thus the whole question of imperialism, as it was debated in the late nineteenth century by pro-imperialists and anti-imperialists alike, carried forward the binary typology of advanced and backward (or subject) races, cultures, and societies. John Westlake's *Chapters on the Principles of International Law* (1894) argues, for example, that regions of the earth designated as "uncivilized" (a word carrying the freight of Orientalist assumptions, among others) ought to be annexed or occupied by advanced powers. Similarly, the ideas of such writers as Carl Peters, Leopold de Saussure, and Charles Temple draw on the advanced/backward binarism[3] so centrally advocated in late-nineteenth-century Orientalism.

Along with all other peoples variously designated as backward, degenerate, uncivilized, and retarded, the Orientals were viewed in a framework constructed out of biological determinism and moral-political admonishment. The Oriental was linked thus to elements in Western society (delinquents, the insane, women, the poor) having in common an identity best described as lamentably alien. Orientals were rarely seen or looked at; they were seen through, analyzed not as citizens, or even people, but as problems to be solved or confined or—as the colonial powers openly coveted their territory—taken over. The point is that the very designation of something as Oriental involved an already pronounced evaluative judgment, and in the case of the peoples inhabiting the decayed Ottoman Empire, an implicit program of action. Since the Oriental was a member of a subject race, he had to be subjected: it was that simple. The *locus classicus* for such judgment and action is to be found in Gustave Le Bon's *Les Lois psychologiques de l'évolution des peuples* (1894).

But there were other uses for latent Orientalism. If that group of ideas allowed one to separate Orientals from advanced, civilizing powers, and if the "classical" Orient served to justify both the Orientalist and his disregard of modern Orientals, latent Orientalism also encouraged a peculiarly (not to say invidiously) male conception of the world. I have already referred to this in passing during my discussion of Renan. The Oriental male was considered in isolation from the total community in which he lived and which many Orientalists, following Lane, have viewed with something resembling contempt and fear. Orientalism itself, furthermore, was an exclusively male province; like so many professional guilds during the modern period, it viewed itself and its subject matter with sexist blinders. This is especially evident in the writing of travelers and novelists: women are usually the creatures of a male power-fantasy. They express unlimited sensuality, they are more or less stupid, and above all they are willing. Flaubert's Kuchuk Hanem is the prototype of such caricatures, which were common enough in pornographic novels (e.g., Pierre Louys's *Aphrodite*) whose novelty draws on the Orient for their interest. Moreover the male conception of the world, in its effect upon the practicing Orientalist, tends to be static, frozen, fixed eternally. The very possibility of development, transformation, human movement—in the deepest sense of the word—is denied the Orient and the Oriental. As a known and ultimately an immobilized or unproductive quality, they come to be identified with a bad sort of eternality: hence, when the Orient is being approved, such phrases as "the wisdom of the East."

Transferred from an implicit social evaluation to a grandly cultural one, this static male Orientalism took on a variety of forms in the late nineteenth century, especially when Islam was being discussed. General cultural historians as respected as Leopold von Ranke and Jacob Burckhardt assailed Islam as if they were dealing not so much with an anthropomorphic abstraction as with a religio-political culture about which deep generalizations were possible and warranted: in his *Weltgeschichte* (1881–1888) Ranke spoke of Islam as defeated by the Germanic-Romanic peoples, and in his "Historische Fragmente" (unpublished notes, 1893) Burckhardt spoke of Islam as wretched, bare, and trivial.[4] Such intellectual operations were carried out with considerably more flair and enthusiasm by Oswald Spengler, whose ideas about a Magian personality (typified by the Muslim Oriental) infuse *Der Untergang des Abendlandes* (1918–1922) and the "morphology" of cultures it advocates.

What these widely diffused notions of the Orient depended on was the almost total absence in contemporary Western culture of the Orient as a genuinely felt and experienced force. For a number of evident reasons the Orient was always in the position both of outsider and of incorporated weak partner for the West. To the extent that Western scholars were aware of contemporary Orientals or Oriental movements of thought and culture, these were perceived either as silent shadows to be animated by the Orientalist, brought into reality by him, or as a kind of cultural and intellectual proletariat useful for the Orientalist's grander interpretative activity, necessary for his performance as superior judge, learned man, powerful cultural will. I mean to say that in discussions of the Orient, the Orient is all absence, whereas one feels the Orientalist and what he says as presence; yet we must not forget that the Orientalist's presence is enabled by the Orient's effective absence. This fact of substitution and displacement, as we must call it, clearly places on the Orientalist himself a certain pressure to reduce the Orient in his work, even after he has devoted a good deal of time to elucidating and exposing it. How else can one explain major scholarly production of the type we associate with Julius Wellhausen and Theodor Nöldeke and, overriding it, those bare, sweeping statements that almost totally denigrate their chosen subject matter? Thus Nöldeke could declare in 1887 that the sum total of his work as an Orientalist was to confirm his "low opinion" of the Eastern peoples.[5] And like Carl Becker, Nöldeke was a philhellenist, who showed his love of Greece curiously by displaying a positive dislike of the Orient, which after all was what he studied as a scholar.

A very valuable and intelligent study of Orientalism—Jacques Waardenburg's *L'Islam dans le miroir de l'Occident*—examines five important experts as makers of an image of Islam. Waardenburg's mirror-image metaphor for late-nineteenth- and early-twentieth-century Orientalism is apt. In the work of each of his eminent Orientalists there is a highly tendentious—in four cases out of the five, even hostile—vision of Islam, as if each man saw Islam as a reflection of his own chosen weakness. Each scholar was profoundly learned, and the style of his contribution was unique. The five Orientalists among them exemplify what was best and strongest in the tradition during the period roughly from the 1880s to the interwar years. Yet Ignaz Goldziher's appreciation of Islam's tolerance towards other religions was undercut by his dislike of Mohammed's anthropomorphisms and Islam's too-exterior theology and jurisprudence; Duncan Black Macdonald's interest in Islamic piety and orthodoxy was vitiated by his perception of what he considered Islam's heretical Christianity; Carl Becker's understanding of Islamic civilization made him see it as a sadly undeveloped one; C. Snouck Hurgronje's highly refined studies of Islamic mysticism (which he considered the essential part of Islam) led him to a harsh judgment of its crippling limitations; and Louis Massignon's extraordinary identification with Muslim theology, mystical passion, and poetic art kept him curiously unforgiving to Islam for what he regarded as its unregenerate revolt against the idea of incarnation. The manifest differences in their methods emerge as less important than their Orientalist consensus on Islam: latent inferiority.[6]

Waardenburg's study has the additional virtue of showing how these five scholars shared a common intellectual and methodological tradition whose unity was truly international. Ever since the first Orientalist congress in 1873, scholars in the field have known each other's work and felt each other's presence very directly. What Waardenburg does not stress enough is that most of the late-nineteenth-century Orientalists were bound to each other politically as well. Snouck Hurgronje went directly from his studies of Islam to being an adviser to the Dutch government on handling its Muslim Indonesian colonies; Macdonald and Massignon were widely sought after as experts on Islamic matters by colonial administrators from North Africa to Pakistan; and, as Waardenburg says (all too briefly) at one point, all five scholars shaped a coherent vision of Islam that had a wide influence on government circles throughout the Western world.[7] What we must add to Waardenburg's observation is that these scholars were completing, bringing to an ultimate concrete refinement, the tendency since the sixteenth and seventeenth centuries to treat the Orient not only as a vague literary problem but—according to Masson-Oursel—as "un ferme propos d'assimiler adéquatement la valeur des langues pour pénétrer les moeurs et les pensées, pour forcer même des secrets de l'histoire."[8]

I spoke earlier of incorporation and assimilation of the Orient, as these activities were practiced by writers as different from each other as Dante and d'Herbelot. Clearly there is a difference between those efforts and what, by the end of the nineteenth century, had become a truly formidable European cultural, political, and material enterprise. The nineteenth-century colonial "scramble for Africa" was by no means limited to Africa, of course. Neither was the penetration of the Orient entirely a sudden, dramatic afterthought following years of scholarly study of Asia. What we must reckon with is a long and slow process of appropriation by which Europe, or the European awareness of the Orient, transformed itself from being textual and contemplative into being administrative, economic, and even military. The fundamental change was a spatial and geographical one, or rather it was a change in the quality of geographical and spatial apprehension so far as the Orient was concerned. The centuries-old designation of geographical space to the east of Europe as "Oriental" was partly political, partly doctrinal, and partly imaginative; it implied no necessary connection between actual experience of the Orient and knowledge of what is Oriental, and certainly Dante and d'Herbelot made no claims about their Oriental ideas except that they were corroborated by a long *learned* (and not existential) tradition. But when Lane, Renan, Burton, and the many hundreds of nineteenth-century European travelers and scholars discuss the Orient, we can immediately note a far more intimate and even proprietary attitude towards the Orient and things Oriental. In the classical and often temporally remote form in which it was reconstructed by the Orientalist, in the precisely actual form in which the modern Orient was lived in, studied, or imagined, the *geographical space* of the Orient was penetrated, worked over, taken hold of. The cumulative effect of decades of so sovereign a Western handling turned the Orient from alien into colonial space. What was important in the latter nineteenth century was not *whether* the West had penetrated and possessed the Orient, but rather *how the* British and French felt that they had done it.

The British writer on the Orient, and even more so the British colonial administrator, was dealing with territory about which there could be no doubt that English power was truly in the ascendant, even if the natives were on the face of it attracted to France and French modes of thought. So far as the actual space of the Orient was concerned, however, England was really there, France was not, except as a flighty temptress of the Oriental yokels. There is no better indication of this qualitative difference in spatial attitudes than to look at what Lord Cromer had to say on the subject, one that was especially dear to his heart:

> The reasons why French civilisation presents a special degree of attraction to Asiatics and Levantines are plain. It is, as a matter of fact, more attractive than the civilisations of England and Germany, and, moreover, it is more easy of imitation. Compare the undemonstrative, shy Englishman, with his social exclusiveness and insular habits, with the vivacious and cosmopolitan Frenchman, who does not know what the word shyness means, and who in ten minutes is apparently on terms of intimate friendship with any casual acquaintance he may chance to make. The semi-educated Oriental does not recognise that the former has, at all events, the merit of sincerity, whilst the latter is often merely acting a part. He looks coldly on the Englishman, and rushes into the arms of the Frenchman.

The sexual innuendoes develop more or less naturally thereafter. The Frenchman is all smiles, wit, grace, and fashion; the Englishman is plodding, industrious, Baconian, precise. Cramer's case is of course based on British solidity as opposed to a French seductiveness without any real presence in Egyptian reality.

> Can it be any matter for surprise [Cromer continues] that the Egyptian, with his light intellectual ballast, fails to see that some fallacy often lies at the bottom of the Frenchman's reasoning, or that he prefers the rather superficial brilliancy of the Frenchman to the plodding, unattractive industry of the Englishman or the German? Look, again, at the theoretical perfection of French administrative systems, at their elaborate detail, and at the provision which is apparently made to meet every possible contingency which may arise. Compare these features with the Englishman's practical systems, which lay down rules as to a few main points, and leave a mass of detail to individual discretion. The half-educated Egyptian naturally prefers the Frenchman's system, for it is to all outward appearance more perfect and more easy of application. He fails, moreover, to see that the Englishman desires to elaborate a system which will suit the facts with which he has to deal, whereas the main objection to applying French administrative procedures to Egypt is that the facts have but too often to conform to the ready-made system.

Since there is a real British presence in Egypt, and since that presence—according to Cromer—is there not so much to train the Egyptian's mind as to "form his character," it follows therefore that the ephemeral attractions of the French are those of a pretty damsel with "somewhat artificial charms," whereas those of the British belong to "a sober, elderly matron of perhaps somewhat greater moral worth, but of less pleasing outward appearance."[9]

Underlying Cromer's contrast between the solid British nanny and the French coquette is the sheer privilege of British emplacement in the Orient. "The facts with which he [the Englishman] has to deal" are altogether more complex and interesting, by virtue of their possession by England, than anything the mercurial French could point to. Two years after the publication of his *Modern Egypt* (1908), Cromer expatiated philosophically in *Ancient and Modern Imperialism*. Compared with Roman imperialism, with its frankly assimilationist, exploitative, and repressive policies, British imperialism seemed to Cromer to be preferable, if somewhat more wishy-washy. On certain points, however, the British were clear enough, even if "after a rather dim, slipshod, but characteristically Anglo-Saxon fashion," their Empire seemed undecided between "one of two bases—an extensive military occupation or the principle of nationality [for subject races]." But this indecision was academic finally, for in practice Cromer and Britain itself had opted against "the principle of nationality." And then there were other things to be noted. One point was that the Empire was not going to be given up. Another was that intermarriage between natives and English men and women was undesirable. Third—and most important, I think—Cromer conceived of British imperial presence in the Eastern colonies as having had a lasting, not to say cataclysmic, effect on the minds and societies of the East. His metaphor for expressing this effect is almost theological, so powerful in Cromer's mind was the idea of Western penetration of Oriental expanses. "The country," he says, "over which the breath of the West, heavily charged with scientific thought, has once passed, and has, in passing, left an enduring mark, can never be the same as it was before."[10]

In such respects as these, nonetheless, Cromer's was far from an original intelligence. What he saw and how he expressed it were common currency among his colleagues both in the imperial Establishment and in the intellectual community. This consensus is notably true in the case of Cromer's viceregal colleagues, Curzon, Swettenham, and Lugard. Lord Curzon in particular always spoke the imperial lingua franca, and more obtrusively even than Cromer he delineated the relationship between Britain and the Orient in terms of possession, in terms of a large geographical space wholly owned by an efficient colonial master. For him, he said on one occasion, the Empire was not an "object of ambition" but "first and foremost, a great historical and political and sociological fact." In 1909 he reminded delegates to the Imperial Press Conference meeting at Oxford that "we train here and we send out to you your governors and administrators and judges, your teachers and preachers and lawyers." And this almost pedagogical view of empire had, for Curzon, a specific setting in Asia, which as he once put it, made "one pause and think."

> I sometimes like to picture to myself this great Imperial fabric as a huge structure like some Tennysonian "Palace of Art," of which the foundations are in this country, where they have been laid and must be maintained by British hands, but of which the Colonies are the pillars, and high above all floats the vastness of an Asiatic dome.[11]

With such a Tennysonian Palace of Art in mind, Curzon and Cromer were enthusiastic members together of a departmental committee formed in 1909 to press for the creation of a school of Oriental studies. Aside from remarking wistfully that had he known the vernacular he would have been helped during his "famine tours" in India, Curzon argued for Oriental studies as part of the British responsibility to the Orient. On September 27, 1909, he told the House of Lords that

> our familiarity, not merely with the languages of the people of the East but with their customs, their feelings, their traditions, their history and religion, our capacity to understand what may be called the genius of the East, is the sole basis upon which we are likely to be able to maintain in the future the position we have won, and no step that can be taken to strengthen that position can be considered undeserving of the attention of His Majesty's Government or of a debate in the House of Lords.

At a Mansion House conference on the subject five years later, Curzon finally dotted the i's. Oriental studies were no intellectual luxury; they were, he said,

> a great Imperial obligation. In my view the creation of a school [of Oriental studies—later to become the London University School of Oriental and African Studies] like this in London is part of the necessary furniture of Empire. Those of us who, in one way or another, have spent a number of years in the East, who regard that as the happiest portion of our lives, and who think that the work that we did there, be it great or small, was the highest responsibility that can be placed upon the shoulders of Englishmen, feel that there is a gap in our national equipment which ought emphatically to be filled, and that those in the City of London who, by financial support or by any other form of active and practical assistance, take their part in filling that gap, will be rendering a patriotic duty to the Empire and promoting the cause and goodwill among mankind.[12]

To a very great extent Curzon's ideas about Oriental studies derive logically from a good century of British utilitarian administration of and philosophy about the Eastern colonies. The influence of Bentham and the Mills on British rule in the Orient (and India particularly) was considerable, and was effective in doing away with too much regulation and innovation; instead, as Eric Stokes has convincingly shown, utilitarianism combined with the legacies of liberalism and evangelicalism as philosophies of British rule in the East stressed the rational importance of a strong executive armed with various legal and penal codes, a system of doctrines on such matters as frontiers and land rents, and everywhere an irreducible supervisory imperial authority.[13] The cornerstone of the whole system was a constantly refined knowledge of the Orient, so that as traditional societies hastened forward and became modern commercial societies, there would be no loss of paternal British control, and no loss of revenue either. However, when Curzon referred somewhat inelegantly to Oriental studies as "the necessary furniture of Empire," he was putting into a static image the transactions by which Englishmen and natives conducted their business and kept their places. From the days of Sir William Jones the Orient had been both what Britain ruled and what Britain knew about it: the coincidence between geography, knowledge, and power, with Britain always in the master's place, was complete. To have said, as Curzon once did, that "the East is a University in which the scholar never takes his degree" was another way of saying that the East required one's presence there more or less forever.[14]

But then there were the other European powers, France and Russia among them, that made the British presence always a (perhaps marginally) threatened one. Curzon was certainly aware that all the major Western powers felt towards the world as Britain did. The transformation of geography from "dull and pedantic"—Curzon's phrase for what had now dropped out of geography as an academic subject—into "the most cosmopolitan of all sciences" argued *exactly* that new Western and widespread predilection. Not for nothing did Curzon in 1912 tell the Geographical Society, of which he was president, that

> an absolute revolution has occurred, not merely in the manner and methods of teaching geography, but in the estimation in which it is held by public opinion. Nowadays we regard geographical knowledge as an essential part of knowledge in general. By the aid of geography, and in no other way, do we understand the action of great natural forces, the distribution of population, the growth of commerce, the expansion of frontiers, the development of States, the splendid achievements of human energy in its various manifestations.
>
> We recognize geography as the handmaid of history.... Geography, too, is a sister science to economics and politics; and to any of us who have attempted to study geography it is known that the moment you diverge from the geographical field you find yourself crossing the frontiers of geology, zoology, ethnology, chemistry, physics, and almost all the kindred sciences. Therefore we are justified in saying that geography is one of the first and foremost of the sciences: that it is part of the equipment that is necessary for a proper conception of citizenship, and is an indispensable adjunct to the production of a public man.[15]

Geography was essentially the material underpinning for knowledge about the Orient. All the latent and unchanging characteristics of the Orient stood upon, were rooted in, its geography. Thus on the one hand the geographical Orient nourished its inhabitants, guaranteed their characteristics, and defined their specificity; on the other hand, the geographical Orient solicited the West's attention, even as—by one of those paradoxes revealed so frequently by organized knowledge—East was East and West was West. The cosmopolitanism of geography was, in Curzon's mind, its universal importance to the whole of the West, whose relationship to the rest of the world was one of frank covetousness. Yet geographical appetite could also take on the moral neutrality of an epistemological impulse to find out, to settle upon, to uncover—as when in *Heart of Darkness* Marlow confesses to having a passion for maps.

> I would look for hours at South America, or Africa, or Australia, and lose myself in all the glories of exploration. At that time there were many blank spaces on the earth, and when I saw one that looked particularly inviting on a map (but they all look that) I would put my finger on it and say, When I grow up I will go there.[16]

Seventy years or so before Marlow said this, it did not trouble Lamartine that what on a map was a blank space was inhabited by natives; nor, theoretically, had there been any reservation in the mind of Emer de Vattel, the Swiss-Prussian authority on international law, when in 1758 he invited European states to take possession of territory inhabited only by mere wandering tribes.[17] The important thing was to dignify simple conquest with an idea, to turn the appetite for more geographical space into a theory about the special relationship between geography on the one hand and civilized or uncivilized peoples on the other. But to these rationalizations there was also a distinctively French contribution.

By the end of the nineteenth century, political and intellectual circumstances coincided sufficiently in France to make geography, and geographical speculation (in both senses of that word), an attractive national pastime. The general climate of opinion in Europe was propitious; certainly the successes of British imperialism spoke loudly enough for themselves. However, Britain always seemed to France and to French thinkers on the subject to block even a relatively successful French imperial role in the Orient. Before the Franco-Prussian War there was a good deal of wishful political thinking about the Orient, and it was not confined to poets and novelists. Here, for instance, is Saint-Marc Girardin writing in the *Revue des Deux Mondes* on March 15, 1862:

> La France a beaucoup à faire en Orient, parce que l'Orient attend beaucoup d'elle. Il lui demande même plus qu'elle ne peut faire; il lui remettrait volontiers le soin entier de son avenir, ce qui serait pour la France et pour l'Orient un grand danger: pour la France, parce que, disposée a prendre en mains la cause des populations souffrantes, elle se charge le plus souvent de plus d'obligations qu'elle n'en peut remplir; pour l'Orient, parce que tout peuple qui attend sa destinée de l'étranger n'a jamais qu'une condition précaire et qu'il n'y a de salut pour les nations que celui qu'elles se font elles-mêmes.[18]

Of such views as this Disraeli would doubtless have said, as he often did, that France had only "sentimental interests" in Syria (which is the "Orient" of which Girardin was writing). The fiction of "populations souffrantes" had of course been used by Napoleon when he appealed to the Egyptians on their behalf against the Turks and for Islam. During the thirties, forties, fifties, and sixties the suffering populations of the Orient were limited to the Christian minorities in Syria. And there was no record of "l'Orient" appealing to France for its salvation. It would have been altogether more truthful to say that Britain stood in France's way in the Orient, for even if France genuinely felt a sense of obligation to the Orient (and there were some Frenchmen who did), there was very little France could do to get between Britain and the huge land mass it commanded from India to the Mediterranean.

Among the most remarkable consequences of the War of 1870 in France were a tremendous efflorescence of geographical societies and a powerfully renewed demand for territorial acquisition. At the end of 1871 the Société de géographic de Paris declared itself no longer confined to "scientific speculation." It urged the citizenry not to "forget that our former preponderance was contested from the day we ceased to compete ... in the conquests of civilization over barbarism." Guillaume Depping, a leader of what has come to be called the geographical movement, asserted in 1881 that during the 1870 war "it was the schoolmaster who triumphed," meaning that the real triumphs were those of Prussian scientific geography over French strategic sloppiness. The government's *Journal officiel* sponsored issue after issue centered on the virtues (and profits) of geographical exploration and colonial adventure; a citizen could learn in one issue from de Lesseps of "the opportunities in Africa" and from Gamier of "the exploration of the Blue River." Scientific geography soon gave way to "commercial geography," as the connection between national pride in scientific and civilizational achievement and the fairly rudimentary profit motive was urged, to be channeled into support for colonial acquisition. In the words of one enthusiast, "The geographical societies are formed to break the fatal charm that holds us enchained to our shores." In aid of this liberating quest all sorts of schemes were spun out, including the enlisting of Jules Verne—whose "unbelievable success," as it was called, ostensibly displayed the scientific mind at a very high peak of ratiocination—to head "a round-the-world campaign of scientific exploration," and a plan for creating a vast new sea just south of the North African coast, as well as a project for "binding" Algeria to Senegal by railroad—"a ribbon of steel," as the projectors called it.[19]

Much of the expansionist fervor in France during the last third of the nineteenth century was generated out of an explicit wish to compensate for the Prussian victory in 1870–1871 and, no less important, the desire to match British imperial achievements. So powerful was the latter desire, and out of so long a tradition of Anglo-French rivalry in the Orient did it derive, that France seemed literally haunted by Britain, anxious in all things connected with the Orient to catch up with and emulate the British. When in the late 1870s, the Société académique indo-chinoise reformulated its goals, it found it important to "bring Indochina into the domain of Orientalism." Why? In order to turn Cochin China into a "French India." The absence of substantial colonial holdings was blamed by military men for that combination of military and commercial weakness in the war with Prussia, to say nothing of long-standing and pronounced colonial inferiority compared with Britain. The "power of expansion of the Western races," argued a leading geographer, La Roncière Le Noury, "its superior causes, its elements, its influences on human destinies, will be a beautiful study for future historians." Yet only if the white races indulged their taste for voyaging—a mark of their intellectual supremacy—could colonial expansion occur.[20]

From such theses as this came the commonly held view of the Orient as a geographical space to be cultivated, harvested, and guarded. The images of agricultural care for and those of frank sexual attention to the Orient proliferated accordingly. Here is a typical effusion by Gabriel Charmes, writing in 1880:

> On that day when we shall be no longer in the Orient, and when other great European powers will be there, all will be at an end for our commerce in the Mediterranean, for our future in Asia, for the traffic of our southern ports. *One of the most fruitful sources of our national wealth will be dried up.* (Emphasis added)

Another thinker, Leroy-Beaulieu, elaborated this philosophy still further:

> A society colonizes, when itself having reached a high degree of maturity and of strength, it procreates, it protects, it places in good conditions of development, and it brings to virility a new society to which it has given birth. Colonization is one of the most complex and delicate phenomena of social physiology.

This equation of self-reproduction with colonization led Leroy-Beaulieu to the somewhat sinister idea that whatever is lively in a modern society is "magnified by this pouring out of its exuberant activity on the outside." Therefore, he said,

> Colonization is the expansive force of a people; it is its power of reproduction; *it is its enlargement and its multiplication through space*; it is the subjection of the universe or a vast part of it to that people's language, customs, ideas, and laws.[21]

The point here is that the space of weaker or underdeveloped regions like the Orient was viewed as something inviting French interest, penetration, insemination—in short, colonization. Geographical conceptions, literally and figuratively, did away with the discrete entities held in by borders and frontiers. No less than entrepreneurial visionaries like de Lesseps, whose plan was to liberate the Orient and the Occident from their geographical bonds, French scholars, administrators, geographers, and commercial agents poured out their exuberant activity onto the fairly supine, feminine Orient. There were the geographical societies, whose number and membership outdid those of all Europe by a factor of two; there were such powerful organizations as the Comité de l'Asie française and the Comité d'Orient; there were the learned societies, chief among them the Société asiatique, with its organization and membership firmly embedded in the universities, the institutes, and the government. Each in its own way made French interests in the Orient more real, more substantial. Almost an entire century of what now seemed passive study of the Orient had had to end, as France faced up to its transnational responsibilities during the last two decades of the nineteenth century.

In the only part of the Orient where British and French interests literally overlapped, the territory of the now hopelessly ill Ottoman Empire, the two antagonists managed their conflict with an almost perfect and characteristic consistency. Britain was *in* Egypt and Mesopotamia; through a series of quasi-fictional treaties with local (and powerless) chiefs it controlled the Red Sea, the Persian Gulf, and the Suez Canal, as well as most of the intervening land mass between the Mediterranean and India. France, on the other hand, seemed fated to hover over the Orient, descending once in a while to carry out schemes that repeated de Lesseps's success with the canal; for the most part these schemes were railroad projects, such as the one planned across more or less British territory, the Syrian-Mesopotamian line. In addition France saw itself as the protector of Christian minorities—Maronites, Chaldeans, Nestorians. Yet together, Britain and France were agreed in principle on the necessity, when the time came, for the partition of Asiatic Turkey. Both before and during World War I secret diplomacy was bent on carving up the Near Orient first into spheres of influence, then into mandated (or occupied) territories. In France, much of the expansionist sentiment formed during the heyday of the geographical movement focused itself on plans to partition Asiatic Turkey, so much so that in Paris in 1914 "a spectacular press campaign was launched" to this end.[22] In England numerous committees were empowered to study and recommend policy on the best ways of dividing up the Orient. Out of such commissions as the Bunsen Committee would come the joint Anglo-French teams of which the most famous was the one headed by Mark Sykes and Georges Picot. Equitable division of geographical space was the rule of these plans, which were deliberate attempts also at calming Anglo-French rivalry. For, as Sykes put it in a memorandum,

> it was clear ... that an Arab rising was sooner or later to take place, and that the French and ourselves ought to be on better terms if the rising was not to be a curse instead of a blessing....[23]

The animosities remained. And to them was added the irritant provided by the Wilsonian program for national self-determination, which, as Sykes himself was to note, seemed to invalidate the whole skeleton of colonial and partitionary schemes arrived at jointly between the Powers. It would be out of place here to discuss the entire labyrinthine and deeply controversial history of the Near Orient in the early twentieth century, as its fate was being decided between the Powers, the native dynasties, the various nationalist parties and movements, the Zionists. What matters more immediately is the peculiar epistemological framework through which the Orient was seen, and out of which the Powers acted. For despite their differences, the British and the French saw the Orient as a geographical—and cultural, political, demographical, sociological, and historical—entity over whose destiny they believed themselves to have traditional entitlement. The Orient to them was no sudden discovery, no mere historical accident, but an area to the east of Europe whose principal worth was uniformly defined in terms of Europe, more particularly in terms specifically claiming for Europe—European science, scholarship, understanding, and administration—the credit for having made the Orient what it was now. And this had been the achievement—inadvertent or not is beside the point—of modern Orientalism.

There were two principal methods by which Orientalism delivered the Orient to the West in the early twentieth century. One was by means of the disseminative capacities of modern learning, its diffusive apparatus in the learned professions, the universities, the professional societies, the explorational and geographical organizations, the publishing industry. All these, as we have seen, built upon the prestigious authority of the pioneering scholars, travelers, and poets, whose cumulative vision had shaped a quintessential Orient; the doctrinal—or doxological—manifestation of such an Orient is what I have been calling here latent Orientalism. So far as anyone wishing to make a statement of any consequence about the Orient was concerned, latent Orientalism supplied him with an enunciative capacity that could be used, or rather mobilized, and turned into sensible discourse for the concrete occasion at hand. Thus when Balfour spoke about the Oriental to the House of Commons in 1910, he must surely have had in mind those enunciative capacities in the current and acceptably rational language of his time, by which something called an "Oriental" could be named and talked about without danger of too much obscurity. But like all enunciative capacities and the discourses they enable, latent Orientalism was profoundly conservative—dedicated, that is, to its self-preservation. Transmitted from one generation to another, it was a part of the culture, as much a language about a part of reality as geometry or physics. Orientalism staked its existence, not upon its openness, its receptivity to the Orient, but rather on its internal, repetitious consistency about its constitutive will-to-power over the Orient. In such a way Orientalism was able to survive revolutions, world wars, and the literal dismemberment of empires.

The second method by which Orientalism delivered the Orient to the West was the result of an important convergence. For decades the Orientalists had spoken about the Orient, they had translated texts, they had explained civilizations, religions, dynasties, cultures, mentalities—as academic objects, screened off from Europe by virtue of their inimitable foreignness. The Orientalist was an expert, like Renan or Lane, whose job in society was to interpret the Orient for his compatriots. The relation between Orientalist and Orient was essentially hermeneutical: standing before a distant, barely intelligible civilization or cultural monument, the Orientalist scholar reduced the obscurity by translating, sympathetically portraying, inwardly grasping the hard-to-reach object. Yet the Orientalist remained outside the Orient, which, however much it was made to appear intelligible, remained beyond the Occident. This cultural, temporal, and geographical distance was expressed in metaphors of depth, secrecy, and sexual promise: phrases like "the veils of an Eastern bride" or "the inscrutable Orient" passed into the common language.

Yet the distance between Orient and Occident was, almost paradoxically, in the process of being reduced throughout the nineteenth century. As the commercial, political, and other existential encounters between East and West increased (in ways we have been discussing all along), a tension developed between the dogmas of latent Orientalism, with its support in studies of the "classical" Orient, and the descriptions of a present, modern, manifest Orient articulated by travelers, pilgrims, statesmen, and the like. At some moment impossible to determine precisely, the tension caused a convergence of the two types of Orientalism. Probably—and this is only a speculation—the convergence occurred when Orientalists, beginning with Sacy, undertook to advise governments on what the modern Orient was all about. Here the role of the specially trained and equipped expert took on an added dimension: the Orientalist could be regarded as the special agent of Western power as it attempted policy vis-à-vis the Orient. Every learned (and not so learned) European traveler in the Orient felt himself to be a representative Westerner who had gotten beneath the films of obscurity. This is obviously true of Burton, Lane, Doughty, Flaubert, and the other major figures I have been discussing.

The discoveries of Westerners about the manifest and modern Orient acquired a pressing urgency as Western territorial acquisition in the Orient increased. Thus what the scholarly Orientalist defined as the "essential" Orient was sometimes contradicted, but in many cases was confirmed, when the Orient became an actual administrative obligation. Certainly Cromer's theories about the Oriental—theories acquired from the traditional Orientalist archive—were vindicated plentifully as he ruled millions of Orientals in actual fact. This was no less true of the French experience in Syria, North Africa, and elsewhere in the French colonies, such as they were. But at no time did the convergence between latent Orientalist doctrine and manifest Orientalist experience occur more dramatically than when, as a result of World War I, Asiatic Turkey was being surveyed by Britain and France for its dismemberment. There, laid out on an operating table for surgery, was the Sick Man of Europe, revealed in all his weakness, characteristics, and topographical outline.

The Orientalist, with his special knowledge, played an inestimably important part in this surgery. Already there had been intimations of his crucial role as a kind of secret agent *inside* the Orient when the British scholar Edward Henry Palmer was sent to the Sinai in 1882 to gauge anti-British sentiment and its possible enlistment on behalf of the Arabi revolt. Palmer was killed in the process, but he was only the most unsuccessful of the many who performed similar services for the Empire, now a serious and exacting business entrusted in part to the regional "expert." Not for nothing was another Orientalist, D.G. Hogarth, author of the famous account of the exploration of Arabia aptly titled *The Penetration of Arabia* (1904),[24] made the head of the Arab Bureau in Cairo during World War I. And neither was it by accident that men and women like Gertrude Bell, T.E. Lawrence, and St. John Philby, Oriental experts all, posted to the Orient as agents of empire, friends of the Orient, formulators of policy alternatives because of their intimate and expert knowledge of the Orient and of Orientals. They formed a "band"—as Lawrence called it once— bound together by contradictory notions and personal similarities: great individuality, sympathy and intuitive identification with the Orient, a jealously preserved sense of personal mission in the Orient, cultivated eccentricity, a final disapproval of the Orient. For them all the Orient was their direct, peculiar experience of it. In them Orientalism and an effective praxis for handling the Orient received their final European form, before the Empire disappeared and passed its legacy to other candidates for the role of dominant power.

Such individualists as these were not academics. We shall soon see that they were the beneficiaries of the academic study of the Orient, without in any sense belonging to the official and professional company of Orientalist scholars. Their role, however, was not to scant academic Orientalism, nor to subvert it, but rather to make it effective. In their genealogy were people like Lane and Burton, as much for their encyclopedic autodidacticism as for the accurate, the quasi-scholarly knowledge of the Orient they had obviously deployed when dealing with or writing about Orientals. For the curricular study of the Orient they substituted a sort of elaboration of latent Orientalism, which was easily available to them in the imperial culture of their epoch. Their scholarly frame of reference, such as it was, was fashioned by people like William Muir, Anthony Bevan, D.S. Margolíouth, Charles Lyall, E.G. Browne, R.A. Nicholson, Guy Le Strange, E.D. Ross, and Thomas Arnold, who also followed directly in the line of descent from Lane. Their imaginative perspectives were provided principally by their illustrious contemporary Rudyard Kipling, who had sung so memorably of holding "dominion over palm and pine."

The difference between Britain and France in such matters was perfectly consistent with the history of each nation in the Orient: the British were there; the French lamented the loss of India and the intervening territories. By the end of the century, Syria had become the main focus of French activity, but even there it was a matter of common consensus that the French could not match the British either in quality of personnel or in degree of political influence. The Anglo-French competition over the Ottoman spoils was felt even on the field of battle in the Hejaz, in Syria, in Mesopotamia—but in all these places, as astute men like Edmond Bremond noted, the French Orientalists and local experts were outclassed in brilliance and tactical maneuvering by their British counterparts.[25] Except for an occasional genius like Louis Massignon, there were no French Lawrences or Sykeses or Bells. But there were determined imperialists like Étienne Flandin and Franklin-Bouillon. Lecturing to the Paris Alliance française in 1913, the Comte de Cressaty, a vociferous imperialist, proclaimed Syria as France's own Orient, the site of French political, moral, and economic interests—interests, he added, that had to be defended during this "âge des envahissants impérialistes"; and yet Cressaty noted that even with French commercial and industrial firms in the Orient, with by far the largest number of native students enrolled in French schools, France was invariably being pushed around in the Orient, threatened not only by Britain but by Austria, Germany, and Russia. If France was to continue to prevent "le retour de l'Islam," it had better take hold of the Orient: this was an argument proposed by Cressaty and seconded by Senator Paul Doumer.[26] These views were repeated on numerous occasions, and indeed France did well by itself in North Africa and in Syria after World War I, but the special, concrete management of emerging Oriental populations and theoretically independent territories with which the British always credited themselves was something the French felt had eluded them. Ultimately, perhaps, the difference one always feels between modern British and modern French Orientalism is a stylistic one; the import of the generalizations about Orient and Orientals, the sense of distinction preserved between Orient and Occident, the desirability of Occidental dominance over the Orient—all these are the same in both traditions. For of the many elements making up what we customarily call "expertise," style, which is the result of specific worldly circumstances being molded by tradition, institutions, will, and intelligence into formal articulation, is one of the most manifest. It is to this determinant, to this perceptible and modernized refinement in early-twentieth-century Orientalism in Britain and France, that we must now turn.

NOTES

1. Friedrich Nietzsche, "On Truth and Lie in an Extra-Moral Sense," in *The Portable Nietzsche*, ed. and trans. Walter Kaufmann (New York: Viking Press, 1954), pp. 46–7.
2. The number of Arab travelers to the West is estimated and considered by Ibrahim Abu-Lughod in *Arab Rediscovery of Europe: A Study in Cultural Encounters* (Princeton, NJ: Princeton University Press, 1963), pp. 75–6 and passim.
3. See Philip D. Curtin, ed., *Imperialism: The Documentary History of Western Civilization* (New York: Walker & Co., 1972), pp. 73–105.
4. See Johann W. Fück, "Islam as an Historical Problem in European Historiography since 1800," in *Historians of the Middle East*, ed. Bernard Lewis and P.M. Holt (London: Oxford University Press, 1962), p. 307.
5. Ibid., p. 309.
6. See Jacques Waardenburg, *L'Islam dans le miroir de l'Occident* (The Hague: Mouton & Co., 1963).
7. Ibid., p. 311.
8. R. Masson-Oursel, "La Connaissance scientifique de l'Asie en France depuis 1900 et les variétés de l'Orientalisme," *Revue Philosophique* 143, nos. 7–9 (July–September 1953): 345.
9. Evelyn Baring, Lord Cromer, *Modern Egypt* (New York: Macmillan. Co., 1908), 2: 237–8.
10. Evelyn Baring, Lord Cromer, *Ancient and Modern Imperialism* (London: John Murray, 1910), pp. 118, 120.
11. George Nathaniel Curzon, *Subjects of the Day: Being a Selection of Speeches and Writings* (London: George Allen & Unwin, 1915), pp. 4–5, 10, 28.
12. Ibid., pp. 184, 191–2. For the history of the school, see C.H. Phillips, *The School of Oriental and African Studies, University of London, 1917-1967: An Introduction* (London: Design for Print, 1967).
13. Eric Stokes, *The English Utilitarians and India* (Oxford: Clarendon Press, 1959).
14. Cited in Michael Edwardes, *High Noon of Empire: India under Curzon* (London: Eyre & Spottiswoode, 1965), pp. 38–9.
15. Curzon, *Subjects of the Day*, pp. 155–6.
16. Joseph Conrad, *Heart of Darkness*, in *Youth and Two other Stories* (Garden City, NY: Doubleday, Page, 1925), p. 52.
17. For an illustrative extract from de Vattel's work, see Curtin, ed., *Imperialism*, pp. 42–45.
18. Cited by M. de Caix, *La Syrie*, in Gabriel Hanotaux, *Histoire des colonies françaises*, 6 vols. (Paris: Société de l'histoire nationale, 1929–33), 3: 481.
19. These details are to be found in Vernon McKay, "Colonialism in the French Geographical Movement," *Geographical Review* 33, no. 2 (April 1943): 214–32.
20. Agnes Murphy, *The Ideology of French Imperialism, 1817-1881* (Washington: Catholic University of America Press, 1948), pp. 46, 54, 36, 45.
21. Ibid., pp. 189, 110, 136.
22. Jukka Nevakivi, *Britain, France, and the Arab Middle East, 1914-1920* (London: Athlone Press, 1969), p. 13.
23. Ibid., p. 24.
24. D.G. Hogarth, *The Penetration of Arabia: A Record of the Development of Western Knowledge Concerning the Arabian Peninsula* (New York: Frederick A. Stokes, 1904). There is a good recent book on the same subject: Robin Bidwell, *Travellers in Arabia* (London: Paul Hamlyn, 1976).
25. Edmond Bremond, *Le Hedjaz dans la guerre mondiale* (Paris: Payor, 1931), pp. 242 ff.
26. Le Comte de Cressaty, *Les Intérêts de la France en Syrie* (Paris: Floury, 1913).

CHAPTER 7

THE WEST AND THE REST: DISCOURSE AND POWER

Stuart Hall

DISCOURSE AND POWER

This article will examine the formation of the languages or "discourses" in which Europe began to describe and represent the *difference* between itself and the "others" it encountered in the course of its expansion. We are now beginning to sketch the formation of the "discourse" of "the West and the Rest." However, we need first to understand what we mean by the term "discourse."

What Is a "Discourse"?

In commonsense language, a discourse is simply "a coherent or rational body of speech or writing; a speech, or a sermon." But here the term is being used in a more specialized way. By "discourse," we mean a particular way of *representing* "the West," "the Rest," and the relations between them. A discourse is a group of statements which provide a language for talking about—i.e. a way of representing—a particular kind of knowledge about a topic. When statements about a topic are made within a particular discourse, the discourse makes it possible to construct the topic in a certain way. It also limits the other ways in which the topic can be constructed.

A discourse does not consist of one statement, but of several statements working together to form what the French social theorist Michel Foucault (1926–84) calls a "discursive formation." The statements fit together because any one statement implies a relation to all the others: "They refer to the same object, share the same style and support 'a strategy ... a common institutional ... or political drift or pattern'" (Cousins and Hussain, 1984, pp. 84–5).

One important point about this notion of discourse is that it is not based on the conventional distinction between thought and action, language and practice. Discourse is about the production of knowledge through language. But it is itself produced by a practice: "discursive practice"—the practice of producing meaning. Since all social practices entail *meaning*, all practices have a discursive aspect. So discourse enters into and influences all social practices. Foucault would argue that the discourse of the West about the Rest was deeply implicated in practice—i.e. in how the West behaved towards the Rest.

To get a fuller sense of Foucault's theory of discourse, we must bear the following points in mind.

1. A discourse can be produced by many individuals in different institutional settings (like families, prisons, hospitals, and asylums). Its integrity or "coherence" does not depend on whether or not it issues from one place or from a single speaker or "subject." Nevertheless, every discourse constructs positions from which alone it makes sense. Anyone deploying a discourse must position themselves *as if* they were the subject of the discourse. For example, we may not ourselves believe in the natural superiority of the West. But if we use the discourse of "the West and the Rest," we will necessarily find ourselves speaking from a position that holds that the West is a superior civilization. As Foucault puts it, "To describe a ... statement does not consist in analyzing the relations between the author and what he [*sic*] says ... ; but in determining what position can and must be occupied by any individual if he is to be the subject of it [the statement]" (Foucault, 1972, pp. 95–6).
2. Discourses are not closed systems. A discourse draws on elements in other discourses, binding them into its own network of meanings. Thus [...] the discourse of "Europe" drew on the earlier discourse of "Christendom," altering or translating its meaning. Traces of past discourses remain embedded in more recent discourses of "the West."
3. The statements within a discursive formation need not all be the same. But the relationships and differences between them must be regular and systematic, not random. Foucault calls this a "system of dispersion": "Whenever one can describe, between a number of statements, such a system of dispersion, whenever ... one can define a regularity ... [then] we will say ... that we are dealing with a *discursive formation*" (Foucault, 1972, p. 38).

These points will become clearer when we apply them to particular examples, as we do later in this article.

Discourse and Ideology

A discourse is similar to what sociologists call an "ideology": a set of statements or beliefs which produce knowledge that serves the interests of a particular group or class. Why, then, use "discourse" rather than "ideology"?

One reason which Foucault gives is that ideology is based on a distinction between *true* statements about the world (science) and *false* statements (ideology), and the belief that the facts about the world help us to decide between true and false statements. But Foucault argues that statements about the social, political, or moral world are rarely ever simply true or false; and "the facts" do not enable us to decide definitively about their truth or falsehood, partly because "facts" can be construed in different ways. The very language we use to describe the so-called facts interferes in this process of finally deciding what is true and what is false.

For example, Palestinians fighting to regain land on the West Bank from Israel may be described either as "freedom fighters" or as "terrorists." It is a fact that they are fighting; but what does the fighting *mean*. The facts alone cannot decide. And the very language we use—"freedom fighters/terrorists"—is part of the difficulty. Moreover, certain descriptions, even if they appear false to us, can be *made* "true" because people act on them believing that they are true, and so their actions have real consequences. Whether the Palestinians are terrorists or not, if we think they are, and act on that "knowledge," they in effect become terrorists because we treat them as such. The language (discourse) has real effects in practice: the description becomes "true."

Foucault's use of "discourse," then, is an attempt to sidestep what seems an unresolvable dilemma—deciding which social discourses are true or scientific, and which false or ideological. Most social scientists now accept that our values enter into all our descriptions of the social world, and therefore most of our statements, however factual, have an ideological dimension. What Foucault would say is that knowledge of the Palestinian problem is produced by competing discourses—those of "freedom-fighter" and "terrorist"—and that each is linked to a contestation over power. It is the outcome of *this* struggle which will decide the "truth" of the situation.

You can see, then, that although the concept of "discourse" sidesteps the problem of truth/falsehood in ideology, it does *not* evade the issue of power. Indeed, it gives considerable weight to questions of power since it is power, rather than the facts about reality, which makes things "true": "We should admit that power produces knowledge.... That power and knowledge directly imply one another; that there is no power relation without the correlative constitution of a field of knowledge, nor any knowledge that does not presuppose and constitute ... power relations" (Foucault, 1980, p. 27).

Can a Discourse Be "Innocent"?

Could the discourse which developed in the West for talking about the Rest operate outside power? Could it be, in that sense, purely scientific—i.e. ideologically innocent? Or was it influenced by particular class interests?

Foucault is very reluctant to *reduce* discourse to statements that simply mirror the interests of a particular class. The same discourse can be used by groups with different, even contradictory, class interests. But this does *not* mean that discourse is ideologically neutral or "innocent." Take, for example, the encounter between the West and the New World. There are several reasons why this encounter could not be innocent, and therefore why the discourse which emerged in the Old World about the Rest could not be innocent either.

First, Europe brought its own cultural categories, languages, images, and ideas to the New World in order to describe and represent it. It tried to fit the New World into existing conceptual frameworks, classifying it according to its own norms, and absorbing it into western traditions of representation. This is hardly surprising: we often draw on what we already know about the world in order to explain and describe something novel. It was never a simple matter of the West just looking, seeing, and describing the New World/the Rest without preconceptions.

Secondly, Europe had certain definite purposes, aims, objectives, motives, interests, and strategies in setting out to discover what lay across the "Green Sea of Darkness." These motives and interests were mixed. The Spanish, for example, wanted to

1. get their hands on gold and silver;
2. claim the land for Their Catholic Majesties; and
3. convert the heathen to Christianity.

These interests often contradicted one another. But we must not suppose that what Europeans said about the New World was simply a cynical mask for their own self-interest. When King Manuel of Portugal wrote to Ferdinand and Isabella of Spain that "the principal motive of this enterprise [da Gama's voyage to India] has been ... the service of God our Lord, and our own advantage" (quoted in Hale, 1966, p. 38)—thereby neatly and conveniently bringing God and Mammon together into the same sentence—he probably saw no obvious contradiction between them. These fervently religious Catholic rulers fully believed what they were saying. To them, serving God and pursuing "our advantage" were not necessarily at odds. They lived and fully believed their own ideology.

So, while it would be wrong to attempt to reduce their statements to naked self-interest, it is clear that their discourse was molded and influenced by the play of motives and interests across their language. Of course, motives and interests are almost never wholly conscious or rational. The desires which drove the Europeans were powerful; but their power was not always subject to rational calculation. Marco Polo's "treasures of the East" were tangible enough. But the seductive power which they exerted over generations of Europeans transformed them more and more into a myth. Similarly, the gold that Columbus kept asking the natives for very soon acquired a mystical, quasi-religious significance.

Finally, the discourse of "the West and the Rest" could not be innocent because it did not represent an encounter between equals. The Europeans had outsailed, outshot, and outwitted peoples who had no wish to be "explored," no need to be "discovered," and no desire to be "exploited." The Europeans stood, vis-à-vis the Others, in positions of dominant power. This influenced what they saw and how they saw it, as well as what they did not see.

Foucault sums up these arguments as follows. Not only is discourse always implicated in *power,* discourse is one of the "systems" through which power circulates. The knowledge which a discourse produces constitutes a kind of power, exercised over those who are "known." When that knowledge is exercised in practice, those who are "known" in a particular way will be subject (i.e. subjected) to it. This is always a power-relation. (See Foucault, 1980, p. 201.) Those who produce the discourse also have the power to *make it true*—i.e. to enforce its validity, its scientific status.

This leaves Foucault in a highly relativistic position with respect to questions of truth because his notion of discourse undermines the distinction between true and false statements—between science and ideology—to which many sociologists have subscribed. These epistemological issues (about the status of knowledge, truth, and relativism) are too complex to take further here. However, the important idea to grasp now is the deep and intimate relationship which Foucault establishes between discourse, knowledge, and power. According to Foucault, when power operates so as to enforce the "truth" of any set of statements, then such a discursive formation produces a "regime of truth."

Let us summarize the main points of this argument. Discourses are ways of talking, thinking, or representing a particular subject or topic. They produce meaningful knowledge about that subject. This knowledge influences social practices, and so has real consequences and effects. Discourses are not reducible to class-interests, but always operate in relation to power—they are part of the way power circulates and is contested. The question of whether a discourse is true or false is less important than whether it is effective in practice. When it is effective—organizing and regulating relations of power (say, between the West and the Rest)—it is called a "regime of truth."

REPRESENTING "THE OTHER"

So far, the discussion of discourse has been rather abstract and conceptual. The concept may be easier to understand in relation to an example. One of the best examples of what Foucault means by a "regime of truth" is provided by Edward Said's study of Orientalism. In this section, I want to look briefly at this example and then see how far we can use the theory of discourse and the example of Orientalism to analyze the discourse of "the West and the Rest."

Orientalism

In his book *Orientalism*, Edward Said analyzes the various discourses and institutions which constructed and produced, as an object of knowledge, that entity called "the Orient." Said calls this discourse "Orientalism." Note that, though we tend to include the Far East (including China) in our use of the word "Orient," Said refers mainly to the Middle East—the territory occupied principally by Islamic peoples.

Also, his main focus is French writing about the Middle East. Here is Said's own summary of the project of his book:

> My contention is that, without examining Orientalism as a discourse, one cannot possibly understand the enormously systematic discipline by which European culture was able to manage—and even produce—the Orient politically, sociologically, militarily, ideologically, scientifically and imaginatively during the post-Enlightenment period. Moreover, so authoritative a position did Orientalism have that I believe no one writing, thinking, or acting on the Orient could do so without taking account of the limitations on thought and action imposed by Orientalism. In brief, because of Orientalism, the Orient was not (and is not) a free subject of thought and action. This is not to say that Orientalism unilaterally determines what can be said about the Orient, but that it is the whole network of interests inevitably brought to bear on (and therefore always involved in) any occasion when that peculiar entity "the Orient" is in question.... This book also tries to show that European culture gained in strength and identity by setting itself off against the Orient as a sort of surrogate and even underground self. (Said, 1985, p. 3)

We will now analyze the discourse of "the West and the Rest," as it emerged between the end of the 15th and 18th centuries, using Foucault's ideas about "discourse" and Said's example of "Orientalism." How was this discourse formed? What were its main themes—its "strategies" of representation?

The "Archive"

Said argues that "In a sense Orientalism was a library or archive of information commonly ... held. What bound the archive together was a family of ideas and a unifying set of values proven in various ways to be effective. These ideas explained the behaviour of Orientals; they supplied Orientals with a mentality, a genealogy, an atmosphere; most important, they allowed Europeans to deal with and even to see Orientals as a phenomenon possessing regular characteristics" (Said, 1985, pp. 41–2). What sources of common knowledge, what "archive" of other discourses, did the discourse of "the West and the Rest" draw on? We can identify four main sources:

1. **Classical knowledge:** This was a major source of information and images about "other worlds." Plato (c. 427–347 B.C.) described a string of legendary islands, among them Atlantis which many early explorers set out to find. Aristotle (384–322 B.C.) and Eratosthenes (c. 276–194 B.C.) both made remarkably accurate estimates of the circumference of the globe which were consulted by Columbus. Ptolemy's *Geographia* (2nd century A.D.) provided a model for map-makers more than a thousand years after it had been produced. Sixteenth-century explorers believed that in the outer world lay, not only Paradise, but that "Golden Age," place of perfect happiness and "springtime of the

human race," of which the classical poets, including Horace (65–8 B.C.) and Ovid (43 B.C.–A.D. 17), had written.

The 18th century was still debating whether what they had discovered in the South Pacific was Paradise. In 1768 the French Pacific explorer Bougainville renamed Tahiti "The New Cythera" after the island where, according to classical myth, Venus first appeared from the sea. At the opposite extreme, the descriptions by Herodotus (484–425 B.C.) and Pliny (A.D. 23–79) of the barbarous peoples who bordered Greece left many grotesque images of "other" races which served as self-fulfilling prophecies for later explorers who found what legend said they would find. Paradoxically, much of this classical knowledge was lost in the Dark Ages and only later became available to the West via Islamic scholars, themselves part of that "other" world.

2. **Religious and biblical sources:** These were another source of knowledge. The Middle Ages reinterpreted geography in terms of the Bible. Jerusalem was the center of the earth because it was the Holy City. Asia was the home of the Three Wise Kings; Africa, that of King Solomon. Columbus believed the Orinoco (in Venezuela) to be a sacred river flowing out of the Garden of Eden.
3. **Mythology:** It was difficult to tell where religious and classical discourses ended and those of myth and legend began. Mythology transformed the outer world into an enchanted garden, alive with misshapen peoples and monstrous oddities. In the 16th century, Sir Walter Raleigh still believed he would find, in the Amazon rainforests, the king "El Dorado" ("The Gilded One") whose people were alleged to roll him in gold which they would then wash off in a sacred lake.
4. **Travellers' tales:** Perhaps the most fertile source of information was travellers' tales—a discourse where description faded imperceptibly into legend. The following 15th century German text summarizes more than a thousand years of travellers' tales, which themselves often drew on religious and classical authority:

In the land of Indian there are men with dogs' heads who talk by barking [and] ... feed by catching birds.... Others again have only one eye in the forehead.... In Libya many are born without heads and have a mouth and eyes. Many are of both sexes.... Close to Paradise on the River Ganges live men who eat nothing. For ... they absorb liquid nourishment through a straw [and] ... live on the juice of flowers.... Many have such large underlips that they can cover their whole faces with them.... In the land of Ethiopia many people walk bent down like cattle, and many live four hundred years. Many have horns, long noses and goats' feet.... In Ethiopia towards the west many have four eyes ... [and] in Eripia there live beautiful people with the necks and bills of cranes.... (quoted in Newby, 1975, p. 17)

A particularly rich repository was Sir John Mandeville's *Travels*—in fact, a compendium of fanciful stories by different hands. Marco Polo's *Travels* was generally more sober and factual, but nevertheless achieved mythological status. His text (embellished by Rusticello, a romance writer) was the most widely read of the travellers' accounts and was instrumental in creating the myth of "Cathay" ("China," or the East generally), a dream that inspired Columbus and many others.

The point of recounting this astonishing mixture of fact and fantasy which constituted late medieval "knowledge" of other worlds is not to poke fun at the ignorance of the Middle Ages. The point is (a) to bring home how these very different discourses, with variable statuses as "evidence," provided the cultural framework through which the peoples, places, and things of the New World were seen, described, and represented; and (b) to underline the conflation of fact and fantasy that constituted "knowledge." This can be seen especially in the use of analogy to describe first encounters with strange animals. Penguins and seals were described as being like geese and wolves respectively; the tapir as a bull with a trunk like an elephant, the opossum as half-fox, half-monkey.

A "Regime of Truth"

Gradually, observation and description vastly improved in accuracy. The medieval habit of thinking in terms of analogies gave way to a more sober type of description of the fauna and flora, ways of life, customs, physical characteristics, and social organization of native peoples. We can here begin to see the outlines of an early ethnography or anthropology.

But the shift into a more descriptive, factual discourse, with its claims to truth and scientific objectivity, provided no guarantees. A telling example of this is the case of the "Patagonians." Many myths and legends told of a race of giant people. And in the 1520s, Magellan's crew brought back stories of having encountered, in South America, such a race of giants whom they dubbed *patagones* (literally, "big feet"). The area of the supposed encounter became known as "Patagonia," and the notion became fixed in the popular imagination, even though two Englishmen who visited Patagonia in 1741 described its people as being of average size.

When Commodore John Byron landed in Patagonia in 1764, he encountered a formidable group of natives, broad-shouldered, stocky, and inches taller than the average European. They proved quite docile and friendly. However, the newspaper reports of his encounter wildly exaggerated the story, and Patagonians took on an even greater stature and more ferocious aspect. One engraving showed a sailor reaching only as high as the waist of a Patagonian giant, and The Royal Society elevated the topic to serious scientific status. "The engravings took the explorers' raw material and shaped them into images familiar to Europeans" (Withey, 1987, pp. 1175–6). Legend had taken a late revenge on science.

This is where the notion of "discourse" came in. A discourse is a way of talking about or representing something.

It produces knowledge that shapes perceptions and practice. It is part of the way in which power operates. Therefore, it has consequences for both those who employ it and those who are "subjected" to it. The West produced many different ways of talking about itself and "the Others." But what we have called the discourse of "the West and the Rest" became one of the most powerful and formative of these discourses. It became the dominant way in which, for many decades, the West represented itself and its relation to "the Other." In this article, we have traced how this discourse was formed and how it worked. We analyzed it as a "system of representation"—a "regime of truth." It was as formative for the West and "modern societies" as were the secular state; capitalist economies; the modern class, race, and gender systems; and modern, individualist, secular culture—the four main "processes" of our formation story.

Finally, we suggest that, in transformed and reworked forms, this discourse continues to inflect the language of the West, its image of itself and "others," its sense of "us" and "them," its practices and relations of power towards the Rest. It is especially important for the languages of racial inferiority and ethnic superiority which still operate so powerfully across the globe today. So, far from being a "formation" of the past, and of only historical interest, the discourse of "the West and the Rest" is alive and well in the modern world. And one of the surprising places where its effects can still be seen is in the language, theoretical models, and hidden assumptions of modern sociology itself.

REFERENCES

Cousins, M., and Hussain, A. 1984. *Michel Foucault*. London: Macmillan.

Foucault, M. 1972. *The Archeology of Knowledge*. London: Tavistock.

Foucault, M. 1980. *Power/Knowledge*. Brighton: England, Harvester.

Hale, J.R., et al. 1966. *Age of Exploration*. The Netherlands: Time-Life International.

Mandeville, Sir J. 1964. *The Travels*. New York: Dover.

Newby, E. 1975. *The Mitchell Beazley World Atlas of Exploration*. London: Mitchell Beazley.

Said, E.W. 1985. *Orientalism: Western Concepts of the Orient*. Harmondsworth: England, Penguin.

Withey, L. 1987. *Voyages of Discovery: Captain Cook and the Exploration of the Pacific*. London: Hutchinson.

FURTHER READING

Barakan, Elazar. 1996. *The Retreat of Scientific Racism: Changing Concepts of Race in Britain and the United States between the World Wars*. Cambridge: Cambridge University Press.

This book examines the handling of the concept of race in both anthropology and biology, comparing American and British approaches. It traces the move away from focusing on physical traits to focusing on social conditions as determinants of behaviour. The author argues that changing social conditions throughout the 20th century have been more influential in the decline of scientific racism than any scientific considerations.

Memmi, Albert. 1965. *The Colonizer and the Colonized*. Boston: Beacon Press.

First published in 1957, this is one of the classics in the field, one that made public the detrimental affect of colonization on the colonizer as well as the colonized. Although in most parts of the world the older exigent forms of colonization have long since disappeared, there are still many regions where colonization is rationalized by both overt and covert forms of racism.

Watson, Peter. 2005. *Ideas: A History From Fire to Freud*. London: Weidenfeld & Nicolson. Section 21, "The 'Indian' Mind: Ideas in the New World," and section 33, "The uses and Abuses of Nationalism and Imperialism."

These two readings from this recent survey of the history of ideas examine the origins of many of the ideas surveyed by Jahoda, Smedley, and Said in this section. Watson offers a non-ideological perspective focusing on their historical context and treating them as noteworthy and influential in the history of ideas.

PART 1C

THINKING THROUGH RACE IN THE 21st CENTURY

Part 1C introduces a number of theoretical debates about race and racialization, with articles by thinkers from a variety of perspectives, drawing on sociological, spatial, political, and other orientations representing varied academic disciplines, traditions, and discourses from Asia, Africa, Canada, Europe, and the United States, among others. The chapters also address how racialization takes on a religious character and the complexities that arise when religion is used to structure the racialization of societies from Islamic, Hindu, and Jewish perspectives. From the historical use of Christianity as a religion of conquest and its implication in the cultural genocide of indigenous populations, especially in the Americas, as invoked in the discussion about the white settler colonial projects (Razack), to anti-Semitism (Banton), which defined the most ignoble events of the 20th century, to the reassertion of a pugnacious form of orientalism—Islamophobia—in the post-Cold War period (Mazrui) and the rise of Hindu nationalism as an oppressive form (Bhatt), religion has structured processes of racialization between majorities and minorities and among minorities making up otherwise subordinate populations. To a lesser degree, the chapters also take up the tension between race and class. But this is mostly hinted at in the explorations of contemporary forms of racialization, especially in metropolitan labour markets increasingly dependant on migrant labour from racialized populations of the global South. This migration flow raises questions about the evolving nature of racism as a tool of exclusion and marginalization in the epicentres of globalized economies in the North.

We begin with Miles and Torres (1996) who pose the essential question of the chapter, regarding the validity and value of race as a concept and an explanatory category. Drawing on long-standing polemics with other academics, they rhetorically ask the question, Do races exist? And if not, what use is an analytical framework that assumes their existence? Their chapter challenges what they see as the essentialism of "race" within the dominant "race relations" paradigm, widely used as a policy and academic framework utilizing race as an analytical category (Banton 1967). Pointing to the double meaning contained in Cornell West's early 1990s title *Race Matters* (1994), they interrogate the notion that "race" is useful, arguing that the tendency among social scientists to reify race for the purposes of understanding how processes of racialization persist and have material meaning directly leads to the reproduction of the very phenomenon many claim to oppose—validating racialization. They lean heavily on the findings of the 1950s UNESCO scientific task force of prominent world scientists (assembled within the context of the obligation to affirm the Universal Declaration of Human Rights) that rejected the concept of race as a biological phenomenon. That the eminent scientists' panel could not establish genetic distinctions among human beings suggests to Miles and Torres that to maintain the concept of race poses a conundrum for social scientists—how to continue to use race as a category when its biological foundation cannot be sustained. They suggest that a simple solution would be to take seriously the high-profile refutation of the ideology of race and abandon the use of race as a social-scientific analytical tool.

Taking their argument at face value and rejecting race as an analytical category, though, raises questions about a prevalent process—racialization, which, by their own admission, structures oppression and exclusion. What, then, to do about the fact that "race," while not a biological fact, has social significance? The rest of their chapter seeks to address itself to this challenge.

Drawing on an ongoing cross-Atlantic dialogue (Miles and Torres argue that the use of race as an analytical category is more prevalent in North America because of the specific history of black/white relations), they offer the possibility of using race as an "idea" as opposed to an analytical concept. To them, this approach gives race the due symbolic value necessary to understand its role in constituting hierarchies of oppression, without falling into the trap of essentializing it—in essence, they assume the racism-as-ideology position, an abstract taken-for-granted assumption of racism as a process that structures experience but is in itself not real.

The chapter represents a debate between those such as Miles and Torres, who take the position that racial categorization traps one in the race relations paradigm and undermines the explanatory power of racialization, and others such as Wellman (1993), hooks (1990), West (1994), Essed (1991), and Omi and Winant (1993), who are either ambivalent about the claim or find it limiting. Those in the latter group argue for retaining race as an explanatory concept, saying that social science needs a concept of race to make sense of the structuring of exclusion and oppression that arises from racialization. Miles and Torres refute this position as, among other things, ahistorical and wedded to white racism as the salient form of racism, rejecting the existence of any other forms of racism (such as anti-Semitism). They suggest that the position implicates academics as collaborators in the perpetuation of a process that gives symbolic meaning to a discredited concept, arguing that the 20th-century use of race in academic and popular contexts has only served to reproduce a socially constructed category that has no scientific basis but is repeatedly reproduced to perilous consequences.

Writers such as Omi and Winant (1994) agree with Miles and Torres about the limited application of the concept of race and its corollary, race relations, as a framework that assumes race as structuring exclusionary hierarchies, especially when deployed within the black/white context in both colonial and contemporary periods. However, they see a danger in the potential to perpetuate a type of denial about the prevalence of racism if we delegitimate the concept of race. They see this manifested in the immobilization of the memories of racism as emerged in Europe in the post-war period when continental Europeans erased the discourses of racism and racialization in favour of discourses of "colour blindness" reinforced by the idea of "one race, the human race." They argue that the resulting forms of popular amnesia do not eliminate racialization and racially hierarchical structures, as the discourse on "new racism" shows. They see the antipathy towards "race" as informed by a preference for other forms of exploitation that Miles and Torres would rather emphasize, such as class and gender, which Omi and Winnant argue are mutually constitutive and reinforcing in structuring exclusion. For them, the negation of race as a category is not an academic exercise since it may well lead to the invalidation of racism and racialization as bases for understanding historical processes of exploitation and exclusion, even in the face of the racialized nature of social relations in metropolitan societies.

Miles and Torres disagree, believing that maintaining race as an "idea" or a social construct is sufficient. But others see this approach as not fully accounting for the materiality of racialization and the prevalence of "race" as deeply entrenched in social relations, or what Omi and Winant claim is the social impact of the longevity of the concept of "race." Although Miles and Torres argue that historical studies show that societies have "simply" invoked the idea of race to construct "explanations for events and processes," it remains unclear why societies keep going back to "race" if its value is only symbolic. Race has a materiality that, while not biologically sustainable, is increasingly immutable.

Sherene Razack's 2002 chapter best illustrates the materiality of "race," as it goes beyond the symbolic representation that Miles and Torres suggest in its effort to materialize "race" in its colonial context. The chapter points to the spatiality of racialization in a critical project aimed at "unmapping" the processes of white supremacy and its deployment of political, economic, and social power in structuring racialized hierarchies, especially in white settler colonies, such as Canada, the USA, Australia, and New Zealand. Razack seeks to investigate "how place becomes race" and race becomes imbued with such social and historical meaning that it helps create empires. She is concerned about how processes that are racially implicated, such as conquest, colonization, and cultural genocide, acquire a benign character through the mythologies of white settlement as a process of civilization. The deeply racist validation of violent settler processes of displacement and dispossession assumes the mythology of the land as uninhabited, an empty space willing and inviting, perhaps even beckoning as a woman in skimpy clothing is said to invite rape. The subsequent acts of development do not erase the stench of the original plunder, although it is masked by the claims of nation-building that become racialized as exclusively European, negating the labour and exploitation of the people of colour who toiled as cheap labour on the railways as they covered the confiscated land, on the farms, in the mines, and in the factories, or the aboriginal peoples dispossessed of their commercial trade and starved through economic exclusion.

Razack argues that sustaining the geographical claim of having built a nation with boundaries and international standing, and an economy to support it, requires a mythology of white settler nationalism and its white supremacist logic that assumes white resourcefulness, ingenuity, and hardwork to create something out of nothing. This, then, is the object of Razack's "unmapping": recovering the existence of aboriginal peoples and other racialized peoples in order to better grasp the impact of the racialization project not just on the original inhabitants of a white settler colony such as Canada, but also its racialized immigrants. She argues that "to contest white people's primary claim to the land and to the nation requires making visible Aboriginal nations whose lands were stolen and communities imperilled."

Both Banton and Mazrui tackle race and religion in their chapters. It is not always possible to distinguish forms of religious discrimination from other types of discrimination. That is especially the case when dealing with a people subject to varied forms of oppression and exclusion that transcend religion. Thus Banton's chapter, originally published in 1992, explores whether there is value in characterizing religious discrimination against Jews—anti-Semitism—as racist. Banton argues against the "exceptionality" of anti-Semitism on the grounds that all forms of discrimination have common features and so the focus should be less on characteristics and more on the identification of the cause. In that vein, he is inclined to focus on the economic and social causes of discrimination as opposed to the psychological (e.g., hatred). But this characterization misses the emotional scars that arise from the memory of the atrocities suffered by the victims of anti-Semitism in repeated pogroms in history and eventually in the Jewish Holocaust. There is a specificity to those events that sets them apart from the experience of economic exploitation. Likewise, there is a specificity to the dehumanizing experience of the Atlantic slave trade and the enslavement of Africans in the Americas not captured by the reduction of the experience to labour exploitation, an element integral to it. Yet this recognition does not resolve the issue of whether anti-Semitism is a specific form of racism per se.

If characterizing action as racist allows for naming acts for the purpose of societal sanction, then there may be value in identifying a historical hostility towards an identified religious group specifically in order to mobilize or sustain societal or state-based remedies. This would apply to Islamophobia and other more recently articulated forms as anti-black racism as well. Banton also suggests that the labels "anti-Semitism" and "racism" have become powerful weapons of the oppressed, because they imply a moral high ground on the part of the victim and pathology on the part of the perpetuator. There are those that argue that the distinction between hostility towards Jews and opposition to the policies of the state of Israel has blurred. Banton says this began with the creation of the state of Israel as an international remedy for historical anti-Semitism. International complicity in the Nazi murder of millions of Jews made action to address anti-Semitism an imperative, but anti-Semitism was not vanquished, and new manifestations of it have emerged. So while Banton may not agree, maintaining the category of anti-Semitism as a particular form of racism could be important in organizing protection against repeating the crimes of the past.

Mazrui's chapter, on the other hand, situates the emergence of religion as a prominent basis for distinguishing state and social action in the context of international events in the post–Cold War period. The re-emergence of long suppressed parochial bases of social mobilization gives religion new social currency. But it also identifies religion as a target of Western antipathy in the post-Communist period and a possible basis for a new clash of civilizations. It is these concerns, the politicization of Islam by its adherents as well as its adversaries, on which Mazrui focuses. With the increasing political salience of Islamophobia in the time of the "long war against terror," we also see the re-assertion of white supremacy and the civilizing mission imbued in the calls for a new imperial posture for those whose resolve is to pacify Islamic populations as the only way of ensuring the national security of Western or non-Islamic populations. The ideological conjuncture between racialization of religion and the clash of civilizations seems more apparent today than when Mazrui wrote, in the aftermath of the first Gulf War; in the context of the "long war," it seems more real and potentially enduring.

Mazrui identifies the new world order/post–Cold War period as racialized in character in the absence of both the transracial socialist ideology that led to Eastern European support for Third World liberation movements under the Cold War order and the anti-Communist alliances between industrialized capitalist states and Islamic states. He argues that the dominant world order alignments relate to the schism between the Christian West and the Muslim South.

Mazrui argues that the new world order's military victims have been predominantly Muslim as the major international fault lines have shifted from East/West or socialism/capitalism to Christian West versus Islamic South. The end of the Cold War ended inter-white rivalries and allowed for the emergence of a pan-European order on a global level. In the post–Cold War period, white socialists are less likely to support black liberation movements or anti-imperialist movements as a new global tribalism emerges as a reassertion of white supremacy in international politics. At the same time, Mazrui argues, Western antipathy towards Islam has become more pronounced, with anti-Islamism taking the place of the anti-Communism of the Cold War period.

In the contemporary period, this antipathy is also fuelled by the increased significance of terrorism, the weapon of choice for some militarily weak Muslim populations, and the vulnerability of Western populations to the potential politicization of oil supply. It is this antipathy that has evolved into new forms of Islamophobia in action and structured a global apartheid system. What distinguishes the anti-terror campaign is its anti-Islamic character, with this new enemy acting as a replacement for the anti-Communism of the Cold War period. While Mazrui argues that this is not a shift from ideology to race as the basis for the fundamental stratifications in the new world order, as suggested by the clash of civilizations rhetoric, he sees the new order taking on a religio-racial caste character, with race a more salient basis for international state action or non-action (American-led action against Iraqi aggression versus non-action against Serbian aggression in Bosnia, for example). A particular example is the Western posture, only partially informed by the fear of terrorism, but representing a clear resolve not to allow Muslim states to go nuclear. The aspirations of Pakistan, Iran, Libya, and Egypt to joining the nuclear club, which includes Israel, pose a particular threat to Western powers and are a cause for imperial adventures aimed at the Islamic Middle East.

For Mazrui, the most significant feature that has emerged in the post–Cold War, post-ideological stalemate period, is a new pan-European nationalism that unites populations of European heritage at the global level, a form of tribalism partly defined by an anti-Islamic identity. It has structured a highly racialized global order under which arrangements such as previous transracial coalitions against imperialism and strategic anti-communist alliances have become increasingly remote.

Mazrui's observations fit with Balibar's assessment of the rise of a new form of racism in continental Europe, a form of racism that shares the antipathy towards Islam that Mazrui talks about. Balibar's focus on the evolving deployment of race in response to "new threats" to Eurocentric ethnicity in France and indeed Europe—especially by nationalist political formations—provides a new and contemporary dimension of the debate on the concept of race. What Balibar suggests is that a new form of racism has emerged in the post-Cold War period to coincide with the multicultural nature of Europe's metropolitan centres. Balibar identifies the global-local articulation of social relations of race in a manner that points to the transnational realities of the early 21st century as increasingly racialized, but in a way that shifts away from a biological foundation towards a cultural one. The reality of the South-North internationalization of population movements informs Balibar's formulation and the transnational character of the form of racism emerging with it.

An obvious question arises as to whether any of this is as new as Balibar's label, "neo-racism," would suggest. His argument hangs on what he sees as the historical and geographical specificity of the emergence, as well as the cultural turn it assumes. He points particularly to the use of immigration as a "substitute" for race in the development of a consciousness that supports or sustains social closure in French society, enabling what he calls "racism without races." In this formulation, racial superiority is maintained through notions of European civilizational superiority, on the one hand, and the insurmountability of the cultural divisions between those of European lineage and "others," on the other. Cultural difference, previously the very basis for anti-racist action, then becomes naturalized and formalized as a basis for what Taguieff (1995) has referred to as "differentialist racism"—a form of racism based on the validity of difference that otherwise underpins contemporary popular notions of diversity, multiculturalism, and anti-racism. But again, as Banton's chapter suggests, a racism that does not have a genetic basis has previously existed in other forms, notably those based on religious distinctions. Anti-Semitism is an enduring example, leading a list to which Islamophobia can be safely added today.

Balibar's argument can be extended to suggest that neo-racism represents new conceptions of race and racialization in ways that are less traditional, as we see with Bhatt's chapter dealing with Hindu natonalism as a form of indigenist neo-racism. While Balibar's focus is on transnational social relations, Bhatt is looking at how national lore is resurrected and constructed in ways that theoretically undermine the project of "diversity" and "multiculturalism" by asserting notions of cultural absolutism among South Asian communities. In this instance, race becomes deployed not only as a political force, but also as a reactionary ideology that informs right-wing political projects by traditional victims of racism—racialized populations themselves. Bhatt's contribution focuses on the Hindutva nationalist movement in India (and among the Indian diaspora abroad) and its deployment of the race concept based on heredity as a cultural phenomenon, as opposed to a biological one. He explores parallels between these "subordinate" group uses of the race concept and the white supremacist deployment of civilizational modes, suggesting that the deployments of "myths of origin, tropes of breeding, cultivation, blood and lineage" amount to a form of "monocultural neoracism." He concludes then that the uses and abuses of the race concept in Hindutva are very close to those in Western "race thinking," certainly much closer than is usually assumed or imagined. On this basis, we can also see how the Hindutva modes would travel transnationally, from India to Europe, presenting a convergence of the instrumentality of neo-racism from above and below that could provide it validity for the exclusions it imports.

REFERENCES

Banton, M. 1967. *Race Relations*. London: Tavistock.

Essed, P. 1991. *Understanding Everyday Racism: An Interdisciplinary Theory*. Newbury Park, CA: Sage.

Gilroy, P. 1987. *"There Ain't No Black in the Union Jack": The Cultural Politics of Race and Nation*. London: Hutchinson.

Goldberg, D.T. 1990. *Anatomy of Racism*. Minneapolis: University of Minnesota Press.

hooks, b. 1990. *Yearning: Race, Gender, and Cultural Politics*. Boston: South End Press.

Omi, M., and M. Winant. 1993. "On the Theoretical Status of the Concept of Race." In *Race, Identity and Representation*, ed. C. McCarthy and W. Crichlow. New York: Routledge.

———. 1994. *Racial Formation in the United States: From the 1960s to the 1990s*, 2nd. ed. New York: Routledge.

Taguieff, P. 1995. *Les Fins de l'antiracisme*. Paris: Michalon.

Wellman, D. 1993. *Portraits of White Racism*, 2nd. ed. Cambridge: Cambridge University Press.

West, C. 1994. *Race Matters*. New York: Vintage Books.

CHAPTER 8

DOES "RACE" MATTER? TRANSATLANTIC PERSPECTIVES ON RACISM AFTER "RACE RELATIONS"

Robert Miles and Rudy Torres

> The discourse promoting resistance to racism must not prompt identification with and in terms of categories fundamental to the discourse of oppression. Resistance must break not only with *practices* of oppression, although its first task is to do that. Resistance must oppose also the *language* of oppression, including the categories in terms of which the oppressor (or racist) represents the forms in which resistance is expressed. (Goldberg 1990:313–14)

In April 1993, one year after the Los Angeles civil unrest, a major US publisher released a book with the creatively ambiguous title *Race Matters* by the distinguished scholar Cornel West. The back cover of the slightly revised edition published the following year categorized it as a contribution to both African American studies and current affairs. The latter was confirmed by the publisher's strategy of marketing the book as a "trade" rather than as an "academic" title: this was a book for the "American public" to read. And the American public was assured that they were reading a quality product when they were told that its author had "built a reputation as one of the most eloquent voices in America's racial debate."

Some two years later, the *Los Angeles Times* published an article by its science writer under the headline "Scientists Say Race Has No Biological Basis." The opening paragraph ran as follows:

> Researchers adept at analyzing the genetic threads of human diversity said Sunday that the concept of race—the source of abiding cultural and political divisions in American society—simply has no basis in fundamental human biology. Scientists should abandon it.

And on the same day (20 February 1995), the *Chronicle of Higher Education* reproduced the substance of these claims in an article under the title "A Growing Number of Scientists Reject the Concept of Race." Both publications were reporting on the proceedings of the American Association for the Advancement of Science in Atlanta.

If "the concept of race ... simply has no basis in fundamental human biology," how are we to evaluate Professor West's assertion that "Race Matters"? If "race" matters, then "races" must exist! But if there are no "races," then "race" cannot matter. These two contributions to public political debate seem to reveal a contradiction. Yet within the specific arena of academic debate there is a well-rehearsed attempt to dissolve the contradiction, which runs as follows. It is acknowledged that, earlier this century, the biological and genetic sciences established conclusively in the light of empirical evidence that the attempt to establish the existence of different types or "races" of human beings by scientific procedures had failed. The idea that the human species consisted of a number of distinct "races," each exhibiting a set of discrete physical and cultural characteristics is therefore false, mistaken. The interventions reported as having been made in Atlanta in February 1995 only repeat what some scientists have been arguing since the 1930s. Yet the fact that scientists have to continue to assert these claims demonstrates that the contrary is still widely believed and articulated in public discussion.

Because this scientific knowledge has not yet been comprehensively understood by "the general public" (which not only persists in believing in the existence of "races" as biologically discrete entities but also acts in ways consistent with such a belief), it is argued that social scientists must employ a *concept* of "race" to describe and analyze these beliefs, and the discrimination and exclusion that are premised on this kind of classification. In other words, while social scientists know that there are no "races," they also know that things believed to exist (in this case "races") have a real existence for those who believe in them and that actions consistent with the belief have real social consequences. In sum, because people believe that "races" exist (i.e. because they utilize the *idea* of "race" to comprehend their social world), social scientists need a *concept* of "race."

Or do they? This chapter will explore the reasons why this question needs to be asked. It will also answer it by suggesting that social scientists do not need to, and indeed should not, transform the *idea* of "race" into an analytical category and use "race" as a *concept*. Pre-eminent amongst the reasons for such an assertion is that the arenas of academic and political discourse cannot be clinically separated. Hence Professor West, in seeking to use his status as a leading Afro-American scholar to make a political intervention in current affairs by arguing that "Race Matters," is likely to legitimate and reinforce the widespread public belief that "races" exist irrespective of his views on this issue. For if this belief in the existence of "races" was not widespread, there would be no news value in publishing an article in a leading daily US newspaper that claims that "Race Has No Biological Basis."

CRITICIZING "RACE" AS AN ANALYTICAL CATEGORY

We begin this exploration by crossing the Atlantic in order to consider the issue as it has been discussed in Britain since the early 1950s. As we shall see, the development of the British discussion has in fact been influenced substantially by the preconceptions and language employed in the US: the use of "race" as an analytical category in the social sciences is a transatlantic phenomenon.

It is now difficult to conceive, but forty years ago no one would have suggested that "Race Matters" *in* Britain. The idea of "race" was employed in public and political discussion, but largely only in order to discuss "the colonies": the "race problem" was spatially located beyond British shores in the British Empire and especially in certain colonies, notably South Africa. It is relevant to add that this too had not always been so. During the nineteenth and early twentieth centuries, it was widely believed that the population of Britain was composed of a number of different "races" (e.g., the Irish were identified as being "of the Celtic race") and, moreover, migration to Britain from central and eastern Europe in the late nineteenth century was interpreted using the language of "race" to signify the Jewish refugees fleeing persecution (e.g., Barkan 1992:15–165). But, as the situation in the port city of Liverpool after the First World War suggested (e.g., Barkan 1992:57–165), the language of "race" used to refer to the interior of Britain was to become tied exclusively to differences in skin colour in the second half of the twentieth century. What, then, was the "race" problem that existed beyond the shores of Britain?

Briefly expressed, the problem was that, or so it was thought, the colonies were spatial sites where members of different "races" (Caucasian, White, African, Hindoo, Mongoloid, Celts: the language to name these supposed "races" varied enormously) met and where their "natures" (to civilize, to fight, to be lazy, to progress, to drink, to engage in sexual perversions, etc.) interacted, often with tragic consequences. This language of "race" was usually anchored in the signification of certain forms of somatic difference (skin colour, facial characteristics, body shape and size, eye colour, skull shape) which were interpreted as the physical marks which accompanied, and which in some unexplained way determined, the "nature" of those so marked. In this way, the social relations of British colonialism were explained as being rooted simultaneously in the biology of the human body and in the cultural attributes determined by nature.

But the "race" problem was not to remain isolated from British shores, to be contained there by a combination of civilization and violence. All Her Majesty's subjects had the right of residence in the Motherland, and increasing numbers of them chose to exercise that right as the 1950s progressed. Members of "coloured races," from the Caribbean and the Indian subcontinent in particular, migrated to Britain largely to fill vacancies in the labour market but against the will of successive governments (Labour and Conservative) who feared that they carried in their cheap suitcases not only their few clothes and personal possessions but also the "race problem" (e.g., Joshi and Carter 1984, Solomos 1989, Layton-Henry 1992). By the late 1950s, it was widely argued that, as a result of "coloured immigration," Britain had imported a "race" problem: prior to this migration, so it was believed, Britain's population was "racially homogeneous," a claim that neatly dispensed with not only earlier racialized classifications of both migrants and the population of the British Isles but also the history of interior racisms.

The political and public response to immigration from the Caribbean and the Indian subcontinent is now a well-known story (e.g., Solomos 1989, Layton-Henry 1992), although there are a number of important by-ways still to be explored. What is of more interest here is the academic response. A small number of social scientists (particularly sociologists and anthropologists) wrote about these migrations and their social consequences using the language of everyday life: *Dark Strangers* and *The Colour Problem* were the titles of two books that achieved a certain prominence during the 1950s, and their authors subsequently pursued distinguished academic careers. Considered from the point of view of the 1990s, these titles now seem a little unfortunate, and perhaps even a part of the problem insofar as they employ language that seems to echo and legitimate racist discourses of the time.

But can the same be said for two other books that became classic texts within the social sciences: Michael Banton's *Race Relations* (1967) and John Rex's *Race Relations in Sociological Theory* (1970)? Both were published in the following decade and were widely interpreted as offering different theoretical and political interpretations of the consequences of the migration to, and settlement in, Britain of British subjects and citizens from the Caribbean and the Indian subcontinent. And indeed they did offer very different analyses. Notably, Rex sought to reinterpret the scope of the concept of racism to ensure that it could encompass the then contemporary political discourses about immigration. Such discourse avoided any direct references to an alleged hierarchy of "races" while at the same time referring to or implying the existence of different "races." Banton interpreted this shift in discourse as evidence of a decline in racism, a conclusion that was to lead him to eventually reject the concept of racism entirely (1987).

But what is more remarkable is that, despite their very different philosophical and theoretical backgrounds and conclusions, they shared something else in common. Both Banton and Rex mirrored the language of everyday life, incorporated it into academic discourse and thereby legitimated it. They agreed that Britain (which they both analyzed comparatively with reference to the US and South Africa) had a race relations problem, and Rex in particular wished to conceptualize this problem theoretically in the discipline of sociology. In so doing, both premised their arguments on the understanding that scientific knowledge proves that "races" do not exist in the sense widely understood in everyday common sense discourse: if "race" was a problem, it was a social and not a biological problem, one rooted in part at least in the continued popular belief in the existence of "races." Indeed, John Rex had been one of the members of the team of experts recruited by UNESCO to officially discredit the continuing exploitation of nineteenth-century scientific knowledge about "race" by certain political groups and to educate the public by making widely known the more recent conclusions of biological and genetic scientists (Montagu 1972).

The concept of "race relations" seemed to have impeccable credentials, unlike the language of "dark strangers," for example. This is in part because the notion was borrowed from the early sociology of the "Chicago School" in the US which, amongst other things, was interested in the consequences of two contemporaneous migrations: the early twentieth-century migration from the southern to the northern states of "Negroes" fleeing poverty (and much more besides) in search of wage labour and the continuing large-scale migration from Europe to the US. As a result of the former migration, "Negro" and "white races" entered, or so it was conceptualized, into conflicting social relations in the burgeoning industrial urban areas of the northern states and sociologists had named a new field of study. "Coloured migration" to British cities after 1945 provided an opportunity for sociologists to import this field of study into Britain: Britain too now had a "race relations" problem.

Moreover, for Rex at least, "race relations situations" were characterized by the presence of a racist ideology. Hence, the struggle against colonialism could now be pursued within the Mother Country "herself: by intervening in the new, domestic race relations problem on the side of the colonized victims of racism, one could position oneself against the British state now busily seeking a solution to that problem through the introduction of immigration controls intended specifically to prevent "coloured" British subjects from entering the country. Such was the rush to be on the side of the angels that few, if any, wondered about what the angels looked like and whether there was any validity in the very concept of angel.

There was a further import from the US that had a substantial impact on the everyday and academic discourses of race relations in the late 1960s and early 1970s in Britain: the struggle for civil rights and against racism on the part of "the blacks" in the US (the notion of "Negro" had now run its course and, like "coloured" before it, it had been ejected into the waste-bin of politically unacceptable language). This movement had the effect of mobilizing not only many blacks in Britain but also many whites politically inclined towards one of several competing versions of socialist transformation. And if radical blacks were busy "seizing the time" in the names of anti-racism and "black autonomy," there was little political or academic space within which radically-inclined white social scientists could wonder about the legitimacy and the consequences of seizing the language of "race" to do battle against racism. For it was specifically in the name of "race" that black people were resisting their long history of colonial oppression: indeed, in some versions of this vision of liberation, contemporary blacks were the direct descendants and inheritors of the African "race" which had been deceived and disinherited by the "white devils" many centuries ago. In this "race war," the white race was soon to face the day of judgement.

Possession of a common language and associated historical traditions can blind as well as illuminate. It is especially significant that both the Left and the Right in Britain looked across the Atlantic when seeking to analyze and to offer forecasts about the outcome of the race relations problem that both agreed existed within Britain. The infamous speeches on immigration made by the MP Enoch Powell in the late 1960s and 1970s contained a great deal of vivid imagery, refracting the current events in US cities and framing them as prophecies of what was inevitably going to happen in due course in British cities if the "alien wedge" was not quickly "repatriated." At the same time, the Left drew political inspiration from the black struggle against racism and sought to incorporate aspects of its rhetoric, style, and politics. Hence, while there was disagreement about the identity of the heroes and the villains of race relations in the US, there was fundamental agreement that race relations there provided a framework with which to assess the course of race relations in Britain. Even legislation intended to regulate race relations and to make racialized discrimination illegal refracted the "American experience."

As a result, the academic response to the race relations problem in Britain was largely isolated both from the situations elsewhere in Europe—and particularly in northwest Europe which was experiencing a quantitatively much more substantial migration than that taking place in Britain—and from academic and political writing about those situations. Two features of those situations are pertinent to the argument here.

First, the nation states of northwest Europe had recently experienced either fascist rule or fascist occupation, and therefore had suffered the direct consequences of the so-called "final solution to the Jewish question" which sought to eliminate the "Jewish race." Hence, the collective historical memory of most of the major cities of northwest Europe was shaped by the genocide effected against the Jews and legitimated in the name of "race," even if that historical memory was now the focus of denial or repression. Second, this experience left the collective memory especially susceptible to the activities of UNESCO and others seeking to discredit the idea of "race" as a valid and meaningful descriptor. Hence, the temporal and spatial proximity of the Holocaust rendered its legitimating racism (a racism in which the idea of "race" was explicit and central) an immediate reality: in this context, few people were willing to make themselves vulnerable to the charge of racism, with the result that suppressing the idea of "race," at least in the official and formal arenas of public life, became a political imperative.

The political and academic culture of mainland northwest Europe has therefore been open to two developments which distinguish it from that existing in the British Isles. First, in any debate about the scope and validity of the concept of racism, the Jewish experience of racism is much more likely to be discussed, and even to be prioritized over any other. Second, the idea of "race" itself became highly politically sensitive. Its very use as a descriptor is more likely to be interpreted in itself as evidence of racist beliefs and, as a result, the idea is rarely employed in everyday political and academic discussion, at least not in connection with domestic social relations. However, in Britain, given the combination of the colonial migration and the multiple ideological exchange with the US, there were far fewer constraints on the everyday use of the idea of "race" and on a redefinition of the concept of racism. As a result, the latter came to refer exclusively to an ideology held by "white" people about "black" people which was rooted in colonial exploitation and in capitalist expansion beyond Europe.

Having recognized the relative distinctiveness of the political and academic space in northwest Europe and then having occupied that space, one can view those social relations defined in Britain and the US as race relations from another point of view. For there is no public or academic reference to the existence of race relations in contemporary France or Germany. It then becomes possible to pose questions that seem not to be posed from within these intimately interlinked social and historical contexts. What kinds of social relations are signified as race relations? Why is the idea of "race" employed in everyday life to refer only to certain groups of people and to certain social situations? And why do social scientists unquestioningly import everyday meanings into their reasoning and theoretical frameworks in defining "race" and "race relations" as a particular field of study? As a result, what does it mean for an academic to claim, for example, that "race" is a factor in determining the structure of social inequality or that "race" and gender are interlinked forms of oppression? What is intended and what might be the consequences of asserting as an academic that "race matters"?

These are the kinds of questions that one of the present authors has been posing for nearly fifteen years (e.g., Miles 1982, 1984, 1989), influenced in part by the important writing of the French theorist Guillaumin (1972, 1995). The answers to these questions lead to the conclusion that one should follow the example of biological and genetic scientists and refuse to attribute analytical status to the *idea* of "race" within the social sciences, and thereby refuse to use it as a descriptive and explanatory *concept*. The reasoning can be summarized as follows (cf. Miles 1982:22–43; 1993:47–9).

First, the idea of "race" is used to effect a reification within sociological analysis insofar as the outcome of an often complex social process is explained as the consequence of some thing named "race" rather than of the social process itself. Consider both the recent publication of *The Bell Curve* (1994) by Richard J. Hernstein and Charles Murray and the authors' common assertion that "race" determines academic performance and life chances. The assertion can be supported with statistical evidence that demonstrates that, in comparison with "black people," "white people" are more likely to achieve top grades in school and to enter the leading universities in the US. The determining processes are extremely complex, including amongst other things parental class position, active and passive racialized stereotyping, and exclusion in the classroom and beyond. The effects of these processes are all mediated through a previously racialized categorization into a "white/black" dichotomy which is employed in everyday social relations. Hence, it is not "race" that determines academic performance; rather, academic performance is determined by an interplay of social processes, one of which is premised on the articulation of racism to effect and legitimate exclusion. Indeed, given the nineteenth-century meanings of "race," this form of reification invites the possibility of explaining academic performance as the outcome of some quality within the body of those racialized as "black."

Second, when academics who choose to write about race relations seek to speak to a wider audience (an activity which we believe to be fully justified) or when their writings are utilized by non-academics, this unwittingly legitimates and reinforces everyday beliefs that the human species is constituted by a number of different "races," each of which is characterized by a particular combination of real or imagined physical features or marks and cultural practices. When Professor West seeks to persuade the American public that "Race Matters," there is no doubt that he himself does not believe in the existence of biologically defined "races," but he cannot control the meanings attributed to his claim on the part of those who identify differences in skin colour, for example, as marks designating the existence of blacks and whites as discrete "races." Unintentionally, his writing may then come to serve as a legitimation not only of a belief in the existence of "race" as a biological phenomenon but also of racism itself. He could avoid this outcome by breaking with the race relations paradigm.

Third, as a result of reification and the interplay between academic and common sense discourses, the use of "race" as an analytical concept incorporates a notion which has been central to the evolution of racism into the discourse of antiracism, thereby sustaining one of the conditions of the reproduction of racism within the discourse and practice of antiracism.

For these reasons, the idea of "race" should not be employed as an analytical category within the social sciences, and it follows from this that the object of study should not be described as race relations. Hence, we reject the race relations problematic as the locus for the analysis of racism. But we do not reject the concept of racism. Rather, we critique the race relations problematic in order to retain a concept of racism which is constructed in such a way as to recognize the existence of a plurality of historically specific racisms, not all of which employ explicitly the idea of "race." In contrast, the race relations paradigm refers exclusively to either black/white social relations or social relations between "people of colour" and "white people," with the result that there is only one racism, the racism of whites which has as its object and victim people of colour (e.g., Essed 1991). Moreover, as is increasingly recognized in the academic literature of the past decade, many recent and contemporary discourses which eschew use of the idea of "race" nevertheless advance notions that were previously a referent of such an idea. We can only comprehend contemporary discourses that dispense with the explicit use of the idea of "race" and those discourses which naturalize and inferiorize white populations if we rescue the concept of racism from the simultaneous inflation and narrowing of its meaning by the intersection of the academic and political debates that have taken place in Britain and the US since the end of the Second World War.

REFLECTIONS ON THE RACIALIZATION OF THE US BY THE AMERICAN ACADEMY

When one views the contemporary academic debate about racism in the US both from this analytical position and from Europe, one is struck by the following things. First, when compared with the mid- and late 1960s, it is now an extremely contested debate, and one in which many voices are heard arguing different positions. On the one hand, writers such as Wellman (1993) continue to assert that racism remains the primary determinant of social inequality in the US, while on the other writers such as Wilson claim that the influence of racism has declined substantially, to the point where it cannot be considered to be a significant influence on current structures of inequality (1987). Between these two positions, one finds writers such as West who assert that the continuing impact of racism has to be assessed in terms of its relationship with the effects of class, sexism, and homophobia (e.g., 1994:44). Moreover, it is a debate in which the voices of "Afrocentrists" (e.g., Karenga 1993) and "black feminists" (e.g., hooks 1990) have become extremely influential over the past two decades, while at the same time a "black" conservative intellectual tradition has emerged and attracted increasing attention (e.g., Sowell 1994).

Second, it remains a debate in which it is either largely taken for granted or explicitly argued that the concept of racism refers to an ideology and (in some cases) a set of practices, of which black people are the exclusive victim: racism refers to what "white" people think about and do to "black" people. While the concept of institutional racism goes further by eschewing any reference to human intentionality, it retains the white/black dichotomy in order to identify beneficiary and victim. Thus the scope of the concept of racism is very narrowly defined: the centrality of the white/black dichotomy denies by definition the possibility that any group other than white people can articulate, practise or benefit from racism and suggests that only black people can be the object or victim of racism.

Some of West's writing illustrates this difficulty. He clearly distinguishes himself from those he describes as black nationalists when he argues that their obsession with white racism obstructs the development of the political alliances that are essential to effecting social changes, changes that will alleviate the suffering of black people in the US, and that white racism alone cannot explain the socio-economic position of the majority of black Americans (1994:82, 98–99). Moreover, he goes so far as to suggest that certain black nationalist accounts "simply mirror the white supremacist ideals we are opposing" (1994:99). Yet he seems reluctant to identify any form of racism other than white racism. In his carefully considered discussion of what he describes as "Black-Jewish relations," he employs a distinction between black anti-Semitism and Jewish anti-black racism (1994:104; see also Lerner and West 1995:135–56) which suggests that these are qualitatively different phenomena: Jews articulate racism while blacks express anti-Semitism. This interpretation is reinforced by his assertion that black anti-Semitism is a form of "xenophobia from below" which has a different institutional power when compared with "those racisms that afflict their victims from above" (1994:109–110) even though he claims that both merit moral condemnation.

A similar distinction is implicit in the recent writing of Blauner (1992) who, partly in response to the arguments of one of the present authors, has revised his position significantly since the 1960s. Blauner returns to the common distinction between "race" and ethnicity, arguing that the "peculiarly modern division of the world into a discrete number of hierarchically ranked races is a historic product of Western colonialism" (1992:61). This, he argues, is a very different process from that associated with ethnicity. Hence, Blauner refrains from analyzing the ideologies employed to justify the exclusion of Italians and Jews in the US in the 1920s as racism: these populations are described as "white ethnics" who were "viewed racially" (1992:64). Concerning the period of fascism in Germany, Blauner refers to genocide "where racial imagery was obviously intensified" (1992:64), but presumably the imagery could never be intensified to the point of warranting description as racism because the Jews were not "black." Yet, as we shall see shortly in the case of West's writing, Blauner comes very close to breaking with the race relations problematic when he argues that

> Much of the popular discourse about race in America today goes awry because ethnic realities get lost under the racial umbrella. The positive meanings and potential of ethnicity are overlooked, even overrun, by the more inflammatory meanings of race. (1992:61)

Third, it is a debate which is firmly grounded in the specific realities of the history and contemporary social structure of the US, or rather a particular interpretation of those particular realities. It is perhaps not surprising therefore that scholars of racism in the US have shown so little interest in undertaking comparative research, although there are important exceptions. Some comparative work has been undertaken which compares the US with South Africa (e.g., van den Berghe 1978; Fredrickson 1981), and a comparison between the US and England achieved prominence some twenty years ago (Katznelson 1976; for a recent analysis, see Small 1994). More recently, the "neo-conservative" Sowell (1994) has chosen a comparative international arena to demonstrate what he sees as the explanatory power of his thesis, although it is arguable whether this constitutes a contribution to the sociology of racism. But the vast bulk of work on racism by scholars in the US focuses on the US itself. This may be explained as the outcome of a benign ethnocentrism, but one wonders whether it is not also a function of the limited applicability of a theory of racism that is so closely tied to the race relations paradigm and a black/white dichotomy that it has limited potential to be used to analyze social formations where there is no "black" presence.

Yet there is evidence of an increasingly conscious unease with this race relations paradigm and the black/white dichotomy. For example, as we have already noted, West argues in a recent book that "race matters":

> Race is the most explosive issue in American life precisely because it forces us to confront the tragic facts of poverty and paranoia, despair and distrust. In short, a candid examination of *race* matters takes us to the core of the crisis of American democracy. (1994:155–56)

But he also argues that it is necessary to formulate new frameworks and languages in order not only to comprehend the current crisis in the US but also to identify solutions to it (1994:11). Indeed, he asserts that it is imperative to move beyond the narrow framework of "dominant liberal and conservative views of race in America," views which are formulated with a "worn-out vocabulary" (1994:4). But it seems that West does not accept that the idea of "race" itself is an example of this exhausted language, for he employs it throughout with apparently little hesitation, despite the fact that he believes that the manner in which "we set up the terms for discussing racial issues shapes our perception and response to these issues" (1994:6). Later in the book, he seems to be on the verge of following through the logic of this argument to its ultimate conclusion when he argues that the Clarence Thomas/Anita Hill hearings demonstrate that "the very framework of racial reasoning" needs to be called into question in order to reinterpret the black freedom struggle not as an issue of "skin pigmentation and racial phenotype" but, instead, as an issue of ethics and politics (1994:38). And yet West cannot follow through the logic of this argument to the point of acknowledging that there cannot be a place for the use of "race" as an analytical concept in the social sciences.

But there is a transatlantic trade in theories of racism and this is now a two-way trade. Some scholars in the US are not only aware of debates and arguments generated in Europe (including those contributions which question some of the key assumptions that characterize the debate in the US), but some have also acknowledged and responded to one of the present authors, who has criticized both the use of "race" as an analytical concept and the way in which the concept of racism has been inflated (e.g., Miles 1982, 1989, 1993). Recent contributions by Wellman (1993), Blauner (1992), Omi and Winant (1993, 1994), and Goldberg (1993) all refer to and comment on these arguments, with varying degrees of enthusiasm. Interestingly, they all seem to ignore the writing of Lieberman and his associates (e.g., Lieberman 1968; Reynolds 1992) in the US, who argue for a position which overlaps in important respects the one outlined here.

Goldberg offers perhaps the most complex and thoughtful response in the course of a wide-ranging and, in part, philosophically inspired analysis of contemporary racisms and of the conceptual language required to analyze them. His important analysis requires a more extended evaluation than is possible in the limited space available here, so we have chosen to focus instead on the work of Omi and Winant. This is in part because their writing has already had considerable influence in both the US and Britain, partly because of the way in which some of their key concepts have parallels in the equally influential work of Gilroy (1987). And this influence is deserved. There is much to admire and to learn from their theoretical and conceptual innovations. We prefer to employ a concept of *racialized* formation (rather than racial formation), but we agree that racialized categories are socially created, transformed, and destroyed through historical time (1994:55). We can recognize that it is essential to differentiate between "race" (although we do not use "race" as a *concept* but rather we capture its use in everyday life by referring to the *idea* of "race") and the concept of racism, a distinction that allows us to make a further distinction between racialization and racism (although Omi and Winant refer to this as a distinction between racial awareness and racial essentialism; compare Omi and Winant 1994:71 with Miles 1989: 73–84). And we also agree that it is essential to retain the concept of racism to identify a multiplicity of historically specific racisms, with the consequence that there is "nothing inherently white about racism" (Omi and Winant 1994:72; see also 1994:73, and compare with Miles 1989:57–60; 1993). Wellman (1993:3) is simply mistaken when he claims that Miles argues that racism is not a useful concept.

It is important to highlight these areas of agreement prior to considering Omi and Winant's defence of the use of the idea of "race" as an analytical concept in the social sciences in order to indicate both the innovations that they have effected within the discussion in the US about racism and their failure to pursue the logic of these innovations to their ultimate conclusion. Partly as a result of their emphasis upon the way in which the idea of "race" has been socially constructed and reconstructed, there is now a debate within the literature in the US about the theoretical and analytical status of the idea of "race." Other scholars in the US have made important contributions to the development of this debate, notably Lieberman (1968), Fields (1990), and Roediger (1994). Fields' work is especially significant because it reaches a conclusion that is close to that reached by one of the present authors (see Miles 1982; 1993:27–52). Omi and Winant have criticized Fields' conclusions in the course of defending their continued use of "race" as analytical concept and it is therefore important to reflect upon the arguments and evidence that they have employed.

Omi and Winant offer two criticisms of the position that the idea of "race" should be analyzed exclusively as a social or ideological construct (1993:5). First, they suggest that it fails to recognize the social impact of the longevity of the concept of "race." Second, they claim that, as a result of this longevity, "race is an almost indissoluble part of our identities," a fact that is not recognized by those who argue that "race" is an ideological construct. They are mistaken on both counts. The writing of Miles highlights the historical evolution of the meanings attributed to the idea of "race" and, for example in his discussions of colonialism and of the articulation between racism and nationalism, stresses the way in which the idea of belonging to the "white race" was central to the construction of the identity of the British bourgeoisie and working class (1982, 1993). Indeed, these claims can be refuted simply by citing a quotation from Fields (1990:118) that Omi and Winant themselves reproduce (1993:5). Fields writes:

> Nothing handed down from the past could keep race alive if we did not constantly reinvent and re-ritualise it to fit our own terrain. If race lives on today, it can do so only because we continue to create and re-create it in our social life, continue to verify it, and thus continue to need a social vocabulary that will allow us to make sense, not of what our ancestors did then, but of what we choose to do now.

Thus Fields certainly does not deny that in the contemporary world people use the idea of "race" to classify themselves and others into social collectivities and act in ways consistent with such a belief, actions which collectively produce structured exclusion. And, hence, Omi and Winant's critique is shown to be vacuous. Fields' key objective is to critique the way in which historians invoke the idea of "race" to construct explanations for events and processes in the past, and her critique applies equally to the work of sociologists such as Omi and Winant who have reinvented and re-ritualized the idea of "race" to fit their own terrain within the academy (which is after all only one more arena of social life). Let us examine how Omi and Winant reinvent and thereby reify the idea of "race" in the course of their sociological analysis. Consider the following claim: "One of the first things we notice about people when we meet them (along with their sex) is their race" (1994:59). Elsewhere, they argue that "To be raceless is akin to being genderless. Indeed, when one cannot identify another's race, a microsociological 'crisis of interpretation' results ..." (1993:5). How are we to interpret this assertion? While they also claim that "race is ... a socially constructed way of differentiating human beings" (1994:65), the former assertion is at the very least open to interpretation as suggesting that "race" is an objective quality inherent in a person's being, that every human being is a member of a "race," and that such membership is inscribed in a person's visible appearance. It is in the interstices of such ambiguity that the idea of "race" as a biological fact does not just "live on" but is actively recreated by social scientists in the course of their academic practice.

This argument commonly stimulates incomprehension on the part of scholars in the US, who echo arguments employed in some critiques of this position in Britain. Thus, it is often said, "How can you deny analytical status to the idea of race and ultimately the existence of race when blacks and whites are so obviously different and when all the evidence demonstrates that their life chances differ too?" In responding to this question, it is necessary first to problematize what it takes for granted, specifically that the "black/white" division is *obvious*. The quality of *obviousness* is not inherent in a phenomenon, but is the outcome of a social process in the course of which meaning is attributed to the phenomenon in a particular historical and social context. The meaning is learnt by those who are its subject and object. They therefore learn to habitually recognize it, and perhaps to pass on this signification and knowledge to others, with the result that the quality of obviousness attributed to the phenomenon is reproduced through historical time and social space.

Skin colour is one such phenomenon. Its visibility is not inherent in its existence but is a product of signification: human beings identify skin colour to *mark* or symbolize other phenomena in a historical context in which other significations occur. When human practices include and exclude people in the light of the signification of skin colour, collective identities are produced and social inequalities are structured. It is for this reason that historical studies of the meanings attributed to skin colour in different historical contexts and through time are of considerable importance. And it is in relation to such studies that one can enquire into the continuities and discontinuities with contemporary processes of signification which sustain the obviousness of skin colour as a social *mark*. Historically and contemporarily, differences in skin colour have been and are signified as a mark which suggests the existence of different "races." *But people do not see "race": rather, they observe certain combinations of real and sometimes imagined somatic and cultural characteristics which they attribute meaning to with the idea of "race."* A difference of skin colour is not essential to the process of marking: other somatic features can be and are signified in order to racialize. Indeed, in some historical circumstances, the absence of somatic difference has been central to the powerful impact of racism: the racialized "enemy within" can be identified as a threatening presence even more effectively if the group is not "obviously different" because "they" can be imagined to be everywhere.

Omi and Winant reify this social process and reach the conclusion that all human beings belong to a "race" because they seek to construct their analytical *concepts* to reproduce directly the common sense ideologies of the everyday world. Because the idea of "race" continues to be widely used in everyday life in the US (and Britain) to classify human beings and to interpret their behaviour, Omi and Winant believe that social scientists must employ a *concept* of race. This assumption is the source of our disagreement with them. We argue that one of the contemporary challenges in the analysis of racisms is to develop a conceptual vocabulary that explicitly acknowledges that people use the *idea* of "race" in the everyday world while simultaneously refusing to use the idea of "race" as an analytical *concept* when social scientists analyze the discourses and practices of the everyday world. It is not the *concept* of "race" that "continues to play a fundamental role in structuring and representing the social world" (Omi and Winant 1994:55) but rather the *idea* of "race," and the task of social scientists is to develop a theoretical framework for the analysis of this process of structuring and representing which breaks completely with the reified language of biological essentialism. Hence, we object fundamentally to Omi and Winant's project of developing a critical theory of the *concept* of "race" (1993:6–9) because we also recognize the importance of historical context and contingency in the framing of racialized categories and the social construction of racialized experiences (cf. Omi and Winant 1993:6): we believe that historical context requires us to criticize all concepts of "race," and this can be done by means of a concept of racialization. Omi and Winant's defence of the concept of "race" is a classic example of the way in which the academy in the US continues to racialize the world.

Furthermore, the concept of racialization employed by Omi and Winant is not fully developed, nor do they use it in a sustained analytical manner, because it is grounded in "race relations" sociology, a sociology that reifies the notion of "race" and thereby implies the existence of "racial groups" as monolithic categories of existence. Additionally, they fail to take into account the impact of the social relations of production within the racialization process. We, on the other hand, advance the position that the process of racialization takes place and has its effects in the context of class and production relations and that the idea of "race" may indeed not even be explicitly articulated in the racialization process (see Miles 1989, 1993).

CONCLUSION

West begins the first essay in his book *Race Matters* with a reference to the Los Angeles riots of April 1992. He denies that they were either a "race riot or a class rebellion." Rather, he continues,

> ... this monumental upheaval was a multi-racial, trans-class, and largely male display of social rage.... Of those arrested, only 36 percent were black, more than a third had full-time jobs, and most claimed to shun political affiliation. What we witnessed in Los Angeles was the consequence of a lethal linkage of economic decline, cultural decay, and political lethargy in American life. Race was the visible catalyst, not the underlying cause. (1994:3–4)

And he concludes by claiming that the meaning of the riots is obscured because we are trapped by the narrow framework imposed by the dominant views of "race" in the US.

The *Los Angeles Times* Opinion Editor, Jack Miles, rendered a different version of the narrow framework of the black/white dichotomy. In an essay in the October 1992 issue of the *Atlantic Monthly* entitled "Blacks vs Browns," Miles suggested that Latinos were taking jobs that the nation, by dint of the historic crimes committed against them, owed to African Americans. He blamed Latinos for the poverty in African American communities—a gross misattribution of responsibility—while reinforcing "race" as a relevant category of social and analytical value. His confusion was revealing: the "two societies, one black, one white—separate and unequal" dichotomy made famous by the 1968 report of the National Advisory Commission on Civil Disorders cannot provide an analytical framework to deconstruct the post-Fordist racialized social relations of the 1990s.

The meaning of West's argument is constructed by what is not said as much as by what is. There is a silence about the definition of "race riot": presumably, the events of April 1992 would have been a race riot if the principal actors had been "blacks" and "whites." Hence, West refers only to "race" as the visible catalyst: Rodney King was "obviously black" and the policemen who arrested him were "obviously white." But the riots themselves did not fit the race relations paradigm because the rioters and those who became the victims of the riot were not exclusively blacks and whites. Indeed, as the media were framing the events of April 1992 in black/white terms in the great melodrama of race relations, the first image across the airwaves was of men atop a car waving the Mexican flag! Thus, "Hispanic" may signify presumptively as "white" in the ethno-"racial" dynamics that rest on a system of neat racialized categories, but this has little to do with the popular understanding and experience of Latinos. The outcome of such practices has led to superficial analysis of the full impact of the riots within the context of a changing political economy. The analytical task is therefore to explain the complex nature of the structural changes associated with the emergence of the post-Fordist socio-economic landscape and the reconfigured city's racialized social relations.

Perhaps half of the businesses looted or burned were owned by Korean Americans and another third or so were owned by Mexican Americans/Latinos and Cuban Americans. Those engaged in the looting and burning certainly included African Americans, but poor, recent, and often undocumented immigrants and refugees from Mexico and Central America were equally prominent. Of those arrested, 51% were Latinos and 36% were African Americans. And, of those who died in the civil unrest, about half were African Americans and about a third were Latinos. All this is only surprising if one begins with the assumption that the events were or could have been "race riots." But such an assumption is problematic for two reasons.

First, academics, media reporters, and politicians "conspired" to use the vocabulary of "race" to make sense of the Los Angeles riots because it is a central component of everyday, commonsense discourse in the US. And when it became overwhelmingly apparent that it was not a black/white riot, the language of "race" was nevertheless unthinkingly retained by switching to the use of the notion of "multiracial" in order to encompass the diversity of historical and cultural origins of the participants and victims. Therefore while the race relations paradigm was dealt a serious blow by the reality of riots, the vocabulary of "race" was retained. But—and here we find the source of West's unease—the idea of "race" is so firmly embedded in common sense that it cannot easily encompass a reference to Koreans or Hispanics or Latinos, for these are neither black nor white. It is thus not surprising that pundits and scholars such as West stumble over "racial" ambiguity. The clash of racialized language with a changing political economy presents challenges for scholars and activists alike.

Second, if one had begun with an analysis grounded simultaneously in history and political economy rather than with the supremely ideological notion of race relations, one would have quickly concluded that the actors in any riot in central Los Angeles would probably be *ethnically* diverse. Large-scale inward migration from Mexico and Central America and from southeast Asia into California has coincided with a restructuring of the Californian economy, the loss of major manufacturing jobs, and large-scale internal migration within the urban sprawl of "greater" Los Angeles, with the consequence that the spatial, ethnic, and class structure that underlay the Watts riots of 1965 had been transformed into a much more complex set of relationships. The most general conditions were structural in nature, and thus the decline and shift in the manufacturing base in Los Angeles was not unique but represented a shift in the mode of capital accumulation worldwide (from Fordist to Flexible). In order to analyze those relationships, there is no need to employ a concept of "race": indeed, its retention is a significant hindrance. But it is also necessary to draw upon the insights consequent upon the creation of the concept of *racisms*. The complex relationships of exploitation and resistance, grounded in differences of class, gender, and ethnicity, give rise to a multiplicity of ideological constructions of the racialized Other. For, while the idea of "race" does not matter outside the process of racialization, to which academics are active contributors, the racisms employed in Los Angeles and elsewhere to naturalize, inferiorize, exclude, and sustain privilege certainly *do* matter.

REFERENCES

Banton, M. (1967). *Race Relations*. London: Tavistock.

———. (1987). *Racial Theories*. Cambridge: Cambridge University Press.

Barkan, E. (1992). *The Retreat of Scientific Racism: Changing Concepts of Race in*

Britain and the United States Between the Wars. Cambridge: Cambridge University Press.

van den Berghe, P.L. (1978). *Race and Racism: A Comparative Perspective*. New York: John Wiley.

Blauner, B. (1992). "Talking Past Each Other: Black and White Languages of Race," *The American Prospect* 10: 55–64.

Essed, P. (1991). *Understanding Everyday Racism: An Interdisciplinary Theory*. Newbury Park, Cal.: Sage.

Fields, B.J. (1990). "Slavery, Race and Ideology in the United States of America," *New Left Review* 181: 95–118.

Fredrickson, G.M. (1981). *White Supremacy*. New York: Oxford University Press.

Gilroy, P. (1987). *"There Ain't No Black in the Union Jack": The Cultural Politics of Race and Nation*. London: Hutchinson.

Goldberg, D.T. (1990). "The Social Formation of Racist Discourse." In D.T. Goldberg (ed.), *Anatomy of Racism*. Minneapolis: University of Minnesota Press.

———. (1993). *Racist Culture: Philosophy and the Politics of Meaning*. Oxford: Blackwell.

Guillaumin, C. (1972). *L'Idéologie Raciste*. Paris: Mouton.

———. (1995). *Racism, Sexism, Power and Ideology*. London: Routledge.

hooks, b. (1990). *Yearning: Race, Gender and Cultural Politics*. Boston: South End Press.

Joshi, S., and Carter, B. (1984). "The Role of Labour in the Creation of a Racist Britain." *Race and Class* 25(3): 53–70.

Karenga, M. (1993). *Introduction to Black Studies*. Los Angeles: University of Sankore Press.

Katznelson, I. (1976). *Black Men, White Cities*. Chicago: University of Chicago Press.

Layton-Henry, Z. (1992). *The Politics of Immigration*. Oxford: Blackwell.

Lerner, M., and West, C. (1995). *Jews and Blacks: Let the Healing Begin*. New York: G.P. Putnam's Sons.

Lieberman, L. (1968). "The Debate Over Race: A Study in the Sociology of Knowledge." *Phylon* 39: 127–41.

Miles, R. (1982). *Racism and Migrant Labour: A Critical Text*. London: Routledge and Kegan Paul.

———. (1984). "Marxism versus the 'Sociology of Race Relations.'" *Ethnic and Racial Studies* 7(2): 217–37.

———. (1989). *Racism*. London: Routledge.

———. (1993). *Racism After "Race Relations."* London: Routledge.

Montagu, A. (1972). *Statement on Race*. London: Oxford University Press.

Omi, M., and Winant, M. (1993). "On the Theoretical Status of the Concept of Race." In C. McCarthy and W. Crichlow (eds.), *Race, Identity and Representation*. New York: Routledge.

———. (1994). *Racial Formation in the United States: From the 1960s to the 1990s*, 2nd. ed. New York: Routledge.

Rex, J. (1970). *Race Relations in Sociological Theory*. London: Weidenfeld and Nicolson.

Reynolds, L.T. (1992). "A Retrospective on 'Race': The Career of a Concept." *Sociological Focus*. 25(1): 1–14.

Roediger, D. (1994). *Towards the Abolition of Whiteness: Essays on Race, Politics and Working Class History*. London: Verso.

Small, S. (1994). *Racialized Barriers: The Black Experience in the United States and England in the* 1980s. London: Routledge.

Solomos, J. (1989). *Race and Racism in Contemporary Britain*. London: Macmillan.

Sowell, T. (1994). *Race and Culture: A World View*. New York: Basic Books.

Wellman, D. (1993). *Portraits of White Racism*, 2nd. ed. Cambridge: Cambridge University Press.

West, C. (1994). *Race Matters*. New York: Vintage Books.

Wilson, W.J. (1987). *The Truly Disadvantaged*. Chicago: University of Chicago Press.

CHAPTER 9

WHEN PLACE BECOMES RACE

Sherene H. Razack

In 1983, commenting on section 97 (b) of the *Indian Act*, which made it an offence for a person to be intoxicated on an Indian reserve, a judge of the Manitoba Court of Appeal commented that its logic was both spatial and racial: "Place becomes race," he concluded succinctly of the now repealed section.[1] This book explores *how* place becomes race through the law. The authors examine drinking establishments, parks, slums, classrooms, urban spaces of prostitution, provincial parliaments, the location of mosques, and national borders, exploring how such spaces are organized to sustain unequal social relations and how these relations shape spaces. To highlight our specific interest in how the constitution of spaces reproduces racial hierarchies, we examine the spatial and legal practices required in the making and maintaining of a white settler society.

A white settler society is one established by Europeans on non-European soil. Its origins lie in the dispossession and near extermination of Indigenous populations by the conquering Europeans. As it evolves, a white settler society continues to be structured by a racial hierarchy. In the national mythologies of such societies, it is believed that white people came first and that it is they who principally developed the land; Aboriginal peoples are presumed to be mostly dead or assimilated. European settlers thus *become* the original inhabitants and the group most entitled to the fruits of citizenship. A quintessential feature of white settler mythologies is, therefore, the disavowal of conquest, genocide, slavery, and the exploitation of the labour of peoples of colour. In North America, it is still the case that European conquest and colonization are often denied, largely through the fantasy that North America was peacefully settled and not colonized.

For example, delivering the prestigious Massey lectures for the year 2000, the well-known Canadian scholar Michael Ignatieff takes to task Aboriginal leader Ovide Mercredi and Aboriginal scholar and judge Mary Ellen Turpel for using the term "settler-colonials" when referring to the Europeans who colonized Canada: "To speak this way, as if settlement were merely a form of imperial domination, is to withhold recognition of the right of the majority to settle and use the land we both share." In this view, violent colonization simply did not happen:

> Throughout centuries of collaboration between newcomers and aboriginal nations, Native peoples have always accepted, with varying degrees of willingness, the fact that being first possessors of the land is not the only source of legitimacy for its use. Those who came later have acquired legitimacy by their labours; by putting the soil under cultivation; by uncovering its natural resources; by building great cities and linking them together with railways, highways, and now fibre-optic networks and the Internet. To point out the legitimacy of non-aboriginal settlement in Canada is not to make a declaration about anyone's superiority or inferiority, but simply to assert that each has a fair claim to the land and that it must be shared.[2]

Mythologies or national stories are about a nation's origins and history. They enable citizens to think of themselves as part of a community, defining who belongs and who does not belong to the nation. The story of the land as shared and as developed by enterprising settlers is manifestly a racial story. Through claims to reciprocity and equality, the story produces European settlers as the bearers of civilization while simultaneously trapping Aboriginal people in the pre-modern, that is, before civilization has occurred. Anne McClintock has described this characterization of Indigenous populations as one which condemns them to anachronistic space and time.[3] If Aboriginal peoples are consigned forever to an earlier space and time, people of colour are scripted as late arrivals, coming to the shores of North America long after much of the development has occurred. In this way, slavery, indentureship, and labour exploitation—for example, the Chinese who built the railway or the Sikhs who worked in the lumber industry in nineteenth-century Canada—are all handily forgotten in an official national story of European enterprise.

The national mythologies of white settler societies are deeply spatialized stories. Although the spatial story that is told varies from one time to another, at each stage the story installs Europeans as entitled to the land, a claim that is codified in law. In the first phase of conquest, we see the relationship between law, race, and space in the well-known legal doctrine of *terra nullius*, or empty, uninhabited lands. As Dara Culhane has shown in the case of British colonialism, already inhabited nations "were simply legally *deemed to be uninhabited* if the people were not Christian, not agricultural, not commercial, not 'sufficiently evolved' or simply in the way." In land claim cases launched by Aboriginal nations in Canada, Culhane points out, when Aboriginal people "say today that they have had to go to court to prove they exist, they are speaking not just poetically, but also *literally*."[4]

When more European settlers arrive and the settler colony becomes a nation, a second installment of the national story begins to be told. In Canada, this is the story of the "empty land" developed by hardy and enterprising European settlers. In our national anthem, Canadians sing about Canada as the "True North Strong and Free," an arctic land unsullied by conquest. This land, as both Carl Berger and Robert

Shields have shown, is imagined as populated by white men of grit, a robust Northern race pitting themselves against the harshness of the climate. "These images," Carl Berger points out, "denote not merely geographical location or climactic condition but the combination of both, moulding racial character."[5]

The imagined rugged independence and self-reliance of the European settlers are qualities that are considered to give birth to a greater commitment to liberty and democracy. If Northern peoples are identified with strength and liberty, then Southern peoples are viewed as the opposite: degenerate, effeminate, and associated with tyranny.[6] Racialized populations seldom appear on the settler landscape as other than this racial shadow; when they do, as David Goldberg writes, they are "rendered transparent ... merely part of the natural environment, to be cleared from the landscape—urban and rural—like debris."[7] In the Canada of the national mythology, there are vast expanses of open, snow-covered land, forests, lakes, and the occasional voyageur (trapper) or his modern-day counterpart in a canoe. So compelling is this spatial vision of pristine wilderness that a contemporary advertising campaign for Stanfield's underwear is able to proclaim: a Canadian is someone who knows how to make love in a canoe.

In the 1990s there is a third, equally spatialized development of the national story. The land, once empty and later populated by hardy settlers, is now besieged and crowded by Third World refugees and migrants who are drawn to Canada by the legendary niceness of European Canadians, their well-known commitment to democracy,[8] and the bounty of their land. The "crowds" at the border threaten the calm, ordered spaces of the original inhabitants. A specific geographical imagination is clearly traceable in the story of origins told in anti-immigration rhetoric, operating as metaphor but also enabling material practices such as the increased policing of the border and of bodies of colour.

The September 11, 2001, terrorist attacks on the World Trade Center in New York City and on the Pentagon in Washington (attacks in which over three thousand people lost their lives) have deeply intensified the policing of bodies of colour. Like the United States, Canada has proposed an *Anti-Terrorism Act*[9] that will give sweeping powers to police to identify, prosecute, convict, and punish suspected terrorists. With terrorist activity broadly defined, a person can be arrested without a warrant and detained for more than twenty-four hours solely on the basis that the police have suspicions of terrorist activity. Already many men of Arab descent or who are Arab looking have been detained indefinitely, often in solitary confinement. The incarceration of Japanese Canadians in camps during the Second World War [...] readily comes to mind.

With its purpose to give the state a chance to sort out who is a terrorist and who is not, the *Anti-Terrorism Act* draws inspiration from a number of existing and proposed changes to Canada's *Immigration Act* that established a two-tier structure of citizenship. For example, the Act penalizes Convention refugees without documents (in contravention of the United Nations 1951 Convention and the 1967 Protocol Relating to the Status of Refugees) and requires them to wait three years before enjoying the benefits of full citizenship. Politicians justify the penalty on the grounds that the original inhabitants have a legitimate right to defend themselves from the massive influx of foreign bodies who possess few of the values of honesty, decency, and democracy of their "hosts." Refugees, it is argued, must be given time to learn respect for Canadian culture, and original citizens must be given time to know who they can trust.[10]

To contest white people's primary claim to the land and to the nation requires making visible Aboriginal nations whose lands were stolen and whose communities remain imperilled. It entails including in the national story those bodies of colour whose labour also developed this land but who are not its first occupants. It is to reveal, in other words, the racialized structure of citizenship that characterizes contemporary Canada. The contributors to this book propose to undertake this by unmapping the primary claim. "To unmap," Richard Phillips notes, is not only to denaturalize geography by asking how spaces come to be but also "to undermine world views that rest upon it."[11] Just as mapping colonized lands enabled Europeans to imagine and legally claim that they had discovered and therefore owned the lands of the "New World," unmapping is intended to undermine the idea of white settler innocence (the notion that European settlers merely settled and developed the land) and to uncover the ideologies and practices of conquest and domination.

In unmapping, there is an important relationship between identity and space. What is being imagined or projected on to specific spaces and bodies, and what is being enacted there? Who do white citizens know themselves to be and how much does an identity of dominance rely upon keeping racial Others firmly *in place*? How are people kept in their place? And, finally, how does place become race? We ask these questions here in the fervent belief that white settler societies can transcend their bloody beginnings and contemporary inequalities by remembering and confronting the racial hierarchies that structure our lives.

In tracking dominance spatially, this book joins in the virtual explosion of books in the 1990s that pay attention to the material and symbolic constitution of actual spaces. It is perhaps true, as some have speculated, that the popularity of spatial theory has something to do (ironically) with the colonial mastery that maps and concrete spaces provide.[12] We feel in control and anchored in something real when we can think and talk about a specific street, town, or region.[13] Spatial theory lends itself to so much "specificity," I tell my graduate class on Race, Space, and Citizenship, seizing the opportunity to encourage theory grounded in an empirical base. But the attraction to the concrete is also bound up with the hope that we can pin down something about racialization processes that are directly experienced as spatial. When police drop Aboriginal people outside the city limits leaving them to freeze to death, or stop young Black men on the streets or in malls, when the eyes of shop clerks follow bodies of colour, presuming them to be illicit, when workplaces remain relentlessly white in the better paid jobs and fully "coloured" at the lower levels, when affluent areas of the city are all white and poorer areas are mostly of colour, we experience the spatiality of the racial order in which we live.

The geographical turn in critical theory may falsely reassure us that we have mapped how white supremacy works, yet it promises a stronger connection between everyday life and scholarship, and a closer connection to radical politics. The contributors hope that our engagement with spatial theory will yield insight into the multiple ways in which whites secure their dominance in settler societies. For the most part, we focus on the geographical spaces of Canada, inviting others who consider both Canadian and other geographies to examine the role of Canadian law in producing and sustaining a racial social order.

It must be said at the outset that our focus on racial formations is automatically a focus on class and gender hierarchies as well. Racial hierarchies come into existence through patriarchy and capitalism, each system of domination mutually constituting the other. The lure of a spatial approach is precisely the possibility of charting the simultaneous operation of multiple systems of domination. As Edward Soja explains in *Postmodern Geographies*, "the spatiality of social life is stubbornly simultaneous, but what we write down is successive because language is successive."[14] To consider, for example, the multiple systems that constitute spaces of prostitution, we must talk about the economic status of women in prostitution, the way in which areas of prostitution are marked as degenerate space that confirms the existence of white, respectable space, the sexual violence that brings so many young girls to prostitution, and so on. Yet, beginning with any one practice privileges a particular system and leaves the impression that it is that system that is pre-eminent. A spatial analysis can help us to see the operation of all the systems as they mutually constitute each other.

POINTS OF ENTRY: SPACE AS AN OBJECT OF STUDY

What an interdisciplinary collection on space such as this one gains from geography must be clarified from the start. The academic world is still largely discipline bound: geographers sometimes think they own the concepts associated with space, legal scholars guard the gates to the study of the law, and sociologists lay claim to social identities and social inequality as their own objects of study. The gate keeping is not merely a turf war, that is, a contest over who has the right to teach and write about whom and where. Rather, each discipline has approached its "proper" objects of study with specific questions in mind. Further, each has its own critical traditions. Borrowing from a variety of disciplines increases the risk that something of the depth of these scholarly projects will be lost. Geographers have not failed to express their concern that those of us eager to assume the language of geography sometimes end up taking as our "unexamined grounding a seemingly unproblematic, common sense notion of space as a container, a field, a simple emptiness in which all things are 'situated' or 'located.'"[15]

The risk, duly noted here, is that non-geographers are not well qualified to engage in spatial theory. While we acknowledge from the start a partial and incomplete access to each discipline, we deliberately reject the boundaries created by them. If there is anything we have learned about racial projects it is that they come into being and are sustained through a wide number of practices, both material and symbolic. The study of the creation of racial hierarchies demands nothing less than the tools of history, sociology, geography, education, and law, among other domains of knowledge. In an effort to delineate the interdisciplinary approach that is the basis of this book, I provide below an outline of the core ideas that have engaged the contributors, providing the reader with a kind of schematic guide to the starting points we each had in mind and offering an indication of the limits contained here.

SPACE AS A SOCIAL PRODUCT

To question how spaces come to be, and to trace what they produce as well as what produces them, is to unsettle familiar everyday notions. Space seems to us to be empty. Either we fill it with things (houses, monuments, bridges) or nature fills it with trees, a cold climate, and so on. Space, in this view, is innocent. A building is just a building, a forest just a forest. Urban space seems to evolve naturally. We think, for example, that Chinatowns simply emerged when Chinese people migrated in sufficient numbers to North America and decided to live together. Slums and wealthy suburbs seem to evolve naturally. In the same way that spaces appear to develop organically, so too the inhabitants of spaces seem to belong to them. If the slum or the housing project has a disproportionate number of Black or Aboriginal people, it is thought to be simply because such people lack the education and training to obtain the jobs, and thus the income, that would enable them to live in a wealthy suburb. Perhaps, we often reason, poor districts are simply occupied by recently arrived immigrants who will, in time, move up to more affluent spaces.

If we reject the view that spaces simply evolve, are filled up with things, and exist either prior to or separate from the subjects who imagine and use them, then we can travel along two theoretical routes. First, we can consider the materiality of space, for example, the fact that a large number of workers must be housed somewhere. The buildings in which they live, perhaps the rooming houses built by their wealthy bosses, become a particular kind of space which we might say was shaped by capitalism and the class system. Here space is the result of unequal economic relations. A second approach is to consider the symbolic meaning of spaces. The rooming houses of the workers mean something specific in our context. Perhaps they represent poverty to us and enable us to understand ourselves as located in a social system where status derives from one's position in the means of production.

By itself, each of these approaches to understanding space is limited, as Henri Lefebvre argues. A theory of space, he maintains, has to cut through the dominant notion of space as innocent and as more real "than the 'subject,' his thought and his desires [sic]," but it also had to avoid reducing space to the status of a "message" (what it can tell us about social relations) and the inhabiting of it to the status of a "reading" (deciphering the codes of social space and how we perform it).[16] To treat space this way is to remain on a purely descriptive level that does not show the dialectical relationship between spaces and bodies. It does not show how the symbolic and the material work through each other to constitute a space.

Lefebvre's project, as Eugene McCann observed, "was to write a history of space by relating certain representations of space to certain modes of production through time."[17] Lefebvre saw, for instance, that capitalism relied upon and produced what he called "abstract space," which, McCann notes, is commodified and bureaucratized space arranged in the interests of capital and produced as a concerted attempt to define the appropriate meaning of public space and what citizens can do in it. Lefebvre proposes the concept of social space, as indistinguishable from mental and physical space, and as containing the social relations of production and reproduction. In his widely cited formulation, Lefebvre identified three elements (perceived, conceived, and lived space) in the production of social space.

First, perceived space emerges out of spatial practices, the everyday routines and experiences that install specific social spaces. For example, the daily life of a tenant in a government-sponsored housing project includes the rhythm of daily life (the buses one must take to work, the spaces through which one must walk), how people know themselves in it, as well as how they are known in it, and what the space accomplishes in relation to other spaces. Through these everyday routines, the space comes to perform something in the social order, permitting certain actions and prohibiting others. Spatial practices organize social life in specific ways. In the case of the housing project, it organizes, among other things, who will be able to walk in green spaces and who will not.

Second, conceived space entails representations of space, that is, how space is conceived by planners, architects, and so on. Here we might consider how the housing project was initially conceptualized, perhaps as a cleaning up of slums and a collecting of the poor into units that are centralized in the city but nonetheless peripheral to it.[18] Third, lived space is space "directly lived through its associated images and symbols, and hence the space of 'inhabitants' and 'users,' but also of some artists and perhaps of those, such as a few writers and philosophers who describe and aspire to do more than describe."[19] For the tenant, the housing project may be experienced as racialized space in which communities of colour both experience their marginal condition and resist it. Perhaps people gather on street corners to socialize, defying the containment offered by the buildings and imagining them instead as symbols of community. In lived space (representational space), the users of the space interpret perceived space (spatial practices), and conceived space (representations of space).

In her study of the homeless body, Samira Kawash offers a compelling example of how we might consider space as a social product by attending to the social hierarchies that sustain and are sustained by the idea of abstract public space. Drawing on Rosalyn Deutsche's analysis of how exclusions from public space are officially justified by representing the space as a unity that must be protected from conflict (in effect, Lefebvre's abstract space), Kawash discusses Deutsche's example of the padlocking after dark of a public park in New York. The padlocked park produces as illegitimate the homeless who might use the park to sleep, while neighbourhood groups in favour of the padlocking are produced as legitimate users and natural owners of public space.[20]

The homeless body is constituted as "the corporeal mark of the constitutive outside of the realm of the public."[21] That is, it is through this body that we know who is a citizen and who is not. Through its presence as a material body that occupies space, but as one that is consistently denied space through a series of violent evictions, the homeless body confirms what and who must be contained in order to secure society. The war on the homeless, evident in so many cities in the last few years (including the passage of restrictions on sleeping in public space, on begging, "bum-proof" bus shelters, and restrictions on "squeegee kids" in public space), must be seen as "the production of an abject body against which the public body of the citizen can stand."[22]

It is important to note how symbolic and material processes work together to produce these respectable and abjected bodies. When public toilets are systematically closed, the homeless have no choice but to perform bodily functions in public, a produced mark of degeneracy that only confirms who is respectable. The violent evictions that produce the homeless body are therefore a "constitutive violence"; they make possible subjects who are legitimate and those who are not.[23] Kawash's exploration of the production of the illegitimate homeless body makes it clear that the production of space is also the production of excluded and included bodies, an aspect of the production of space illustrated in the work of Michel Foucault.

THE BODY IN SPACE

It is from Michel Foucault that many of us learned to think about the production of subjects in space. In his work, we encounter the body marked as degenerate and its opposite, the bourgeois body marked as respectable. Foucault believed that space was fundamental in any exercise of power.[24] Foucault begins his analysis with the establishment in the seventeenth century of "enormous houses of confinement,"[25] of the Hôpital Général for housing the poor and the unemployed, the asylums for the insane, and extends it to prisons and schools to consider what was meant by the physical segregation of marginal populations, an exclusionary practice characteristic of the liberal state. He proposed that the bourgeois citizen of the state, the figure who replaced the earlier orders, distanced himself from the aristocracy and the lower orders of this earlier hierarchy by developing an identity premised on close control over the manner of living. The new citizen subject was a figure who, through self-control and self-discipline, achieved mastery over his own body. The self-regulating bourgeois subject had to be spatially separated from the degeneracy, abnormalcy, and excess that would weaken both him and the bourgeois state. Bodies that crossed "the frontier of bourgeois order"[26] were segregated, not for the purpose of punishment, but for moral regulation. The poor and the unemployed, housed in the Hôpital Général were to be trained not to be idle; asylums set themselves the task of producing moral subjects cleansed of everything that opposed the essential virtues of the society; prisons revolved around a political technology of the body, morally reforming inmates.

What sets the period of the establishment of states and citizen subjects in the eighteenth century apart from previous periods in Europe is the treatment of the body as object and target of power on a scale that did not exist before. While in every society there were constraints, prohibitions, and obligations on the body, what was new, according to Foucault, was the practice of exercising upon the body such micro processes as disciplining bodies to produce "subjected and practised bodies, 'docile' bodies." In the school, the barracks, the hospital, or the workshop, "the smallest fragment of life" becomes subject to minute calculation, "a codification that partitions as closely as possible time, space, movement." Timetables, specific, repeated movements, continual examinations, penalties for latenesses, absences, inattention: all these capture and fix individuals, placing them in a field of surveillance. Discipline "makes individuals" but the making requires a "mechanism that coerces by means of observation." Architecture had to render visible people's movement and conduct and thus to convey that one was always seen and known: "This infinitely scrupulous concern with surveillance is expressed in the architecture by innumerable petty mechanisms." By means of such surveillance, two kinds of bodies are produced: the normal and the abnormal body, the former belonging to a homogenous social body, the latter exiled and spatially separated.[27]

Kathleen Kirby elaborates on the individual body's relationship to space in the social/spatial configurations described above. Focusing on the respectable body, she argues, as Foucault did, that Enlightenment individualism is "inextricably tied to a specific concept of space and the technologies invented for dealing with that space."[28] Kirby explains how the bourgeois citizen, the Enlightenment individual, and the figure Kirby calls "the Cartesian subject" are reducible to the same graphic schema: "The 'individual' expresses a coherent, consistent, rational space paired with a stable, organized environment."[29] Cartography (the science of mapping), Kirby observes, both expresses this new subjectivity and enables it to exist. The subject who maps his space and thereby knows and controls it, is also the imperial man claiming the territories of others for his own; the inventor of *terra nullius*. The Cartesian or the mapping subject achieves his sense of self through keeping at bay and in place any who would threaten his sense of mastery. Maps sought to measure, standardize, and bind space, keeping the environment on the outside. Mapping the "New World" enabled Samuel de Champlain, for instance, to feel himself master of the lands he would eventually claim for the king of France. Only occasionally revealing himself to be overwhelmed by a landscape he does not know, Champlain, at such moments, considers the land itself (and its inhabitants) as inherently chaotic and unstable.[30] His sense of self is directly derived from controlling rigid boundaries and specific practices of knowledge production to create racial space, that is, space inhabited by the racial Other.

Kirby's account of the Cartesian subject in space, a subject privileged enough to choose to be in unfamiliar landscapes, may be usefully contrasted with Radhika Mohanram's account of its opposite, the Black body. Mohanram describes the two bodies in terms of their racial and spatial attributes: "First, whiteness has the ability to move; second, the ability to move results in the unmarking of the body. In contrast, blackness is signified through a marking and is always static and immobilizing."[31] To explain how the two bodies are imagined in a racial social order, Mohanram uses a text of the anthropologist Lévi-Strauss in which he explains human intellectual activity and compares two ways of knowing—that of the engineer and the bricoleur (handyman)[32] Although Lévi-Strauss does not suggest that one way of knowing is a more primitive form of thought than the other, Mohanram shows how, in Lévi-Strauss's narrative, the engineer is white and male, a figure who is able to connect the laws of physics and chemistry in anthropological discourse, while the bricoleur is the native, the indigenous scientist who uses intuition, imagination, and signs to know the world. The engineer has science to guide him; the bricoleur has intuition. Significantly, while the bricoleur can only classify perceived differences, the engineer's scientific system enables him to classify things not yet seen.

Thinking of Mary Louise Pratt's description of the European naturalists and cartographers who roamed Europe's colonies classifying plants and making maps with their scientific knowledge, and thus creating a European discourse about a non-European world,[33] Mohanram reflects on how the bricoleur, a pre-capitalist and pre-modern figure, is tied to place while the engineer, located within capitalism and modernity, has the freedom to roam. Noting the same two figures in Alfred Cosby's book *Ecological Imperialism*, where Europeans are described as shaping the environment of the Americas to their advantage, Mohanram comments that the European settler becomes the disembodied Universal Subject, "a subject who is able to take anyone's place." The Indigene, on the other hand, remains "immobile against the repeated onslaught of the settler."[34] For the settler, it is through movement from European to non-European space that he comes to know himself, a journey that materially and symbolically secures his dominance.

GENDER, TRANSGRESSION, AND JOURNEYS THROUGH SPACE

We know the black body by its immobility and the white body by its mobility. However, bodies are gendered and when we speak of subjects coming to know themselves in and through space, we are speaking of identity-making processes that are profoundly shaped by patriarchy. It is not only that men and women come to know themselves as dominant or subordinate in different ways. It is also that dominant masculinities and femininities exist symbiotically. In *Mapping Men and Empire*, Richard Phillips examines Victorian adventure stories showing, in the case of Robert Ballantyne's novels, how the journeys of male heroes through nineteenth-century Canada enable their coming to manhood through encounters with the rugged Canadian wilderness and its "wild Indians." Heroic boys learn the "rough life" and return home to women and civilization confirmed in their mastery and ready to assume the responsibilities of patriarchs. Careful to note that readers have agency when they enter into such fantasies, what Phillips nonetheless underlines is the process through which individuals gain a sense of self in and through space, by moving from civilized to liminal and back again to civilized space.

Liminal space is the border between civilized and primitive space, the space inhabited by savages whom civilized men vanquish on every turn. The subject who comes to know himself through such journeys first imagines his own space as civilized, in contrast to the space of the racial Other; second, he engages in transgression, which is a movement from respectable to degenerate space, a risky venture from which he returns unscathed; and third, he learns that he is in control of the journey through individual practices of domination. In the boys' adventure stories, white masculinity is confirmed when the boy hero punches out an Indian who is cruel to dogs.[35] Here the young white boy comes to know himself as white and in control, and as possessing superior values, a knowledge gained through the bodies and spaces of the racial Other. He also learns his place through white girls and women who stand as the marker of home and civility.

As Radhika Mohanram observes, it is as "feminine women" that white women are co-opted into imperial ventures as keepers of the imperial hearth.[36] Thus for white girls, Phillips points out, confined to domestic and enclosed material space, journeys into liminal space and contact with the Other in adventure stories required a gender transgression. Paradoxically, refusing their gender-specific imperial role in the home and undertaking such an imperial journey enabled girls to understand themselves as part of the colonial project and as potential settlers.

The journeys through the metaphorical space of the adventure stories have their material expression. Young white boys and girls learned something of who they were through such stories and the stories promoted popular support for imperialism. Phillips is rightfully emphatic, however, in noting that the novels of colonial culture did not "cause" colonialism.[37] The novels suggest the relationship between space, identity, and racial domination, a relationship I describe as a racial journey into personhood. Today, the identity-making processes of such journeys are evident in women's participation in development work in the Third World, where, as development workers, women of the First World can know themselves as autonomous, competent, and good through their interactions with Third World peoples and their efforts to "help" them.[38] Their development activities fix the natives, confining them to their environment and mode of thought and making them available to be assisted into modernity.[39] We might also see a racial journey into personhood taking place when Northern peacekeepers leave their own "civilized" spaces determined to save Southern nations from their own chaos.[40]

The identity-making processes at work in journeys from respectable to degenerate space are multiple and gendered. The processes described above do not show what the spaces might mean to the subordinate person in the encounter, for example. How might the Indian in Ballantyne's Canadian adventure stories experience the encounter differently from the young white boys? To return to Kathleen Kirby's example of Samuel de Champlain, when Champlain is lost, the land is experienced as chaotic, wild, and untamed, something it would not have seemed to the Aboriginal nations whom Champlain encountered. As well, we cannot presume that subordinate peoples were merely dominated. There is a spatiality to their resistance, which we do not take up to any great extent in this book.

SPACE AND INTERLOCKING SYSTEMS OF OPPRESSION

To interrogate bodies travelling in spaces is to engage in a complex historical mapping of spaces and bodies *in relation*, inevitably a tracking of multiple systems of domination and the ways in which they come into existence in and through each other. Spatial theorists have not generally used an interlocking approach. For example, in many anthologies devoted to gender and space,[41] woman remains an undifferentiated category with an occasional article on women of colour as a variation on the original model. That race, gender, and class hierarchies structure (rather than simply complicate) each other is not considered. For example, in their work on the segregation of large numbers of women into poorly paid jobs in Worcester, Massachusetts, Susan Hanson and Geraldine Pratt focus on the social and economic geographies of women's lives as compared with men's lives. They note that occupational segregation begins at home, that suburbs make it difficult to combine work and home, and that neighbourly networks facilitate participation in the workforce.[42] These patterns largely apply to white women, something the authors do not interrogate. More significantly, the patterns are themselves embedded in an economy in which, for example, Black women clean the houses of white suburban women. Had Hanson and Pratt considered how their locality was historically produced as a white space, exploring for instance how it comes to be that 70 per cent of the largely white working-class population has lived there for forty years, they might have seen how the gendered conditions they explore are profoundly shaped by a racial economy.

Similar erasures are evident in work on geography and disability. For example, in her review of the edited collection *Mind and Body Spaces: Geographies of Illness, Impairment and Disability*, Sheila Gill identifies what is elided when the category of analysis is an uncomplicated notion of disability. Articles in this collection discuss, among other topics, the ableism of nineteenth-century architecture theory, the spatial dimensions of the "mental deficiency" asylum, and the moral topography of intemperance yet pay no attention to the context of imperial expansion and colonialism. The result is that "mental deficiency" in nineteenth-century Canada is understood as largely unconnected to the eugenics movement and to the making of a white Canada. That a disproportionate number of new immigrants were confined to the asylums and a vigorous discourse about preserving the health of the white race was in place do not interrupt the text's central raceless narrative about "feeblemindedness."[43]

Race also strangely disappears in some geographical work on cities in spite of the fact that difference is a sustained feature of urban spaces and geographers have long paid attention to how the city is experienced differently.[44] Jane Jacobs explains how this erasure of race is most likely to happen. Many of the spatial features of cities, including gentrification, mega-developments, large malls, and heritage buildings are understood primarily as hallmarks of postmodernity. That is, it is clear that globalization has resulted in the growth of international cities in which financial activities are concentrated. Cities are characterized increasingly by a polarization of labour—young professionals in the information and financial sectors on one end and large pools of migrant labour in the service sector on the other. Inequalities are understood here as class inequalities, sometimes complicated by race (for example, the argument that people of colour are overrepresented in the lower levels of the labour market).

Such monocausal explanations, Jacobs argues, ignore the way that "postmodernity manufactures difference in service of its own consuming passions." Older racial orders are reshaped and revitalized in the new globalized conditions. To keep imperialism in sight, Jacobs recommends a closer attention to how spaces are mapped together. "Imperialism," she reminds us, "in whatever form, is a global process—it occurs across regions and nations—but even in its most marauding forms it necessarily takes hold in and through the local."[45] Her reminder is an important one, not only because it instructs us to explore how spaces are linked but also because it insists that we abandon monocausal explanations in favour of those that pay attention to interlocking systems of oppression.

Two steps mark our interlocking approach. First, we examine how the systems mutually constitute each other, an analysis aided by Jacobs's advice to map how spaces are linked. Second, we pursue how all the systems of domination operate at the local level, a task facilitated by attending to material and symbolic constitution of specific spaces. Our goal is to identify legal and social practices that reproduce racial hierarchies. For us, a spatial approach is one way, among others, to uncover processes of racialization. The concept we have all worked with is simply expressed by Radhika Mohanram: racial difference is also spatial difference.[46] Making the same point, David Goldberg writes: "Racisms become institutionally normalized in and through spatial configuration, just as social space is made to seem natural, a given, by being conceived and defined in racial terms."[47]

To denaturalize or unmap spaces, then, we begin by exploring space as a social product, uncovering how bodies are produced in spaces and how spaces produce bodies. This, in turn, entails an interrogation of how subjects come to know themselves in and through space and within multiple systems of domination. We draw on spatial theorists, including, but not limited to, Lefebvre, Foucault, and on a wide range of postcolonial scholars (Mohanram, Phillips, Kirby, and others). Additionally, each chapter draws on scholars who consider colonial space, city space, suburban space, institutional space, and so on. What ties the collection together, however, is the central idea of national space, in this instance, the space of a white settler society. Our concern is to tell the national story as a racial and spatial story, that is, as a series of efforts to segregate, contain, and thereby limit, the rights and opportunities of Aboriginal people and people of colour.

*****

These nine chapters, which cover two coasts of Canada, its Prairies, and the borders between Canada and the United States and the United States and Mexico, show us in intricate detail how the law is used to protect the interests of white people. Each author challenges the racelessness of law and the amnesia that allows white subjects to be produced as innocent, entitled, rational, and legitimate. We are encouraged to ask on what basis our emancipatory projects lie and are reminded not to forget history. The chain of events that begins with eviction and moves through "burials, denials, and complicities through time" must be resurrected. We must find ways to move beyond law's insistence on abstract individuals without histories. The tracing of the constitution of spaces through law and the mapping of the hierarchical social relations they create and sustain is one way of beginning. *Race, Space, and the Law* proposes some initial methodologies for this work of denaturalization, the work of asking how spacial divisions by race come into existence and are sustained.

NOTES

1. *R. v. Hayden*, Manitoba Court of Appeal, Monnin C,J,M., Hall and Philp JJ.A. Judgment delivered by Hall J.A. *Western Weekly Reports* [1983] 6 W.W.R. at 659.

2. Michael Ignatieff, *The Rights Revolution* (Toronto: House of Anansi Press, 2000), pp. 123–4.
3. Anne McClintock, *Imperial Leather: Race, Gender and Sexuality in the Colonial Contest* (New York: Routledge, 1995), p. 130.
4. Dara Culhane, *The Pleasure of the Crown: Anthropology, Law and First Nations* (Burnaby, BC: Talonbooks, 1998), p. 48.
5. Carl Berger, "The True North Strong and Free," in Peter Russell, ed., *Nationalism in Canada* (Toronto: McGraw-Hill, 1966), p. 5; Robert Shields, *Places on the Margins: Alternative Geographies of Modernity* (New York: Routledge, 1991), p. 162.
6. Berger, "The True North Strong and Free," p. 5.
7. David Goldberg, *Racist Culture: Philosophy and the Politics of Meaning* (Oxford: Blackwell Publishers, 1993), p. 186.
8. Ignatieff, *The Rights Revolution*, p. 10.
9. "Government of Canada Introduces Anti-Terrorism Act," Department of Justice Canada, <http://canada.justice.gc.ca/ en/news/nr/2001/doc_27785.html>, November 13, 2001.
10. Sherene H. Razack, '"Simple Logic': Race, the Identity Documents Rule and the Story of a Nation Besieged and Betrayed," *Journal of Law and Social Policy* 15 (2000), pp. 181–209.
11. Richard Phillips, *Mapping Men and Empire: A Geography of Adventure* (New York: Routledge, 1997), p. 143.
12. Steve Pile and Michael Keith, eds., *Geographies of Resistance* (New York: Routledge, 1997), p. 6.
13. See, for example, N. Smith and C. Katz, "Grounding Metaphor: Towards a Spatialized Politics," in Michael Keith and Steve Pile, eds., *Place and the Politics of Identity* (New York: Routledge, 1993), pp. 67–83, discussed in David Morley, *Home Territories: Media, Mobility and Identity* (New York: Routledge, 2000), pp. 7–8.
14. Edward W. Soja, *Postmodern Geographies: The Reassertion of Space in Critical Social Theory* (London: Verso Press, 1989), p. 247.
15. Julie Kathy Gibson-Graham, "Postmodern Becomings: From the Space of Form to the Space of Potentiality," in Georges Benko and Ulf Strohrnayer, eds., *Space and Social Theory* (Oxford: Blackwell Publishers, 1997), p. 307, discussing N. Smith and C. Katz, "Grounding Metaphor: Towards a Spatialized Politics," in Keith and Pile, eds., *Place and the Politics of Identity*, pp. 67–83.
16. Henri Lefebvre, *The Production of Space*, trans. Donald Nicholson-Smith (Oxford: Blackwell Publishers, 1991), p. 7.
17. Eugene J. McCann, "Race, Protest, and Public Space: Contextualizing Lefebvre in the US City," *Antipode* 31,2 (1999), p. 169.
18. Goldberg, *Racist Culture*, p. 198.
19. Lefebvre, *The Production of Space*, p. 39.
20. Samira Kawash, "The Homeless Body," *Public Culture* 10,2 (1998), p. 323.
21. Ibid., p. 329.
22. Ibid., p. 325.
23. Ibid., pp. 332, 337.
24. Michel Foucault, "Space, Power, Knowledge," interview with Paul Rabinow, trans. Christian Hubert, in Paul Rabinow, ed., The Foucault Reader (New York: Pantheon, 1984) p. 252.
25. Foucault, "Madness and Civilization," in Rabinow, ed., *The Foucault Reader*, p. 124.
26. Ibid., p. 131.
27. Ibid., pp. 181–2, 184, 189, 191.
28. Kathleen Kirby, "Re:Mapping Subjectivity: Cartographic Vision and the Limits of Politics," in Nancy Duncan, ed., *Body Space: Destabilizing Geographies of Gender and Sexuality* (New York: Routledge, 1996), p. 44.
29. Ibid.
30. Ibid., p. 48.
31. Radhika Mohanram, *Black Body: Women, Colonialism, and Space* (Minneapolis: University of Minnesota Press, 1999), p. 4.
32. A bricoleur undertakes odd jobs and is a jack of all trades. Since the term as used in Lévi-Strauss has no English equivalent, it is usually not translated. Lévi-Strauss uses bricolage to describe a characteristic feature of mythical thought. David Macey, *The Penguin Dictionary of Critical Theory* (London: Penguin, 2000), p.52.
33. Mary Louise Pratt, *Imperial Eyes: Travel Writing and Transculturation* (New York: Routledge, 1992).
34. Mohanram, *Black Body*, pp. 11, 14, 15; Alfred W. Crosby, *Ecological Imperialism: The Biological Expansion of Europe, 900-1900* (Cambridge: Cambridge University Press, 1986).
35. Phillips, *Mapping Men and Empire*, p. 60.
36. Mohanram, *Black Body*, p. 167.
37. Phillips, *Mapping Men and Empire*, p. 68.
38. Barbara Heron, "Desire for Development: The Education of White Women as Development Workers" (Ph.D. diss., University of Toronto, 1999).
39. Arjun Appadurai, "Putting Hierarchy in Its Place," *Cultural Anthropology* 3,1 (1988), pp. 36–49. See also Mohanram, *Black Body*, p. 11, for a discussion of Appadurai.
40. Sherene H. Razack, "From the 'Clean Snows of Petawawa': The Violence of Canadian Peacekeepers in Somalia," *Cultural Anthropology* 15,1 (2000), pp. 127–63.
41. See, for example, Erica Carter, James Donald, and Judith Squires, eds., *Space and Place: Theories of Identity and Location* (London: Lawrence and Wishart, 1993); Gillian Rose, *Feminism and Geography: The Limits of Geographical Knowledge* (Minneapolis: University of Minnesota Press, 1993); Doreen B. Massey, *Space, Place and Gender* (Minneapolis: University of Minnesota Press, 1994); Women and Geography Study Group, *Feminist Geographies: Explorations in Diversity and Difference* (Harlow: Longman, 1997); Rosa Ainley, ed., *New Frontiers of Space, Bodies and Gender* (New York: Routledge, 1998); Elizabeth Kenworthy Teather, *Embodied Geographies: Space, Bodies and Rites of Passage* (New York: Routledge, 1999).
42. Susan Hanson and Geraldine Pratt, *Gender, Work, and Space* (New York: Routledge, 1995).

43. Sheila Gill, review of *Mind and Body\Spaces: Geographies of Illness, Impairment and Disability*, edited by Ruth Butler and Hester Parr, *Revue Canadienne Droit et Société/Canadian Journal of Law and Society* 15,2 (2000), pp. 228–34.
44. Ruth Fincher and Jane M. Jacobs, "Introduction," in Ruth Fincher and Jane M. Jacobs, eds., *Cities of Difference* (London: The Guilford Press, 1998), p. 2.
45. Jane M. Jacobs, *Edge of Empire: Postcolonialism and the City* (New York: Routledge, 1996), pp. 33–4.
46. Mohanram, *Black Body*, p. 3.
47. Goldberg, *Racist Culture*, p. 185.

SELECTED BIBLIOGRAPHY

Berger, Carl. "The True North Strong and Free." In Peter Russell, ed. *Nationalism in Canada*. Toronto: McGraw-Hill, 1966.

Carter, Erica, James Donald, and Judith Squires, eds. *Space and Place: Theories of Identity and Location*. London: Lawrence and Wishart, 1993.

Culhane, Dara. *The Pleasure of the Crown: Anthropology, Law and First Nations*. Burnaby, BC: Talonbooks, 1998.

Fincher, Ruth, and Jane M. Jacobs, eds. *Cities of Difference*. London: The Guilford Press, 1998.

Goldberg, David. *Racist Culture: Philosophy and the Politics of Meaning*. Oxford: Blackwell Publishers, 1993.

Heron, Barbara. "Desire for Development: The Education of White Women as Development Workers." PhD Dissertation, The Ontario Institute for Studies in Education of University of Toronto, 1999.

Jacobs, Jane M. *Edge of Empire: Postcolonialism and the City*. New York: Routledge, 1996.

Kawash, Samira. "The Homeless Body." *Public Culture* 10,2 (1998).

Kirby, Kathleen. "Re-Mapping Subjectivity: Cartographic Vision and the Limits of Politics." In Nancy Duncan, ed. *Body Space: Destabilizing Geographies of Gender and Sexuality*. New York: Routledge, 1996.

Lefebvre, Henri. *The Production of Space*. Trans. Donald Nicholson-Smith. Oxford: Blackwell Publishers, 1991.

McCann, Eugene J. "Race, Protest, and Public Space: Contextualizing Lefebvre in the US City." *Antipode* 31,2 (1999), pp. 163–84.

McClintock, Anne. *Imperial Leather: Race, Gender and Sexuality in the Colonial Contest*. New York: Routledge, 1995.

Mohanram, Radhika. *Black Body: Women, Colonialism, and Space*. Minneapolis: University of Minnesota Press, 1999.

Phillips, Richard. *Mapping Men and Empire: A Geography of Adventure*. New York: Routledge, 1997.

Pile, Steve, and Michael Keith, eds. *Geographies of Resistance*. New York: Routledge, 1997.

Pratt, Mary Louise. *Imperial Eyes: Travel Writing and Transculturation*. London: Routledge, 1992.

Rabinow, Paul, ed. *The Foucault Reader*. New York: Pantheon, 1984.

Razack, Sherene. "From the 'Clean Snows of Petawawa': The Violence of Canadian Peacekeepers in Somalia." *Cultural Anthropology* 15,1 (2000), pp.127–63.

———. "'Simple Logic': Race, the Identity Documents Rule and the Story of a Nation Besieged and Betrayed." *Journal of Law and Social Policy* 15 (2000), pp.181–209.

Rose, Gillian. *Feminism and Geography: The Limits of Geographical Knowledge*. Minneapolis: University of Minnesota Press, 1993.

Soja, Edward W. *Postmodern Geographies: The Reassertion of Space in Critical Social Theory*. London: Verso Press, 1989.

CHAPTER 10

IS THERE A "NEO-RACISM"?

Etienne Balibar

To what extent is it correct so speak of a neo-racism? The question is forced upon us by current events in forms which differ to some degree from one country to another, but which suggest the existence of a transnational phenomenon. The question may, however, be understood in two senses. On the one hand, are we seeing a new historical upsurge of racist movements and policies which might be explained by a crisis conjuncture or by other causes? On the other hand, in its themes and its social significance, is what we are seeing only a *new* racism, irreducible to earlier "models," or is it a mere tactical adaptation? I shall concern myself here primarily with this second aspect of the question.[1]

First of all, we have to make the following observation. The neo-racism hypothesis, at least so far as France is concerned, has been formulated essentially on the basis of an internal critique of theories, of discourses tending to legitimate policies of exclusion in terms of anthropology or the philosophy of history. Little has been done on finding the connection between the newness of the doctrines and the novelty of the political situations and social transformations which have given them a purchase. I shall argue in a moment that the theoretical dimension of racism today, as in the past, is historically essential, but that it is neither autonomous nor primary. Racism—a true "total social phenomenon"—inscribes itself in practices (forms of violence, contempt, intolerance, humiliation and exploitation), in discourses and representations which are so many intellectual elaborations of the phantasm of prophylaxis or segregation (the need to purify the social body, to preserve "one's own" or "our" identity from all forms of mixing, interbreeding or invasion) and which are articulated around stigmata of otherness (name, skin colour, religious practices). It therefore organizes affects (the psychological study of these has concentrated upon describing their obsessive character and also their "irrational" ambivalence) by conferring upon them a stereotyped form, as regards both their "objects" and their "subjects." It is this combination of practices, discourses and representations in a network of affective stereotypes which enables us to give an account of the formation of a racist community (or a community of racists, among whom there exist bonds of "imitation" over a distance) and also of the way in which, as a mirror image, individuals and collectivities that are prey to racism (its "objects") find themselves constrained to see themselves as a community.

But however absolute that constraint may be, it obviously can never be cancelled out as constraint *for its victims*: it can neither be interiorized without conflict (see the works of Memmi) nor can it remove the contradiction which sees an identity as community ascribed to collectivities which are simultaneously denied the right to define themselves (see the writings of Frantz Fanon), nor, most importantly, can it reduce the permanent excess of actual violence and acts over discourses, theories and rationalizations. From the point of view of its victims, there is, then, an essential dissymmetry within the racist complex, which confers upon its acts and "actings out" undeniable primacy over its doctrines, naturally including within the category of actions not only physical violence and discrimination, but words themselves, the violence of words in so far as they are acts of contempt and aggression. Which leads us, in a first phase, to regard shifts in doctrine and language as relatively incidental matters: should we attach so much importance to justifications which continue to retain the same structure (that of a denial of rights) while moving from the language of religion into that of science, or from the language of biology into the discourses of culture or history, when in practice these justifications simply lead to the same old acts?

This is a fair point, even a vitally important one, but it does not solve all the problems. For the destruction of the racist complex presupposes not only the revolt of its victims, but the transformation of the racists themselves and, consequently, *the internal decomposition of the community created by racism*. In this respect, the situation is entirely analogous, as has often been said over the last twenty years or so, with that of sexism, the overcoming of which presupposes both the revolt of women and the break-up of the community of "males." Now, racist theories are indispensable in the formation of the racist community. There is in fact no racism without theory (or theories). It would be quite futile to inquire whether racist theories have emanated chiefly from the elites or the masses, from the dominant or the dominated classes. It is, however, quite clear that they are "rationalized" by intellectuals. And it is of the utmost importance that we enquire into the function fulfilled by the theory-building of academic racism (the prototype of which is the evolutionist anthropology of "biological" races developed at the end of the nineteenth century) in the crystallization of the community which forms around the signifier, "race."

This function does not, it seems to me, reside solely in the general organizing capacity of intellectual rationalizations (what Gramsci called their "organicity" and Auguste Comte their "spiritual power") nor in the fact that the theories of academic racism elaborate an image of community, of original identity in which individuals of all social classes may recognize themselves. It resides, rather, in the fact that the theories of academic racism mimic scientific discursivity by basing themselves upon visible "evidence" (whence the essential importance of the stigmata of race and in particular of bodily stigmata), or, more exactly, they mimic the way in which scientific discursivity articulates "visible facts" to "hidden causes" and thus connect up with a spontaneous process of theorization inherent in the racism of the masses.[2] I shall therefore venture the idea that the racist complex inextricably combines a crucial function of *misrecognition* (without which the violence would not be tolerable to the very people engaging in it) and a "will to know," a violent *desire for* immediate *knowledge* of social relations. These are functions which are mutually sustaining since, both for individuals and for social groups, their own collective violence is a distressing enigma and they require an urgent explanation for it. This indeed is what makes the intellectual posture of the ideologues of racism so singular, however sophisticated their theories may seem. Unlike for example theologians, who must maintain a distance (though not an absolute break, unless they lapse into "gnosticism") between esoteric speculation and a doctrine designed for popular consumption, historically effective racist ideologues have always developed "democratic" doctrines which are immeditately intelligible to the masses and apparently suited from the outset to their supposed low level of intelligence, even when elaborating elitist themes. In other words, they have produced doctrines capable of providing immediate interpretative keys not only to what individuals are *experiencing* but to what they *are* in the social world (in this respect, they have affinities with astrology, characterology and so on), even when these keys take the form of the revelation of a "secret" of the human condition (that is, when they include a *secrecy effect* essential to their imaginary efficacity: this is a point which has been well illustrated by Leon Poliakov).[3]

This is also, we must note, what makes it difficult to *criticize* the content and, most importantly, the influence of academic racism. In the very construction of its theories, there lies the presupposition that the "knowledge" sought and desired by the masses is an elementary knowledge which simply justifies them in their spontaneous feelings or brings them back to the truth of their instincts. Bebel, as is well known, called anti-Semitism the "socialism of fools" and Nietzsche regarded it more or less as the politics of the feeble-minded (though this in no way prevented him from taking over a large part of racial mythology himself). Can we ourselves, when we characterize racist doctrines as strictly demagogic theoretical elaborations, whose efficacity derives from the advance response they provide for the masses' desire for knowledge, escape this same ambiguous position? The category of the "masses" (or the "popular") is not itself neutral, but communicates directly with the logic of a naturalization and racization of the social. To begin to dispel this ambiguity, it is no doubt insufficient merely to examine the way the racist "myth" gains its hold upon the masses; we also have to ask why other sociological theories, developed within the framework of a division between "intellectual" and "manual" activities (in the broad sense), are unable to fuse so easily with this desire to know. Racist myths (the "Aryan myth," the myth of heredity) are myths not only by virtue of their pseudo-scientific content, but in so far as they are forms of imaginary transcendence of the gulf separating intellectuality from the masses, forms indissociable from that implicit fatalism which imprisons the masses in an allegedly natural infantilism.

We can now turn our attention to "neo-racism." What seems to pose a problem here is not the *fact* of racism, as I have already pointed out—practice being a fairly sure criterion (if we do not allow ourselves to be deceived by the denials of racism which we meet among large sections of the political class in particular, which only thereby betrays the complacency and blindness of that group)—but determining to what extent the relative novelty of the language is expressing a *new* and lasting articulation of social practices and collective representations, academic doctrines and political movements. In short, to use Gramscian language, we have to determine whether something like a hegemony is developing here.

The functioning of the category of *immigration* as a substitute for the notion of race and a solvent of "class consciousness" provides us with a first clue. Quite clearly, we are not simply dealing with a camouflaging operation, made necessary by the disrepute into which the term "race" and its derivatives has fallen, nor solely with a consequence of the transformations of French society. Collectivities of immigrant workers have for many years suffered discrimination and xenophobic violence in which racist stereotyping has played an essential role. The interwar period, another crisis era, saw the unleashing of campaigns in France against "foreigners," Jewish or otherwise, campaigns which extended beyond the activities of the fascist movements and which found their logical culmination in the Vichy regime's contribution to the Hitlerian enterprise. Why did we not at that period see the "sociological" signifier definitively replace the "biological" one as the key representation of hatred, and fear of the other? Apart from the force of strictly French traditions of anthropological myth, this was probably due, on the one hand, to the institutional and ideological break which then existed between the perception of immigration (essentially European) and colonial experience (on the one side, France "was being invaded," on the other it "was dominant") and, on the other hand, because of the absence of a new model of articulation between states, peoples and cultures on a world scale.[4] The two reasons are indeed linked. The new racism is a racism of the era of "decolonization," of the reversal of population movements between the old colonies and the old metropolises, and the division of humanity within a single political space. Ideologically, current racism, which in France centres upon the immigration complex, fits into a framework of "racism without races" which is already widely developed in other countries, particularly the Anglo-Saxon ones. It is a racism whose dominant theme is not biological heredity but the insurmountability of cultural differences, a racism which, at first sight, does not postulate the superiority of certain groups or peoples in relation to others but "only" the harmfulness of abolishing frontiers, the incompatibility of life-styles and traditions; in short, it is what P.A. Taguieff has rightly called a *differentialist racism*.[5]

To emphasize the importance of the question, we must first of all bring out the political consequences of this change. The first is a destabilization of the defences of traditional anti-racism in so far as its argumentation finds itself attacked from the rear, if not indeed turned against itself (what Taguieff excellently terms the "*turn-about effect*" of differentialist racism). It is granted from the outset that races do not constitute isolable biological units and that in reality there are no "human races." It may also be admitted that the behaviour of individuals and their "aptitudes" cannot be explained in terms of their blood or even their genes, but are the result of their belonging to historical "cultures." Now anthropological culturalism, which is entirely orientated towards the recognition of the diversity and equality of cultures—with only the polyphonic ensemble constituting human civilization—and also their transhistorical *permanence*, had provided the humanist and cosmopolitan anti-racism of the post-war period with most of its arguments. Its value had been confirmed by the contribution it made to the struggle against the hegemony of certain standardizing imperialisms and against the elimination of minority or dominated civilizations—"ethnocide." Differentialist racism takes this argumentation at its word. One of the great figures in anthropology, Claude Lévi-Strauss, who not so long ago distinguished himself by demonstrating that all civilizations are equally complex and necessary for the progression of human thought, now in "Race and Culture" finds himself enrolled, whether he likes it or not, in the service of the idea that the "mixing of cultures" and the suppression of "cultural distances" would correspond to the intellectual death of humanity and would perhaps even endanger the control mechanisms that ensure its biological survival.[6] And this "demonstration" is immediately related to the "spontaneous" tendency of human groups (in practice national groups, though the anthropological significance of the political category of nation is obviously rather dubious) to preserve their traditions, and thus their identity. What we see here is that biological or genetic naturalism is not the only means of naturalizing human behaviour and social affinities. At the cost of abandoning the hierarchical model (though the abandonment is more apparent than real, as we shall see), *culture can also function like a nature*, and it can in particular function as a way of locking individuals and groups a priori into a genealogy, into a determination that is immutable and intangible in origin.

But this first turn-about effect gives rise to a second, which turns matters about even more and is, for that, all the more effective: if insurmountable cultural difference is our true "natural milieu," the atmosphere indispensable to us if we are to breathe the air of history, then the abolition of that difference will necessarily give rise to defensive reactions, "interethnic" conflicts and a general rise in aggressiveness. Such reactions, we are told, are "natural," but they are also dangerous. By an astonishing volte-face, we here see the differentialist doctrines themselves proposing to *explain racism* (and to ward it off).

In fact, what we see is a general displacement of the problematic. We now move from the theory of races or the struggle between the races in human history, whether based on biological or psychological principles, to a theory of "race relations" within society, *which naturalizes not racial belonging but racist conduct*. From the logical point of view, differentialist racism is a meta-racism, or what we might call a "second-position" racism, which presents itself as having drawn the lessons from the conflict between racism and anti-racism, as a politically operational theory of the causes of social aggression. If you want to avoid racism, you have to avoid that "abstract" anti-racism which fails to grasp the psychological and sociological laws of human population movements; you have to respect the "tolerance thresholds," maintain "cultural distances" or, in other words, in accordance with the postulate that individuals are the exclusive heirs and bearers of a single culture, segregate collectivities (the best barrier in this regard still being national frontiers). And here we leave the realm of speculation to enter directly upon political terrain and the interpretation of everyday experience. Naturally, "abstract" is not an epistemological category, but a value judgement which is the more eagerly applied when the practices to which it corresponds are the more concrete or effective: programmes of urban renewal, anti-discrimination struggles, including even positive discrimination in schooling and jobs (what the American New Right calls "reverse discrimination"; in France too we are more and more often hearing "reasonable" figures who have no connection with any extremist movements explaining that "it is anti-racism which creates racism" by its agitation and its manner of "provoking" the mass of the citizenry's national sentiments).[7]

It is not by chance that the theories of differentialist racism (which from now on will tend to present itself as the *true anti-racism* and therefore the true humanism) here connect easily with "crowd psychology," which is enjoying something of a revival, as a general explanation of irrational movements, aggression and collective violence, and, particularly, of xenophobia. We can see here the double game mentioned above operating fully: the masses are presented with an explanation of their own "spontaneity" and at the same time they are implicitly disparaged as a "primitive" crowd. The neo-racist ideologues are not mystical heredity theorists, but "realist" technicians of social psychology....

In presenting the turn-about effects of neo-racism in this way, I am doubtless simplifying its genesis and the complexity of its internal variations, but I want to bring out what is strategically at stake in its development. Ideally one would wish to elaborate further on certain aspects and add certain correctives, but these can only be sketched out rudimentarily in what follows.

The idea of a "racism without race" is not as revolutionary as one might imagine. Without going into the fluctuations in the meaning of the word "race," whose historiosophical usage in fact predates any re-inscription of "genealogy" into "genetics," we must take on board a number of major historical facts, however troublesome these may be (for a certain anti-racist vulgate, and also for the turn-abouts forced upon it by neo-racism).

A racism which does not have the pseudo-biological concept of race as its main driving force has always existed, and it has existed at exactly this level of secondary theoretical elaborations. Its prototype is anti-Semitism. Modern anti-Semitism—the form which begins to crystallize in the Europe of the Enlightenment, if not indeed from the period in which the Spain of the *Reconquista* and the Inquisition gave a statist, nationalistic inflexion to theological anti-Judaism—is *already* a "culturalist" racism. Admittedly, bodily stigmata play a great role in its phantasmatics, but they do so more as signs of a deep psychology, as signs of a spiritual inheritance rather than a biological heredity.[8] These signs are, so to speak, the more revealing for being the less visible and the Jew is more "truly" a Jew the more indiscernible he is. His essence is that of a cultural tradition, a ferment of moral disintegration. Anti-Semitism is supremely "differentialist" and in many respects the whole of current differentialist racism may be considered, from the formal point of view, *as a generalized anti-Semitism*. This consideration is particularly important for the interpretation of contemporary Arabophobia, especially in France, since it carries with it an image of Islam as a "conception of the world" which is incompatible with Europeanness and an enterprise of universal ideological domination, and therefore a systematic confusion of "Arabness" and "Islamicism."

This leads us to direct our attention towards a historical fact that is even more difficult to admit and yet crucial, taking into consideration the French national form of racist traditions. There is, no doubt, a specifically French branch of the doctrines of Aryanism, anthropometry and biological geneticism, but the true "French ideology" is not to be found in these: it lies rather in the idea that the culture of the "land of the Rights of Man" has been entrusted with a universal mission to educate the human race. There corresponds to this mission a practice of assimilating dominated populations and a consequent need to differentiate and rank individuals or groups in terms of their greater or lesser aptitude for—or resistance to—assimilation. It was this simultaneously subtle and crushing form of exclusion/inclusion which was deployed in the process of colonization and the strictly French (or "democratic") variant of the "White man's burden." I return in later chapters to the paradoxes of universalism and particularism in the functioning of racist ideologies or in the racist aspects of the functioning of ideologies.[9]

Conversely, it is not difficult to see that, in neo-racist doctrines, the suppression of the theme of hierarchy is more apparent than real. In fact, the idea of hierarchy, which these theorists may actually go so far as loudly to denounce as absurd, is reconstituted, on the one hand, in the practical application of the doctrine (it does not therefore need to be stated explicitly), and, on the other, in the very type of criteria applied in thinking the difference between cultures (and one can again see the logical resources of the "second position" of meta-racism in action).

Prophylactic action against racial mixing in fact occurs in places where the established culture is that of the state, the dominant classes and, at least officially, the "national" masses, whose style of life and thinking is legitimated by the system of institutions; it therefore functions as a undirectional block on expression and social advancement. No theoretical discourse on the dignity of all cultures will really compensate for the fact that, for a "Black" in Britain or a "*Beur*" in France, the assimilation demanded of them before they can become "integrated" into the society in which they already live (and which will always be suspected of being superficial, imperfect or simulated) is presented as progress, as an emancipation, a conceding of rights. And behind this situation lie barely reworked variants of the idea that the historical cultures of humanity can be divided into two main groups, the one assumed to be universalistic and progressive, the other supposed irremediably particularistic and primitive. It is not by chance that we encounter a paradox here: a "logically coherent" differential racism would be uniformly conservative, arguing for the fixity of *all* cultures. It is in fact conservative, since, on the pretext of protecting European culture and the European way of life from "Third Worldization," it utopianly closes off any path towards real development. But it immediately reintroduces the old distinction between "closed" and "open," "static" and "enterprising," "cold" and "hot," "gregarious" and "individualistic" societies—a distinction which, in its turn, brings into play all the ambiguity of the notion of culture (this is particularly the case in French!).

The difference between cultures, considered as separate entities or separate symbolic structures (that is, "culture" in the sense of *Kultur*), refers on to cultural inequality within the "European" space itself or, more precisely, to "culture" (in the sense of *Bildung*, with its distinction between the academic and the popular, technical knowledge and folklore and so on) as a structure of inequalities tendentially reproduced in an industrialized, formally educated society that is increasingly internationalized and open to the world. The "different" cultures are those which constitute obstacles, or which are established as obstacles (by schools or the norms of international communication) to the acquisition of culture. And, conversely, the "cultural handicaps" of the dominated classes are presented as practical equivalents of alien status, or as ways of life particularly exposed to the destructive effects of mixing (that is, to the effects of the material conditions in which this "mixing" occurs).[10] This latent presence of the hierarchic theme today finds its chief expression in the priority accorded to the individualistic model (just as, in the previous period, openly inegalitarian racism, in order to postulate an essential fixity of racial types, had to presuppose a differentialist anthropology, whether based on genetics or on *Völkerpsychologie*): the cultures supposed implicitly superior are those which appreciate and promote "individual" enterprise, social and political individualism, as against those which inhibit these things. These are said to be the cultures whose "spirit of community" is constituted by individualism.

In this way, we see how the *return of the biological theme* is permitted and with it the elaboration of new variants of the biological "myth" within the framework of a cultural racism. There are, as we know, different national situations where these matters are concerned. The ethological and sociobiological theoretical models (which are themselves in part competitors) are more influential in the Anglo-Saxon countries, where they continue the traditions of Social Darwinism and eugenics while directly coinciding at points with the political objectives of an aggressive neo-liberalism.[11] Even these tendentially biologistic ideologies, however, depend fundamentally upon the "differentialist revolution." What they aim to explain is not the constitution of races, but the vital importance of cultural closures and traditions for the accumulation of individual aptitudes, and, most importantly, the "natural" bases of xenophobia and social aggression. Aggression is a fictive essence which is invoked by all forms of neo-racism, and which makes it possible in this instance to displace biologism one degree: there are of course no "races," there are only populations and cultures, but there are biological (and biophysical) causes and effects of culture, and biological reactions to cultural difference (which could be said to constitute something like the indelible trace of the "animality" of man, still bound as ever to his extended "family" and his "territory"). Conversely, where pure culturalism seems dominant (as in France), we are seeing a progressive drift towards the elaboration of discourses on biology and on culture as the external regulation of "living organisms," their reproduction, performance and health. Michel Foucault, among others, foresaw this.[12]

It may well be that the current variants of neo-racism are merely a transitional ideological formation, which is destined to develop towards discourses and social technologies in which the aspect of the historical recounting of genealogical myths (the play of substitutions between race, people, culture and nation) will give way, to a greater or lesser degree, to the aspect of psychological assessment of intellectual aptitudes and dispositions to "normal" social life (or, conversely, to criminality and deviance), and to "optimal" reproduction (as much from the affective as the sanitary or eugenic point of view), aptitudes and dispositions which a battery of cognitive, sociopsychological and statistical sciences would then undertake to measure, select and monitor, striking a balance between hereditary and environmental factors.... In other words, that ideological formation would develop towards a "post-racism." I am all the more inclined to believe this since the internationalization of social relations and of population movements within the framework of a system of nation-states will increasingly lead to a rethinking of the notion of frontier and to a redistributing of its modes of application; this will accord it a function of social prophylaxis and tie it in to more individualized statutes, while technological transformations will assign educational inequalities and intellectual hierarchies an increasingly important role in the class struggle within the perspective of a generalized techno-political selection of individuals. In the era of nation-enterprises, the true "mass era" is perhaps upon us.

NOTES

1. It was only after writing this article that Pierre-André Taguieff s book, *La Force du préjugé. Essai sur le racisme et ses doubles* (La Découverte, Paris, 1988), became known to me. In that book he considerably develops, completes and nuances the analyses to which I have referred above, and I hope, in the near future, to be able to devote to it the discussion it deserves.
2. Colette Guillaumin has provided an excellent explanation of this point, which is, in my opinion, fundamental: "The activity of categorization is *also* a *knowledge activity*.... Hence no doubt the ambiguity of the struggle against stereotypes and the surprises it holds in store for us. Categorization is pregnant with knowledge as it is with oppression." (*L'Idéologie raciste. Genèse et langage actuel*, Mouton, Paris/The Hague, 1972, pp. 183 *et seq.*)
3. L. Poliakov, *The Aryan Myth: A History of Racist and Nationalist Ideas in Europe*, transl. E. Howard, Sussex University Press, Brighton, 1974; *La Causalité diabolique: essais sur l'origine des persécutions*, Calmann-Lévy, Paris, 1980.
4. Compare the way in which, in the United States, the "Black problem" remained separate from the "ethnic problem" posed by the successive waves of European immigration and their reception, until, in the 1950s and 60s, a new "paradigm of ethnicity" led to the latter being projected on to the former (cf. Michael Omi and Howard Winant, *Racial Formation in the United States*, Routledge & Kegan Paul, London, 1986).
5. See in particular his "Les Présuppositions définitionnelles d'un indéfinissable: le racisme," *Mots*, no. 8, 1984; "L'Identité nationale saisie par les logiques de racisation. Aspects, figures et problèmes du racisme différentialiste," *Mots*, no. 12, 1986; "L'Identité française au miroir du racisme différentialiste," *Espaces 89, L'identité française*, Editions Tierce, Paris, 1985. The idea is already present in the studies by Colette Guillaumin. See also Véronique de Rudder, "L'Obstacle culturel: la différence et la distance," *L'Homme et la société*, January 1986. Compare, for the Anglo-Saxon world, Martin Barker, *The New Racism: Conservatives and the Ideology of the Tribe*, Junction Books, London, 1981.
6. This was a lecture written in 1971 for UNESCO, reprinted in *The View from Afar*, transl. J. Neugroschel and P. Hoss, Basic Books, New York, 1985; Cf. the critique by M. O'Callaghan and C. Guillaumin, "Race et race ... la mode 'naturelle' en sciences humaines," *L'Homme et la société*, nos. 31–2, 1974. From a quite different point of view, Lévi-Strauss is today attacked as a proponent of "anti-humanism" and "relativism" (cf. T. Todorov, "Lévi-Strauss entre universalisme et relativisme," *Le Débat*, no. 42, 1986; A. Finkielkraut, *La Défaite de la pensée*, Gallimard, Paris, 1987). Not only is the discussion on this point not closed; it has hardly begun. For my own part, I would argue not that the doctrine of Lévi-Strauss "is racist," but that the racist theories of the nineteenth and twentieth centuries have been constructed

within the conceptual field of humanism; it is therefore impossible to distinguish between them on the basis suggested above (see my "Racism and Nationalism," chapter 3 in *Race, Nation, Class: Ambiguous Identities* [London and New York: Verso, 1991]).

7. In Anglo-Saxon countries, these themes are widely treated by "human ethology" and "sociobiology." In France, they are given a directly culturalist basis. An anthology of these ideas, running from the theorists of the New Right to more sober academics, is to be found in A. Béjin and J. Freund, eds., *Racismes, antiracismes*, Méridiens-Klincksieck, Paris, 1986. It is useful to know that this work was simultaneously vulgarized in a mass-circulation popular publication, *J'ai tout compris*, no. 3, 1987 ("Dossier choc: *Immigrés: demain la haine*" edited by Guillame Faye).

8. Ruth Benedict, among others, pointed this out in respect of H.S. Chamberlain: "Chamberlain, however, did not distinguish Semites by physical traits or by genealogy; Jews, as he knew, cannot be accurately separated from the rest of the population in modern Europe by tabulated anthropomorphic measurements. But they were enemies because they had special ways of thinking and acting. 'One can very soon become a Jew ...' etc." (*Race and Racism*, Routledge & Kegan Paul, London, 1983 edn., pp. 132 *et seq.*). In her view, it was at once a sign of Chamberlain's "frankness" and his "self-contradiction." This self-contradiction became the rule, but in fact it is not a self-contradiction at all. In anti-Semitism, the theme of the inferiority of the Jew is, as we know, much less important than that of his irreducible otherness. Chamberlain even indulges at times in referring to the "superiority" of the Jews, in matters of intellect, commerce or sense of community, making them all the more "dangerous." And the Nazi enterprise frequently admits that it is an enterprise of *reduction* of the Jews to "subhuman status" rather than a consequence of any *de facto* subhumanity: this is indeed why its object cannot remain mere slavery, but must become extermination.

9. See *Race, Nation, Class*, chapter 3, "Racism and Nationalism."

10. It is obviously this subsumption of the "sociological" difference between cultures beneath the institutional hierarchy of Culture, the decisive agency of social classification and its naturalization, that accounts for the keenness of the "radical strife" and resentment that surrounds the presence of immigrants in schools, which is much greater than that generated by the mere fact of living in close proximity. Cf. S. Boulot and D. Boyson-Fradet, "L'Echec scolaire des enfants de travailleurs immigrés," *Les Temps modernes*, special number: "L'Immigration maghrébine en France," 1984.

11. Cf. Barker, *The New Racism*.

12. Michel Foucault, *The History of Sexuality*, vol. 1, *An Introduction*, transl. Robert Jurley, Peregrine, London, 1978.

CHAPTER 11

THE RELATIONSHIP BETWEEN RACISM AND ANTISEMITISM

Michael Banton

In 1975 the United Nations General Assembly voted by seventy-five to thirty-five to adopt Resolution 3379 which "determines that Zionism is a form of racism and racial discrimination." It has sometimes been suggested that antisemitic feelings lay behind this Resolution. But only a moment's reflection is needed to appreciate that whether or not Zionism is racism, and whether or not criticism of Israeli policies is antisemitic, depends upon the meanings given to the key terms. Both concepts—racism and antisemitism—have been of great rhetorical value in mobilizing opinion against grievous evils, and both can be used in interpreting the history of these evils. Neither, however, is useful for social analysis or for the designing of counter-measures.

THE UNITED NATIONS

At the end of 1959 there were attacks on Jewish burial grounds and synagogues in West Germany, followed by similar attacks in some other European countries. The concern which they generated led to a proposal in 1961 that the General Assembly should prepare a convention that would impose on those states choosing to accede to it a legal obligation to prevent manifestations of racial and national hatred. Some states argued that it should also cover religious discrimination. But the eventual decision favoured two separate declarations and conventions: one on racial discrimination and one on religions discrimination. Opposition to combining the two came from some of the Arab delegations, and reflected the Arab-Israeli conflict; however, it might have been difficult in any event to cover them both in the same document. Many delegations, particularly those from Eastern Europe, did not consider questions of religion to be as important as those of race.

The International Convention on the Elimination of All Forms of Racial Discrimination was adopted in 1965. In 1970, monitoring the implementation of its provisions by State Parties began. Israel ratified the Convention in 1979. The Declaration on the Elimination of All Forms of Intolerance and of Discrimination Based on Religion or Belief was adopted in 1981. A draft convention which would give, for the ratifying states, legal effect to the principles in the Declaration was prepared in 1967 but its progress has been slow.

When Resolution 3379—declaring Zionism a form of racism—was proposed, one particular charge was that the Israeli Law of Return discriminated on racial grounds and was in breach of Article 1 (1) of the International Convention which states that racial discrimination:

> shall mean any distinction, exclusion, restriction or preference based on race, colour, descent, or national or ethnic origin which has the purpose or effect of nullifying or impairing the recognition, enjoyment or exercise, on an equal footing, of human rights and fundamental freedoms in the political, economic, social, cultural or any other field of public life.

The charge against the Israeli law seems justified. If in no other way, the Law of Return discriminates on the basis of descent. Article 11 of the Convention offers a procedure whereby a State Party—if it considers that another State Party is not giving effect to the provisions of the Convention—may raise the issue of possible non-compliance. Even if Israel had been a State Party to the Convention in 1975, this procedure could not have been used, since Article 1 (2) states: "This Convention shall not apply to distinctions, exclusions, restrictions or preferences made by a State Party to this Convention between citizens and non-citizens." This exception protects Israel against any charge that the Law of Return breaches the Convention. (It also protects the government of the United Kingdom against charges that its immigration legislation is discriminatory.)

In 1969, the General Assembly designated 1971 as "International Year to Combat Racism and Racial Discrimination" which later developed into the "Decade for Action to Combat Racism and Racial Discrimination" (starting in 1973)—followed later by a "Second Decade." The Programme of Action was the responsibility of the entire General Assembly, not just the State Parties to the International Convention. It therefore offered scope for a resolution against Israel even though that country was not then a party to the Convention.

The vote in favour of the 1975 Resolution was a diplomatic defeat for Israel, and it has provided a basis for many criticisms of that state's policies. The extent to which those criticisms are justified is not at issue here. But the entire episode has been a striking illustration of just how important rhetoric can be in international politics. Any proposition about the nature and form of an "ism" has a flexible character that can be exploited in debate but cannot provide the necessary precision for legal proceedings. Such propositions can also be used persuasively in social analyses which assume that a social pattern can be understood only by placing it in a wider historical context. Thus in *Caste, Class and Race* (New York, 1948), Oliver C. Cox distinguished between antisemitism and racism—he used the phrase "race-prejudice," but in a manner corresponding to the post-1968 meaning of "racism" (p. 393). Antisemitism, he said, is a form of social intolerance directed towards the conversion, expulsion or eradication of a specific minority;

racism, on the other hand, serves to rationalize and justify exploitation. The Jew is hated for being different; black people are expected to remain different—and subordinate.

From this point of view, racism is a historical phenomenon associated with the expansion of the capitalist world; it has a definite beginning and therefore can have a definite end. Some Jews might interpret antisemitism as having a definite historical meaning, albeit a very different one: namely, proof that the Jews are indeed the chosen people. One early Zionist thinker, Leon Pinsker, describing the status of Jews in Gentile societies, presented antisemitism in just that way when he argued: "He must be blind indeed who will assert that the Jews are not *the chosen people*, the people chosen for universal hatred." Since many people find it difficult to accept that human history has no meaning other than that which is read into it, propositions which promise to explain history can have enormous appeal.

THE GROUNDS OF DISCRIMINATION

The concept of intent is central to criminal law in most countries. Thus, it is not intrinsically wrong to walk out of a shop with goods that have not been paid for, but it is an offence to knowingly deprive someone of his or her property. Discrimination has not been criminalized in every country; in some it has been made a civil wrong. But whatever form the prohibition takes, it usually rests on a concept close to that of intent—namely, that there have been unlawful grounds for a particular action. It is not wrong to dismiss workers who happen to be black or Jewish, but it is wrong to dismiss them *because* they are black or Jewish, i.e. on the grounds of ethnic origin.

The International Bill of Human Rights declares that such rights must be available "without distinction of any kind, such as race, colour, sex, language, religion, political or other opinion, national or social origin, property, birth or other status." Not every country prohibits all these forms of discrimination. The United Kingdom, for example, prohibits discrimination on grounds of race, colour, sex and national origin in Great Britain; whereas in Northern Ireland it prohibits discrimination on grounds of sex, religion and political belief only, maintaining that there is no need to prohibit racial discrimination there. The prohibitions cover both direct and indirect discrimination—that is, both actions stemming from an unlawful purpose and those having an unlawful effect.

There are some ambiguities in the present international law against discrimination, as well as possible inconsistencies between direct and indirect discrimination. For example, it seems clear that, within the territory controlled by the State of Israel, there is discrimination against Arabs: they are treated less favourably because they are Arabs. But is this on racial, religious or political grounds? It could be very difficult for a court to decide. This difficulty should not, however, be used as a basis for complaint about the law on human rights. It should rather be seen as an indication of how hard it is to draft laws against discrimination. Given the nature of the problem, it might be a source of satisfaction that so much progress has already been made. The International Convention on the Elimination of All Forms of Racial Discrimination was drafted with an eye to the gross violations of human rights occurring at that time, the 1960s, in South Africa and in the Deep South of the United States, where the lines of discrimination were drawn very clearly. It will take time to adapt it to the different circumstances of the Middle East, to East Asia, to the Hindu caste system and to the discrimination suffered by the indigenous peoples of South America.

When the Universal Declaration of Human Rights came to the UN General Assembly for adoption, four Muslim states abstained from voting because of Article 18 which declares that the right to freedom of thought includes a person's right "to change his religion or belief." The Muslims averred that their co-religionists did not have a right to abandon their faith. This objection influenced the drafting of the International Declaration on the Elimination of All Forms of Intolerance and of Discrimination Based on Religion or Belief, and led to the complaint that the Declaration failed to protect a right acknowledged earlier. Communist delegates also argued that the use of the word "religion" did not explicitly extend the principle of tolerance to atheists, so the first reference to "religion" was expanded to read "religion or whatever belief of his choice." From the believers' standpoint, there is a fundamental difference between a divine order they are not free to dispute or qualify, and a human right which lies on the same plane as other human rights, all of which have to be simultaneously accommodated. The difficulties experienced by several western legislatures in coming to terms with differing beliefs about abortion are another example of the same conflict.

In the court-room or the lecture hall it may be possible to distinguish religious discrimination from discrimination on the grounds of race or political opinion; but in everyday life such distinctions may not be so obvious. The intensity of caste-based discrimination in some parts of India is illustrated by a recent report of an incident in which a young man and a young woman of different castes fell in love; this so scandalized some of the villagers that they forced the fathers of these two young people to kill them in a public assembly. Whether this was religious discrimination or some other kind seems almost irrelevant compared to the enormity of the conduct. The political philosophy of Hitler's Nazis elaborated a particular idea of race as part of its interpretation of the human past and its future; displaying many features of religion itself, Nazism was set against traditional Christian beliefs. Many terrorists (Armenian, Basque, Irish, Palestinian, Sikh, Tamil, etc.) dedicate their lives to upholding a faith in their nation's historic rights—sometimes in spite of knowing that most of their compatriots do not share their convictions. In recent times, some white South Africans and some Israeli settlers have gunned down people whose very presence they thought incompatible with their group's historic destiny; according to some definitions, such behaviour would also count as a form of terrorism. These examples may be contentious. They are adduced simply to call into question any assumption that religion can easily be distinguished from other grounds of discrimination.

Religious belief is often said to impose upon believers obligations of a non-negotiable character. Yet for some people beliefs about race and political opinion are just as inflexible; while others who consider themselves religious accept that the tenets of their faith have to be reinterpreted in the light of changing circumstances. Since these circumstances include a very pressing need to live in peace with others of different faiths, some are ready to engage in dialogues and develop mutual understanding.

Such considerations indicate that, since Jews can be discriminated against on a number of grounds other than those of race, there is no merit in regarding antisemitism as a form of racism. Indeed, it could be said that the notion of antisemitism became obsolete with the foundation of the State of Israel since it is often difficult to distinguish hostility towards Jews from hostility towards Israeli policies.

THE SOURCES OF DISADVANTAGE

Discrimination is not the only cause of inequality between groups. Its importance can be measured by a consideration of racial disadvantage—that is, any form of handicap associated with assignment to a racial group. The evidence of such handicaps are well displayed in the labour market, in the under-representation of women and members of ethnic minorities in preferred occupations. This situation might arise simply because such persons have not applied for these positions—casual observation would suggest that in Britain the number of Jews who want to become engineers is proportionately' much lower than the number who want to become doctors or lawyers.

A category of persons may also be under-represented when for some reason their labour is less highly valued. There are four principal reasons why the services of members of a minority race may be less valuable: nature, experience, motivation and investment. First, people in some groups may be of different physical stature or health and, on average, less suited to heavy work, for example. Second, immigrant workers may have less experience than native workers in the use of equipment; they may be less skilled and have less knowledge about how to perform tasks. Third, motivations vary. Refugees, for example, may be less career-orientated than economic migrants and native workers because their aspirations are set upon return to their home country. Minority workers may believe (perhaps with justification) that they have little chance of obtaining certain jobs and never apply for them—an example of supply being affected by perceptions of demand. Fourth, groups differ in their attitudes towards children. In some, parents like to have many children (a reflection of circumstances in their country of origin); in others, parents prefer to have fewer children and to invest more of their time, emotional energy and money on their upbringing so that they enter the labour market with more valuable skills.

Discrimination occurs when an employer has less demand for the services of some category of workers even though, objectively, their labour is equally valuable. The three main reasons for this are taste, risk and profit.

It is customary to speak of consumers exercising taste when they buy one sort of product rather than another, whether the product be a foodstuff, a brand of petrol or an item of clothing. But if people selling houses want to sell to purchasers from the same group as themselves, that too is an expression of taste. If it is a white person who wants to sell to another white, and a black person offers a higher price than any white person is willing to pay, there must come a point at which the vendor agrees to a sale. If whites would pay, say, £100,000 and the black person has to bid up to £110,000 in order to buy, the difference of £10,000 represents the price which the vendor puts upon his or her taste; for the purchaser it represents a "colour tax." The concept of taste can be applied in other situations. Workers of one racial group may resist the recruitment of workers of another because of their taste for associating only with their own kind, and so on.

Risk arises when information is lacking about the consequences that will result from an action. Buyers and sellers do not know how a market will react to future considerations. They are short of information about probable futures; it takes time and money to get the facts which would help them make the predictions on which their policies will have to depend. They will be averse from taking risky decisions when the consequences of mistakes will be costly. Engaging minority workers may seem just such a risk, and if the employer never engages any he will never find out whether his initial assumption was correct. Since some discrimination results from estimates about differential frequencies of risk associated with different groups, and since the same argument applies to the recruitment of women workers, what has been called the statistical theory of racism and sexism has been developed.

If employers want to make the maximum profit, they cannot afford to bother about the economically irrelevant characteristics of their customers or employees. But many employers are not that set on profit, and most markets fall very far short of perfect competitiveness. The simplest example is that of a monopoly—one seller, many buyers—in which the seller is able to exploit a position of power in order either to charge a higher price or to be less efficient. Another example is a monopsony—one buyer, many sellers—such as the South African mining industry in which employers, seeking black labour, established a common recruiting agency to enlist workers at standard rates, paying them less than they would have done had they been bidding against one another. Having created a monopsony, they benefited from the greater bargaining power it gave them. South Africa has offered an example of a triangular relationship between the (white) employer, the higher-paid (white) section of the labour force and the lower-paid (black) section which was, until recently, forbidden to form trade unions. Because the higher-paid section had greater bargaining power it could get a greater share of the wages bill and therefore profit from its position of strength. State regulation of the labour market permitted the two white sections to profit from the black section's weaker position. How that profit was (and is) divided is an empirical issue to be investigated case by case, but the example does illustrate the way in which the search for profit can lead to discrimination and thereby to disadvantage.

This sort of analysis can be extended to other markets, like housing and, to some extent, the health services and education; but it must always be remembered that markets are embedded in political processes. It is governments that decide what can be bought and sold, and according to what rules. There is a plausible argument that ideologues who want to maintain racial, religious or political boundaries fear markets because they can dissolve such boundaries. For example, if people are permitted to put a price on their tastes when selling houses, they may breach an established pattern of segregation. Therefore segregationists will try either to restrict their freedom of action or threaten them with dire consequences for ignoring the prejudices of others. A series of studies of local communities in the Deep South of the United States in the 1930s showed how whites were brought up to regard any move towards social equality between blacks and whites as positively immoral; for them, certain kinds of contact with blacks were considered harmful. Any white person who stepped out of line could be subjected to tremendous pressure—and any black person could be killed. It was possible for a poor white to rent a house from a black landlord but the relationship had to be strictly commercial and open to public scrutiny. Differences of wealth could not threaten the colour line. A market analysis needs to be extended to explain the constraints upon transactions, and how it is that some markets adjust to racial boundaries.

An account of the relationship between racism and antisemitism should cover questions of disadvantage, including the relationship between racial discrimination and discrimination against Jews. The above discussion sketches the outlines of the argument that all forms of group disadvantage (including those based on sex or gender) have common features and can be explained by the use of a body of general concepts. Discrimination is a normal feature of social life, since it can be observed in some form wherever groups exist. When there are opportunities for gain, patterns of discrimination can be elaborated to an extent that is contrary to the economic interests even of those who believe that they benefit from them. The cultural representation of group differences may conceal this. All societies will include individuals with psychopathological tendencies; these may find a release in group hostilities, and may be more influential where discrimination is institutionalized. Because of differing circumstances, instances of group hostility necessarily have some unique features, but minority members are sometimes inclined to exaggerate the uniqueness of their group's suffering. The social scientist seeks the general causes of discrimination and hatred within the more powerful groups by studying psychology and economic relationships. The starting point of analysis is the identification of cause, not the characteristics of victims. Generalizations about antisemitism are misleading if they imply that hostility towards Jews is of a special kind.

THE PRESENT AND THE PAST

Addressing the German Parliament in May 1985, Richard von Weiszacker, President of the Federal Republic, said:

> Whoever closes his eyes to the past becomes blind to the present.... Precisely because we seek reconciliation, we must remember that reconciliation without remembering is impossible. Every Jew, wherever he may be, has internalized the experience of the millions of murders, not only because people cannot forget such horror, but also because the memory belongs to the Jewish faith.

The force of that statement is not lessened by the observation that the memory of suffering is important to other groups as well. It recalls a conversation with a black scholar in the United States. Referring to recent calculations that the number of Africans caught up in the Atlantic slave trade were fewer than previously thought, he said: "The Jews say that six million died in the camps; we say that twelve million came in the ships." To him, it was important that the suffering be remembered not just by the descendants of the victims but also by the descendants of those who had been responsible. The accusation of racism has carried a heavy emotional charge because so many white people feel as guilty about how whites have treated blacks during the past four hundred years as about present economic disparities. It might be worthwhile sometime to study the nature of this sentiment more closely and to compare it with Gentile guilt about antisemitism.

Racism and antisemitism are ideas used today to define patterns in the abuse of human rights in the past, and to stimulate action designed to reduce the likelihood of their being repeated in the future. Before 1968, "racism" designated a doctrine but thereafter its significance was broadened to incorporate attitudes and practices. This extension brought many positive benefits. At the United Nations it contributed powerfully to a massive mobilization against *apartheid*, the policies of the South African government, and for decolonization of Angola, Mozambique, Namibia and Zimbabwe. It led to a much greater than expected number of accessions to the International Convention on the Elimination of All Forms of Racial Discrimination—more than might have been achieved had states appreciated the comprehensiveness of the Convention's definition of racial discrimination.

Within particular states, the idea of racism has entered the public consciousness. A 1991 opinion poll in Britain found that 97 per cent of the white respondents were willing to answer the question "Do you think Britain as a society is very racist, fairly racist, fairly non-racist or completely non-racist?" Sixty-seven per cent considered Britain to be racist to some extent, which is evidence of a major change over the last twenty-five years.

The idea of racism has provided the foundation for an attack on some of the conditions which generate discrimination. For example, it has been used to encourage school teachers to develop less ethnocentric approaches in the classroom. The underlying moral concern can be appreciated better by comparing recent attitudes towards racism with those towards crime—also a normal feature of human societies. People accept that there will always be crime and that policies must simply aim to keep it in check, balancing restraints against freedoms. The same might be said of discrimination but racism is understood as something pathological which could and should be eliminated. It is not excused in the way that crime is excused.

One difficulty in conceiving of racism as an impersonal force is the link between the noun "racism" and the adjective "racist," now in such common use. The concept has become an epithet. The accusation of racism is disabling. The accuser claims a moral superiority; the accused has not so much to defend an action as to demonstrate a purity of intention, which is necessarily difficult since all persons—accusers as well as accused—are impelled by a medley of motivations and associations. The black scholar referred to earlier insisted that no black person should ever criticize another black person in public. When it was objected that criticism could then come only from whites, and that there would therefore be a suspicion that it was racially motivated, he replied that this could not be helped. Solidarity was essential to the black cause. Partly because of this outlook some blacks in responsible positions have abused their powers. Whites have been afraid to criticize them for fear of being called "racist"; blacks have been silent because of the demand for solidarity.

Parallels with the accusation of antisemitism are weak however. Gentiles have not felt equally guilty about the past mistreatment of Jews. Responsibility for the Holocaust has been pinned on Germans, on Nazis and on those who collaborated with the Nazis. The silence of the world while the "Final Solution" was being attempted has been excused by professions of ignorance of what was going on at the time, and the pressures of war-time priorities.

A CONCLUSION

Nothing is gained by defining antisemitism as a form of racism. They are both political ideas used in interpreting experience and in organizing protection against the repetition of past evils. They have stimulated attempts to understand the factors in human society which give rise to—and magnify—group hostilities, but neither racism nor antisemitism belongs in the battery of analytical concepts of social science which are useful in identifying the causes of hostility or in planning measures to reduce disadvantage. Both of them are emotion-laden, especially for the victims of group hostility. Both tend to be eurocentric, reflecting particular events in the history of Europe and of European expansion into Africa and the Americas, so that people in other regions of the world sometimes conclude that such issues are not their concern. Both racism and antisemitism relate to hateful experiences; their contemplation easily leads to pessimism.

The last half-century's international struggle to define and protect human rights offers an escape from this conceptual cul-de-sac. The relative success of the human rights movement offers hope for a better future. It seeks to cultivate values that can be acknowledged in all regions of the world, and it can be guided by research into the factors which threaten human rights. Three-quarters of the world's states, as parties to the International Convention on the Elimination of All Forms of Racial Discrimination, have accepted an obligation to provide legal remedies for racial discrimination. In several countries recently, antisemitic writings have been condemned by courts which, while recognizing the right to freedom of expression, have held that the exercise of that right must not infringe the human rights of Jewish citizens. In the twenty-first century, concern with racism and antisemitism will increasingly be brought within the new framework constructed by the movement for human rights.

POSTSCRIPT

An illustration of some of the difficulties attaching to references to antisemitism in international bodies was provided at the 41st session of the United Nations Committee for the Elimination of Racial Discrimination in 1992. The Report of the Committee to the General Assembly concerning the 10th periodic report of Austria states at paragraph 185: "Some members expressed concern over the results of a Gallup Poll conducted in Austria in 1991 in which up to 20 per cent of those interviewed did not recognize the equal rights of Jews in economic life." The response of the state representative appears in paragraph 192: "As for anti-Semitism, the only danger came from organized antisemitic organizations or movements and not from individuals who were free to hold whatever opinions they wished regarding Jews." The Committee's "concluding observations" on the Austrian report read "The Committee was disturbed to learn that in Austria, as in other parts of Europe, there were signs of an increase in racism, xenophobia and anti-Semitism, and readiness to ignore the rights of members of ethnic groups, including Jews."

The concluding observations were adopted only after an animated discussion which involved 14 of the 18 members of the Committee and which took longer than might be expected. I served as Country Rapporteur for the consideration of the Austrian report and in this capacity proposed a set of concluding observations which included: "The Committee was disturbed to learn that, according to a Gallup Poll conducted in 1991, significant numbers of Austrians did not recognize the equal rights of Jews in economic life." This was challenged by one of my colleagues as representing my views only. He said that he was not disturbed by the results of a mere opinion poll; until recently the Chancellor of Austria had been Jewish. Moreover an opinion poll on antisemitism covered not only Jews, but also Arabs—as the Gallup Poll would know. Some members did not wish to single out Austria; others thought there were good reasons to do so. Some nationals of Asian and African countries say that antisemitism (i.e. hostility towards Jews just because they are Jews) is a purely European phenomenon, so that it is acceptable to refer to antisemitism only if it is clear that it refers to Europe alone. Some felt that the result of the discussion was to weaken an observation that should have been stronger. In due course a public record of the Committee's 951st meeting will be available through the UN information centre.

CHAPTER 12

GLOBAL APARTHEID? RACE AND RELIGION IN THE NEW WORLD ORDER

Ali A. Mazrui

Now that secular ideological divisions between the East and West have declined in relevance, are we witnessing the re-emergence of primordial allegiances? Are we witnessing new forms of *retribalization* on the global arena—from Natal in South Africa to Bosnia and Herzegovina, from Los Angeles to Slovakia? In Europe, two levels of retribalization are discernible. In Eastern Europe, *microretribalization* is particularly strong. Microretribalization is concerned with microethnicity, involving such conflicts as Serbians versus Croats, Russians versus Ukrainians, and Czechs versus Slovaks.

On the other hand, Western Europe shows strides in regional integration despite hiccups as the 1992 referendum in Denmark against the Maastricht Treaty. Regional integration can be *macroretribalization* if it is race-conscious. Macroretribalization can be the solidarity of white people, an arrogant pan-Europeanism greater in ambition than anything seen since the Holy Roman Empire.

Is the white world closing ranks in Eastern Europe and the West? Will we see a more united, and potentially more prosperous, white world presiding over the fate of a fragmented and persistently indigent black world in the twenty-first century? Put in another way, now that apartheid in South Africa is disintegrating, is there a global apartheid in the process of formation? With the end of the Cold War, is the white world closing ranks at the global level—in spite of current divisions within individual countries such as Yugoslavia? Is the danger particularly acute between black and white people?

In addition to the black-white divide in the world, Muslim countries, in particular, may have reason to worry in the era after the Cold War. Will Islam replace communism as the West's perceived adversary? Did the West exploit the Gulf War of 1991 to put Islam and its holiest places under the umbrella of Pax Americana? It is to these issues that we turn.

BETWEEN IDEOLOGY AND RACE

There was a time when the white people of the Soviet Union colonized fellow white people of Eastern Europe while at the same time Soviet weapons and money aided black liberation. In other words, Moscow was an imperial power in Europe and a liberating force in Africa. At the global level, alliances for or against imperialism did not coincide with racial differences. Indeed, the liberation of black people from white minority governments in Africa would probably have been delayed by at least a generation without the support of white socialist governments during the days of the Cold War.

The end of the Cold War ended inter-white rivalries in the Third World. On the positive side, this meant an earlier end to African civil wars. The war in Eritrea would not have lasted thirty years had there been no external material support and encouragement. The war in Angola would not have lasted a decade and a half if the Cold War had ended sooner. Similar things can be said of the war in Mozambique, which was a child of external racist manipulation.

On the negative side, former members of the Warsaw Pact lost all interest in supporting Third World causes. Leninist anti-imperialism seems to be as dead as other aspects of Leninism. V.I. Lenin added to Marxism some elements that are responsible for the present crisis of socialism worldwide. These factors included a vanguard party; democratic centralism; statism; and Marxism as an ideology of development, which in the end failed to deliver economic goods.

But Lenin also rescued Marxism from ethnocentrism and racism. Karl Marx's historical materialism once applauded British imperialism in India as a force that was destroying older precapitalist Hindu forms, propelling the country towards capitalism as a higher phase. Friedrich Engels also applauded French colonization of Algeria as two steps forward in the social evolutionary process. In other words, Engels and Marx were so Eurocentric that their paradigm legitimated European imperialism.

It was Lenin, however, who put European imperialism on trial with his book, *Imperialism: The Highest Stage of Capitalism*.[1] From then on, Marxism-Leninism became one of the major anti-imperialist forces of twentieth-century history. Now that even Marxists in Eastern Europe are de-Leninized, socialist anti-imperialism has declined. White socialists are far less likely to support black liberation today than they were two or three decades ago. De-Leninization strengthened the bonds between white socialists and white imperialists. For now, the process of de-Leninization is quite comprehensive. What were once Africa's comrades in arms against colonialism are now collaborators with apartheid in South Africa.

The demise of Leninism in Eastern Europe resulted in the decline of antiracism and anti-imperialism as well. Some Eastern European countries in 1990 moved almost obscenely toward full resumption of relations with the apartheid regime in South Africa before the racist structure had begun to be dismantled. Some newly democratized Eastern European countries started to violate international sanctions against Pretoria even before they held their first multiparty elections. The Soviet Union in 1990 used a subsidiary of a South African company, DeBeers, to market diamonds for Moscow—

something that would have been unthinkable before *glasnost* and *perestroika*. Liberalization among the former Warsaw Pact members meant their greater readiness to do business with the world's leading racist regime, Pretoria.

BETWEEN IDEOLOGY AND RELIGION

Meanwhile, another tilt was taking place—not a shift from ideology to race, but a transition from anticommunism to anti-Islamism. Western fears of Islam are centuries older than Western fears of communism. But in recent times, Western anti-Islamic tendencies were ameliorated by the indisputable superiority in technological and military power held by the West. Western nervousness about Islam was also ameliorated by the West's need for Muslim allies in its confrontation with the Soviet Union and the Warsaw Pact.

Three things occurred in the last quarter century to affect this shift. First, some elements in the Muslim world learned that those who are militarily weak have one strategy of last resort against the mighty—terrorism. They became convinced that terrorism was no worse than any other kind of warfare; if anything, it killed far fewer civilians than conventional, let alone nuclear, warfare.

As the fear of communism receded in the 1980s, however, the West felt freer to be tough about terrorism from the Muslim world. Libya was bombed. Syria was put into diplomatic cold storage. US ships went to the Persian Gulf in the midst of the Iran-Iraq War to intimidate Iran and protect Kuwaiti ships. In the process, the United States shot down an Iranian civilian airliner and killed all—over three hundred passengers—on board.

Second, if terrorism becomes the weapon of the militarily weak, nuclear weapons are for the technologically sophisticated. While some elements of the Muslim world were experimenting with terrorism and guerrilla warfare, others explored the nuclear option and other weapons of mass destruction. Ancient Western worries about Islam were rekindled. Egypt must be bribed to sign the Nuclear Nonproliferation Treaty whether or not Israel complied. Pakistan must be stopped from acquiring a nuclear capability. And Iraq must be given enough rope to hang itself over Kuwait so that all Iraqi weapons of mass destruction could then be destroyed.

The third reason for Western anxiety about Islam was the importance of Muslim oil for Western industry. Although Western technological power was still preeminent and undisputed, its dependence on Middle Eastern oil made it vulnerable to political changes in the Muslim world—changes of the magnitude of the revolution in Iran or of Iraq's annexation of Kuwait.

It seems almost certain that Muslims became the frontline military victims of the new world order while Blacks became the frontline economic victims of this emerging global apartheid. Muslims, especially in the Middle East, felt the firing power of US guns and US-subsidized Israeli planes. Blacks felt the deprivations of economic exploitation and neglect.

The military victimization of Muslims took either the direct form of Western bombing, as in the war against Iraq, or the surrogate Western aggression of heavily subsidizing Israel without adequately criticizing its repressive and military policies. There have also been Western double standards of crying "foul" when Muslim killed Muslim (as when Arab Iraqis repressed Kurds), but remaining apathetic when the Indian array committed atrocities in Kashmir.

Was the Gulf War against Iraq part of global apartheid? Aspects of the war were certainly ominous including Soviet submissiveness to the United States, Western hegemony in the United Nations, the attempted recolonization of Iraq after the war, and Western insensitivity to the killing of over two hundred thousand Iraqis. It was not a war; it was a massacre. Admittedly, it was triggered by Iraq's unforgivable aggression against Kuwait. But Bush, in turn, was more keen on saving time than saving lives. He refused to give sanctions enough time, even if it meant killing hundreds of thousands of Iraqis.

The coalition against Iraq was multiracial. Its leadership was decidedly and unmistakably white. Bush regarded the war against Iraq as the first major war of the new world order. Perhaps one day we will also lament the Gulf War as the first major war of the era of global apartheid. Just when we thought apartheid in South Africa was over, apartheid on a global scale reared its ugly head.

The apparent demise of Soviet and East European anti-imperialism hurt the Muslim world in other ways. When a US ship shot down an Iranian civilian airliner over international airspace, the new Soviet Union under Gorbachev did not attempt to rally the world against this act of manslaughter committed by Americans. Would the Iranian airliner have been shot down if there was a chance that European passengers were on board? Would Soviets have been silent if Soviet citizens were aboard? Moscow said it was deliberately not going to follow the accusatory precedent set by the United States in 1983 when Washington led the world in vigorously denouncing the Soviet Union's shooting down of a Korean civilian airliner. When the Soviets shot down South Korea's Flight 007, the Cold War was still on. Many of the passengers killed were Westerners, including a US Congressman. The United States served as the conscience of the world. But when a US battleship shot down the Iranian airliner, the Cold War was ending, there was no reason to believe that any Westerners or Soviet citizens were on board, and the USSR refused to serve as the conscience of the world and to denounce this fatal "accident."

If there is global apartheid in formation, how will it affect the European Soviet Union in relation to the Asian Soviet Union? One out of five citizens of the former USSR was a Muslim, and the Muslim pace of natural reproduction was much faster than that of non-Muslims. One future scenario could be an alliance between the Russian Federation and the Muslim republics. Indeed, the possibility of a Muslim president of the USSR was already in the cards, although with much reduced power. Gorbachev even considered appointing a Muslim vice president.

No less likely a scenario is one in which the European parts of what used to be the Soviet Union would align more closely to the newly integrated Western Europe, while the Muslim parts of the former USSR developed relationships with the rest of the Muslim world and Third World. Pakistan is now seeking new markets in places such as Uzbekistan and may open a consulate there. Turkey is seeking a new role in that part of the Muslim world. Such a trend would once again reinforce global apartheid. There is even a risk that the former Muslim republics would become Russian Bantustans, "backyards" with even less power than they had before.

But not all aspects of the newly emerging global apartheid may be detrimental to Muslim interests globally. After all, the new world order is predicated on the foundation of Pax Americana. An imperial system values stability and peace (hence the "pax'), but on its own imperial terms. Objectively, the main obstacle to peace in the Middle East since the 1970s is Israel. Will Pax Americana not only force Israel and the Arabs to the negotiating table, but compel them to consider exchanging land for peace as well? Indeed, will the Gulf War against Iraq turn out to be the undoing of Israel as we have so far known it?

Before he went to war against Iraq, George Bush vowed that there was no linkage between the Gulf crisis and the wider Arab-Israeli conflict. Almost as soon as the war was over, Secretary of State James Baker started a series of diplomatic trips in order to start a peace process in the Arab-Israeli conflict. There was de facto linkage. The Gulf War that Bush and his allies launched was not really a war; it was a massacre. On the other hand, Desert Storm temporarily made Bush so strong in domestic politics that he was able to stand up to the pro-Israeli lobby and defy the Israeli prime minister. George Bush may turn out to be the toughest president on Israel since Eisenhower. Are there signs that the Gulf War may turn out to be the beginning of the political undoing of the old, defiant Israel after all?

Israel's political decline in Washington, although modest, may be due to two very different factors: the end of the Cold War and the new US-Arab realignments following the Gulf War. The end of the Cold War, as indicated, reduced the strategic value of Israel to the United States. It also increased Syria's desire to be friends with the United States. Israel may become a less intimate friend to the United States; Syria has already become less objectionable as an adversary to the United States. The Gulf War provided a test for US-Syrian realignment. Damascus and Washington moved closer as a result of the Gulf War.

Most commentators focused on the political and economic losses the Palestinians sustained as a result of the Gulf War. Few noted that this was balanced, at least to some degree, by the political losses sustained by Israel as a result of a new US-Arab realignment and by the popularity of George Bush in the aftermath of the war. The popularity was great enough to withstand the criticism of the pro-Israeli lobby, at least for one year.

On the other hand, the end of the Cold War also reduced the strategic value of Pakistan to the Western world. Pressures on Pakistan to conform to Western prescriptions have already increased and its nuclear credentials have become even more of an issue in its relations with the United States. As far as the West is concerned, Islam must on no account be nuclearized. This means (1) stopping Pakistan from developing nuclear capability, (2) destroying Iraq's capacity in weapons of mass destruction, (3) neutralizing Egypt by getting it to sign the Nuclear Non-Proliferation Treaty, (4) coopting Syria into pro-Western respectability, and (5) preventing Qaddafy from buying nuclear credentials.

On the other hand, the United States' conventional capability—although originally targeted at the Second World of Socialist countries—in reality tended to be used against the Third World. There were disproportionate numbers of Muslim victims. Under the Reagan and Bush administrations the United States (1) bombed Beirut from the sea, (2) invaded Grenada, (3) bombed Tripoli and Bengazi in Libya, (4) hijacked an Egyptian plane in international airspace, (5) shot down an Iranian civilian aircraft in the Gulf and killed all on board, (6) invaded Panama and kidnapped General Manuel Noriega, and (7) bombed Iraqi cities as part of an anti-Saddam coalition. More than two-thirds of the casualties of US military activity since the Vietnam War were Muslims, amounting to at least a quarter of a million, and possibly half a million, Muslim deaths.

BETWEEN IDEOLOGY AND ECONOMICS

If the first military victims of global apartheid were disproportionately Muslims, the first economic victims of global apartheid may be Blacks. The good news is that Europe, in spite of Yugoslavia and the fragmentation of the Soviet Union, is carrying forward the torch of continental unification and regional integration. The bad news is that countries such as France, often "champions of African interests" in world affairs, are beginning to turn their eyes away from Africa toward Europe.

In the struggle against old style narrow nationalism and the nation-state, Western Europe led the way. The Treaties of Rome created the European Economic Community (EEC) in March 1957 and set the stage for wider regional integration. In 1992, an enlarged European Community achieved even deeper integration as more walls between members disappeared (or came down). The former German Democratic Republic was reunited with the Federal Republic of Germany as part of this wider Europe. And the newly liberated Eastern European countries are seeking new links with the European Community, further eroding narrow nationalism and enlarging regional integration. Yugoslavia and the Soviet Union, torn by ethnic separatism, still manifest in the European areas an eagerness to be accepted into the wider European fraternity. The decline of socialist ideology throughout Eastern Europe is accompanied by a resurgence of primordial culture. Marxism has either died or been de-Leninized, but a pan-European identity is reasserting itself on a scale greater than the Holy Roman Empire.

Marxism-Leninism, while it lasted, was transracial. It made European Marxists seek allies and converts among people of color. But European identity is, by definition, Eurocentric. It increases the chances of pan-Europeanism. The bad news is that pan-Europeanism can carry the danger of cultural chauvinism and even racism.

Anti-Semitism has been on the rise in Eastern Europe as an aspect of this cultural chauvinism. And racism and xenophobia in the reunified Germany have reached new levels. Racism in France took its highest toll among North Africans. And all over Europe, there is a new sense of insecurity among immigrants who are of a darker hue than the local populations; some of the immigrants farther north may even be Portuguese mistaken for Turks or North Africans. Where does xenophobia end and racism begin? An old dilemma once again rears its head.

Then there is the racial situation in the United States with all its contradictions. On the one hand, the country produced the first black governor of a state (Virginia) and the first black mayor of New York City. On the other hand, in 1991 the state of Louisiana produced a startling level of electoral support for David Duke, a former member of the Ku Klux Klan and former advocate of Nazi policies. Duke got a majority of the white votes that were cast, but lost the election because of the other votes. In April 1992, a mainly white jury in California found that beating and kicking of a black suspect (Rodney King) while he was down was not excessive use of force. The verdict sparked some of the worst riots in US history in Los Angeles in which nearly sixty people were killed.

George Bush exploited white racial fears in the presidential electoral campaign of 1988. A television commercial of the Bush campaign exploited to the utmost the image of a black convict, Willie Horton, who had been prematurely "furloughed" in Massachusetts and who killed again. The television commercial was probably a significant factor behind George Bush's victory in the 1988 presidential election.

Meanwhile, the Supreme Court of the United States moves farther and farther to the right, endangering some of the interracial constitutional gains of yesteryear. The new right wing Supreme Court legalized atrocities, ranging from violence by prison wardens to kidnapping by US agents in countries such as Mexico. The economic conditions of the black underclass in the United States are as bad as ever. Poverty, drug abuse, crime, broken homes, unemployment, infant mortality, and now the disproportionate affliction by AIDS are a stubborn part of the black condition in the United States.

The holocausts of the Western hemisphere continue to inflict pain and humiliation on native Americans and descendants of enslaved Africans. Approximately 40 percent of the prisoners on death row in the United States are African Americans. The jails, mortuaries, and police cells still bear anguished testimony to the disproportionate and continuing suffering of US holocausts. In the United States today, there are possibly more male descendants of enslaved Africans in prison than in college.

Equally ominous on a continental scale is the economic condition of Africa. The continent still produces what it does not consume, and consumes what it does not produce. Agriculturally, many African countries have evolved dessert and beverage economies, producing cocoa, coffee, tea, and other incidentals for Northern dining tables. In contrast, Africa imports the fundamentals of its existence from basic equipment to staple foods. In addition, Africa is liable to environmental hazards that lead to drought and famine in certain areas. The Horn of Africa and the Sahel were particularly prone to these ecological deprivations.

The external factors that retarded Africa's economic development included price fluctuations and uncertainties about primary commodities, issues over which Africa had very little say. The debt crisis in Africa is also a major shackle on the pace of development. Although the debts of African countries are modest compared with countries such as Brazil and Mexico, it is important to remember that African economies are not only smaller, but also more fragile than those of the major Latin American states. The West demonstrated more flexibility in recent times about Africa's debt crisis, and some Western countries extended debt forgiveness. Speedy action toward resolving the debt problem would be a contribution in the fight against the forces of global apartheid.

Just as African societies are becoming more democratic, African states exert less influence on the global scene than ever. African people are increasing their influence on their governments just when African countries are losing leverage on the world system. As the African electorate is empowered, the African countries are enfeebled.

Africa's international marginalization does include among its causes the absence of the Soviet bloc as a countervailing force in the global equation. A world with only one superpower is a world with less leverage for the smaller countries in the global system. Africa's marginalization is also a result of the re-emergence of Eastern European countries as rivals for Western attention and Western largesse.

Africa is also being marginalized in a world of such mega-economies as an increasingly unified North America, an increasingly unified European Community, an expanding Japanese economy, and some of the achievements of the member states of the Association of South East Asian Nations (ASEAN). In the economic domain, global apartheid is a starker and sharper reality between white nations and black nations than between white nations and some of the countries of Asia.

In the United Nations and its agencies, Africa is also marginalized, partly because Third World causes have lost the almost automatic support of former members of the Warsaw Pact. On the contrary, former members of the Socialist bloc are now more likely to follow the US lead than to join forces with the Third World. Moreover, the African percentage of the total membership of the UN system is declining. In 1991, five new members were admitted to the UN, none of them African (the two Koreas and three Baltic states). The disintegration of Yugoslavia and the Soviet Union has resulted in at least ten more members. The numerical marginalization of Africa within the world body is likely to continue.

In the financial world, the power of the World Bank and the International Monetary Fund (IMF) not only remains intact, but is bound to increase in the era of global apartheid. It was once said of a British monarch that the power of the king has increased, is increasing and ought to diminish. This philosophy is especially applicable to the power of the World Bank in Africa. Unfortunately, all indications continue to point in the direction of greater escalation of Africa's dependence upon such international financial institutions.

On the other hand, the World Bank sometimes acts as an ambassador on behalf of Africa, coaxing Japan, for example, to allocate more money for African aid. The World Bank may help to persuade Western countries to bear African needs in mind even as the West remains mesmerized by the continuing drama in the former Soviet Union and Eastern Europe. At its best, the World Bank can be a force against the drift towards global apartheid. But at its worst, the World Bank is an extension of the power of the white races over the darker peoples of the globe.

It is virtually certain that German money is already being diverted from Tanzania and Bangladesh toward the newly integrated East Germany, to compensate the Soviet Union for its cooperation with German reunification. Before long, larger amounts of Western money will be going to Poland, Hungary, the Czech and Slovak republics, and the newly independent republics of Lithuania, Latvia, and Estonia.

Western investment in former Warsaw Pact countries may also be at the expense of investment in Africa. Western trade may also be redirected to some extent. Now that white Westerners and Easterners no longer have an ideological reason for mutual hostility, are their shared culture and race acquiring more primary salience? Are we witnessing the emergence of a new Northern solidarity as the hatchets of the Cold War are at last buried? Are Blacks the first economic victims of this global apartheid?

CONCLUSION

Are we witnessing new forms of retribalization and race consciousness just as the more localized apartheid of South Africa is coming to an end? I argued that if there is a new world order, its first economic victims will be black people of Africa, the Americas, Europe, and elsewhere. I also argued that the new world order's first military victims are Muslims; about half a million have been killed by the West or Western-subsidized initiatives since the Vietnam War. Palestinians, Libyans, Iraqis, and Lebanese are among the casualties. Since World War II, far more Muslims have been killed by the West than have citizens of the former Warsaw Pact, from the Suez War of 1956 to the Gulf War of 1991.

One advantage of the old East-West divide was that it was transracial and interracial. White socialist countries supported black liberation fighters militarily against white minority governments in Africa. But now the former Socialist countries are among the least supportive of Third World causes. In the UN, the former communist adversaries are often more cooperative with Washington than are some Western allies. In reality, Paris is more independent of Washington than is Moscow since the Gorbachev revolution.

With regard to this new world order, are there racial and racist differences between the Western response to Iraqi aggression against Kuwait in 1990 and to Serbia's aggression against Bosnia and Herzegovina in 1992? Both Bosnia and Kuwait had prior international recognition as sovereign states. Both had prior historical links with the countries that committed aggression against them, Serbia and Iraq respectively. Bosnia and Serbia had once been part of Yugoslavia; Kuwait and Iraq had once been part of the same province of the Ottoman Empire. Iraq in 1990 had territorial appetites masquerading as a dispute over oil wells between Iraq and Kuwait; Serbia had territorial appetites masquerading as protection of ethnic Serbs in Bosnia.

The West, under the leadership of the Bush administration, said to Iraqi aggression: "This will not stand!" To end Iraqi aggression in Kuwait, the West and its allies bombed Baghdad and Basra. To end Serbian aggression in Bosnia, was the West in 1992 prepared to bomb Belgrade? If not, why not? Did the reasons include racism? Was it all right to bomb Arab populations thousands of miles away, but insupportable to bomb fellow Europeans next door?

The new idea of creating a European army answerable to the European Community, as well as to NATO, also seemed to draw a sharp distinction between "military intervention" outside Europe and "peacekeeping" within Europe.

According to Joseph Fitchett, writing for the *International Herald Tribune*:

> Braving Bush administration objections, France and Germany are proceeding ... to establish a substantial joint military force that could assume functions previously reserved for NATO.
>
> Conceived as the core for a future European army, the proposed Euro-corps is supposed to ready the equivalent of two divisions by 1995 for military intervention outside Europe and for peacekeeping and other, as yet undefined, operations within Europe.[2]

Is there a clear reluctance to shed European blood among some nations, such as France and Britain, which have very recently shed Arab and Muslim blood?

Regarding the war in Bosnia, Anthony Lewis of *The New York Times* said in 1992:

> The Americans and Europeans have plenty of warplanes, based near enough ... to take command of the air.... We could have said to Mr. Milosevic, and still could: Stop

> your aggression at once, or our military aircraft will control your skies. Not just over Dubrovnik or Sarajevo, but over Belgrade.... The failure of nerve and imagination in the face of Serbian aggression is Europe's as well as America's. But Mr. Bush raised expectations so high in the Gulf War that disappointment naturally focused on him. What happened to the man who three days after Iraq grabbed Kuwait said, "This will not stand"?[3]

Was it a "failure of nerve" on the part of the United States or Europe? Or was it a triumph of macroracial empathy? It was easier to remember British planes bombing Baghdad in 1991 than to imagine British planes bombing Belgrade in 1992. And US planes bombing Sarajevo or Dubrovnik in the 1990s in order to save them seems distasteful. It was easier to bomb parts of Kuwait in 1991 and would be easier to rebomb Tripoli and Baghdad in 1992 and 1993.

Long before the end of the Cold War, I had occasion to worry publicly about a "global caste system" in the making. I argued in a book published in 1977 that the international stratification did not have the flexibility and social mobility of a class structure, but had some of the rigidities of caste:

> If the international system was, in the first half of the twentieth century a class system, it is now moving in the direction of rigidity. We may be witnessing the consolidation of a global caste structure.... Just as there are hereditary factors in domestic castes, so there are hereditary elements in international castes. Pre-eminent among those factors is the issue of *race*.... If people of European extraction are the Brahmins of the international caste system, the Black people belong disproportionately to the caste of the untouchables. Between the highest international caste [Whites] and the lowest [Blacks] are other ranks and estates such as Asians.[4]

What prevented this global caste system from becoming global apartheid at that time was, ironically, the Cold War, which divided the white world ideologically. Rivalry between the two white power blocs averted the risk of racial solidarity among the more prosperous whites. The white world was armed to the teeth against each other. This was unlike apartheid in South Africa. At the global level, we had Brahmins at dagger points.[5]

But there is now a closing of ranks among the white peoples of the world. The ethnic hiccups of Yugoslavia and the Soviet Union notwithstanding, and after allowing for Denmark's caution and Britain's relative insularity, the mood in Europe is still toward greater continental union. Pan-Europeanism is reaching levels greater than anything experienced since the Holy Roman Empire. The question that arises is whether this new pan-European force, combined with the economic trend towards a mega-North America, will produce a human race more than ever divided between prosperous white races and poverty-stricken Blacks. Is a global macroretribalization in the making?

The era of global apartheid coincided with the era of a unipolar world—a global system with only one superpower. The declining fear of communism may reactivate an older Western fear of Islam. The location of petroleum disproportionately in Muslim lands, combined with the tensions of the Arab-Israeli conflict, cost the Muslim world upward of half a million lives as a result of military actions by the United States and its allies during the Reagan and Bush administrations. The main victims were Libyans, Iranians, Lebanese, Palestinians, and, most recently, Iraqis.

Race and religion remain potent forces in global affairs. Historically, race has been the fundamental divisive factor between Westerners and people of African descent almost everywhere. Religion has been the fundamental divisive factor between Westerners and people of Muslim culture almost everywhere. Was the collapse of the Berlin Wall in 1989 the beginning of the racial reunification of the white world? Did the Gulf War of 1991 put the holiest places of Islam under the imperial umbrella of Pax Americana? Is the twentieth century getting ready to hand over to the twenty-first century a new legacy of global apartheid? The trends are ominous, but let us hope that they are not irreversible.

NOTES

1. V.I. Lenin, *Imperialism: The Highest Stage of Capitalism* (New York: International Publishers, 1939).
2. Joseph Fitchett, "Paris and Bonn to Form the Nucleus of a 'Euro-corps,'" *International Herald Tribune* (14 May 1992).
3. Anthony Lewis, "What Was That About a New World Order?" *International Herald Tribune* (18 May 1992).
4. Ali A, Mazrui, *Africa's International Relations: The Diplomacy of Dependency and Change* (Boulder, CO: Westview Press, 1977): 7–8.
5. Gernot Kohler used the concept of "global apartheid" in a working paper published for the World Order Models Project (Gernot Kohler, *Global Apartheid*, New York: World Order Models Project, Institute for World Order, Working Paper No. 7, 1978). His definition of apartheid did not require a fundamental solidarity within the privileged race. My definition does.

CHAPTER 13

THE LORE OF THE HOMELAND: HINDU NATIONALISM AND INDIGENIST "NEORACISM"

Chetan Bhatt

INTRODUCTION

Conventional Western paradigms of race and ethnic relations sociology, as well as the political practices of anti-racism, have undergone significant internal evaluation over the last decade. This has been partly the result of the political conflicts over varieties of authoritarian anti-racism and identity politics since the mid-1980s. Sociological paradigms around race and class have also been interrogated and developed in a number of feminist interventions over the same period (Solomos and Back 1996). Many of the recent debates on globalisation and European integration have shifted emphasis away from some of the more parochial aspects of ethnic and race relations sociology of the last two decades. However, perhaps the most significant challenge to the theorisation of "race" or racism, the ethnographic assessment of minority communities or the policy framework of multicultural pluralism has been the rise since the mid-1980s of ethnic and cultural absolutist movements in South Asian communities in the UK. The impact of the Rushdie affair is well known, and established the vulnerable nature of the secularism that was inherent in the projects of "Asian" or "black" politics. The affair also exposed an absence in political sociology of a serious and sustained consideration of the specificity of the politics of the South Asian experience in the UK, especially in a way that did not reduce the latter to an ethnography of cultural habits or to "black anti-racism." If there has been a rapid, though uneven move away from the secular politics of black liberation and anti-racism towards issues of primarily religious and ethnic difference, it is still the case that "race" has retained an importance for some black political formations. For example, a concept of "race," and a claim about the value of "racial" attributes is as important for some varieties of Afrocentricity as it is for the right-wing, neo-nazi and racist political formations that are animating contemporary European politics.

This essay explores the importance of "race thinking" in the new Hindu authoritarian religious movements that are dominating both Indian politics and the Hindu diaspora. These movements are variously labelled "Hindu nationalism," the sangh parivar,[1] the Hindutva movement or "Hindu cultural nationalism." Their particular formations of "race" may be very different from western scientific or cultural "racial" paradigms. Because of the relative unfamiliarity within mainstream western sociology of South Asian politics and history, and in particular the substantive historical, political and cultural configurations of Hinduisms, the essay is broadly introductory. Much can be learned from the experience of religious and ethnic conflict in India during and since the colonial period. Many of the political languages of multiculturalism, secularism, diversity and discrimination that are important in the west have a longer pedigree in South Asian politics and administration and indeed have been fundamental to (and fundamentally contested in various ways) in Indian politics. The depth of the debates in India about these matters can inform discussions of these issues in progressive British multicultural sociology and political theory. It also needs remembering that multiculturalist discourse itself arose in the period of colonial administrative theory and practice, especially in the New World, South Asia and central Africa. Many of its older languages survive in surprisingly similar forms in contemporary western race and ethnic relations theory.

The Hindutva movement condenses numerous themes about ethnogenesis, religious authoritarianism, cultural absolutism, the nature of secular postcolonial citizenship, majority-minority relations, and "racial" and ethnic hatred that often appear separately in other examples of contemporary religious and ethnic conflict. In this sense, Hindutva ideology can represent a universal example of the numerous directions that absolutist and totalitarian ideologies can travel in the late modern period. Similarly, in describing Hindutva ideology using conventional theoretical paradigms, none of the analytical concepts of "race," racism, religion, ethnicity or culture on their own suffice, but all are deeply relevant in a combination that perhaps requires a new description, as perhaps do many other contemporary "absolutist ideologies of indigenism."

Hindutva ideology presents a highly overdetermined ontology of *ethnos* and *xenos*. There is, for example, a powerful hereditarian "race concept" in Hindutva but this has little to do with western scientific racism proper. It is instead related to, and often indistinguishable from a separate hereditarian discourse of culture, religion and ethnicity. If the opposition between biology and culture has often been used to analytically situate western racisms, it is important to consider how "culture" already contains powerful epistemic resources that can provide for a sentimentalist racism that is never obliged to take actual biology or science seriously but can still contain a hereditary or genetic core, the latter frequently articulated through primordial origin myths, and the tropes of breeding, cultivation, blood and lineage. This kind of "racism"[2] is virtually definitive of Hindutva discourse (Jaffrelot 1995, Bhatt 1997). There is a different equally relevant Hindutva "civilisational-nationalist" discourse that need not necessarily be hereditarian, but can convincingly be called "racist," and in many ways presents a paradigmatic case of "monocultural neoracism." There is yet another purely "metaphysical ethnology" that arises in Hindutva ideology (Bhatt 1999). In this sense, the Hindutva movement has created a distinctive ontology of selves and others that is not easily captured by many of the theoretical discourses typically used to analyse racism. We shall however see later that the relations between Hindutva and western "race thinking" are historically closer and deeper than is usually imagined.

An assessment is presented below that some South Asian ideological formations have come close in form and content to versions of classical fascism and Nazism. This may seem a stark judgment, especially when applied to some of the political formations arising from minority communities who may already face structural discrimination or "racial" inequality in the west. The ethical challenge is indeed to keep equally abreast of both issues in all their dense historical and social complexity and without reducing each to the other. In doing so, it is necessary to move away from a distinct "metaphysics of innocence" (an explicit disavowal of the capacity for ethical judgement that travels beyond the rhetorical labour that is required to uphold the unity of one's ownmost identity or being), that accompanies much discussion of the victims of racism and discrimination and engage in a deeper and more reflexive consideration of the global and national processes of South Asian community formation and representation that by and large overwhelm the binary syntax of racism and anti-racism. Indeed, it is precisely the normative location of those communities within the nexus of British racial discourse (or sociological racialisation) that has prevented more comprehensive assessments of some of the far right-wing movements and networks that claim to represent those communities.

It finally needs emphasising that the discussion below is about Hindu nationalism, and not about vernacular, cultural, historical or ascetic forms of Hinduism, or their attendant beliefs and practices in South Asian communities. However, some general points about the relation between Hindutva and Hinduism are necessary. The Hindutva movement has attempted to blur the distinctions between its novel ideology and historical Hinduisms in general, and has mobilised various strategies of obfuscation and indigenist claims about incommensurability to achieve this. In doing so, the Hindutva movement reproduces a grand epistemology about Hinduism that fundamentally subverts the methods of history and historical sociology. In this view, Hinduism or its essence is in some fundamental way unchanging and primordial (Hindutva is indeed based on this "essence"). The extraordinarily complex histories of sects, caste development and change, and the social, political and cultural processes that eventually led in the modern period to the idea of Hinduism are grossly simplified and reified—in essence, they are stagnated. The similarity with western thinking (for example, Marxism) about South Asian social formations during the colonial period is obvious. In this Hindutva conception, ideas such as brahminism, sanatana dharma ("the eternal religion") and so forth are detached from the historical processes in which they developed and mobilised as self-evident signifiers of a contemporary identity. In this sense, "Hinduism" becomes an abstraction, an empty but normative signification of something that exists above and beyond the histories of societies and cultures. The temporal schemes of Hindu mythology are applied to contemporary histories (indeed, a realism is claimed for mythic temporalities). The Hindutva movement also supplies other grand linear historiographies, one of which, like James Mill, simply divides Indian history into ancient (Vedic-Aryan), medieval (Muslim-Mughal) and modern (colonial British) hermetic periods (Thapar 1996a). Much of the structure and power of Hindutva discourse is derived by intentionally blending (and confusing) mythic, archaeological, medieval, colonial and contemporary time, space and event.

A second aspect of Hindutva methodology has included reliance on some traditional Hindu conceptual schemes and tropes, especially, but not exclusively, selective components of brahminism. Within many forms of traditional Hinduism, its many texts, symbols, myths and iconography are subject to compounded and variant meanings. In the cultural ecology of traditional Hinduism, conceptions of mythic, historical and contemporary times and spaces can cohabit the same intellectual universe without contradiction. That these layered religious and secular concepts may be seen, from an external gaze, to accumulate epistemological or ontological anomalies is viewed as irrelevant to their purposes. This is a distinctive characteristic of many Hinduisms: through processes of accretion, conflict, epistemic breaks, interpolation, fabulations, refabulations and retellings, Hinduism invests its symbols (in the broadest sense) with a vast number of meanings that remain together in a shifting hermeneutic and semiotic alliance. This is a self-conscious process (rather than a consequence of linguistic theory) which is sometimes referred to as periphrasis, but in an important sense it is its opposite: a symbol is invested with a large number of mundane and metaphysical aspects that are known, in various hybrid, syncretistic ways by Hindus who may otherwise belong to differing sects.[3]

Hindutva exploits these characteristics around time, space, event, symbol and myth by appropriating the symbols of Hinduism and rearticulating their various layered cultural and religious meanings into a politically ordered, "syndicated" and homogeneous Hinduism (Thapar 1991). This has also been identified as a key characteristic of the history of brahminism, which mobilised similar strategies to incorporate within itself, hegemonise, politically exploit or reach a complex syncretic negotiation with other movements, such as Buddhism, Jainism and the numerous bhakti (devotional) sects. Consequently, the Hindutva movement has been interpreted by some writers as a legacy of the same historical tendency within dominant forms of brahminism (Lele 1995). It certainly is the case that the Hindutva movement has been brahmin-led and dominated, and reliant on north-Indian brahminic metaphysics or ideals (such as the glorification of Vedic and Upanishadic religion and sanatana dharma) rather than other metaphysical narratives produced by other castes and sects, including dalit movements.

THE HINDUTVA FAMILY

Hindu nationalism has a long and complex ideological history that owes much to the formation of, and indigenous Indian negotiation with, European Romantic and British colonial knowledges about Indian social formations, their cultural and epistemic products, their histories and their antiquity. In their paradoxical way, the antecedents of Hindu nationalism are located precisely in that period from the mid-eighteenth to the late-nineteenth-century Europe, and in that divergence between Enlightenment secular rationality and Romantic affective primordialism whose product was itself an unsettled "secular nationalism," the latter phrase perhaps capturing a key instability within modernity.

However, the birth of contemporary Hindu nationalism is usually traced to, and just after, the inter-war period, from 1916–25, during which two organisations, the Hindu Mahasabha (The Great Assembly of Hindus) and its "semi-rival," the Rashtriya Swayamsevak Sangh (RSS, the National Volunteer-Servers Organisation) were formed. Hindu nationalism's key, but by no means only ideologue was Vinayak Damodar Savarkar, an anti-colonial revolutionary hero and founder of the Mahasabha, who in 1923 presented the novel idea of Hindutva, the essence or "beingness" of a Hindu. Hindutva was a hereditarian conception, born from the time the intrepid Aryans entered India and whose "blood commingled" with that of the original inhabitants of India.[4] For Savarkar, a Hindu could be defined as someone who considers India as their fatherland, motherland and holy-land and "who inherits the blood of that race whose first discernible source could be traced back" to the Vedic Aryans (Savarkar [1923] 1989: 115).

Savarkar's formulation of Hindutva considerably influenced Keshav Baliram Hedgewar, the founder of the paramilitary Rashtriya Swayamsevak Sangh (RSS, formed in 1924) as well as Madhav Golwalkar, the RSS's second leader. Golwalkar extended strands of Hindutva to develop an extraordinarily modern, Nazi-like racial idea of Hinduness, most clearly elaborated in his *We—or our nationhood defined* (1939).[5] The RSS is the core ultra-nationalist organisation of the Hindutva movement and has about 2.5 million members in India. It has emphasised since its beginning a novel organisational method that owes practically nothing to Hindu traditions. This is the shaka, a regimented and regulated system of boy-scout discipline involving physical games and exercise, nationalist ideological inculcation and martial arts. The RSS recruits its members from among young and very young boys, reflecting a conscious "catch them young" policy. It has a distinctive uniform based on the British colonial police uniform—khaki shorts, white shirt, black cap—which evokes variously both considerable amusement and fear. Its supreme emblem, "the true preceptor," is the saffron flag. This is saluted as a symbol of the Hindu nation with a bodily gesture that cannot but invoke for an onlooker the period of the 1930s and 1940s in Germany. The RSS has developed several mantras that extol the glory of a united Hindu society or nation. It celebrates six main festivals (*utsavs*) a year, several of which are traditional Hindu festivals, but the traditional pedagogies of these festivals are heavily slanted towards the secular-nationalist concerns of the sangh: political unity and social cohesion among Hindus, a celebration of Hindu strength and nationhood, and worship of the nation and motherland. It would be extremely difficult to conceptualise the cultural, symbolic and ideological content of RSS philosophy as anything other than anti-traditional, especially its explicit secular deification of nation and nationalism. Its organisational structure is hierarchical, centralised and based on the principle of *ek chalak anuvartita* (devotion to the One Supreme Leader). An obsession with organisation and discipline sums up the RSS's quotidian philosophy. However, its wider aim is to literally take individual after individual "and mould them for an organised national life."

> The ultimate vision of our work, which has been the living inspiration for all our organisational efforts, is a perfectly organised state of our society wherein each individual has been moulded into a wider ideal of Hindu manhood and made into the living limb of the corporate personality of society. (Golwalkar 1966: 61)

Deendayal Upadhyaya, an RSS member and one of the founders of the Jana Sangh political party, precursor to the contemporary Bharatiya Janata Party (BJP) developed many of Savarkar's and Golwalkar's ideas into a simplistic corporatist social and political philosophy, Integral Humanism, which became increasingly important from the mid-1960s. This defined an ideal social order as an organic unity (based on *ekatmata*, "the unifying principle" or "oneness") in which *karna* ("desire," especially bodily desire) and *artha* ("wealth," but including political and economic instrumental need), are to be subsumed under the greater principle of *dharma* ("natural law," order and duty) for the ideal of *moksha* ("salvation" or liberation) (Upadhyaya 1991). Integral Humanism now forms the main ideological plank of the contemporary BJP and is based on a view of the ideal social formation as one regulated by Hindu *dharma* (religion, ethical code) which is seen as transcendent and prior to the exigencies of the state and civil society. As in Golwalkar's mystical cultural nationalism, Upadhyaya's philosophy stresses the *a priori* nature of the cultural-dharmic field which exists above and beyond the social and political histories of nations and societies and is indeed the condition for them. Integral Humanism also emphasises an organicist view of the social formation and state–civil society relations, the latter, and indeed all social relations, to be conceived of as non-conflictual and non-contradictory if *dharmic* principles are followed.

The RSS created several other organisations of which the Vishwa Hindu Parishad (VHP, World Hindu Council), formed in the 1960s and representing a federation of Hindu religious leaders, and the BJP created in 1980 out of the RSS remnants of the Jana Sangh, are the most important. From the 1960s onwards, and especially from the early 1980s, one can speak of the formation of a mass far-right-wing Hindu social movement which perhaps reached its peak in the successful campaign to destroy the medieval Mughal mosque, the Babri masjid, in 1992. In 1998, the BJP formed India's government under a broad, shaky coalition and entered the world's political stage by ordering the explosion of five nuclear devices, including allegedly a thermonuclear device, at the Pokharan test site in northern India.[6]

Aside from its political successes, the Hindutva movement has developed formidable, in several respects unique, cultural and ideological strategic practices in Indian civil society that have not been matched by recent secular movements. The emphasis on slow patient work in civil society should be noted, and indeed the RSS often calls itself the largest voluntary organisation in the world. Its self-conscious and deep cultural strategy attempts to intervene in the detail of the ecology, vernacular practices and beliefs of everyday Hinduisms, to reconstitute these into a new habitus, a way of practising and thinking about Hinduism and its relation to the life-world that reappears as innate, natural and instinctive, despite its historical newness and fabrication. The Vedas, Puranas and epics become palimpsests, simplified icons of the new Hinduism. An attempt is made to rearticulate many vernacular Hinduisms, and their epics, myths or devotionalism into a political (that is, a secular) idiom in a way that seeks to fundamentally alter the cultural meanings and symbolic import of religious forms and artefacts. These "neotraditional" methods aim to make their intended subjects not more religious but more political.

The complex and compounded histories of Hinduisms, Buddhism, Sikhism, Jainism and South Asian Islam over several millennia, as well as the complexities of the economic, social, political and cultural formations in the Indian sub-continent are shielded from followers in favour of a monologic view of history and of the social formation as an elementary, easily intelligible totality made up of just Hindus and just minorities, and the conflicts between the latter. The parameters of state or civil society are reduced to ones solely of religious belonging. Culture is a simple inventory of the cultural artefacts that tell stories of a golden age or a glorious and endless war. The familiar temporal scheme of many ethnic absolutist movements is also evident. "Historicity," and "a revenge against history" are customary tropes. History is typically imagined as commencing from an ancient primordial and sublime origin, a temporally illegible utopia that falters because of Hindu failure in faith, or external aggression or both. This is followed by a period of medieval (Muslim) or modern (British) degradation and oppression and a long unflinching war that drives time forward. The present dystopian moment is one of Hindu renewal and identity formation. Futurity is closed with the establishment of a perfected and powerful Hindu utopia.

War metaphors are central to the political language of the Hindutva movement. The movement has identified the domestic "enemies" that have placed "Hindu society under siege"—communism ("Soviet Imperialism"), western influences ("Christian" or "Western Imperialism" or "Macaulayism") and Muslims ("Islamic Imperialism"). India's Muslim population is already articulated as a minority that has been *appeased* for too long by previous governments. India's traditional military adversaries, the belligerent and aggressive Pakistan, as well as China, are joined by Bangladesh, the latter seen in Hindutva political language as a source of Islamic "demographic aggression" against, and "infiltration" of, India (because of Bangladeshi migration into India). The extremely volatile situation in Kashmir is already conceivable as a war by proxy.

The "anti-imperialist" rhetoric of Hindu nationalism, as in many varieties of Islamism, is less to do with the history of British economic imperialism and political domination. Apart from its banning after the murder of Gandhi, and its paramilitary activities in the Punjab during Partition, the RSS was conspicuously absent from the Indian liberation movement that it now seeks to own. Its anti-imperialism is however related to a xenophobic religious-cultural indigenism that is to be cultivated against what are seen as foreign influences. It is also axiomatic that Hindu nationalism reduces all social identities and social, economic and political processes to bare religious signifiers—Hindu and Muslim/Christian, the former conceived of as tolerant, peaceful and inclusive of all Hindu sects, which are seen to include Buddhism, Jainism and Sikhism, and the latter as monolithic, intolerant and violent. This disembedding of complex major or quotidian social, cultural and political processes and identities into pure religious signifiers of self and other is a familiar authoritarian strategy in which the democratic ideals of people, citizenship and individual autonomy are reconstituted into antagonistic, permanently separate religious collectives (Panikkar 1997). It also raises a deeper question about why modern democracies tend to problematise minorities. Hindu nationalism also undertakes the familiar metaphoric substitution of the nation by the idea of the national, or social or human body; conversely, minorities, especially Muslims, are seen as a polluting presence within that body. Consequently, Hindu nationalism is dangerously obsessed with Muslim demography, reproduction and fertility (see, for example, Lal 1990). Within the Hindutva repertoire of blood and belonging, Muslims are for the most part Hindus "whose original Hindu blood has been unaffected by alien adulteration" but who have betrayed their original faith or were coerced into Islam, and now constitute the traitorous fifth column in the Hindu nation. This ambiguity about blood, allegiance and betrayal is suggestively primordial. It is also extremely similar to Serbian (and Croat) nationalist discourses about Bosnian, Croat or Albanian Muslims who have transgressed their "original" Slavic or Croat "blood heritage."

"Global" Hindutva

A significant feature of Hindu nationalism has been its international network and form of organisation. The RSS and the VHP have established an organisational presence in over 150 countries, virtually everywhere that Hindus have settled because of indentured labour, migrant labour, economic migration, as refugees or through the more recent professional economic migration of NRIs (non-resident Indians) to the US and Canada. (In RSS hagiography, the first overseas *sangh shaka* was formed aboard a ship of South Asian migrants and labourers heading from Bombay to Kenya in 1946, and the first non-Indian *shaka* formed in Keyna the following year.) In the west, the RSS, the VHP and the supporters of the BJP are extremely (USA) or relatively (UK and Europe) well organised. However, the sociological features of Hindutva in Britain and the US are dissimilar, and related to the different processes of migration and settlement, as well as the different socio-economic characteristics of South Asian communities in the respective countries. US Hindutva is primarily organised through the VHP (the latter being perhaps the main RSS platform) and the Overseas Friends of the BJP (OFBJP). Its key feature is "silicon Hindutva," the relatively large influence of Hindu nationalism and RSS-VHP ideology on professional, educated and relatively wealthy American NRIs and their families, especially physicists and computer scientists. Indeed, the key US Hindutva activists are natural scientists. Youth and children are involved in RSS activities through the distinctively American summer camp tradition or through various Hindu Students Councils at various US campuses. The US Hindutva phenomenon reflects a characteristic global process of ultra-nationalism by a reltively young community of professionals and students that has chosen to leave India, and yet supports financially the Hindutva movement "at home" and attempts to dominate the representation of Hindus or India in the US media and within political fora. In both areas it has been very successful.

In the UK, the Hindutva movement, first organisationally established in 1973 (though it is claimed that the first *sangh shaka* was formed in the mid-1960s), has been subject to a longer more complex and varied process of South Asian community formation and settlement and the rise of communal-religious conflict in recent years. Both the RSS and the VHP are well established in the UK. Perhaps their most important events were the Virat Hindu Sammelan organised in Milton Keynes in 1989 and attended by some 50,000 Hindus, as well as their Hindu Sangam in Bradford in 1984. The RSS's current UK structure reflects the centralist structure of its Indian parent. This includes the idiosyncratic titles and tiers that RSS members and officers have: executives (*sanghchalak*), organisers (*karyawahas*), guides/intellectuals (*bauddhiks*), teachers (*mukya shikshaks*), probationary officers (*vistaraks*) and full-time officers (*pracharaks*). The RSS women's affiliate in the UK, the Rashtriya Sevika Samiti, has a parallel national structure. The RSS has branches across the UK, and several regional offices. It is organised by region (*vibhag*), city (*nagar*) and local branch (*shaka*) level. There are over 20 regular *shakas* as well as *sevika samitis* in London (mainly in west London, Brent, Newham and Essex). Organisationally, the RSS is strongest in the South East and Midlands, though with a strong presence in Bradford, Oldham, Manchester and Bolton. Attendance at its regular *shakas* is fairly low, ranging from 15 at a local *shaka* or *samiti* to 150 at a city level event involving both men and women. However, at public events, the RSS can muster a much larger attendance of local Hindus, invited Asian guests and other local dignitaries, the latter typically local councillors and officers. In some areas, the RSS has managed to cultivate extremely strong and regular associations with the local authority, the city council, education authorities or political parties. The National Hindu Students Federation (NHSF), which, like many of its US counterparts, uses a key RSS corporate slogan ("A vision in action") is still fairly small in comparison with other student bodies. It is dominated by RSS-Hindutva philosophy and several officers of its central executive are RSS members or younger RSS officers, including RSS *vistaraks*. It receives its instructions from the RSS and its main officers indeed meet at RSS head offices. Its political orientation can be gauged from the title of one of its leaflets—*The smokescreen of 'Asian Unity'*—establishing a Hindu youth agenda (NHSF 1996). During the campaigns in the mid-1990s by the National Union of Students against the activities of the fringe Islamic fundamentalist Hizb ut Tahrir, the NHSF joined Jewish and gay student groups in demanding its banning. A key claim in their national campaign against the "religious persecution" of Hindu university students was the forced conversion to Islam of young Hindu women by the Hizb—a curious transplantation of an Indian VHP agenda onto UK campuses.

The political concerns of the RSS family in the UK and US have revolved around several main themes: the authoritarian policing of the popular representation of Hinduism; the organisational, cultural, historical and national representation of Hindu communities in official public and policy fora; the desecularisation of the languages of minority South Asian political negotiation; the assertion of one particular kind of militant Hindu identity with self-evident needs that have to be articulated, typically antagonistically in diverse political processes; and the mobilisation of community support for BJP-RSS-VHP ventures in India. The RSS has faced little sustained political opposition in the UK except for activities of the small South Asian secular left, some strands within the women's movement and, indirectly, by progressive and syncretic South Asian youth cultures whose transgressions, "blasphemies" and "sin" they increasingly seek to discipline, even though such Semitic concepts are typically alien to Hinduisms. Hindu nationalist sensitivities about the representation of Hindu icons, texts, symbols and especially deities are particularly acute and it would not be surprising if the authoritarian surveillance of the representation of images, idols and text came to dominate much of their activism in the UK, just as it has with many Islamist groups. Indeed the equivalence and convergence in political activism and language between ostensibly adversarial fundamentalisms, Christian, Jewish, Islamic or Hindu, is a key sociological feature.

Cultural Incommensurability and the Field of Intellectual Production

One dominant aspect of the political projects of many fundamentalist movements is the claim that their conceptual and epistemic schemes are unique and not capable of translation and comprehension from a "foreign" or "western" gaze. These absolutist claims about cultural incommensurability are remarkably similar to those made within many recent western postmodern or postcolonial theoretical writings. Religious fundamentalism has indeed provided the empirical example for the most obscurantist varieties of cultural and epistemic relativism in some contemporary multicultural theory. However, it needs emphasising that apart from its many epistemological problems, claims about cultural incommensurability can never be self-evident but are an intrinsic part of the political strategy employed by fundamentalist movements to disavow the legitimacy of oppositional political critiques. The claim is made that reason and rationality, arbitrarily identified as "western," cannot legitimately provide a foundation for the critique of Hindu nationalism since the latter, in the form of its metaphysical spirituality, exists prior to the emergence of reason itself (Bhatt 1997).

Cultural incommensurability and its sibling strategy, the self-conscious cultivation of epistemic vagueness in core political concepts, is a key tactic of the Hindutva movement. However, despite the consistent and vigorous claims of the Hindutva movement that concepts such as "*dharma*" and "*rashtra*" are untranslatable into western concepts of "religion" and "nation-state or "nationalism," many of the aims of Hindutva movement are based on very familiar modern-authoritarian political conceptions. The Hindutva movement is primarily a majoritarian movement that demands, to differing degrees, an exclusive Hindu *rashtra* or Hindu nation-state which provides the precepts for the obligations of citizenship for all those, including all minorities, who live within the national territory. A Hindu *rashtra* is frequently, though not always, conceived to be genuinely secular and reflecting simply the "Hindu ethos," "Hindu civilisation" or Hindu *dharma* that has moulded and shaped the lives of Hindus, Buddhists, Jains and Sikhs over a period seen to be commencing from some ineffable, primordial moment. In this register, Hindu *dharma* is presented as secular and non-discriminatory. Consequently, it is frequently claimed that Hinduism and the Hindu nation-state are the basis for a genuine secularism. The Indian Supreme Court in its wisdom indeed made the appalling judgement in the mid-1990s that Hindutva was, like Hinduism, intrinsically secular (M. Rama Jois 1996).

Dharma is a key trope in Hindu nationalist political language. Its meaning is held to be both ineffable and totalising and this is central to the manner of its use by the Hindutva movement. It is also monotonously claimed that *dharma* is unique and untranslatable from a foreign gaze. In many varieties of Hinduism, *dharma* has compounded meanings that include religion, religious law (as in jurisprudence), a religious code of conduct, way of life, an ethics, or more broadly the natural order of things, "natural law," the righteous path, following the ordinances of sacred revelation or tradition, "the way things are" or "the way things ought to be." There are many sect and subcaste *dharmashastras*[7] ("law books") that can govern or inform the lives of Hindus to widely varying degrees. In the practical lives of Hindus, *dharma* is more mundane. In many (north Indian) Hindu sects or subcastes, *dharma* can define rules for, for example, caste mixing and marriage, birth and death rites, gender relations, food and the compulsion to respect one's parents. It is a fundamentally religious, typically ritualistic conception. However, in Hindu nationalism it is disingenuously claimed to be secular since *dharma* is held to be the basis for Hinduism's unique traditional tolerance and reverence for all paths towards the Ineffable. The typical religious source used by many secularists and Hindu nationalists alike, is Rig Veda 1:164:46, "It is of one existence that the sages speak in many ways."[8] However, arguably, "tolerance" was an attribute ascribed to Hinduism, and against Islam, in the modern colonial period, and was dependent on the reformative strands of modern Hinduism that eventually culminated in Gandhianism. Similarly, the ahistoricised conception of *dharma* promoted in Hindu nationalism is a distinctly brahminic one, the ideal of *sanatana dharma*, the eternal ethical order of things. These ideas of Hindu *dharma* are claimed to be unique, and Hinduism is held to be a unique code for human and natural existence that cannot be compared with other religious traditions. Hinduism in this view is a complete universal order for life,[9] whereas Christianity and Islam are simply religious ideologies.

Hinduism, in this sense, is articulated in the Hindutva movement as not a religion at all but an eternally valid ethical code, a distinct orientation to the temporal and spiritual world, the natural social and political order, the fulfilment of civilisation and a world-view for humankind. It cannot, therefore, be compared with or comprehended by external western or Islamic paradigms. If Hinduism (Hindu *dharma*) can be conceptualised not as a religion but as an incommensurable civilisational ethos, a further claim can be made that Hinduism is itself a tolerant genuinely secular way of being and not a religion as such. Descriptions such as fundamentalism, fascism, authoritarianism can be dismissed as western concepts that are inapplicable to Hinduism (see for example Goel [1983] 1994a, Frawley 1995a). Consequently, state and civil society can be *dharmic* and secular, even as all citizens can be compelled to live by Hindu *dharma* and love and adulation for the Hindu nation.

This kind of holistic revolutionary conservatism is not, however, simply the package of prejudice and exclusivist identity politics that emerges in its political languages. The Hindutva movement has cultivated its own "field of intellectual production: (Bourdieu 1991). Whatever the critical rational evaluation of its intellectual content, Hindu nationalism is a deeply intellectual enterprise and it would be a fundamental error to reduce its intellectual and cultural strategy to "chauvinism" or propaganda, or to reduce its political trajectory to only that of seeking elected power or political representation. In Hindu nationalism one can speak of the creation of a major revisionist project around nation, state, civil society, culture, religion, ethnicity, metaphysics and human origins. Its form is manifest in the now incalculably large body of literature produced or fundamentally influenced by far-right-wing Hindu nationalist ideologues. This has attempted to breach the boundaries and methods of research and verification within several intellectual disciplines, including social and cultural history, ancient and medieval history, archaeology, philosophy and metaphysics, anthropology, sociology, political science, religious studies, natural science and mathematics, education and pedagogy, astronomy, linguistics, comparative philology and human geography. In the process the Hindutva movement has managed to carve out a characteristic intellectual field. This has a typically antagonistic conceptual border (anti-secular, anti-Muslim, anti-marxist, anti-western) that is necessary for its reproduction. Its intellectual content is reproduced by a relatively large and international orbit of writers and critics. Its political languages and academic-nationalist thematics are discrete, distinguishable, and broadly unified. Its intellectual disagreements occur within its own field and mutually reinforce the field itself, but much of the core and productive nationalist content and its "thematic and lexical ramifications" are shared.

THE LONG NINETEENTH CENTURY

The intellectual antecedents of both the Hindutva movement and of many modern Hinduisms are complex and related to several ideological currents, prominent from the mid-1850s that were concerned to re-present, and in many ways recreate Hinduism in relation to modern political and social systems during a period of colonial domination. There are several aspects of this complex and diverse period of the mid-nineteenth-century "Hindu Renaissance" that are worth noting briefly because they have important contemporary resonances. This period can also be viewed as reconstructive of certain strands of especially, but not exclusively, elite, brahminic or higher-caste Hindu thinking. In the face of the challenge and ethical claims of colonial Christianity, several mostly elite organisations undertook the project of demonstrating the ethical content or superiority of an intellectual Hinduism that was concerned to shed what was perceived as its polytheism and idolatry and its backward practices regarding the status of women and the injustice of the caste system. Both the liberal Brahmo Samaj (1828) and the "fundamentalist" Arya Samaj (1875) can be seen as representative of some of these strands.

As important was the necessity of negotiating with key political concepts that made a modernist Hinduism thinkable: nation, the people, citizenship, self-determination, representation, equality, autonomy, state and civil society. Put differently, how could elite Hinduism reconstruct itself within the framework of modern procedural, bureaucratic, scientific and technical rationality? How could Hinduism simultaneously negotiate both secular rationality and affective nationalism in a period of colonial and imperial domination? Perhaps the third important strand was an intense negotiation with, and recovery of, important philosophical aspects of Vedic and Upanishadic Hinduism, which elite Hinduism could use to develop an epistemic and ethical resource both for modernity and against western colonial modernity. A related and powerful syncretic current from within the nineteenth century "Hindu Renaissance" that continued to resonate deeply in numerous, otherwise antagonistic conceptions of modern Hinduism in this century was the belief not only in the universality of Hinduism but of its relevance outside India. Hinduism was not necessarily superior to other religious or ideological systems, though that claim was (and is) enunciated often enough, but rather that its metaphysical resources and epistemic and ethical systems, especially those of tolerance, peace, pluralism, and organicist reverence for all of creation provided a foundational example for all other ideological and political systems. Hinduism's revelation was the *a priori* for all other religious systems. Hinduism in some fundamental way could not be compared to any other religion, just as India was a country unlike any other. In this register, deeply resonant in the contemporary Hindutva movement, Hinduism was the seat of all religion and revelation, just as India was the cradle of all civilisation.

The Aryas: Philology and Ethnology

Another important though often ambiguous strand emerged during the nineteenth century that was concerned with the recovery of the Hindu present by cultivating its primordial past. This was quite fundamentally reliant on the discoveries from the mid-eighteenth century of both British philology and Germany Indology. The contemporary Hindutva movement also closely follows the epistemic trajectory of early Indology, expressed through that early German love affair with India during the late eighteenth century, in the period during and after the French revolution. Charles Wilkins's translation of Sanskrit and Sir William Jones's discovery in the 1780s of the philological similarities between Greek, Latin and archaic Sanskrit, and his discussions of the antiquity and perfection of the Sanskrit language and its grammar, provided rich material for those who sought a new, non-Biblical, and importantly a non-Semitic, non-Hebraic origin for "the obscurer portions" of European, especially German history and civilisation (Poliakov 1974). In Germany and to a lesser degree France, from the eighteenth century onwards, this became a major justification for the fascination with India.

Frederick Schlegel's *On the language and wisdom of the Indians* (Schlegel 1849), published in 1808, contained several key points that were to become so effective later: India received the primordial revelation (and, he added, the primordial errors); world civilisation emerged either from Indian migration out of India or from Indian influence; Greek, Latin, Hebraic and Arabic language and mythology are already both superseded and captured in Sanskrit and in the Vedic religion; Indian spiritual and mystical reverence for a "northern place" was the basis for Indian outward migration, which led ultimately to the formation of the Teutonic races in northern Europe.[10]

For Schlegel the Teutons were descendants of the primordial Indians (for his brother August Wilhelm, Germany was the "orient of Europe"). Similar themes were to differing degrees embraced by other writers. India was seen as the site of the first revelation (Herder) or civilisation (Kant, among numerous Enlightenment thinkers, including the encylopaedists). Hinduism's key concepts, such as "metempsychosis" provided other writers with a "pessimistic immortalism" which was contrasted with life-denying ethics of Judaeo-Christianity (Schopenhauer). However, much of this "arche-philology" became immensely complicated towards the late eighteenth century. Max Muller, the British-German Indologist, had in the mid-1800s argued comprehensively for the popularisation of "the technical term, Aryan" to refer to the group of languages which Frederick Schlegel had earlier called "Indo-Germanic" and Franz Bopp had called "Indo-European" (various other names were popular in Britain, including "Japhetic," "Sanskritic" or "Mediterranean"). "Aryan," which was borrowed from the archaic Sanskrit *arya*[11] and the Zend Avestan *airya*, "had the advantage of being short, and being of foreign origin lending itself more easily to any technical definition" (Muller 1881: 205). Muller also explicitly and often inadvertently created a convergence between the *arya* language and the *arya* people, itself reflective of a problematic disciplinary equivalence between comparative philology and ethnology that was to have such horrifying consequences in this century. Some of this was based on translations of the Rig Veda which, it was claimed, showed the Aryans as both a warrior race and one that was distinctly organised on racial-colour and "nobility"[12] hierarchies (caste). The *aryas*, it was claimed, had a definitive xenology whose victims were the ("dark-skinned, stub-nosed") *dasyus*, *mlecchas* ("foreigners" or "barbarians") and other non-*arya* speaking groups (Thapar 1996a).

The third, and perhaps consequential focus was on the origins of the Aryans. Schlegel's original lineage was increasingly modified (a project that continues to today) and the primordial Aryan homeland moved westwards and northwards out of India proper and settled variously in Persia, the Caucasus, the Russian steppe, "Atlantis," Lithuania or the Balkans generally, the Mediterranean or Greece, Germany, Scandinavia, Eire and even the North Pole.[13] Max Muller, exasperated by many of these debates, retracted his earlier discussions of the Aryans as a racial rather than a linguistic group, and was eventually to conclude that the primordial Aryan linguistic homeland was "somewhere in Asia" (Muller 1888: 127). However, Aryanist thinking had already travelled widely and by the mid 1800s in the hands of Joseph Arthur de Gobineau, became a fully-fledged theory of white Aryan-noble racial supremacy. In the case of Houston Stewart Chamberlain, Wagner and the Bayreuth Circle, it became a vicious anti-semitism (Mosse 1966), a refraction of an earlier metaphysics in which the Judeo-Christian and the Hindu-Buddhist were antagonistically polarised (Schopenhauer 1890).

Aryanism and Hindutva

The importance of Aryanism for the contemporary Hindutva movement has been highlighted by the Indian historian Romila Thapar (1996b). A distinctive variety of Aryanist thinking, often metonymically linked to a separate hereditarian discourse, aspects of which were already embedded in many varieties of Hinduism, became an important current from the late nineteenth century in colonial India itself. Hindu discussions about Aryan origins are probably best represented in the speeches and writings of the nationalist activist and spiritualist Aurobindo Ghose during the early part of this century. Aurobindo, a spiritual source of emulation for both the Hindutva movement and for some remarkably reactionary strands of a burgeoning "New Age evolutionism" (Danino and Nahar 1996), stated that Aryans were autochthonous to India and the theory of an Aryan migration into or invasion of India was a British colonialist myth that sought to deny India's unique, superlative nature.

However, Hindutva appropriations of Aryanism only really became important after the 1930s. For the founders of the contemporary Hindutva movement, western Aryanism presented an obvious epistemic problem. The evidences of English and German comparative linguistics and Indology suggested Aryans entered from outside physical India, and hence the idea of an immemorial originary cultural hearth in which the physical land, culture and people intermingled to give rise to Hindu civilisation is already disturbed at its origin by a founding presence which is alien to the land. In the 1920s Savarkar indeed initially argued for a hybrid origin for Vedic civilisation: it was the mixture of the blood of the Aryans and the people they encountered that gave rise to Vedic-Hindu civilisation, though evidently only the Aryan blood was of any consequence. Savarkar articulated the birth of Vedic civilisation through a Lamarckian conception whereby the physical land and environment impressed upon, and was conversely affected by the Aryan people so as to instil a unique *hereditary* quality to land, culture and people. Savarkar provided an archetypal genealogy of cultural hearth and reverence for the land, imagined as the first and best land of the Aryans. The essence of Aryan culture was *hindutva*, the "beingness" of a Hindu that defines a common nation (*rashtra*), race (*jati*) and civilisation (*sankskriti* culture). Hindutva is transmitted patrilinearly by blood and apprehended by a *feeling*, a structure of emotion that makes a Hindu realise his or her true connection with the sublime civilisation of the Vedic Aryans (Savarkar [1923] 1989). Savarkar's powerful "race concept" combines land, heredity, affect, an ancestral blood community, and an originary Vedism. But, at least in its earlier form, it still depended on an external invasive event.

In later Hindutva writers, just as in Aurobindo's writings, this hybrid, syncretic Aryan origin for Hinduism is simply rejected and, in a fundamentally instructive move, Schlegel's (and indeed the Enlightenment's) original thesis is resurrected. For Golwalkar, the RSS's second and perhaps most important "Supreme Guide and Philosopher," the idea of an Aryan invasion of India was a product of colonialism, aimed to denigrate Hindus. Against this view, Golwalkar stated that Hindus had existed in India from time immemorial: "Undoubtedly ... we Hindus have been in undisputed and undisturbed possession of this land for over 8 or even 10 thousand years before the land was invaded by any foreign race." (Golwalkar [1939] 1944)

FROM LANGUAGE TO ARCHAEOLOGY

[...] It is exactly around these issues the Hindutva movement and its western New Age[14] apologists have forcefully intervened over the last few years in an imposing revisionist project that has regenerated an epistemic obsession with primordial Aryanism in many Hindutva or Hinducentric circles (Gupta 1996; Singh 1995; Sethna 1989, 1992; Talageri 1993a, 1993b; Rajaram 1995; Rajaram and Frawley 1997; Shendge 1996; Danino and Nahar 1996; Kak 1989 and 1992; Feuerstein, Kak and Frawley 1995). The rewriting of history, both medieval[15]and ancient, has become a dominant theme in the literary outpourings of the Hindutva movement, as well as of other Hinducentric efforts. The project appropriated by the Hindutva movement may well be dependent on a recent intellectual reassessment of India's and Pakistan's antiquity in which more recent archaeological and geographical discoveries might suggest that the Indus Valley civilisations were both more extensive and older than may have been assumed. However, the pace of actual archaeological scholarship, the possibilities of rethinking Indian antiquity against western colonial distortions, and the speculations and fancies of Hindu nationalists have become mixed up in these recent interventions. The Hindutva movement has instead attempted to set the agenda for debate and create "commonsense" worldviews about India's and Pakistan's antiquity that shortcut the methods of traditional scholarship, and which would have relied, in different circumstances, on a necessary mobilisation of the whole critical intellectual process itself.

It is in the interests of the Hindutva movement to claim, despite the archaeological and linguistic evidence to the contrary, that the Indus Valley civilisation was Aryan in language, culture, ethnicity and "nobility," Vedic in religion, and Sanskritic in civilisation. Several other consequences immediately follow, for such claims imply that Aryans were autochthonous and not usurpers, that a fundamentally Aryan civilisation was the first world civilisation, that all other civilisations were its direct or indirect products, that the differentiations between Indo-Aryan and other Indian languages are colonial racist fabrications, and that, instead, all Indian languages and cultural products are essentially derived from one ethnic, indigenous, non-invasive Aryan culture and civilisation. This, of course, also provides a far greater lineage for Hinduism, and confirms not only its primordial antiquity, but its superlative and original genesis in that first civilisational hearth, "the best land of the Aryans." The congruence of this Aryan "prehistory" with that developed in early German orientalism, and its exact mirroring in the western racial Aryanism that animated the pre-Nazi and Nazi periods, is less important than the general Aryan primordialism that all these tendencies share.

Much of this unsettled Hindutva Aryanist thinking, which can itself be cloaked in volkish "anti-racist" and "anti-imperialist" rhetoric, illustrates how *varieties of Aryanism* are important to contemporary politics, and that Aryanism continues to be a resource for origin myths that are not completed by the kind of specifically western white Aryanism that dominated Europe, and especially Germany, earlier this century. In late modernity, authoritarian movements have arisen again that seek to ideologically combine an organic and holistic natural social order, a purified nationality, a primeval mysticism, and a belief in a superlative civilisation that was created by an ancestral community of blood.

NOTES

I would like to thank John Solomos, Jane Hindley and Parita Mukta for comments on an earlier draft.

1. Or just "sangh," whose meaning sits suggestively between "organisation" and "society."
2. The term "racism" is used in describing aspects of Hindutva discourse throughout the essay despite its very different meanings in many contemporary western debates about "race" and racism. This is acknowledged to be a deeply problematic area and its taxonomic difficulties are symptomatic of a wider epistemic shift that is necessary in thinking through a range of absolutist ideologies of primordial indigenism.
3. "Sect" is a misleading term in relation to branches of Hinduism, or varieties of Hindu belief and practice, but is used for convenience.
4. Savarkar's genesis of Hindutva is worth contrasting with, for example, Gobineau's or Houston Stewart Chamberlain's or Alfred Rosenberg's view of the racial degradation of the Aryans once their blood mixed with that of the original Indians.
5. It is likely that Golwalkar's *We* ... was a paraphrasing of Savarkar's brother, Babarao's earlier work.
6. The appeal to religious sensibilities during the nuclear tests should be noted. The tests, like those undertaken in the 1970s, were conducted on Buddha purnima. The Vishwa Hindu Parishad has declared the test site holy and is planning to build there a temple to the Mother God-

dess (*shaktipeeth*, a "seat of strength") that symbolises India's resurgence as a nuclear power. "We are no longer eunuchs," declared the Shiv Sena. Some parivar activists wanted to distribute sand from the site throughout India as a religious symbol and offering, though this idea was abandoned because of possible harmful radiation. If the literal worship and deification of nuclear bombs whose only purpose is mass human destruction seems obscene, it also illustrates how far the contemporary representatives of Hinduism have travelled from Hinduism itself. The inevitable claim that nuclear weapons are traditional to Hinduism was also made: the fire god Agni in the Vedas was proof, it was said, that the ancient Hindus possessed nuclear bombs, *India Abroad* 22.S.98.

7. The *Manu Dharmashastra* is often held to be the archaic basis for many other (north Indian Hindu) *dharmic* regulations that may use, or oppose, its precepts. But the point is that *dharma* is an abstract term for an extremely widely varying series of caste or subcaste, sect and regional regulations.
8. The full verse (Griffith translation, 1896) is: "They call him Indra, Mithra, Varuna, Agni, and he is heavenly nobly-winged Garutman. To what is One [Reality], sages give many a title [name]: they call it Agni, Yama, Matarisvan.'
9. This exact claim is, of course, also made in Islamist and other fundamentalist movements.
10. This critical idea of the mountainous cold north derived from an interpretation of the Rig Veda and the reverence with which the Aryans held mountains, possibly the Himalayas, has influenced numerous writers, up to the present period. Kant held this cradle to be Tibet, and later writers assumed the Caucasus. A north pole origin for the Aryans gained currency from various interpretations of the Rig Veda and was pronounced again this century by Tilak, a founder and leader of the Indian National Congress.
11. The word *arya* occurs over 30 times in the ancient Sanskrit Rig Veda, and may have been used in this and in the ancient Persian Zend Avesta as a description of self by the putative groups who composed the original versions of these texts. It is also used much more freely in later Indian Buddhist texts to describe a quality, usually considered to be "noble."
12. What it translated as "nobility" or "noble" in western thinking requires a much fuller discussion than can be provided here, especially because the western use of the concept of nobility has been so fundamentally important in the histories of "race thinking." Similarly, the ease with which aristocratic ideals, nobility, culture and hierarchy are translated into their archaic Hindu counterparts (and vice versa) require much further elaboration. "Nobility" is also of considerable importance for Hindutva apologists for the caste system and for arya xenology.
13. Childe (1926) is an earlier overview, useful for illustrating both an abhorrence of racism and a warrior or dynamic quality to the Aryan. For the current state of debate on Aryan origins and homeland, see Mallory (1989). Renfrew (1987) is perhaps the main scholarly western advocate for an Indian Aryan homeland. The recent, numerous Indian and Hindutva contributions are discussed below, and tend to argue for an Aryan primordial homeland in the east, especially in northern- or central-eastern India.
14. The relation between some syncretic western spiritual movements and varieties of deep conservatism, including racism and racial Aryanism, are considerable. The transmutation of some strands of the New Thought movement and some strands of Theosophy in the earlier parts of this century into a specifically Aryan religion, Ariosophy, which formed the epistemic content for Nazism's natural religion has been brilliantly described by Goodrick-Clarke (1985). It is important to note the marriage between the far-right Hindutva ideology and western New Ageism in the works of writer like David Frawley (1994, 1995a, 1995b), who is both a key apologist for the Hindutva movement and author of various New Age books on Vedic astrology, oracles and yoga. Similarly, Subhash Kak, a collaborator on a work that is both distinctively New Ageist and rehearses the Hindutva obsession with a arya-Vedic primordialism (Feuerstein, Kak and Frawley 1995), is also a Hindu nationalist writer who has a substantial publications record on Aryans in *Mankind Quarterly*, perhaps the most important academic racist eugenicist journal in the west.
15. The revision of medieval Indian history is at least as important to the Hindutva project, and in many respects far more important for its immediate political purposes than the obsession with ancient India, but cannot be discussed here for reasons of space. However, it should be noted that historical revisionism around the medieval, especially Mughal period constitutes a monumental project for the Hindutva movement. The project is single-minded in its desire to demonstrate that the medieval period was one of Muslim religious conquest and oppression of non-aggressive and tolerant Hindus. Virtually everything disagreeable within Hinduism is traced to this period and viewed as either as a consequence of Islamic rule or as an intrinsic attribute of Islam that has polluted Hinduism. This includes caste and caste discrimination, tribe formation, purdah, harems, bonded labour systems, corruption, poverty, women's oppression, educational backwardness, obscurantism, alongside the more typical discussions of religious oppression of Hindus, genocide, minorityism and so forth (Lal 1992, 1994, 1995; Rai 1993, 1994). Everything considered agreeable with Hinduism, especially wars that can be reinterpreted from the gaze of the present as simply "heroic Hindu resistance against Muslim invaders," is celebrated within this historical revisionism. See Goel [1983] 1994a.

REFERENCES

Bhatt, C. 1997. *Liberation and Purity.* London: UCL Press.

Bhatt, C. 1999. "Ethnic absolutism and the authoritarian spirit." *Theory, Culture and Society* 16(2).

Bourdieu, P. 1991. *The Political Ontology of Martin Heidegger.* Cambridge: Polity.

Childe, V.G. 1926. *The Aryans*. London: Kegan Paul.

Danino, M., and Nahar, S. 1996. *The Invasion That Never Was*. Mysore: Mira Aditi.

Dhavalikar, M.K. 1995. *Cultural Imperialism: Indus Civilisation in Western India*. New Delhi: Books and Books.

Feuerstein, G., Kak, S., and Frawley, D. 1995. *In Search of the Cradle of Civilisation*. Wheaton, Ill.: Quest.

Frawley, D. 1994. *The Myth of the Aryan Invasion of India*. New Delhi: Voice of India.

Frawley, D. 1995a. *Hinduism: the Eternal Tradition*. New Delhi: Voice of India.

Frawley, D. 1995b. *Arise Arjuna: Hinduism and the Modern World*. New Delhi: Voice of India.

Gautier, F. 1994. *The Wonder That Is India*. New Delhi: Voice of India.

Goel, S.R. [1983] 1994a. *Defence of Hindu Society*. New Delhi: Voice of India.

Goel, S.R. 1994b. *Heroic Hindu Resistance to Muslim Invaders*. New Delhi: Voice of India.

Golwalkar, M.S. [1939] 1944. *We, Or Our Nationhood Defined*, second edn. Nagpur: Bharat Publications.

Golwalkar, M.S. 1966. *Bunch of Thoughts*. Bangalore: Vikrama Prakashan.

Goodrick-Clarke, N. 1985. *The Occult Roots of Nazism*. New York: New York University Press.

Gupta, S.P. 1996. *The Indus-Saraswati Civilisation: Origins, Problems, Issues*. Delhi: Pratibha Prakashan.

Jaffrelot, C. 1995. "The idea of the Hindu race." In P. Robb, ed., *The Concept of Race in South Asia*. Delhi: Oxford University Press.

Jois, M.R. 1996. *Supreme Court Judgment on Hindutva: An Important Landmark*. New Delhi: Suruchi Prakashan.

Kak, S.C. 1989. "Indus writing," *Mankind Quarterly* 30: 113–118.

Kak, S.C. 1992. "The Indus tradition and the Indo-Aryans," *Mankind Quarterly* 32: 195–213.

Lal, K.S. 1990. *Indian Muslims—Who Are They?* New Delhi: Voice of India.

Lal, K.S. 1992. *The Legacy of Muslim Rule in India*. New Delhi: Aditya Prakashan.

Lal, K.S. 1994. *Muslim Slave System in Medieval India*. New Delhi: Aditya Prakashan.

Lal, K.S. 1995. *Growth of Scheduled Tribes and Castes in Medieval India*. New Delhi: Voice of India.

Lele, J. 1995. *Hindutva: The Emergence of the Right*. Madras: Earthworm Books. Mallory, J.P. 1989. *In Search of the Indo-Europeans: Language, Archaeology, Myth*. London: Thames & Hudson.

Mosse, G.L. 1966. *The Crisis of German Ideology*. London: Weidenfeld & Nicholson.

Muller, F.M. 1881. *Selected Essays on Language, Mythology and Religion*, vol. I. London: Longmans, Green & Co.

Muller, F.M. 1888. *Biographies of Words and The Home of the Aryas*. London: Longmans, Green & Co.

Panikkar, K.N. 1997. *Communal Threat Secular Challenge*. Madras: Earthworm Books.

Poliakov, L. 1974. *The Aryan Myth: A History of Racist and Nationalist Ideas in Europe*.

London: Chatto Heinemann.

Rai, B. 1993. *Demographic Aggression Against India*. Chandigarh: B.S. Publishers.

Rai, B. 1994. *Is India Going Islamic?* Chandigarh: B.S. Publishers.

Rajaram, N.S. 1995. *The Politics of History: Aryan Invasion Theory and the Subversion of Scholarship*. New Delhi: Voice of India.

Rajaram, N.S., and Frawley, D. 1997. *Vedic Aryans and the Origins of Civilisation*. New Delhi: Voice of India.

Renfrew, C. 1987. *Archaeology and Language*. Cambridge: University Press.

Savarkar, V.D. [1923] 1989. *Hindutva—Who is a Hindu?* sixth edn. Bombay: Veer Savarkar Prakashan.

Schlegel, F. 1849. *Aesthetic and Miscellaneous Works* London: Henry G. Bohn.

Schopenhauer, A. 1890. *Studies in Pessimism* London: George Allen & Unwin.

Sethna, K.D. 1989. *Ancient India in a New Light* New Delhi: Aditya.

Sethna, K.D. 1992. *The Problem of Aryan Origins From an Indian Point of View*, second edn. New Delhi: Aditya Prakashan.

Shendge, M.J. 1996. *The Aryas: Facts without Fancy or Fiction*. New Delhi: Abhinav.

Singh, B. 1995. *The Vedic Harappans*. New Delhi: Aditya Prakashan.

Solomos, J., and Back, L. 1996. *Racism and Society*. London: Macmillan.

Talageri, S.G. 1993a. *Aryan Invasion Theory and Indian Nationalism*. New Delhi: Voice of India.

Talageri, S.G. 1993b. *The Aryan Invasion Theory: A Reappraisal*. New Delhi: Aditya Prakashan.

Thapar, R. 1991. "A historical perspective on the story of Rama." In S. Gopal, ed., *The Anatomy of a Confrontation*. New Delhi: Penguin.

Thapar, R. 1996a. *Ancient Indian Social History: Some Interpretations*. London: Sangarn.

Thapar, R. 1996b. "The theory of Aryan race and India: history and polities." *Social Scientist* 24, 1–3, Jan-Mar.

Upadhyaya, D. 1991. *Ideology and Perception, Part. II: Integral Humanism*. New Delhi:

Suruchi Prakashan.

Wheeler, M. 1963. *Early India and Pakistan to Ashoka*. London: Thames & Hudson.

FURTHER READING

Dipboye, Robert L., and Adrienne Colella, eds. 2005. *Discrimination at Work: The Psychological and Organizational Bases*. Mahwah, NJ: Lawrence Erlbaum Associates.

Discrimination at Work is an eclectic compilation of research, theories, and perspectives on discrimination in the workplace. As a part of the Organizational Frontier Series, this volume explores workplace discrimination at the individual, group, and organizational levels, identifying its manifestations based on race and ethnicity, religion, sexual orientation, age, disability, personality, as well as physical appearance. The result is a comprehensive volume that integrates the varied disciplines, literatures, and bodies of research that address workplace discrimination, and lays the foundation for a general model for an important issue.

Gilroy, Paul. 1987. *"There Ain't No Black in the Union Jack": The Cultural Politics of Race and Nation*. London: Hutchinson.

Gilroy demonstrates the enormous complexity of racial politics in England today. Exploring the relationships among race, class, and nation as they have evolved over the past 20 years, he highlights racist attitudes that transcend the left-right political divide. He challenges current sociological approaches to racism as well as the ethnocentric bias of British cultural studies.

Goldberg, David Theo. 1990. *Anatomy of Racism*. Minneapolis: University of Minnesota Press.

This collection of essays discusses the persistent and multifarious nature of racism. By exposing the historical as well as the contemporary forms of racist practices, discourses, and expressions, the author shows that racism, though constantly undergoing transformations, remains a significant constant. The implications for social identity are highlighted and collective resistance and opposition to racism are voiced.

Miles, Robert. 1989. *Racism*. New York: Routledge

In *Racism*, Miles powerfully depicts the evolution and expansion of the dynamic concept of racism. From debates on "racism as ideology" to debates on "institutional racism" and the "new racism," Miles illuminates the central place of the concept in historical and contemporary capitalist societies. He argues that racism is best seen as an "ideology," and that while it does not describe a biological or material fact, the concept should continue to be used in sociological analysis.

UNESCO. 1980. *Sociological Theories: Race and Colonialism*. Paris: UNESCO.

In this volume, various authors address the concept of race within the context of traditional and contemporary sociological theories. Drawing on the theories of Weber, Marx, and Durkeim, as well as pluralist, rational choice, and dependency theories, the authors in this volume show how race is integral to the ways in which societies have been structured in particular historical periods.

Winant, Howard. 1994. *Racial Conditions: Politics, Theory, Comparisons*. Minneapolis: University of Minnesota Press.

This book addresses the gaps in our understanding of contemporary racial dynamics and develops a powerful theoretical approach to the vast subject of race. The author argues that race cannot be understood as a "social problem" or as a "survival" of earlier, more benighted ages. The key to Winant's analysis is racial formation theory, an approach he refines and advances as he considers a wide range of contemporary controversies in racial theory and politics. Among these are the relationship between race and class, as well as the racial dimensions of gender, diaspora, colonialism, and fascism.

PART 2

EXPERIENCES OF COLONIALISM AND RACISM

PART 2A

INDIGENEITY AND COLONIALISM

Indigenous peoples are among the most disadvantaged on earth. Given that they are the most diverse grouping of humanity and constitute a large percentage of the global population, how can such a grouping—one so diverse that it defies simple definition—be so uniformly disadvantaged, occupying the bottom of most qualify of life indicators boasted about by the nation-states within which indigenous peoples continue to reside? The answer lies in another experience common to all indigenous peoples: colonization. All of today's indigenous peoples have experienced, and continue to experience, colonization in one form or another. Historically, colonizing powers dominated territories belonging to others and conceptualized these occupant societies as "others." Placed in juxtaposition with these colonizing societies, indigenous peoples were positioned as inferior societies with inferior religion, language, and morals, and, as such, without civilization (see part 1B). The conceptualization of the indigene or the "Native" as inferior was required to justify the exploitation of their labour, lands, and other resources, as well as to justify their exclusion from any substantial benefits of the colonial economy. The racialization of colonial societies was entrenched as the "Natives" were eventually either incorporated into the state apparatus as wards or forced to occupy remote areas as marginalized minorities. The economic and social exclusion of indigenous peoples served as a particular form of racialization and remains an enduring feature of the national character of so-called democratic nation-states with indigenous populations within their borders. In this section, we explore the present situation and its more complex past by highlighting the role of disease epidemics, the subsequent impact of economic globalization, the representation of contemporary indigeneity by dominant society, and the politicization of Saami (the indigenous peoples of Norway and Sweden).

The first reading in this section, "Settling In"—part of Noble David Cook's *Born to Die*—traces the genocidal impact of diseases brought by colonizers on indigenous peoples in the South American and Caribbean regions. Cook argues that indigenous societies were conquered not by the natural superiority of explicit colonial strategies, but rather by the devastating impact of compound epidemics—i.e., multiple disease epidemics that followed closely in the same time and space. Surviving the initial wave of disease often simply delayed an inevitable death to the second, third, or fourth waves. Essentially, Cook argues that colonial subjugation was made possible not because the colonizing powers possessed superior technology or more advanced civilizations, but because their arrival introduced pathogens to which indigenous populations held no immunity. According to Cook, even brief exposure to such diseases was enough to devastate indigenous populations.

Sometimes, understanding the decline of indigenous societies—however we define that term—is not so easy. In "The Guaraní: The Economics of Ethnocide," Richard Robbins uses the example of the Guaraní of Paraguay to demonstrate how, in the post-contact era, an indigenous group created and maintained a successful, economically and culturally sustainable relationship with European traders and colonialists, even within a larger system of colonial relations. However, in recent years this relationship has suffered at the hands of the seemingly insatiable needs of an economic globalization far more concerned with ecologically damaging but profitable commodity farming. Such ideologies and attendant policies have created a situation of economic dependence in which the Guaraní's traditional land base has been destroyed such that they are forced either to change the kinds of crops they grow or, alternatively, to sell their labour to those who have done so.

A powerful myth of modern nation-states is that conquest and colonialism contained the seeds of the destruction and eventual extinction of indigenous societies. This myth was so powerful that it anchored many of the moral justifications upon which these conquests relied. Such justifications relied heavily on a "split stereotype," which either idealized indigenous peoples as living in a paradise, or dismissed them as backward or barbaric. Both constructions relied on the latent assumption that indigenous peoples would be unable to bear the weight of conquest/colonization (although, ironically, indigenous societies themselves were blamed for this inability). In "The Indians Are Coming to an End," Matthew Restall challenges such simplistic, stereotypical arguments, suggesting instead that indigenous societies were as complex as those of Western conquerors; he thus launches a critique through a careful and nuanced presentation of the various and heterogeneous ways in which indigenous peoples resisted and adapted to colonization.

The readings in this section demonstrate that the indigenous resistance has many facets, as well as a number of common characteristics. One of the latter, brought out by Trond Theun in his article on the Saami of Norway, is the necessity of indigenous people to continually explain themselves to outsiders. Whether sympathetic observers or opponents of the indigenous cause, outsiders somehow feel the necessity to pose the "who," "how," and "why" questions to indigenous individuals and collectivities. Asking who they are, and why they think that their rights as distinctive peoples should be acknowledged, is a tactic that forces indigenous peoples to continually explain themselves and defend their position before they can make any headway in their pursuit of justice and equity. From the same mindset that poses these questions comes the obligation for indigenous people to explain the politicization of their collective identity as peoples. Theun observes that the Saami possessed a clear sense of their peoplehood as far back as 1862.

CHAPTER 14

SETTLING IN: EPIDEMICS AND CONQUEST TO THE END OF THE FIRST CENTURY

Noble David Cook

The following extract explores the impact of various diseases on Indigenous Peoples in South America and the Caribbean in the first century after contact with the colonizers.

COMPOUND EPIDEMICS OF 1576–1591

Epidemics that closely followed earlier ones appear to have done the most severe damage, and the 1576 to 1591 series was one of the deadliest. People already weakened by a bout with the first sicknesses were swept away quickly when they came down with a subsequent malady. As one approaches the end of the century, the documentary record improves. Indeed, the epidemic series of 1576–80 is one of the best documented for Mexico, in part because of the efforts of Spanish royal officials to comply with Philip II's order to compile the geographical descriptions (*relaciones geográficas*) for each province. According to Borah and Cook, the agricultural year 1575–76 had been marked by drought, crop failure, and famine.[1] The epidemic first appeared in August 1576, according to the Chimalpahin source, and by October the number of cases was declining. It appeared again early in 1577 and continued to April. The following year seemed to be free of disease, but illness resurfaced in 1579 in conjunction with other sicknesses.[2] Other similar patterns of flare-ups followed by abatements characterize the epidemic in central Mexico, with some areas being spared during one passage only to be hit in a subsequent onslaught. Such a pattern could easily be a consequence of the existence of two, even three or more different disease factors, thus complicating analysis of the series. Observers note that by the end of the half decade, most regions of Mexico and Guatemala had come under the influence of these deadly infections.

Disease was also a factor in reducing the number of Amerindian peoples to the south in Nicaragua during the same period. The best modern study of the situation in the region is by Newson, who found evidence that *romadizo,* or catarrh, hit Nicaragua in 1578. Both native Americans and Europeans were infected, but mortality was generally low for both groups. Pneumonic plague may have been present in Guatemala at the time, and a Honduran epidemic may have been a minor localized outbreak of the same disease. Newson also found documentation for an unidentified epidemic reported to have taken 300 lives in Nicaragua (1573) in only 20 days.[3]

In the Andes the 1570s were not as deadly for Amerindians as in Mesoamerica, but the following decade was. Speed of disease dissemination depends on a number of factors, of which population density is one important component. The higher the population density, the more rapid the spread of infectious community diseases. Native American depopulation in the years immediately after contact, and the dispersed settlement pattern found throughout most of the central Andes, led Spanish officials to attempt to congregate the Indians into villages. Clerics and bureaucrats had advocated concentration of people earlier, and Francisco Pizarro had even made a half-hearted attempt in the late 1530s. But instability and civil wars had prevented systematic application of the process through the mid-1550s. Beginning in the early 1570s, Viceroy Francisco de Toledo's resettlement program (*reducciones*) in the viceroyalty of Peru was designed to create a Christian Utopia in the New World. Where earlier Andean residents had lived scattered in small communities of a few families, spread across the landscape, Toledo brought them together into villages of several thousand inhabitants, where they could be more closely watched, indoctrinated, and taxed. It was one of the most successful urban planning efforts in the Americas, and many of the towns established by the viceroy continue into the 20th century. But unwittingly, the viceroy established the conditions necessary for a new epidemic crisis by sharply increasing population density in an urban context. Quickly, Toledo's living Utopia turned into a death trap for the Amerindian peoples of the Andes.

Within a decade after the *reducciones* had been established, a devastating series of epidemics passed through the Andes; it proved to be one of the most severe to hit the west coast of South America in the era and was just as disastrous as the one in central Mexico in the early 1550s. The duration and sharp impact of the 1585–91 crisis indicates that two, perhaps three or more, disease factors were operating. Indeed, sifting through the extensive evidence exposes the difficulty in dating the termination of one epidemic and the inception of another. The first seems to have afflicted Peru in 1585. According to Montesinos, smallpox and measles reached Cuzco in the form of a *peste universal* in 1585.[4] One city resident described the ailment as "high fevers with mumps" and claimed that thousands died in the city. The council of Huamanga (modern Ayacucho) closed the road with Cuzco to prevent the spread of the contagion, suggesting that the epidemic was moving westward.[5] What was described as *dolor de costado,* or pleurisy, was present at the same time, and the illness came with such force that those who were stricken suffered intensely. The epidemic recurred in Cuzco in 1590, with many Indian and creole victims. Father Barrasa in 1586 wrote about a smallpox epidemic in which young people were attacked with a merciless fury that reaped numerous victims. Native Americans were especially hard hit in this sweeping pandemic that stretched from Cartagena on the Gulf Coast of New Granada to Chile.[6] About 3,000 perished in Lima from the epidemic in 1586, mostly Indians, but many Blacks died too. As the rash healed, victims fell to "catarrh and cough," likely influenza or pneumonia, with the children and elderly the principal victims. Lima, with its population of approximately 14,262 in 1600, lost about 20 percent of its inhabitants to the 1586 onslaught. The city's Jesuits mourned six out of 60 of their own who died in the Lima house, so the death rate for the Jesuits was about half that of the population at large. In the Indian Hospital of Santa Ana, 14 to 16 died each day for a period of two months; the consequence was that "an innumerable quantity of Indians died."[7]

Andean South America was probably infected through the port and slave center of Cartagena de Indias, just as had happened in the 1558 Colombian epidemic outbreak. Old World disease could have been introduced in the normal course of the human trade, or might have been the result of infections carried by the crew of the expedition of Sir Francis Drake. Drake had departed from Plymouth, England, on 14 September 1585, with about 2,300 men. The fleet stopped on 17 November at the port of Santiago in the Portuguese Cape Verde Islands. The residents of the town fled, and the English stole anything of value they could lay hands on. Unfortunately, they carried away far more than they realized: "There was adjoining to their greatest church an hospital, with as brave rooms in it, and in as goodly order as any man can devise; we found about 20 sick persons, all negroes, lying of very foul and frightful diseases. In the hospital we took all the bells out of the steeple and brought them away with us." They took more than church bells; they took the peal of death, for on 1 December, two days after leaving the islands, disease flared among the crew with a vengeance. Victims broke out with a "rash of small spots" and suffered high fever. Drake stopped at Dominica, traded with Indians, sailed on and attacked the Spanish city of Santo Domingo, then continued and took the port of Cartagena, occupying it for six weeks in early 1586. The attacking force in mid-March 1586 consisted of about 1,000 men. Continuing to be plagued by disease, Drake's forces passed sickness on to the permanent residents, who suffered greatly from its effects. Weakened by the disease, the English gave up and headed home, but may have also transferred disease to St. Augustine. By the time the fleet set sail for the return to England, 750 men had perished, three-quarters of them from the fever taken in the Cape Verde Islands. Dobyns believes that the Drake group suffered from a vectored disease; because Europeans suffered too, it was not measles or smallpox but more likely typhus. Had it been bubonic plague, it would have probably been diagnosed accurately, for Spanish physicians had seen the plague all too frequently in Europe in the 16th century and could easily identify it.[8]

Alchon records the initial appearance of disease in Quito in or following 1585, and then chronicles the 1587 Quito outbreak in detail. In February 1587, the native American confraternity of the Holy Cross was so destitute that it was forced to petition the Audiencia to provide funds to help cure and bury those stricken by the disease. First noticed in July 1587, the epidemic continued for nine seemingly interminable months. A contemporary reported that 4,000 died during a brief three months; many victims were children.[9] According to the geographical report, the elements were "typhus, smallpox and measles ... innumerable people, Creoles, men and women, children and Indians" died.[10] The epidemic lingered in the Ecuadorian highlands well into 1590. Before the series of diseases subsided in 1591, "they left behind a trail of death and destruction unsurpassed by even the 1558 outbreak. In fact, the sharpest drop in Quito's native American population during the 16th century, at least as far as is presently known, occurred between 1560 and 1590; the epidemics of 1585–91 were primarily responsible."[11]

The Colombian disease experience of 1588 is also well documented. Castellanos noted that the epidemic came by way of an infected female slave who had been brought from Mariguita on the coast.[12] The infection was present in Cartagena in 1588 and spread quickly throughout Colombia. Castellanos reported especially high mortality for "boys, girls, youth." Almost all informants from Colombia indicate smallpox as the principal component. One contemporary said that the 1553 bout was "one of the most unfortunate that the natives have experienced." It took more than a third of the population, striking Spaniards as well as Indians.[13]

Bernabé Cobo, who was an eyewitness, reported that the 1588 series covered Popayan and Quito and entered Peru. He traced the source of infection to trade goods imported on ships. It afflicted the black population and caused a "monstrous ugliness in the faces and bodies." Women were especially vulnerable; spontaneous abortions were commonplace in those who were infected: "The fetuses were not expelled from the womb, and they died from the force and the rigor of the fire and torment." Purges and bloodlettings, among the most common cures at the time, were used to combat the contagion, and, if we are to believe Cobo, the condition of many Indians improved with the bleedings.[15]

On 21 March 1589, Peruvian Viceroy Fernando de Torres y Portugal, the Conde de Villar, wrote to Philip II that the epidemic of "smallpox and measles" had reached coastal Trujillo. He had established a commission to block, by quarantine, the southward drift of contagion and to assist those who fell ill. On 19 April, he wrote that in

> the epidemic of smallpox and measles that began to hit the province of Quito, and from which some people have begun to die, the natives are receiving particular injury ... following it is a pestilential typhus.... In the highland provinces there has arrived, at almost the same time, another sickness of cough and *romadizo* with fevers, from which in Potosí more than ten thousand Indians have sickened, as well as some Spaniards. Up until now there has not been noticeable harm either in Cuzco or Huancavelica.

Physicians Hierónymo Enriquez and Francisco Franco Mendoza advised the viceroy to recommend the use of sugar, oil, honey, raisins, and meat to help block infection. The all-too-common practice of bleeding was also cited as a useful tool to save those who were sick. The viceregal recommendation to burn the clothing of those who died was an important positive step to slow the contagion. It was precisely what the Conde de Villar had ordered in Seville at the beginning of the 1580s as an effort to block passage of the plague. Nonetheless, also on 19 April, the viceroy wrote that smallpox and measles already had done their damage in Quito, where they had "destroyed and killed a great number of Indians." It had reached Cuenca, Paitá, and finally Trujillo. In spite of the best efforts of the medical commission, the sickness reached Lima in June 1589, and by the end of the year it struck Cuzco.[15]

The Jesuit Provincial in Lima described victims in frightful detail: "Virulent pustules broke out on the entire body that deformed the miserable sick persons to the point that they could not be recognized except by name." Dobyns found that "the pustules obstructed nasal passages and throats, impeding respiration and food ingestion, occasioning some deaths from these complications. Many survivors lost one or both eyes."[16] The symptoms described in Cuzco parallel those of Lima. The epidemic arrived around mid-September, in spite of cutting transportation across the Apurimac bridge, halting the flow of wine into the city, and conducting many religious celebrations to ward off the approaching pestilence. The author of a Cuzco annal reported ulcerated lips, eyes, and throats, with "tumors, callous excrescences or itchy scabs or very nasty pustules." It was virtually impossible to prevent those afflicted from scratching themselves, and Cuzco's small-pox victims were marked with "monstrous ugliness in faces and bodies." It is little wonder that most of those with the disease fell into profound depression.[17]

The epidemic series greatly devastated Arequipa, where it erupted in 1589. Joralemon identifies the Arequipa outbreak as "a combination of fulminating and malignant confluent (*variola major*) smallpox." He noted that typical mortality in this combination is 30 percent. Infants tended to be affected most by the disease: "as recently as 1885 the case mortality for ages 0–4 was 60 percent."[18] The symptoms in adult cases in general were described in detail by Dobyns:

> The onset of the disease brought severe headaches and kidney pains. A few days later, patients became stupefied, then delirious, and ran naked through the streets shouting. Patients who broke out in a rash had a good chance to recover, reportedly, while those who did not break out seemed to have little chance. Ulcerated throat extinguished the lives of many patients. Fetuses died in the uterus. Even patients who broke out in a rash might lose chunks of flesh by too sudden movement.[19]

Viceroy Villar on 11 May 1589 wrote Philip II that the illness was becoming less virulent in Peru's north and apologized that he had been unable to send more reports on local conditions "because everyone is ill and those who are well are very busy curing them." The sickness was spreading and recently had reached Lima, but at the time the viceroy reported to the monarch there were still few deaths, and most of those who did succumb were Blacks and native Americans. "But the illness is so general that there is scarcely a person in the place who is not touched with it." By the middle of June, epidemic-related deaths in Lima had soared. On 13 June, the viceroy wrote the king that "catarrhal smallpox and measles" were worse in the capital. His description of disease susceptibility is informative: "People have died in this city, among them natives and Blacks and mulattos and Spaniards born here, and now it has spread to those from Castile." All became sick, and mortality affected all ages in this compound series. On 16 June, the viceroy lamented that disease had again hit Trujillo with renewed fury and that many natives and "even Creoles and Spaniards died" from "catarrh and pleurisy."[20] Dobyns believes that influenza moved from Lima into Peru's north, following the disease that produced the symptoms of a rash. But in Lima the rash bearing the sickness followed influenza. By 28 June, Viceroy Conde de Villar sent an inspector to the communities of Surco, Lati, and Luringancho to set up hospitals supplied with beds and well stocked with medicines; on 12 July, he named a surgeon for a tenure of six months to cure the ill in San Juan de Matocana, San Gerónimo de Surco, and San Mateo de Guanchor.[21]

Mortality levels from the compound epidemics were as high as any previous ones, perhaps even higher, because during these years, not one epidemic but two or three coincided. If one suffered from one disease and survived, then was infected by a subsequent disease, the body's forces were incapable of fighting the second infection successfully. In the border districts between the Audiencias of Lima and Quito, deaths were exceptionally high. Native chiefs of the Jaén and Yaguarsongo districts reported in 1591 that, especially in the smallpox series, it was well known that in the valley of Jaén and province only 1,000 of an original 30,000 Indians remained. [22]

The epidemic series afflicted highland Charcas, too. Thanks to some exceptionally well-preserved records, Evans was able to study in detail one native-American community, Aymaya, from 1583 to 1623, and estimate mortality levels. The normal number of annual burials among the Aymaya in the 1580s was in the twenties. In 1590 the number exploded to 194, slightly over 10 percent of the community's population, based on Evans's estimate of about 1,800 as the total population of the Aymaya on the eve of the epidemic. Of these deaths, 147 were listed in the registers as having been precipitated by smallpox. About 45 percent of deaths were of children under 10, again a reflection of the terrible impact of smallpox on the young. There were very few deaths among males over 40 during the 1590 smallpox epidemic. This suggests that the cohort above the age of 40 had experienced, or had at least been exposed to, one or more smallpox epidemics that had extended through the region in the decades before 1550.[23]

Most components of the series assailed the entire Andean region, ultimately flowing into Chile, where both Spaniards and Araucanian Indians were infected.[24] The 1585–91 epidemic series also invaded the upper Amazon basin and may have drifted downstream. We have noted the impact on Jaen, where the native population of 30,000 dropped to 1,000. Yaguarsongo and Pacamoros were hit hard. Between 1585 and 1586, "pestilence" and "*enfermedades*" were reported in Loyola and Santiago de las Montañas. In Cangasa the population fell by more than a third. All these population centers have relatively easy access to the lower stretches of the montaña and the Amazon basin beyond. Unfortunately, measurement of the impact of disease in the Amazon basin is difficult, the consequence of inadequate documentation. The early descriptions of the expeditions of Francisco de Orellana (1541–42) and Pedro de Ursúa, and Lope de Aguirre (1560–61) make no comment regarding poor health conditions in the places the explorers visited.

Foreign disease was inadvertently introduced to the peoples of the southeastern part of what became the United States, La Florida, many times during the course of the 16th century. The ill members of Sir Francis Drake's English fleet, as we have seen, carried sickness to Florida in 1586 on their way home from Cartagena in the Indies. Though much weakened by disease, the English stopped briefly, from 27 May to 2 June, and sacked the fortified port of St. Augustine on the Florida coast. According to the log of the *Primrose*, "The wilde people at first comminge of our men died verie fast and said amongest themselues, It was the Englisshe God that made them die so faste."[25] Four years later, another epidemic seemed to carry native victims to the grave. Royal accountant Bartolomé de Argüelles wrote to the Crown on 12 May 1591 that "this last year there was among them a mortality and many died, and also part of this cabildo and fortress was affected."[26] This epidemic, perhaps linked to the series that so seriously afflicted Mesoamerica and the Andean region, was probably separate from any sickness introduced by Drake.

Furthermore, epidemic disease struck Amerindians near the Raleigh colony on the coast of the Carolinas in 1587. Thomas Harriot reported that after the English had toured hostile native-American settlements, "people began to die very fast, and in many in short space; in some townes about twentie, in some fourtie, in some sixtie, and in one sixe score." As Harriot said, this, in proportion to the size of the town, was substantial. "The disease also was so strange that they neither knew what it was, nor how to cure it; the like by report of the oldest men in the countrey never happened before, time out of mind."[27] Apparently no serious ill effects were experienced by the approximately 100 Englishmen there at the time.

During the 16th century, the native peoples of the Americas experienced one disaster after another. The Europeans brought not only their arms for conquest but also their plants and animals and their pathogens. It was not a single infection that came, but one, then another, a third, a fourth, and more. Just as the outsiders settled and became colonists, Old World diseases settled in, and some gradually became endemic. Taken together, the various epidemics resulted in a huge loss of life and led to relatively easy subjugation of an entire hemisphere. Of the several pandemics to sweep the Americas in the 16th century, three series stood out in the popular mind as watersheds. In Mesoamerica, Juan Bautista Pomar, who compiled the history of Tetzcoco, emphasized the three major killers: those in 1520, 1545, and 1576. For him the first plague was the most deadly. In the same vein, Diego Muñoz Camargo wrote in the 1580s of the impact of disease on Tlaxcala: "I say that the first [1520] ought to be the greatest because there were more people, and the second [1545] was also very great because the land was very full [of people], and this last one [1576] was not as great as the first two.[28] The sequence was similar in Andean America, although the third pandemic wave was especially devastating there because of the quick succession of highly mortal pathogens. Debilitated and convalescing peoples easily fell victim to fresh new infections.

NOTES

1. Borah and Cook, *Essays in Population History*, 2:115.
2. Prem, "Disease Outbreaks in Central Mexico," p. 42.
3. Newson, *Indian Survival in Nicaragua*, p. 247.
4. Lastres, *Historia de la medicina peruana*, 2:76–77.
5. Dobyns, "Andean Epidemic History," p. 501.
6. Lastres, *Historia de la medicina peruana*, 2:77.
7. Dobyns, "Andean Epidemic History," pp. 501–502; José Toribio Polo, "Apuntes sobre las epidemias del Perú," *Revista Histórica* 5(1913):50–109; Lastres, *Historia de la medicina peruana*, 2:77.
8. Dobyns, "Andean Epidemic History," p. 505; Alfred Crosby, *The Columbian Exchange. Biological and Cultural Consequences of 1492* (Westport, CT: Greenwood Press. 1972); David Beers Quinn, ed., *The Roanoke Voyages, 1584–1590*, 2 vols. (London: Hakluyt Society, 1955), 1:378.
9. Alchon, *Native Society and Disease*, p. 40.
10. Jiménez de la Espada, *Relaciones geográficas*, 3:70.
11. Suzanne Austin Browne, "Effects of Epidemic Disease," p. 56.
12. Villamarín and Villamarín, "Sabana de Bogotá," pp. 119–121.
13. María del Carmen Borrego Plá, *Cartagena de Indias en el siglo XVI* (Seville: Escuela de Estudios Hispano-americanos, 1983), p. 406; Villamarín and Villamarín, "Sabana de Bogotá," pp. 119–122.
14. Lastres, *Historia de la medicina peruana*, 2:77.
15. Dobyns, "Andean Epidemic History," p. 505; Alchon, *Native Society and Disease*, pp. 41–43; Roberto Levillier, ed., *Gobernantes del Perú. Cartas y papeles, siglo XVI*, 14 vols. (Madrid: Sucesores de Rivadeneyra, 1925), 11:207–208.
16. Dobyns, "Andean Epidemic History," p. 507; Polo, "Apuntes," p. 56.
17. Dobyns, "Andean Epidemic History," p. 508; Polo, "Apuntes," pp. 16–17.
18. Donald Joralemon, "New World Depopulation and the Case of Disease," *Journal of Anthropological Research* 38(1982):121.

19. Dobyns, "Andean Epidemic History," p. 507; Jiménez de la Espada, *Relaciones geográficas*, 3:70; Archivo General de Indias, Lima 32.
20. Levillier, *Gobernantes del Perú*, 11:221, 284, 285–286.
21. Dobyns, "Andean Epidemic History," p. 506; Polo, "Apuntes," pp. 58–62.
22. Alchon, *Native Society and Disease*, p. 42; Archivo General de Indias, Seville, Quito.
23. Brian Evans, "Death in Aymaya of Upper Peru," in *Secret Judgments*, ed. Cook and Lovell, pp. 142–158.
24. Dobyns, "Andean Epidemic History," p. 508.
25. Quinn, *Roanoke Voyages*, 1:306.
26. University of Florida, P.K. Younge Collection, 33; Archivo General de Indias, Santo Domingo 229.
27. Quinn, *Roanoke Voyages*, 1:378.
28. McCaa, "Spanish and Nahuatl Views," p. 428.

CHAPTER 15

THE GUARANÍ: THE ECONOMICS OF ETHNOCIDE

Richard H. Robbins

It is difficult for any member of the culture of capitalism to take an unbiased view of indigenous peoples, that is not to view such groups as backward, undeveloped, economically depressed, and in need of civilizing. This, of course, is the way indigenous peoples have been portrayed for centuries. Theodore Roosevelt (cited Maybury-Lewis 1997:4), famous for his campaign to conserve nature, said, "The settler and pioneer have at bottom had justice on their side; this great continent could not have been kept as nothing but a game preserve for squalid savages."

In the 19th century, "scientific" theories of evolution and racial superiority allowed people to rationalize the enslavement, confinement, or destruction of indigenous peoples. As late as the 1940s, British anthropologist Lord Fitzroy Raglan (cited Bodley 1990:11), who was to become president of the Royal Anthropological Institute, said that tribal beliefs in magic were a chief cause of folly and unhappiness. Existing tribes were plague spots: "We should bring to them our justice, our education, and our science. Few will deny that these are better than anything which savages have got." While many of these attitudes have changed, indigenous peoples still tend to be seen as needy dependents or victims, largely incapable of helping themselves. We tend to see their destruction as a consequence of their weakness, rather than of patterns of behavior and exploitation built into the culture of capitalism.

It may help to change that view if instead of seeing indigenous peoples as needy dependents living largely outmoded ways of life, we consider the resemblance between indigenous societies and a modern, socially responsible corporation that carefully manages its resources, provides well for its workers, and plans for the long term rather than the short term. Looking at indigenous societies in this way may help us better appreciate why they don't survive. The fact is that environmentally and socially responsible corporations do not fare well in the capitalist world; they fail not because of any inherent weakness but because they become targets for takeovers by individuals or groups who, after taking the corporation over, quickly sell off the carefully managed resources solely to make a quick profit, leaving the corporation in ruin and its workers unemployed.

Take the fate of the Pacific Lumber Company. The family-owned company was known as one of the most environmentally and economically sound companies in the United States. It pioneered the practice of sustainable logging on its large holdings of redwoods and was generous to its employees, even overfunding its pension plan to ensure that it could meet its commitments. Furthermore, to ensure the security of its employees, it had a no-layoff policy. Unfortunately, the very features that made the company a model of environmental and social responsibility also made it a prime target for corporate raiders. After they took control of the company in the late 1980s, they doubled the cutting rate on company lands, drained $55 million of the $93 million pension plan, and invested the remaining $38 million in a life insurance company that ultimately failed (Korten 1995:210). And the fate of Pacific Lumber is not unique.

Indigenous peoples possess all the characteristics that make them prime targets for takeovers. Like responsible corporations, they have managed their resources so well that those same resources (e.g. lumber, animals, farmlands) become targets for those who have used up theirs or who wish to make a quick profit. The indigenous peoples themselves become expendable, or themselves become resources to be exploited. To illustrate, let's look at the case of the Guaraní as described by Richard Reed (1997).

HISTORY AND BACKGROUND

Most of the 15,000 Guaraní are settled in the rainforests of eastern Paraguay; they live in 114 communities ranging from three to four houses to over 100 families. They are a minority population in a country in which most citizens are *mestizo* or *criollos*, descendants of Europeans who married Guaraní.

When Europeans arrived, over 1,000,000 Guaraní and related groups lived in the area stretching from the Andes to the Atlantic Ocean. The Guaraní welcomed the first conquistadors, joining them in carving out trade routes to the Andes. The earliest reports of travellers indicate that the Guaraní system of production and standard of living were successful. In 1541 the region's first governor, Cabeza de Vaca (cited Reed 1997:8), noted that the Guaraní

> [a]re the richest people of all the land and province both for agriculture and stock raising. They rear plenty of fowl and geese and other birds, and have an abundance of game, such as boar, deer, and dantes (anta), partridge, quail and pheasants; and they have great fisheries in the river. They grow plenty of maize, potatoes, cassava, peanuts and many other fruits; and from the trees they collect a great deal of honey.

In addition to their economic success, the Guaraní were a relatively egalitarian society in which a person's place in society was determined by kinship. Leadership was usually determined by age, although political leaders had little or no power of coercion over others.

The Guaraní engaged European markets soon after

contact, managing to combine their traditional subsistence activities of swidden agriculture and hunting and gathering with the collection of commercial products from the forests such as yerba mate, a naturally growing tea, animal skins, and honey. Anthropologists call this combination of productive activities *agroforestry,* the active management of foest resources for long-term production.

To understand agroforestry as practiced by the Guaraní, we need to understand a little about the nature of tropical rainforests. They are the most diverse biosystems on Earth, containing half the recorded species in the world, although only about 15 percent of these species have even been discovered. They are also among the most fragile ecosystems. A rainforest is a layered system. The top layer, or canopy, is provided by large trees protecting the layers underneath it, with each species of plant or animal in lower layers dependent on the others, and all surviving on a very thin layer of soil.

Guaraní agroforestry focuses on three activities: horticulture, hunting and gathering, and commercial tree cropping. The agriculture is shifting or swidden agriculture, in which small areas of the forests are cut and burned, the ash providing a thin layer of nutrients for the soil. These areas are planted until spreading weeds and decreased yields force the farmer to move to a new plot. The old plot is not abandoned but planted with banana trees and manioc, crops that need little care and which produce for up to four years. In this way land is gradually recycled back into tropical forest. Furthermore, these plots provide forage for deer, peccary, and other animals, which the Guaraní trap or shoot.

Fishing is another source of protein. Usually the Guaraní fish with poison. They crush the bark of the timbo tree and wash it through the water, leaving a thin seal on top of the water. They wait for the water to be depleted of oxygen and the stunned fish float to the surface. The Guaraní also fish with hook and lines. Other food sources include honey, fruit, the hearts of palm trees, and roots gathered from the forest floor.

Finally, to earn cash, the Guaraní collect yerba mate leaves, animal skins, oils, and food. In these activities the Guaraní use the forest extensively but not intensively. For example, they will cut leaves from all yerba trees but take only the mature leaves from each tree every three years, thus promoting the plants' survival. In addition, since the Guaraní harvest from a number of ecological niches and since their consumption needs are modest, they never overexploit a commodity to earn cash.

Thus the Guaraní use the forest to supplement their other subsistence activities, integrating this resource into their production system. It is a production system that is modeled after that of the rainforest itself; by incorporating trees, the system preserves or recreates the forest canopy necessary for the survival of plants and animals below it. The surviving diversity of crops and animals ensures the recycling of nutrients necessary for their maintenance. In fact, as Richard Reed (1997:15) noted, "agroforestry often increases ecological diversity."

Agroforestry differs markedly from the typical exploitive forest activities in the culture of capitalism, such as intensive agriculture, lumbering, and cattle raising, activities modeled after factory production. First, indigenous production systems are diverse, allowing forest residents to exploit various niches in the forest without overexploiting any one niche. Second, unlike intensive agriculture, lumbering, or cattle raising, the Guaraní production system depends on the resources of plants and animals themselves rather than on the nutrients of the forest soils. Thus by moderate use of the soils, water, canopy, and fauna of the forest the Guaraní ensure that the whole system continues to flourish. Third, Guaraní production techniques lend themselves to a pattern of social relations in which individual autonomy is respected and in which activities do not lend themselves to a division of labour that lends itself to status hierarchy. The basic work unit is the family, with both men and women involved in productive labour—farming, gathering food, and collecting commercial products—and reproductive labour—child care, food preparation, and the construction and maintenance of shelters.

Fourth, unlike the activities of the culture of capitalism, the Guaraní mode of production is neither technology- nor labour-intensive. The Guaraní spend about 18 percent of their time in productive activities; one-third of that is devoted to horticulture, slightly less to forest subsistence activities, and about 40 percent to commercial activities. Another 27 percent of their time is devoted to household labour. In all, about half their daylight time is spent working; the rest is devoted to leisure and socializing. Reed said that the Guaraní workday is approximately half that of a typical European worker.

Finally, unlike capitalist production, which is tightly integrated into the global system, Guaraní production allows them a great deal of autonomy from the larger society. When prices for their products are too low, the Guaraní stop selling; if prices on store goods are too high, the Guaraní stop buying. Thus they do not have to rely on commercial markets; their stability is in their gardens, not their labour.

This autonomy can be attributed in part to the Guaraní's modest consumption needs. Food accounts for about 40 percent of the average family's monthly market basket—about two kilograms of rice, pasta, and flour; one kilogram of meat, a half liter of cooking oil, and a little salt. Cloth and clothing is the next most important purchase, perhaps a new shirt or pants (but not both) each year. Another one-fifth of the budget is spent on tools, such as machetes and axes, and an occasional luxury, such as tobacco, alcohol, or a tape recorder. Thus, as Reed (1997:75) noted, the Guaraní engage the global economic system without becoming dependent on it.

CONTEMPORARY DEVELOPMENT AND GUARANÍ COMMUNITIES

Guaraní culture and their system of adaptation are, however, being threatened. Since the 1970s, the rate of forest destruction in Paraguay has increased dramatically as forests are cleared to make way for monocultural agriculture and cattle ranching. As a result, Guaraní house lots stand exposed on open landscapes and families are being forced to settle on the fringes of *mestizo* towns. Reed made the point that it is not market contact or interethnic relations that are destroying the Guaraní; they have participated in the market and interacted with *mestizo* townspeople for centuries. Rather, it is a new kind of economic development spawned by the needs of the global economy.

After decades of little economic growth, in the 1970s the Paraguayan economy began to grow at the rate of 10 percent per year. This growth was fueled by enormous expansion of agricultural production, particularly cotton, soy, and wheat. Most of this growth came at the expense of huge tracts of rainforest felled to make way for the new cultivation. As Reed said, since 1970 every effort has been made to convert the land of eastern Paraguay into fields for commodity production. A number of things contributed to rainforest destruction.

First, roads built into the forests for military defense against Brazil contributed to the influx of settlers into the rainforest. Second, large-scale, energy-intensive agriculture displaced small farmers, who flooded to the cities in search of work.

This created pressures on these populations to find work or land, but rather than redistribute the vast tracts of cleared land held by wealthy cattle ranchers to peasants, the government chose to entice poor peasants into the forests with land-distribution programs. Between 1963 and 1973, 42,000 families had been given land; between 1973 and 1976, 48,000 families were given a total of 4,000,000 hectares of land.

A third factor was international finance. The oil boom of the 1970s, along with changes in currency, allowed core institutions to go on a lending spree as people sought ways to reinvest their profits. Like most other peripheral countries, Paraguay borrowed heavily in the 1970s to build roads, hydroelectric projects, and other things they believed necessary to build an industrial economy. The money that came into the country from the World Bank and other financial institutions needed to be reinvested by Paraguayan financiers, and some invested in farms and cattle ranches in the forests. Finally, to repay the loans, the country needed to raise funds, which it did by expanding agricultural growth in export crops, putting further demands on the rainforest.

The process of environmental destruction soon followed. For example, the Guaraní group Reed worked with (the Itanaramí) suffered their first major incursion in 1972, when the government cut a road into their forest. It was built partly to control the border with Brazil, but it also allowed logging in what had been impenetrable forests. Loggers brought in bulldozers to cut road directly to the hardwood trees. Lumber mills were positioned along the roads and the cut lumber was trucked to the capital city, where it was shipped to the United States, Argentina, and Japan. As Reed (1997:85) said, the forests that had provided the Guaraní with shelter and subsistence were cut down so that consumers in the United States, Europe, and Japan could enjoy furniture and parquet floors.

The roads also brought into the Guaraní forest impoverished Paraguayan families in search of land that they illegally cut to create fields in the forests, fields that will bear crops only for a short time before losing their fragile fertility. To complicate matters, Brazilian peasants, many displaced by large-scale agricultural projects in their own country, crossed the border seeking land on which to survive. The area even became home to a Mennonite community seeking to escape the pressures and problems of the larger world.

On the heels of these colonists came agribusiness concerns clearing more forest on which to raise soy and cotton. Within months of their arrival, thousands of hectares of forest were cut down and replaced by fields of cash crops. The road that had brought in the military, loggers, and peasant colonists was now used to haul out produce for foreign markets and for cattle drives to deliver meat to consumers across South and North America.

Thus in the same way that corporate raiders seize responsible corporations to turn a quick profit, often destroying them in the process, people seeking a profit from the lands of the Guaraní quickly destroyed the forest. The logging companies cut the trees that provided the canopy for the forests as well as the trunks on which vines such as orchids and philodendron climbed. Without the protective cover of the large trees, the enormous diversity of life that thrived beneath the canopy was no longer viable. Faunal populations declined immediately because their habitat was being destroyed and because they were being hunted to extinction by the new settlers. With the flora and fauna decimated, all that remained was a fragile layer of topsoil, which the harsh sunlight and rains quickly reduced to its clay base.

The rate of forest destruction was enormous. From 1970 to 1976, Paraguayan forests were reduced from 6.8 million to 4.2 million hectares. Half of the remaining forest was cut by 1984, and each year thereafter another 150,000–200,000 hectares has fallen to axes and bulldozers. At this rate, the Paraguayan forests will be gone by the year 2025.

More to the point for this discussion, with the rainforest went the way of life of the Guaraní. When Reed first began working with the Itanaramí in 1981, they were isolated in the forest, living largely as they had for centuries. By 1995 they were on a small island of forest in an "ocean of agricultural fields."

The Guaraní had no legal title to the land they have inhabited for centuries, such title being claimed by the nation-state; those who bought the land from the government assume they have both a legal and moral right to remove any people occupying the land. Even when Guaraní were allowed to retain their houseplots, their traditional system of agroforestry was impossible because their forest was being destroyed and they were forced to seek new and smaller plots. Furthermore, the settlers destroyed their hunting stock, so the Guaraní quickly came to depend for meat on the occasional steer slaughtered by ranchers in the towns, for which the Guararí had to pay cash. But the ranchers destroyed the stands of yerba mate, a source of cash for the Guaraní, that they had cultivated for centuries.

Gradually, with their traditional production system destroyed, the Guaraní were forced to enter the market economy as cotton or tobacco growers or as wage labourers on the lands they had sustained for centuries. Those who entered the agricultural sector found that the new system of farming was capital-intensive and required inputs of fertilizers, herbicides, and insecticides. Families went into debt, becoming dependent on *mestizo* merchants and lenders. Those who chose to work found that wages were often too low to support a family, forcing several or all family members to work. Furthermore, labour required people to travel outside their communities so that even those families who managed to gain access to land on which to garden had little time for it. Since wage labour demands the strongest workers, it is often the youngest and strongest who must leave their communities.

There are other effects. Illness and disease became more prevalent. Suicide, virtually unknown previously in Guaraní communities, increased from a total of six in 1989 to three suicides per month in the first half of 1995. The leadership system collapsed, as religious leaders who earned their authority through their ability to mediate disputes found themselves helpless to mediate the new problems that arose between Guaraní and *mestizo* or government bureaucrats. Today the government appoints community leaders, to make it easier for them to control and negotiate with Guaraní communities. These new leaders derive their power from assistance programs that funnel resources to the Guaraní, but which many leaders use to reward friends and relatives, and punish non-kin and enemies.

In sum, the debt assumed by the Paraguayan government to foster economic expansion and the resulting expansion of capital-intensive farming and cattle ranching in the 1980s disrupted Guaraní society more than had four centuries of contact; as a result its members are dispersing and assimilating into the larger society. It would be easy to condemn the Paraguayan government, and other governments whose indigenous peoples are being destroyed. Yet the nation-states are only doing what capital controllers are supposed to do: they are choosing modes of production and ways of life that will bring the greatest immediate monetary return.

REFERENCES

Bodley, John H. 1985. *Anthropology and Contemporary Human Problems*, 2nd ed. Mountain View: Mayfield Publishing.

Bodley, John H. 1990. *Victims of Progress*, 3rd ed. Mountain View: Mayfield Publishing.

Korten, David C. 1995. *When Corporations Rule the World.* Hartford: Kumarian Press.

Maybury-Lewis, David. 1997. *Indigenous Peoples, Ethnic Groups, and the State.* Boston: Allyn & Bacon.

Reed, Richard. 1997. *Forest Dwellers, Forest Protectors: Indigenous Models for International Development.* Boston: Allyn & Bacon.

CHAPTER 16

THE INDIANS ARE COMING TO AN END: THE MYTH OF NATIVE DESOLATION

Matthew Restall

In 1539, Jerusalem was attacked by three Christian armies at once. One was an imperial force led by Charles V, Holy Roman Emperor and king of Spain, accompanied by his brother, the king of Hungary, and French king Francis I. This army had come as reinforcements for a separate Spanish army led by the Count of Benavente. The third attacking force was the army of New Spain, led by Viceroy Mendoza. The battle raged for hours, until the Muslim defenders of Jerusalem finally capitulated. Their leader, "the Great Sultan of Babylon and Tetrarch of Jerusalem," was none other than "the Marqués del Valle, Hernando Cortés."

This battle did not actually take place in the Middle East, but in the vast central plaza of Tlaxcala, the Nahua city-state whose alliance with Cortés had proved crucial to his defeat of the Mexica empire almost two decades earlier. The mock battle, part of a day-long series of plays and battles, was staged on Corpus Christi day by the Tlaxcalans, with the possible assistance of Franciscan friars. One of the friars witnessed the spectacle and wrote an account of it, published soon after in Motolinía's *History of the Indians of New Spain*.[1]

While a mock battle in which the victorious armies are led by the Spanish king, the colonial Mexican viceroy, and a Spanish count prominent in colonial Mexican affairs might seem to be a celebration of the Spanish Conquest of Mexico, Tlaxcala's theatrical "Conquest of Jerusalem" was hardly that. Cortés (played by a native Tlaxcalan actor) was not the victor in the drama, but the Sultan, doomed to defeat—and the captain general of the Moors was Pedro de Alvarado, the second most prominent Spaniard in the fall of Tenochtitlan and the subsequent conqueror of highland Guatemala. As the losers, Cortés and Alvarado requested mercy and baptism, and admitted that they were the "natural vassals" of the Tlaxcalan—played Charles V—an interesting inversion of the conquistadors' claim that natives were naturally subject to Spaniards.[2] As possible insurance against Cortés's reacting negatively to his role in the play, the Tlaxcalans had the army of New Spain led by a Tlaxcalan playing the viceroy, don Antonio de Mendoza, with whom Cortés was in dispute in 1539 (resulting in Cortés's sailing to Spain later that year).[3]

The parts in the play were all played by Tlaxcalans. It was Tlaxcalan warriors, in their thousands, who took Jerusalem, just as 18 years earlier thousands of them had taken Tenochtitlán. And whereas the Tlaxcalans playing soldiers in the European armies all wore the same bland uniforms, the Tlaxcalans of the army of New Spain dressed as themselves—in the traditional multicolored costumes of the city-state's warriors, complete with feathered headdresses, "their richest plumage, emblems, and shields" (in the words of the Franciscan observer). The setting for the play was Tlaxcala's impressive new plaza, the size of four football fields, whose buildings, still under construction, became part of the elaborate scenery. An important aspect of the festival's political context was Tlaxcala's age-old rivalry with the Mexica, as the play was put on in part to trump a similar spectacle staged four months earlier in Mexico City and centered on an imaginary Spanish "Conquest of Rhodes" that was a thinly disguised Mexica reconquest of Mexico.[4] The "Conquest of Jerusalem" was thus a Tlaxcalan creation intended to glorify Tlaxcala's recent triumphs and current status as an important, if not the most important, *altepetl* or central Mexican city-state.

Called "the most spectacular and intellectually sophisticated theatrical event" of its time, Tlaxcala's 1539 Corpus Christi celebration is an especially rich illustration of the genre.[5] But it was by no means the only such festival in 16th-century Mexico, or indeed in colonial Spanish America. Throughout the colonies in Mesoamerica and the Andes, plays, dances, and mock battles were staged by native communities. Many persist to this day. All placed complex local spins on a mix of traditional native ritual performance and various elements of Spanish theatrical tradition. The effect, if not the purpose, of such festivals was to reconstruct the Conquest not as a historical moment of defeat and trauma, but as a phenomenon that transcended any particular historical moment and was transcended in turn by that local native community. These festivals were not commemorations of something lost, but celebrations of community survival, micropatriotic integrity, and cultural vitality.[6] Festivals of reconquest therefore represent the first of the seven indicators of Conquest-era and post-Conquest native vitality.

The second such indicator consists of other expressions of native denial or inversion of defeat. An extraordinarily rich body of sources illustrating this phenomenon with respect to Mesoamerica is contained within the genre referred to by scholars as the primordial title, or *título*. The *título* was a community history that promoted local interests, particularly related to land ownership, often those of the local dynasty or dominant noble families. Such documents were written down alphabetically, in native languages, all over Mesoamerica during the colonial period—but especially in the 18th century when land pressures mounted due to population growth among Spaniards and natives alike. Late-colonial *títulos* drew upon earlier sources, both written and oral, representing continuities from pre-Conquest histories and often including accounts of the Spanish invasion.[7] Maya accounts of the

Conquest contained in *títulos* from Yucatan reveal that there was no single, homogeneous native view; perspectives were determined largely by differences of class, family, and region. Most of the Maya elite, however, tended to downplay the significance of the Conquest by emphasizing continuities of status, residency, and occupation from pre-Conquest times. Mayas placed the Spanish invasion, and the violence and epidemics it brought, within the larger context of history's cycles of calamity and recovery, relegating the Conquest to a mere blip in their long-term local experience.[8]

Another example of the localized nature of native responses to the Conquest came from the Valley of Oaxaca, in southern Mexico. In the 1690s, a legal dispute over land erupted between two native communities in the valley, one Nahua, the other Mixtec. In court, both submitted *títulos* to prove their cases, each complete with a brief Conquest account. The Nahua version of events of the 1520s asserted that Nahua warriors had come down to Oaxaca from central Mexico in response to a plea from the Zapotecs, who needed help defending themselves from the cannibalistic Mixtecs. Cortés approved the mission, but when he came to Oaxaca in the wake of Nahua victory, he and the Nahuas fell out and fought. The Nahuas won this battle too, and after this, the "original conquest," they settled in the valley on land granted to them.

In contrast, the Mixtec version claimed that Cortés came to the valley first, where he was welcomed by the Mixtecs, who gave Spaniards some land on which to settle. The trouble began when Cortés returned with a group of Nahuas, who started a fight and were soundly defeated by the Mixtecs. With Cortés as peace broker, the Mixtecs graciously allowed the Nahuas to settle in the valley. The boundaries of the land they were given were, not surprisingly, less generous in the Mixtec *título* than in the Nahua version.

In both versions, local community—or micropatriotic—identities remain paramount. There is no acceptance of the colonial division of peoples into Spaniards and "Indians," nor is there an acceptance of the Conquest as either a Spanish initiative or a primarily Spanish triumph. Native defeat is not only denied, but inverted. Even the phrase "native defeat" is meaningless from a community perspective that views all outsiders in more or less the same way, whether they be Spaniards, Mixtecs, Nahuas, or Zapotecs—or even people of the same language group who live in a separate town.[9]

The third indicator of native vitality during the Conquest was the role played by natives as allies in the campaigns that followed the major wars of invasion. Although in the long run these campaigns usually (but not always) resulted in the spread of Spanish colonial rule, in the short run they often constituted local native exploitation of the Spanish presence to advance regional interests. For example, the armies of Nahua warriors who waged campaigns in what is now northern Mexico, southern Mexico, Yucatan, Guatemala, and Honduras helped create the colonial kingdom of New Spain and were led by Spanish captains. But the vast majority of those who fought were Nahuatl-speakers under their own officers. Many of them remained as colonists in new colonial towns such as Oaxaca, Santiago (Guatemala), Merida, and Campeche, and their culture and language made a permanent mark on these regions. As symbolized by place-names in highland Guatemala to this day, Nahuatl became a lingua franca in New Spain. In many ways, these campaigns were a continuation of the Mexica expansionism that had gone almost unchecked for a century before the Spanish invasion.[10]

A slightly different type of example is that of the Chontal Maya expansion of the late 16th century under their king, Paxbolonacha. His simultaneous colonial identity was as don Pablo Paxbolon, the region's governor. Although the Chontal Mayas's first major contact with Spaniards was as early as 1525, not until the 1550s did the region become fully incorporated into the nearest Spanish colony, Yucatan. Beginning in the 1560s, and running continuously until his death in 1614, Paxbolon engaged in campaigns against neighbouring Maya communities that had yet to be incorporated into the colony or that had slipped out of colonial control. The Spanish presence on most of these expeditions was minimal or nonexistent. Although Paxbolon had a license from Merida permitting him to round up refugees and "idolaters," a Chontal Maya *título* written during his rule recorded such campaigns before and after the Spanish invasion, revealing the colonial ones to be little more than continuations of age-old slaving raids.[11]

Paxbolon's expansionism was a localized phenomenon, but so were all cases of native military activity after the Spanish invasion—from Nahua campaigns after the fall of the Mexica empire to campaigns by Andean warriors for decades after the capture and execution of Atahuallpa. Local circumstances produced regional variations, but the general pattern reveals considerable native military activity during the Conquest and after it was supposedly over, not always directed against Spaniards but often pursued to advance local native interests.

The historian Charles Gibson, in his seminal study of colonial Tlaxcala, remarked that there were times when "Indians accepted one aspect of Spanish colonization in order to facilitate their rejection of another.[12] This situation is illustrated by the role often played by native elites, whose partial and complex collaboration in Conquest and colonial agendas represents the fourth anti-desolation indicator. At the highest level of native leadership, that of the Mexica and Inca emperors, such collaboration served only to buy time. But while Moctezuma and Atahuallpa lived, even as captives, their policies of collaboration and appeasement served to save native lives and prevent full-scale wars. The Moctezuma of myth—invented by Franciscans and Tlatelolcans and perpetuated by modern historians from Prescott to Tuchman—was no artful collaborator. But the real Moctezuma was the most successful ruler the Mexica empire had known; "the most dynamic, the most aggressive, the most triumphantly self-confident of all," in Fernández-Armesto's words, Moctezuma "outstripped all predecessors" with campaigns that ranged over some 150,000 square miles and continued even after Cortés had taken up residence in Tenochtitlán. Cortés later claimed to have captured Moctezuma soon after reaching the city, but it is clear from descriptions of the emperor's activities in other Spanish and native sources that his arrest did not take place for months. Meanwhile, the Mexica ruler spun a web of confusion around the Spaniards, who remained unsure right up to their disastrous and bloody escape from Tenochtitlán whether to expect submission, deadly duplicity, or open hostility.[13] Atahuallpa's capture was more immediate, but even as a captive he was able to plot and strategize, temporarily containing the Spaniards and using them to win his own war against his brother.

The high status of Moctezuma and Atahuallpa made them unsuited in the long run for the roles of puppet rulers and condemned them to death at the hands of Spaniards. Lesser native rulers, however, were able to negotiate their way out of captivity and execution, or avoid imprisonment altogether, and be confirmed in office by the colonial authorities. Don Pablo Paxbolon is a good example of such a ruler who was able to maintain this dual status throughout his long reign/rule, partly because his small kingdom was of relatively little interest to Spaniards. In contrast, Manco Inca Yupanqui's kingdom attracted so much Spanish attention that he soon rebelled against his dual status. As well as being Inca (meaning "emperor") by right of succession, Manco was confirmed in office as regent of Peru by the Spaniards in 1534 and was supposed to function as a puppet of the colonial regime (see figure 16.1). But by 1536, the conditions of compromise had become too onerous, and the abuse of the Inca's family and retainers by the Pizarros and their associates had become intolerable. Manco fled the capital of Cuzco, raised an army, and laid siege to the city for a year before retreating into the Andes, where an independent Inca kingdom lasted until 1572. Meanwhile, in 1560, Manco's son Titu Cusi became Inca, later becoming baptized and negotiating a rapprochement with the Spanish. Although his brother, Tupac Amaru, and other family members were executed in 1572 as rebels, Titu Cusi, his descendents, and other members of the Inca nobility were able to maintain considerable economic and political status within colonial Peru for centuries.[14]

Figure 16.1 "Manco Inca, raised up as Inca king," in *Nueva corónica y buen gobierno*, by don Felipe Huaman Poma de Ayala (1615).

Figure 16.2 "The Xiu Family Tree," probably by Gaspar Antonio Chi (c. 1557), updated by don Juan Xiu (c. 1685).

Inca survival paralleled in many ways the perpetuation of status by Moctezuma's relatives and descendents. While they lacked their pre-Conquest political clout, their local social and economic significance was underpinned by confirmation of titles and honours by the Spanish crown.[15] Likewise, most of the highest-ranking noble Maya families, as a result of protracted negotiations through a Conquest decades long, succeeded in preserving their local status as community rulers in return for accepting Spanish political authority at a regional level. The Spanish governor of Yucatan became the *halach uinic* (provincial ruler), but the noblemen of dynasties such as the Cocom, Pech, and Xiu remained as *batabob* (local rulers or town governors) for the next three centuries.

The Xiu were among the most powerful noble families in Yucatan before and after the Conquest.[16] Figure 16.2 illustrates through the medium of a family tree the perpetuation of the Xiu dynasty's sense of historical legitimacy through the Conquest period. The semi-mythical founding couple are supposed to have lived centuries before the Conquest, while the named individuals run from the 15th to 17th centuries. Drawn in the 1550s by Gaspar Antonio Chi, and updated over a century later by a member of one branch of the family, the tree exhibits a complex mix of Maya, Nahua, and Spanish cultural elements. The image evocatively exhibits the blend of change and continuity, compromise and survival that underscored elite native adaptation to colonial rule.

Most of the Xiu noblemen named in figure 16.2 served as *batabob*, illustrating the flourishing of the native municipal community from the 16th to 18th centuries—the fifth indicator of post-invasion native vitality. One of the native mechanisms of adaptation to colonial rule that fostered the golden age of the native town was the ready adoption of the Spanish *cabildo* (town council). Spaniards imposed the *cabildo*'s election, offices, and functions on native towns early in the colonial period—or at least, Spaniards assumed they did. In fact, native elites only appeared to create Spanish-style *cabildos*. Their "elections," if held at all, were but a veneer covering traditional factional maneuvers and cycles of power sharing. Spanish titles such as *alcalde* (judge) and *regidor* (councilman) were adopted, but the numbers, rankings, and functions of the officers followed local traditions, while many *cabildos* contained officers with pre-Conquest titles. In some cases, municipal governors were Spanish-appointed, but in many more instances native governors continued to function as they had before the Conquest, even keeping pre-colonial titles, ruling for life and passing the positions on to their sons.[17]

While Spaniards viewed native *cabildos* as products of colonialism, natives initially adopted the framework of the *cabildo* as a superficial change and then soon came to view it as a local institution rather than a colonial one. This double perception is another example of Double Mistaken Identity, whereby both Spaniards and natives viewed the same concept or way of doing something as rooted in their own culture. In this way, the native borrowing of Spanish cultural elements did not represent native culture loss or decline, but rather adaptability and vitality (the sixth indicator of post-Conquest native cultural vitality). Natives tended to view borrowings—be they Spanish words, concepts, ways of counting, of worship, of building houses, or of town planning—not as loans but as part of community practice and custom. They viewed them not as Spanish, nor even as native, but as local. And they were able to do this because of the integrity and flourishing of semi-autonomous municipal communities. By the end of the colonial period, there was little about native culture in most of Spanish America that (in James Lockhart's words) "could safely be declared to have been entirely European or entirely indigenous in origin. The stable forms that emerged in the long run often owed so much to both antecedents, with many elements having been similar from the beginning and others now interwoven and integrated, that identifying what belonged to which antecedent becomes to a large extent impossible, and even beside the point."[18]

Just as the violence and drama of the Spanish invasion gave way to gradual cultural change, so did the immediate tragedy of native population decline give way in the long run to opportunities of various kinds. The Andean chronicler Huaman Poma warned in 1615 that the "Indians are coming to an end," and in demographic terms, a century after Spaniards began their conquests on the American mainland, this almost seemed a real possibility. The rapid decline in the Native American population, beginning in 1492 and continuing well into the 17th century, has been called a holocaust. In terms of absolute numbers and the speed of demographic collapse—a drop of as many as 40 million people in about a century—it is probably the greatest demographic disaster in human history.[19]

But the decline was not a holocaust in the sense of being the product of a genocide campaign or a deliberate attempt to exterminate a population. Spanish settlers depended upon native communities to build and sustain their colonies with tribute, produce, and labour. Colonial officials were extremely concerned by the demographic tragedy of Caribbean colonization, where the native peoples of most islands became extinct within a few decades. That concern mounted with evidence of massive mortality on the mainland during—and even preceding—Spanish invasions. What Spaniards did not fully understand was the degree to which disease caused this disaster. The arguments of a vocal minority—of whom Las Casas remains the best known—that colonial brutality was the principal cause of the natives seeming to "come to an end" were taken seriously by the crown. As a result, edicts were regularly passed that were designed to protect natives from colonial excesses. Their impact was limited, but they reflected the important fact that Spaniards needed Native Americans to survive and proliferate, even if this was only so they could be exploited.

The combination of population decline and Spanish colonial dependence upon a shrinking—and then very slow-growing—native population actually provided opportunities for the survivors. One type of opportunity was political. The relative stability of the ruling elite in Yucatan, and the few instances of upstart families acquiring power as a result, was not paralleled everywhere in Spanish America. In the Riobamba region of colonial Quito, for example, the pre-Inca elite and the surviving families among the local Inca nobility vied for power within the crucible of the Conquest and colonial rule. The situation was skillfully manipulated by the Duchiselas, a family that was prominent in the area before the Inca conquest, but not a ruling dynasty. The family welcomed the 1534 Spanish expedition under Sebastián de Benalcázar and as a result was granted a local lordship. By the 1570s, they had parlayed this into the governorship of the town of Yaruquies. Over the next two centuries, the Duchiselas consolidated considerable regional political power, established a land-based family fortune, and largely succeeded in inventing the dynasty's deep-rooted historical legitimacy.[20]

The Duchisela family fortune was land based, and by the early 17th century its patriarch, don Juan, and his wife, dona Isabel Carrillo, owned almost a thousand hectares of land. Indeed, land was another arena of native opportunity in the Conquest's wake. Contrary to common belief, Spaniards did not come to the Americas to acquire land. The goal of conquistadors was to receive an *encomienda*, a grant of native tribute and labour—not land. The Spanish pressure on native communities to give up or sell land was not serious until later in the colonial period. In the 16th century there was a great deal more land available to natives than before the Conquest. And with the advent of iron and steel tools and a new array of crops and domesticated animals, there were new opportunities for working that land.[21]

To be sure native peoples in 16th-century Spanish America faced epidemics of lethal disease and onerous colonial demands. But they did not sink into depression and inactivity because of the Conquest. Instead they tenaciously sought ways to continue local ways of life and improve the quality of life even in the face of colonial changes and challenges. Furthermore, the decline in population did not mean that native culture declined in some or any sense. Native cultures evolved more rapidly and radically in the colonial period as a result of exposure to Spanish culture and the need to adapt to new technologies, demands, and ways of doing things. But as historians of late-medieval Europe have observed, when populations were periodically decimated by plagues and epidemics, this did not result in culture loss.

All of this is ignored by the myth of native desolation, which subsumes into "nothingness" the complex vitality of native cultures and societies during and after the Conquest.[22] As Inga Clendinnen puts it, the mythic or "conventional story of returning gods and unmanned autocrats, of an exotic world paralyzed by its encounter with Europe, for all its coherence and its just-so inevitabilities, is in view of the evidence like Eliza's progression across the ice floes: a matter of momentary sinking balances linked by desperate forward leaps."[23]

NOTES

1. Motolinía, *Historia*, 1979 [1541]: *trat.* I, chap. 15; Harris, *Aztecs, Moors, and Christians*, 2000:132–47.
2. As Harris observes; *Aztecs, Moors, and Christians*, 2000:144.
3. Harris, *Aztecs, Moors, and Christians*, 2000:137. A further dimension to the slighting of Cortés in the drama is the fact that the governor of Tlaxcala in 1539 was don Luis Xicotencatl, nephew of the Axayacatzin Xicotencatl who had led Tlaxcalan resistance against Cortés in 1519, had reluctantly joined the allied cause in 1521 and then, when he seemed uncooperative, had been hanged by Cortés in Texcoco that year (Gómara, *Cortés*, 1964 [1552]: 100–16; Gibson, *Tlaxcala*, 1952: 98–100; Thomas, *Conquest*, 1995: 490–91; Harris, *Aztecs, Moors, and Christians*, 2000:139).
4. The exception to the actors being Tlaxcalans was a fictional Caribbean native army, defeated in the middle of the play in their attempt to take Jerusalem. These actors were Otomi natives—reflecting Tlaxcalan insight into colonial Caribbean history and their perception of Caribbean and Otomi natives in a different category from Tlaxcalans (a difference we would define as that between semi-sedentary and sedentary peoples). Harris, *Aztecs, Moors, and Christians*, 2000:140–41, 136, 135.
5. Harris, *Aztecs, Moors, and Christians*, 2000:134.
6. Bricker, *The Indian Christ*, 1981: 129–54; Hill, *Colonial Cakchiquels*, 1992: 1–8; Cohen, "Danza de la Pluma," 1993; Rappaport, *Cumbe Reborn*, 1994:145–66; Restall, *Maya Conquistador*, 1998: 46, 193–94 n53; Harris, *Aztecs, Moors, and Christians*, 2000.
7. See Restall, "Heirs to the Hieroglyphs," 1997, which includes a fairly comprehensive bibliography of *título* studies. *Títulos* continue to be discovered and published, enriching our understanding of the native views of the Conquest described above; see Colom et al., *Testamento y Título*, 1999.
8. Restall, *Maya Conquistador*, 1998.
9. The only presentation and study of these *títulos* is Sousa and Terraciano, "Original Conquest," 2003; also see Terraciano, *The Mixtecs*, 2001: 336–38.
10. Fernández-Armesto in Prescott, *Conquest of Mexico*, 1994: xxx; Hassig, *Aztec Warfare*, 1988; Hill, *Colonial Cakchiquels*, 1992; Dakin and Lutz, *Nuestro Pesar*, 1996.
11. AGI, *Mexico* 97; 138; 2999; Restall, *Maya Conquistador*, 1998: 53–76; Scholes and Roys, *Maya-Chontal Indians*, 1948: 142–290.
12. Gibson, *Tlaxcala*, 1952: 191; also quoted by Harris, *Aztecs, Moors, and Christians*, 2000: 139.
13. Fernández-Armesto, "'Aztec' Auguries," 1992: 298; Prescott, *Conquest of Mexico*, 1994: xxix; Hassig, *Aztec Warfare*, 1988; Brooks, "Construction of an Arrest," 1995.
14. Cieza de León, *Peru*, 1998 [1550]: 447–66; Sarmiento, *History of the Incas*, 1907 [1572]: 258–61; Prescott, *Conquest of Peru*, 1847, II: chaps. 1–3; Wachtel, *Vision of the Vanquished*, 1977: 169–84; Himmerich y Valencia, "Siege of Cuzco," 1998; Wood, *Conquistadors*, 2000: 155–85.
15. As illustrated in an important and fascinating series of documents of the 1530s to 1620s, most of them petitions to the king from Mexica royalty and other nobles, preserved in the AGI and recently published in Pérez-Rocha and Tena, *La nobleza indígena*, 2000. Complementary sources are the records of legal actions taken over lands and noble privileges by doña Isabel Moctezuma, the emperor's daughter, in the 1540s to 1560s, published in Pérez-Rocha, *Privilegios en Lucha*, 1998. Doña Isabel's descendents received government pensions until 1934, and in 2000 began a legal campaign to have the pensions reinstated (Lloyd, "The Scholar," 2002).
16. They were prominent members of what I have elsewhere termed Yucatan's "dynastic dozen"; Restall, "People of the Patio," 2001: 351–58, 366–68. The collection of documents known as the Xiu Papers, of which figure 16.2 is a part, were recently published for the first time, as Quezada and Okoshi, *Papeles de los Xiu*, 2001.
17. For this argument laid out with Maya evidence, see Restall, *Maya World*, 1997: 51–83; for treatments of native *cabildos* in other regions, see Spalding, *Huarochirí*, 1984: 216–26; Haskett, *Indigenous Rulers*, 1991; Stern, *Peru's Indian Peoples*, 1993: 92–96; and Terraciano, *The Mixtecs*, 2001: 182–97.
18. Lockhart, *Of Things*, 1999: 98. Also see Restall, "Interculturation," 1998: 141–62.
19. Cook, *Born to Die*, 1998. Note that there is much disagreement on the size of native populations in the ancient Americas, with estimates on 16th-century losses varying above and below the middle-ground figure of 40 million. But even at, say, 25 million, the death toll was still greater than Europe's Black Death, for example.
20. See Powers, "Battle of Wills," 1998: 183–213.
21. For readings on this issue with respect to central Mexico and Yucatan, for example, see Harvey, *Land and Politics*, 1991; Lockhart, *The Nahuas*, 1992: 141–202; Horn, *Postconquest Coyoacan*, 1997: 111–165; and Restall, *Maya World*, 1997: 169–225.

22. "Nothingness" is Le Clézio's term *(Mexican Dream*, 1993: 5)
23. Clendinnen, "'Fierce and Unnatural Cruelty,'" 1991: 19.

REFERENCES

Primary Archival Source and its Abbreviation

AGI Archive General de las Indias, Seville, Spain

Primary and Secondary Published Sources

Bricker, Victoria R. 1981. *The Indian Christ, the Indian King: The Historical Substrate of Maya Myth and Ritual*. Austin: University of Texas Press.

Brooks, Francis J. 1995. "Motecuzoma Xocoyotl, Hernán Cortés, and Bernal Díaz del

Castillo: The Construction of an Arrest," in *Hispanic American Historical Review* 75:2: 149–83.

Cieza de León, Pedro de. 1998. *The Discovery and Conquest of Peru* [ca. 1550]. Alexandra Parma Cook and Noble David Cook, eds. Durham: Duke University Press.

Clendinnen, Inga. 1987. *Ambivalent Conquests: Maya and Spaniard in Yucatan, 1517–1570*. Cambridge: Cambridge University Press.

Clendinnen, Inga. 1991. "'Fierce and Unnatural Cruelty': Cortés and the Conquest of Mexico," in *Representations* 33, Winter. (Reprinted in *New World Encounters*. Stephen Greenblatt, ed., 12–47. Berkeley: University of California Press, 1993).

Clendinnen, Inga. 1991. *Aztecs: An Interpretation*. Cambridge: Cambridge University Press.

Cohen, Jeffrey H. 1993. "Danza de la Pluma: Symbols of Submission and Separation in a Mexican Fiesta," in *Anthropological Quarterly* 66: 149–58.

Colom, Alejandra, et al., eds. 1999. *Testamento y Título de los Antecesores de los Señores de Cagcoh (San Cristóbal Verapaz)*. Guatemala City: Universidad del Valle de Guatemala.

Cook, Noble David. 1998. *Born to Die: Disease and the New World Conquest, 1492–1650*. Cambridge: Cambridge University Press.

Dakin, Karen, and Christopher H. Lutz. 1996. *Nuestro Pesar, Nuestra Aflicción: Memorias en lengua náhuatl enviadas a Felipe II por indigenas del valle de Guatemala hacia 1572*. Mexico City: Universidad Nacional Autónoma de Mexico and CIRMA.

Fernández-Armesto, Felipe. 1992. "'Aztec' Auguries and Memories of the Conquest of Mexico," in *Renaissance Studies* 6:3–4, 287–305.

Gibson, Charles. 1952. *Tlaxcala in the Sixteenth Century*. New Haven: Yale University Press.

Gómara, Francisco López de. 1964. *Cortés: The Life of the Conqueror by His Secretary*. Lesley Byrd Simpson, ed. (trans. of *Istoria de la conquista de Mexico* [1552]). Berkeley: University of California Press.

Harris, Max. 2000. *Aztecs, Moors, and Christians: Festivals of Reconquest in Mexico and Spain*. Austin: University of Texas Press.

Harvey, H.R., ed. 1991. *Land and Politics in the Valley of Mexico: A Two Thousand Year Perspective*. Albuquerque: University of New Mexico Press.

Haskett, Robert. 1991. *Indigenous Rulers: An Ethnohistory of Town Government in Colonial Cuernavaca*. Albuquerque: University of New Mexico Press.

Hassig, Ross. 1988. *Aztec Warfare: Imperial Expansion and Political Control*. Norman: University of Oklahoma Press.

Hill, Robert M., II. 1992. *Colonial Cakchiquels: Highland Maya Adaptation to Spanish Rule, 1600–1700*. Fort Worth: Harcourt Brace.

Himmerich y Valencia, Robert. 1998. "The 1536 Siege of Cuzco: An Analysis of Inca and Spanish Warfare," in *Colonial Latin American Historical Review* 7:4 (Fall): 387–418.

Horn, Rebecca. 1997. *Postconquest Coyoacan: Nahua-Spanish Relations in Central Mexico, 1519–1650*. Stanford: Stanford University Press.

Jones, Grant D. 1998. *The Conquest of the Last Maya Kingdom*. Stanford: Stanford University Press.

Le Clézio, J.M.G. 1993. *The Mexican Dream. Or, The Interrupted Thought of Amerindian Civilizations* (trans. of *Le rêve mexicain*). Chicago: University of Chicago Press.

Lloyd, Marion. "The Scholar as P.I.: A Historian Takes on the Case of Moctezuma's Heir," in *The Chronicle of Higher Education* (12 April 2002), p. A14 (accessed online).

Lockhart, James. 1992. *The Nahuas After the Conquest*. Stanford: Stanford University Press.

Lockhart, James. 1999. *Of Things of the Indies: Essays Old and New in Early Latin American History*. Stanford: Stanford University Press.

Motolinía, fray Toribio de. 1979. *Historia de los indios de la Nueva Espana* [1541]. Edmundo O'Gorman, ed. Mexico City: Pornia.

Pérez-Rocha, Emma. 1998. *Privilegios en lucha: La información de doña Isabel Moctezuma*. Mexico City: Instituto National de Antropologia e Historia (Colección científica).

Pérez-Rocha, Emma, and Rafael Tena. 2000. *La nobleza indígena del centro de México después de la conquista*. Mexico City: Institute Nacional de Antropología e Historia (Colección obra diversa).

Powers, Karen Vieira. 1998. "A Battle of Wills: Inventing Chiefly Legitimacy in the Colonial North Andes," in *Dead Giveaways: Indigenous Testaments of Colonial Mesoamerica and the Andes*. Susan Kellogg and Matthew Restall, eds., 183–214. Salt Lake City: University of Utah Press.

Prescott, William H. 1847. *History of the Conquest of Peru*. 2 vols. Philadelphia: Lippincott & Co.

Prescott, William H. 1909. *The Conquest of Mexico* [1843]. London: Dent.

Prescott, William H. 1994. *History of the Conquest of Mexico* [1843]. Introduction by Felipe Fernandez-Armesto. London: The Folio Society.

Quezada, Sergio, and Tsubasa Okoshi Harada. 2001. *Papeles de los Xiu de Yaxá, Yucatán*. Mexico City: Universidad Nacional Autonóma de México.

Rappaport, Joanne. 1994. *Cumbe Reborn: An Andean Ethnography of History.* Chicago: Chicago University Press.

Restall, Matthew. 1997. *The Maya World: Yucatec Culture and Society, 1550–1850.* Stanford: Stanford University Press.

Restall, Matthew. 1997. "Heirs to the Hieroglyphs: Indigenous Writing in Colonial Mesoamerica," in *The Americas* 54:2 (October): 239–67.

Restall, Matthew. 1998. *Maya Conquistador.* Boston: Beacon Press.

Restall, Matthew. 1998. "Interculturation and the Indigenous Testament in Colonial Yucatán," in *Dead Giveaways: Indigenous Testaments of Colonial Mesoamerica and the Andes.* Susan Kellogg and Matthew Restall, eds., 141–62. Salt Lake City: University of Utah Press.

Restall, Matthew. 2001. "The People of the Patio: Ethnohistorical Evidence of Yucatec Maya Royal Courts," in *Royal Courts of the Ancient Maya, Volume 2: Data and Case Studies.* Takeshi Inomata and Stephen D. Houston, eds., 335–90. Boulder: Westview.

Sarmiento de Gamboa, Pedro. 1907. *History of the Incas* [1572]. Sir Clements Markham, ed. London: Hakluyt Society.

Scholes, France V., and Ralph L. Roys. 1948. *The Maya-Chontal Indians of Acalan-Tixchel: A Contribution to the History and Ethnography of the Yucatan Peninsula.* Washington: Carnegie Institution. (Reprinted by University of Oklahoma Press, 1968).

Sousa, Lisa M., and Kevin Terraciano. 2003. "The Original Conquest of Oaxaca: Nahua and Mixtec Accounts of the Spanish Conquest," in *Ethnohistory* 50: 2.

Spalding, Karen. 1984. *Huarochirí: An Andean Society Under Inca and Spanish Rule.* Stanford: Stanford University Press.

Stern, Steve J. 1993. *Peru's Indian Peoples and the Challenge of Spanish Conquest: Huamanga to 1640.* 2nd ed. Madison: University of Wisconsin Press.

Terraciano, Kevin. 2001. *The Mixtecs of Colonial Oaxaca: Ñudzahui History, Sixteenth through Eighteenth Centuries.* Stanford: Stanford University Press.

Thomas, Hugh. 1995. *Conquest: Montezuma, Cortés, and the Fall of Old Mexico.* New York: Simon and Schuster.

Wachtel, Nathan. 1977. *The Vision of the Vanquished: The Spanish Conquest of Peru through Indian Eyes, 1530–1570.* Hassocks, UK: Harvester Press. (Translation of *La vision des vaincus. Les Indiens du Pérou devant la conquête espagnol 1530–1570.* Paris: Gallimard, 1971.)

Wood, Michael. 2000. *Conquistadors.* Berkeley and London: University of California Press and the BBC.

CHAPTER 17

SAAMI AND NORWEGIANS: SYMBOLS OF PEOPLEHOOD AND NATIONHOOD

Trond Thuen

INTRODUCTION

Except for the outburst of rebellion against the state which occurred during the Alta conflict, Saami political emancipation can hardly be conceived as a nationalist, that is a separatist, movement. Even on that occasion, those few who proposed that "Saami should be masters in their own house" never specified their aspirations beyond the level of political slogans; they were far from being representative. As Part Three will demonstrate, Saami ethnopolitical voices express diverging perspectives on the status of Saami culture, rights, and organizations within the Norwegian political system. The oppression of cultural distinctiveness, in particular the Saami language, with the aim of assimilating the Saami population between 1860 and 1960, produced a widespread ambivalence and even antagonism towards those who propagated Saami cultural and political interests, and thus confronted their Norwegian social environment as well as Norwegian governmental institutions. There has been, and still is, a scepticism concerning the politicization of Saami ethnic identity, which is intimately linked to ambivalences of identity management. The questions "who is Saami?" and "what does it mean to be a Saami?" are commonly conceived as being political, implicating the question "where do I belong in the ethnopolitical landscape?"

In an influential article, Eidheim (1971:68–82) presented a model comprising two basic aspects of the idiomatic recodification inherent in the Saami ethnic incorporation during the 1960s: *complementarization* and *dichotomization*. The first depicts interethnic (Saami-Norwegian) transactions serving "to facilitate the establishment of interethnic relations based on equality" (*op. cit.*:79), and the second emphasizes intraethnic (Saami-Saami) transactions engendering a dichotomization of the two groups "so that Lappish [i.e. Saami] ethnic designata can be shared and made objects of transactions of incorporation by Lappish people" (ibid.:79). These concepts emphasize aspects of ethnopolitical incorporation that are basic to the emancipatory efforts of ethnic minorities everywhere. Saami themselves recognize that their cultural manifestations contrast with those of the Norwegians on a comparable and even a complementary basis, and that their Norwegian counterparts increasingly have come to accept this self-ascription; this implies that they share a sense of peoplehood founded on this relationship. Their shared sense of distinctiveness is not, in other words, based on any set of "objective" criteria of cultural differences *per se*, but on their symbolic relevance in communicating ethnic belonging and dissimilarity.

Whether these qualities of peoplehood should also be extended to encompass a sense of nationhood is another question, however. If so, it would entail a recurring denial of any sharing of national symbols with the Norwegians as well as consistently evaluating pan-Saami relationships over and above relationships with Norwegians. As I will argue, this does not seem to be the case. There are allegiances and evaluations shared with the Norwegians which attest to the fact that Saami ethnopolitical aspirations do not encompass any purpose of separating from the Norwegian nation-state.

POLITICIZATION OF PEOPLEHOOD

Conventions about how ethnic identity is constituted and signalled may be regarded as manifest or latent communicative opportunities corresponding to idioms which may be adopted or rejected by individuals in their ongoing presentations of self. As demonstrated in the last chapter, their application is either mandatory or optional, largely dependent on how well the ascription of ethnic status from others corresponds to self-identification, how skilled one is in performances customarily associated with a specific ethnic identity, and how extensive and relevant is the public knowledge of a person's origin of descent. In this respect, Saami ethnic identity differs from Norwegian in that Saami-ness may be undercommunicated or even abandoned, whereas Norwegian identity derives from origin and does not command any specific performances other than language (which has to be idiomatically correct, not "broken"). Norwegian identity can hardly be substituted for any other ethnic identity. These considerations apply to individual challenges of identity management. However, we should also consider the differences between Norwegian-ness and Saami-ness, which concern their respective "national" symbols. What are the characteristics of Saami images of peoplehood that constitute their collective and encompass belonging? To what extent are they considered separate from, and complementary to, Norwegian nationhood, and to what extent do shared idioms of common nationhood exist?

The opening of the Saami Assembly in Karasjohka in October 1989 marked an important official upgrading of the status of the Saami as an Aboriginal people within the Norwegian society and state system. The opening was celebrated with greetings from Norwegian authorities, Saami organizations on a Nordic level, and first and foremost by the Norwegian king, King Olav V, who officially performed the solemn inauguration. The occasion visualized an important step in the evolution of a Saami peoplehood, and at the same time demonstrated a major change in the ethnopolitical relationship between the Saami people and the Norwegian nation-state. The institution is an innovation within the Norwegian polity inasmuch as the Norwegian Parliament has bestowed upon one segment of Norwegian citizens the opportunity to recruit a representative assembly through a general election organized and supervised by the government. In fact, Saami electoral boards authorized the elected representatives. The Saami Assembly has a consigned authority to voice its opinion on any issue that it deems relevant to its constituency, and may have its authority extended to include decisive control over issues later to be negotiated. During the first period (1989–1993), the government has transferred to it a number of specific administrative responsibilities, and the politicization of Saami peoplehood has entered a new phase: it has reached a level of officially recognized complementarity to the Norwegian peoplehood.

As one symbol of Saami peoplehood, the Saami Assembly may be compared to other symbols of this peoplehood as they relate to features of cultural diversities within the Saami population and to the varying identity ascriptions of Saami-ness relative to the Norwegian nationhood encompassing it. To corroborate my assumption that Saami political aspirations aim at some measure of self-determination within the Norwegian national system rather than separation from it, I will depict some images of the Saami-Norwegian relationship exposed at events prior to the establishment of the Saami Assembly.

Tensions between divergent conceptions of how the future relationship between these two peoples should be managed permeates Saami ethnopolitics, creating internal political rivalry. However, none of the contesting factions within the Saami polity have adopted a one-sided ideology on the question of integration within Norwegian nationhood or separation from it. The issue seems too complex to invite a non-compromising stand, and its complexity reflects the long-lasting history of Saami-Norwegian relationships, which has been experienced differently by various categories of the ethnic minority. Like many other ethnic minorities, the Saami present images of peoplehood that differ markedly when notions on the grass-roots level are compared to those prevalent within the elite.

The very concept of "a Saami people" may have originated among intellectuals early in this century, but the organization of collective movements has a longer history. There were protests against missionaries, priests, sheriffs, merchants, and farmers, caused by their encroachment on Saami territories, the eradication of their religious beliefs and symbols, the destructive effects of alcohol, and the closure of borders which excluded reindeer from their habitual pastures. Religious revivals occurred in the late 18th century and had a major outburst in the "Kautokeino rebellion" of 1852; this may have been more of a social protest than a "religious delusion" or "mental delirium," as it was explained by Norwegian authorities at the time. Since about 1860, protests were also launched against the school authorities which from that time ordered a complete eradication of the Saami language in the schools.[1]

In his history of the Saami coastal community of Kvænangen in Northern Troms, Bjørklund cites a local Saami protest against a Norwegian farmer's appropriation of a field of special grass used in footwear (*sennagras*), which they always considered as their common property:

> [We], the common people of Kvænangen, hereby authorize these men [two elected representatives] to do on our behalf anything that seems legal and necessary in this case, so that we may know how to behave, and, if necessary, even go to His Majesty the King of Norway to ask our gracious King to protect us, *who are the aboriginal inhabitants of this country*, against our oppressors, so that we may keep our use and rights in peace, like we used to do from ancient times in hundreds of years; or is it really so that we shall have to leave this country forced by the encroachments of our adversaries? Signed by 101 persons in 1862 (Bjørklund 1985:278–279, my translation).

The Saami lost their case, but irrespective of who formulated it, it is a remarkable testimony of a local Saami community's early self-conception as a people. It also alludes to a theme to which we shall return: the king as superimposed protector.

Around the turn of the last century, the national movement in Norway was paralleled by a Saami ethnopolitical mobilization. From 1906 to 1912, Isak Saba, a Saami teacher who also wrote the Saami national anthem, represented rural districts in Finnmark in the Norwegian Parliament. A Saami newspaper, edited by another Saami teacher, Anders Larsen, appeared from 1904 to 1911. Their demands were particularly directed at the abolishment of a clause in the law on the sale of state-owned land in Finnmark, which claimed that buyers commanded the Norwegian language, and they also protested against the "Norwegianization" of the school system. In principle, they argued a policy of ethnic equality. A second effort at parliamentary representation on a basis independent of Norwegian political parties was unsuccessfully made in 1921 (Finnmark) and 1924 (Nordland). Between 1905 and 1920, several Saami local and regional associations were founded, and in 1917 and 1921 national meetings held in Trondheim were also attended by Saami from Sweden. However, a national, permanent organization was not established (Otnes 1970). In 1948 the reindeer owners founded their own national organization, the NRL. But, as we have seen, the idea of a separate and general Saami national organization and a uniting program of Saami claims and interests does not surface again until the late 1950s.

How to relate to Norwegian political parties and organizations was a pervasive problem for the Saami movement. After Saba, their spokesmen opted to cooperate with the Labour movement but did not succeed even there in gaining acceptance for a Saami program (Minde 1984). As farmers' and fishermen's organizations developed and gained influence over governmental policies, Saami also joined and tried to make their voices heard.[2]

The political and economic climate did not encourage the development of a genuine Saami national movement, whether inside the Norwegian nation-state or on a Nordic basis. Instead, they sought protection of their cultural distinctiveness (language, reindeer breeding) within the Norwegian nationhood. It has only been since the 1970s that an image of an extended self-government has developed, starting with some unspecified declarations and developing into a more coherent claim of decisive power, which, according to some voices (Stordahl 1987), went further than what the Saami Rights Committee proposed at the time.

Changing political aspirations are also revealed in a collective self-ascription. The application of terms denoting a group's cohesiveness and aspirations to advanced status within the political realm of the encompassing political system is of course itself a question of the symbolic presentation of self. The change in labels for Saami peoplehood illustrates this. Throughout the 1970s the NSR used the term "the Saami minority," but the tendency in later years has been to replace it with "the Saami people" and even "the Saami nation." The "minority" label suggested an acceptance of that status and did not just denote the existing asymmetrical relationship. The change corresponds to, and is probably inspired by, the adoption of "nation" by other Aboriginal peoples, such as the Assembly of First Nations in Canada, which strongly emphasizes the status of original (pre-colonial), self-governing entities as the justification for future legal and political independence. And not surprisingly, the term "nation" is dismissed by the integrationist ethnopolitical opposition to the NSR and the Saami Assembly since it implies a separatist stance.

The enrolment of the Saami for participation in an election of their own political organization could be seen as the first step towards building a nation. Their claim of land rights implying some control of resource management within a specified territory, and a measure of self-government implying the right to decide on their own public affairs, would be the minimum preconditions for the development of a Saami nation and nationhood. Aside from internal antagonism on these issues, which basically concerns the question of self-ascription of Saami versus Norwegian identity, the problem is also a practical one. Not only is the demarcation of their territory problematic, but as they are also the subjects of different state jurisdictions, this would make the creation of an encompassing Saami nation a rather distant aim, if politically accomplishable at all.

When conceptualized as an alternative to the nation-states in which they now live, the notion of a "pan-Saami" nationhood is hardly conceivable to Saami political leadership. Rather, their political task is conceptualized as the development of self-determination within the respective national state borders that intersect Saami settlement areas. Consequently, their efforts to determine their political space are aimed at demarcating it for the political and administrative authorities of governmental agencies on the central and lower levels of ministries, provinces, and municipalities. In these efforts they seek acceptance from the top level of the political system, notably from the national parliament.

State borders physically intersect the Saami society: they represent obstacles to traffic between communities that traditionally enjoyed close contact, and after 1917 completely prohibited interaction between Eastern Finnmark and the Kola peninsula. In other parts, traditional adaptations such as reindeer breeding are subject to agreements between the state governments, according to which pastures on the other side of the border have limited access for a limited number of animals. Equally important is the subdivision engendered among the Saami because they have to relate to different governments and are treated according to policies which are part of the general understanding and acceptance of their interests. The Saami, encapsulated within different state jurisdictions, are exposed to diverging administrative regimes and state policies, which halt the formation of an encompassing Saami political community. As a consequence, the achievements of their national organizations within the realms of a particular nation-state are considered important and attract the most interest and demand the most effort. It is within the nation-state that particular claims have an addressee and concrete amendments can be gained. Coordinated Nordic efforts are typically aimed at symbolic statements of unity of culture and peoplehood, and are rarely backed by concrete demands or strategies for specific pan-Saami achievements. The Nordic Saami Council (established 1956) is an umbrella organization for the national associations of the NSR and the NRL in Norway, the *Same Ätnam* and the Swedish Saami Association in Sweden, and the Saami Assembly in Finland, and arranges a Nordic Saami Conference every third year. In 1980, it adopted a program of basic principles for the definition of Saami political aims and interests; the first read: "We Saami are one people, and the national borders shall not break up the community of our people."

New perspectives on the prospects of pan-Saami unification were presented, derived from the ideology of regionalism emerging within the European Union (EU). However, following plebiscites in 1994, Sweden and Finland joined the EU while Norway stayed outside. The general idea was that the corrosion of state borders would vitalize cultural links across those borders and encourage the establishment of stronger organizational links between peoples who had hitherto been separated by them.

STRUCTURAL CHARACTERISTICS OF THE EXTRA-LOCAL SAAMI SOCIETY

The problem of developing a pan-Saami nationhood is of course a reflection of the historical state-building processes in Scandinavia. Traditionally, relationships between Saami communities have been stronger with other Saami to the east, on the other side of the Norwegian-Swedish border, than with adjacent communities on a north-south axis. This is reflected in the distribution of Saami dialects. Dialect differences between the northern and southern parts of their settlement area are greater, to the extent that they are not mutually comprehensible, whereas communities on a west-east line belong to the same dialect area. In a real sense, then, national borders cut across the Saami settlement area and reduce or prohibit east-west connections, for instance for cross-border reindeer nomadism, which can only be maintained by limited inter-state agreements.

The cohesiveness of Saami peoplehood is perhaps best conceptualized as a network of social relationships with zones of varying density. The extensive resource utilization by reindeer husbandry facilitates and encourages social interaction over vast areas; it has served to develop an extensive network of social exchange, which compensated for the isolation that geographical distance and topographical barriers would otherwise have engendered. In addition, individuals and families have to some extent traditionally switched between varying niche exploitations. Nomads have resorted to a sedentary adaptation when their reindeer husbandry failed, and sedentary individuals and families have become nomads when prospects invited them to do so (Paine 1964, 1981). Bilateral and affinal kinship relations have made the transitions easy. Demographic investigations reveal that the stability of the sedentary population has not usually been very strong. The roots of local populations in many communities usually do not extend over more than three or four generations. This is in marked contrast to the immigrant Norwegian farming population in inner Troms, where pioneers settled during a 40- to 50-year period starting just before the turn of the 18th century. For this population, the concept of an "organic" relationship between lineage of descent and the farm and its cultivated area is very solid (Bårnes 1991). This contrast between the extensive, combined, and mobile use of a number of resources on one hand and the permanent adaptation to a geographically limited area on the other articulates a difference in cultural preferences and skills. It should also be related to the problem of retaining land ownership and control among the Saami after the introduction of a state registration of farm plots and absentee land ownership in the 18th century. Whether Saami geographical mobility was enforced as a consequence of the loss of land or as a strategy for a varied and complex resource utilization, the existence of a large number of kin in close and distant localities was a major asset as well as an adaptational prerequisite. Market relations and congregational gatherings at particular times of the year also cemented the linkages between partners within this extensive network.

The characteristics of a Saami traditional peoplehood may be visualized, then, as an informal network bound together by consanguine and affinal relations, trade and gift exchange, and religious faith. These fields of interaction partly overlapped, partly subdivided the population into entities with characteristic dialects, congregational divergences, and economic pursuits. But these variations were subcultural in character compared to the distinctiveness of their relationship to the Norwegian society. Although interethnic relations also developed, they were limited and constrained by the mutual perception of difference. As state authorities changed from a position of control and taxation to one of governmental responsibility for economic development and social welfare, Norwegians learned to enjoy their citizenship within a national realm sustained by an ideology of unity, whereas Saami cohesive networks were made obsolete by new forms of communication, trade, and production as well as by their emerging dependency on bureaucracies of an extra-local kind (Paine 1958, 1962, 1965).

SYMBOLS OF PEOPLEHOOD AND THEIR VARYING INTERPRETATIONS

The single event that most decisively engendered a change in the governmental apprehension of Saami ethnopolitical rights was the hunger strike of 1979. The Alta-Kautokeino project highlighted the question of Saami land claims and Aboriginal status on an unprecedented scale. The hunger strike was an unequalled demonstration of the power relationship prevailing between the Norwegian state and the Saami people, as interpreted by the public and the mass media. The significational impact was achieved by the juxtaposition of metonymic signs relating the two parties to the specific confrontational situation: the *lavvo* (reindeer herder's tent) erected in front of the *parliament building* in Oslo. The hunger strikers demonstrated a strong conviction in the legitimacy of their cause by their chosen form of action, *starvation*, while at the same time exhibiting their lack of power; state authorities demonstrated their power of jurisdiction and their physical strength by surrounding the hunger strikers with *police*. The *urban scene* contrasted with the *nature-dependent* and *exotic* Saami.

This juxtaposition aroused massive support from the Norwegian public in the South, but the reaction was considerably more varied among the Saami population. Although some applauded the hunger strikers for their perseverance and determination, a number of other voices disqualified them on the grounds that they were not at all representative of the Saami population, neither by their emphasis on reindeer nomadism nor by their political message. Some who disparaged them would agree with protesting against the damming, but disagree on the political means used; some would accept the project since it had been decided by the Norwegian Parliament, following regular decision-making procedures within the Norwegian political system. A number of Saami condemned the hunger strike and the Alta road blockade as an illegitimate challenge of Norwegian democratic institutions, as a rejection of the political system to which every citizen owed allegiance, whereas for the majority of the general public the authorities lost their credibility by enforcing this unfair treatment of a tiny minority's legitimate claim to survive ethnically and culturally within the Norwegian society. Introducing the Saami on the Norwegian political agenda reopened a division among the Saami concerning their peoplehood as well as their relationship to the encompassing political system and its national symbols. In the way it challenged supreme Norwegian institutions, it was conceptualized as an act of separation from the Norwegian national community, which these Saami considered deserved their allegiance as well. In the short run, the Saami ethnopolitical offensive proved counterproductive in creating Saami unity.

Investigations which followed proposed recommendations that included a constitutional amendment: "It is incumbent on the government authorities to take the necessary steps to enable the Saami population to safeguard and develop their language, their culture and their societal life."[3] On the basis of its interpretation of international legal principles, the committee stated that "[t]here is no doubt that the Saami population comprises a people in a political and sociological sense." But concerning the implications of peoplehood, the committee had reservations:

> ... [the] Saami minority in Norway cannot invoke any of the principles of the right of self-determination of all peoples as they are formulated in current conventions. In this respect, the position of the Saami people is different from that of the Inuit population in Greenland—where the area and its population are distinctly separate, geographically, historically and culturally, from the "mother country," and where the area has, moreover, for many years had the explicit status of a colony—even though there are points of resemblance between the Saami and the Inuits [sic] in other respects (Kommunaldepartementet, n.d.:15).

However, the committee found support for the principle of positive discrimination, particularly in Article 27 of the UN International Covenant on Civil and Political Rights:

> The conclusion of our report is that Article 27 probably imposes an obligation on the various states to provide economic support to enable the minority groups virtually to use their own language and other aspects of their culture. As regards quantification of this obligation, it should be presumed that the states are under an obligation to implement measures whereby a reasonable degree of equality is attained with regard to allowing a minority to enjoy its own culture in relation to the rest of society (ibid.: 16).

These considerations formed the basis for the committee's recommendation of the constitutional amendment cited above. Again, Saami committee representatives were divided on the issue of constitutional reference to the Saami, namely whether the continued existence of a Saami people and culture required an acknowledgment within a legislation codifying Norwegian nationhood.

Another event which signified divergences of Saami attitudes towards Norwegian national symbols occurred one year before the hunger strike. In 1978 the NSR, the main Saami organization at that time, was invited to send its chairman to the 75th anniversary of King Olav V. At the annual assembly, the NSR board announced that it had turned down the invitation, allegedly because the organization could not afford to send its chairman to Oslo when there was already a lack of funds for other urgent needs. However, a number of representatives at the annual assembly considered it an offensive act to challenge the king: he was a national symbol not only for Norwegians, but also for Saami. It was argued that the invitation was by itself a token of acknowledgement of the Saami as a people. The opposition signalled their discontent with the board's decision by exiting from the organization. They later joined with other Saami who had long considered the NSR to be too much of a "separatist" and "extremist" organization to be representative of the Saami, and founded a rival organization, the SLF (the Saami National Association) (Stordahl 1982), which explicitly stated that SLF should work on the basis of the principles of the Norwegian constitution and show deference and respect for the king and his government, Parliament, and other public authorities in a democratic fashion. This extraordinary avowal of Norwegian national and governmental allegiance should be interpreted as a distancing from the NSR, which, by implication, was accused of alienating the Saami from their nation-state membership.

Again, we can observe the symbolic prominence of certain national emblems, notably the king. The guiding principle of the SLF's policy has been to promote Saami interests from within established institutions, contending that they are Saami *and* Norwegians. This contention, whether implicitly or explicitly stated, should be interpreted in two interrelated ways: a) that the Saami are Norwegian citizens as well, and the ordinary institutions of the Norwegian political system guarantee their equal treatment and participation in the democratic process of government; and b) although they consider themselves Saami, many of them do not feel like having an exclusive Saami identity as opposed to a Norwegian. They argue that they are of "mixed" origin, and their culture is influenced by the Norwegian to the extent that they differ more from those who exhibit an obvious Saami identity (for instance, reindeer breeders) than from Norwegians in the North. Therefore, the ethnic border is not significant. Rather, Saami should be considered to be marginal in a geographical sense as are many Norwegians, and there is no need for an antagonistic relationship between Saami and Norwegians when regional development and a firmer basis for the existing settlement pattern are the main concerns for both parties. There is also a deeply felt fear among many Saami that the antagonism of the past should be reinvoked. To them, the notion of "positive discrimination" brings to mind a situation where Saami are given special access to resources which Norwegians equally evaluate and depend upon for their livelihood; they fear that this situation will provoke Norwegian resentment.[4]

As previously mentioned, the SLF members of the Saami Rights Committee opposed the idea of a directly elected Saami Assembly. However, when the institution was finally adopted by the Norwegian Parliament, and in particular when it was given symbolic value by the king's act of inauguration, the SLF chairman greeted the Saami Assembly by taking the king's presence to be a token of the future friendly relationship between the two categories of Norwegian citizens. The interpretation of the occasion may have differed among other Saami participants. What had started as a juxtaposition 10 years earlier in Oslo was now transformed into some kind of equivalence, even complementarity. It was no longer weakness confronting power in the Norwegian capital, but symbols of peoplehood displayed in Karasjohka, "capital of the Saami."[5] It could even be seen as the embryo of nationhood: an organizational tool had been created that could be developed further into an institution for the management of self-determination within those areas of public administration that most decisively concerned the Saami, which was obviously the aim of the majority of its representatives.

Still, some notion of Norwegian nationhood is retained. There seems to be no wish to disregard the legally and symbolically significant principle that states that the Saami Assembly derives its mandate from the Saami Act adopted by the Norwegian Parliament. A balance must be kept between Saami political aspirations and Norwegian nationhood, inspired by a deeply anchored allegiance towards Norwegian nationhood which many Saami do not feel is incompatible with their feeling of Saami peoplehood.

THE KING: EMBLEM OF JOINT NATIONHOOD?

The personification of Norwegian nationhood that the king represents is a master symbol which derives its importance from its quality of lending itself to different interpretations. As noted earlier, it is plausible that the effects of "Norwegianization" on a large proportion of the Saami led them to internalize a self-identification of Saami-ness as being of a lesser value than Norwegian-ness. To them, its signification would mean an ultimate guarantee that Saami are fully accepted as Norwegian citizens while sustaining their identity as Saami. They would not demand any separate treatment by the state beyond that which pertains to subcultural variations within the Norwegian population as long as this acknowledgement of equivalence is sustained. The formal position of the king, above antagonism within the nation-state and independent of shifting governments, has a special significance: he is also above ethnic difference. He may even have his own political will and act as a corrective to government or to Norwegian condescension toward Saami. To others, and here those self-conscious Saami who have continuously demanded that the acknowledgement of Saami political rights be contingent upon their Aboriginal status are included, the king embodies a strong symbol of nationality, but without much political power of his own. His presence is a manifestation of the governmental acknowledgment of a complementary status for the Saami as a people in their own right. His performance of the inauguration was significant not only as an expression of governmental and parliamentary approval of the Saami Assembly as an exceptional institution, but also by the impression they knew that this act would have on the Saami and the Norwegian populations at large.

In the mind of Norwegians, the position of the late King Olav V can hardly be underestimated, and there is no reason to assume that as part of the Norwegian image of nationhood this was not equalled by the one held by Saami. In this respect, then, we envisage nationhood as encompassing the two peoplehoods. Since this leaves the Saami without any overarching symbol of their own nationhood, would it mean that they are inevitably bound to see their minority position confirmed? No one other than a Saami would recognize any particular symbolic relationship between the king and the category of Norwegian citizens, the Saami. As suspected by their opposition, it would not have been politically inconsistent for the NSR leadership to reject the invitation in 1978 on more than pragmatic grounds. It is perhaps more than a curiosity that the Saami newspaper *Ságat* argued, prior to the inauguration of the Saami Assembly in 1989, that the king should consider wearing a Saami costume (a *kofte*) on the occasion in order to symbolize his status as sovereign of the two peoples. It was further argued, obviously as a curiosity, that he even had the right to wear it in terms of ethnicity, since he had "Saami blood in his veins." The newspaper referred to the old Norse saga in which King Harald Fairhair, the founder of the Norwegian kingdom in the ninth century, had a number of sons with the daughter of a Saami "chief." Through one of these sons the Norwegian royal dynasty in the Middle Ages was infused with "Saami blood." An old Saami had compared the "strength" of Saami blood to the effect of a drop of ink in a glass of water: the water turns black, but a drop of water in a glass of ink has no effect[6].

Why do Saami, seemingly irrespective of political allegiance and conception of future prospects for their people, regard the King of Norway as "their" king as well? I suggest two explanations: first, to Norwegians the king-image is an image of their national belonging, whereas to the Saami it is, in addition, an image of a relationship between the two categories of citizens. Grammar is important here, and I propose the following distinctions:

TABLE 17.1

"King of Norway"	
Norwegian codification King of the Norwegians	*Saami codification* King of Norwegian citizens (Norwegians and Saami)
Norwegian king	King of the Saami, but not Saami king (but may be of "mixed" origin?)

Second, we should recognize in this overarching emblem something more than a metonym in its ordinary sense of a condensed symbol. In hereditary monarchies, sovereigns are not elected: they are not personally installed by the majority or the power elite to rule over the minority(ies), although historically that may have occurred. They are "above" ethnicity, although they belong culturally to one category (prior to the creation of the nation-state they belonged to an "international" aristocracy). They may even be accepted and venerated for using symbols that are considered exclusive to the other category, as when on special occasions members of the royal family (usually female) dress in native costume. Such mixing of ethnic signs would otherwise be considered as a kind of sacrilege, since they are used for constituting ethnicity: when the rule is that only Saami wear Saami costume, anyone in such costume signals that s/he wishes to be recognized as a Saami.[7] Royal persons seemingly do not blur the message; they are recognized as who and what they are anyhow, and their use of the costume might be considered a device for ceremonial definition of specific occasions, and, as *Ságat* argued, "It would represent an appraisal of the traditional Saami costume which might make it easier to restore it from oblivion in Norwegianized Saami areas."[8] The monarch is not merely a symbol rendered meaningful by "his" people, but an agent giving meaning to his "peoples." He can be a good or bad king, a failure or an inspiration. Although he has little formal political power, he may still be considered a supreme judge of politics, and on certain occasions may actually perform his role in a way that renders particular meaning to decisive events (as King Haakon VII did when he refused to abdicate after the German attack and occupation of Norway in 1940, although asked by the Parliament).

THE RELEVANCE OF ETHNICITY: PAROCHIAL OR PAN-SAAMI?

The challenge of any ethnopolitical movement is to translate the everyday experiences of an ethnically suppressed category into a common fate to be changed by their concerted efforts. Attention should be given to the range of interethnic experiences and their relationship to differences in the expression of Saami identity. Simplified, these differences may be conceptualized as

1. those who identify as Saami as an obvious, unquestionable reality (reindeer breeders as the prototype);
2. those who identify as Saami because denying it would be unthinkable, despite experiencing stigmatization. A number of these Saami, particularly the younger generation, are converting their self-image from shame to pride, and joining the Saami ethnopolitical movement;
3. those who reckon themselves to be "both Saami and Norwegians" who may be on the way to an assimilated status, but may also find some advantage and future in cultivating their Saami relationship; and
4. those who do not identify as Saami any more, who live in communities that for all practical purposes would seem to be assimilated, or have moved away from their Saami home community to a career leading them out of the Saami and into Norwegian society.

The Saami ethnopolitical movement, having regained its momentum in the 1960s after an impasse since the 1920s, had to face these varying identifications and try to translate them into an encompassing ethnopolitical perspective in which these inward-directed and parochial codifications of Saami-ness could merge. They were confronted with scepticism and rejection: Saami nationhood was a theoretical construction by academics who did not have a proper understanding of the grass-roots problems and identity conceptions of the ordinary Saami (Eidhelm 1971, Ingold 1974). And in a sense, these allegations were real. Laestadian congregations have been and still are a central focus of Saami identification in many Saami communities, and there is little correspondence between their religious philosophy and the aspirations of the ethnopolitical movement (Torp 1986). The Laestadian confrontation with the majority society is based on a paradigm other than that of power and self-determination. It is a religious opposition: the state-operated Lutheran Church and its clergy have wrongly interpreted the holy message of salvation and taken control of the sinful individual's access to God. This access can only be obtained through confession and forgiveness by the congregation. A Laestadian meeting is a collective enactment of co-identity: "a congregational realization of self ... reached through ecstatic confession."[9] In "mixed" communities, the congregation may consist of individuals of both Saami and Norwegian origin who find in this community a sense of unity and equality against the valuational temptations and the administrative pressures of the outside world (Thuen 1987:80). Their ethos is strongly attached to a defence of their religious values, and if they are provoked to take political action, it will have to be in defence of their religious interests (Steinlien 1984). If connected to ethnopolitical alignments, some of these identifications are transformed into political allegiances such as the SLF and the NSR. But the Saami Assembly might evolve into an institution that will engender ethnopolitical commitments among Saami who do not feel engaged by what they presently consider to be a somewhat theoretical construction.

The identifications listed above do not parallel any divisions found within the Norwegian polity. Here we find political commitments on a scale from liberalist Thatcherism to socialism, with the Labour and Conservative parties as the dominant antagonists. Norwegian-ness is not an issue, but as we have seen, regionalism may be: whenever large investments are planned in one part of the country, some form of "compensation" is often due to another. Norwegian political representatives are accountable to their regional constituencies, and on some occasions their regional balance sheet counts more than their party's ideological responsibilities. Norwegian regionalism has never challenged nationhood, however strong might be the regional voices complaining of unequal distributions of public goods.

As I have argued, Norwegian nationhood (or peoplehood, as it were) depends on, or is expressed through, some regional guise. Spoken Norwegian always has its dialectal style from which natives can tell a person's geographical background, and regional characteristics abound with folk stereotypes. Northerners are traditionally debased, particularly by urbanites in the central eastern region, much as the Norwegian northerners used to debase Saami for their appearance and allegedly broken Norwegian.

In the present context, regional diversities and the parochial aspect of ethnic identification can be summed up: Norwegian nationhood encompasses a number of regional or subcultural variations. Inasmuch as the national "totality" is larger than the sum of these parts and has a quality of its own, this totality is the Norwegian nationhood. It is expressed at ritual occasions (the king's death, Independence Day) and as outbursts of patriotism at international athletics contests, and the monarchy serves to idiomatize it. Saami culture and society also exhibit parallel regional variations, or actually of a more divisive kind (for example, dialect differences of the Saami language). Until the present, however, the Saami "totality" has been more of a construction or a contention than a felt reality lacking those ritual and emblemic forms of expression characteristic of its Norwegian counterpart. And what is more, Saami attitudinal divergences are related to identity management and ascription in a qualitatively different way than how Norwegians feel about their identity or nationhood. Politicization among the Saami concerns ethnic identity and self-identification, which are questions related to nationhood and peoplehood, whereas for Norwegians it concerns more pragmatic interests, however ideologically flavoured.

CONCLUSION

Whereas for Norwegians, state borders correspond with national identity, state borders have split the Saami. Although linkages across the borders separating Norway, Sweden, and Finland have been firm between local Saami populations, and despite the fact that reindeer nomadism through its long-distance movements links otherwise separated Saami communities, the concept of Sápmi—Saamiland—is still very much a fiction. For the Saami, lack of traditional overarching institutions, language and adaptive differences, and the long-lasting state jurisdiction over their territories have effectively prohibited the creation of encompassing national symbols and institutions. And naturally, pressures to assimilate have counteracted the evolution of a general conception of Saami commonality. Common symbols such as a Saami flag have only recently been constructed. A Nordic Saami council has been in existence since 1953, but relative to the Nordic countries its political role has not been substantial. NSR, in signalling its stand on SLF accusations of "separatism" and "extremism," has repeatedly denied that their policy includes a constitutionally independent Sápmi.

While most Saami interpret Norwegian nationhood as deserving their loyalty, the state has been blamed for being ethnically blind. As far as this blindness goes (the allegation might not be completely fair), it has confirmed what its majority inhabitants perceived, that Saami had become so similar to Norwegians that special concerns were uncalled for, and even considered reactionary. Why should Saami be treated differently on ethnic grounds when class differentiation had been declared immoral? Through most of the post-war period, *marginality*, not ethnicity, was considered the main source of inequality. Accordingly, the ethnopolitical task of the Saami movement was to add *ethnic* disqualification to the majority's conceptualization of *economic* deprivation as an illegitimate social differentiation between Norway's citizens.

Saami and Norwegian regional diversities represent two contrasting series of differences, but in addition, as a minority the Saami are split among themselves as to how nationality should be conceptualized. Few, if any, demand separation from the Nordic nation-states. Many are concerned that the articulation of Saami interests does not bring about antagonism on the community level between those Saami and Norwegians equally dependent on the resource base in the north.

Norwegian national symbols, in particular the king and the royal family, but also the Norwegian Parliament after almost unanimously adopting the constitutional amendment and Saami Act, are considered to be overarching and also embrace Saami. The Norwegian Parliament is seen as a watchdog and guarantor of Saami interests against the government. Images of nationhood and common ideals, such as that of the king depicted as a symbol of unity with his people, would be as dear to most Saami as to Norwegians. In fact, a lack of representative Saami national institutions made them seek an ultimate authority for their appeals when suffering ill-treatment from authorities on lower levels, much as ordinary people before representative democracy went to the king in Copenhagen with their complaints. The king could be accorded a position beyond ethnic differences as much as he was considered above other divisions of class and ideology within Norwegian society. The ultimate proof of political extremism within the Saami ethnopolitical movement has been the rejection of the royal family on the grounds that they idiomatized Norwegian-ness *par excellence*. Thus, the opposition within NSR exited and formed SLF in 1978, protesting against the alleged disrespect for the king expressed by NSR "extremists." On the same pretext, the SLF chairman in 1989 greeted the opening assembly of the Saami Assembly to which his organization had been so vehemently opposed, by taking the king's presence as a guarantee for a future harmonious relationship between "the two categories of Norwegians."

In this respect, then, certain prominent emblems of Norwegian nationhood are also venerated by Saami. The king is the symbolic personification of national coexistence, not of majority supremacy. Other experiences testify to this codification, primarily during the German occupation when the test of a good Norwegian was the closing of ranks against collaboration with the enemy. Saami did not score less than Norwegians in that test. The "scorched earth" strategy of the German occupation forces, who destroyed homesteads and production equipment as they retreated from the Soviet army, put Saami and Norwegians literally on the same level as they were evacuated to the south of Norway. The rebuilding during early post-war years added to this experience of sharing the same destiny across ethnic boundaries.

However, although sharing common experiences and evaluating identical national symbols, the Saami were never equivalent to the Norwegians within a plural cultural system. In this respect Saami have been excluded as a nation while being incorporated, on Norwegian terms, into the state. Accordingly, the king may be conceptualized as bringing citizens rather than nationalities together.[10] Saami nationhood may be considered to embrace all Saami living in the four nation-states, but this is an abstract notion as long as no institutional arrangements symbolize this nationhood. The development of an all-embracing political, cultural, and social Saami unity is a challenging image not yet fully introduced on the Saami agenda.

A model for Saami self-determination is still in the making. It seems easier for the government to transfer administrative responsibilities that concern Saami exclusively, such as the allocation of funding for Saami small enterprises and artistic activities, to the Saami Assembly, rather than on issues which concern non-Saami interests, such as resource management as well. But Saami will expectedly have divergent opinions among themselves when it comes to such issues.

In essence, the balance of powers between Saami and Norwegian authorities concerns the future distinction of Saami nationhood relative to the Norwegian: will the dimensions of nationhood that have been missing in the Saami vision of the future Sapmi—territorial demarcation and self-government—be added at some future point? For the moment, this vision is restrained by the Nordic nation-state borders. The Nordic states have made minimal efforts to coordinate their policies on Saami demands.

NOTES

1. Otnes (1970). See also Worsley (1957).
2. In 1989 and 1993 this relationship was turned around: Norwegian political parties formulated Saami programmes and participated in the Saami election. As mentioned, only the Labour Party won any seats.
3. Quotations are from Kommunaldepartementet (n.d.): "Summary of the First report of the Norwegian Saami Rights Committee," which is a translation of the summary of the Norwegian version of the report.
4. This is not without corroboration. In the fall of 1991, the Saami Assembly commented on a proposed amendment of the game act, advising that the management of wildlife and hunting licences should be transferred to Saami agencies in Saami settlement areas which should be given the mandate to rent out hunting permits to non-resident hunters. This proposal was immediately interpreted by the Norwegian Hunters' and Anglers' Association as a Saami effort to monopolize access to and utilization of traditionally "free" resources.
5. Karasjohka's status of capital may be disputed by the neighbouring community of Guovdagealdnu (Kautokelno). If it should deserve that status, it would be contingent upon the localization of the Saami Assembly itself, which was decided on the basis of a fair distribution of central Saami institutions between the two townships.
6. As it turned out, he was dressed in the uniform of the supreme commander of the military forces.
7. Paine (1985: 175). See also Paine (1988a and 1988b).
8. *Ságat*. October 7, 1989.
9. Paine (1985: 175). See also Paine (1988a and 1988b).
10. I owe this formulation to Robert Paine.

REFERENCES

Bårnes, Vibeke B. 1991. "Dølakultur som delkultur. Kontinuitet og en-dring hos ei østnorsk innvandrerbefolkning i Indre Troms." Master's thesis, mimeographed. Tromso: University of Tromsa.

Bjørklund, Ivar. 1985. *Fjordfolket t Kvaenangen*. Oslo: Universitetsforlaget.

Eidheim, Harald. 1971. *Aspects of the Lappish Minority Situation*. Oslo: Universltetsforlaget.

Ingold, Tim. 1974. "Entrepreneur and Protagonist: Two Faces of a Political Career." *Journal of Peace Research*, 11(3):179–88.

Kommunaldepartmentet. n.d. "Summary of the First Report of the Norwegian Sami Rights Committee." Mimeographed. Oslo: Ministry of Municipal Affairs.

Minde, Henry. 1984. "The Saami Movement, the Norwegian Labour Party and Saami Rights." In H. Ahrweiler (ed.), *L'image de l'autre: étrangers, minoritaires, marginaux*, vol. 2. Stuttgart.

Otnes, Per. 1970. *Den samiske nasjon*. Oslo: Pax Forlag.

Paine, Robert. 1958. "Changes in the Ecological and Economic Bases in a Coast Lappish District." *Southwestern Journal of Anthropology*, 14(2):168–88.

Paine, Robert. 1962. "Innlemmelse av et utkantstrok i det nasjonale samfunn." *Tidsskrift for samfunnsforskning*, 3(3):65-82.

Paine, Robert. 1964. "Cultural Demography and Nomad/Sedentary Relations of Reindeer Lapp Groups in Norway and Sweden." Paper read at the VIIth International Congress of Anthropological and Ethnological Sciences, Moscow. Mimeographed.

Paine, Robert. 1965. *Coast Lapp Society II. A Study of Economic Development and Social Values*. Oslo: Universitetsforlaget.

Paine, Robert. 1981. "Til Norges Høyesterett. Uttalelse fra professor Robert Paine som oppnevnt sakkyndig i Samespørsmål og Altavassdraget." Mimeographed.

Paine, Robert. 1985. "Ethnodrama and the "Fourth World": The Saami Action Group in Norway, 1979–81." In N. Dyck (ed.), *Indigenous Peoples and the Nation-State.* St. John's, Newfoundland: Institute of Social and Economic Research, Memorial University.

Paine, Robert. 1988a. "The Persuasions of 'Being' and 'Doing': An Ethnographic Essay." *International Journal of Moral and Social Studies,* 3(1):17-40.

Paine, Robert. 1988b. "Grace out of Stigma: The Cultural Self-Management of a Saami Congregation." *Ethnologia Europeae,* 18:161–78.

Steinlien, Øystein. 1984. "Kulturell endrlng og etnisk kontinuitet. Lsestadianisme som politisk samlingsverdi i en samisk kystbygd." Master's thesis. University of Tromsø.

Stordahl, Vigdis. 1982. "Samer sier nel til Kongen.' En analyse av Norske Samers Rlksforbunds utvlkling og vilkar som etnopolitlsk organisasjon." Master's thesis, University of Tromsø.

Stordahl, Vigdis. 1987. "Sámithing and Sámi Committees—a Useful Political and Administrative Solution for the Sámi in Norway?" In *Self Determination and Indigenous Peoples. Sami Rights and Northern Perspectives.* IWGIA Document no. 58. Copenhagen.

Thuen, Trond. 1987. "One Community—One People? Ethnicity and Demography In a North-Norwegian Community 1865–1930." *Acta Borealia,* 4(l–2):65–84.

Torp, Eivind. 1986. "Fra 'markaflnn' til same. Etnopolltisk mobilisering i en laestadiansk kontekst." Master's thesis. University of Tromsø.

Worsley, Peter. 1957. *The Trumpet Shall Sound: A Study of "Cargo" Cults in Melanesia.* London: MacGibbon and Kee.

FURTHER READING

Blaut, J.M. 1993. *The Colonizer's Model of the World: Geographic Diffusionism and Eurocentric History.* New York: The Guilford Press.

The author challenges the proposition that Western civilization is superior to other civilizations and argues that "West"—a hallmark of more than three centuries of intellectual thought—is an ideology of colonialism. In particular, Blaut explains that the rise of European nation-states as international superpowers is a direct result of the exploitative effects of colonialism itself.

Francis, Daniel. 1992. *The Imaginary Indian: The Image of the Indian in Canadian Culture.* Vancouver: Arsenal Pulp Press.

Using a wide array of popular cultural icons, including paintings, travel writings, and fictional accounts, Daniel Francis explores the ways in which the image of "the Indian" was constructed and entrenched in the consciousness of 19th-century Anglo-Canadians. In particular, he explores the ways in which the dominant ideology of the "vanishing Indian" impacted the explosion of motifs (many of which were state-sponsored) around "indigeneity" as a respectable art form.

Wolf, Eric. 1997. *Europe and the People without History.* Berkeley: University of California Press.

Using history and anthropology, along with other social sciences, the author offers a Marxian analysis of the imperial expansion of Western Europe and explains how indigenous peoples were incorporated, to their detriment, into capitalist societies. Disciplinarily, Wolf tethers anthropological insights to a global political economy framework in the interests of understanding the complex and myriad ways in which indigenous societies and economies came to be interconnected with larger global/colonial forces.

PART 2B

COLONIALISM, SLAVERY, AND INDENTURED LABOUR

The chapters in this part provide a glimpse of the effects of colonialism and its associated labour forms in different social formations, particularly such labour forms as slavery and indentureship. Readers will see that the effects of these labour forms have been economic, social, cultural, political, psychological, and spiritual. Taken together, these effects have fundamentally shaped societies, the subjectivities of oppressed people, and their relationships with members of dominant groups.

W.E.B. Du Bois, writing at the turn of the 20th century, discussed "double consciousness" in the context of the post-Reconstruction United States. He asks, "How does it feel to be a problem?" Du Bois spoke about "a world which yields [the black man] no true self-consciousness." He argued that the formal freedom from slavery had not brought "real" freedom, in that most African Americans still lived in the shadows of slavery, in utter poverty, with broken homes, having to deal with war, racism, and capitalism. Du Bois argues, "To be a poor man is hard, but to be a poor race in a land of dollars is the very bottom of hardships." He ends with the positive assertion that African Americans have a great deal to offer the country, riches and resources that have come out of struggle and sorrow.

Moving away from the psychological and spiritual, Eric Williams brings home the point that colonialism, specifically the plantation economy in the Caribbean, was at its root an exploitative economic system based on slave labour. The sugar trade was accompanied by the West African slave trade, which was the jurisdiction of various Portuguese, English, French, Dutch, and Swedish companies. Williams writes that the slave trade became "an international free-for-all." Free trade was a matter of great debate in the 17th century as it is today, but in the earlier period it dealt with "slaves as commodities," as well as with consumer products. It was hardly a concern for slave traders that three out of every ten Africans died in the middle passage. Neither was it a concern for plantation owners that one in three Africans died within the first three years after landing. Africans were in fact "objectified." The so-called "triangular trade" involving European traders and shopkeepers, West African traders and enslaved people, and Caribbean plantation owners, filled the coffers of European monarchies, traders, and entrepreneurs.

Next to slave labour, indentured labour represented for plantation owners the next best source of workers. Verene Shepherd's chapter speaks to the experience of thousands of Indians who were brought over to work as plantation labourers in Jamaica from the middle of the 19th century to about 1917. (Even larger numbers of Indian labourers were brought to Trinidad and Guyana.) In addition to the economic, political, and psychological implications of colonialism explored in earlier chapters, this chapter reflects on the social and cultural implications of being colonized and racialized. Shepherd writes of Indian men and women of diverse linguistic, religious, caste, and class origins being "herded" together and being introduced to, yet segregated from, African Jamaicans. "A new kind of 'Indian' identity began to emerge," an Indian-Jamaican identity. Demographic realities affected gender relations and family and household formations in ways that were distinctive from other Caribbean and South American countries. The legacy of these realities remains even today.

CHAPTER 18

OF OUR SPIRITUAL STRIVINGS

W.E.B. Du Bois

O water, voice of my heart, crying in the sand,
All night long crying with a mournful cry,
As I lie and listen, and cannot understand
The voice of my heart in my side or the voice of the sea,
O water, crying for rest, is it I, is it I?
All night long the water is crying to me.
Unresting water, there shall never be rest
Till the last moon droop and the last tide fail,
And the fire of the end begin to burn in the west;
And the heart shall be weary and wonder and cry like the sea,
All life long crying without avail,
As the water all night long is crying to me.

Arthur Symons.

 [1]

Between me and the other world there is ever an unasked question: unasked by some through feelings of delicacy; by others through the difficulty of rightly framing it. All, nevertheless, flutter round it. They approach me in a half-hesitant sort of way, eye me curiously or compassionately, and then, instead of saying directly, How does it feel to be a problem? they say, I know an excellent colored man in my town; or, I fought at Mechanicsville;[2] or, Do not these Southern outrages make your blood boil? At these I smile, or am interested, or reduce the boiling to a simmer, as the occasion may require. To the real question, How does it feel to be a problem? I answer seldom a word.

And yet, being a problem is a strange experience,—peculiar even for one who has never been anything else, save perhaps in babyhood and in Europe. It is in the early days of rollicking boyhood that the revelation first bursts upon one, all in a day, as it were. I remember well when the shadow swept across me. I was a little thing, away up in the hills of New England, where the dark Housatonic[3] winds between Hoosac and Taghkanic to the sea. In a wee wooden schoolhouse, something put it into the boys' and girls' heads to buy gorgeous visiting-cards—ten cents a package—and exchange. The exchange was merry, till one girl, a tall newcomer, refused my card,—refused it peremptorily, with a glance. Then it dawned upon me with a certain suddenness that I was different from the others; or like, mayhap, in heart and life and longing, but shut out from their world by a vast veil. I had thereafter no desire to tear down that veil, to creep through; I held all beyond it in common contempt, and lived above it in a region of blue sky and great wandering shadows. That sky was bluest when I could beat my mates at examination-time, or beat them at a foot-race, or even beat their stringy heads. Alas, with the years all this fine contempt began to fade; for the worlds I longed for, and all their dazzling opportunities, were theirs, not mine. But they should not keep these prizes, I said; some, all, I would wrest from them. Just how I would do it I could never decide: by reading law, by healing the sick, by telling the wonderful tales that swam in my head,—some way. With other black boys the strife was not so fiercely sunny: their youth shrunk into tasteless sycophancy, or into silent hatred of the pale world about them and mocking distrust of everything white; or wasted itself in a bitter cry, Why did God make me an outcast and a stranger in mine own house? The shades of the prison-house closed round about us all: walls strait and stubborn to the whitest, but relentlessly narrow, tall, and unscalable to sons of night who must plod darkly on in resignation, or beat unavailing palms against the stone, or steadily, half hopelessly, watch the streak of blue above.[4]

After the Egyptian and Indian, the Greek and Roman, the Teuton and Mongolian, the Negro is a sort of seventh son,[5] born with a veil,[6] and gifted with second-sight in this American world,—a world which yields him no true self-consciousness, but only lets him see himself through the revelation of the other world. It is a peculiar sensation, this double-consciousness,[7] this sense of always looking at one's self through the eyes of others, of measuring one's soul by the tape of a world that looks on in amused contempt and pity. One ever feels his twoness,—an American, a Negro; two souls, two thoughts, two unreconciled strivings; two warring ideals in one dark body, whose dogged strength alone keeps it from being torn asunder.

The history of the American Negro is the history of this strife,—this longing to attain self-conscious manhood, to merge his double self into a better and truer self. In this merging he wishes neither of the older selves to be lost. He would not Africanize America, for America has too much to teach the world and Africa. He would not bleach his Negro soul in a flood of white Americanism, for he knows that Negro blood has a message for the world. He simply wishes to make it possible for a man to be both a Negro and an American, without being cursed and spit upon by his fellows, without having the doors of Opportunity closed roughly in his face.[8]

This, then, is the end of his striving: to be a co-worker in the kingdom of culture, to escape both death and isolation, to husband and use his best powers and his latent genius. These powers of body and mind have in the past been strangely wasted, dispersed, or forgotten. The shadow of a mighty Negro past flits through the tale of Ethiopia the Shadowy and of Egypt the Sphinx. Throughout history, the powers of single black men flash here and there like falling stars, and die sometimes before the world has rightly gauged their brightness. Here in America, in the few days since Emancipation, the black man's turning hither and thither in hesitant and doubtful striving has often made his very strength to lose effectiveness, to seem like absence of power, like weakness. And yet it is not weakness,—it is the contradiction of double aims. The double-aimed struggle of the black artisan—on the one hand to escape white contempt for a nation of mere hewers of wood and drawers of water, and on the other hand to plough and nail and dig for a poverty-stricken horde—could only result in making him a poor craftsman, for he had but half a heart in either cause. By the poverty and ignorance of his people, the Negro minister or doctor was tempted toward quackery and demagogy; and by the criticism of the other world, toward ideals that made him ashamed of his lowly tasks. The would-be black *savant* was confronted by the paradox that the knowledge his people needed was a twice-told tale to his white neighbors, while the knowledge which would teach the white world was Greek to his own flesh and blood. The innate love of harmony and beauty that set the ruder souls of his people a-dancing and a-singing raised but confusion and doubt in the soul of the black artist; for the beauty revealed to him was the soul-beauty of a race which his larger audience despised, and he could not articulate the message of another people. This waste of double aims, this seeking to satisfy two unreconciled ideals, has wrought sad havoc with the courage and faith and deeds of ten thousand thousand people,—has sent them often wooing false gods and invoking false means of salvation, and at times has even seemed about to make them ashamed of themselves.

Away back in the days of bondage they thought to see in one divine event the end of all doubt and disappointment; few men ever worshipped Freedom with half such unquestioning faith as did the American Negro for two centuries. To him, so far as he thought and dreamed, slavery was indeed the sum of all villainies, the cause of all sorrow, the root of all prejudice; Emancipation was the key to a promised land of sweeter beauty than ever stretched before the eyes of wearied Israelites.[9] In song and exhortation swelled one refrain—Liberty; in his tears and curses the God he implored had Freedom in his right hand. At last it came,—suddenly, fearfully, like a dream. With one wild carnival of blood and passion came the message in his own plaintive cadences:—

> "Shout, O children!
> Shout, you're free!
> For God has bought your liberty!"[10]

Years have passed away since then,—ten, twenty, forty; forty years of national life, forty years of renewal and development, and yet the swarthy spectre sits in its accustomed seat at the Nation's feast. In vain do we cry to this our vastest social problem:—

> "Take any shape but that, and my firm nerves
> Shall never tremble!"[11]

The Nation has not yet found peace from its sins; the freedman has not yet found in freedom his promised land. Whatever of good may have come in these years of change, the shadow of a deep disappointment rests upon the Negro people,—a disappointment all the more bitter because the unattained ideal was unbounded save by the simple ignorance of a lowly people.

The first decade was merely a prolongation of the vain search for freedom, the boon that seemed ever barely to elude their grasp,—like a tantalizing will-o'-the-wisp, maddening and misleading the headless host. The holocaust of war, the terrors of the Ku-Klux Klan,[12] the lies of carpetbaggers,[13] the disorganization of industry, and the contradictory advice of friends and foes, left the bewildered serf with no new watchword beyond the old cry for freedom. As the time flew, however, he began to grasp a new idea. The ideal of liberty demanded for its attainment powerful means, and these the Fifteenth Amendment gave him.[14] The ballot, which before he had looked upon as a visible sign of freedom, he now regarded as the chief means of gaining and perfecting the liberty with which war had partially endowed him. And why not? Had not votes made war and emancipated millions? Had not votes enfranchised the freedmen? Was anything impossible to a power that had done all this? A million black men started with renewed zeal to vote themselves into the kingdom. So the decade flew away, the revolution of 1876 came,[15] and left the half-free serf weary, wondering, but still inspired. Slowly but steadily, in the following years, a new vision began gradually to replace the dream of political power,—a powerful movement, the rise of another ideal to guide the unguided, another pillar of fire by night after a clouded day. It was the ideal of "book-learning"; the curiosity, born of compulsory ignorance, to know and test the power of the cabalistic letters of the white man, the longing to know. Here at last seemed to have been discovered the mountain path to Canaan; longer than the highway of Emancipation and law, steep and rugged, but straight, leading to heights high enough to overlook life.

Up the new path the advance guard toiled, slowly, heavily, doggedly; only those who have watched and guided the faltering feet, the misty minds, the dull understandings, of the dark pupils of these schools know how faithfully, how piteously, this people strove to learn. It was weary work. The cold statistician wrote down the inches of progress here and there, noted also where here and there a foot had slipped or some one had fallen. To the tired climbers, the horizon was ever dark, the mists were often cold, the Canaan was always dim and far away. If, however, the vistas disclosed as yet no goal, no resting-place, little but flattery and criticism, the journey at least gave leisure for reflection and self-examination; it changed the child of Emancipation to the youth with dawning self-consciousness, self-realization, self-respect. In those sombre forests of his striving his own soul rose before him, and he saw himself,—darkly as through a veil;[16] and yet he saw in himself some faint revelation of his power, of his mission. He began to have a dim feeling that, to attain his place in the world, he must be himself, and not another. For the first time he sought to analyze the burden he bore upon his back, that dead-weight of social degradation partially masked behind a half-named Negro problem. He felt his poverty; without a cent, without a home, without land, tools, or savings, he had entered into competition with rich, landed, skilled neighbors. To be a poor man is hard, but to be a poor race in a land of dollars is the very bottom of hardships. He felt the weight of his ignorance,—not simply of letters, but of life, of business, of the humanities; the accumulated sloth and shirking and awkwardness of decades and centuries shackled his hands and feet. Nor was his burden all poverty and ignorance. The red stain of bastardy, which two centuries of systematic legal defilement of Negro women had stamped upon his race, meant not only the loss of ancient African chastity, but also the hereditary weight of a mass of corruption from white adulterers, threatening almost the obliteration of the Negro home.

A people thus handicapped ought not to be asked to race with the world, but rather allowed to give all its time and thought to its own social problems. But alas! while sociologists gleefully count his bastards and his prostitutes, the very soul of the toiling, sweating black man is darkened by the shadow of a vast despair. Men call the shadow prejudice, and learnedly explain it as the natural defence of culture against barbarism, learning against ignorance, purity against crime, the "higher" against the "lower" races.[17] To which the Negro cries Amen! and swears that to so much of this strange prejudice as is founded on just homage to civilization, culture, righteousness, and progress, he humbly bows and meekly does obeisance. But before that nameless prejudice that leaps beyond all this he stands helpless, dismayed, and well-nigh speechless; before that personal disrespect and mockery, the ridicule and systematic humiliation, the distortion of fact and wanton license of fancy, the cynical ignoring of the better and the boisterous welcoming of the worse, the all-pervading desire to inculcate disdain for everything black, from Toussaint[18] to the devil,—before this there rises a sickening despair that would disarm and discourage any nation save that black host to whom "discouragement" is an unwritten word.

But the facing of so vast a prejudice could not but bring the inevitable self-questioning, self-disparagement, and lowering of ideals which ever accompany repression and breed in an atmosphere of contempt and hate. Whisperings and portents came borne upon the four winds: Lo! we are diseased and dying, cried the dark hosts; we cannot write, our voting is vain; what need of education, since we must always cook and serve? And the Nation echoed and enforced this self-criticism, saying: Be content to be servants, and nothing more; what need of higher culture for half-men? Away with the black man's ballot, by force or fraud,—and behold the suicide of a race! Nevertheless, out of the evil came something of good,— the more careful adjustment of education to real life, the clearer perception of the Negroes' social responsibilities, and the sobering realization of the meaning of progress.

So dawned the time of *Sturm und Drang*:[19] storm and stress to-day rocks our little boat on the mad waters of the world-sea; there is within and without the sound of conflict, the burning of body and rending of soul; inspiration strives with doubt, and faith with vain questionings. The bright ideals of the past,—physical freedom, political power, the training of brains and the training of hands,—all these in turn have waxed and waned, until even the last grows dim and overcast. Are they all wrong,—all false? No, not that, but each alone was over-simple and incomplete,—the dreams of a credulous race-childhood, or the fond imaginings of the other world which does not know and does not want to know our power. To be really true, all these ideals must be melted and welded into one. The training of the schools we need to-day more than ever,—the training of deft hands, quick eyes and ears, and above all the broader, deeper, higher culture of gifted minds and pure hearts. The power of the ballot we need in sheer self-defence,[20]—else what shall save us from a second slavery? Freedom, too, the long-sought, we still seek,—the freedom of life and limb, the freedom to work and think, the freedom to love and aspire. Work, culture, liberty,—all these we need, not singly but together, not successively but together, each growing and aiding each, and all striving toward that vaster ideal that swims before the Negro people, the ideal of human brotherhood, gained through the unifying ideal of Race; the ideal of fostering and developing the traits and talents of the Negro, not in opposition to or contempt for other races, but rather in large conformity to the greater ideals of the American Republic, in order that some day on American soil two world-races may give each to each those characteristics both so sadly lack. We the darker ones come even now not altogether empty-handed: there are to-day no truer exponents of the pure human spirit of the Declaration of Independence than the American Negroes; there is no true American music but the wild sweet melodies of the Negro slave; the American fairy tales and folk-lore are Indian and African; and, all in all, we black men seem the sole oasis of simple faith and reverence in a dusty desert of dollars and smartness. Will America be poorer if she replace her brutal dyspeptic blundering with light-hearted but determined Negro humility?[21] or her coarse and cruel wit with loving jovial good-humor? or her vulgar music with the soul of the Sorrow Songs?

Merely a concrete test of the underlying principles of the great republic is the Negro Problem, and the spiritual striving of the freedmen's sons is the travail of souls whose burden is almost beyond the measure of their strength, but who bear it in the name of an historic race, in the name of this the land of their fathers' fathers, and in the name of human opportunity.

And now what I have briefly sketched in large outline let me on coming pages tell again in many ways, with loving emphasis and deeper detail, that men may listen to the striving in the souls of black folk.

NOTES

1. The verse is Arthur Symons, "The Crying of Waters." The music is a Negro spiritual, "Nobody Knows the Trouble I've Seen." In every chapter but the last, Du Bois uses this structure of epigraphs: a passage of verse (usually from an American or European poet, but in one case from the Bible and in another from the *Rubaiyat of Omar Khayyam*), followed by a bar of music from the songs of American slaves. On the significance of this structure, especially the choice and origins of the spirituals, see Eric J. Sundquist, *To Wake the Nations: Race in the Making of American Literature* (Cambridge, Mass.: Harvard University Press), 490–539.
2. Mechanicsville was a Civil War battle fought on June 26, 1862, just east of Richmond, Virginia.
3. Housatonic is the river that flows through Great Barrington, Massachusetts.
4. In a composition he wrote as an undergraduate at Harvard, Du Bois may have expressed resentment that had been prompted by this childhood experience. Entitled "The American Girl," the essay describes the girl as an "eye-sore" whose face is "more shrewd than intelligent, arrogant than dignified, silly than pleasant, and pretty than beautiful." See Herbert Aptheker, ed., *Against Racism: Unpublished Essays, Papers, Addresses, 1887–1961, W.E.B. Du Bois* (Amherst: University of Massachusetts Press, 1985), 20. "The shades of the prison-house closed round us all" explicitly echoes William Wordworth's ode "Intimations Of Immortality From Recollections Of Early Childhood," lines 67-68. [...]
5. The figure of the seventh son carries multiple meanings. Apparently revising Hegel's philosophy of history, Du Bois adds the Negro to Hegel's story of six world-historical peoples (see pp. 12–13). In African American folklore, the seventh son is said to be distinguished in some way, to be able to see ghosts, and to make a good doctor. See Newbell Niles Puckett, *Folk Beliefs of the Southern Negro* (New York: Dover, 1969); Elsie Clews Parsons, *Folk-Lore of the Sea Islands, South Carolina* (Cambridge, Mass.: American Folklore Society, 1923); and Melville Herskovitz, *The Myth of the Negro Past* (1941; reprint, Boston: Beacon Press, 1958).
6. In African American folklore, a child born with a caul, a veil-like membrane that sometimes covers the head at birth, is said to be lucky, to be able to tell fortunes, and to be a "double-sighted" seer of ghosts. In some West African folk traditions, a child born with a caul is thought to possess a special personality endowed with spiritual potency. For biblical allusions to the veil, see Exodus 34.33–35; 2 Corinthians 13.13–18; Matthew 27.51; Hebrews 6.19, 10.20; and Isaiah 25.7. Also see the sources in note 5 of this chapter.
7. For an introduction to the literature on double consciousness, see Dickson D. Bruce Jr., "W.E.B. Du Bois and the Idea of Double Consciousness," *American Literature* 64 (June 1992): 299–309. [...]
8. Du Bois in this passage echoes the most prominent philosophers and poets writing in the European romantic tradition (such as William Blake, Samuel Taylor Coleridge, Friedrich Schiller, and Georg Wilhelm Friedrich Hegel) by promoting the creation of a unified self that synthesizes and preserves diverse elements. Though the American Negro was captured in Africa and forced into slavery in America, he knows no nostalgia for an African "self' that was untainted by the experience of America. Rather, his is a quest for a better, truer, and more encompassing self, the search for a mode of integrity that merges his African and newly acquired American identities yet retains them as distinct. On the romantic philosophers and poets, see M.H. Abrams, *Natural Supernaturalism* (New York: Norton, 1971).
9. Du Bois envisions blacks in America as the Old Testament Jews (Israelites) who have yet to escape the land of their captivity (Egypt) and enter the promised land (Canaan). On the late-nineteenth-century tradition of African American religious and political thought that gives rise to this imagery, see David W. Wills, "Exodus Piety: African-American Religion in an Age of Immigration," in *Minority Faiths and the American Protestant Mainstream*, ed. David O'Brien and Jonathan Sarns (Urbana: University of Illinois Press, 1998).
10. From the Negro spiritual "Shout, O Children!"
11. Shakespeare, *Macbeth*, 3.4.102–3.
12. The Ku Klux Klan is the white fraternal terrorist organization created in 1866 by Confederate veterans in Pulaski, Tennessee. Its members altered the Greek word for circle, *kuklos*, and invented their name. During Reconstruction in the South, the Klan engaged in widespread violence against blacks and their white Republican supporters.
13. Carpetbaggers were northern politicians and businessmen who moved to the South after the Civil War, allegedly to exploit the devastation of the South and the political vacuum left by the defeat of the Confederacy.
14. The Fifteenth Amendment to the US Constitution passed Congress in February 1869 and was ratified by the states in March 1870. It provided that voting rights "shall not be denied ... on account of race, color, or previous condition of servitude." The Fifteenth Amendment was a moderate measure; it did not specifically outlaw qualifications tests for the right to vote. But it did represent the federal government's key role as guarantor of rights during Reconstruction.
15. In the disputed presidential election of 1876, Republican Rutherford B. Hayes defeated Democrat Samuel J. Tilden. In three southern states, Louisiana, Florida, and South Carolina, the voting returns were disputed, with fraud and intimidation charged by both sides. The election was settled by a congressional committee that declared Hayes

the winner in the three contested states as well as by a political compromise (known as the Compromise of 1877) between the two parties. The "revolution" refers to southern Democratic threats to secede from the Union or march on Washington, D.C., early in the crisis. This "revolution" also represented the abandonment of the freedpeople in the South by the Republican Party.

16. See 1 Corinthians 13.12: "For now we see through a glass, darkly; but then face to face: now I know in part; but then shall I know even as also I am known."
17. Du Bois alludes to the belief, prevalent in the nineteenth century, that there exist several races of human beings that can be ranked hierarchically. For example, Count Arthur de Gobineau, in his *Essay on the Inequality of Human Races* (1853–1855), held that the white race possessed qualities (such as love of freedom, honor, and spirituality) that made it superior to the yellow and black races.
18. Toussaint L'Ouverture (1746–1803) was the leader of the Haitian revolution of 1791. A former slave, he became a brilliant general, led the forces that overthrew French rule in Sainte Domingue, and established himself as ruler of the new government by 1796. Toussaint was eventually captured by the French and died in France in 1803.
19. Literally in English, "storm and stress," the term *Sturm und Drang* was used for a literary movement in Germany during the last quarter of the eighteenth century. In general, the writings of the Sturm und Drang movement were intensely personal, emphasizing emotional experience and spiritual struggle. The work that perhaps best captures the spirit of the movement is Johann Wolfgang von Goethe's novel *Die Leiden des Jungen Werthers* (*The Sorrows of Young Werther*), published in 1774.
20. Appealing to the necessity of self-defense to justify an extension of the franchise was common in the nineteenth century and echoed utilitarian arguments for democracy made by philosophers Jeremy Bentham and James Mill. On Bentham's and Mill's views, see C.B. Macpherson, *The Life and Times of Liberal Democracy* (Oxford: Oxford University Press, 1977), 23-43.
21. Du Bois echoes the commencement speech he delivered at Harvard in June 1890, "Jefferson Davis as a Representative of Civilization." The speech describes the contrast between the brutal civilization of Jefferson Davis, president of the Confederacy, and the personal submissiveness of the Negro. See Aptheker, *Against Racism*, 14–16. Also see page 125 in chapter 8 of *Souls*.

SELECTED BIBLIOGRAPHY

Aptheker, Herbert, ed. *Against Racism: Unpublished Essays, Papers, Addresses. 1887–1961, W.E.B. Du Bois*. Amherst: University of Massachusetts Press, 1985.

Sundquist, Eric J. "Swing Low: *The Souls of Black Folk*." In *To Wake the Nations: Race in the Making of American Literature*. Cambridge: Harvard University Press, 1993.

CHAPTER 19

CAPITALISM AND SLAVERY

Eric Williams

"There is nothing which contributes more to the development of the colonies and the cultivation of their soil than the laborious toil of the Negroes." So reads a decree of King Louis XIV of France, on August 26, 1670. It was the consensus of seventeenth-century European opinion. Negroes became the "life" of the Caribbean, as George Downing said of Barbados in 1645. The "very being" of the plantations depended on the supply of Negroes stated the Company of Royal Adventurers of England trading to Africa to King Charles II in 1663. Without Negroes, said the Spanish Council of the Indies in 1685, the food needed for the support of the whole kingdom would cease to be produced and America would face absolute ruin. Europe has seldom been as unanimous on any issue as it has been on the value of Negro slave labour.

In 1645, before the introduction of the sugar economy, Barbados had 5,680 Negro slaves, or more than three able-bodied white men to every slave. In 1667, after the introduction of the sugar industry, the island, by one account, contained 82,023 slaves, or nearly ten slaves to every white man fit to bear arms. By 1698 a more accurate estimate of the population gave the figures as 2,330 white males and 42,000 slaves, or a ratio of more than eighteen slaves to every white male.

In Jamaica the ratio of slaves to whites was one to three in 1658, nearly six to one in 1698. There were 1,400 slaves in the former year, 40,000 in the latter. The ratio of slaves and mulattoes to whites increased from more than two to one in Martinique in 1664 to more than three to one in 1701. The coloured population amounted to 2,434 in 1664 and 23,362 in 1701. In Guadeloupe, by 1697, the coloured population outnumbered the whites by more than three to two. In Grenada in 1700 the Negro slaves and mulattoes were more than double the number of whites. In the Leeward Islands and in St. Thomas the whites steadily lost ground.

By 1688 it was estimated that Jamaica required annually 10,000 slaves, the Leeward Islands 6,000, and Barbados 4,000. A contract of October, 1675, with one Jean Oudiette, called for the supply of 800 slaves a year for four years to the French West Indies. Four years later, in 1679, the Senegal Company undertook to supply 2,000 slaves a year for eight years to the French Islands. Between 1680 and 1688 the Royal African Company supplied 46,396 slaves to the British West Indies, an annual average of 5,155.

The Negro slave trade became one of the most important business enterprises of the seventeenth century. In accordance with sixteenth-century precedents its organisation was entrusted to a company which was given the sole right by a particular nation to trade in slaves on the coast of West Africa, erect and maintain the forts necessary for the protection of the trade, and transport and sell the slaves in the West Indies. Individuals, free traders or "interlopers," as they were called, were excluded. Thus the British incorporated the Company of Royal Adventurers trading to Africa, in 1663, and later replaced this company by the Royal African Company, in 1672, the royal patronage and participation reflecting the importance of the trade and continuing the fashion set by the Spanish monarchy of increasing its revenues thereby. The monopoly of the French slave trade was at first assigned to the French West India Company in 1664, and then transferred, in 1673, to the Senegal Company. The monopoly of the Dutch slave trade was given to the Dutch West India Company, incorporated in 1621. Sweden organised a Guinea Company in 1647. The Danish West India Company, chartered in 1671, with the royal family among its shareholders, was allowed in 1674 to extend its activities to Guinea. Brandenburg established a Brandenburg African Company, and established its first trading post on the coast of West Africa in 1682. The Negro slave trade, begun about 1450 as a Portuguese monopoly, had, by the end of the seventeenth century, become an international free-for-all.

The organisation of the slave trade gave rise to one of the most heated and far-reaching economic polemics of the period. Typical of the argument in favour of the monopoly was a paper in 1680 regarding the Royal African Company of England. The argument, summarised, was as follows: firstly, experience demonstrated that the slave trade could not be carried on without forts on the West African Coast costing £20,000 a year, too heavy a charge for private traders, and it was not practicable to apportion it among them; secondly, the trade was exposed to attack by other nations, and it was the losses from such attacks prior to 1663 which had resulted in the formation of the chartered company; thirdly, the maintenance of forts and warships could not be undertaken by the Company unless it had an exclusive control; fourthly, private traders enslaved all and sundry, even Negroes of high rank, and this led to reprisals on the coast; finally, England's great rival, Holland, was only waiting for the dissolution of the English company to engross the entire trade.

The monopolistic company had to face two opponents: the planter in the colonies and the merchant at home, both of whom combined to advocate free trade. The planters complained of the insufficient quantity, the poor quality, and the high prices of the slaves supplied by the Company; the latter countered by pointing out that the planters were heavily in debt to it, estimated in 1671 at £70,000, and, four years later, at £60,000 for Jamaica alone. The British merchants claimed that free trade would mean the purchase of a larger number of Negroes, which would mean the production of a larger quantity of British goods for the purchase and upkeep of the slaves.

The controversy ended in a victory for free trade. On July 5, 1698, Parliament passed an act abrogating the monopoly of the Royal African Company, and throwing open the trade to all British subjects on payment of a duty of ten per cent *ad valorem* on all goods exported to Africa for the purchase of slaves.

The acrimonious controversy retained no trace of the pseudo-humanitarianism of the Spaniards in the sixteenth century, that Negro slavery was essential to the preservation of the Indians. In its place was a solid economic fact, that Negro slavery was essential to the preservation of the sugar plantations. The considerations were purely economic. The slaves were denominated "black ivory." The best slave was, in Spanish parlance, a "piece of the Indies," a slave 30 to 35 years old, about five feet eleven inches in height, without any physical defect. Adults who were not so tall and children were measured, and the total reduced to "pieces of the Indies." A contract in 1676 between the Spaniards and the Portuguese called for the supply of 10,000 "tons" of slaves; to avoid fraud and argument, it was stipulated that three Negroes should be considered the equivalent of one ton. In 1651 the English Guinea Company instructed its agent to load one of its ships with as many Negroes as it could carry, and, in default, to fill up the ship with cattle.

The mortality in the Middle Passage was regarded merely as an unfortunate trading loss, except for the fact that Negroes were more costly than cattle. Losses in fact ran quite high, but such concern as was evinced had to deal merely with profits. In 1659, a Dutch slaver, the *St. Jan*, lost 110 slaves out of a cargo of 219—for every two slaves purchased, one died in transit to the West Indies. In 1678, the *Arthur*, one of the ships of the Royal African Company, suffered a mortality of 88 out of 417 slaves—that is, more than 20 per cent. The *Martha*, another ship, landed 385 in Barbados out of 447 taken on the coast—the mortality amounted to 62, or a little less than 15 per cent. The *Coaster* lost 37 out of 150, a mortality of approximately 25 per cent. The *Hannibal*, in 1694, with a cargo of 700 slaves, buried 320 on the voyage, a mortality of 43 per cent; the Royal African Company lost £10 and the owner of the vessel 10 guineas on each slave, the total loss amounting to £6,560. The losses sustained by these five vessels amounted to 617 out of a total cargo of 1,933, that is, 32 per cent. Three out of every ten slaves perished in the Middle Passage. Hence the note of exasperation in the account of his voyage by the captain of the *Hannibal*:

> No gold-finders can endure so much noisome slavery as they do who carry Negroes; for those have some respite and satisfaction, but we endure twice the misery; and yet by their mortality our voyages are ruin'd, and we pine and fret our selves to death to think we should undergo so much misery, and take so much pains to so little purpose.

The lamentations of an individual slave trader or sugar planter were drowned out by the seventeenth-century chorus of approbation. Negro slavery and the Negro slave trade fitted beautifully into the economic theory of the age. This theory, known as mercantilism, stated that the wealth of a nation depended upon its possession of bullion, the precious metals. If, however, bullion was not available through possession of the mines, the new doctrine went further than its Spanish predecessor in emphasising that a country could increase its stock by a favourable balance of trade, exporting more than it imported. One of the best and clearest statements of the theory was made by Edward Misselden, in his *Circle of Commerce*, in 1623:

> For as a pair of scales is an invention to show us the weight of things, whereby we may discern the heavy from the light ... so is also the balance of trade an excellent and politique invention to show us the difference of weight in the commerce of one kingdom with another: that is, whether the native commodities exported, and all the foreign commodities imported do balance or over-balance one another in the scale of commerce.... If the native commodities exported do weigh down and exceed in value the foreign commodities imported, it is a rule that never fails that then the kingdom grows rich and prospers in estate and stock: because the overplus thereof must needs come in in treasure.... But if the foreign commodities imported do exceed in value the native commodities exported, it is a manifest sign that the trade decayeth, and the stock of the kingdom wasteth apace; because the overplus must needs go out in treasure.

National policy of the leading European nations concentrated on achieving a favourable balance of trade. Colonial possessions were highly prized as a means to this end; they increased the exports of the metropolitan country, prevented the drain of treasure by the purchase of necessary tropical produce, and provided freights for the ships of the metropolis and employment for its sailors.

The combination of the Negro slave trade, Negro slavery and Caribbean sugar production is known as the triangular trade. A ship left the metropolitan country with a cargo of metropolitan goods, which it exchanged on the coast of West Africa for slaves. This constituted the first side of the triangle. The second consisted of the Middle Passage, the voyage from West Africa to the West Indies with the slaves. The triangle was completed by the voyage from the West Indies to the metropolitan country with sugar and other Caribbean products received in exchange for the slaves. As the slave ships were not always adequate for the transportation of the West Indian produce, the triangular trade was supplemented by a direct trade between the metropolitan country and the West Indian islands.

The triangular trade provided a market in West Africa and the West Indies for metropolitan products, thereby increasing metropolitan exports and contributing to full employment at home. The purchase of the slaves on the coast of West Africa and their maintenance in the West Indies gave an enormous stimulus to metropolitan industry and agriculture. For example, the British woollen industry was heavily dependent on the triangular trade. A parliamentary committee of 1695 emphasised that the slave trade was an encouragement to Britain's woollen industry. In addition, wool was required in the West Indies for blankets and clothing for the slaves on the plantations.

Iron, guns and brass also figured prominently in the triangular trade and the ancillary West Indian trade. Iron bars were the trading medium on a large part of the West African coast, and by 1682 Britain was exporting about 10,000 bars of iron a year to Africa. Sugar stoves, iron rollers, nails found a ready market on the West Indian plantations. Brass pans and kettles were customarily included in the slave trader's cargo.

*****

Barbados was the most important single colony in the British Empire, worth almost as much, in its total trade, as the two tobacco colonies of Virginia and Maryland combined, and nearly three times as valuable as Jamaica. The tiny sugar island was more valuable to Britain than Carolina, New England, New York and Pennsylvania together. "Go ahead, England, Barbados is behind you," is today a stock joke in the British West Indies of the Barbadian's view of his own importance. Two and a half centuries ago, it was no joke. It was sound politics, based on sound economics. Jamaica's external trade was larger than New England's as far as Britain was concerned; Nevis was more important in the commercial firmament than New York; Antigua surpassed Carolina; Montserrat rated higher than Pennsylvania. Total British trade with Africa was larger than total trade with Pennsylvania, New York and Carolina. In 1697 the triangular trade accounted for nearly ten per cent of total British imports and over four per cent of total British exports. Barbados alone accounted for nearly four per cent of Britain's external trade.

Mercantilists were jubilant. The West Indian colonies were ideal colonies, providing a market, directly as well as indirectly, through the slave trade, for British manufactures and foodstuffs, whilst they supplied sugar and other tropical commodities that would otherwise have had to be imported from foreigners or dispensed with entirely. The West Indies thus contributed to Britain's balance of trade in two ways, by buying Britain's exports and by rendering the expenditure of bullion on foreign tropical imports unnecessary. On the other hand, the mainland colonies, Virginia and Maryland, and, to a lesser extent, Carolina excepted, where the conditions of labour and production duplicated those of the West Indies, were nuisances; they produced the same agricultural commodities as England, gave early evidence of competing with the metropolitan countries in manufactured goods as well, and were rivals in fishing and shipbuilding.

The British economists enthused. Sir Josiah Child in his *New Discourse of Trade* in 1668, wrote:

> The people that evacuate from us to Barbados, and the other West India Plantations ... do commonly work one Englishman to ten or eight Blacks; and if we keep the trade of our said plantations entirely to England, England would have no less inhabitants, but rather an increase of people by such evacuation, because that one Englishman, with the Blacks that work with him, accounting what they eat, use and wear, would make employment for four men in England ... whereas peradventure of ten men that issue from us to New England and Ireland, what we send to or receive from them, doth not employ one man in England.

In 1690, Sir Dalby Thomas stated that every white man in the West Indies was one hundred and thirty times more valuable to Britain than those who stayed at home:

> Each white man, woman, and child, residing in the sugar plantations, occasions the consumption of more of our native commodities, and manufactures, than ten at home do—beef, pork, salt, fish, butter, cheese, corn, flour, beer, cyder, bridles, coaches, beds, chairs, stools, pictures, clocks, watches; pewter, brass, copper, iron vessels and instruments; sail-cloth and cordage; of which, in their building, shipping, mills, boiling, and distilling-houses, field-labour and domestic uses, they consume infinite quantities.

Charles Davenant, perhaps the ablest of the seventeenth-century economists, estimated at the end of the century that Britain's total profit from trade amounted to two million pounds. Of this figure the plantation trade accounted for £600,000, and the re-export of plantation produce for £120,000. Trade with Africa, Europe and the Levant brought in another £600,000. The triangular trade thus represented a minimum of 36 per cent of Britain's commercial profits. Davenant added that every individual in the West Indies, white or Negro, was as profitable as seven in England.

What the West Indies had done for Seville in Spain in the sixteenth century, they did for Bristol in England and Bordeaux in France in the seventeenth. Each town became the metropolis of its country's trade with the Caribbean, though neither Bristol nor Bordeaux enjoyed the monopoly that had been granted to Seville. In 1661 only one ship, and that ship a Dutch one, came to Bordeaux from the West Indies. Ten years later twelve ships sailed from that port to the West Indies, and six returned from there. In 1683 the number of sailings to the sugar islands had risen to twenty-six. La Rochelle for a time eclipsed Bordeaux. In 1685 forty-nine ships sailed from that port to the West Indies. Nantes also was intimately connected with West Indian trade; in 1684 twenty-four ships belonging to the port were engaged in West Indian trade.

As a result of the triangular trade Bristol became a city of shopkeepers. It was said in 1685 that there was scarcely a shopkeeper in the city who had not a venture on board some ship bound for Virginia or the West Indies. The port took the lead in the struggle for the abrogation of the Royal African Company's monopoly, and in the first nine years of free trade shipped slaves to the West Indies at the rate of 17,883 a year. In 1700 Bristol had forty-six ships in the West Indian trade.

The basis of this astounding commercial efflorescence was the Negro slaves, "the strength and sinews of this western world." In 1662 the Company of Royal Adventurers trading to Africa pointed to the "profit and honour" that had accrued to British subjects from the slave trade, which King Charles II himself described as that "beneficial trade ... so much importing our service, and the enriching of this Our Kingdom." According to Colbert in France, no commerce in the world produced as many advantages as the slave trade. Benjamin Raule exhorted the Elector of Prussia, on October 26, 1685, not to be left behind in the race: "Everyone knows that the slave trade is the source of the wealth which the Spaniards wring out of the West Indies, and that whoever knows how to furnish them slaves, will share their wealth. Who can say by how many millions of hard cash the Dutch West India Company has enriched itself in this slave trade!" At the end of the seventeenth century all Europe, and not England only, was impressed with the words of Sir Dalby Thomas: "The pleasure, glory and grandeur of England has been advanced more by sugar than by any other commodity, wool not excepted."

The Negro slave trade in the eighteenth century constituted one of the greatest migrations in recorded history. Its volume is indicated in the following table, prepared from various statistics that are available.

TABLE 19.1

Years	Colony	Importation	Average importation per year
1700–1786	*Jamaica*	*610,000*	*7,000*
1708–1735 & 1747–1766	*Barbados*	*148,821*	*3,100*
1680–1776	*Saint-Domingue*	*800,000*	*8,247*
1720–1729	*Antigua*	*12,278*	*1,362*
1721–1730	*St. Kitts*	*10,358*	*1,035*
1721–1729	*Montserrat*	*3,210*	*357*
1721–1726	*Nevis*	*1,267*	*253*
1767–1773	*Dominica*	*19,194*	*2,742*
1763–1789	*Cuba*	*30,857*	*1,143*
1700–1754	*Danish Islands*	*11,750*	*214*

Average annual importations do not provide a complete picture. In 1774 the importation into Jamaica was 18,448. In fourteen of the years 1702–1775, the annual importation exceeded 10,000. Imports into Saint-Domingue averaged 12,559 in the years 1764–1768; in 1768 they were 15,279. In 1718 Barbados imported 7,126 slaves. During the nine months in which Cuba was under British occupation in 1762, 10,700 slaves were introduced. The British introduced 41,000 slaves in three years into Guadeloupe whilst they were in occupation of the island during the Seven Years' War.

These large importations represented one of the greatest advantages which the slave trade had over other trades. The frightful mortality of the slaves on the plantations made annual increments essential. Consider the case of Saint-Domingue. In 1763 the slave population amounted to 206,539. Imports from 1764 to 1774 numbered 102,474. The slave population in 1776 was 290,000. Thus, despite an importation of over one hundred thousand, without taking into account the annual births, the increase of the slave population in thirteen years was less than 85,000. Taking only importations into consideration, the slave population in 1776 was 19,000 less than the figure of 1763 with the importations added, and the imports for one year are not available.

A much clearer illustration of the mortality is available for Barbados. In 1764 there were 70,706 slaves in the island. Importations to 1783, with no figures available for the years 1779 and 1780, totalled 41,840. The total population, allowing for neither deaths nor births, should, therefore, have been 112,546 in 1783. Actually, it was 62,258. Thus, despite an annual importation for the eighteen years for which statistics are available of 2,324, the population in 1783 was 8,448 less than it was in 1764, or an annual decline of 469. [...]

Thus, after eight years of importations, averaging 4,424 a year, the population of Barbados was only 3,411 larger. 35,397 slaves had been imported; 31,897 had disappeared. In 1770 and 1771 the mortality was so high that the importation in those years, heavy though it was, was not adequate to supply the deficit. Half the population had had to be renewed in eight years.

In 1703 Jamaica had 45,000 Negroes; in 1778, 205,261, an average annual increase from all causes of 2,109. Between 1703 and 1775, 469,893 slaves had been imported, an average annual importation of 6,807. For every additional slave in its population, Jamaica had had to import three. The total population in 1778, excluding births and based only on imports, should have been 541,893, and that figure excludes imports for 1776, 1777 and 1778. Allowing 11,000 a year for those three years, the total population in 1778 should have been 547,893. The actual population in that year was less than forty per cent of the potential total.

Economic development has never been purchased at so high a price. According to one of the leading planters of Saint-Domingue, one in every three imported Negroes died in the first three years. To the mortality on the plantations must be added the mortality on the slave ships. On the slave ships belonging to the port of Nantes in France, that mortality varied from 5 per cent in 1746 and 1774 to as high as 34 per cent in 1732. For all the slave cargoes transported by them between 1715 and 1775, the mortality amounted to 16 per cent. Of one hundred Negroes who left the coast of Africa, therefore, only 84 reached the West Indies; one-third of these died in three years. For every 56 Negroes, therefore, on the plantations at the end of three years, 44 had perished.

The slave trade thus represented a wear and tear, a depreciation which no other trade equalled. The loss of an individual planter or trader was insignificant compared with the basic fact that every cargo of slaves, including the quick and the dead, represented so much industrial development and employment, so much employment of ships and sailors, in the metropolitan country. No other commercial undertaking required so large a capital as the slave trade. In addition to the ship, there was its equipment, armament, cargo, its unusually large supply of water and foodstuffs, its abnormally large crew. In 1765 it was estimated that in France the cost of fitting out and arming a vessel for 300 slaves was 242,500 livres. The cargo of a vessel from Nantes in 1757 was valued at 141,500 livres; it purchased 500 slaves. The cargo of the *Prince de Conty*, of 300 tons, was valued at 221,224 livres, with which 800 slaves were purchased.

Large profits were realised from the slave trade. The *King Solomon*, belonging to the Royal African Company, carried a cargo worth £4,252 in 1720. It took on 296 Negroes who were sold in St. Kitts for £9,228. The profit was thus 117 per cent. From 1698 to 1707 the Royal African Company exported from England to Africa goods to the value of £293,740. The Company sold 5,982 Negroes in Barbados for £156,425, an average of £26 per head. It sold 2,178 slaves in Antigua for £80,522, an average of £37 per head. The total number of Negroes imported into the British islands by the Company in these years was 17,760. The sale of 8,160 Negroes in Barbados and Antigua, less than half the total imports into all the islands, thus realised 80 per cent of the total exports from England. Allowing an average price of £26 per head for the remaining 9,600 Negroes, the total amount realised from the sale of the Company's Negroes was £488,107. The profit on the Company's exports was thus 66 per cent. For every three pounds' worth of merchandise exported from England, the Company obtained two additional pounds by way of profit.

The Negroes taken on by the *Prince de Conty* on the coast of Africa averaged 275 livres each; the survivors of the Middle Passage fetched 1,300 livres each in Saint-Domingue. In 1700 a cargo of 238 slaves was purchased by the Danish West Indies at prices ranging from 90 to 100 rixdollars. In 1753 the wholesale price on the coast of Africa was 100 rixdollars; the retail price in the Danish West Indies was 150 to 300 rixdollars. In 1724 the Danish West India Company made a profit of 28 per cent on its slave imports; in 1725, 30 per cent; 70 per cent on the survivors of a cargo of 1733 despite a mortality in transit of 45 per cent; 50 per cent on a cargo of 1754. It need occasion no surprise, therefore, that one of the eighteenth-century slave dealers admitted that, of all the places he had lived in, England, Ireland, America, Portugal, the West Indies, the Cape Verde Islands, the Azores, and Africa, it was in Africa that he could most quickly make his fortune.

The slave trade was central to the triangular trade. It was, in the words of one British mercantilist, "the spring and parent whence the others flow"; "the first principle and foundation of all the rest," echoed another, "the mainspring of the machine which sets every wheel in motion." The slave trade kept the wheels of metropolitan industry turning; it stimulated navigation and shipbuilding and employed seamen; it raised fishing villages into flourishing cities; it gave sustenance to new industries based on the processing of colonial raw materials; it yielded large profits which were ploughed back into metropolitan industry; and, finally, it gave rise to an unprecedented commerce in the West Indies and made the Caribbean territories among the most valuable colonies the world has ever known.

Examples must suffice. In 1729 the British West Indies absorbed one-quarter of Britain's iron exports, and Africa, where the price of a Negro was commonly reckoned at one Birmingham gun, was one of the most important markets for the British armaments industry. In 1753 there were 120 sugar refineries in England—eighty in London, twenty in Bristol. In 1780 the British West Indies supplied two-thirds of the six and a half million pounds of raw cotton imported by Britain. Up to 1770 one-third of Manchester's textile exports went to Africa, one-half to the West Indian and American colonies. In 1709 the British West Indies employed one-tenth of all British shipping engaged in foreign trade. Between 1710 and 1714, 122,000 tons of British shipping sailed to the West Indies, 112,000 tons to the mainland colonies. Between 1709 and 1787, British shipping engaged in foreign trade quadrupled; ships clearing for Africa multiplied twelve times and the tonnage eleven times.

The triangular trade marked the ascendancy of two additional European ports in the eighteenth century, Liverpool in England and Nantes in France, and further contributed to the development of Bristol and Bordeaux, begun in the seventeenth century. [...]

Liverpool's exports to Africa in 1770 read like a census of British manufactures: beans, brass, beer, textiles, copper, candles, chairs, cider, cordage, earthenware, gunpowder, glass, haberdashery, iron, lead, looking glasses, pewter, pipes, paper, stockings, silver, sugar, salt, kettles.

In 1774 there were eight sugar refineries in Liverpool. Two distilleries were established in the town for the express purpose of supplying slave ships. There were many chain and anchor foundries, and manufacturers of and dealers in iron, copper, brass and lead in the town. In 1774 there were fifteen roperies. Half of Liverpool's sailors were engaged in the slave trade, which, by 1783, was estimated to bring the town a clear annual profit of £300,000. The slave trade transformed Liverpool from a fishing village into a great centre of international commerce. The population rose from 5,000 in 1700 to 34,000 in 1773. It was a common saying in the town that its principal streets had been marked out by the chains, and the walls of its houses cemented by the blood, of the African slaves. The red brick Customs House, blazoned with Negro heads, bore mute but eloquent testimony to the origins of Liverpool's rise by 1783 to the position of one of the most famous—or infamous, depending on the point of view—towns in the world of commerce.

*****

Magnum est saccharum et prevalebit! Great is sugar, and it will prevail! Mercantilists were jubilant. The colonies, wrote Horace Walpole, were "the source of all our riches, and preserve the balance of trade in our favour, for I don't know where we have it but by the means of our colonies." An annual profit of 7s per head was sufficient to enrich a country, said William

Wood; each white man in the colonies brought a profit of over seven pounds, twenty times as much. The Negro slaves, said Postlethwayt, were "the fundamental prop and support" of the colonies, "valuable people," and the British Empire was "a magnificent superstructure of American commerce and naval power on an African foundation." Rule Britannia! Britannia rules the waves. For Britons never shall be slaves.

But the sons of France arose to glory. France joined in the homage to the triangular trade. "What commerce," asked the Chamber of Commerce of Nantes, "can be compared to that which obtains men in exchange for commodities?" Profound question! The abandonment of the slave trade, continued the Chamber, would be inevitably followed by the ruin of colonial commerce; "whence follows the fact that we have no branch of trade so precious to the State and so worthy of protection as the Guinea trade." The triangular trade was incomparable, the slave trade precious, and the West Indies perfect colonies. "The more colonies differ from the metropolis," said Nantes, "the more perfect they are.... Such are the Caribbean colonies: they have none of our objects of trade; they have others which we lack and cannot produce."

But there were discordant notes in the mercantilist harmony. The first was opposition to the slave trade. In 1774, in Jamaica, the very centre of Negro slavery, a debating society voted that the slave trade was not consistent with sound policy, or with the laws of nature and of morality. In 1776 Thomas Jefferson wrote into the Declaration of Independence three paragraphs attacking the King of England for his "piratical warfare" on the coast of Africa against people who never offended him, and for his veto of colonial legislation attempting to prohibit or restrain the slave trade. The paragraphs were only deleted on the representations of the states of South Carolina, Georgia and New England. Two petitions were presented to Parliament, in 1774 and 1776, for abolition of the slave trade. A third, more important, was presented in 1783 by the Quakers. The Prime Minister, Lord North, complimented them on their humanity, but regretted that abolition was an impossibility, as the slave trade had become necessary to every nation in Europe. European public opinion accepted the position stated by Postlethwayt: "We shall take things as they are, and reason from them in their present state, and not from that wherein we could hope them to be.... We cannot think of giving up the slave-trade, notwithstanding my good wishes that it could be done."

The second discordant note was more disturbing. Between 1772 and 1778, Liverpool slave traders were estimated to have lost £700,000 in the slave trade. By 1788 twelve of the thirty leading houses which had dominated the trade from 1773 had gone bankrupt. Slave trading, like sugar production, had its casualties. A slave trader in 1754, as his supreme defence of the slave trade, had adumbrated that "from this trade proceed benefits, far outweighing all, either real or pretended mischiefs and inconveniencies." If and when the slave trade ceased to be profitable, it would not be so easy to defend it.

The third discordant note came also from the British colonies. The British Government's ambition was to become the slave carriers and sugar suppliers of the whole world. Britain had fought for and obtained the *asiento*. The supply of slaves to foreign nations became an integral part of the British slave trade. Of 497,736 slaves imported in Jamaica between 1702 and 1775, 137,114 had been re-exported, one out of every four. In 1731, imports were 10,079; re-exports, 5,708. From 1775 to 1783, Antigua imported 5,673 slaves and re-exported 1,972, one out of every three. Jamaica resorted to its seventeenth-century policy, an export tax on all Negroes re-exported. In 1774, the Board of Trade, on the representation of the slave traders of London, Liverpool and Bristol, disallowed the law as unjustifiable, improper and prejudicial to British commerce, pointed out that legislative autonomy in the colonies did not extend to the imposition of duties upon British ships and goods or to the prejudice and obstruction of British commerce, and reprimanded the Governor of the island for dereliction of duty in not stopping efforts to "check and discourage a traffic ... beneficial to the nation."

SELECTED BIBLIOGRAPHY

Davenant, Charles. *Discourse on the Trade and Publick Revenues of England*. London, 1698. (There are other useful writings of Davenant, all of which can be found in C. Whitworth (ed.), *The Political and Commercial Works of Charles Davenant*, London, 1781).

Postlethwayt, M. *The National and Private Advantages of the African Trade considered*. London, 1746.

——. *The Universal Dictionary of Trade and Commerce*, London, 1751.

——. *Great Britain's Commercial Interest explain'd and improv'd*. London, 1759.

——. *The African Trade, the Great Pillar and Support of the British Plantation Trade in North America*. London, 1765.

Thomas, Sir Dalby. *An Historical Account of the Rise and Growth of the West India Colonies, and of the Great Advantages they are to England, in respect to Trade*. London, 1690.

Wood, W. *A Survey of Trade*. London, 1718.

——. *The Importance of the Sugar Colonies to Great Britain*. London, 1731.

——. *Some Considerations humbly offer'd upon the Bill now depending in the House of Lords, relating to the Trade between the Northern Colonies and the Sugar-Islands*. London, 1732.

CHAPTER 20

PRELUDE TO SETTLEMENT: INDIANS AS INDENTURED LABOURERS

Verene Shepherd

According to A. E. Smith, "... the system of indentured servitude was the most convenient system next to slavery by which labour became a commodity to be bought and sold."[1] Its applicability to colonial requirements had been suggested as early as 1582 by Sir George Peckham[2] and, indeed, had its precedent in the ancient institution of apprenticeship. In the case of Jamaica, indentureship pre-dated the abolition of African slavery, having been applied to white servants in the seventeenth century. It was extended to immigrants imported between 1835 and 1916. It was, however, most extensively applied to the Indians.

The system of Indian indentureship not only provided the basis for the development of a settled Indian community in Jamaica, but also had far-reaching implications for the later history of Indian settlers. In the passage from Indian village to the immigration depot, the long sea voyage and then residence on a Jamaican plantation, the indentured labourer went through a series of profound shifts in his or her social environment. These inevitably facilitated cultural change.

In the first place, as Benedict noted with reference to Mauritius, Indian labourers were herded together with little regard to regional origin, caste, religion or linguistic group.[3] This led to intra-culturation between different Indian groups which might not have had contact prior to their arrival in the Caribbean, so that a new kind of "Indian" identity began to emerge. Second, contact with managers and other workers on the estate, no matter how limited, started the process of inter-culturation to both Euro- and Afro-creole norms, though this became more pronounced later. Third, though the estate managers maintained a degree of residential and occupational separation between Indians and Afro-Jamaicans, inevitably the juxtaposition of the two groups led to some social contact and, at the very least, the formation of perceptions about the ethnic other. These perceptions, which frequently took a racially stereotyped form, themselves played a part in the formation of an Indo-Jamaican ethnic identity. This came about both in terms of how Indians felt they were perceived by others and sometimes in an enlarged sense of difference from their Afro-Jamaican neighbours. Fourth, the very patterns of work on the plantation were socially and psychologically transforming. The person who set out from village India was part of a caste society whose way of life had changed little over the past centuries. On the plantation began the complex process of change from peasant to proletarian.

In reviewing the experience of indentureship and its implications for the settlement period, this chapter examines the origins of the indentured workers who came to Jamaica, their demographic composition and the salient features of how the indentureship system affected their lives as workers on the estates.

I. ORIGINS OF INDIAN INDENTURED SERVANTS

[...] The process of recruitment was similar for all colonies and, as it has been amply described elsewhere,[4] only a brief account is given here. Recruitment was carried out by men licensed by the Protector of Emigrants, but employed by Sub-Agents who manned the up-country depots at which emigrants were assembled prior to their journey to Madras or Calcutta for embarkation. Licensed recruiters often appointed assistants —*Kutty Maistries* in Madras, *Arkatias* in North India—who travelled around the villages to obtain recruits. Recruiters were paid by commission. Though perhaps the only practicable method of payment, this was accompanied by many abuses which at times led to the cancellation of licences. Unlicensed recruiters, however, often operated undetected.[5]

*****

In general, the pattern of recruitment for other Caribbean colonies was not vastly different, except that by the time that places such as the Windwards began to import Indians, competition with the Assam tea gardens had caused recruitment to shift away from the "Hill Coolies." Jamaica, Trinidad, Guyana and Suriname tapped the same areas, though the source of emigrants was not always the same for each colony for each year. In most cases, the demand for Trinidad and Guyana was filled first, leaving recruiters for Jamaica and Suriname to fill their quota as best they could. This was a reflection of the fact that Jamaica was less popular as a destination for Indians. Repatriation was inefficient and wages were lower than in other colonies.

This brief survey of the areas of recruitment reveals that the Indians who came to Jamaica did not represent a homogeneous group. They came from different linguistic and cultural zones. On the estates, therefore, Tamil and Hindi speakers, Hindus and Muslims would meet with creole Jamaicans and learn the lingua franca of the estate—an early area of cultural adaptation.

II. DEMOGRAPHIC COMPOSITION OF THE INDENTURED INDIANS

[...] Muslims (referred to at times in the Emigration Passes as "Musalmans") formed only a minority of the immigrants introduced to Jamaica and the rest of the Caribbean. Of the 607 imported on the *Indus* in 1907, only 93 were Muslims.[6] Planters were not keen on their importation and only in a few cases did they form the majority on any shipment.[7] Reporting on the arrival of the *Rhine* from Calcutta in 1899 the Protector remarked that there was an unusually large number of "Musalmans" amongst the shipment. This fact he lamented on the grounds that "... these invariably cause trouble among the rest on the properties to which they are allotted."[8] [...]

The most significant demographic characteristic of Indian immigrants to Jamaica and the rest of the diaspora was the disproportionate number of males. This was despite an ordinance stipulating a ration of 40 females to every 100 males and the higher commission paid for the recruitment of females.[9] There were a few years (1892 and 1893 were exceptions) when the obligatory number of women was obtained for emigration. Several reasons have been advanced to explain the failure. First, planters seemed to have preferred to import married women accompanying their husbands. The majority of women opting for emigration, however, were single women (some being widows and women kidnapped in the pilgrim centres) whose dispatch to the colonies was discouraged unless they formed part of an emigrating family. The planters saw women as desirable immigrants only in the light of their ability to satisfy the domestic and sexual needs of male workers and would support single women only if they formed permanent attachments to male labourers on arrival. The feeling was that "a woman who is not occupied otherwise than in cooking her husband's food is more likely to get into mischief." This was an euphemism for "sexual mischief", the planters being of the view that single women were generally prostitutes and "women of doubtful character."[10] However, despite planter preference, the majority of women imported to the region were single—often disguised as married women, emigrating with professing "husbands" and "children."[11] This latter fact means that any figure relating to the number of married women dispatched to the colonies in any one year must be treated with caution. There must be doubts, for example, over the unusually high proportion of married women on the 1893 shipment to Suriname—67%, compared to 45% to Guyana and 27% to Jamaica.[12] [...] This low percentage for Jamaica was replicated in other years. On the *Indus* of 1905 for example, only 29% of the 217 women were married and accompanied by spouses.[13] A similar trend was observed on the *Indus* in 1906 where out of 442 emigrants, 114 were women. Out of the 114, 38 were married and 76 single.[14] Whether married or single, women were underrepresented on each shipment down to 1916—a trend set from the earliest importation of 1845 when out of 261 immigrants only 28, or 11%, comprised women.[15] Indeed, it would be safe to say that women comprised less than one-third of each shipload of immigrants imported to Jamaica from the 1880s.

A second reason for the low importation of women was that up to 1910, no family with more than two children was allowed to emigrate. The view was that large numbers of children increased the risk of epidemics at the depot and on board the ships and the planters were unwilling to incur maintenance expenses for large numbers of children. Thus, up to 1913, no commissions were paid for the recruitment of children under 12. However, in an effort to increase the proportion of women in the colonies, recruiters were given financial incentives for the recruitment of girls after 1913. This, though, had little effect. Up to 1916, when Jamaica obtained the last shipment of Indian immigrants, no significant improvement was noted in the proportion of women dispatched to the island. Combined with the much smaller numbers of Indians in Jamaica, this sexual disparity no doubt played a role in the greater prevalence of Indians marrying outside their group than occurred in Trinidad or Guyana.

III. THE INDENTURESHIP EXPERIENCE

(a) Allocation to Estates, Work and Wages

Between 1845 and 1916, an estimated 37,000 Indian immigrants entered the island and served their period of indentureship on properties located primarily in the parishes of St. Andrew, St. Mary, Portland, Clarendon, Westmoreland, St. Catherine and St. Thomas-in-the-East (simply St. Thomas after 1867). After their arrival in the island (first at Port Royal and then on to various disembarkation depots) immigrants were dispatched in carts, schooners or by rail to the properties on which they were to serve out their indentures. These were the ones who after examination by the Medical Board on arrival were found to be "fit for service" and who were then issued with certificates of indenture. Despite the length and rigours of the journey from India—particularly before the use of steam ships in 1906—those rejected as "unfit" were remarkably few.[16]

In the early years of immigration, Indians seem to have been allocated to estates in batches of about 20, but between 1891 and 1916 some estates received as few as four and others as many as 63 from single shipments. [...] The geographical distribution of immigrants indicated by the parish breakdown was replicated on other shipments. In comparison to Trinidad and Guyana where much larger numbers of Indians were densely concentrated, in Jamaica a much smaller number was widely dispersed, though there were concentrations in areas of high sugar and banana production. Thus, in Jamaica, the land area into which Indians were absorbed—particularly after their employment on banana estates—was larger than in Trinidad and

Guyana where estates were concentrated in comparatively smaller ecological zones.[17] The patterns in Martinique and Guadeloupe were much like that of Jamaica.[18] Commenting on the implications of this pattern of settlement for the maintenance of a strong ethnic/cultural identity, Erlich noted that "... whatever strengths existed in the small number that came were shattered by the small numbers in which they were parcelled out."[19] Even when there was the possibility of movement off the estates into villages and the increase of the Indian population by natural means or the addition to their numbers through further importations, there were other factors militating against any significant growth in the Indian population in the island. These included repatriation, the lack of continuous importations and socio-economic factors frustrating the evolution of "Indian villages."

On the estates, Jamaican proprietors employed a variety of measures in an effort to render Indian immigrants a more controllable labour force than Afro-Jamaican labourers. The main strategy was, of course, to secure Indian labourers under indentured contracts. The rationale for such contracts was that when labour was not sufficiently cheap and servile, the free play of market forces had to be interrupted and an element of extra-economic compulsion introduced. Planters constantly agitated for longer contracts, though at first the British Government only allowed one-year contracts. By 1850 the Government had relented sufficiently to allow three-year contracts; this was because Indians from the 1845–47 batches had generally refused to re-indenture after the first year. The provision had been that after serving out the first contract year they were at liberty to enter into contracts for periods not exceeding one year with any planter for whom they wished to work. By 1848, for example, it was clear that a lack of supervision and the Indians' understandable disinclination to renew their contracts posed problems for the proprietors. A parish-by-parish survey conducted by the press in that year revealed that a large number had become vagrants and mendicants and that poverty was widespread among them.[20] These factors combined with reactions to the Sugar Duties Act of 1846 led to the suspension of immigration in 1848. In the 1850s, however, there were renewed calls for the resumption of Indian immigration—but under more stringent control and longer contracts. Importations restarted in 1860 and by 1862, five-year contracts were general throughout the region. This was confirmed by section 30 of Jamaica Law 23 of 1879 which clarified and amplified earlier laws and with minor adjustments regulated Indian immigration to Jamaica. Sections 41 and 43 of the Law provided that at the expiration of this five-year period immigrants could enter into fresh contracts of one-year duration in each case. They could choose their employers the second time round. Nevertheless, while such second contracts were in force, "Second Term Coolies," as re-indentureds were called, were subject to the provisions of the immigration laws just as if they were under indenture.

Up to 1921, indentured and "time-expired" Indians worked side by side on the estates; and until re-indentureship was abolished by Law 20 of 1891, a small percentage of "time-expired" immigrants regularly renewed their contracts. In supporting the abolition of re-indenture, the Protector indicated that few Indians in Jamaica made use of this provision because it was not a necessary condition for securing employment—at least not in times of buoyancy in the main economic sectors. [...] In times of economic depression, however, "time-expireds" were the first to suffer. At such times the availability of surplus Afro-Jamaican labourers and the obligation to hire indentured servants deprived the ex-indentured labourer of work.

Before the beginning of the period of contract, each labourer was issued with agricultural implements, cooking utensils and a suit of clothing. Trousers were made out of oznaburgh and shirts out of striped Holland or flannelette. Women's clothes were made from brown calico and striped Holland. This represented a further break in tradition and the demise of the dhoti and sari for many. New immigrants were supplied with rations, for the first few months but thereafter, provided food out of their wages.[21]

On sugar estates, indentured labourers worked in gangs supervised by either an Indian or Afro-Jamaican headman or "driver." Indian "drivers" were selected solely on the basis of their ability to implement plantation routine—not according to caste or religion. Thus low castes could be placed over high caste, Muslims over Hindus, and so on—factors which forced inter-ethnic interaction. Indian labourers naturally preferred Indian headmen or sirdars, who, according to Chimman Lai and James McNeil "... are more cheerfully obeyed if the latter are sure that the former's control is exercised with the full knowledge and approval of the employer."[22]

The classification of gangs followed closely that of slavery, with strength and physical condition, age and gender being important criteria for the worker's allocation. Thus the weeding gang was invariably composed of the less physically able, and some women. At times there was also an invalid gang comprising children and convalescents. In Jamaica the criterion of "race" was also applied. Planter preference for Afro-Jamaican labourers for heavier tasks, combined with the stereotype of the physically weak Indian, caused certain gangs to consist heavily of blacks; correspondingly, certain tasks referred to as "womens' work" tended to be assigned specifically to Indians—male or female.[23] However, the list of tasks performed by Indian labourers [...] including digging stumps, preparing the land, planting and reaping indicates that ethnic factors in allocating work were not absolute. For instance, contrary to popular belief, Indian labourers were employed in sugar factory work.[24]

Work on banana plantations and livestock pens was less regimented, but even on these units the gang system often prevailed. On banana plantations, a similar stereotype regarding the physical capacity of the Indian directed "delicate work" such as pruning bananas, to Indian labour gangs. Other tasks on banana estates ranged from hoeing grass, billing, forking and trenching to heading and carting. Greater dependence on Indian labourers in Trinidad and Guyana meant that such stereotypes could not be allowed to have any significant impact on the allocation of work.

The Indian's life—whether employed on pen, sugar estate or banana plantation—was arranged according to the schedule devised by the plantation. Neither routine nor tasks bore any relationship to caste or religion.[25] About the only restriction which respected caste and religious sensibilities was the direction that Hindus should not be given jobs which involved the handling of meat. Governor Manning claimed that none were so employed in Jamaica,[26] but as Indians worked on livestock farms it is unclear whether this denial was accurate.[27]

During their first three months in the colony, immigrants were required to do nine hours of day labour for six days a week. In Jamaica labourers were paid at the rates of 1/6d a day for men of 16 years and upwards and 9d per day for women and children between the ages of 12 and 16. Wages in Trinidad and Guyana were only slightly higher. In Trinidad, a minimum wage of 1/1d a day was stipulated in the indenture contract. [...][28]

The rates for tasks on banana estates also varied but generally some were more remunerative than others. Cutting, heading, wrapping and carting fruits were the highest paying tasks while among the lowest paid were hoeing and fencing. As cocoa cultivation was generally interspersed with banana cultivation, the Indians also were engaged in pruning and picking cocoa. The wages for these activities were low. [...] Such low wages affected the Indians' ability to leave the estates for village settlement.

Wage rates were not always promptly paid; neither did the employers always pay the correct wage rates or provide jobs to enable the immigrants to earn sufficient wages. This was despite the responsibility of the Protector of Immigrants to ensure that the correct rates were paid. [...]

(b) Accommodation on the Estate

Indentured immigrants were housed in barracks on the estates on which they worked. As in Guyana and Trinidad, the fact that Indians were housed separately from Afro-Jamaicans was a most important factor for the encouragement of Indian cultural retention.[29] Barracks in Jamaica were similar to those in other colonies and were essentially long ranges of buildings divided into rooms of 120 square feet with a covered verandah five feet in width. Detached huts were also found in Jamaica. The mean height of rooms was from nine feet upwards. Floors were boarded and raised from 18 to 24 inches above ground level. In some cases rammed earth raised well above the ground was used. Regulations were laid down to ensure proper ventilation and latrine facilities for the occupants of these buildings,[30] but despite the constant warnings of Medical Officers who visited each estate monthly, these regulations were not always carried out. Indeed, sanitation around the barracks was so poor that immigrants were constantly plagued with ankylostomiasis.[31]

(c) Medical Care

A multiplicity of laws were established to govern immigrants' health experiences under the system of indenture. At first, estates maintained their own hospitals. After 1869, the system of treating patients in estate hospitals in Jamaica was abandoned. Thus Jamaican estates were less elf-enclosed than those in Guyana which were more self-sufficient. The abandonment of estate hospitals was not welcomed by all. It was thought, for example, that the treatment of minor ailments in the hospitals increased the number of days labourers were absent from work and facilitated malingering.[32] The Acting Protector, F.N. Isaacs, suggested in 1914 that to offset this tendency, the Medical Department should furnish each estate with dressings and medicines with simple directions for their use. This could be administered for minor ailments by a "responsible" person.[33]

*****

The main illnesses for which immigrants were admitted to hospital were anaemia, ulcers, malaria and phititis. These diseases weakened victims considerably and caused them to be readmitted frequently to hospital. Abas Ali of Agualta Vale Estate in St. Mary, for example, was admitted to hospital for malaria 20 times between 1906 and 1909. The high incidence of illness revealed in the statistics speaks of human misery, but the loss of labour through sickness was also a serious problem for the employers. As usual, though, it was the employers who were able to mitigate the situation to their own advantage. Large numbers of immigrants had their period of indenture extended to take account of periods of sickness; very few were freed on account of ill-health.

(d) Control and Resistance

In addition to contracts, estate residency and gang labour, Jamaican proprietors made extensive use of penal clauses and restrictive labour laws to render Indians a "controllable" work force. These regulations represented an elaborate system of coercion which included laws curtailing freedom of movement outside the estates. In order to lodge a complaint against an employer, for example, the immigrant first had to obtain permission from that same employer to leave the estate and go to the Protector of Immigrants' office. The rationale for this attempt to confine Indians within the physical boundaries of the estate was that like slaves before them,

Indians were prone to marronage and had to be restrained from such "vagabond" instincts. A number of punitive devices were also imposed upon indentured workers for what were deemed "offences against the labour law." Such offences included "unlawful" absence from work, downright refusal to labour, "wilful indolence," feigned illness and general malingering. Punishment for such offences ranged from the extra-legal methods of floggings to heavy fines and imprisonment. Furthermore, time spent in prison was simply added to the length of immigrants' indentures. Contrary to the once prevalent myth of the "docile coolie," there is much evidence that Indians in Jamaica as in other receiving colonies, employed a variety of strategies both to resist and to register their disaffection with repressive aspects of the system,

This has added another dimension to resistance studies in the region. While still dominated by a focus on slave resistance, the historiography reflects the increasing attention being paid to protest among indentured labourers. [...] It is not an easy task to determine whether all forms of non-cooperation on the part of indentured immigrants constituted resistance.[34] [...]

The myth of the docile Indian, in Jamaica, was shattered by the frequency of malingering, "wilful indolence," unlawful absence from work and downright refusal to work. According to Law 23 of 1879 (Section 95 (15)), these offences were regarded as serious breaches of contract and conviction made the labourer liable up to a £3 fine. The fact that such offences formed a large percentage of the cases brought before the Resident Magistrate and the Protector of Immigrants in each year attests to the fact that the threat of fines did not deter the Indians. In 1914-15 alone, a total of 256 cases of wilful indolence were brought before the Resident Magistrates and the Protector. Many employers described the Indians as incorrigible idlers who would never reform even though they were continually punished. However, this did not deter employers and the courts from making extensive use of the labour laws and their penalties. As the Protector of Immigrants, Charles Doorly, admitted, punishment was very often only applied, "...by way of setting an example to others on the property who perhaps are not too zealously inclined."[35]

Refusal to work and "unlawful" absence also accounted for a number of the cases before the Protector and the Magistrates. In 1914-15, 123 cases of downright refusal to work were recorded and 70 cases of "unlawful" absence. Careful records of "unlawful" absence were kept. [...] When compared to the total number of indentured workers, however, these percentages become less significant. In fact, between 1911 and 1916, only 1.55 days on average were lost per year on account of absence from work. [...]

More violent signs of discontent were organised strikes, riots and protest marches to the Protector of Immigrants or to the police station.

Strikes, riots and protest marches occurred throughout the indentureship period, though they were more marked in the twentieth century. These were usually spontaneous and localised and never reached the proportion of planned island-wide revolts. The usual reasons for strikes, riots and protest marches were non-payment of wages or the failure of employers to pay wages on time, disputes over task work, dissatisfaction with the headmen, disputes over rations and ill-treatment. In some cases, violence accompanied strikes. In all cases, the aim of action was to gain better working conditions for all indentured servants and force employers to conform to the terms of contracts. [...]

The Indian leaders of these riots, strikes or protest marches were usually seasoned immigrants. Walter Rodney has reported the planter view that fresh arrivals were more malleable, which was why the planters favoured the continual influx of new Indian immigrants. [36]

Political resistance was resorted to when other methods had failed. In theory, immigrants had access to the courts for legal redress for grievances, and they did sometimes take their employers to court for breaches of the "beneficent" clauses of the immigration ordinances. In theory, too, the magistrates were obliged to move against planters who breached their legal obligations. However, the reality was that immigrants regularly went before the courts as victims of a legal system which brought the force of the law directly on the side of the planters. Indeed, in Jamaica, only in very isolated cases were employers convicted and fined, as for example, in 1913, when the overseer of an estate in Portland was prosecuted for assaulting an Indian worker.[37] [...]

However, neither personal intransigence nor collective resistance brought about the abolition of indentureship or any greater freedom for the indentured population. Despite the frequency of desertion, no free extra-estate communities developed which could "have formed the basis of residential separation. Freedom came through the expiration of contracts and the ten-year compulsory period of residence, through release from indenture on account of disability or by commutation of the unexpired portion of indentures. Between 1907 and 1915 it was recorded that the annual average release from indenture because of physical disability was 4%. Some of those released from indenture settled in the island adding to the resident population. Abolition of the system of indentureship, however, had to await developments in India.

(e) Abolition of Indentureship

Whilst the conditions of indentured labourers in Jamaica and other colonies was the subject of much official investigation from the 1870s to 1913, such recommendations as were made after these investigations only brought about certain minor changes and did not seriously affect the essential nature of the system. Indeed, even some of the attempts to bring about minor improvement were frustrated. [...]

Ultimately, it took the concerted efforts of Mahatma Gandhi, C.F. Andrews and Gokhale to bring about the demise of the system of indentured labour migration in 1917. As the details of that effort have been well documented elsewhere, and as they are necessarily external to Jamaica, they will not be recounted here.[38] However, what is less well known is that economic factors in Jamaica had already led to the cessation of immigration in 1916, although Guyana and Trinidad continued their importations.

Consequently, the news from India of the proposed abolition of indentured immigration was not received in Jamaica with any great alarm and engendered no great public comment in the press.[39] [...]

Indentureship was, then, an inescapable experience in the lives of Indian immigrants in the Caribbean. It operated similarly in all colonies and therefore was not a crucial variable in the observed differences in the cultural adaptation of Indians in Jamaica and in other receiving colonies such as Trinidad and Guyana. The plantation experience began the process of indigenization. However, though it provided the first contact with Afro-Jamaicans, its arrangements for residential separation helped to foster some Indian cultural retention in the non-working hours. At the same time, however, the nature of the estates as "total institutions," organised to deliver regimented labour, had a severe impact on Indian culture, particularly on language, dress and family life. And though the impact of the estate was not ineradicable, as the experience of Indians in Trinidad and Guyana shows, there was no similar pattern of movement off the estates in Jamaica. In Trinidad and Guyana it was this which led to the development of communities organised around Indian cultural patterns, albeit modified. It will be seen that such communities, which greatly facilitated cultural retention, did not develop in Jamaica.

NOTES AND REFERENCES

1. A.E. Smith, *Colonists in Bondage: White Servitude and Convict Labor in America, 1607-1706* (Chapel Hill: University of North Carolina Press, 1947), p. 4.
2. Ibid.
3. B. Benedict, *Indians in a Plural Society: A Report on Mauritius* (London: HMSO, 1961), p. 26.
4. See for example, H. Tinker, *A New System of Slavery: The Export of Indian Labour Overseas, 1830-1920* (Oxford: Oxford University Press, 1974), and P. Saha, *Emigration of Indian Labour, 1834-1900*, New Delhi: People's Publishing House, 1970.
5. See CO 571/3 "Notes on Colonial Emigration."
6. CGF 1B/9/141 Papers of the SS *Indus*, 1907.
7. CGF 1B/SM43, Nominal Roll, SS *Mutlah*, 1913.
8. *Governor's Report on the Blue Book, 1898-99* (Kingston: Gov't. Printing Office, 1899).
9. In 1914, for example, 60 rupees were paid for male recruits and 100 rupees for each female. See CO 571/3. Emigration Agent Gibbes to the Under-Secretary of the State in the Colonial Office.
10. See V.A. Shepherd, "Indian Women in Jamaica, 1845-1945," in F. Birbalsingh (ed.), *Indenture and Exile: The Indo-Caribbean Experience* (Toronto: Tsar Press, 1989), pp. 100-107, and CO 571/3, Gibbes to the Under-Secretary.
11. Shepherd, p. 100.
12. IORE 4 vii A(l)1893.
13. CGF IB/9/34 and 38, Papers of the *Indus*, 1905.
14. CGF 1B/9/35B, Papers of the *Indus*, 1906.
15. CGF IB/9/3, Papers of the *Blundell*. 1845. See also V. A. Shepherd, "Aspects of the condition of Indian Female Plantation Workers in Jamaica During the Indentureship and Post-Indentureship Periods," unpublished paper submitted for R. Reddock (ed.), *Reader on Plantation Women* (forthcoming).
16. Small sailing ships and barques were used up to 1906. These ranged from 500 to 1,000 tons. One of the smallest ships to Jamaica was the *Wentworth* which was 521 tons. The *Mullah*, one of the largest, was 2,153 tons. Sailing ships took up to six months to arrive in the colonies with a resultant high mortality rate. Seventy-five of the 308 passengers despatched on the *Rajasthan* in 1860 died. The *Humber* of 1872 recorded a 13% death rate. By 1910, however, better medical supervision and steam ships had cut the journey and the mortality rate. The latter ranged between 1 and 4% by 1916.
17. A.S. Erlich, "History, Ecology and Demography in the British Caribbean: An Analysis of East Indian Ethnicity," *Southwestern Journal of Anthropology* 27, no. 2 (1971), pp. 173-176.
18. E. Moutoussamy, "Indianness in the French West Indies," in Birbalsingh (ed.), *Indenture and Exile*, p. 28.
19. Erlich, p. 176.
20. CO 142/7, *Morning Journal*, 3 Aug. 1847 and 15 May 1847. See also Parliamentary Paper No. 399, Vol. XLV, 1847-48.
21. CGF IB/9/17, "Laws operating in 1903 for the treatment of Coolies," Immigration Office, 6 March 1903.
22. Gt. Britain Parliament, 1915. *Report of Chimman Lal and James McNeil on East Indian Immigration* (London: HMSO, 1915), p. 213.
23. Sanderson Commission, Evidence of Sir Arthur Blake, Governor, 6 May 1909, Sec. 2637.
24. J. Weller, *East Indian Indenture in Trinidad* (Rio Piedras, Puerto Rico: Institute of Caribbean Studies, 1967), p. 3.
25. B. Brereton, "The Experience of Indentureship, 1845-1917," in J. La Guerre (ed.), *Calcutta to Caroni: The East Indians of Trinidad* (Port of Spain: Longman Caribbean, 1974), p. 29.
26. Sec. 50, Law 23, 1879.
27. Ibid.
28. CSO IB/5/11/5, Jamaica Legislative Council Debates, Session of 24 Oct. 1912.
29. W. Rodney, *A History of the Guyanese Working People, 1881-1905* (London: Heinemann Educational Books Ltd., 1981), p. 17.

30. Ibid., p. 201.
31. This disease was caused by the hookworm which developed in the intestines of the person afflicted and was indicated by an anaemic condition. It was spread by the ova in the faeces of the afflicted person. Fully 75% of the working classes of India suffered from this debilitating and often fatal disease.
32. *Report of Chimman Lal and James McNeil*, p. 202. Also CGF 1B/9/28, Isaacs to the Managers of Estates, 17 April 1914.
33. Protector of Immigrants, Isaacs, to the Manager of Estates, 1914.
34. G.M. Frederickson and C. Lasch, "Resistance to Slavery," *Civil War History* 13 (1967), pp. 315–329.
35. Protector of Immigrants' Report, Jamaica, 1910–11.
36. Rodney, *A History of the Guyanese Working People*, p. 155.
37. PIR 1913–1914.
38. Correspondence No. 20, Protector of Immigrants Papers, Jamaica Archives, Protector to the Colonial Secretary, n.d., 1902.
39. Tinker, *A New System of Slavery*, p. 194.

BIBLIOGRAPHY

Primary Sources

I. Manuscripts

Public Record Office, London

Selected volumes from the following classes:
CO 571: Immigration Correspondence

Jamaica Archives

CSO 1B/S/11/1 to 22, Legislative Council Debates

CSO 1B/5/75 to 77, Original Correspondence and Copies of Original Correspondence from the Colonial Secretary's Office

CGF 1B/9,1845–1950, Immigration Department Papers of the Protector of Immigrants.

II. Printed

Parliamentary Papers

India Office Library and Records

PP Vol. XLV, (353), 1847–48

Reports and Papers

Gt. Britain. Parliament, 1915. *Report by James McNeil and Chimman Lal on East Indian Emigration*. London: HMSO, 1915.

Government of India

IOR Collection V/24/1208-14, 1875–1916, Annual Reports on Emigration from the Port of Calcutta.

Government of Jamaica

Jamaica Annual Reports (which included Reports of the Immigration Department), 1879–1938.

Newspapers, Serials and Yearbooks

Newspapers

Morning Journal

Secondary Sources

Books

Benedict, B. *Indians in a Plural Society: A Report on Mauritius*. London: HMSO, 1961.

Birbalsingh, F. (ed). *Indenture and Exile: The Indo-Caribbean Experience*. Toronto: Tsar Press, 1989.

Brereton, B. *A History of Modern Trinidad, 1783-1962*. Kingston, Port of Spain, London: Heinemann Educational Books Ltd., 1981.

Rodney, W. *A History of the Guyanese Working People, 1881-1905*. Kingston, Port of Spain, London: Heinemann Educational Books Ltd., 1981.

Saha, P. *Emigration of Indian Labour, 1834-1900*. New Delhi: Peoples Publishing House, 1970.

Smith, A.E. *Colonists in Bondage: White Servitude and Convict Labour in America, 1607-1776*. USA: University of North Carolina Press, 1947.

Tinker, H. *A New System of Slavery: The Export of Indian Labour Overseas, 1830-1920*. London: Oxford University Press, 1974.

Weller, J.A. *The East Indian Indenture in Trinidad*, Caribbean Monograph Series, No. 4. Puerto Rico: Institute of Caribbean Studies, University of Puerto Rico, 1968.

Articles

Erlich, A.S., "History, Ecology, and Demography in the British Caribbean: An Analysis of East Indian Ethnicity." *Southwestern Journal of Anthropology* 27, 2 (1971).

Frederickson, G.M., and Lasch, C. "Resistance to Slavery." *Civil War History* 13 (1967).

Shepherd, V.A. "Aspects of the Condition of Indian Female Plantation Workers in Jamaica During the Indentureship and Post-Indentureship Period." In R. Reddock (ed.), *Reader in Plantation Women*, forthcoming.

FURTHER READING

Bhaba, Homi. 2002. "Of Mimicry and Man: The Ambivalence of Colonial Discourse." In *Race Critical Theories: Text and Context*, ed. Philomena Essed and David Theo Goldberg. Malden, MA: Blackwell Publishers.

Bhaba combines psychological perspectives with post-colonial concerns in the formation of subjectivities and inter-subjectivities. He illustrates that colonialism had an effect not only at the economic and political level, but also at the level of psycho-social existence. The colonial project of assimilating the "native" was never complete insofar as difference between the colonizer and the colonized was maintained in order to preserve colonial power. The partial imitation of British men that colonialism produced—what Bhaba calls the "mimic man"—turned out to be a "menace" because his ambivalence preserved a space for subversion. What happened to "mimic woman" has been theorized by other writers.

Fanon, Frantz. 1963. *The Wretched of the Earth*. New York: Grove Press Inc.

This is an English translation of Fanon's work on colonization and decolonization in Africa, with a preface by Jean-Paul Sartre. In this work, Fanon discusses in detail the political, economic, cultural, and mental health effects of colonialism, colonial war, and violence on the colonized. Chapters deal with the inherent polarization between the colonizer and the colonized ("settlers" and "natives"), as well as the stark violence perpetrated against the latter by the former through the state apparatus and its individual representatives. Fanon argues that power relations in the colony are different from those in the "mother" country in that ruling is done through force alone, not through consent. Colonization produces two worlds in the colonies, one in which the "settler" lives and the other in which the "native" lives; the two are presented as diametrical opposites (by the colonial regime), with the former embodying everything that is good and virtuous and the latter embodying that which is evil and inferior. Fanon then explores the effects of such social and political arrangements on the subjectivities of the colonized through a class analysis. In particular, he engages in a fascinating exploration of the position of bourgeois African intellectuals and their separation from the rank and file. He discusses the economic, political, and cultural limitations of the post-colonial situation when this national intellectual class takes over the government. In contrast, he argues for the revolutionary potential of the peasantry in such countries.

Fanon, Frantz. 1967. *Black Skin, White Masks*. New York: Grove Press

This is an English translation of Fanon's seminal text in which he explores the psychological effects of colonialism and racism on the black man, predominantly from his own subject position. Fanon contends that colonization and racism produce a desire in the black man to be white. In chapters two and three, he discusses the impact of these dynamics on intimate relations between blacks and whites, the former chapter dealing with the relationship of the woman of colour and the white man. The book also includes critiques of other contemporary writers, as well as considerations of the black man's struggles to discover his identity in a white-dominated world. Fanon takes the provocative position of arguing that what is represented as blackness is a white construct. This work provides a rare and early revelation of the intersections of colonialism, racism, psychology, and intimacy, one that has spawned many other contemporary writings in related areas.

Mehta, Brinda. 2004. *Diasporic (Dis)Locations: Indo-Caribbean Women Writers Negotiate the Kala Pani*. Kingston, Jamaica: University of West Indies Press.

This book focuses on the experiences and literary expressions of Indian Hindu women who braved the treacherous Kala Pani (Atlantic Ocean) to lead new lives marked by indentureship in the Caribbean. For many this was a flight from Hindu patriarchal family relations to lives of relative social, economic, and sexual "freedom," particularly in the context of the demographic imbalance in which women were a minority among indentured labourers. This book examines the expression of diasporic Indian womanhood in recent critical and creative writings by Indo-Caribbean women.

Tharu, Susie. 1999. "Tracing Savitri's Pedigree: Victorian Racism and the Image of Women in Indo-Anglian Literature." In *Recasting Women: Essays in Indian Colonial History*, ed. Kumkum Sangari and Sudesh Vaid. New Brunswick, NJ: Rutgers University Press.

In the post-colonial tradition of Fanon and Bhaba, Tharu throws light on the subjectivities of colonized women, in particular upper-class and upper-caste Hindu women from Bengal, the seat of British colonial power in India. In this critical essay, the author deconstructs a number of Indo-Anglian nationalist writings by women in the context of British colonial domination. She argues that, in an effort to dispute racist and Orientalist constructions of Indian women and men—for instance, the stereotype of them as weak and immoral—Indo-Anglian writers constructed heroines who embodied Victorian virtues of chastity, purity, and freedom in a way that was typically associated with European women. Indeed, the combination of indigenous purity, sacrifice, and spiritual strength were portrayed as vital for the defeat of colonialism. However, the author argues that in this process of constructing the feminine figure of the martyr, patriarchy was not completely dismantled; there was an assertion of racial equality (and thus a confirmation of the idea of race); and there was an obfuscation of the exploitation of ordinary men and women, lest a negative light be thrown on Indians.

PART 3

RACE, RACISM, AND INSTITUTIONS

PART 3A

RACISM IN THE EDUCATION SYSTEM

In the following chapters, Celia Haig-Brown, Carmel Borg and Peter Mayo, and George J. Sefa Dei explore the impact of racism and colonialism on education. They demonstrate that the socially constructed meanings of race operate in ways that disenfranchise, essentialize, and misrepresent the realities of the First Nations of Canada, Arabs and Africans in Malta, and African Canadians. The authors argue that there is a need for education to expose students to the ways in which colonization and imperialism have operated to racialize, and in the process subjugate, exploit, assimilate, and make invisible the existence of these populations. The process of assimilation and the "denial of difference" (Dei) have been facilitated, historically and currently, by school systems in which the textbooks and other resources make the existence of racialized students invisible.

In the first reading, Haig-Brown discusses how Canada's "Founding Nation" narrative only tells the story of the colonizers—the English and French—even though aboriginal people "have always been here." She argues that as long as the "Founding Nations" narrative continues, Canadian students will not be getting an education that enables them to work toward changing that "learned ignorance" about aboriginal people. Haig-Brown suggests that a good start in working toward that change would be to answer these fundamental questions: "Whose traditional lands are you on at this moment? What do you know of the past and present of the peoples who traditionally dwelt here? Whose interests are served when you cannot answer these questions?" Haig-Brown documents how today, aboriginal peoples are working with governments and public school administrators to make needed changes in school systems, including recruiting aboriginal teachers, curriculum developers, and culturally sensitive non-aboriginal supporters.

In writing about the educational situation in Malta, Borg and Mayo describe how Malta's British colonial past operates in today's school system, contributing to a situation in which the school curricula, textbooks (some of which are still printed in England), and other materials help to produce Eurocentric "systems of knowledge." The authors also explain how Islamophobia and xenophobia function in the society—and in school texts—to instill fear of Malta becoming an Islamic state, even though the Maltese population is made up of people of both Arabic and European backgrounds. Borg and Mayo argue for an anti-racist approach to education in which educators, with the understanding that "racism is socially constructed, and can therefore be reversed," take into account the local context—that is, the history, "indigenous knowledge," and lived experiences of the people and students that the education is expected to serve.

George Dei in his discussion of how difference, specifically race difference, is often denied in academic discourses and educational practices, makes a case for employing anti-racist practices in order to make race and the racialized experiences of students visible. He interrogates the ways in which race is denied and the reasons for its denial, arguing that "strategic essentialism" is useful in keeping race at the centre of anti-racist practices. Dei makes an important contribution in explaining how to understand social oppression more broadly while keeping race at the centre of anti-racist politics.

In a way, all three chapters in this section deal with anti-racism as an approach to counteract the racism and concomitant racialization that education perpetuates. They argue for an education that critically engages students in understanding the historical and contemporary realities of their lives. An anti-racist pedagogy can help students comprehend how, to use Borg and Mayo's terminology, the "debtor's syndrome"—the idea that people who are owed are often hated, especially if they are "other" or different—operates; and with that knowledge, both students and educators can develop a dialectical relationship between past and present, thereby transforming both the education system and the society generally, with the hope of fostering interethnic and interracial solidarity.

CHAPTER 21

RESISTANCE AND RENEWAL: FIRST NATIONS AND ABORIGINAL EDUCATION IN CANADA

Celia Haig-Brown

> First Nations education must go beyond the bounds of being only for First Nations. Our place in this land must be understood by all Canadians so that we might work together toward building a more harmonious world.
>
> Verna J. Kirkness, Cree Nation, 1992.

> But there cannot be peace or harmony unless there is justice.
>
> Royal Commission on Aboriginal Peoples, 1996.

In this country, educators as well as the general public remain, for the most part, vastly ignorant of the history of relationships between Aboriginal peoples and the nonnative majority. North Americans of immigrant ancestry, whether they have come to this continent more recently or were born here, have been allowed to become citizens with little knowledge of an issue foundational to the new nations imposed upon the lands. Within Canada, for example, the very phrase "the founding nations" most often bypasses First Nations to focus on England and France. In keeping with this presentation of history, schools have generally failed to develop appropriate cultural space for Aboriginal students, with often tragic consequences for the students and for the society which loses them through its inability or refusal to respond.

SOME TERMS

To begin our discussion, some words about terminology. In rapidly changing political times, labels take on marked significance, their changes reflecting some of the concerns with which people are struggling. The words Aboriginal, Indigenous, First Nations, Native, and Indian are used in different places and by different people to refer to themselves or others as the descendants of the original inhabitants of these lands. Aboriginal is a term which simply means from the original people. Indigenous means "occurring naturally in a particular place," the dictionary tells us. First Nations is a politically charged term encompassing a trilogy: 1) primacy of place, 2) a political entity with structures of governance and, 3) through its plural form, a multiplicity of peoples and cultures forming these political entities. Native, which indicates that people are born in that place, is seen as somewhat ambiguous because of the claims of many people of immigrant ancestry who have been born in North America to be native. The capitalisation of the word is usually what distinguishes its application to Aboriginal people from the more general usage. Finally, Indian refers to people who are defined and governed by a set of federal laws called the Indian Act. The definition has been the site of considerable controversy over the years. It excludes many people of Aboriginal ancestry, among them the Métis. While based on a lost European's misnomer, this term has taken on social and historical significance to become a part of the daily vocabulary of many people of Aboriginal ancestry. Increasingly people are choosing to identify themselves according to the particular Nation or band of which they are a part. Patricia Monture-Angus writes:

> I am a member of the Ho-Dee-No-Sau-Nee Confederacy.... For many years, our nations were known as the Iroquois. But this is not how we call ourselves. There are six nations which make up the Ho-Dee-No-Sau-Nee Confederacy. We are the Seneca, Oneida, Onondaga, Cayuga, Mohawk, and Tuscarora. I do not like to say that I am a Mohawk woman. A friend recently told me that she had been taught that Mohawk means "man-eater" in one of the European languages.... That is not what being "Indian" means to me. I am a proud member of my nation and that is a good way to be (1995, 30).

NOT DISAPPEARING

Despite efforts which colonizers have made over time and continue to make to obliterate the collective memories and the current presence of Aboriginal people, they are not disappearing. In the *Globe and Mail*'s November 23, 1996 cover story on the Minister of Indian Affairs' response to the Report of the Royal Commission on Aboriginal Peoples, the Minister says: "There has to be an understanding that they [Aboriginal people] won't disappear unless their issues are addressed." The Minister, and by implication too many Canadian people, remain caught in assimilationist ideology expecting Aboriginal people to disappear. Initial efforts were made very much by design; some recent moves are driven as much by ignorance. That being said, the ramifications of Bill C-31 regarding Indian status appear to indicate another effort on the part of the federal government to absorb Indians into what Duncan Campbell Scott called "the body politic." Aboriginal peoples have been here since time immemorial and continue to work to regain their rightful places as well as full recognition of their continuing presence on their traditional lands. Aboriginal peoples often state in English translation of their languages that they have been in these territories "since time immemorial." As Kwakwaka'wakw leader Gloria Cranmer-Webster puts it succinctly, "We have always lived here" (National Film Board 1993). For those people who subscribe to a European interest in attempting precision where only speculation is possible, there have been many carbon-dated examples of the existence of the ancestors of Aboriginal people here in North America since times before any written records. The English word "prehistory," which refers to a time before written history and which is used to give scientific credibility to this time, appears to have some equatability to the phrase, used in the transmission of oral histories, "since time immemorial." The new nations, existing as an overlay of the primary Aboriginal nations, serve as a constant reminder of the fruits of colonization. The question becomes how can peoples throughout the land begin to address the collective amnesia and the racism which accompanies and contributes to such forgetfulness?

One is also faced with the question how it is that so many of us are allowed *not* to know some things which seem so obvious and so central once they are stated. Whose traditional lands are you on at this moment? What do you know of the past and present of the peoples who traditionally dwelt here? Whose interests are served when you cannot answer these questions? How might we all address a continuing lack that Canada's education systems have been unable or unwilling to remedy: a consideration of the places of Aboriginal people in this country?

Rather than take my word for this learned ignorance, I present you with some voices from the university where I teach as examples of this permission *not* to know. A few years ago, I gave introductory lectures on Aboriginal education in a number of classes of students in their fifth year of a concurrent program in education which leads them to two degrees—one in education and the other in arts or science. These students then have spent at least seventeen years in our educational institutions; they are some of the best schooled young people in our country. Three students' comments, used with their permission, follow:

> (1) Today was the only day in all of my education classes that the topic of Native peoples was discussed. Unfortunately, it has been my experience that we have overlooked this issue and have instead focused solely on the broader issue of multiculturalism. Although multicultural issues are important topics in our schools, neglecting the issue of Native peoples or simply encompassing them into the realm of multiculturalism makes a very strong negative statement about Canada's First Nations.
>
> (2) I have always seen myself as someone who tries to understand and learn about other cultures in order to better myself as a person living in a multicultural society. This lecture brought me down to earth in a sense that I realised that I do not know more than the bare essentials about Native culture.
>
> (3) This is the first I've ever heard about the residential schools, and as I am studying Anne Frank's diary in another course, I could not help thinking that residential schools have been as detrimental to Native people as the Holocaust was for Jews and others affected by the disaster.... I will admit that because of my ignorance, my sympathy for the struggles of First Nations people was minimal. I have heard more about the Native people with alcohol related issues who receive free tuition to university than I have heard what has happened to them to make them so desperate. I have not heard as often that European settlers brought alcohol to the Native people and that tuition is not free. Schooling is financed using money that belongs to the First Nations people for centuries. This money is owed to them as a form of compensation for their land.

These young people are not exceptional. They have been part of a program which makes a sincere effort to address the diverse backgrounds of the students in Ontario schools and yet manages to ignore Aboriginal peoples. And they are not the only generation to have been allowed such ignorance.

A FRACTURED CIRCLE

After many years of working with Aboriginal people and learning and teaching about Aboriginal education in courses such as Social Issues in Education, Anthropology of Education and Foundations of Education, I have developed a model as a way of thinking about Aboriginal education in Canada. Like all models, it constrains thinking as it informs; its usefulness pales even as it coheres. I chose to focus on four aspects: traditional education; federally supported residential schools; integration into provincially funded public schools; and Aboriginal control. While I initially conceived of the components in a chronological, linear arrangement, as I worked with them, I came to see that there is no distinct beginning and end to what I then called stages of First Nations education. On the other hand, the four points configured in a circle of relations allowed their interconnections to remain evident. The following graphic, A Fractured Circle, is an effort to depict the relationship of some salient moments of Aboriginal education in tradition and in Canada. It is an effort to depict the disruption when world views collide and cultures move on from there, inextricably interlinked, inescapably affected one by the other. It also shows that even as the assaults on Aboriginal cultures were at their strongest, the circle, although fractured, was never broken.

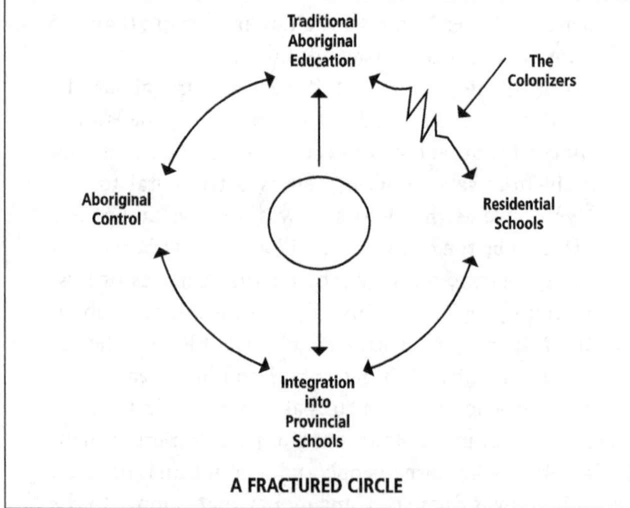

A FRACTURED CIRCLE

As I have mentioned above, I originally considered these four points on the circle distinct stages of Aboriginal education. I now see them as aspects interpenetrating and interrelated in many ways. For example, if one is to consider traditional education, it is not separate from the other aspects, but rather it is an understanding which continues to inform Aboriginal education in its various iterations. Some people currently focus on traditions and have little to do with institutional education; some work in and around public schools or in Band-controlled situations and look to tradition for contributions to a curriculum development respectful of Aboriginal cultures and their histories. A Band-controlled school is one located most often on a reserve, i.e. a small piece of the traditional land of a people or an unrelated piece allotted by the federal government to a particular group of Indians as defined by the Indian Act. Representatives of the Band have varying degrees of control over the personnel and the curriculum of the school. The main student body comprises children of Band members. One of the oldest Band-controlled schools in Canada, located at Peguis Reserve in Manitoba, has been under Band direction since 1977 (Archibald et al. 1994, 11).

What is traditional education? I have kept a quote attributed anonymously to an Aboriginal educator, which says, "There's more to traditional education than some Mickey Mouse courses in moccasin making." Traditionally, in keeping with conceptions of the world in which all exists in relation to all else, traditional education lasts a lifetime. Jeanette Armstrong writes that it is "a natural process occurring during everyday activities ... ensuring cultural continuity and survival of the mental, spiritual, emotional and physical well-being of the cultural unit and of its environment" (cited in Kirkness 1992, 7). In a related vein, Carl Urion says, "Traditional knowledge is living knowledge" (cited in Stewart-Harawira 2005, 35). Although there are particular life passages which call for temporary separation from parts of the community—such as the time of a woman's first menses—there is no discrete separation of children from others for instruction over an extended period of time, either daily or for defined period of years. Integral to each day and each life, community members take responsibility for passing on needed skills and understandings as events come to pass within the community. Whether learning the ways of the fisher, the ways to conduct a ceremony or a witnessing, or the ways to prepare hides or meat and gather berries, community members work together, each taking on the responsibilities appropriate to their abilities and knowledge. Watching and trying, children and adults are expected to participate in daily work and other activities in the ways that their developing competencies allow them. The use of the present tense throughout this passage is to alert the reader to the fact that these traditions continue to be part of many Aboriginal peoples' lives.

Although nations across North America vary significantly in the details of traditional education, and its persistence today, there are some striking similarities among groups in terms of beliefs and values. Vicki English-Currie, cautioning against any romantic notions of perfect and idyllic life, writes of these educational values as evident in her upbringing as a member of the Blackfoot Nation in what is now called Alberta:

> At the gatherings, there was no separation of the children and the adults. It was an extended family; even community members could become involved. All of the talk was comprehensible so the children were included in the conversation, although the adults did most of the talking.... I remember spending many days walking with my grandfather in the woods or down the road. Many of the stories he told me were turned into a life-lasting informal education of values (1990, 48).

She goes on to say:

> The Indian people's non-directive approach is a way of guiding offspring. It determined a basis for a future lifestyle. We matured rapidly and we became adept at determining our own actions and making our own decisions, while being sensitive to the expectations of the collective and of our elders (50).

Into this established form of education, the European came making demands for change. With residential schools established as the most effective means for accomplishing the changes European wanted, the traditional forms of education persisted only for the children who were lucky enough to avoid the schools or to spend at least some of their time with their families and communities. In the schematic above, I have conceptualized the residential schools as a rupture with the traditions Aboriginal people defined: it is the thunder bolt from outside that fractures the circle as Aboriginal peoples and the European colonizers clash over values and lifestyles. As the generations attending the schools increased through to the 1960s and 70s, it became increasingly difficult for community members to be educated into the traditions of the people. As this chapter unfolds, however, it becomes clear that the traditions have persisted in ever changing and dynamic forms through a tenacity of those who resisted the ways of the colonizers.

One of the reasons that Europeans ventured out into the world in various directions was an interest in pursuing what they considered to be the roots of their now superior society. In 1774, a frequently quoted letter demonstrates this attitude in its inclusion of "observations about the various kinds of apes and men in accordance with the eighteenth century postulate of a great chain of being stretching from the simplest forms of life to the most developed (the white European being a little lower than the angels)" (Banton 1987, 50). In 1859, Charles Darwin published *The Origin of Species* in which he theorizes evolution with its notions of the struggle for existence and natural selection of the species most suited to particular environments. People interested in human organizations and their developments used Darwin's theory in ways that he never intended. Social Darwinists believed that the theory could be "carried into sociology by substituting social groups for organisms.... Society was for them a rather vague universe of social groups in conflict.... Gumplowicz and Ratzenhofer identified them with racial groups" (Timasheff 1957, 70). Herbert Spencer is often cited as the person providing the impetus for social Darwinism which assumed that Europeans' complex societies were at a pinnacle of the "civilized races." In this conceptualization, the other so-called races of the world were deemed to represent the less developed primitive precursors of this superior "race" of men.

> ... by the late nineteenth century white-skinned Canadians were very much inclined to look down on people of different hues for several reasons. New strains of scientific racism such as Social Darwinism, [and] the influence of British imperialist attitudes ... combined to influence Euro-Canadian society strongly in a racist manner (Miller 1996, 185).

An examination of current school and university curricula in much of Canada demonstrates that assumptions of European superiority continue to be an organizing force in the way that we select the content to which we expose the children and adults in our educational institutions. When members of a society with these beliefs meet with the original peoples of the Americas, there can only be disruption. Most Aboriginal societies are based in a respect for difference and a recognition that the people outside the nation can never become like them. As the chiefs of Fort Rupert said to anthropologist Franz Boas in a speech published in 1896,

> We want to know whether you have come to stop our dances and feasts as other missionaries and agents who live among our neighbours tried to do. We do not want anybody here who will interfere with our customs. Is this the white man's land? We are told that it is the Queen's land but, no, it is ours. Where was the Queen when our god gave the land to my grandfather and told him, This will be yours? Do we ask the white man, Do as the Indian does? No, we do not. Why then do you ask us, Do as the white man does? Let the white man observe his law; we shall observe ours. Now if you are come to forbid us to dance, leave us; if not, you will be welcome (National Film Board 1993).

The efforts to train Aboriginal people to become like Europeans were never based in the kind of respect for difference which the passage above demonstrates. Starting in a limited way in 1620 in New France (Miller 1996, 39) and reaching what Aboriginal people might refer to as the Dark Ages during the late 1800s and well into the second half of the twentieth century, these schools wrecked havoc on traditions of Aboriginal cultures in almost every way imaginable.

RESIDENTIAL SCHOOLS

The Province of Canada in 1847 published a report based on the ideas of Egerton Ryerson which formed the basis for future directions in policy for Indian education and which, with Confederation, strongly influenced the development of schooling for Native people. (Prentice and Houston 1975, 218). Clearly expressed is the perception of superiority of the European culture, the need "... to raise them [the Indians] to the level of the whites," and the ever-increasing pressure to take control of land out of Indian hands. At the same time the contradictory need to isolate Indians from the evil influences of white society is acknowledged. The general recommendations of the report were that Indians remain under the control of the Crown rather than the provincial authority, that efforts to Christianize the Indians and settle them in communities be continued, and finally that schools, preferably manual labour ones, be established under the guidance of missionaries (Prentice and Houston 1975, 220). Cultural oppression was becoming written policy. Within the discussion of the recommendations is the following comment:

> Their education must consist not merely of the training of the mind, but of a weaning from the habits and feelings of their ancestors, and the acquirements of the language, arts and customs of civilized life (Prentice and Houston 1975, 220).

What clearer statement of an effort to destroy a culture could exist? The necessity of minimizing parental influence, another tool of cultural destruction, is further developed by Rev. Peter Jones, a Native convert to Christianity, in the same report:

> It is a notorious fact, that the parents in general exercise little or no control over their children, allowing them to do as they please. Being thus left to follow their own wills, they too frequently wander about the woods with their bows and arrows, or accompany their parents in their hunting excursions (Prentice and Houston 1975, 221)

The activities described were one of the main forms of traditional education for Native people: children learned by observing and following their parents and by doing the tasks expected of adults.

Following the establishment of the Indian Act of 1876, a consolidation of existing legislation, the government commissioned N.F. Davin to report on industrial schools established for Native people in the United States. Out of his report came the strong recommendations which resulted in the establishment of many residential schools across Canada. In the introduction to the report, Davin made references to President Grant's policy on the Indian question:

> The industrial school is the principal feature of the policy known as "aggressive civilization" (Davin 1879, 1).

Other comments show that some of Davin's attitudes were reinforced by politicians involved with schools for Native people in the US. One point which frequently arose in discussions of Native education was that working with adults or children in day schools was ineffective.

> The experience of the United States is the same as our own as far as the adult Indian is concerned. Little can be done with him.... The child, again, who goes to a day school learns little, and what he learns is soon forgotten, while his tastes are fashioned at home, and his inherited aversion to toil is in no way combatted (Davin 1879, 2).

Positively endorsing the notion of residential schools for Indians in Canada, Davin's final comment is "... if anything is to be done with the Indian, we must catch him very young (12).

In 1887, L. VanKoughnet, then Deputy Superintendent General of Indian Affairs, again stressed the need for schools for Native children. He wrote to the Right Honourable John A. Macdonald:

> That the country owes to the poor Indian to give him all that will afford him an equal chance of success in life with his white brother, by whom he has been supplanted (to use no stronger expression) in his possessions, goes without saying, and the gift for which we pray on his behalf, with a view to the discharge of this just debt, is the education of his children in such a way as will put beyond question their success in after life (VanKoughnet 1887, 1).

This report recommended the establishment of day schools. By 1920 amendments to the Indian Act included compulsory school attendance of Indian children and industrial or boarding schools for Indians (Miller and Lerchs 1978, 115). Following these amendments were other minor ones relating to education. It is interesting to note that in 1920 in the House of Commons discussion of changes to the Indian Act, Deputy Superintendent General Duncan Campbell Scott stated clearly the idea that Indian cultures as such were to be eliminated.

> ... Our object is to continue until there is not a single Indian in Canada that has not been absorbed into the body politic and there is no Indian question, and no Indian department, that is the whole object of this Bill. (Miller and Lerchs 1978, 114)

Not until 1946 was there serious possibility for change in this attitude and in the expressed intent of Department of Indian Affairs policy. J. Allison Glen, Minister of Mines and Resources, declared: "The Indian ... should retain and develop many of his Native Characteristics, and ... ultimately assume the full rights and responsibilities of democratic citizenship" (Miller and Lerchs 1978, 130). Also in 1946 discussions began for complete revamping of the Indian Act. For the first time, and only after initial strong resistance by committee members, Native input was actually permitted. Andrew Paull, President of the North American Indian Brotherhood, appeared before the Special Joint Committee. He was highly critical of the committee's lack of Indian representation. He condemned the existing Act as "an imposition, the carrying out of the most bureaucratic and autocratic system that was ever imposed upon any people in this world of ours" (Special Joint Committee 1947, 247). He spoke strongly for Indian self-government, and finally he commented that what was needed was

> ... to lift up the morale of the Indians in Canada. That is your first duty. There is no use in passing legislation about this or that if you do not lift up the morale of the people. The only way you can lift up the morale of any people is to let the members look after themselves and look after their people (427).

His words fell upon deaf ears.

In 1947, anthropologist Diamond Jenness told the Committee what it wanted to hear. His "Plan for Liquidating Canada's Indian Problems within 25 Years" (Special Joint Committee 1947, 310–311) recommended the abolition of Indian reserves and the establishment of an integrated educational system as the basis for assimilation. The never-ceasing attempt by the now dominant majority society to make the Indian disappear continued unabashed through this revision of the Indian Act. "The new Indian Act did not differ in many respects from previous legislation" (Miller and Lerchs 1978, 149). It did, however, serve as the beginning of the end for many residential schools because it allowed for Indian attendance in the public school system.

A CASE STUDY: KAMLOOPS INDIAN RESIDENTIAL SCHOOL

A more detailed examination of the establishment of one residential school in British Columbia exemplifies what went on across the country. George Manuel, the Secwepemc leader and author writes, "All areas of our lives which were not occupied by the Indian agent were governed by the priest" (Manuel and Posluns 1974, 63). Such was the case with the residential school. While the government espoused assimilation of the Indian through Christianization and civilization, it turned the doing of the task over to the religious orders—priests and teachers.

The Oblates of Mary Immaculate was founded in 1812 by Eugene de Mazenod in France. He sought to improve the quality of priests and of religious instruction while asking members of the order to emphasize self-spiritual regeneration, strict observation of the rules of the order and, secondarily, preaching to the poor. Original involvement with North America came in response to a request from the bishop of Montreal. From there, a small group of Oblates moved west, arriving in Oregon in 1847. Here, the philosophies which were to guide much of the Oblate missionary work in British Columbia were put into action. In his "Instructions on Foreign Missions" de Mazenod had written:

> Every means should therefore be taken to bring the nomad tribes to abandon their wandering life and to build houses, cultivate fields and practise the elementary crafts of civilized life (Whitehead 1981, 118).

Second only to insisting that the Native people abandon their own religious beliefs and take up Christianity was the push for them to abandon their migratory lifestyle. From a practical point of view, it proved very difficult to minister to people who were frequently on the move.

Fort Kamloops, a North West Company trading post founded in 1812 and, since time immemorial, an important site of winter homes for the Secwepemc, was a logical site for the establishment of a mission. Father Demers, an Oblate, was the first missionary to visit the Kamloops area in 1842. In 1878, Father Grandidier was appointed rector and bursar of the permanent St. Louis Mission. The original church and mission were located two and a half miles west of the present city centre. Father Lejacq served as supervisor from 1880 to 1882 and was succeeded by Father Lejeune in 1883. Although the Oblates previously had been operating a school for the children in a different location, in 1893 they took control of the permanent residential school. Father A.M. Carion served as the director of the school and, with some time away, remained in charge until 1916. While the priests were frequently busy travelling to preach to the Native bands of the area, their policies served to control the direction of the school. Father Carion, in a report from Kamloops Indian Residential School, states:

> We keep constantly before the mind of the pupils the object which the government has in view ... which is to civilize the Indians and to make them good, useful and law-abiding members of society. A continuous supervision is exercised over them, and no infraction of the rules of morality and good manners is left without due correction (Cronin 1960, 215).

The prime objectives of the Oblates were to control the lives of the Native people spiritually and in terms of lifestyle. Although their impact on Native people was very different from the whiskey trade and profit-seeking exploitation of some Europeans, it was exploitation in that the Oblates created a growing need for themselves in the Native people's lives. Because the missionaries had more extensive knowledge of Jesus Christ than Native people, once converted, they had to rely on this source of spirituality. Only priests could say Mass and offer the sacraments essential to the practising Catholic.

In British Columbia, the missionaries and governments worked hand in hand to deal with the Indian "problem." Government must have seen the religious order's efforts to control as most beneficial. Rather than sending soldiers and guns to control the lives of the owners of the land, the governments had the missionaries who influenced the Native people to limit their movements, take up an agrarian lifestyle, and abandon their culture.

The Oblates noticed that they were much more effective with Native people who had not been involved with the corruptive influences of some white traders. In 1861, Father Chirouse wrote:

> ... I find it much more difficult to reclaim and teach those who are brought much in contact with the evil-disposed and immoral among the whites than is the case with those who are differently situated (Cronin 1960, 139).

This recognition led to an even stronger push for control of Native people's lives. It was seen as an advantage to separate the Native people from the white settlements and, in the beginning, even from the English language. In a letter to Father Lejeune in 1892, L.N. Saintonge states:

> I agree with you that to teach English to the Indian is too much of a task. Besides they always learn it too soon for their own good. Unfortunately, when the Indians come to know English, they are more disposed to have relations with the whites, and you know what the result is of their intercourse. No, no, teach them no English. Let them learn it how they may, and as late as possible.

Although his words suggest that acquisition of English is inevitable, one can assume that he hopes to have Christianity ingrained before exposure to evil influences.

Despite its good intentions, this desire for control over Native people partially through segregation and more directly through the destruction of their traditional lifestyle reveals the invasive nature of the Oblates' work. References to "my Indians" are frequent and this possessiveness, while showing attachment to the people, also belittles and relegates the people to being possessions of another human being. Paulo Freire, in his discussion of cultural invasion, refers to well-intentioned professionals who invade not as a deliberate ideology but as an expression of their upbringing (1970, 154). He goes on to point out that cultural invasion "always involves a parochial view of reality, a static perception of the world and the imposition of this world view upon another" (159). Robin Fisher summarizes missionary efforts as follows:

> Because the missionaries did not separate Western Christianity and Western civilization, they approached Indian culture as a whole and demanded a total transformation of the Indian proselyte. Their aim was the complete destruction of the traditional integrated Indian way of life. The missionaries demanded even more far-reaching transformation than the settlers and they pushed it more aggressively than any other group of whites. (1977, 144–145)

Education was seen as a primary tool in effecting this transformation. In a vein similar to the government's notion of "getting them while they are young," the Oblates saw tremendous possibilities in the establishment of residential schools. Here the students could be isolated from the cultural influences of their parents and a daily, systematic inculcation of Christian theory and practice became possible. Attempts to control became close to absolute in that students were expected to attend from August to June and visits from home were strictly limited. In a reversal of Saintonge's recommendation, the use of English became mandatory. Through efforts to prohibit the Native languages, the very base of culture was attacked.

In Kamloops, the permanent residential school was built on land purchased by the government at the edge of what is now the Kamloops Indian Reserve. It was across the river from the town, providing the separation deemed optimal. In addition, it was several miles from the Indian village itself. The government had refused to purchase the buildings owned by the Oblates some miles away, because it was felt that they were asking too much money. In 1890, three two-storey wooden buildings were completed at the present site, now owned by the Kamloops Indian Band, and provided separate dormitories for boys and girls, a living area for teachers, classrooms, and a play area.

After a faltering start under the guidance of lay teacher Michael Hagan, the school was taken over by the Oblates in 1893. The Sisters of St. Ann also played a major role in working with the girls. Sister Mary Joachim started at the school in 1890, left shortly after, but returned in 1894 when the Oblates had taken over and remained until her death in 1907 (Kamloops Souvenir Edition 1977, 8). In 1923, the new brick building was completed to replace the one destroyed by fire. Throughout most of its operation until its closure in 1966, the KIRS was guided by the Oblates assisted by the Sisters of St. Ann. In the usual male-female hierarchy within the Church, the Oblate priests controlled policy and served as administrators while the Sisters were expected to work obediently as teachers, child care workers, and supervisors along with the Oblate brothers, the labourers of the order.

Most students who attended the school fell within the governmental jurisdiction called the Kamloops Agency. This area included the southern Shuswap Bands of Bonaparte, ChuChua, Skeetchestn, Kamloops, Adams Lake, Chase, Neskonlith, and several bands of Thompson Indians of the Nicola Valley. People from the Nicola Valley could choose to send children to St. Joseph's School in Lytton if they were Protestant and to St. Louis Mission in Kamloops if they were Catholic. In addition, some children from the Chilcotin and coastal bands attended the school. Following the 1916 McKenna-McBride Commission hearings, day schools were built on several reserves located some distance from Kamloops. Rising birth rates and enforced attendance after 1920 provided students not only for these schools but also an increasing number for the residential school.

THE PEOPLE

The Secwepemc whose children enrolled at the Kamloops residential school in 1893 had little experience with the formal European style of schooling offered by the Oblates. They saw childhood and schooling as an inseparable part of the on-going process of life and living.

> The methods used to teach skills for everyday living and to instill values and principles were participation and example. Within communities, skills were taught by every member, with Elders playing a very important role. Education for the child began at the time he or she was born. The child was prepared for his role in life whether it be hunter, fisherman, wife, or mother. This meant that each child grew up knowing his place in the system.... Integral to the traditional education system was the participation of the family and community as educators (Jack 1985, 9).

While warning of the danger of generalizing, Mary Ashworth (1979) says of traditional education amongst the diverse tribal groups in British Columbia:

> Education was the responsibility of all and it was a continuous process. Parents, grandparents and other relatives naturally played a major role, but other members of the tribe particularly the elders helped to shape the young people (6).

In the early part of this century, James Teit, an ethnographer who learned the Shuswap language and spent his life working with Native people of the Central Interior of British Columbia, wrote extensively of the Shuswap people's traditional lifestyle. Children had few responsibilities or duties until they reached puberty. Although he does not comment in detail on Shuswap childhood, Teit points out that children of the Thompson, a closely related tribe to the South, had few restrictions. They had to rise early, wash frequently in cold water and limit their play after sunset. Shuswap children also participated in a complex ceremony twice a year called "whipping the children" in which they were encouraged to overcome fear and ultimately demonstrate courage (Teit 1900, 308–309). Other than that, puberty was the time of focus on training. Girls were assisted by a grandmother, mother or aunt and spent a year in isolation practising all the work which a woman must do. Boys, isolating themselves for shorter periods of time, followed a similar pattern when their voices changed or they dreamed of women, arrows, and canoes, but their training could last several years (Teit 1909, 587–590). In addition to this specialized training, in the evenings elders spent much time telling stories which emphasized ethical concepts and myths important to the people. Frequently time was spent addressing the young people directly.

> These were the times when the old people would address the young, and then they would admonish them to follow the rules of proper ethical conduct (617).

The startling differences between Shuswap education and that of the residential school are numerous. Education with the Shuswap was a responsibility shared by family and community. Only at puberty did children remove themselves from the community for any length of time. Generally education was on-going, not focussed specifically on young people. The myths and stories told by the elders were directed not only at children but were a part of the life-blood of the community. With the residential school, children were removed from their community, placed in large groups and expected to follow a tight schedule. The adults with whom they had contact had very definite ideas about the children's need for changes in language, beliefs, and lifestyle.

Across the country, similar schools came into being. Children were taken away from their parents, sometimes for months and even years at a stretch, as the newly arrived colonisers attempted to impose and perpetuate what they saw as their superior ways onto the children. The methods employed in efforts to civilize and Christianize Aboriginal peoples and especially the children in the residential schools were generally repressive and dehumanizing. Children were punished for speaking their languages and forbidden to practice their cultural ways. Shirley Bear who attended a school in Prince Albert just north of Saskatoon said, some "of the staff were pretty mean too and did things that were not right—such as pulling ears, slapping heads and hitting knuckles" (in Miller 1996, 324). In and outside the schools, Aboriginal spirituality was deemed to be the Devil's work. As one residential school survivor states:

> He [the priest] would just get so carried away; he was punching away at that old altar rail ... to hammer it into our heads that we were not to think or act or speak like an Indian. And that we would go to hell and burn for eternity if we did not listen to their way of teaching (Sophie, cited in Haig-Brown 1988, 54).

From 1884 to 1951 (Tennant 1990, 52, 122), the potlatch, an economic system which included dances and feasting was outlawed; this legal control was later extended to any gathering of Indians which seriously affected the people's ability to address land claims and treaty issues.

For the most part the students attending the schools were being asked to become like white people only to perform menial, gender specific jobs or lead a life of dependency. Edward Ahenakew, a member of the Cree Nation, a residential school graduate and an ordained minister uses a fictional elder's account of the schools to give his critique of them. Decrying the lives claimed through diseases spread at the schools, he says:

> As for those who do live, who survive and who graduate from the school at the age of eighteen, during every day of their training they have acted under orders. Nothing they did was without supervision. They did not sweep a floor, wash dishes, clean stables, without first being told to do so, and always there would be a member of the staff to show them each step. They never needed to use their own minds and wills. They came to think it would be wrong if they went their own way. Now discipline and expediency in life are good, but will and initiative are better (1973, 133).

The details of residential schools are well documented elsewhere (see for example Johnston 1988; Haig-Brown 1988; Knockwood 1992; Miller 1996). Suffice it to say that their legacy persists. Closed for the most part by the late 1970s, there are many ongoing ramifications of these institutions. Recent media publicity surrounding church and federal government efforts to begin to redress charges of physical and sexual abuse have brought the schools to the attention of many members of the Canadian public. The impact on the minds, bodies and hearts of people who were taught for years that their ways of life were abominable in the eyes of God may be less easily identified but cut as deeply. Aboriginal people—even those in generations or as individuals who did not attend the schools—most often have relatives or friends who have felt their impact and whose trauma reaches out to those closest to them.

RESISTANCE

Almost from the beginning of the residential schools, Aboriginal people made efforts to resist them. (See for examples, Redford 1979; Haig-Brown 1995, 50–76.) From refusing to send children to attending government hearings in order to present grievances and concerns about them, the people indicated that they saw education as a powerful and useful tool but that they did not see the necessity of abandoning their own ways in order to assume the power of the "white man's" education. One might consider their attitude to be indicative of an assumption that biculturalism and multiculturalism was an advantage not a detriment. Serious questioning about the schools came to a head in the 1946–48 hearings in Ottawa for the purpose of revising the Indian Act. The Indian Act, which has been referred to by some as Canada's apartheid law, is a separate set of federal legislation which pertains to those defined by the government to be "Indians." This definition has been a source of endless conflict based in such inequities as the Section 12 (l)b, which until 1985 determined that an Indian woman who married a white man became a non-Indian and a non-Indian woman who married an Indian man became an Indian entitled to all the rights and benefits as well as the restrictions of an Indian in Canada. Changing that piece of legislation was the result of unceasing work on the part of Aboriginal women from across the country. As Patricia Monture-Angus writes: "It is interesting to understand that the first formal (that is to say under the corporate laws of Canada) organizing of Aboriginal women occurred around the issue of state oppression and not around so-called women's issues (violence against women and children, rape, custody, daycare, employment equity and so on)" (1995, 181).

Among the many other issues discussed during the 1946–48 hearings, presentations were made regarding the residential schools, their shortcomings and the disappointments they had wrought. Although some also spoke favourably about them, the outcome of the discussions was the beginning of the end of the schools. In amendments to the Indian Act which resulted from these hearings and in new provincial agreements established with the federal government—but significantly without the direct involvement of Aboriginal people—it became possible for Indian children, upon the payment of a tuition fee, to attend public schools.

One might assume that once Aboriginal children had access to the public schools, their aspirations for formal education in a respectful environment could be realized. This was not the case and when one examines the current levels of ignorance of Aboriginal peoples and lands which permeate today's schools, some of the answers for students' lack of success become evident. In 1967, in his *Survey of the Contemporary Indians of Canada*, Hawthorn and others documented the now infamous statistic which haunts those who work in Aboriginal education. Between kindergarten and graduation, Indian students were experiencing—creating—a 97% drop out rate from public schools. It is noteworthy that the recommendations from the Hawthorn Report are quoted in their entirety in Verna Kirkness's 1992 report on First Nations schools across Canada. She makes it clear that these recommendations were still applicable twenty-five years later and that very few of them had been satisfactorily addressed. As some nonnative and Aboriginal Canadian educators continued their struggles with an inability to provide a satisfactory schooling experience for Aboriginal students, Aboriginal parents and policy makers decided that this was the time to act.

Partly in response to the Hawthorn report and more directly in response to the White paper of the Trudeau government which sought a solution to what the bureaucrats had come to call the "Indian problem," members of the National Indian Brotherhood prepared a landmark document for presentation to the federal government. Written in 1972, *Indian Control of Indian Education* remains one of the clearest statements of direction for the future and dissatisfaction with the past that has been written. Calling for local control and parental responsibility, the authors of the policy pointed out that integration into the public schools was a one way street:

> Integration in the past twenty years has simply meant the closing down of Indian schools and transferring Indian students to schools away from their Reserves, often against the wishes of the Indian parents. The acceleration with which this program has developed has not taken into account the fact that neither Indian parents and children, nor the white community: parents, children and schools, were prepared for integration, or able to cope with the many problems which were created....
>
> In the past, it has been the Indian student who was asked to integrate: to give up his [sic] identity, to adopt new values and a new way of life. This restricted interpretation of integration must be radically altered if future education programs are to benefit Indian children (1972, 25).

Calling for teachers with cross-cultural training and sensitivities, a curriculum which reflects the reality of Aboriginal students, and schooling which honours the fundamental values and attitudes of First Nations, the document remains a beacon of possibility for all children. It says: "It is essential that all Canadian children of every racial origin have the opportunity during their school days to learn about the history, customs and culture of this country's original inhabitants and first citizens" (2).

A CIRCLE OF HEALING

In relation to the circle this document is a marker in the efforts at healing the rupture which colonization has wrought. A new circle, A Circle of Healing, is one which, through an honest and open examination of the legacy of residential schools in all their complexities, unmasks the genocidal breaks with traditional education. The document above and the three-volume comprehensive study of First Nations education across Canada, *Tradition and Education: Towards a Vision of Our Future* (1988), developed by the Assembly of First Nations, calls for precisely these changes. When schools can acknowledge the place of Aboriginal peoples since time immemorial, in history, and in the current context of Canadian society, the children will have an opportunity to grow into the fullness of our history. It is not all nice, but it is important that it is known rather than hidden. Through coming to understand the silences and the pain of people whose cultures have been under attack for up to five centuries, Canadians together can know themselves a little more.

In 1997, Newfoundland "celebrated" the arrival of John Cabot in "New Founde Land," a land which was known to the Beothuks for thousands of years. The organizing committee for the celebrations indicated that "Native leaders will offer their perspective on the impact of European settlement in North America" (*John Cabot 500th Anniversary Celebrations* 1997). The Beothuks who were hunted by the settlers and others to extinction were not there to speak Was their memory honoured and respected throughout the time of the remembrance and did the children learn more of the ways of our ancestors so that they can become part of a country and a world which recoils with the same horror at its own history as it does at genocide in Rwanda and Nazi Germany? Through efforts to tell truth, healing becomes possible; through deception, contrived half-truths and outright lies, the ruptures can only continue. Patricia Monture-Angus, while cautioning that First Nations meanings are "are not the same as the ways known to the dominant society" (31), uses respect and truth interchangeably. The Assembly of First Nations (1988) and the Report of the Royal Commission on Aboriginal Peoples (1996) argue for truth telling and the reparation which must accompany it. The second circle shown below shows the possibilities that exist with healing.

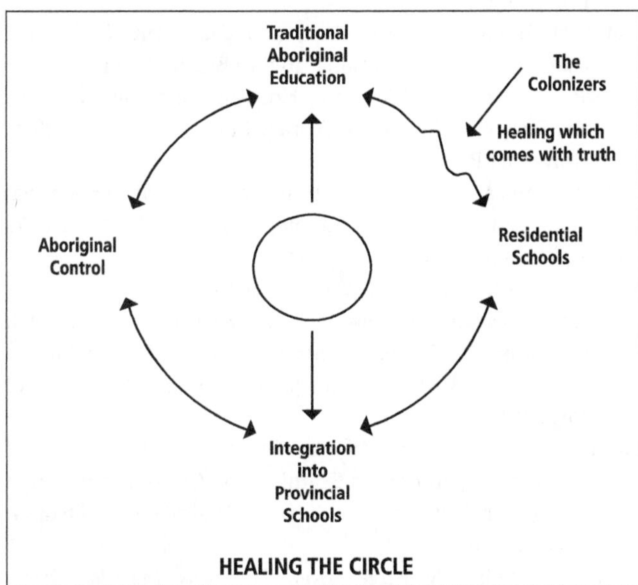

HEALING THE CIRCLE

Following years of devastation through disease and community disruption, the population of Aboriginal people in Canada is increasing. A federal report from 1985 comments that "by 1991, it is estimated that one out of two new entrants to the Manitoba and Saskatchewan labour force will be of Native ancestry" (Deputy Prime Minister 1985, 5). Increasing numbers of Aboriginal people are locating within the cities across Canada. Urion (1992, 3) reports, "half a million aboriginal people in Canada live away from reserves, 45% of them 19 years old or younger." They are asking that the schools they attend treat Aboriginal people within them with a respect that acknowledges the traditions of the lands on which the cities are founded. Reiterating the notions of local control and parental responsibility which are central to the *Indian Control of Indian Education* document of 1972, the Royal Commission on Aboriginal Peoples reports:

> In the main, Aboriginal peoples want two things from education:
>
> They want schools to help children, youth and adults learn the skills they need in order to participate fully in the economy.
>
> They want schools to help children to develop as citizens of Aboriginal nations—with the knowledge of their languages and traditions as necessary for cultural continuity (Canada 1996, 82).

Aboriginal people are working with public schools to address the needed changes with more and more Aboriginal teachers, curriculum developers and culturally-sensitive non-Aboriginal supporters contributing their expertise. Schools and other educational institutions with considerable Aboriginal control are being developed across the country. In the cities, cultural survival schools such as Joe Duquette High School in Saskatoon, Wandering Spirit School in Toronto, and the Plains Indian Survival School in Calgary have taken on the role of teaching the students some of the truths not available to them in mainstream schools. These schools exist in a complex historical and social context of Aboriginal people and their education in what is now called Canada. Sol Sanderson, a president of the Federation of Saskatchewan Indians, writes of the history of schooling in that province:

> For some time we have recognized the critical importance of having our own educational institutions to counteract the influence of Canadian educational institutions on our young people, who are being alienated from their own communities and heritage. As Indian people we have been expected to change spiritually, culturally, and otherwise to conform to Canadian expectations (1984, 156).

Never losing sight of whose land we are on, we know which peoples have been here since time immemorial, in a time when the buffalo were plentiful and long before the horses which Hollywood stereotypes summon to mind, long before the coming of white men and women. I conclude this chapter with the following words from Dr. Verna Kirkness:

> It is the challenge to today's peoples to correct the situation created over three hundred years of attempted assimilation. To achieve this, the First Nations children of today must know their past, their true history, in order to understand the present and plan for the future. First Nations cultures must once again be respected and the traditional values must again be held in high esteem (1992, 103).

REFERENCES

Ahenakew, Edward. 1973. *Voices of the Plains Cree*, edited and introduced by Ruth M. Buck. Toronto: McClelland and Stewart Limited.

Archibald, Jo-ann. 1984. "Locally Developed Native Studies Curriculum: An Historical and Philosophical Rationale." Presented to the International Conference of the Mokakit Indian Education Research Association. London: University of Western Ontario.

Ashworth, Mary. 1979. *The Forces Which Shaped Them*. Vancouver: New Star Books.

Archibald, Jo-ann, and Celia Haig-Brown, with Verna Kirkness, Rhonda Olson, Cheryl Cochrane, and Val Friesen. 1994. *Kisti Notin: Peguis Central School*. Toronto: Canadian Education Association.

Assembly of First Nations (AFN). 1988. *Tradition and Education: Towards a Vision of Our Future*. Vols. 1–3. Ottawa: Queen's Printer.

Banton, Michael. 1987. "The Classification of Races in Europe and North America: 1700–1850." *International Social Science Journal* 39(1):32–46.

Cronin, Kay. 1960. *Cross in the Wilderness*. Vancouver: Mitchell Press.

Deputy Prime Minister. 1985. *Report of the Ministerial Task Force on Native Programs*. (The Buffalo Jump of the 1980s). April 12, 1985. (Photocopy from library of the First Nations House of Learning, UBC, Vancouver.)

Davin, Nicholas F. 1879. *Report on Industrial Schools for Indians and Halfbreeds*. Ottawa, March 14. PABC RG 10 Vol. 6001 File 1-1-1, Pt. 1.

English-Currie, Vicki. 1990. "The Need for Re-evaluation in Native Education." In *Writing the Circle: Native Women of Western Canada*, ed. Jeanne Perreault and Sylvia Vance, 47–60. Edmonton: NeWest Publishers Limited.

Fisher, Robin. 1977. *Contact and Conflict*. Vancouver: University of British Columbia Press.

Freire, Paulo. 1970. *Pedagogy of the Oppressed*. New York: Continuum.

Haig-Brown, Celia. 1988. *Resistance and Renewal: Surviving the Indian Residential School*. Vancouver: Tillacum Library.

———. 1995. *Taking Control: Power and Contradiction in First Nations Adult Education*. Vancouver: University of British Columbia Press.

Jack, Rita. 1985. "Legacy of the Indian Residential School." *Secwepeme Cultural Arts Magazine* 1(1):9.

John Cabot 500th Anniversary Celebrations. 1997. Brochure. PO Box 1997, St. John's, NF, Canada A1C 5R4.

Johnston, Basil H. 1988. *Indian School Days*. Toronto: Key Porter Books.

Kamloops Souvenir Edition. 1977. Kamloops Indian Residential School, May 21. Secwepemc Cultural Education Society.

Kirkness, Verna J. 1978. *Evaluation Report of Indians in Federal and Provincial Schools in Manitoba*. Ottawa: Department of Indian Affairs and Northern Development.

———. 1981. "The Education of Canadian Indian Children," *Child Welfare*, July–August 60:7.

———. 1985. "Indian Teachers—A Key to Progress." Address to University of Saskatoon, February 27.

Kirkness, Verna J., with Sheena Selkirk Bowman. 1992. *First Nations and Schools: Triumphs and Struggles*. Toronto: Canadian Education Association.

Knockwood, Isabelle. 1992. *Out of the Depths: The Experiences of Mi'kmaw Children at the Indian Residential School at Shubenacadie, Nova Scotia*. Lockeport, NS: Roseway Publishing.

Manuel, George, and Michael Posluns. 1974. *The Fourth World: An Indian Reality*. Toronto: Collier-MacMillan.

Miller, J.R. 1996. *Shingwauk's Vision: A History of Native Residential Schools*. Toronto: University of Toronto Press.

Miller, Kahn-Tineta, and George Lerchs. 1978. *The Historical Development of the Indian Act*. Ottawa(?): Treaties and Historical Research Branch, PRE Group, Indian and Northern Affairs.

Monture-Angus, Patricia. 1995. *Thunder in My Soul: A Mohawk Woman Speaks*. Halifax: Fernwood Publishing.

National Film Board of Canada. 1993. "Potlatch." In *First Nations: The Circle Unbroken*, produced by Gary Marcuse and Svend Erik Erikson.

National Indian Brotherhood. 1972. *Indian Control of Indian Education*. Ottawa: National Indian Brotherhood.

Prentice, Alison L., and Susan E. Houston. 1975. *Family, School and Society In Nineteenth-Century Canada*. Toronto: Oxford University Press.

Redford, James. 1979–80. "Attendance at Indian Residential Schools in British Columbia, 1890–1920." *BC Studies* 44(Winter):41–56.

Sanderson, Sol. 1984. "Preparations for Indian Government in Saskatchewan." In *Pathways to Self-Determination: Canadian Indians and the Canadian State*, ed. Leroy Little Bear, Menno Boldt, and J. Anthony Long, 152–158. Toronto: University of Toronto Press.

Special Joint Committee of the Senate and the House of Commons Appointed to Examine and Consider the Indian Act. 1947. *Minutes of Proceedings and Evidence* No. 1. Ottawa: King's Printer.

Stewart-Harawira, Makere. 2005. *The New Imperial Order: Indigenous Responses to Globalization*. London: Zed Books.

Teit, James. 1909 [1975]. *The Shuswap*. New York: AMS Press.

———. 1900 [1975]. *The Thompson Indians of British Columbia*. New York: AMS Press.

Tennant, Paul. 1990. *Aboriginal Peoples and Politics: The Indian Land Question in British Columbia, 1849–1989*. Vancouver: University of British Columbia.

Timasheff, Nicholas S. 1955, 1957. *Sociological Theory: Its Nature and Growth*. New York: Random House.

Urion, Carl. 1992. "Editorial: Big Pictures and Paradoxes." *Canadian Journal of Native Education* 19(1):1–6.

VanKoughnet, L. 1887. *Letter to John A. MacDonald*. Ottawa, August 26. PABC RG 10 Vol. 6001 File 1-1-1, Pt. 1.

Whitehead, Margaret. 1981. *The Cariboo Mission: A History of the Oblates*. Victoria: Sono Nis Press.

CHAPTER 22

TOWARD AN ANTIRACIST AGENDA IN EDUCATION: THE CASE OF MALTA

Carmel Borg and Peter Mayo

One of the main features of the present historical conjuncture, the intensification of globalization, has brought in its wake not only the mobility of capital but also mass mobility of potential labor power across the globe—two types of mobility that do not occur on a level playing field. In a mode of production always characterized by uneven levels of industrial development (see Marx and Engels 1998), people in the subaltern part of the North–South axis move up north in search of pastures new. The specter of the violent colonial process the old continent initiated has come back with a vengeance to haunt it. This process is exacerbated by the fact that highly industrialized countries require certain types of labor and that this requirement cannot be met via the internal labor market, despite high levels of unemployment in these countries (Apitzsch 1995, 68). The process of mobility of persons from South to North is therefore great.

With southern Europe witnessing mass immigration from North Africa, the Mediterranean plays an important role in this process, serving, in the view of many, as "a kind of Rio Grande" (Richter-Malabotta 2002, 73). Like other countries of the Mediterranean, Malta is firmly caught up in the throes of this mobility process. Sharing with many countries of the region a history of having been an exporter of labor power to several parts of the world, ironically including North Africa but, most particularly, former British colonies of settlement (Attard 1983, 1989, 1999), Malta has been witnessing an influx of immigrants from different parts of Africa and, most particularly, North Africa. Racism against blacks and Arabs, previously played down in the media, is now here for all to see.

Racism has hitherto been given lip service in the discourse, concerning oppression, throughout the islands forming the Maltese archipelago. This can be seen from the fact that the literature dealing with different forms of privilege and oppression in Malta rarely deals with the subject. Class and gender analyses feature prominently in sociological texts produced in Malta (see Sultana 1992, 1997; Sultana and Baldacchino 1994; Darmanin 1992; Baidacchino and Mayo 1997), but in-depth studies on racism are few and far between. In fact, the only monograph-length text to date appeared a few years ago (Calleja 2000). This text certainly fills a void concerning Maltese analysis of social difference and identity. As far as educational literature is concerned, the only article on antiracist education to date appeared in a professional journal (Borg 2002).

ISLAMOPHOBIA

A recent extremely popular television program tackled the issue on two occasions, one in 1999 and one in 2003, both sparking considerable debate in a section of the Maltese press. This debate was characterized by the expression of a particular form of racism—Islamophobia—which is rampant worldwide and has traditionally been a feature of the southern European, or "Latin arc," context. This phenomenon has to be viewed against a southern European historic backdrop featuring periods of Arab domination, which left indelible marks on the culture of these places, and long periods of European colonization marked by Christian wars against the Saracen other. This is true of the Maltese islands, which were under Arab domination for at least three hundred years. This process of domination naturally had its effect on the islands. One of its most tangible legacies is the native Maltese language, which is a derivative of Arabic with an influx of romance words. It is also written in a European script. The legacy is also evident in several Maltese surnames (e.g., Abdilla, Caruana, Saliba) and in most place-names (Rabat, Marsa, Zebbug, Mdina). The period of Arab domination was followed by a lengthy process of European rule, which consolidated Catholicism as the dominant belief system throughout the islands. This process includes (1) the Sicilian period, (2) the period when the islands were ruled by the Order of St. John of Jerusalem, and, finally, (3) the British period (which followed two years of French occupation under Napoleon). Catholicism was consolidated during the first two periods. The British period of colonization started in 1800 and officially came to an end in 1964 with the country's independence, though British forces remained in Malta until 1979.

THE SARACEN OTHER

The period of European colonization left a strong Eurocentric imprint on the islands and its inhabitants. A substantial part of this period was characterized by war between European powers, acting as the bulwarks of Christendom, and the Ottoman Empire. Malta was caught up in these wars, especially during its period of rule by the Order of St. John (often referred to as the Knights of Malta), who had settled in Malta after losing the island of Rhodes to the Turks. The events of 1565, when the islands successfully repelled an invasion by Turkish troops, are commemorated every year. Images and anecdotes connected with these events are an important feature of Maltese popular lore. The iconography in works of art commissioned by the Order of St. John also reflected an antagonism toward the Saracen. This type of iconography is nowhere more apparent than at St. John's co-Cathedral in Valletta, one of the island's major artistic attractions that was also the order's church. The Ottoman adversary is represented, in this iconography, as the other (Borg and Mayo 2000a,b). As always, and using Edward Said's (1978) terms, the iconography reflects an assumption of positional superiority, in the construction of alterity, by those who commission the work. Each sculpted figure of the Saracen other, at St. John's, constitutes an integral feature of the cathedral's ostentatious high baroque setting. The figures referred to here are specifically those of the Turkish slaves supporting the ornate wooden pulpit and the marble slaves shouldering the weight of Grand Master Nicholas Cottoner's monument. One of the latter slave figures brings to mind the typically Western construction of Caliban, the Shakespearean figure which, in conventional Western literary criticism, often prompts commentators to refer to the nature–nurture debate. What we come across here is an exotic representation not only of the Saracen other but, more generally, the non-European. The figure fits the popular Western construction of the non-European, the African in particular, represented as a deficient figure ripe for European missionary intervention. This type of image is a recurring one in the predominantly Roman Catholic country that is Malta. It features prominently in holy pictures and much of the Church's other iconography.

The baroque marble figure of the young Turkish slave, in the Cottoner Monument at St. John's, is reproduced on the front cover of Calleja's book, *Aspects of Racism in Malta*. Given the argument (centering around the issue of Islamophobia) that Calleja carries forward in this book, the choice of such an illustration strikes us as being very apt. In these artistic representations, the Saracen is also demonized, rendered the personification of all that is dark and therefore evil or irrational. This distortion has all the features of the (mis)representation of the other, "based on scientific proof" (Fanon 1963, 296)—decried by Frantz Fanon in *The Wretched of the Earth*. Of course, in Fanon's text, it is the colonized Algerian subject who constitutes alterity.

Given such a racist and Islamophobic representation of the other in both high and popular culture, not only in Malta but throughout southern Europe (e.g., the Sicilian marionettes featuring the Crusader and the Ottoman "predator"), it is not surprising that anything associated with Islam becomes the object of repudiation in the Maltese psyche. As a result, the much-despised Turk is replaced by the feared neighboring Arab, Islam being the common denominator. As Calleja (2000) points out:

> Apart from the international media's systematic campaigns against Arab interests, there is some popular Maltese cultural mythology that compounds these prejudices. Maltese have been nurtured ... to associate the Arabs and Islam with hostility and oppression. We have popular myths about Count Roger who liberated Malta from the Arabs and numerous other myths about Arab raids on Malta. This continued with the Knights of Malta who annihilated all historical evidence of our Arab culture and Islamic religion. We thus construe an image based on a variety of stereotypical assumptions that Arabs are hostile, violent, untrustworthy and totally incompatible with our standards and values and must hence be "kept out" both physically and attitudinally. (44)

MISCONCEPTIONS

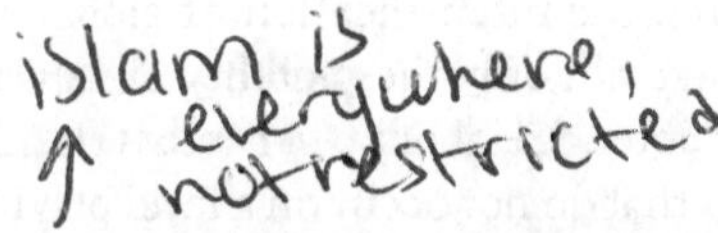

One point that emerges from this type of racism, predicated on Islamophobia, is an astounding lack of basic knowledge concerning Islam and the Arab world. The two are conflated, when it should be common knowledge that Islam is a world religion that knows no ethnic, racial or geographical boundaries. It makes its presence felt everywhere (Shaykh 'Abd al Wahid Pallavicini 1998). One can find Islamic communities in Malta, the United Kingdom and Italy, just to give three examples. These communities do not consist exclusively of people who would be referred to as "migrants" but also include people coming from families who have been, say, British or Italian for several generations. Ahmed Moatassime underlines that the Arabs, strictly speaking, constitute a minority (approximately one-fifth) among millions of Muslims (Moatassime 2000, 113).

Lack of basic knowledge of the culture of those constructed as other is manifest in the Maltese media, which constructs Arabs as either terrorists or drug dealers. In the latter case, the media focuses exclusively on those caught, at Malta's International Airport, importing drugs, without going beyond the surface to investigate such matters as who really lies behind the operation. Furthermore, such media as school textbooks are often guilty of distorting the culture of *alterity*. We come across distortions as serious as that found in a much-used secondary school history textbook (Education Department of Malta 1976, 129). We are shown the picture of a man sporting a beard and wearing a turban purporting to represent the prophet Mohammed. Distortions such as these border on ignorance of and lack of sensitivity toward the religious values of others. It should, after all, be common knowledge that the Qu'ran prohibits representations of the Prophet and God.

Of course, these distortions are found not only in Malta but elsewhere, as Mahmoud Salem Elsheikh (1999, 47) clearly demonstrates with regard to school texts used in Italy.

While such distortions are reprehensible per se, they become all the more offensive given that the Maltese school population is increasingly becoming multiethnic as a result of the influx of foreigners in Malta. For instance, an Arab community has been present in Malta since the early 1970s, when the then Labor government forged strong ties between Malta and certain Arab states, Libya in particular. Furthermore, in addition to the presence of Muslims in Maltese schools, there was a period between the 1970s and mid-1980s when a number of Arab teachers, many of whom were Muslim, taught Arabic in Maltese state schools. The Arabic language was rendered a compulsory subject in schools by the then Labor government. It is reasonable to assume that the more multiethnic an environment becomes, the greater the contestation that takes place with respect to the politics of representation. It was, in fact, an Egyptian colleague, a teacher of Arabic, who first brought the distortion in the history textbook to the attention of one of the chapter authors when this author was a teacher of English in a Maltese secondary state school.

Distortions are also found in early Maltese literature, where the term "Turk" is often used interchangeably with Muslim. The imagery generated by the eighteenth- and nineteenth-century literature dealing with the "traditional enemy" (read: Turks) is that of "sons of Mohammed," who regarding the Maltese as "wicked," were bent on "enslaving" Malta to convert it to Islam and to replace the Bible with the Qu'ran. They are also depicted as rapists bent on destroying whatever they found in the villages (Cassola 2000). This reflects the pervasive image of the predator in southern European culture. For many years, this literature was compulsory reading for students at different levels of the Maltese educational system.

EUROCENTRIC CURRICULA

Of course, there is much to argue about the politics of representation in texts used in Maltese schools. One rarely comes across texts in Maltese schools which provide illustrations revealing an ethnic mix. This is often compounded by the fact that, in the case of English language reading texts, the state is still using textbooks (e.g., the graded Ladybird reading books) published in England several decades ago. These textbooks are therefore not reflective of the multiethnic and multiracial contestation and ferment that characterized British society in later years. Furthermore, little seems to be done in the way of rendering courses at Maltese educational institutions less Eurocentric. A classic example here would be *Systems of Knowledge*, introduced as a compulsory area in 1987 at sixth form level. It was originally criticized for attaching little importance to the writings of authors who do not fall within the male Eurocentric framework (and this despite the presence of a huge corpus of African literature available in English). *Systems of Knowledge* was also criticized for being similar in conception to the Great Books and the process of cultural literacy advocated in the United States by Allan Bloom and E.D. Hirsch, respectively (see Borg et al. 1995). A reviewer of the current *Systems of Knowledge* official textbook provides a very positive appraisal of the work. He nevertheless makes the point that the book "could usefully have devoted more systematic attention to the implications of its own boundaries, and to the fact that its orientations are exclusively Eurocentric" (Grixti 1996, 210). He goes on to state, "More could have been made of the fact that other cultural, artistic, intellectual and technological traditions were developed in non European contexts, and that some of the most stimulating developments in art and thought often resulted from contact between different cultural traditions" (Grixti 1996, 210).

ARAB AND ISLAMIC CONTRIBUTIONS

There is often a tendency, when dealing with the Mediterranean, to concentrate exclusively on the southern European and particularly the Greco-Roman traditions, ignoring the other civilizations that have emerged in the African part of the region. These civilizations have also made tremendous contributions to the development of European civilization (see e.g., Lê Thánh Khôi 1999, 444; 2000, 58), a point stressed by Predrag Matvejevic, who states that one cannot construct a Europe without reference to its "infancy and adolescence," namely, the formative influence of the Mediterranean (Matvejevic 1997, 119). The Mediterranean, of course, comprises the Arab and Islamic civilizations. Elsheikh (1999) regards the antagonism shown in Europe toward these civilizations as indicative of what he calls "the debtor's syndrome": "the person to whom one is indebted is constantly a hated person; particularly if the creditor, as in this case, is a strange body, rejected by the collective consciousness, hated by the political, social, cultural and religious institutions. If anything, the rage against the creditor, in these circumstances, becomes an almost moral duty and a necessary condition for the survival of that society" (literal translation by one of the authors, from Elsheikh 1999, 38).

In misrepresenting Arabs and Islam, Maltese texts and mass media obscure Western culture's indebtedness to those other civilizations that are often denigrated in Western regimes of truth. Of course, this denigration becomes a feature of "common sense" that is manifest in a variety of ways.

There is much to be said, in this context, about popular Maltese expressions. These include such expressions as "Am I black?" (*Mela jien iswed?*) uttered to express resentment at being excluded or overlooked. Other expressions represent Jews and Arabs in a pejorative light.

The ever-increasing presence of Arabs in Malta has also led to expressions of fear concerning the "threat" they are supposed to pose to the preservation of the "Maltese identity," the "Maltese culture" and the country's "Catholic values." As is often the case, we are confronted with an essentialist and totalizing discourse that negates the existence of multiple cultures and identities within a single society. There seems to be little recognition of the fact that there are no fixed identities, a point painstakingly underlined by the Vietnamese author Lê Thánh Khôi (1999, 2000) through a detailed historical overview of the intermeshing of cultures in the Mediterranean. It is a point that underscores the problematic nature of the term "race" itself. As Robert Miles has argued, "owing to interbreeding and large-scale migrations, the distinctions between 'races,' identified as dominant gene frequencies, are often blurred" (quoted in Virdee and Cole 2000, 52–53).

As Carlos Alberto Torres (1998) eloquently states, "Recognition of the complexities posed by the process of hybridization and the notion of multiple identities in the social and the psychological construction of the pedagogical subject should challenge any attempt to essentialize differences based on race, gender, class, nationality, ethnic, religious and sexual preferences" (254).

XENOPHOBIA

Columnists and opinion leaders often express the fear that the Arab population in Malta would grow to such an extent that Malta would eventually become an Islamic state, and therefore lose its "identity" in the process. The following excerpt from an opinion column, entitled "Slay the Infidel," which appeared in the *Malta Independent*, is typical of this position:

> History has taught us that Islam has always spread at the cost of the culture of the people whose lands it has occupied. In larger countries, it would take centuries for Muslim proliferation to make a quantifiable impact. Thus the political aim would not be identified for a long while yet. But Malta is a drop in the ocean where ramifications will be felt much sooner because of its limitations. The race for conquest, if such a conquest is intended, will be quick. Worse, like a stealthy predator, it will be upon us before we know what has hit us. (Zammit Endrich 1999)

Reference to the situation of women in certain parts of the Arab world is often made to justify this xenophobic attitude toward Arabs and Islam. Furthermore, the fear of Arabs and blacks has often led to very blatant and obscene acts of racism that take the form of shops and bars occasionally displaying notices barring Arabs from entering. There have been allegations that bouncers at entertainment spots have been discriminating against certain potential patrons on the grounds of race. It was reported in *The Times*, a Maltese English-language daily newspaper, on November 25, 1999, that a "man of Nigerian origin is considering filing a constitutional case, claiming racial discrimination against the owners of a Paceville [Malta's main entertainment center for young people] night club after black people were allegedly turned away on two occasions recently because of their skin colour" (Galea Debono 1999a, 4). The *Malta Independent on Sunday*, of August 8, 1999, reported a similar incident concerning blacks (Balzan 1999, 1) while *The Times* (Malta) reported a similar complaint by a French professor of Arab origin who felt that he was being discriminated against, when denied entry to a Paceville nightclub, because he was "Arab-looking" (Galea Debono 1999b, 14).

Furthermore, a section of the Maltese broadcasting media has given prominence to the publication, in 1999, of a book by Norman Lowell, a far-right candidate for the 2004 European parliamentary elections, entitled *Credo*. We are not in a position to go into the details of this book since, in keeping with our political convictions, we deliberately refuse to look at its contents. The evidence from the TV discussion programs suggests that this book expounds concepts on a range of subjects, including race and disability, that smack of neo-Nazi "master race" theories. The author's ideas were, for the most part, decried in the course of the programs. This notwithstanding, the prominence given by TV stations to this book suggests that authors of outrageously racist works constantly prove attractive to the media in its search for the sensational and the "provocative."

LACK OF ANTIRACIST LEGISLATION

The foregoing is indicative of the fact that the gradual development of Maltese society into a multiethnic and multiracial one is marked by tensions that generate a racism which assumes different forms, some subtle and others not so subtle. These acts of racism have occurred with impunity for a long time given that it is only recently that there has been legislation allowing for the prosecution of those inciting racial hatred in Malta, even though there has been pressure for the enactment of antiracist legislation emanating from left-wing groups such as Graffiti.

Furthermore, the former Maltese prime minister is on record as having said that, although Malta's "constitutional principles do not allow racism and there are measures against it," he believes that "the time has come for racism to be made a criminal offense" (Chetcuti 1999, 1). The Graffiti group took the prime minister up on his word and, apart from organizing an activity against racism on July 22, 2000, wrote a letter to the prime minister (signed by the group's general secretary and circulated through e-mail), dated July 19, 2000, expressing their concern at the growing racism and xenophobia in Malta. The group refers in this letter to the publication of *Credo* and the allegations that Africans are being denied access to nightclubs in Paceville. There is also reference, in the letter, to one specific case involving an African who was allegedly beaten up by bouncers at a particular locality in the area. The group also refers to a study by Anthony Abela (forthcoming), from the University of Malta's Department of Sociology, which demonstrates empirically that "intolerance" is rife in Malta in various aspects of life including attitudes toward foreigners. They cite statistics from this study which indicate that 28 percent of Maltese do not want to live in proximity to Muslims, 21 percent consider the presence of Jews to be undesirable, 19 percent are averse to the presence of people of other races, while 16 percent do not want immigrants or foreign workers in the country. The letter calls on the government to introduce legislation against racism and xenophobia.

While there is a pressing need for further antiracist legislation, there is an equal need for progressive transformative action concerning race and ethnicity in different spheres and sites of practice. This chapter focuses on education, the area being conceived of here in its broader context. We argue for an antiracist agenda in education. We now attempt to identify the elements that make up an antiracist agenda in education in Malta and Gozo.

TOWARD AN ANTIRACIST AGENDA IN MALTESE EDUCATION

Two major characteristics of recent media debates on racism were the misuse and abuse of terminology and the lack of understanding of the complex nature of the subject. Panels that included educationists showed limited understanding of the language associated with antiracist projects. With sporadic exceptions, lack of familiarity with the terminology restricted the discussions to commonsense knowledge and spontaneous outbursts, rather than deep analysis. Moreover, different forms of racisms were rendered banal through a totalizing discourse, thereby defrauding the public of a serious debate on the different facets of and routes to racism.

A learning community that is committed to resisting racism cannot afford to refrain from gaining familiarity with the glossary concerning this type of oppression. Educators who have a good grasp of the terminology will automatically understand the complex nature of racism and will be in a position to comment in a complex way on the multiple nature of this form of oppression.

ANTIRACIST EDUCATION: KEY CHARACTERISTICS

Effective antiracist educational programs reflect the perspective that racism is socially constructed and therefore can be reversed. Since most racisms are manufactured within particular contexts, good antiracist programs are sensitive to the particular demographics of the geographic area in which the programs are situated. This means that it is important to address the complexities of racism by including all targeted groups within a given context. It also means that antiracist pedagogies should be reinvented within a lived space to include indigenous knowledges.

Another element that normally characterizes good antiracist programs is their praxial stance. Praxis-oriented programs consider advocacy, action and mobilization as complementary to analysis. Finally, good antiracist programs shun insularity. There is a link between racisms and global capitalism. As a result, participants need to understand how racisms come packaged in cheap products and services.

THE NEW NATIONAL MINIMUM CURRICULUM FOR MALTA: A GOOD START

The new National Minimum Curriculum (NMC), published by the Ministry of Education in December 1999, is inspired by an educational agenda that sets out to socialize students into a pluralistic, democratic and socially inclusive society. As a result, the document, which provides a framework for compulsory Maltese education from the first year of kindergarten (age 3) to the end of the secondary years (age 16), constitutes a good reference point for local educators and learning communities interested in developing an antiracist pedagogy within a scholastic environment.

The National Minimum Curriculum is sensitive to the fact that multiculturalism and therefore diversity and difference are facts of Maltese life. The term "multiculturalism" is here used in its broader sense (see McLaren 1997; Torres 1998). This immediate and concrete social reality demands that "the educational system should enable students to develop a sense of respect, cooperation, and solidarity among cultures" (Ministry of Education 1999, 24). According to the NMC, the development of such crucial skills should help students "better understand individual, local and regional differences and should enable them to live a productive and meaningful life in a context characterized by socio-cultural diversity" (Ministry of Education 1999, 24).

For the above project to materialize, the local educational community should discard methods of teaching built on the illusion that classrooms constitute homogeneous groups. According to the NMC, the community should embrace "a pedagogy based on respect for and the celebration of difference" (Ministry of Education 1999, 30).

Awareness, respect, affirmation and celebration of differences, including bio-differences (see O'Sullivan 1999), are not abstract concepts but concrete experiences that have to be accessed very early in a child's life. The National Minimum Curriculum asserts that, from an early age, children should participate in an educational process which helps them "identify, appreciate and celebrate the physical, intellectual, emotional and social characteristics as well as their differences; enable children to develop a sense of co-operation; promote respect for human rights and the rights of other species" (Ministry of Education 1999, 74). The technological infrastructure is conceived of as an important asset in the antiracist agenda. According to the NMC, "communications technology and information technology can help draw our students closer to other students located in different parts of the world" (Ministry of Education 1999, 27–28).

An educational program intended to imbue students with an antiracist mentality cannot distance itself from historical analysis of how racisms are created, reproduced and hegemonized by privileged groups/communities/nations. Moreover, the acknowledgment of and high regard for different cultures depends on the appreciation of the different facets of life within different countries and regions. The National Minimum Curriculum recognizes the need for students to enrich their cultural capital in this regard. In a section dealing with educational objectives (Ministry of Education 1999, 47–70), the document encourages schools to familiarize students with "the culture, history and different religions of the Mediterranean and Malta's history viewed within this regional context ... [and] with the culture, history and different religions of Europe" (50).

In addition to this Euro-Mediterranean dimension, the NMC underscores the need to "ensure that the country can avail itself of a nucleus of people who have a mastery of languages deemed strategically important. These include Chinese, Japanese, Russian and Arabic" (Ministry of Education 1999, 82). Also stressed is the need for students to know more about "the characteristics of the most important religions and how each one of them attempts to answer the same fundamental questions concerning human existence" (Ministry of Education 1999, 52). The areas of knowledge, among many others, provide the informative backdrop for the promotion of greater interest in, understanding of, and empathy and solidarity with societies and cultures.

Educators in Malta who are willing to help in creating an educational context that is culturally pluralistic and antiracial in character should find, in the National Minimum Curriculum, the basic ingredients for a pedagogy that can lead students to confront cultural territorialism. The drafters of this document were particularly sensitive to the fact that the previous National Minimum Curriculum, published between 1989 and 1990, smacked of Eurocentrism (for an analysis of this document, with respect to issues concerning race, class, gender and disability, see Borg et al. 1995). Eurocentrism contradicts the commitment toward genuine and critical multiculturalism, and destroys the possibility for students to understand racism and oppression within themselves and society. In fact, a Eurocentric curriculum supports, in an active or passive way, the perceived "superior" qualities of Western thought and traps students within a cultural fortress. This is an offshoot of or variation on what is often termed "Fortress Europe," centering around an essentialist and outdated fixed notion of what constitutes the "European," a notion that does not reflect the contemporary reality of a Europe characterized by multiracial/ethnic difference.

This cultural fortress breeds in students the mental attitude that whatever is good, advanced, progressive and sophisticated originates in the West. It keeps them trapped within their perceived and preset cultural boundaries, not allowing them to cross the racial and ethnic divides. To adapt a sentence from Henry Giroux, we would argue that, in crossing these borders, they can begin to "challenge" the white and Eurocentric racism to which their "body has grown accustomed" (Giroux 1998, 150). The challenge here is that of moving from a Eurocentric toward a "multicentric" curriculum, to borrow George Sefa Dei's term (Dei 1997). The traditionally subaltern would thus be encouraged to move, in the words of bell hooks (1994), from "margin to centre" (Dei 1997, 81–82). The traditionally subordinated ethnic groups would be allowed possibilities to become major actors in the curriculum and not simply adjuncts to a cast formed of people from the dominant ethnic group (Dei 1997, 83).

EDUCATIONAL PROGRAMS IN SCHOOLS

A genuine antiracist project in schools does not create new subjects. Where there is a commitment toward this pedagogy, all stakeholders within the learning community are perceived as responsible for the concretization of the project. In this way, the school avoids creating "cultural islands" that are incompatible with and/or contradict each other.

An educational program characterized by an avowedly antiracist stance needs to be sensitive to the process of human development. In the context of early childhood education, the program should be concrete in orientation, that is to say, it should be close to the immediate life of the children. The development of self-esteem helps individual pupils appreciate friends and adults who form part of their lives. Through the promotion and development of self-esteem, the emotional infrastructure weaves itself with the concrete and visible experience of difference. The concrete experience in this phase of the human continuum manifests itself physically, as well as in different national costumes, cuisine, traditional celebrations, music, dance and other forms of expressive arts. This is only an initial step and we recognize that a genuine antiracist education requires much more than this. We must ensure that all ethnicities, including those of the dominant groups, are included in this process. Furthermore, we must constantly oppose the tendency to exoticize minority ethnic group cultures. As Blair and Cole (2000) point out, with respect to "multicultural" education in Britain:

> The exoticization of minority ethnic group cultures and customs merely served to reinforce the notion that these cultures were indeed "Other" and drew the boundary more firmly between "Them," the "immigrants" or "foreigners," and "Us," the "real" British. Needless to say, this approach itself came under severe criticism as a form of education that was said to be tokenistic and failed to address the real problems of schools and of communities within them. (Blair and Cole 2000, 70)

The aesthetic and tactile environments, which are so crucial at the early childhood level, should be particularly sensitive to the issue of difference. Accurate information about racial and cultural differences and similarities should be evident in the visuals, stories and activity tables and corners, made available to children as part of the learning experience.

At the primary level (ages 5–11), the educational program should continue to build on the process initiated in early childhood. At the primary level, children familiarize themselves with international children's literature and with the history and development of local and regional traditions. Exposure to this literature would, hopefully, enable children to learn how different cultures, societies and communities respond to fundamental human needs. A primary-level program should also help students develop: a positive attitude toward cultures; the will to learn from the experiences of different cultures; and the will to resist different forms of prejudices, intolerance and discrimination. This attitudinal change, together with the basic knowledge, should facilitate the process of developing the necessary skills in cooperation, dialogue, critical thinking, problem solving, conflict resolution and empathy, among other skills. Without the development of these skills, the antiracist project at the primary level will remain a mere academic exercise.

At the secondary level (ages 12–16), concrete experience remains the focal point around which an antiracist pedagogy revolves. The strengthening and consolidation of critical and reflective thinking should lead to the program becoming more praxis-oriented in nature. This means that the personal and social experience of students is scrutinized in the hope that such self-reflection would lead to personal transformation and concrete action. In more specific terms, an antiracist pedagogy at the secondary level should help students:

- Realize how a racial/ethnic identity is created
- Reflect on how they may be unconsciously or actively participating in the racist project
- Understand how they are introduced to and socialized in the racist cultures
- Familiarize themselves with the basic terminology used in describing and arguing against racism
- Familiarize themselves with the experience of ethnic and racial groups present in Malta
- Realize the historical and current link between racism and imperialism
- Realize how racism can intersect with other forms of oppression
- Realize their role as change agents and cultural workers
- Engage in concrete action

At different points of the scholastic journey, students affirm their own identity, confront themselves, analyze and problematize their prejudices, intolerance and cultural ignorance, celebrate difference and become actively engaged in antiracist action.

TEACHER EDUCATION

Teachers who fail to admit the problem of racism in Malta and/or do not think that the means of confronting this problem should include educational intervention will most probably resist attempts to develop an antiracist project in their school. In a context marked by initial resistance or outright rejection, a dialogical approach is key.

A good way for one to start an antiracist project in a school is through action research. This type of research would enable teachers to examine their knowledge of and attitudes toward different ethnic and racial groups and their level of awareness with regard to the different facets of Maltese racism. The results should provide an ideal context for dialogue with teachers.

A school community that feels that there is the right cultural infrastructure to initiate an antiracist project can regard the school's development plan as its initial point of departure. The antiracist project should form an integral part of the school's overarching vision and strategy. The inclusion of an antiracist agenda in the school's development plan accords the project a sense of permanence.

The program of teacher preparation should be inspired and informed by the data obtained through action research and by the dialogue that ensues. While the program should target the specific needs of the educational community, international literature that reports on such projects generally suggests that teachers should be helped to:

- Develop greater awareness of their identity
- Examine their personal knowledge, attitudes and experiences
- Study the link between personal experience and systemic racism
- Examine the link between personal and institutional racism
- Realize how different forms of oppression intersect with and complicate the problem of racism
- Examine how racisms are rationalized
- Examine how Eurocentrism defines what is best
- Analyze different models of multicultural and antiracist pedagogies
- Engage in antiracist projects

Teacher antiracist education should not stop at the end of the aforementioned program. Ongoing preparation, in the form of dialogical and reflective meetings, should sustain the project. Simultaneously, schools need to invest in books and materials that address the foregoing issues.

CONCLUSION: REDEMPTIVE MEMORY

In all the above programs of antiracist education, one can make use of reflective and redemptive (in Walter Benjamin's sense) memory work (Simon 1992; McLaren and Da Silva 1993). This work can possibly encourage a dialectical relationship between reminiscences of a past characterized by massive Maltese emigration (involving members of the teachers' and students' families) and a present marked by increasing immigration. The program can provide historical accounts and evoke memories of the perpetration of racist attitudes toward Maltese migrants who, together with other Mediterranean people and Asians, were often regarded by the receiving authorities (see, for example, what occurred in Canada as the result of a 1910 immigration act) as "undesirable aliens" (Attard 1989, 68).

This aspect of antiracist education can take different forms. This pedagogy can take the form of theater, especially community theater or "theater in education." The inspiration for this idea derives from a dramatic presentation, by a troupe from the Laboratorio Interculturale Comune di Genoa, which took place at Sestri Levante, Liguria, Italy, during an international conference on multicultural education in the Mediterranean (October 22–24, 1998). It involved a juxtaposition of situations reflecting the harsh realities of migration both past and present. The plight of Italians who had migrated to the United States, Argentina and elsewhere, and of Italians from the south moving to the peninsula's northern regions, was juxtaposed against that of Africans (including Arabs) and eastern Europeans, with their personal narratives, moving into Italy (Mayo 2000). Theater and other cultural work along these lines can help develop a dialectical relationship between past and present that can have a redemptive effect on the participants, in the hope of fostering interethnic and interracial solidarity.

NOTE

This chapter draws material from Borg 2002 and Mayo 2000.

REFERENCES

Abela, A.M. Forthcoming. *Values 2000: European Values Studies (Malta 1984–1999)*. Summary of preliminary report submitted to the Government of Malta, September 13, 1999. http://staff.um.edu.mt/aabe2/Report99.htm.

Apitzsch, U. 1995. *Razzismo ed Atteggiamenti Verso gli Immigrati Stranieri: Il Caso della Republica Federale Tedesca* [Racism and Attitudes toward Foreign Immigrants: The Case of the German Federal Republic]. Messina, Malta: University of Messina.

Attard, L.E. 1999. *L-EMIGRAZZJONI Maltija: Is-seklu dsatax u ghoxrin*. Pieta, Malta: pin.

———. 1989. *The Great Exodus (1918–1939)*. Marsa, Malta: PEG Ltd.

———. 1983. *Early Maltese Emigration (1900–1914)*. Valletta, Malta: Gulf Publication.

Baldacchino, G., and P. Mayo, eds. 1997. *Beyond Schooling: Adult Education in Malta*. Msida, Malta: Mireva.

Balzan, S. 1999. "Racism Is Not a Criminal Offense in Malta: 'No Blacks' Rule Imposed in Popular Paceville Bar." *Malta Independent*, August 8, 1.

Blair, M., and M. Cole. 2000. "Racism and Education: The Imperial Legacy." In *Education, Equality and Human Rights: Issues of Gender, "Race," Sexuality, Special Needs and Social Class*, ed. M. Cole, 58–77. London: Routledge/ Falmer.

Borg, C. 2002. "Lejn agenda anti-razzista fl-edukazzjoni" [Toward an Anti-Racist Agenda in Education]. *Education 2000*, 7: 27–29.

Borg, C, J. Camilleri, P. Mayo, and T. Xerri. 1995. "Malta's National Curriculum: A Critical Analysis." *International Review of Education* 41, no. 5: 337–56.

Borg, C, and P. Mayo. 2000a. "Malta." In *Museums and Adult Learning: Perspectives from Europe*, ed. A. Chadwick and A. Stannett. Leicester, UK: NIACE.

———. 2000b. "Museums, Adult Education, and Cultural Politics: Malta." *Education and Society* 18, no. 3: 77–97.

Calleja, M. 2000. *Aspects of Racism in Malta*. Bormla, Malta: Mid-Dlam Ghad-Dawl (Daritama).

Cassola, A. 2000. *The Literature of Malta: An Example of Unity in Diversity*. Sliema, Malta: Minima.

Chetcuti, S. 1999. "Plans to Make Racism a Criminal Offense." *Malta Independent*, August 17, 1.

Darmanin, M., ed. 1992. "Gender and Education." Special issue of *Education* (Malta) 4, no. 4.

Dei, G.S. 1997. *Anti-Racism Education: Theory and Practice*. Halifax, Canada: Fernwood.

Education Department of Malta. 1976. *Grajjiet Malta*, book 1. Valletta, Malta: Education Department.

Elsheikh, M. 1999. "Le omissioni della cultura italiana" [The Omissions of Italian Culture]. In *Islam nella Scuola* [Islam in Schools], ed. I. Siggillino and Franco Angeli, 30–45. Milan: Franco Angeli.

Fanon, Frantz. 1963. *The Wretched of the Earth*. New York: Grove.

Galea Debono, F. 1999a. "Man on Mission to Fight Racism in Malta. Considering Filing Case against Paceville Night Club—But Club Management Denies Any Form of Discrimination against Blacks." *The Times* (Malta), November 25, 4.

———. 1999b. "French Professor Complains of Inhuman Discrimination: 'This Is Worse Than Racism.'" *The Times* (Malta), November 23, 14.

Giroux, Henry. 1998. "Critical Pedagogy as Performative Practice: Memories of Whiteness." In *Sociology of Education: Emerging Perspectives*, ed. C.A. Torres and T.R. Mitchell, 143–53. Albany, NY: SUNY Press.

Grixti, J. 1996. Review of J. Giordmaina, ed., "Systems of Knowledge: A Guide, Book 1: Antiquity and Early Middle Ages, Middle Ages and Renaissance." *Mediterranean Journal of Educational Studies* 1, no. 2: 209–11.

hooks, bell. 1994. *Feminist Theory: From Margin to Center*. Boston: South End.

Lê Thánh Khôi. 2000. "Il Mediterraneo e il Dialogo fra le Civiltà" [The Mediterranean and Dialogue among Civilizations]. In *Un mare di opportunità: Cultura e educazione nel mediterraneo del III millenio* [A Sea of Opportunity: Culture and Education in the Mediterranean of the Third Millennium], ed. G. Pampanini. Rome: Armando Editore.

———. 1999. *Educazione e civiltà: Le società di ieri* [Education and Civilization: Yesterday's Societies], trans. G. Pampanini. Rome: Armando Editore.

Marx, Karl, and Friedrich Engels. 1998. *The Communist Manifesto*. New York: Monthly Review Press.

Matvejevic, P. 1997. Address to the Civil Forum EuroMed. In *Obiettivi e mezzi per il partenariato euromediterraneo: Il forum civile euromed* [Objectives and Means for a Euro-Mediterranean Partnership: The Civil Forum Euromed], ed. Laboratorio Mediterraneo. Naples: Magma.

Mayo, P. 2000. "Globalization, Postcolonialism, and Identity: The Role of Education in the Mediterranean Region." Paper presented at the international course Redefining Cultural

Identities: The Multicultural Contexts of the Central European and Mediterranean Regions, Inter-university Centre, Dubrovnik, May 16.

McLaren, Peter. 1997. *Revolutionary Multiculturalism: Pedagogies of Dissent for the New Millennium*. Boulder, CO: Westview.

McLaren, Peter, and T.T. Da Silva. 1993. "Decentering Pedagogy: Critical Literacy, Resistance and the Politics of Memory." In *Paulo Freire: A Critical Encounter*, ed. Peter McLaren and P. Leonard. New York: Routledge.

Ministry of Education [Malta]. 1999. *Creating the Future Together: National Minimum Curriculum*. Floriana, Malta: Ministry of Education.

Moatassime, A. 2000. "Mediterraneo fra plurilinguismo e pluriculturalita" [The Mediterranean: Between Linguistic Pluralism and Cultural Pluralism]. In *Un mare di opportunità: Cultura e educazione nel mediterraneo del III millenio* [A Sea of Opportunity: Culture and Education in the Mediterranean of the Third Millennium], ed. G. Pampanini. Rome: Armando Editore.

O'Sullivan, E. 1999. *Transformative Learning: Educational Vision for the Twenty-first Century*. London: Zed.

Richter-Malabotta, M. 2002. "Toward a Multicultural Italy." *Journal of Postcolonial Education* 1, no. 2: 69–79.

Said, Edward. 1978. *Orientalism*. New York: Random House.

Shaykh 'Abd al Wahid Pallavicini. 1998. "Identita'e differenze" [Identity and Differences]. Paper presented at the international conference, "Il mare che unisce: Scuola, Europa e Mediterraneo [The Sea That Unites: School, Europe, and the Mediterranean], Sestri Levante, Italy, October 22-24.

Simon, R.I. 1992. *Teaching against the Grain: Texts for a Pedagogy of Possibility*. Toronto: OISE Press.

Sultana, R.G., ed. 1997. *Inside/Outside Schools*. San Gwann, Malta: PEG Ltd.

———. 1992. *Themes in Education*. Msida, Malta: Mireva.

Sultana, R.G., and G. Baldacchino, eds. 1994. *Maltese Society: A Sociological Inquiry*. Msida, Malta: Mireva.

Torres, C. A. 1998. *Democracy, Education, and Multiculturalism: Dilemmas of Citizenship in a Global World*. Lanham, MD: Rowman & Littlefield.

Virdee, S., and M. Cole. 2000. "'Race,' Racism, and Resistance." In *Education, Equality, and Human Rights: Issues of Gender, "Race," Sexuality, Special Needs, and Social Class*, ed. M. Cole. London: Routledge/Falmer.

Zammit Endrich, S. 1999. "Slay the Infidel." *Malta Independent*, July 24, 8.

CHAPTER 23

THE DENIAL OF DIFFERENCE: REFRAMING ANTI-RACIST PRAXIS

George J. Sefa Dei

I. INTRODUCTION: THE DENIAL OF DIFFERENCE

In 1903, W.E.B. Du Bois made the oft-repeated assertion that "the problem of the twentieth century is the problem of the 'color-line'" (see DuBois, 1903, p. 13). Today, many may deny DuBois's statement, and even contend that it is time to move beyond the obsession with "colour and race." DuBois himself assumed that what he called the "colour problem" would be solved by the end of this century. In 1998, as we approach the end of the century the problem is anything but solved. The existing state of affairs is not because anti-racist workers, scholars, community activists still hang on to the race concept. The reality of race is beyond the mere social conditioning of human minds; it encompasses the attribution of real material consequences to racial designations and social practice. There are "punitive and damaging effects of [race] identification" (Ginsberg, 1996, p. 267). [...]

Increasingly, the denial of race continues to inform varied social and institutional contexts. Race is an unsettling issue for many Euro-Americans. In the post–civil rights era it remains a taboo subject (Tatum, 1992). Educators, parents, and decision-makers shy away from discussing race either for fear of offending individuals and groups or in a concealed attempt to deny race privilege. To avoid what some will term "the contentious issue of race," racial difference is simply equated to ethnicity. The fluidity of social identities is at times unwittingly evoked to counter the salience of race in public and academic discussions. Many educators, for example, grow defensive when schooling research focuses on race. The denial of racism in schools may take the simplistic form of "there is no racism here" or "skin colour does not matter" (see Solomon & Levine-Rasky, 1994, 1996; Dei et al., 1997). Race and colour are rendered insignificant as in the "colourblind" approach to schooling. Nonetheless, some students continually complain of low teacher expectations of Black students (James, 1990; Dei et al., 1997). There is the insidious attempt to deracialise students by failing to acknowledge that "racelessness" (Fordham, 1988) is a privilege that is only afforded to White/dominant students (Joyce, 1995).

Clearly, what is missing is a theoretical understanding and concrete acknowledgement of race and difference as providing the contexts for power and domination in society. Individuals will deny racial differences in justifying their failure to challenge race injustice (see Henry & Tator, 1994). And yet, disturbingly, race is evoked when expedient by the dominant group (e.g. the criminalisation of Black youth). At the same time, race is denied when the dominant group is challenged to acknowledge its privileges and power base. The use of code words, a "hallmark" of the New Right, is another example of the myriad ways race can be denied. Words and phrases such as "welfare mothers," "criminals," "foreigners" and "immigrants" have become synonymous with "Black" and minority/minoritised groups in the New Right racial politics (see also Winant, 1997). An open resistance to dealing with race is expressed in the problematic discourse of "competency," "ability," "merit" and "excellence," which are evoked to signify that one group (specifically, the dominant) has a monopoly over these domains.[1]

Henry and Tator's (1994) notion of "democratic racism" perfectly alludes to the everyday rationalisations of racist behaviour in Euro-American society. It is a form of racism that appeals to easy rationalisations without much discomfort. Blacks and racial minorities deserve what they get. Similarly, a "cult of individualism" shields dominant members from acknowledging their social privilege and material advantage (see Scheurich, 1993).[2]

The bland, pluralistic, multicultural talk celebrating "cultural diversity" and/or "cultural difference" fails to affirm the context of power in which differences are produced, and the significance of dislodging such power relations (see also Razack, 1998, pp. 8–10). Critics of anti-racist praxis find solace from a deliberate politics of the modern state driven by the whims and caprices of industrial capital. In fact, anti-racists are confronted with an emerging challenge of speaking of race and equity issues in a political climate of harsh conservativism.[3] To counter this shift to the Right, the critical discourse of race and difference must re-enter public consciousness and academic debates. It demands an unapologetic politics of affirming race and difference and making the case for the "strategic essentialism" of anti-racist practice. Why?

Race hierarchies shape and/or demarcate our schools, communities, workplaces, social practices and lived experiences. Winant (1997) reminds us that "we articulate our anxieties in racial terms: wealth and poverty, crime and punishment, gender and sexuality, nationality and citizenship, culture and power, are all articulated ... primarily though race" (p. 49). There is a "normality" to systemic racism that is tempered with utter abhorrence when we are consciously aware of its existence. Our society is racially stratified. Raced and colonial hierarchies are embedded in institutions, and everyday racism "travels like a virus through institutional structures, policies, practices, relationships, fights and identities" (Fine et al., 1997, p. x).

There is some legitimate concern that perhaps the "meaning" of race/colour and the significance of the term have been extensively problematised in the theoretical sense to jeopardise the struggle for race justice and equity. The absence of an intellectual agreement as to what constitutes race should not induce an open repudiation of the term. In fact, Winant (1997) advises that the meaning of race in general has proved flexible to adapt to shifts in social formations. The shifts in early biologistic conceptions of race to the current social, cultural and political parameters has implications for thought and action. But, perhaps more importantly, it is the ambiguities, complexities and nuances of the social (and political) construction of race and difference that need a serious intellectual interrogation. A discursive invocation of racial significance calls for critical praxis. A refusal to "engage in 'race thinking' amounts to a defence of the racial status quo, in which systemic racial inequality and ... discrimination ... are omnipresent" (Winant, 1997, p. 45).

Integrative Anti-racism: An Articulated Understanding of the Interlocking Nature of Oppressions

In this article, I hope to contribute to the reformulation of anti-racism knowledge working with race and difference (see Brandt, 1987). I want to affirm race and social difference. In doing so, I explore the significance and implications of maintaining power in a racialised society along the lines of social difference. I work with Omi and Winant's (1993) idea that race is a fundamental principle of social organisation and social relations in Euro-American contexts. Race is a salient marker of social position and status. My intent is not to render race as a fixed category of identity and experience. It is problematic to apply a race reductionist approach to understanding society. The gaze on race is not to deny or negate other social oppressions, or the complexities of multiplex oppressions. My objective is to highlight the significance of race in understanding social formations.

This article adopts an integrative anti-racism discursive framework (see Dei, 1999) in examining the relational aspects of race and social difference. An integrative analysis articulates the complexities of racial and other social identities. Such analysis responds to the confluence of identities by working with the idea of multiple, intersecting and concurrent oppressions. It critiques the exclusivity and essentialism involved in disconnecting singular sites of oppression. The integrative discourse eschews the "matrix of oppression" (Collins, 1993) and the "simultaneity of oppression" (Brewer, 1993). Facey (1997) also observes that such an approach rejects the "exclusivity of singular constructs in explaining the diversity of experiences of oppressions and provides space for the inter-changeability of oppressions and oppressors" (p. 3). While articulating the intersecting and interlocking nature of social oppressions, integrative anti-racism also critiques the shortcoming of liberal democratic thought that denies the situational and contextual variations in intensities of oppressions.

"Difference" is a site of power and oppression. Difference is also a site of possibility enabling human subjects to work with experience and critical self-reflection for collective political action. There is no "essential subject," nor an "essential autonomy of the individual" (see also James, 1998). In fact, the individual subject is equally a product of history, culture and politics. Experience constructs personal and collective identities. Thus, experience, far from rendering an authoritative voice/subject, is itself an ethnography that must be critically interrogated and reflected upon to reveal biases, truths and limitations in how we make sense of our worlds (see also Butler, 1992; hooks, 1994).

A critical examination of daily human experiences reveals that all social oppressions are inextricably linked. An intersectional and multifactorial analysis is useful in capturing the nuances and complexities of social experiences. It is possible to adhere to the notions of "intersecting oppressions" and "interlocking systems of oppression" and at the same time recognise the persistence and the saliency of particular oppressions at given historical moments. Such approaches to understanding oppressions necessarily assume non-unified, inconsistent and unequal social effects. The study of interlocking oppressions also demonstrates the situational and contextual variations in the intensities of human oppressions.

II. INTERROGATING RACE KNOWLEDGE

There are academic dangers in speaking and writing race. As Fine et al. (1997, p. x) have observed, the development and pursuit of a critical and oppositional discourse to challenge power and dominance opens oneself to assault, misinterpretations, abuse and denial. Conventional academic attacks on anti-racism writings as race reductionism or privileging are examples of strategic misinterpretation. Dominant critiques of critical race theorising and anti-racist practice can be pursued to negate the history of racism in the West. Dominant groups' criticisms of anti-racist politics may also be seen as an incomplete acknowledgement of the history of race knowledge and the scholarship on "difference." There are important lessons for going back to the evolution of the liberal democratic thought which entails developing a familiarity with the history of racisms in the West. As pointed out elsewhere (Dei, 1999), this history is one unbroken chain. When one understands the important role of Immanuel Kant and John Locke, for example, in the development of "thought" in the West, and how their ideas have permeated the fabric of Western society (see Eke, 1997), then we can begin to interrogate Euro-centred definitions of "valid" knowledge and normalcy. As Eke (1997) argues, "[E]nlightenment philosophy was instrumental in codifying and institutionalizing both the scientific and popular European perceptions of the human race" (p. 5).

The numerous writings on race by Hume, Kant and Hegel played a strong role in articulating Europe's sense not only of its cultural but also racial superiority. In "their writings ... 'reason' and 'civilization' became almost synonymous with 'white' people and northern-Europe, while unreason and savagery were conveniently located among non-whites, the 'black,' the 'red' and the 'yellow,' outside Europe" (Eke, 1997, p. 5). The contemporary idea that "social justice" can only be constructed within the context of the "liberal democratic" tradition is equally problematic. The West's paternalistic attitude has blinded scholars to other/alternative formulations of balance, equality and fairness. As social critics observed very long ago, justice is not defined simply by treating everyone equally. The creation of a vision of social justice within the liberal democratic framework ignores the fact that the structure within which the space exists to rupture "stable knowledge" has not altered. It is not simply the space that is at issue; it is the very structure/ideology which is in question (see also Blanford, 1997).

In his critique of the search for absolute objectivity, Turner (1997, p. 3) reminds us that the "object" and "subject" are maintained in a dualistic relationship in order to establish legitimacy of dominant scientific practice and theory. Science claims to "truth" rest within a constant possibility of self-deception. Science reaches its "valid conclusions" not independent of the scientist's own thought processes, social desires and/or political agendas. There is no "absolute" or infallible object or subject exempt from critical analysis. There are no mutually exclusive subjects/objects. In daily social practices, the desire to create and then deny difference rests on a need to establish a dominant power as legitimately superior over the identified "Other." Historically, the creation of knowledge about the racialised and subjugated "Other" has been part of the dominant's strategy to meet defined needs, including the service of capital. A scientist, then, develops her/his theories within a specific historical context, and in relation to the prevailing cultural, political, economic and social discourses. Thus, the science of racism was infused into Christianity, Social Darwinism and capitalism, not because of an inherently adaptable method, but because a "gradual epistemological shift" (Miles, 1989, p. 40) through various paradigms rendered the changes of justification normal and practically invisible.

What is muted in dominant discourses that debate the science of justification of racism, is the admission that "race" itself is a dominant construct articulated through science, and not simply an objective construct wrongly exploited. The question is, what is it about science which facilitates the perniciousness of racism? Furthermore, the controlling paradox of science is that the project of science in creating "knowledge" and "truth" for the West, at the very same stroke transforms the "truth" of subjugated knowledges into myth and fiction. For example, early Nordic, Anglo-Saxon and Greco-Roman stories are "history," while early Mayan, Inuit or Ibo stories are "pre-history"; the North is said to have "creation theories," the South has "creation myths." The disciplines of science create their knowledges out of marginalised cultures. Subjugated history becomes dominant anthropology, subjugated medicine becomes dominant "herbal remedies," subjugated ways of understanding and naming the physical world become dominant science and technology. Science may neither be the ultimate creator or destroyer of knowledge or "truth," it is only able to enhance, deprecate or ignore what has gone before.

Naturalised discourses are created and legitimised as "truth" (i.e. the natural/given order of things), thereby opposing dissenting voices/experiences. The establishment of "absolutes" may be linked to the propensity for easy, uncomplicated readings of the natural order of things. An uncritical discourse of "unqualified subjectivity" can deny the implication of social structures and institutional policy in the continuing subordination of social difference. To the marginalised subject, the colonising practices of dominant knowledge are all too familiar. Knowledge hierarchies combine with forms of social practices to produce and sustain power inequities. For example, conventional race knowledge constructs dominance through the privileging of certain experiences while excluding others. Knowledge about the depravity of marginalised groups is fetishised to produce and reinforce dominant groups as embodiments and arbitrators of normality, truth and merit. Such knowledges come to acquire an objectivity and a naturalness. They are reproduced in public discussions, social practices and identities, institutional structures, policies and relationships. [...]

As Europeans searched for ways to differentiate themselves from their neighbours, they developed a justification of "the superiority of one group over another" based on the supposed superiority of European (White) biology, psychology and spirituality (see Popkin, 1974). That a concept of differentiation was available and in some sense part of the philosophical preoccupation in Europe from the fifteenth to the eighteenth century and onward is pivotal. With the emergence of the Enlightenment and the "science of [hu]man" there was a concomitant emergence of the degeneracy theories and polygenetic theories (Popkin, 1974). These "theories" went on to explain why Black people and Native people, in particular, were different from "Christian Europeans" and why they were inferior. It went on to explain why non-European cultures and land-use were also inferior. This set the framework for the subjugation of people who "looked different" into an ideology of an inalienable "difference" and the conceptualisation of the "Other" (Blanford, 1997).

Yet the very concept of "Othering" not only describes the bifurcation of dominant discourse, but prescribes the legitimacy of European epistemology. Asian, African, Aboriginal cannot become legitimate, because according to Eurocentric definitions they could never become scientific. The only way to "science" is through whiteness. Thus, the process of demarginalisation of the ideas of the "para-normal," the "new-age," "homeopathy" and "astrology" is achieving popular currency and study by moving away from the centre of indigenous knowledges and belief systems towards the periphery of Western science. Hence the popularity of "new agism," the television show *The X-Files*, the interest in the "crop-circles" and renewed belief in astrology. The bifurcation is found throughout all disciplines, the stories of the past are "fiction," the facts of the past are "history." Even philosophy, which has been called "the science of uncertainty," has a content which when proven, is no longer philosophy but a "hard" science (Russell, 1989, pp. 90–91). The replacement of uncertainty in Western knowledge systems echoes the replacement of the subjugated knowledges of colonised people. However, where Western philosophy has a place in the constellation of Western knowledge systems, colonised/subjugated knowledges have never become "scientific," i.e. legitimate, without Western interpretation, analysis and mastery (Trinh, 1989, pp. 40–41).

Therefore, colonialism was not simply the imposition of a physical occupation. It was, more importantly, the destruction of indigenous knowledge systems accompanied by the imposition and internalisation of the colonisers' way of knowing by the colonised. Since this view entailed a devalued view of the self, for the colonised, necessarily it created the tension between indigenous views and imposed views. It is this imposed view or devaluation which, anti-racists argue, continues to this day and which must be transformed. It is why, for example, official school curriculums present a picture of all history viewed from the context of the dominant. This view presupposes the veritability of presentations. In other words, there is an unbroken chain of thought which to this day forms the fabric of the "liberal democratic state." It is systematically interwoven into the structure of societal institutions, particularly the educational system. That the curriculum of our schools is "narrow" is not a matter of chance.

III. TOWARDS A POLITICS OF AFFIRMATION: IS THERE A SPACE FOR ANTI-RACISM KNOWLEDGE?

Taylor (1994) argues that there are a number of reasons why alternative voices and experiences should be part and parcel of the public curriculum/official knowledge. He argues that previously silenced groups are currently fighting for recognition. The need for this recognition emerges not only because of the omission of other voices and experiences but largely because this view, by the existing structure, is negative and demeaning. However, what is most profound about Taylor's discussion is that he links this need to the Fanonnian conceptualisation of the process of liberation. Taylor suggests, then, that like liberation from colonial occupation, there must be a way to transform the *status quo* and find a basis for incorporating alternative and critical views. This process of intellectual liberation does not simply appear out of a vacuum. It is a response to the history of slavery, colonialism and imperialism which was occurring well before the fifteenth century (see also Popkin, 1974). It is in these contexts that minority calls for critical race and anti-racist knowledge and practice may be understood.

Anti-racism is an intellectual discourse as well as an educational advocacy for social change. Anti-racism moves the heart of social science discourse beyond narrow questions of interpretations and meaning to strategies for political and social action. Certain questions are crucial in this regard: how do we create space for divergent and oppositional voices to exist? How can we alter the very structures through which knowledge is produced and spread both internally and globally? How do we create and nurture different prisms/perspectives in the varying contexts from which we operate in our daily lived practices? How can we move beyond the search for "harmony" to a redistribution of responses and power in society? These questions call for critical reflections using personal and collective experiences and knowledges. For an educator, these questions also mean that effective teaching and learning demands a clear positioning of one's politics, as well as an enunciation of a political project.

(a) Dealing with the Race Concept

The interrogation and production of knowledge for social change is not without competing interests and claims. The politics of integrative anti-racism is defined in terms of developing an educational strategy for meaningful social change. Anti-racism acknowledges race and difference as being "performative" (see Austin, 1970). This has implications for discussing the intellectual relevance of the race concept in public and academic discourses.

Miles and Torres have enthused that the idea of race has no analytical status and the use of the race concept is "likely to legitimize and reinforce the widespread public belief that 'race' exists" (Miles & Torres, 1996, p. 26). In fact, very long ago, Du Bois (1965) argued that we might concede the existence of races in discussions "knowing well that no scientifically accurate definition of these races could be made which would not leave most of [hu]mankind outside the limits" (p. 116). As Zack (1997) remarks, "the social reality of race is often physical in a way that overpowers the lack of biological foundation, which renders the lack of a scientific foundation for the concept of race a mere theoretical truth" (p. 2).

The academic concern with race extends beyond its epistemological value or the lack thereof. Zack (1997) notes that "essentialism in racial theory has entailed a false idea of inherited racial essences that are biological, cultural or both" (p. 2). This important critique does not deny the analytical and empirical status of race. It serves to caution against seeing race as "pure races." It also serves to acknowledge that race assigns, as well as denies, identity. Race can be a "strategically deployed 'construction' responding to the systemic injustice cultivated as a by-product of categorical thinking in search of purity" (Miles, 1997, p. 142). Race is more than a theoretical concept. It is also an idea that governs social relations. If it was merely a concept, we could abandon it. Race cannot fully be comprehended within the logic of "science" or "biology." What may be understood as "biological" could also be a social construction. Race, as Kevin Miles (1997) observes, is not simply to be comprehended as a discourse of the body. Critical race theorising moves beyond the limits of science and metaphysical discourse in accounting for race and difference.

Turner (1997) argues that a "common justification for eliminating the term 'race' from sociological discourse is by virtue of the concept's scientific untenability. Yet a fairly widespread acknowledgment of this scientific untenability has not made objective concepts of race disappear from the dominant/common discourse, e.g. media" (p. 9). Race cannot be rejected simply because of the failure of biological sciences to identify, confirm or prove its (race) existence. Rather, as Kevin Miles (1997) further reminds us, it is science that has to be critiqued (if not discredited) for its failure to account for race.

Throughout human history, race has been invented, reinvented and performed to achieve certain social and political goals. Individuals and groups authentically claim racial identities to engage in racist practices and to rationalise and sustain institutional racism. Thus, although race has no scientific meaning, it has a "pragmatic [and political] meaning that depends on what is valued in concrete situations in which ideas of race are invented or applied" (Zack, 1997, p. 4). Within our communities, the idea and concept of race is used to establish advantage and privilege, as well as disadvantage and injury. And, performing race to seek material advantage only ensures that those disadvantaged in the process will similarly evoke race to seek justice and remedy. An example is the political discourse about the need for Black and minority staff representation given the glaring absences of these bodies in our teaching academies. Therefore, while race cannot be understood in terms of biological or cultural essences, race meanings continue to emerge in new forms and contexts, to be given new situations and relations of power.

The use of language in discursive practice is to speak to reality as much as creating social reality. Stone (1995, p. 391) reminds us of W.I. Thomas's poignant words that "if [people] define situations as real, they are real in their consequences." Rather than deny race, it is worthwhile to work to dismantle the fixed and stratified constructions of race, and to dissociate conventional meanings from race. In Euro-American society race, like all forms of identities, has textually and politically mediated meanings. Identity is itself a social construction based on common-sense understandings of "self" and "society." Individuals and groups assume a racial identity to make sense of their worlds. Heywood (1997) points out that the "identity" which "individuals assume to make sense of the social world, actually gives the individual a sense of 'empowerment'" (p. 1). Race identity is personal, social/communal and political.

(b) The "Saliency of Race" and Critical Anti-racism Analysis

There are varied interpretations and understandings of the notion of "saliency." For example, the notion of salience can gesture to the situational and contextual variations in intensities of oppressions. In other times, salience can denote a conscious political practice of seeing race as an important entry point to progressive politics. It speaks of the ability to make certain choices as we engage in political action for change. It also attests to how personal histories and experiences may position each of us to articulate the saliency of a particular oppression at certain situations. Thus, the notion of saliency does not necessarily imply an additive approach nor quantitative measure to understanding oppressions. But the saliency of race may well rest on the fact that race is a pressing and persistent social issue in our communities today. These observations are crucial in order that the theoretical articulation of the saliency of race in anti-racist political practice is not misunderstood. There are limitations in accentuating differences (whether social or cultural) without recognising power and the embedded power differences, and what these mean for political practices. For subjugated and minoritised peoples, seeing and accentuating "difference" in myriad ways that move beyond material benefits/consequences to concerns about cultural and symbolic affirmation and the legitimacy of particular histories and identities is crucial to social survival.

The critique of "race hierarchy" or "race privileging" that is levelled against critical anti-racism practice fails to acknowledge the fact that the notion of "saliency" is a means to reach the goals of political action for race equity and justice. For the racialised subject, race identity is defined as salient and performed to demand justice, and to resist oppression. For example, within school systems, students' expression of self and collective identities encompass multiple social locations (race, class, gender and sexuality). Yet minoritised Black youth strategically adopt a politicised racial identity that is expressed in the act of becoming/performing "Black" (see Ibrahim, 1997; Dei, 1997). These students link identity and learning in three significant aspects: to demand/create a space they call their "own"; to interrogate, critique and engage conventional academic knowledge and schooling; and to define and acquire the requisite social skills (see also Dei & James, 1998). While Black students see the self as having multiple identities, they also see the embodiment of race as salient in North American schooling contexts. To a large measure, the idea of multiple identities can be a metaphor of everyday social life and experience, while the saliency of race alludes to a particular social context and the ensuing political pragmatism.

In my writings on anti-racism, I work with the notion of "saliency of race" (see Dei, 1996). It is acknowledged that race is a useful analytical category. Its saliency rests on the fact that race has powerful currency in Euro-American society. Race language is used to differentiate people. Our society is structured along racial, gender, class and sexual lines. As Winant (1994, p. 271) has repeatedly alluded, the meaning of race pervades social life, affecting individual and collective identities, as well as social structures. Admittedly, it is always very tempting to deny the site from which we oppress, subordinate or gain privilege. As a Black male teaching at a

Canadian institution of higher learning, I have often denied my gender and middle-class privilege. But I also find something curious: the assertion of race and racism often evokes the most visceral of responses by some members of the dominant group. The social markers—race, ethnicity, class, gender, sexuality—are all social constructs. Yet I have also noticed that it is only race that is sometimes put in inverted commas, as in "race." For me, the commatisation of race is nothing short of "academic gymnastics" (Mire, 1998). The academic explanation that race does not have scientific validity or that it is not a useful analytical tool can be worn out to the victim of racism.

The idea of the "saliency of race" is one of the distinguishing aspects of the discourse of "critical anti-racism." As argued elsewhere (Gillborn, 1995a; Dei, 1996, 1999), critical anti-racism draws on broader definitions of race and racism, extending beyond skin colour as the only signifier of difference. Skin colour is a most important signifier of racial identity. Through the racial signification of skin colour, individuals and groups are marked and classified for differential and preferential treatment (see Omi & Winant, 1993). In a racialised society, skin colour drives and maintains a degree of saliency and persistence primarily because as a phenotypical characteristic, skin colour is a biological marker conventionally viewed as absolute, fixed and determinate of race. The currency of skin colour is that it is either "a harbinger of inferiority" (Facey, 1997, p. 6) or a mark of valued "property" (Harris, 1993).

Skin colour is an important criterion around which to politically engage questions of fairness and equity, particularly in relation to the material redistribution of wealth. Skin colour has been, and continues to be, an important marker of privilege and punishment. The permanence of skin colour as marker of difference cannot be overemphasised. Yet skin colour is not the only important signifier of difference. There are other important markers that would support the contention that no one has ever been one thing (to paraphrase Edward Said [1993]). Thus, in articulating the "saliency of race," it is useful to mention the new forms of cultural racisms that extend beyond skin colour differences. Cultural racism relies on often contradictory and arbitrary markers of distinction among groups and individuals. This is where the process of "racialisation," that is, racialising groups for different and unequal treatment on the basis of supposedly biological, phenotypical and cultural characteristics becomes significant (Miles, 1989; Li, 1990)—for example, the use of language, culture and religion as new markers of difference for unequal treatment (power, privilege and subordination) (Goldberg, 1993).

Critical anti-racism asserts that a discussion about racism should not be restrictive to "White racism," but must explore the myriad ways racism is manifested in society (Gillborn, 1995b). The new social markers or indicators of difference can today be seen in discourses around language, politics, culture, religion and social difference (see also Macchiusi, 1992). However, these racist discourses still stem and emanate from "White racism," from the discourse of the dominant White society which has prescribed what is normal, acceptable, and what is not. In other words, whoever is engaging in the racism, it (racism) is still fully entrenched in dominant White (Christian) ideology. Furthermore, critical anti-racism asserts that racial minorities cannot simply be presented as "victims," "powerless" and "subordinated" in the study of race relations and conflict. Their histories of resistance struggles against myriad forms of social domination (e.g. race, class, gender and sexual oppressions) contain important lessons for anti-racism praxis for social change.

(c) Intersecting and Interlocking Oppressions: Integrative Anti-racism Analysis

Whereas race *is* an important entry point in an anti-racism work, the relational aspects of difference cannot be denied. There are axes of difference that we need to explore to fully understand the "simultaneity of oppressions," or multiplex oppressions. As already discussed, a genuinely transformative anti-racism politics must recognise the situational and contextual variations in intensities of oppressions. Such academic/discursive and political approaches are not intended to privilege or deny other forms of oppression. Turner (1997) rightly argues that fundamental intersections and foundations do exist and that "theorizing on these intersections/foundations may inform subversive praxis in the cause of social justice" (p. 1). Integrative anti-racism studies, by interrogating the exclusivities and essentialisms involved in the singular discussion of social positioning, offer an interlocking analysis of oppressions.

"Integrative anti-racism acknowledges our multiple, shifting and often contradictory identities and subject positions ... [it] rejects meta-narratives or grand theories ... in effect, calls for multiplicative, rather than additive, analysis of social oppression" (Dei, 1996, p. 70). Critical anti-racism advocates for social change in which race is acknowledged as a central axis of power, and racist inequities are ameliorated. The politics of anti-racism demands that race come first, that its salience is primary even when other dimensions of oppression coexist with racial ones. For the anti-racism worker, a decision to speak of the saliency of race is a political one. It beholds that a consciousness about race and racial identities can and must exist even in a transracial coalition politics searching for a common ground for social change.

The distinction between "intersecting oppressions" and "interlocking oppressions" is crucial in emphasising the situational and contextual nature of oppressions and political practice. This distinction can be specified in two areas: first, at the level or point of articulation (e.g. identifying a locus and structures of oppressions), and second, at the level of discursive and political practice. The idea of inseparability is eschewed by an "interlocking" approach, as opposed to the possibility of according separate analytical status/space depending on situations and contexts, for which "intersections" argue. "Intersectionality" has one aspect of identity as a foundational base through which other oppressions are read as interconnected. For example, dominant discourses eschewing "Black criminality" and those pathologising Black families for youth "educational failures and underachievement" in North America are primarily raced. It does not mean there are no nuances in terms of class and gender and sexual intersections. This oppressive discourse can be understood through the lens of race and how race intersects with class, gender and sexuality. However, understanding the segmentation of the labour force and workplace harassment calls for an examination of the interlocking nature of social oppressions such as racism, misogyny, classism and homophobia, religious bigotry, ableism and linguistic chauvinism. Informing this framework is the understanding that race, gender, class, sexuality, religion, ability and language are sites of difference, as well as loci of oppressions. And the structures through which they are articulated, such as law, education, and government are, ultimately, interrelated and interdependent. To push against one site of oppression in complete isolation only serves to reinforce the focus of oppression on other sites.

At the level of discursive and political practice, a distinction is made between intersectional and interlocking oppressions. By way of illustrating intersectional versus interlocking discursive analysis and political practice, let us consider the following examples. The concept of "intersection" means more than reinscribing the additive analysis of "race, gender, class" which follows White scholars' admissions of privilege, and pledge to examine their own complicity in dominance (Agnew, 1996, p. 3). Yet such pledges are not often found throughout the body of these confessional works, and even more rarely lead to political action. The scholars make the connections of how their relative locations of privilege and subordination intersect, as they attempt to work this conscious knowledge into their work. However, little attention is paid to the material consequences of publishing "Whiteness" when the socio-economic differential between dominant and marginalised scholars is still glaring. Intersectionality then becomes a discursive, analytical, restorative, and deconstructive framework that aims to "disrupt the tendencies to see race and gender as exclusive or separable categories" and link "current concepts with their political consequences" (Crenshaw, 1993, p. 114). Intersectionality, thus, is a framework through which cases of discrimination may be analysed and contextualised in legal, economic and political arenas.

In contrast, an interlocking analysis goes further to critically challenge the players and policies that perpetuate the cycle of oppression. An interlocking analysis is a political, constructive and, most importantly, transformative framework that exposes how subject locations are secured by the dominant power and articulated through the disempowerment of the subordinated. For example, in Canada, historically, many different loci of oppression have been at work in the Indian Act. The Act disenfranchised an Aboriginal woman and her children when she married a "non-status" man, while the children of a "status" man and his "non-status" wife would be entitled to all of his birth rights (including legal benefits and land rights) (Monture-Angus, 1995; Prentice et al., 1988, pp. 396–397).[4] The interlocking approach would bring forward the claims, motives and competing interests of all the relevant stakeholders, such as the women themselves, and their children, conflicts among the elders, and hereditary and traditional chiefs, the Government's exploitation of the conflict, and the justice system's complicity in providing a legal framework for inequality. Interlocking lines of inquiry would also focus on the women's need to find a remedy, the oppositional forces at work, and how Aboriginal women could be empowered in social action for themselves and their communities. [...]

In effect, an interlocking analysis examines the linkage between material forces and social ideologies in producing difference and social change. It entails drawing on the crucial distinction between the origins and functions of social oppression. In the context of race and difference, the ideology of racism cannot be solely interpreted in the material conditions of existence. We need to explicate the ideology underlying human enslavement and the ideology of human inferiority/superiority that underlie social oppressions.[5] The widening manipulation and control of global resources by the North is a major concern for all progressive social forces. Neo-Marxist economic analysis of society offers important lessons in terms of how race, gender and class and sexual differences intersect to fulfil the needs of capital. Northern global hegemony is organised around class, gender, race, ethnicity and sexual struggles and tensions. But the explication of such analysis cannot be conducted in a way that denies or simply subsumes the significance of race under questions of materiality. A comprehensive understanding of the role of ideology that brings spirituality and consciousness to material practices is relevant. [...]

IV. CONCLUSION

In concluding this article I will offer a few notes on the implications of race and difference for rethinking schooling and education in North America. A discussion of race and schooling must appropriately be anchored in the existing critical literature examining current and historical roles of the state in public education in general. The pioneering works of Paul Willis (1977), Bowles & Gintis (1976), Michael Apple (1986, 1989), Henry Giroux (1981, 1983), McCarthy (1990) and Michelle Fine (1991), among many others, are significant points of reference and departure. These works have moved our thinking away from conventional views that focused on family-school relations, conceptualising homes and families as sites and sources of student educational problems and pathologies. These critical theorists view schools as "contested public spheres" (Fine, 1993, p. 682), as political sites for the reproduction of power and social inequality (see also Apple & Weis, 1983). More importantly, the authors see structural poverty, racism, sexism and social and cultural differences as consequential to the schooling outcomes of (particularly) minority youth. It is argued that structural processes of schooling and education provide unequal opportunities, and create differential outcomes, particularly for racial minority students and those from marginalised socio-economic family backgrounds (see also Willis, 1977, 1983).

The ongoing denials of race and difference, however, necessitate a new politics of affirmation for those directly injured or harmed by a racial divide and/or racist actions in institutional settings. Within schools, for example, marginalised youths are conscious of their social positions because race, ethnicity, gender, class and sexuality have all become important signifiers of power and difference. It is through the signifiers of race and class that the sorting functions of schools are performed in Euro-American contexts. Race difference, in particular, is continually associated with negative meanings and connotations. Discourses about rights, citizenship, nationhood are defined by race and other assumed characteristics. To the marginalised and subordinated youth, a resistant politics of positive (solution-oriented) affirmation of race and difference is a legitimate way to deal with their forced marginality in the educational setting. Unfortunately, missing from current liberal democratic critiques of society is the interrogation of discourses of nationhood, definitions of citizenship and rights, and the way resistance politics unfold as marginalised groups seek to redress race injustice.

Identity is tied to questions of social and political change. Race identity is crucial in progressive politics for educational change. This is because students do not go to school as disembodied youth. They are seen as raced, gendered, classed and sexualised subjects. The denial of race difference only serves to justify the status quo and its inherent systemic bias and disadvantage to non-dominant groups. Social practices and cultural representations are significant for understanding how identities are claimed through the identifications that youth make in schools. Race, gender, class and sexual identities are linked to schooling in very powerful ways. Therefore, critical anti-racism must deal with the axes of difference and the bland talk of multicultural education that fails to confront the fundamental question of power.

Dei (1998) opines that the current discourse of "social justice for all" that permeates much of conservative and liberal and neo-liberal theorising and politics of educational change is very seductive. Yet the discourse of "social justice" does not adequately grasp the severity of the issues as faced by identified disadvantaged and minoritised groups. It is this concern that propels race-centric theorising and politics. Many times the liberal discourse of social justice is evoked to mute and/or trivialise the continuing history of racism in the West.[6]

In order to deal with the prevailing silence over race and equity issues, anti-racism has a fundamental role in schools and institutional settings. No doubt, the success of anti-racism educational praxis demands concerted efforts on the part of all progressive-minded students, teachers, administrators, parents and community activists. Yet collaborative action does not simply mean that anti-racist workers speak the "language" dominant groups want to hear. The resistance to the language of anti-racism should not mean eschewing terms such as race and anti-racism in favour of terms more palatable for dominant audiences. We need to work from the alternative position that it is relevant and useful to hear oppositional voices and critical language as part of the necessary process of dealing with equity, justice and social change. This means that we must all make that personal and collective effort to listen and hear the voices of pain, suffering and hurt, and where necessary reward resistance. As academics we run the risk of being theoretically radical, practically liberal and fiscally conservative. Even for academics change must come from within; transformative socio-political action begins with the examination of our selves and the strategies we employ to make sense of the world.

A valid approach to educational transformation would be to introduce the ideals of social justice into several levels of education simultaneously (see Lund, 1998). Nonetheless, it is important for educators initially to acquire a basic understanding that race and difference provide the context for power and domination in society. The teachings of integrative anti-racism offer this important philosophical and conceptual understanding. We should be sceptical of the neo-liberal language of "social justice" when presented in a way that fails to name race, racism and anti-racism in stark terms. The need to "teach tolerance" and the discourse of "social justice for all" should not mean a downplaying of the political implications of race and social difference. A critical observer of Euro-American public schools will find it hard to ignore the differential educational outcomes for students by race, class and gender differences. The repudiation of race and the denial of difference only serve to reinforce the mistrust that many racially minoritised youth have of dominant institutions (e.g. schools, courts, media). Arguably then, in improving educational outcomes for all social groups, any successful strategy for educational change will have to be accountable to, and empowering for, the specific groups whose knowledges, experiences and histories have been marginalised in educational systems in the Euro-American context.

NOTES

1. Within specific Canadian contexts, the defence of the principle of meritocracy opines that to enforce employment equity is to hire the "unqualified." This serves as a powerful resistance to anti-racism change.
2. A clear example of the "cult of individualism" is the blurring of the important conceptual distinction between "blaming victims" and "asking people to take responsibility" when accounting for minority educational failures. In asking families to take responsibility for their children's education there is the all too familiar quick slippage into blaming and pathologising Black families (see Dei et al., 1997).

3. In Ontario, for example, the provincial government is relinquishing its roles and responsibilities to marginalised groups for equity and justice. The state operates without acknowledging the differential outcomes of capitalist industrial developments for diverse racial groups.
4. Originally intended to preside over the assimilation of Aboriginal peoples in Canada, the Ministry of Indian Affairs and the Indian Act cover a wide range of issues from land and reserve rights to education, citizenship, and taxation. They arc primarily responsible for determining what legal status and access to federal services Aboriginal peoples may claim. In rights continuum, there are several legal categories of "Indian," "status Indian," "Inuit," "Métis" (a recognised mixed-race category) and "non-status Indian," where the last category is all but excluded from legal recognition (Monture-Angus, 1995).
5. For example, a key historical question is: was there a racial ideology that guided the exploitation of African labour beyond the perception that Africans were "better workers"? Why were Blacks considered the cheap source of paid labour? After the American Revolution, why were Blacks chosen for menial work instead of the unemployed white settlers (see also Facey, 1997, p. 12). The argument that Blacks were more adapted to the sun begs the question. Positing and interrogating these questions would not negate the fact that, today, the reproduction of racism is largely through what can be termed the "trope of economics"/capitalist ideology.
6. It shows a lack of understanding to argue erroneously that a race-centric analysis, for example, reduces the Black/African experiences solely as a response to European racism. Race and skin colour are important criteria around which to politically engage questions of fairness and educational equity.

REFERENCES

Agnew, V. (1996) *Resisting Discrimination: women from Asia, Africa, and the Caribbean and the women's movement in Canada* (Toronto, University of Toronto Press).

Apple, M. (1986) *Teachers and Texts: a political economy of class and gender relations in education* (New York, Routledge & Kegan Paul).

Apple, M. (1989) American realities: poverty, economy and education, in L. Weis, E. Farrar & H.G. Petrie (Eds.) *Dropouts from School*, pp. 205–223 (New York, State University of New York Press).

Apple, M. & Weis, L. (1983) *Ideology and Practice in Schooling: a political and conceptual introduction*. (Philadelphia, PA, Temple University Press).

Austin, J.L. (1970) Performative utterances, in J.O. Urmson (Ed.), *Philosophical Papers*, 2nd edn, pp. 233–252 (Oxford, Clarendon Press).

Blanford, B. (1997) Notes on the relevance of Afrocentric knowledge, unpublished paper, Department of Sociology and Equity Studies in Education, Ontario Institute for Studies in Education, University of Toronto.

Bowles, S. & Gintis, H. (1976) *Schooling in Capitalist America* (New York, Basic Books).

Brandt, G. (1987) *The Realization of Anti-Racist Teaching* (London, Falmer).

Brewer, R.M. (1993) Theorizing race, class and gender: the new scholarship of black feminist intellectuals and black women's labour, in M. James & A.P.A. Baize (Eds.) *Theorizing Black Feminisms: the visionary pragmatism of black women*, pp. 13–30 (London, Routledge).

Butler, J. (1992) Experience, in J. Butler & J. Scott (Eds.) *Feminists Theorize the Political* (London, Routledge).

Collins, P.H. (1993) Toward a new vision: race, class and gender as categories of analysis and connection, *Race, Sex and Class*, 1, pp. 25–45.

Crenshaw, K. (1993) Beyond racism and misogyny: black feminists and 2 live crew, in M. Matsuda (Ed.), *Words that Wound: critical race theory, assaultive speech, and the First Amendment*, pp. 111–132 (Boulder, CO, Westview Press).

Dei, G.J.S. (1996) *Anti-racism Education: theory and practice* (Halifax, Fernwood Publishing).

Dei, G.J.S. (1997) Race and the production of identity in the schooling experiences of African-Canadian youth, *Discourse*, 18, pp. 241–257.

Dei, G.J.S. (1998) "Why Write Black?" On the Role of Afrocentric Discourse in Social Change and Public Education, *Canadian Journal of Education*, 23(2), pp. 200–208.

Dei, G.J.S. (1999) Towards an anti-racism discursive framework, in A. Calliste & G.J.S. Dei (Eds.) *Anti-racism and Critical Race, Gender and Class Studies* (Toronto, University of Toronto Press).

Dei, G.J.S., Mazzuca, J., McIsaac, E. & Zine, J. (1997) *Reconstructing Drop-out: a critical ethnography of the dynamics of black students' disenagement from school* (Toronto, University of Toronto Press).

Dei, G.J.S. & James, I.M. (1998) "Becoming black": African-Canadian youth and the politics of negotiating racial and racialized identities, *Race, Ethnicity and Education*, 1, pp. 91–108.

Dei, G.J.S., Hall, B. & Goldin-Rosenberg, D. (Eds.) (1998) *Indigenous Knowledge in Global Contexts: multiple readings of our world* (Toronto, University of Toronto Press).

DuBois, W.E.B. (1903) *The Souls of Black Folks* (New York, Penguin Books).

DuBois, W.E.B. (1965) *The World and Africa: an inquiry into the part which Africa has played in world history* (New York, International Publishers).

Eke, E.C. (Ed.) (1997) *Race and the Enlightenment: a reader* (London, Blackwell).

Facey, M. (1997) Race and work: a critical-historical review, unpublished paper, Department of Sociology and Equity Studies in Education, Ontario Institute for Studies in Education, University of Toronto.

Fine, M. (1991) *Framing Dropouts: notes on the politics of an urban public high school* (New York, State University of New York Press).

Fine, M. (1993) Apparent involvement: reflections on parents, power and urban schools, *Teachers College Record*, 94, pp. 682–710.

Fine, M., Powell, L., Weis, L. & Wong, L.M. (1997) Preface, in M. Fine, L. Weis, L. Powell & L. Mun Wong (Eds.) *Off White: readings on race, power and society*, pp. vii–xii (New York, Routledge).

Fordham, S. (1988) Racelessness as a factor in black students' school success: pragmatic strategy or pyrrhic victory? *Harvard Educational Review*, 58, pp. 54–84.

Gillborn, D. (1995a) Racism, modernity and schooling: new directions in anti-racist theory and practice, paper presented at the Annual Meeting of the American Educational Research Association, San Francisco, 18–22 April.

Gillborn, D. (1995b) *Racism and Anti-racism in Real Schools* (Philadelphia, PA, Open University Press).

Ginsberg, E.K. (Eds.) (1996) *Passing and the Fictions of Identity* (Durham, NC, Duke University Press).

Giroux, H. (1981) *Ideology and Culture and the Process of Schooling* (Philadelphia, PA, Temple University Press).

Giroux, H. (1983) *A Theory of Resistance in Education: a pedagogy for the opposition* (South Hadley, MA, Bergin & Harvey).

Goldberg, D.T. (1993) *Racist Culture: philosophy and the politics of meaning* (Oxford, Blackwell).

Harris, C. (1993) Whiteness as property, *Harvard Law Review*, 106, pp. 1710–1791.

Henry, F. & Tator, C. (1994) The ideology of racism—"Democratic racism," *Canadian Ethnic Studies*, 26(2), pp. 1–14.

Heywood, D. (1997) Reinventing imagined communities: "ethnic" and "racial" identities as sites of resistance, unpublished paper, Department of Sociology and Equity Studies in Education, Ontario Institute for Studies in Education, University of Toronto.

hooks, b. (1994) *Teaching to Transgress: education as the practice of freedom* (New York, Routledge).

Ibrahim, A. (1997) Becoming black: race, language, culture and the politics of identity: African students in a Franco-Ontarian high school, unpublished PhD dissertation, Department of Sociology and Equity Studies in Education, Ontario Institute for Studies in Education, University of Toronto.

James, C. (1990) *Making It: black youth, racism and career aspirations in a big city* (Oakville, ON, Mosaic Press).

James, I.M. (1998) Reclaiming the ancestors' quilt: black women in the law networking for social change, unpublished MA thesis, Department of Sociology and Equity Studies in Education, Ontario Institute for Studies in Education, University of Toronto.

Joyce, M. (1995) Class communication, "Principles of anti-racism education," Department of Sociology in Education, Ontario Institute for Studies in Education, University of Toronto, Toronto, Spring.

Leah, R. (1995) Anti-racism studies: an integrative perspective, *Race, Gender and Class*, 2, pp. 105–122.

Li, P. (1990) Race and ethnicity, in P. Li (Ed.) *Race and Ethnic Relations in Canada*, pp. 3–17 (Toronto, Oxford University Press).

Lund, D. (1998) Social justice and public education: a response to George J. Sefa Dei, *Canadian Journal of Education*, 23(3), pp. 191–199.

Macchiusi, J. (1992/93) The origins of racism and the rise of biological determinism, *Paradox of Racism, Prize Winning Essays*, 6, pp. 53-63 (Toronto, York University).

McCarthy, C. (1990) *Race and Curriculum: social inequality and the theory and politics of difference in contemporary research on schooling* (Basingstoke, Falmer Press).

Miles, K.T. (1997) Body badges: race and sex, in N. Zack (Ed.) *Race/Sex: their sameness, difference and interplay*, pp. 133–144 (New York, Routledge).

Miles, R. (1989) *Racism* (London, Tavistock).

Miles, R. & Torres, R. (1996) Does race matter?: transatlantic perspectives on racism after race relations, in V. Amit-Talai & C. Knowles (Eds.) *Re-situating identities: the politics of race, ethnicity and culture*, pp. 1–18 (Peterborough, ON, Broadview Press).

Mire, A. (1998) Class communication, "Indigenous knowledges and decolonization: pedagogical implications," Department of Sociology in Education, Ontario Institute for Studies in Education, University of Toronto, Toronto, Spring.

Monture-Angus (-O'Kanee), T. (1995) *Thunder in My Soul: A Mohawk woman speaks* (Halifax, Fernwood Publishing).

Omi, W. & Winant, H. (1993) On the theoretical concept of race, in C. McCarthy & H. Crichlow (Eds.) *Race, Identity and Representation in Education*, pp. 3–10 (New York, Routledge).

Popkin, R.H. (1974) The philosophy bases of modern racism, in C. Walton & J.P. Anton (Eds.) *Philosophy and the Civilizing Arts*, pp. 126–165 (Athens, OH, University Press).

Prentice, A.L. et al. (1988) *Canadian Women: a history* (Toronto, Harcourt Brace Jovanovich).

Razack, S. (1998) *Looking White People in the Eye: gender, race and culture in courtrooms and classrooms* (Toronto, University of Toronto Press).

Russell, B. (1989) *The Problems of Philosophy* (Oxford, Oxford University Press).

Said, E. (1993) *Culture and Imperialism* (New York, Alfred A. Knopf).

Scheurich, J.J. (1993) Toward a white discourse on white racism and RESPONSES, *Educational Researcher*, 22, pp. 5–16.

Solomon, P. & Levine-Rasky, C. (1994) *Accommodation and Resistance: educators' response to multicultural and anti-racist education*. Report to the Department of Canadian Heritage (North York, ON, Department of Canadian Heritage/York University).

Solomon, P. & Levine-Rasky, C. (1996) Transforming teacher education for an antiracism pedagogy, *Canadian Review of Sociology and Anthropology*, 33, pp. 337–360.

Stone, J.H. (1995) Race, ethnicity and the Welsenian legacy, in J.H. Stanfield (Ed.) *Theories of Ethnicity*, pp. 391–406 (Thousand Oaks, CA, Sage Publications).

Tatum, B.D. (1992) Talking about race, learning about racism: the application of racial identity development theory in the classroom, *Harvard Educational Review*, 62, pp. 1–24.

Taylor, C. (1994) The politics of recognition, in A. Guttman (Ed.) *Multiculturalism*, pp. 25–73 (Princeton, NJ, Princeton University Press).

Trinh, T.M. (1989) *Woman, Native, Other: writing, postcoloniality and feminism* (Bloomington, IN, State University Press).

Turner, I. (1997) *Silencing Weesageechak: racism and the search for absolute objectivity, unpublished paper*, Department of Sociology and Equity Studies in Education, Ontario Institute for Studies in Education, University of Toronto.

Wilus, P. (1977) *Learning to Labour* (Farnborough, Saxon House).

Willis, P. (1983) Cultural production and theories of reproduction, in L. Barton & S. Walker (Eds.) *Race, Class and Education* (London, Croom Helm).

Winant, H. (1994) Racial formation and hegemony: global and local implications, in A. Rattansi & S. Westwood (Eds.) *Racism, Modernity and Identity*, pp. 266–289 (London, Polity Press).

Winant, H. (1997) Behind blue eyes: whiteness and contemporary US radical politics, in M. Fine, L. Weis, L. Powell & L. Mun Wong (Eds.) *Off White: readings on race, power and society*, pp. 40–53 (New York, Routledge).

Zack, N. (1997) Introduction: aim, questions, and overview, in Naomi Zack (Ed.) *Race/Sex: their sameness, difference and interplay*, pp. 1–10 (New York, Routledge).

FURTHER READING

Campbell, Carl. 1992. *Colony and Nation: A Short History of Education in Trinidad and Tobago, 1834–1986.* Kingston, Jamaica: Ian Randle Publishers.

This book reports in brief (134 pages) on the development of education system in the twin island states of Trinidad and Tobago in the Caribbean. Starting from the time of slavery and ending with the 1980s, Campbell tells the story of the role that colonialism has played in schooling and education in these former British colonies. While there are similarities with the development of education in many of the former British Caribbean colonies, the settlement of Trinidad and the post-slavery population—comprising of Africans, Indian indentured labourers, and smaller numbers of Chinese and Europeans—make for important differences in post-colonial Trinidad and Tobago.

Jarvie, Grant, ed. 1991. *Sport, Racism, and Ethnicity.* London: Falmer.

In this edited book, Jarvie and his contributors explore the role of race in the identity formation, race consciousness, participation, and achievement of racial minorities in relation to sports and recreational activities. They examine male and female athletes' experiences with racism in Britain, Canada, South Africa, and the United States, as well as how sports influence the academic performance and outcome of minority, particularly black and Asian, students.

Karumanchery, Leeno, ed. 2005. *Engaging Equity: New Perspectives on Anti-racist Education.* Calgary: Detselig Enterprises Ltd.

This anthology consists of 10 chapters, the last of which is written by the author. In this chapter, he addresses the need for developing a process of education that is equitable for minority students. Each contributor addresses the effects of systemic/institutional racism on the schooling and education of students and teachers in Canada, the United States, and Britain.

Lee, Stacey J. 2001. "More than 'Model Minorities' or 'Delinquents': A Look at Hmong American High School Students." *Harvard Educational Review* 71(3): 505–528.

In this article, Lee challenges the popular stereotype of Asians as high-achieving "model minorities." With data from her ethnographic study of 1.5- and second-generation Hmong American students, Lee discusses the variations that exist among these two generations of students in terms of how their relationships with the dominant society, family and economic circumstances, perceptions of their opportunities, and educational experiences affect their attitudes toward school. Based on her findings, Lee suggests possible ways in which schools "can better serve these students."

Lynn, Marvin. 2004. "Inserting the 'Race' into Critical Pedagogy: An Analysis of 'Race-Based Epistemologies.'" *Educational Philosophy and Theory* 36(2): 153–165.

In this article, the author addresses the critical question of whether critical pedagogy as an approach in education adequately incorporates issues of race and racism. He reveals what both critical pedagogy and Afrocentricity (with its focus on race) have in common—among other things, both can be referred to as *"epistemologies of transformation and liberation"* operating from the vantage point of oppressed people and people of colour.

McCarthy, Cameron, Warren Crichlow, Greg Dimitriadis, and Nadine Dolby, eds. 2005. *Race, Identity, and Representation in Education.* 2nd ed. New York: Routledge.

This very popular edited collection features authors who work in many different educational settings, mainly in the United States but also in Canada and Australia. This second edition also gives consideration to the discourse of race in the post-9/11 context. Authors take up issues such as multiculturalism, identity, whiteness, imperialism, showing the complexity, fluidity, and contradictions of race in relation to the educational experiences of students.

PART 3B

RACISM AND EMPLOYMENT

The chapters in this section address an essential part of the experience of racialized groups in metropolitan societies, both past and present—the search for employment. Work is central to the process of citizenship, and thus the inequalities to which racialized minorities are subjected undermine their ability to aspire to full citizenship, creating a condition of social exclusion that threatens the entire society by weakening the glue that should keep society together.

The section begins with Cheryl Teelucksingh and Grace-Edward Galabuzi, who present quantitative evidence to show that in the early 21st century racial discrimination continues to deny members of racialized groups[1] the attainment of their full potential in the Canadian labour market. Racial discrimination in employment is manifested in the patterns of differential access to employment, differential labour market mobility, and income inequality for racialized groups and recent immigrants. The authors use quantitative data on income, unemployment, and occupational and sectoral segregation, as well as qualitative data on the differential labour market experiences of internationally trained skilled workers, to discuss the extent of racial discrimination in employment and its implications for the life chances of racialized Canadians and for public policy.

In addressing the unequal access to Canada's labour market experienced by members of racialized groups in that country, Teelucksingh and Galabuzi argue that in a liberal democratic society such as Canada racial discrimination in employment is an affront to the principle of equality for all citizens. It has implications for the victimized minority group as well as the majority since it represents an inefficient way to allocate scarce human resources and imposes an economic cost on the Canadian economy as a whole. Not only does it rob the economy of a valuable resource and diminish the competitiveness of Canadian businesses at home and abroad, it also saps the self-esteem of racialized minorities, leading to conditions of poverty that undermine social cohesion.

Philomena Essed's chapter extends the discussion of racism in the workplace to the everyday activities that define the existence of racialized citizens in the Netherlands. Essed's exploration includes identifying the impact of racialization on the processes of entry into the labour market and mobility within it, as well as its impacts on the conditions of work and the quality of working life. She presents the example of Rosa, a geriatrician in training, who feels strong pressures to assimilate into Dutch society, only to suffer the indignities of a marginalized existence all the same because of the social significance of race and gender in everyday life. Essed argues that structures and processes of racialization play out in both the macro and micro dimensions of the lived experiences of racialized people, and particularly women who are subject to both racial discrimination and patriarchy. She presents Rosa's life as defined by exclusion, underestimation, and inequality, all representing forms of oppression felt daily as they assault her dignity and material aspirations.

In the final chapter, Tomás Almaguer puts these experiences of racialized hierarchies in a historical context with his discussion of white supremacy in California. Examining key features of anti-Chinese racism in late 19th- and early 20th-century California, within the context of an emerging industrial white working class feeling insecure about its place in a changing world and only too ready to lean on white supremacy as a crutch, Almaguer suggests that the antagonisms and conflicting interests of white capitalists and white workers were worked out through processes that often resorted to anti-Chinese hostility expressed by both sides. From time to time, American capitalists sought to utilize cheap Chinese labour only to provoke a backlash felt not by the white capitalists but by Chinese labourers, who were at once exploited by white capitalists and victimized by the intra-class competitive racism manifest in the stereotypical characterization of Chinese immigrants as infantile, docile, lying, irresponsible, thieving, and lazy. While these characterizations were clearly inconsistent with the workers that white capitalists sought to hire, in direct competition with white workers, the incongruence did not shake the dominant perceptions of the Chinese. In fact, it simply affirmed what Almaguer calls the "'negroization' of the Chinese stereotype." The Chinese came to be described by attributes used to similarly slander blacks as irrational, savage, lustful, and morally inferior heathens.

Almaguer does not identify any moments when the subordinate populations of Chinese and blacks sought to mobilize jointly to confront this spectre of racism, except that the small business classes in each group sought to exhibit a form of class consciousness that had them reproduce the class distance that the white capitalists maintained from their own working classes. Thus, while race was historically a key basis for social stratification, it did not negate class and often worked through it to intensify capital accumulation by encouraging competitive racism between Chinese and European workers.

NOTE

1. "Racialized groups" here refers to persons other than aboriginal people who are non-Caucasian in race or not white in colour. Racialized categories include Chinese, South Asian, black, Arab/West Asian, South East Asian, Filipino, Latin American, Japanese, Korean, and Pacific Islanders (based on the Federal Employment Equity Act definition of visible minorities).

CHAPTER 24

WORKING PRECARIOUSLY: THE IMPACT OF RACE AND IMMIGRANT STATUS ON EMPLOYMENT OPPORTUNITIES AND OUTCOMES IN CANADA

Cheryl Teelucksingh and Grace-Edward Galabuzi

INTRODUCTION

The purpose of this report is to draw attention to the issue of racial discrimination in employment and its impact on the status of racialized group members in a changing Canadian labour market. We argue that the position of individuals in the Canadian labour market is determined not only by their productive capacity but also by their group affiliation and that it varies from group to group.

Labour market attachment is critical to the livelihood and identity formation of individuals and groups, but also their ability to claim a sense of belonging and full citizenship. This is especially true of historically socially excluded groups such as racialized groups.

The early twenty-first-century shift towards flexible deployment of labour and flexible accumulation on a global scale has converged with the focus on the knowledge-based economy and the growth of the racialized population to amplify the impact of racial discrimination in employment on the groups. The growth in the population of racialized groups far outpaced the growth in the rest of the Canadian population over the last decade of the twentieth century with a major source of that growth being increased racialized immigration.

While Canadian public policy has placed a premium on occupational skills and educational attainment, historical structures of discrimination in employment seem to have impeded the labour market success of the better educated and expanding proportion of the Canadian population that is racialized. Social indicators such as higher rates of poverty, sectoral and occupational concentrations along racial lines, high unemployment and underemployment, and a failure of educational attainment to translate into comparable occupational status and compensation suggest the need to revisit a concern that seems to have faded in the minds of mainstream observers of the Canadian labour market.

The intensified racial stratification of Canada's labour market under neo-liberal restructuring has led some to observe that what was once described as an ethnic Canadian vertical mosaic is now colour coded.

These developments call renewed attention to the need for equity in employment since they have an adverse impact on the lives of racialized group members, their communities and ultimately, given their population growth rates, the productivity of the Canadian economy.

We present some evidence to show that in the early twentieth century, racial discrimination continues to deny racialized group members the attainment of their full potential in the Canadian labour market. As the data show, it is manifested in the patterns of differential access to employment, differential labour market mobility and income inequality for racialized groups and other highly racialized groups such as recent immigrants.

METHODOLOGY

Using quantitative data on income, unemployment, and occupational and sectoral segregation, and qualitative data on the differential labour market experiences of internationally trained skilled labour, we discuss the extent of racial discrimination in employment and its implications for the life chances of racialized Canadians and for public policy. Comparative data is drawn from the 1996 and 2001 Canadian Census as well as Survey of Labour and Income Dynamics (SLID) and Human Resources and Skills Development (formerly HRDC) sectoral employment data by race, gender, immigration status and educational attainment. In this report, we consider five key aspects of the experience of racialized group members and recent immigrants in the Canadian labour market to determine the prevalence of racial discrimination in employment as a feature of the Canadian labour market in the early twenty-first century. These include:

- The employment income of racialized and nonracialized groups
- The labour market participation of the groups based on employment and unemployment rates
- The sectoral distribution of the group to establish whether there are patterns of concentration in particular sectors
- The ability of racialized and non-racialized groups to convert their human capital investment in the form of education into occupational status and income
- The experience of recent immigrants, 75% of whom are racialized, with access to professions and trades

We conclude that racial discrimination is evident in the experience of racialized group members in the Canadian labour market, and secondly that its significance has grown with the increase in the numbers of racialized group members in the Canadian population, a trend that seems only likely to escalate.

BACKGROUND

Discrimination in employment has been documented for over a century, yet the study of racial discrimination in employment in Canada is a more recent enterprise. It was not until the 1984 Parliamentary Committee report "Equality Now" that racial discrimination in employment became a prominent part of contemporary scholarship.

In the Report of the Equality in Employment Commission (1984) which identified racial discrimination as part of the phenomenon of discrimination in employment in Canada, Judge Rosalie Abella defined discrimination in employment as "practices or attitudes that have, whether by design or impact, the effect of limiting an individual or group's right to opportunities generally available because of attributed rather than actual characteristics."

According to the Commission Report, discrimination represents an arbitrary barrier standing between a person's ability and his or her opportunity to demonstrate it. While discrimination occurs in different ways at different times and in different places, the one constant is that the persistence of barriers that disproportionately affect certain groups is a signal that the practices that lead to this adverse impact are discriminatory.

All things being equal, in a market economy, the value of labour should derive from its marginal productivity and equally productive persons should both be compensated equally and have equal opportunities for mobility.

Yet the reality is that, in the Canadian labour market, there are widely documented differential outcomes that occur along racial and gender lines, suggesting a more complex, differentiated and even hierarchical labour market. Racial discrimination occurs in a variety of ways. To begin with, race acquires a social significance attached to certain biological features which become the basis for categorizing distinct groups of people. Then the social process of racialization imbues these categories with value, leading to socio-economic practices that reflect and reinforce those values. It is these practices that are responsible for the differential treatment that privileges some and oppresses other members of society.

For the purposes of this report, racial discrimination in employment refers to two forms of practices that deny racialized group members equality of opportunity in the Canadian labour market and secure an advantage for non-racialized groups.

Economic discrimination is said to occur when employers, unable to assess the ability of members of a group, make generalized assumptions about the worth of their human capital, as may be the case when the value of qualifications from a certain country or region is considered unclear.

Exclusionary discrimination occurs when members of a group are not hired or paid commensurate wages, or once hired, not promoted regardless of their skills and experience. In both cases, it is the outcome, not the intent that is the standard as established by the Supreme Court of Canada. In *Andrews v. Law Society of British Columbia*, the Court clearly identified discrimination as the: "distinction which, whether intentional or not but based on grounds relating to personal characteristics of an individual or group, has an effect which imposes disadvantages not imposed upon others or which withholds or limits access to other members of society."

In emphasizing the negative impact of discrimination, the Court seemed to depart from the then conventional approaches to labour market discrimination. In much of the human resource management discourse at the time, discrimination was considered a function of the free exchange of labour and wages, subject to competitive market forces, to the exclusion of influences from other institutions in society. This was especially true of what is known as the human capital approach, popular with neo-classical economists, who are more comfortable talking about statistical discrimination as opposed to systemic discrimination. Yet these practices have never been innocuous or without consequence for individuals, communities and the Canadian nation.

For racialized groups, a survey of key indicators such as occupational status and sectoral participation, income levels, employment and unemployment rates, and access to professions and trades points to patterns of racially distinctive experiences.

Evidence contained in this paper suggests strongly that the differential outcomes identified can be attributed to racially discriminatory systemic practices such as:

- Differential treatment in recruitment, hiring and promotion
- Extensive reliance on non-transparent forms of recruitment such as word of mouth which reproduce and reinforce existing networks
- Differential valuation or effective devaluation of internationally obtained credentials
- Use of immigrant status as a proxy for lower quality of human capital

CHANGES IN DEMOGRAPHICS

In the early twenty-first century, racialized groups represent a key source of human resources for the Canadian labour market. Already, 70% of net new entrants into the labour force are immigrants, 75% of whom are racialized. By 2011, 100% of net new entrants will come from this group, making the issue of racial discrimination critical to their integration into the Canadian labour market and to the success of the Canadian economy (HRDC, 2002). The percentage of racialized groups in the Canadian population, which was under 4% in 1971, grew to 9.4% by 1991, and reached 13.4% by 2001. In the last census period, 1996–2001, racialized group population growth outpaced Canadian population, 24.6% versus 3.9%.

Racialized group population is projected to rise to 20% by 2016 partly based on its current rate of growth. Between 1996 and 2001, the working age racialized population rose by 24.6% while the racialized male proportion of the labour market grew by 28.7% and racialized female proportion by 32.3%. According to the 2001 Census, the racialized group working age population growth was highest in Ontario (28%) and significant in British Columbia (26.6%), Alberta (22.5%), New Brunswick (18.0%), Quebec (14.7%) and only declining in Prince Edward Island (-22.6%). This compares to the general percentage change of Canada (3.9%), Ontario (6%), British Columbia (10.2%), Alberta (-1.4%), New Brunswick (-1.4%), Quebec (1.1%).

Much of that growth can be attributed to immigration, with significant increases from Asia and the Middle East. Given Canada's continued reliance on immigration for population growth and labour market needs, and the escalating process of globalization, these trends are likely to persist. Canada's racialized population is mainly concentrated in urban centres, with nearly three quarters (73%) living in Canada's three largest cities in 2001 and accounting for significant proportions of the populations of those municipalities—Toronto (43%), Vancouver (49%) and Montreal (23%).

In 2001, racialized group members made up 19% of the population of Ontario, Canada's largest province. That share is projected to rise to 25% by 2015. In 2001, British Columbia had the highest proportion of racialized group members in its population at 22%. While 68% of Canada's racialized group members are immigrants, a significant proportion, 32%, are Canadian-born. It is significant to note that the growth of the racialized population far outpaced that of the Canadian population in general over the last census period—1996–2001—and especially in the urban areas and the provinces of Alberta (23%), British Columbia (27%), Ontario (28%), and Quebec (15%). The size of the racialized population will continue to be an important consideration for labour market and other public policy because it is concentrated in urban Canada, which is the engine of Canada's economy.

SOME IMPLICATIONS OF CANADA'S CHANGING RACIAL PROFILE

Canada's changing demographics have far reaching implications for how the Canadian economy is organized and whether it can maintain its position as one of the world's strongest economies. The growth of the racialized population puts the issue of racial discrimination in employment front and centre in the early twenty-first century labour market policy debates.

In a liberal democratic society such as Canada, racial discrimination is an affront to the aspirations of equality. But it also represents an inefficient way to allocate scarce human resources and imposes an economic cost on both the racialized groups and the Canadian economy as a whole. Not only does it rob the economy of a valuable resource in a global environment, it undermines the competitiveness of Canadian business at home and abroad, while the skills of those who are improperly deployed degrade along with their self-esteem.

Along with this scenario, it imposes lives of poverty on the victims of discrimination and increases the budgetary costs associated with dealing with poverty and its impacts on health and social well-being.

With the racialized proportion of the Canadian labour force continuing to grow as projected, with trends showing increases in full-time participation of both male and female racialized workers between 1996 and 2001 far outpacing those of other Canadians, concerns about the hierarchical structures that affect the distribution of opportunity in the labour market can only become more prominent.

As this report shows, by denying racialized men, women and immigrants full access to Canadian labour markets, racial discrimination in employment denies Canada the full benefit of the potential of a growing proportion of Canadians. Left to its devices, racial discrimination in employment will continue to impair the ability of Canada to make the best of its human resources. Perhaps as disturbing is the impact, both on their lives and the Canadian economy, of the devaluation of the human capital of thousands of highly qualified newcomers to Canada, many of them qualified professionals and trades people. These skilled immigrants are attracted from their home countries by an aggressive immigration policy which promises the potential to improve their lives and be successful contributors to a modern economy and multicultural society. Many then find themselves relegated to precarious employment in low wage sectors and low end occupations because barriers in the Canadian economy deny them the opportunity to attain employment and compensation commensurate with their training and experience (Brouwer, 1999; Reitz, 2001; Li, 2003; interviews, 2004).

KEY RESEARCH FINDINGS

Employment Income Attainment of Racialized and Non-racialized Groups

Income inequalities have historically been a reliable measure of racial discrimination in the labour market. The impact of racial discrimination on income distribution can be tracked using employment income data. Our analysis of that data for the period between the two census years, 1996–2001, reveals a persistent double-digit income disparity between racialized and non-racialized individual earners.

During the period, racialized group members and new immigrants experienced a median after-tax income gap of 13.3% and an average after-tax income gap of 12.2%. The gap is highest among male youth (average after-tax income gap 42.3% and median after-tax income gap 38.7%), as well as those with less than high school education (median after-tax income gap 20.6%) and those over 65 years (average income gap 28% and median income gap 21%).

This gap is evident among the university educated (median gap 14.6%) as well as those without post-secondary education (20.6%), suggesting a cross social class factor. But the size of the gap varies among sub-groups and disappears within the family income category—likely because racialized groups have more income earners per average family.

This suggests that while the income gap between racialized and non-racialized individual earners over that period seems to be changing, it remains a significant indicator of racial inequality in the Canadian labour market.

Labour Market Participation of Racialized and Recent Immigrants

Labour market participation rates and rates of unemployment show a continuing gap between the experience of racialized and non-racialized workers. In 2001, while the participation rates for the total population were 80.3%, those for racialized group members were as low as 66% and 75% for immigrants. Racialized groups and immigrants also experienced unequal unemployment rates with the total population rate being 6.7% while the racialized group rate was as high as 12.6%.

Sectoral Distribution for Racialized and Non-racialized Groups

The labour market is segmented along racial lines, with racialized group members over-represented in many low paying occupations with high levels of precariousness while they are under represented in the better paying, more secure jobs. Racialized groups were over-represented in the textile, light manufacturing and service sector occupations such as sewing machine operators (46%), electronic assemblers (42%), plastics processing (36.8%), labourers in textile processing (40%), taxi and limo drivers (36.6%), weavers and knitters (37.5%), fabrics, fur and leather cutters (40.1%), iron and pressing (40.6%).

They were under-represented in senior management (8.2%), professionals (13.8%), supervisors (12%), fire-fighters (2.0%), legislators (2.2%), oil and gas drilling (1.5%), farmers and farm managers (1.2%). One area where they fared better is in the information technology industry, with software engineers (36.3%), computer engineers (30.1%) and computer programmers (27.8%).

Converting Human Capital Investment into Occupational Status and Compensation

Yet another key indicator of racial inequality is the ability of racialized group members to translate their investment in human capital in terms of educational attainment into comparable occupational status and compensation. The shift towards more immigrants from the South has led to a noticeable lag in economic attainment among members of the immigrant groups. This has occurred despite the 1990s emphasis on skilled immigrants in immigration policy. Ironically, as the selection process has become more stringent in response to charges that immigrant quality has declined, a majority of immigrants from the South now come through the independent (skilled) class—over 60% in recent years (Citizenship & Immigration Canada, Facts and Figures, 2002).

For many racialized group members, educational attainment has not translated into comparable labour market access, or workplace mobility. In 2001, racialized group members were over-represented among highly educated categories such as holders of bachelor's, master's and doctorate degrees. However, they were under-represented under the trades and colleges graduates ranks, as well as among those with less than a grade 12–13 education. According to a Conference Board of Canada study, while racialized groups averaged less than 11% of the labour force between 1992 and 2000, they accounted for 0.3% of real gross domestic product growth (GDP). That contrasts with the remaining 89% of the labour force that contributed 0.6%. This disproportionately larger contribution to GDP growth is likely to grow over the 2002–2016 period as the contribution of the rest of the population falls. However, this productivity was not rewarded, as the average wages for racialized groups over that period remained 14.5% lower than that of other Canadians. The Board report concludes that in monetary terms, over the period 1992 to 2016, racialized groups will contribute $80.9 billion in real GDP growth.

Differential Access to Professions and Trades

In the early twenty-first century, an important aspect of the experience of racialized groups in the Canadian labour market is the experience of those whose education is obtained abroad. This category, here referred to as internationally educated professionals and trades people (IEPs), has been growing as Canada's immigration system has moved towards more stringent selection criteria, with emphasis on higher education and market-oriented skills. In the first 3 years of the new millennium, over 60% of the newcomers have university degrees.

Because of their increasingly significant numbers as a proportion of racialized cohort, their experience, while specific, in part explains the failure of racialized group members to translate the educational attainment and experience into higher occupational status, intra- and inter-sectoral mobility and compensation.

It also speaks directly to the failure of the major players—governments, licensing bodies and other regulators, employers, educational institutions, trade unions (and perhaps the IEPs themselves), to devise appropriate policy and program responses to the problem of inequitable access to professions and trades and to ensure a smooth transition for internationally trained professionals and trades people into their fields of expertise.

A successful integration strategy would require a focus on evaluating the competencies of trained immigrants rather than demands for undefined Canadian experience, approximating the value of their human capital based on what source country they are from and proposing to send them without supports to non-urban environments as a condition of their residence. It would mean state-supported efforts to match immigrant skills with the labour market shortages that exist in Canada's regions, provinces and cities, towns and communities. The Canadian government has a history of supporting past immigration with such resources as land for settlement. In this case, however, it has embarked on the selection of highly talented immigrants but assumed no accountability for their successful integration or even bothered to track their progress. Instead, even as it pursues a laissez-faire approach to their integration, it continues to compete for immigrants bearing similar skills, raising troubling questions about the logic of this aggressive immigration policy.

Surprisingly, in the case of the debate on the brain drain to the USA, the federal and provincial governments have responded by implementing taxation and other policy measures aimed at discouraging skilled immigration to the United States. However, despite demands for similar action by IEPs, communities and increasingly employers, equitable access to professions and trades in Canada has remained on the policy backburner. Ironically, in terms of sheer numbers, Canada receives four skilled immigrants to every one that migrates to the USA. Moreover, they are as or even more highly skilled than the ones leaving (Canada attracts more master's and doctoral graduates than it loses), and have chosen to live and work in Canada. Yet the issue of the brain waste has not prompted policy action adequate to the problem.

THE NATURE OF THE PROBLEM

Internationally educated immigrants are supposed to be the future of Canada's increasingly labour-strapped economy. With massive baby boom retirements on the horizon, someone has to pay their pensions and keep the tax dollars flowing for the social programs they will need in their old age.

Canada also promises the IEPs an opportunity to improve their lives and those of their families. It seems like a win-win proposition. This proposition, however, depends on the relatively seamless integration of IEPs into their fields of expertise. Yet, not unlike their predecessors, this group of largely racialized immigrants confronts a Canadian labour market with racial hierarchies, with structures of discrimination that defy the logic articulated above.

With governments in a neo-liberal era committed to deregulating the labour market rather than intervening in failed labour markets to ensure the optimal allocation of human resources, IEPs are impacted by the full weight of subjective decision making on the part of employers. The racial composition of the immigration group began to change in the 1960s, and by the 1980s that process was in full stride. It seemed to coincide with a period during which the state and self-regulating professional and occupational bodies imposed strict administration of rules and regulations in the name of ensuring the public interest, a process that has had the effect of erecting new barriers to entry for many recently immigrated IEPs. While the labour market conditions that precipitated the defensive actions have changed, the regulators have been slow to respond to the growing demands for licensing newcomers.

Furthermore, not all occupations or trades are regulated, and some are more regulated than others, which leads to varied experiences and leaves decisions at the behest of the employers.

Employers' attitudes towards internationally obtained skills and their bearers have been identified as particularly problematic. There is some general agreement around some of the issues that need to be addressed:

- Lack of adequate information about the licensing process, pre- and post-arrival
- Paucity of reliable tools for assessing credentials and other prior learning
- Lack of competency-based licensing and sector-specific language testing
- Inadequate bridging and supplementary training and internship opportunities
- Limited transparency in the licensing process and lack of feedback or an appeal process
- Limited co-ordination between stakeholders

While generally acknowledged, there has been no comprehensive, cross-jurisdictional policy response. Thus, the failure to translate internationally obtained human capital and higher immigrant educational attainment into better labour market performance is partly explained by the existence of systemic barriers to the recognition of international qualifications and prior learning assessment by regulators and employers. That is the conclusion of a number of important Canadian studies dealing with the situation of internationally trained professionals and trades people in the Canadian labour market.

While some argue that skilled immigrants require soft skills, employment-related language training, sector-specific orientation and labour market information in order to be competitive in the labour market, others acknowledge that immigrants face barriers to access to relevant information about licensing procedures both before and after arrival, barriers to obtaining equivalence, recognition and certification of internationally acquired credentials and in obtaining employment in their fields of expertise because of employer attitudes. While there are some common features across the country, the experiences vary from profession and trade as well as province and community.

POLICY RESPONSES

Most of the issues identified herein are within the purview of public policy and can be addressed by governments, in partnership with regulators, educational institutions, assessment agencies, trade unions, employers and service providers.

There is a need to define the public interest as including a focus on equity and economic efficiency. This need has never been greater than it is in this globalized labour market environment. The systemic failure to properly evaluate and accredit prior learning by employers and regulators casts them not as defenders of the public interest but gatekeepers and lacking transparency in the application processes.

Along with the existence of closed trade union shops, these factors make it difficult to review their excise of discretion to eliminate the barriers. The effect is the devaluation and degrading of the skills of vulnerable IEPs, which contributes to documented occupational and wage inequality. Although IEPs, immigrants and racialized communities are organizing to challenge this exercise of power, they are often powerless to stop their victimization and require governments to take the responsibility of enforcing a broader definition of the public interest.

CONCLUSION

While far outpacing the general Canadian population growth, and contributing a majority of new entrants into the labour market, racialized groups and immigrants have not fared well in the labour market in the last census period (1996–2001).

A review of employment income data and labour market participation patterns of racialized groups and recent immigrants, during the last census periods (1996–2001) shows both a double digit income gap between racialized and non-racialized populations in the Canadian labour market, higher unemployment and lower participation rates, and occupational concentrations in the low-income occupations.

These patterns are evident even when educational attainment is taken into account, suggesting that racialized group members and recent immigrants are not able to translate their educational attainment (indeed advantage) into comparable occupational status and compensation. This is partly explained by the experience of internationally educated professionals who face barriers to converting their skills into skilled occupations. There are variations in the size of the gap among sub-groups and it seems to disappear when you consider family income—with racialized groups having more income earners per family. There is a noticeable gap between racialized men and women, suggesting a gendered dimension to the inequality identified. This analysis is confirmed by the findings from interviews with key informants from among settlement sector officials in Vancouver, Calgary, Toronto, Montreal and Halifax, where over 80% of the racialized and recent immigrant population lives. Read together with the unequal unemployment rates, the inability of racialized group members to convert their educational attainment advantage into commensurate occupational status and income, the differential experience of internationally trained racialized group members, and the sectoral concentrations, the findings confirm the racialized groups experience of racial inequality in the Canadian labour market and the persistence of racial discrimination in employment.

The impact of racial discrimination in employment in the early twenty-first century is amplified because of the size of the racialized population but also because the population's contribution to the Canadian economy has grown exponentially over the last two decades. The stakes are high because race continues to be a major factor in the distribution of opportunities in the Canadian labour market and by extension in determining the life chances of racialized peoples and immigrants in Canada. The major difference is that this disadvantage will now translate into a drag on the Canadian economy and the Canadian population as a whole.

SOURCES

Abella, R. *Equality Now: Report of the Commission on Equality in Employment*. Ottawa: Supply and Services Canada, 1984.

Abbott, C. and C. Beach, "Immigrant Earnings Differentials and Birth-Year Effects of Men in Canada: Post-War-1972." *Canadian Journal of Economics*. 26 August 1993, 505–524.

Akbari, A. *The Economics of Immigration and Racial Discrimination: A Literature Survey (1970–1989)*. Ottawa: Multiculturalism & Citizenship Canada, 1989.

———. "Immigrant 'Quality' in Canada: More Direct Evidence of Human Capital Content, 1956–1994." *International Migration Review* 33 (Spring 1999): 156–175.

Alboim, N., R. Finnie and M. Skuterud. *Immigrants' Skills in the Canadian Labour market: Empirical Evidence and Policy Issues*. Mimeo, 2003.

Anisef, P., R. Sweet and G. Frempong. *Labour Market Outcomes of Immigrant and Racial Minority University Graduates in Canada*. CERIS working paper No. 23. CERIS, March 2003.

Arrow, K. "What Has Economics to Say about Racial Discrimination?" *Journal of Economic Perspectives* 12, no. 2 (Spring 1998): 91–100.

Bakan, A., and A. Kobayashi. *Employment Equity Policy in Canada: An Interprovincial Comparison* Ottawa: Status of Women Canada, 2000.

Baker, M. and D. Benjamin. "The Performance of Immigrants in the Canadian Labour Market." *Journal of Labour Economics* 12 (1994): 369–405.

Basran, G.S. and L. Zong "Devaluation of Foreign Credentials as Perceived by Visible Minority Professional Immigrants." *Canadian Ethnic Studies* 30, no. 3 (1998): 6–23.

Beach, C. and C. Worswick, "Is there a Double-Negative Effect on the Earnings of Immigrant Women?" *Canadian Public Policy* 19, no. 1 (1993): 36–53.

Bloom, M. and M. Grant. *Brain Gain: The Economic Benefits of Recognizing Learning Credentials in Canada*. Ottawa: Conference Board of Canada, 2001.

Boyd, M. "Gender, Visible Minority and Immigrant Earnings Inequality: Reassessing and Employment Equity Premise." In *Deconstructing a Nation: Immigration, Multiculturalism and Racism in the 1990s Canada*, ed. V. Satzewich. Toronto: Garamond Press, 1992.

Brouwer, A. *Immigrants Need Not Apply.* Ottawa: Caledon Institute of Social Policy, 1999.

Calleja, D. "Right Skills, Wrong Country." *Canadian Business*, 26 June 2000, www.skillsforchange.org/news/other/canadian_business_news_june_2000.htm.

Canadian Human Rights Commission. *Employment Equity Annual Reports*, 1996–1999.

Citizenship and Immigration Canada. *The Economic Performance of Immigrants: Immigration Category Perspective, 1998.* Ottawa: Government of Canada, 2000.

Citizenship and Immigration Canada. *The Economic Performance of Immigrants: Education Perspective, Strategic Policy, Planning and Research.* Ottawa: Government of Canada, 2000.

Citizenship and Immigration Canada. *Skilled Worker Immigrants: Towards a New Model of Selection.* Ottawa: Government of Canada, 1998.

Citizenship and Immigration Canada. *Facts and Figures 2001.* Ottawa: Government of Canada, 2001.

Conference Board of Canada. *Making a Visible Difference: The Contributions of Visible Minorities to Canadian Economic Growth.* Ottawa: Conference Board of Canada, 2004.

De Voretz, D.J., ed. *Diminishing Returns: The Economics of Canada's Recent Immigration Policy.* Toronto: C.D. Howe Institute, 1995.

Fernando, T. and K. Prasad. *Multiculturalism and Employment Equity: Problems Facing Foreign-Trained Professionals and Trades People in British Columbia.* Vancouver: Affiliation of Multicultural Societies and Services of British Columbia, 1986.

Frenette, M. and R. Morissette. *Will they ever converge? Earnings of immigrants and Canadian-born workers over the last two decades.* Analytical Studies paper No. 215. Ottawa: Statistics Canada, 2003.

Galabuzi, G. *Canada's Creeping Economic Apartheid: The Economic Segregation and Social Marginalization of Racialized Groups.* Toronto: CJS Foundation for Research & Education, 2001.

Grant, H. and R. Oertel. "Diminishing Returns to Immigration? Interpreting the Economic Experience of Canadian Immigrants." *Canadian Ethnic Studies* 30, no. 3 (1998): 57–76.

Harvey, E.B. and B. Siu. "Immigrants' Socioeconomic Situation Compared, 1991–1996." *INSCAN* 15, No. 2 (Fall 2001): 1–3.

Henry, F. and E. Ginsberg. *Who Gets the Job: A Test of Racial Discrimination in Employment.* Toronto: Urban Alliance on Race Relations / Social Planning Council of Metro Toronto, 1985.

Hou, F. and T. Balakrishnan, "The Integration of Visible Minorities in Contemporary Canadian Society." *Canadian Journal of Sociology* 21, no. 3 (1996): 307–326.

House of Commons. *Equality Now! Report of the Special Committee on the Participation of Visible Minorities in Canadian Society.* Ottawa: Government of Canada, 1984.

Human Resources Development Canada. "Recent Immigrants Have Experienced Unusual Economic Difficulties." *Applied Research Bulletin* 7, no. 1 (Winter/Spring, 2001).

Jackson, A. *Is Work Working for Workers of Colour?* Ottawa: Canadian Labour Congress, 2002.

Jain, H. *Employment Discrimination Against Visible Minorities and Employment Equity.* Hamilton: McMaster University, 1988.

Li, P. *Destination Canada: Immigration Debates and Issues.* Toronto: Wall & Thompson, 2003.

———. *Ethnic Inequality in a Class Society.* Toronto: Wall & Thompson, 1988.

———. "The Market Worth of Immigrants' Educational Credential." *Canadian Public Policy* 27, no. 1 (2001): 23–38.

Lundahl, M. and E. Wadensjo. *Unequal Treatment: A Study in the Neo-classical Theory of Discrimination.* New York: New York University Press, 1984.

Mata, F. "The Non-Accreditation of Immigrant Professionals in Canada: Societal Impacts, Barriers and Present Policy Initiatives." Paper presented at Sociology and Anthropology Meetings, University of Calgary, 3 June 1994.

Ontario Ministry of Training, Colleges and Universities. *The Facts Are In: A Study of the Characteristics and Experiences of Immigrants Seeking Employment in Regulated Professions in Ontario.* Toronto: Queen's Printer, 2002.

Pendukar, K. and R. Pendukar. "The Colour of Money: Earnings Differentials among Ethnic Groups in Canada." *Canadian Journal of Economics* 31, no. 3 (1998): 518–548.

Reitz, J.G. "Immigrant Skill Utilization in the Canadian Labour Market: Implications of Human Capital Research." *Journal of International Migration and Integration* 2, no. 3 (Summer 2001): 347–378.

Sangster, D. *Assessing and Recognizing Foreign Credentials in Canada: Employers' Views.* Ottawa: Canadian Labour and Business Centre, 2001.

Siddiqui, H. "Immigrants Subsidize Us by $55 Billion per Year." *Toronto Star*, 14 January 2001.

Stasiulis, D. "Affirmative Action for Visible Minorities and the New Politics of Race in Canada." In *Canada 2000 Race Relations and Public Policy*, ed. O.P. Dwivedi et al. Guelph: University of Guelph, 1989.

Stoffman, D. *Towards a More Realistic Immigration Policy for Canada.* Toronto: C.D. Howe Institute, 1993.

CHAPTER 25

THE INTEGRATION OF RACISM INTO EVERYDAY LIFE: THE STORY OF ROSA N.

Philomena Essed

In discussing the method of understanding accounts of racism, it was shown how Black women expose clues and hidden messages enclosed in situations. Overemphasis on situational evidence, however, and insufficient inference from knowledge of the general processes of racism may depoliticize evidence of racism (Essed, 1990a, 1990b). The reader must bear in mind that reconstructions of events are always embedded in more complex and elaborate clusters of knowledge and social processes. The processes involved in the experience of everyday racism are further addressed in this chapter. For that purpose the focus of analysis moves from heuristics of understanding to understanding as experience and from events to interrelated experiences.

To conceptualize and to analyze racism as a process, it is relevant to look at the different dimensions of experience. In real life personal confrontations with racism merge with the experiences with racism of Black friends and family and others who are not even personally known. Furthermore racism operating in interactions with colleagues, supervisors, fellow students, or shop attendants overlaps and reinforces other experiences with racism, such as viewing negative portrayals of Blacks in the media or large-scale discrimination on the labor market. Racism experienced today reminds one of similar past experiences and influences one's expectations about tomorrow. If one unravels complex processes involving different situations and agents, as well as both personal and vicarious experiences, a coherence between practices and experiences can be revealed. [...] [I]ntrasubjective comparisons are made to give insight into simultaneous and sequential instances of racism in personal biographies. Obviously it would be too time-consuming to analyze in detail the infusion of racism into the everyday experiences of each woman. Therefore, one detailed example is given, based on the accounts of one woman, Rosa N., from the Netherlands.

Rosa N. is a geriatrician in training, the only Black in her group. In some respects her story is typically Dutch. [...] Black women in the Netherlands are subjected to strong pressure to assimilate culturally. They also sketch a more elaborate system of ideological repression, in which dominant consensus operates not only to impede equal participation but also to suppress protest against racism. We will see later that the story of Rosa N. is consistent with those of other Black women. Thus the experience of Rosa N. forms a microcosm of everyday racism. I shall demonstrate that these situations are everyday situations and that each experience acquires meaning relative to other experiences.

To examine whether the reported experiences represent everyday racism, they must be tested against the definition and main features of everyday racism. To recapitulate, everyday racism has been defined as a process in which socialized racist notions are integrated into everyday practices and thereby actualize and reinforce underlying racial and ethnic relations. Furthermore racist practices in themselves become familiar, repetitive, and part of the "normal" routine in everyday life. With these presuppositions in mind, let us now turn to the story of Rosa N.

A FRAGMENTARY REPRESENTATION OF EVERYDAY RACISM

Rosa N. was born in Suriname in 1951. She lost both of her parents before she was 10 years old. Her mother's sister adopted her, and Rosa N. was raised with four other children, all girls. After finishing high school in Suriname, she got a scholarship to study medicine in the Netherlands. After graduation she further specialized in geriatrics. In the period when she was interviewed, she was doing her internship at a modem complex for medical research. Four years earlier she had married a Dutchman, Rob, an architect. The following account, recorded in 1986, represents a moment of reflection upon some of her experiences of racism as a Black woman, trainee, and young doctor. The presentation of the story of Rosa N. is largely faithful to the order in which it was told. This may give us an impression of the way experiences of racism in different contexts and situations are associated and related to each other in accounts of racism in everyday life.

Why tell the story of Rosa N.? In many respects this reconstruction of everyday racism challenges (Dutch) commonsense notions of racism (see also Essed, 1987). Rosa N. has never been physically molested, her life has not been threatened. She hardly has to deal with blatant "bigots." She has not been fired. She has been called a Black "whore" only once. She is gifted, she has a job, and she is pursuing a promising career. She is a "successful Black." So one might ask: What is the problem? The problem is exactly that which is at the heart of everyday racism: the invisibility of oppression and the imperceptibility of Rosa N.'s extraordinary perseverance, despite multiple forms of oppression. Rejection, exclusion, problematization, underestimation, and other inequities and impediments are regularly infused into "normal" life, so that they appear unquestionable. This is a story of oppression in the fabric of everyday life. Some of her experiences are obvious indications of racism. Many others are concealed and subtle. Their understanding requires a certain degree of general knowledge of racism. To prevent any misinterpretations, I will clarify in detail why specific seemingly nonracial experiences can only be explained as forms of racism.

A relevant question concerns why we should believe Rosa N. The idea that Blacks are "too sensitive" is popular enough. Therefore, it may be expected that some readers think she just has a "chip on her shoulder" and that she is just as prejudiced against the Dutch as she thinks the Dutch are against Blacks. Suppose that she perceives racism where it is not present. Theoretically this may be the case, which would imply that Rosa N. has little knowledge of racism. This would mean that she is only expressing her common sense about race to account for a range of negative experiences. These crucial questions must be attended to carefully.

"Common sense" is a problematic notion. However, for my purposes the Gramscian (Gramsci, 1971) interpretation, as applied by Lawrence (1982b) in race relations theory, is relevant. Lawrence (1982b, p. 89) discusses common sense in relation to racist ideologies, which he argues have been elaborated from "taken-for-granted" assumptions. Here my concern is not with "racist ideas" but with "ideas about racism." More specifically it must be emphasized that Black women's notions about racism cannot be seen as "common sense" about racism. These notions are not based in taken-for-granted assumptions but, as I demonstrated earlier (see Chapter 3), comprehension of racism is acquired through deliberate problematization of social reality. Lawrence (1982b, pp. 48–50) argues that common sense is basically unsystematic, inconsistent, and contradictory and that it consists of notions that are taken for granted. In other words, common sense lacks reflective underpinning.

*****

[P]roof that she is careful and knowledgeable may be derived from the consistency of evidence. If Rosa N. has recollected just any negative experience to present as racism, we shall not be able to find consistency and coherence in her story. As noted before, everyday racism does not exist in the singular but only in the plural form, as a complex of mutually related, cumulative practices, and situations. [...]

[T]he Rosa N. story is also consistent in another sense, as may be inferred by the absence of the ultimate attribution error (Pettigrew, 1979). Unlike prejudiced interpreters Rosa N. does not dismiss evidence of positive behavior by dominant group members as a means of sustaining previous expectations about racism. This will be illustrated shortly. [...]

The Story of Rosa N.

> I came to Holland in 1969. My life was hard: work, study. My main friends were Dutch, the typical medical students. I had a time when I started to notice more things, such as, I have no home here, but a Dutch person does. I always had a very close friend—Ida, my father's younger sister. She was able to keep me from feeling lonely, from being homesick for Suriname. We gave each other a lot of support without ever consciously knocking the Dutch. That never entered your mind.

Even when Rosa N. did not explicitly feel different than the Dutch, fellow students reminded her that she was not like the Dutch.

> I can remember once making a phone call in a dorm when a Dutch boy said: "There's Rosa with that laugh of hers." And I thought: What does he mean? Strange! Because I was laughing very loud. But that doesn't happen anymore, only when I'm with Rob. [I felt like] I had to get rid of a lot of the Suriname in me. Not consciously. Not at all. I certainly had to lose a lot of my spontaneity. I think too I might have done it because I was always getting it thrown in my face, like with the boy who said, "Why are you laughing like that?" I must say, I've got some of that back now. I'm rediscovering my own culture. That's fantastic.

As for many other Black women in the Netherlands, the 1980s represents a period in which Rosa N. developed a deeper understanding of racism in her daily experiences. Vague feelings of oppression, of Eurocentrism, and cultural deprivation make way for a focused understanding of related practices of racism. Rosa N. preludes her accounts of a range of situated practices of racism by remembering: "How I loathed the Dutch. I saw all those depressed Moroccans, depressed Turks. And I saw all kinds of discrimination and racism. How people reacted, how people treated you." She continues with some examples:

> We were in a surgery class. It was taught by a plastic surgeon whose name I've forgotten. If it were now, I'd certainly report that man. I was really angry. [He told us about an industrial accident] in a food processing plant where a Turk working on a cutting machine had sliced open his hand. And he even started the story with: "the stupid Turk." Yeah, that's how he started, "the stupid Turk. His hand is not a can!" He said I didn't really have much confidence, but still, I wanted to save the man's hand, because, he said, you know what it costs the Dutch government if that man loses his hand! He gets social security. So, he had to save the man's hand. He showed us another series of slides [about] how he'd operated on the hand. It looked really weird, but he must and he would save that hand, for it would cost the government too much. But eventually, the hand started to die anyway. It looked really terrible. The surgeon left the hand alone until it was completely black, like a hand of coal. His hand was amputated, after all. And then he showed the next picture. Someone's heel gone, that's another stupid foreigner in a factory, he says then. He talks about there being so many accidents. Only with foreigners. And he doesn't understand it, that's just

how he tells the class the story. But he [doesn't add] that it's foreigners who do this kind of work and that they are the highest risk group for having an accident. The students thought it was real funny. They don't really give it much thought, because it arouses a kind of hilarity when it's told that way. Then everyone laughs about it. But I find such humor out of place, actually.

I waited until the man was finished. The lights went on, I told him he shouldn't make remarks like that again because they are offensive, and I chose that attitude because I thought: I must not become uncontrolled, agitated, or aggressive. [...]

And then one time in a general health class, this extremely stupid civil servant blamed the foreigners for overpopulation. I said something about that then, but what struck me was that someone said: oh, there's Rosa with that racism again. And I thought: what a prick! I thought: I'll turn in a complaint. But—and that really disappointed me—when I asked a few people I got on well with if they would testify, the one said, like no, because I have a child and a job I don't want to lose. One girl said she would testify. Then I spoke with my adviser, and he gave me some literature which showed that it has never been demonstrated that foreigners cause overpopulation. I very politely sent the man a letter. He sent such a nasty letter back. It was a totally degrading letter that said more about him than me, because he attacked me on personal points: that I had used my boss's FAX number—while my boss had even approved my letter. That I had not written "personal" on the letter and the secretary and other people had read it.

All these experiences took place when Rosa N. was doing her internship. This is a special situation in which study and work overlap. Thus people who are fellow students in one situation are her colleagues in other situations. Therefore, the distinction between the context of education and work is made only for the purpose of the analysis.

Now at my work, they find me oversensitive, probably because I just can't let certain things pass. And I can absolutely not do that. I do not want to and I will not. So I always respond [against racism], because now I just can't keep quiet. Here's another example. A student [presented] a patient—and I'm the only Surinamese present as doctor. He [introduced the patient with] she is from Suriname. He looked at me and said: sorry. I thought, what's all this? Why in god's name does he say "sorry"?! But to make things worse, when in my confusion I did this [very astonished face], another person started patting me on the back. Then I was completely at a loss.

The patient [being presented] had herpes genitalis. And the student said, oh, yeah, women in Suriname do have more than one man. Then I jumped in immediately with, then everyone in Suriname must have herpes!

*****

Rosa N. mentions that she has been confronted with racism from patients, but, because the patients are ill or demented, she is less worried about this than when it comes from her colleagues:

A patient, a woman told me afterward that during a psychosis, she had thought I was a whore. Then I think once more, yeah, a Black is a whore.... You know, this reminds me of one of the first times that I came into the hospital, I was with [a] demented woman. I gave her my hand. "I don't want the hand of a foreign worker, I don't want that hand." She went on [with] a heap of racist language.

I take a lot of time for things [because] I have the idea that I must work very scrupulously, must not fail. It's the same with everyone, so this isn't so exceptional, but with me there's another dimension. I may not make as many mistakes as the others. I must not do things wrong when with the Dutch. Absolutely not, I don't want to be their lesser. You've got to be better.

In this respect Rosa N. feels that the stress to prove herself as a Black woman is, in fact, the continuation of her past. In comparison with her cousins—the four daughters of her mother's sister—she was darker. She always felt treated as the "nigger" of the family.

*****

Reviewing her life at the hospital, Rosa N. says:

I'm not safe at G. [name of hospital]. Like, I can never in my life bring up the subject of racism. That just can't be, because they'll only trip me up.

If you want to say anything about racism, you've got to state your case very well. Otherwise ... they tackle you and lay down a thousand pieces of evidence to prove the opposite, and they make you ridiculous.

Because I'm Black, I'm more vulnerable [as a woman]. I always have the idea, if men see a Black woman ... then they've got a good chance. You also see this on television. Then there's this stupid commercial where a White man wants a Black [woman], and he plays with her, and suddenly he reaches under her skirt. And then it seems something or the other comes out. I've forgotten what.

The above summary of racism in everyday situations portrays a story in which the woman is constantly fighting against racist opposition—a lonely struggle to keep breathing in a racist climate with an almost overwhelming degree of suppression. In this respect that story of Rosa N. is representative for the story of many other women in the Netherlands. [...] Thus she concludes the interview with the following statement:

> I used to think, when I am a doctor, this will be in the past, then I'll have proved myself, but no such thing. Then the long, hard road begins. Then you start to notice that you aren't there yet, that the fight has just begun. I would really like for it to be over, because I'd like to just be able to live. I'd find it wonderful if I could just feel good with my job and not have a third-rate position in the job. If you spend all your time competing, then it never stops. I participate in this consciously and take care that I don't backslide. I think: just keep it up.
>
> I read at lot more about discrimination now—but then, not so much about Holland, because you don't get any further if you keep on thinking only about they do that and they do that and they do that. Now I would like to know much more about how I can deal with it. My first 10 years in Holland, I found it much too painful to see what was going on in South Africa. The slaughter there. It also has to do with being ready to let that penetrate. I find that positive. I think too that Rob has certainly learned from me. He has learned to look; he gives me support, accepts criticism, while he used to go into a discussion about it.

THE PROCESS OF EVERYDAY RACISM IN THE EXPERIENCE OF ROSA N.

The reader must bear in mind that the story of Rosa N. is not a representation of the whole interview with Rosa N., of which the transcript has 54 pages, but only a compilation of experiences she presented as illustrations of racism. Therefore, one must not see this summary as a general bias against the Dutch, as an indication that she only has negative experiences with the Dutch, or as evidence that she does not know how to distinguish between racism and injustice for other reasons. Space limitations prevent detailed analysis of the experiences not included here, but it may be useful to give a brief impression. On various occasions Rosa N. distinguishes positive aspects of Dutch individuals from practices of racism. To give a few examples: She feels culturally oppressed from the very beginning of her stay in the Netherlands. Yet she has quite positive memories of the group of (Dutch male) friends she spent time with early on. They were "real old fashioned, even brazen in a certain way, but they were also quite straightforward," which is what she "really liked about them." At work she experiences racism from her supervisor in some situations, yet she otherwise appreciates that he is often "very perceptive" about her needs as a trainee. Her comprehension of racism—that is, the fact that she qualifies practices, rather than individuals, as racist—is particularly important. [...]

Rosa N. is also self-critical, as she realizes that on some occasions, in the first period of her stay, she was wrong about the Dutch because she "did not know" enough about their cultural styles and about the way they "socialized among themselves." In other words, Rosa N. realized there were certain gaps in her understanding of Dutch culture that made it difficult to make reliable interpretations of her own experiences with the Dutch. This is consistent with my theory that comprehension of racist events requires knowledge of dominant or subcultural codes of behavior. The consequence is that examples in which Rosa N. was not sure herself whether she was confronted with racism are either excluded or presented with due reservation. Finally, some comments are in order about the criteria against which are assessed the accounts of Rosa N. Her experiences are examples of everyday racism if they are consistent with the definition of (experiences of) everyday racism. Thus it may be assumed that the experiences of Rosa N. represent everyday racism if they are consistent with the following presuppositions:

1. Everyday racism is reflected in different types of experiences.
2. Everyday racism presupposes everyday situations.
3. Everyday racism involves repetitive practices.
4. Experiences of everyday racism are heterogeneous.
5. Everyday racism involves specifications of general processes of racism.

Different Types of Experiences

The story of Rosa N. shows a relatively high frequency of direct experiences of racism. She connects her personal experiences with those of other Blacks and of other oppressed groups such as Turks and Moroccans. [...]

Cognitive experiences. What you feel, know, or believe is happening continuously, or what you expect may happen any day, constitute permanently felt pressures lingering beneath the surface of social reality. Some of these pressures have been activated so many times they are presented as generalized experiences in memory. In the experiences of Rosa N. one of these forms of permanently felt racism is the pressure to assimilate culturally under conditions of Eurocentrism. Apparently she has been harassed or criticized so many times that she has gotten "rid of a lot of the Suriname" in her. Because the Dutch explicitly adhere to the norm of tolerance, pressures on Blacks to assimilate often operate covertly (Jong, 1989). This probably explains why Rosa N. was "not" even "conscious" herself that she was losing much of her genuine cultural identity. [...]

Underestimation is another constant form of racism that must have been activated so many times that Rosa N. feels she cannot afford to be less than perfect. It is interesting to note that Rosa N. is perfectly well aware that all her colleagues work under pressure to perform ("I must not fail. It's the same with everyone, so that is not so exceptional, but with me there is another dimension"). In other words, she is not trying to hide any personal incompetence behind the explanation of racism. She only makes a qualitative difference when she suggests that, if she fails, it will not be seen as personal failure but as failure of a Black woman. In fact Rosa N. points here to a general problem that has been confirmed in many experiments in intergroup attribution (e.g., Hewstone, 1989).

I shall return to the behavioral implications of this important aspect when I discuss dominant group actions against Black women who aspire to achieve and who are competent in their fields.

These three forces of racism experienced by Rosa N. symbolize the framework in which all her other experiences may be placed: (a) *Eurocentrism*; (b) the dominant group impeding the efforts of Blacks to achieve (which is rationalized with, among other things, *attribution of incompetence*); and (c) Whites exercising covert pressure with the aim of enforcing cultural *assimilation*. Eurocentrism marginalizes Blacks; low expectations legitimize marginalization; and pressure to assimilate is a form of control. Assimilation is not just a question of state policy, which is how this is usually identified. This "need for control" (Dijker, 1989, p. 87) expressed by individual members of the dominant group, who demand that Blacks adapt to Dutch ways of living, is a dominant feature of Dutch racism. The story of Rosa N., and as we shall see the stories of other women as well, demonstrate that assimilative forces work through everyday situations and practices. These forms of racism all presuppose that difference is organized hierarchically, whether it concerns culture or structure.

Vicarious experiences. Among the most characteristic differences between the experiences of Black women in the United States and those in the Netherlands are those associated with identification with other groups who are targets of racism. The tendency among Black women in the Netherlands to transcend the boundaries of ethnicity when antiracism is concerned is remarkable in light of the prevailing forces on the side of the dominant group to generate and maintain rigid ethnic differentiation in the context of a pluralist model of society. [...] This can also be inferred from Rosa N., who says about the period when she became "aware" of racism that she "loathed the Dutch" because of the depressed conditions of Turks and Moroccans and all of the kinds of racism she began to recognize. [...] A form of commitment is Rosa N.'s protest against the lectures of a plastic surgeon who jokes about the medical experiment he did on a Turkish worker.

Rosa N. says that no matter how polite specific Whites may be to her because she is a doctor, when they intimidate another Black because he is "just" a worker, "they are doing it to you" too. Rosa N. does not only identify with other targets of racism because she feels a commitment to challenge racism. If this were the case, any active opponent of racism, including Whites, would vicariously experience racism through knowledge of the oppression of Blacks. Individual Blacks also experience racism through the experiences of others because of the very nature of racism. It is not directed against any one person but against every Black. For these reasons, vicarious experiences represent a major component of the experience of everyday racism. The notion of vicarious racism underscores the fact that, in the reproduction of racism, agents and subjects are of secondary importance. Whether or not agents indulge in racist practices depends on many factors, among others the degree of saturation of racist ideologies in the individual's social cognitions, the interests involved, the personality of the agent, and expectations about reactions of Blacks or White group members. However, the characteristics of the situation determine the specific forms racism takes. To give an example, the professor abuses the authority attached to his profession by infusing his teaching with racist statements after he had used the power attached to the medical profession to physically abuse a Turkish patient. Another teacher may do the same in a teaching situation, as can be inferred from the experiences of Rosa N. The content of the racist statements that are made may be determined by other factors, such as the role of the speakers in other situations (the surgeon makes racist remarks related to surgery, and the guest speaker comes with racist ideas developed in the context of his work at the Ministry of Public Health). To avoid misunderstanding the primacy of situation over agents and subject does not mean that racism is just situationally construed. It will be shown in the course of this study that the major forms racism takes are ideologically structured; the specific manifestations of these forms, however, are situationally created.

Comparisons between the direct and the vicarious experiences of Rosa N. show that there are similarities in the forms racism takes. Here particular attention is paid to the pathologizing of Blacks. Various studies have focused on the process by which racist notions of difference translate the behavior of Blacks into "maladjusted" behavior while "maladjusted" behavior becomes subsequently "pathological" behavior (Baratz & Baratz, 1972/1977; Lawrence, 1982a). These notions constitute part of commonsense thinking (Lawrence, 1982b).

Pathologizing is in many respects worse than inferiorizing because pathological behavior needs to be cured for one to become "normal" again. Furthermore, it is relevant to make a distinction between ideas of cultural pathology and attribution to Blacks of pathological personalities. The first form represents cultural deterministic explanations of "social disadvantage." The second form perceives reactions of Blacks to oppression in general or to racism in particular as pathological. This line of thinking is important in the story of Rosa N. as it draws upon the idea that, due to "social deprivation," Blacks develop damaged personalities with symptoms such as "oversensitive" and "overemotional" reactions to their social surroundings.

Rosa N. is repeatedly confronted with Whites who think that her perceptions of racism are pathological. This ideological form of racism structures direct and vicarious experiences and is expressed in specific situations according to the characteristics of the situation and the interests involved. In this process both Black professionals and patients are subjected to the same process of pathologizing so that it becomes legitimate to disqualify Rosa N. as a doctor. The story of Rosa N. holds good illustrations of the intricate relation between acts of racism directed against Rosa N. herself and racism embedded in the way doctors discuss their Black patients in the presence of Rosa N.

*****

Everyday Racism Presupposes Everyday Situations

The story of Rosa N. does not deal with racist ideologies of organized racist or fascist movements. She is just reporting about her day-to-day experiences in routine situations involving "normal" people. Due to her profession a proportionally high number of dominant group members with whom she has to deal in daily interactions belong to the Dutch-educated "elite." Relations between Rosa N. and dominant group members are racialized because they are structured by the wider stratifications in society. However, this racialized dimension, which Rosa N. described so well when she referred to "another dimension" compelling her to pursue perfection, is not constantly activated. Dominant group members may relate to her in a nonracist way in some situations but not in others. The racial dimension of the relationship is activated when racist practices are integrated into the situation. All of the situations in which Rosa N. experiences racism directly constitute routine situations in everyday life. To illustrate I summarize the situations of racism on the job. On the job racism permeates routine situations, formal and informal, through which the institution of a hospital is reproduced:

1. discussing patients with colleagues
2. small talk in the corridors
3. having informal conversation with colleagues
4. having lunch with colleagues
5. discussing patients with the supervisor
6. working with a patient
7. giving a paper in a seminar
8. being disturbed in one's work by the cleaner
9. overhearing the head custodian and the cleaner

Similarly the agents of racism in these situations are part of the natural human fabric of the specific workplace, a medical complex:

1. colleagues: doctors
2. supervisor: doctor
3. patient
4. cleaner
5. head custodian

Recurrent Practices and Heterogeneity of Experiences

Repetition is an indication of the degree of uniformity of practice. [...] In the biography of Rosa N. herself, there is also similarity in the forms of racism she encounters: (a) The same complications arise in similar situations. [...] Also there is repetition of (b) similar forms of racism in different situations. An [...] example concerns the rejection of Surinamese styles of communication by a fellow student in one situation and by Rosa N.'s supervisor in another situation. (c) Similar agents may be involved in similar or in different racist practices. The same colleagues who tolerate racist remarks from the professor during class patronize and pathologize Rosa N. or other Blacks in other situations.

*****

Everyday Racism as Specifications of General Processes of Racism

For practices to occur systematically, there must be certain ideological conditions that both stimulate and legitimize these practices. As stated before, this is not meant to imply that relations between prejudice and discrimination are simple or straightforward. However, the saturation of cognitions with shared notions or consensus on race allows certain practices to happen routinely. This may also be inferred from the experiences of Rosa N. It is explicitly assumed that practices are allowed, rather than that agents always consciously perform racist practices or that others explicitly agree with these practices. Indeed Rosa N. says she also has (situational) allies, among others her husband and a female colleague who she thinks supports her even when she does not take any explicit initiatives against racism. Her boss supported her letter of protest to the representative of the ministry. The tolerance of racism that many other dominant group members display may be a question of indifference, of ignorance, or of mere behavioral conformity (Pettigrew, 1958). In particular in the Netherlands the tradition of establishing harmony through consensus may inhibit individuals from confronting other group members, irrespective of the problem at hand. Whatever the reasons individuals may have, the rule applies that, the more saturated social cognitions are with racist ideological notions, the more likely it becomes that racist cognitions encourage or rationalize specific actions and the more oppressive tolerance of racism becomes. For these reasons it is relevant to reconstruct from the story of Rosa N. the main ideological concepts underlying the racism she experiences.

Problematization. [...] [T]wo structuring concepts underlie ideological racism as reconstructed by Rosa N.: real or imaginary *differences* attributed to Blacks and the subsequent *hierarchical ordering of difference.* Not only is difference organized hierarchically, it is common in—although not only typical of—European thinking for the "superior" to control the "inferior" (Hodge et al., 1975). [...]

Overemphasis on ethnic difference is inherent in various comments and criticisms dominant group members make about (what they presume to be) Surinamese culture. One pertinent example of the fact that difference is inherently perceived in hierarchical terms concerns the situation in which a colleague introduces a patient with "she is from Suriname," after which he immediately looks at Rosa N. and says "sorry." Later the colleague confesses that he apologized because he felt it might have been offensive to his Black colleague to be reminded that she is from the same "inferior background" as the patient.

*****

Another source of problematization Rosa N. experiences derives from the underestimation of Blacks. The idea that

Black people are incapable of intellectual advancement probably combines remnants of racist notions of biological determinism (Blacks as genetically less intelligent) and forms of cultural determinism (attributed low drive to achieve). Furthermore it is likely that gender- and race-based ideologies converge in the practice of underrating Black women (Hall, 1982; Piliawsky, 1982; Tomlinson, 1983). The least harmful example Rosa N. mentions is almost too stereotypical to be true: The cleaner comes in and takes the old White male patient for a doctor and the Black young doctor for the patient.

*****

Rosa N. depicts an atmosphere in which difference is exaggerated, reduced to ethnicity, and subsequently pathologized, the prevailing assumption being that Blacks are "emotional." A very good example of this is the reaction of her supervisor when Rosa N. reacts with sarcasm, and then leaves the session, after blatantly offensive remarks one colleague makes about Black female sexuality. First, the supervisor pathologizes her reaction by suggesting that she probably "did not want to react" in that way. And he adds that she "reacted like that because [she] is a Surinamese." Rosa N. is confronted with various other attempts to pathologize Blackness. Being Black in one situation is interpreted as a "disability," in another as an indication of mental instability ("too emotional"), or in another as a condition to be pitied ("another person started patting me on the back"). The pathologization of Blackness can only partly be explained by the environment in which Rosa N. works. However, it is relevant to briefly consider further ramifications of the attribution to Blacks of emotional instability by (mental) health care professionals.

In addition to general knowledge about racism against Black women in society at large, it is relevant to consider general information about racism (class and gender bias) in (mental) health care (Littlewood & Lipsedge, 1982; Miller & Rose, 1986). The overemphasis on differences functions to reduce ethnic behavior to individual traits to justify psychiatric intervention (Mercer, 1986). The case of the "swinging" Surinamese, who, according to Rosa N., should probably not have been hospitalized at all, is an example of this. Racism nurtures the stereotype of Afro-Caribbean (men) as deviant, aggressive, and "dangerous" and as a group that potentially undermines the existing order. The "swinging" style of the patient fits the dominant model of deviant (Black male) behavior. It is behavior that mocks "bourgeois" norms and values. This suggests that the Black man is pathologized and admitted as a patient not on medical grounds but because of potential "dangerousness." Therefore, pathologizing must also be seen in its function to control opposition to the existing order. I shall come back to containment of opposition in a moment. [...]

Marginalization. If Rosa N. had been a cleaner rather than a doctor in the hospital, her story would have been one of racism structured by class exploitation and of class oppression permeated by racism. Indirectly she is confronted with the impact of class oppression in everyday racism. The head custodian bullies the Black cleaner, but he would never be anything but polite with Dr. N. Her own struggle, as it relates to the structural position of Black women with higher education, is directed more exclusively toward racial and ethnic marginalization. [...] Colleagues express indifference rather than polite, let alone cordial, interest when she engages in casual conversation with them ("I'd also like ... to say what I find nice, pretty or whatever, but they never really go into this").

Often Whites *passively tolerate* and probably hardly even notice *racism*. Let me illustrate: When colleagues insult Rosa N. by considering her *incompetent* to judge a Surinamese patient, none of the participants challenges the insult. It is taken for granted that a White male colleague who has been in Suriname once is more competent. [...]

Containment. Rosa N. is not just a "powerless victim" of racism; neither are agents of racism simply maliciously abusing power. It can be inferred from the story of Rosa N. that power is centrally involved in interracial (ethnic) situations. [...]

Almost half of Rosa N.'s experiences concern processes of containment. This suggests that she encounters a relatively high degree of reluctance to change. The message implied in the *humiliation* of the Black cleaner is that he should accept an inferior position. [...] I speak of *intimidation* when lecturers use racist examples in front of Black students because this situation activates group power. In the act of underrating Rosa N. dominant group members confirm racial consensus that allows these things to be said without sanctions being applied. This is even worse when racist statements are used to induce laughter, which is an explicit way to create approval and tolerance of racism. [...]

The function of intimidation is to "keep Blacks in their place." Later I will return to this important function of containment as it presupposes approval for existing relations between "superior" and "inferior" groups. Many forms of rejection of ethnically specific behavior operate in the same way. Stigmatizing the way you laugh or your enthusiasm about your work is giving the message that different behavior is not appreciated. One could argue that these are trivialities not even worth mentioning. Indeed these are trivialities. That is exactly the problem. We can also look at it in this way: Apparently the dominant group refuses to accept even the most trivial manifestations of difference, because they do not want to deal with them. This confirms my earlier stated presupposition that racism penetrates otherwise insignificant situations in everyday life. This introduces another subtle form of suppression, namely, the act of *patronizing*. In this context Rosa N. recalls how her colleagues made it a point to correct her when they detected a Dutch accent in her pronunciation of a US name.

*****

If dominant group members are tolerant of racism in many other situations, it is not surprising that Rosa N.'s refusal to tolerate racism induces new forms of control. The final step in the process of denial is the incrimination of Blacks (or others) who make a point of opposing racism. Rosa N. is accused of "malice." A colleague who had first compared Blackness to being "disabled" wants the supervisor to do something about Rosa N.'s. "accusing others of racism." [...]

These indications of pathologizing and denial also confirm that Rosa N.'s position is marginal. She is not (considered) part of the in-group, and racism operates to sustain racialized dimensions of social relations. Rosa N. is tolerated as a student and colleague, but she must not expect her colleagues to be sensitive or feel responsible for problems of racism, for they do not acknowledge it to be a problem. The analysis of everyday racism in the life of Rosa N. is not complete. Many other factors may be looked at, such as the specific consequences of racism from people in positions of authority, gender differences in expressions of racism, and conditions for change.

*****

CONCLUSIONS: ROSA N. AND THE SHARED EXPERIENCE OF RACISM

To examine whether the experiences of Rosa N. are consistent with those of other Black women, it is useful first to reiterate some of the earlier findings about the general processes of racism. [...] Earlier I provided a reconstruction of the main descriptive and explanatory concepts included in Black women's general knowledge of racism. This reconstruction reflects highly abstract knowledge and is based empirically in the categorization of statements about the general nature of racism. The structure of Black women's general knowledge of racism reflects the fact that racism consists of general processes (marginalization, problematization, containment) and various subprocesses (e.g., nonacceptance, pathologizing, patronizing). [...]

The general processes and subprocesses of racism as inferred from the story of Rosa N. are the same as those reported by other Black women. Therefore, the story of Rosa N., though unique in its biographical detail, inherently reflects experience shared by other Black women.

REFERENCES

Baratz, J., & Baratz, S. (1977). Black culture on Black terms: A rejection of the social pathology model. In T. Kochman (Ed.), *Rappin' and stylin' out* (pp. 3-16). Urbana: University of Illinois Press. (Original work published 1972.)

Dijker, A. J. (1989). Ethnic attitudes and emotions. In J.P. van Oudenhoven & T.M. Willemsen (Eds.), *Ethinic Minorities* (pp. 73-93). Amsterdam: Swets & Zeitlinger.

Essed, P. (1990a). The myth of over-sensitivity about racism. In I. Foeken (Ed.), *Between selfhelp and professionalism, Part III* (pp. 21-36). Amsterdam: Moon Foundation.

Essed, P. (1990b). Against all odds: Teaching against racism at a university in South Africa. *European Journal of Intercultural Studies, 1*(1), 41-56.

Gramsci, A. (1971). *Selections from prison notebooks*. London: Lawrence and Wishart.

Hall, R.M. (1982). *The classroom climate: A chilly one for women?* (Project on the Status and Education of Women). Washington, DC: Association of American Colleges.

Hewstone, M. (1989). Intergroup attribution: Some implications for the study of ethnic prejudice. In J.P. van Oudenhoven & T.M. Willemsen (Eds.), *Ethnic minorities* (pp. 25-42). Amsterdam: Swets & Zeitlinger.

Hodge, J.L., Struckman, D.K., & Trost, L.D. (1975). *The cultural bases of racism and group oppression*. Berkeley, CA: Two Riders.

Jong, W. de (1989). The development of ethnic tolerance in an inner city area with large numbers of immigrants. In J.P. van Oudenhoven & T.M. Willemsen (Eds.), *Ethnic Minorities* (pp. 139-153). Amsterdam: Swets & Zeitlinger.

Lawrence, E. (1982a). In the abundance of water the fool is thirsty: Sociology and Black "pathology." In Centre of Contemporary Cultural Studies (Birmingham; Ed.), *The empire strikes back: Race and racism in the 70s* (pp. 95-142). London: Hutchinson.

Lawrence, E. (1982b). Just plain common sense: The "roots" of racism. In Centre of Contemporary Cultural Studies (Birmingham; Ed.), *The empire strikes back: Race and racism in the 70s* (pp. 47-94). London: Hutchinson.

Littlewood, R., & Lipsedge, M. (1982). *Aliens & alienists*. Harmondsworth, England: Penguin.

Mercer. K. (1986). Racism and transcultural psychiatry. In P. Miller & N. Rose (Eds.), *The power of psychiatry* (pp. 111-142). Cambridge: Polity.

Miller, P., & Rose, N. (1986). *The power of psychiatry*. Cambridge: Polity.

Pettigrew, T.F. (1958). Personality and sociocultural factors in intergroup attitudes: A cross-cultural comparison. *Journal of Conflict Resolution, 2*, 29-42.

Pettigrew, T.F. (1979). The ultimate attribution error: Extending Allport's cognitive analysis of prejudice. *Personality and Social Psychology Bulletin, 5*(4), 451-476.

Piliawsky, M. (1982). *Exit 13: Oppression and racism in academia*. Boston: South End.

Tomlinson, S. (1983). Black women in higher education: Case studies of university women in Britain. In L. Barton & S. Walker (Eds.), *Race, class and education* (pp. 66-80). London: Croom Helm.

CHAPTER 26

"THEY CAN BE HIRED IN MASSES; THEY CAN BE MANAGED AND CONTROLLED LIKE UNTHINKING SLAVES"

Tomás Almaguer

The consignment of Indians and Mexicans to different "group positions" in the social structure of Anglo California vividly illustrates how the racialization process helped structure the imposition of white supremacy in the state. Although each ethnic group was racialized differently, neither was ever seen as the equal of white Americans; neither ever posed a serious threat to the superordinate racial status or privileged class position of white male immigrants. Indians became a marginal part of the new society while Mexicans were subordinated at the lowest levels of the working class, where they did not pose a serious problem for European Americans. Moreover, both groups remained tied to the precapitalist ranching or hunting and gathering economies of the Mexican period for decades after statehood and did not contend with European-American men who were rapidly being integrated into the capitalist labor market.

White Californians, however, grew rapidly alarmed by the presence of other racialized, non-European groups in the state: African-American, Chinese, and Japanese immigrants. As discussed earlier, the arrival of black slaves during the Gold Rush heightened anxiety among European Americans that slavery might compromise California's prospect of becoming a haven for free white labor. When Chinese immigrants followed blacks into the mining region, whites drew close analogies between black slaves and Chinese "coolies." This relationship was further reinforced by the unfortunate timing of the arrival of the Chinese; they came to California in the midst of mounting sectional conflict over slavery. The replacement, to all intents and purposes, of the African slave trade by the traffic in Chinese "coolies" only reinforced the image of the Chinese as a threat to the status of free white labor.[1]

It is against the backdrop of this class-based controversy among white Americans over the presence of unfree labor in the state, and the displacement of antiblack sentiment onto Asian workers, that the Chinese experience in nineteenth-century California initially unfolds. These concerns, plus widespread anxiety over the Chinese immigrant's ostensible "heathenism" and "savagery," rapidly ignited virulent anti-Chinese sentiment throughout California during the last half of the century.

This chapter examines the major features of this anti-Chinese sentiment, situating it specifically within the context of the emerging class antagonisms and conflicting interests between white capitalists and white workers. Racialized hostility against the Chinese is best understood in light of the way class-based interests among European Americans were defined in relation to this immigrant population. American capitalists sought to utilize Chinese labor whenever possible and profited handsomely from doing so. White workers, on the other hand, railed against the Chinese because of the threat they ostensibly posed to their status as a "free" laboring class. They believed that the Chinese were mere pawns of capitalist interests and other monopolistic forces that relied upon unfree labor. Consequently, white male laborers believed that Chinese workers threatened both their precarious class position and the underlying racial entitlements that white supremacy held out to them and to the white immigrants who followed them into the new class structure.

THE UNWELCOME ARRIVAL OF "JOHN CHINAMAN"

The Chinese immigrants who first arrived in California during the 1850s came from the agricultural district of Kwangtung province in southeastern China. These immigrants were largely an agricultural peasantry drawn to California by either the lure of the Gold Rush or by promises of lucrative employment opportunities made by overseas shipping companies. Within China, overpopulation, floods and other natural catastrophes, and the social dislocation wrought by the Opium Wars and the Taiping Rebellion also stimulated Chinese emigration.[2] Although these immigrants initially were seen as "coolies," they were not actual victims of the coolie trade that enslaved many Chinese nationals at the time.

The vast majority of Chinese who came to California arrived as indentured immigrants through the "credit-ticket system." They were a semifree population who secured passage to America by entering into contract labor arrangements whereby they were bound for a period of time to labor "bosses" in order to repay their debt.[3] They were typically bonded for passage by Chinese merchants in California who then rented them out in gangs of fifty to one hundred men. Alexander Saxton succinctly summarizes the major features of this debt bondage system:

> In effect [the worker] was at the mercy of the American employer, and of the Chinese merchant associations, agents, or contractors, who had arranged his passage from Canton, who hired him out, received his wages, provided his food and protection, and determined when,

> if ever, he would return home again. To complete this circle, an extra-legal but firm understanding between Chinese merchants associations and the Pacific ship operators hindered any Chinese from booking return passage until he had been cleared by the merchant association. It was a tight system, not exactly the same as slavery, but not altogether different.[4]

Although indentured Chinese workers were typically advanced approximately seventy dollars (fifty for passage and twenty for expenses), they were routinely required to repay upward to two hundred dollars.

While most came to the United States as indentured servants, some Chinese immigrants managed to secure the necessary funds for the trip from informal rotating credit associations in south China or from family resources.[5] A few of the first Chinese immigrants were merchants and shopkeepers who later became part the Chinese community's small middle class. This merchant class became a localized ruling elite within San Francisco's Chinatown between 1847 and 1858. According to Stanford Lyman, "Because commercial success was so closely tied to social acceptance and moral probity in America, this elite enjoyed good relations with public officials. Chinatown merchants controlled immigrant associations, dispensed jobs and opportunities, settled disputes, and acted as advocates for Chinese sojourners before white society."[6]

Historian Sucheng Chan also notes that the largest merchants owned import-export businesses and often established political organizations on the basis of homeland ties. According to Chan, "as almost all the imported goods were sold to Chinese—who favored food, clothing, and utensils from China—it was in the interests of these merchants and directors of community associations to help their customers and clients maintain strong ties to China. After all, provisioning their fellow countrymen was the chief source of the merchants' profit, and helping to retain an orientation to the homeland was the main basis of the association leaders' power."[7]

Furthermore, Chan estimates that between 1870 and 1900 approximately 40 percent of the Chinese residing in San Francisco and Sacramento were entrepreneurs and 5 to 12 percent professionals and artisans, while the working-class population comprised less than 50 percent of the urban Chinese. In sharp contrast, 80 percent of the Chinese rural population were farm laborers and service workers, 1 to 3 percent professionals and artisans, and only about 15 percent farmers, labor contractors, and merchants—the "rural elite."[8]

While only a few hundred Chinese immigrants arrived in California during the initial phase of the Gold Rush, by 1851 that number had swelled to 2,716 and by 1852 reached over 20,000. By 1870, approximately three-quarters of the 63,000 Chinese in the United States resided in California, where they comprised 9 percent of the total population.[9] Most of these Chinese immigrants initially settled in rural areas as well as the northern mining region of the state. Only one-quarter of the Chinese population resided in San Francisco by 1870, with other urban centers such as Sacramento, Stockton, and Marysville also having significant Chinese populations. In 1900, however, 45 percent of all Chinese in the state resided in the San Francisco Bay area alone; over two-thirds were already urban dwellers by this date.[10]

A crucial demographic feature of Chinese immigration was that it was overwhelmingly male from the outset. In 1860, for example, only 1,784 of the more than 34,000 Chinese residing in the United States were women—a ratio of one to eighteen. This ratio increased to a high of one to twenty-six in 1890 before settling once again at the 1860 figure in 1900. Even as late as that, there were only 4,522 Chinese women enumerated on the federal census of that year.[11] This accounts for the common reference to the early immigrant population as a "bachelor society."

According to historian Ronald Takaki, Chinese immigrants brought with them three main social organizations that structured their lives in California: the *huiguan* (district associations), the *tongs* (secret societies), and the *fongs* (clans) which were comprised of close family and village members or larger village associations. The latter two organizations were devoted primarily to the provision of illegal goods and services (such as the *tong*'s opium trade, gambling, and prostitution) and to mutual aid activities (such as the *fong*'s maintenance of clubhouses and temples, its transmission of letters to China, and its shipping home of the remains of deceased Chinese).[12]

Takaki maintains that the most important of these organizations was the *huiguan* or district associations from regions such as Toishan, Tanping, or Namhoi in southern China. These associations received immigrants, provided initial housing, secured employment, and administered the "credit-ticket" system.[13] The main district associations in San Francisco during the 1850s were the Sze Yup, Ning Yeung, Sam Yup, Yeong Wo, Hop Wo, and Yan Wo. These organizations came to be known as the Chinese Consolidated Benevolent Association (CCBA) or, more popularly, as the Chinese Six Companies. The CCBA settled interdistrict conflicts and provided important educational and health services to the community.[14] They also played a major role as spokespersons for the Chinese immigrant community. They often hired prominent white attorneys to represent their commercial trade as well as the general interests of the Chinese community.[15] Lacking any meaningful recourse to state and local government, the Chinese Six Companies frequently functioned as a quasi-government for the Chinese community. Indeed as one scholar maintains, the Chinese community was "more like a colonial dependency than an immigrant settlement in an open society."[16]

Sucheng Chan maintains that three fundamental differences between the Chinese-American communities established in the U.S. and the original communities in China profoundly shaped the Chinese immigrant experience in California.

> First, Chinese immigrant communities, though semiautonomous enclaves, were profoundly shaped by forces emanating from the larger society around them. Not only did the Chinese quickly adapt to the functioning of a capitalist economy, they persisted despite legal exclusion and anti-Chinese violence. Second, since few members of gentry families emigrated ... merchants who had a low status in China became the elite in Chinese-American communities by virtue of their ability to deal with whites and to provide for the needs of other Chinese. Finally, as few women emigrated to the United States, Chinese America was virtually a womanless world, especially in rural areas. Consequently, Chinese-American communities were socially incomplete.[17]

THE "DAMNING INFLUENCE" OF THE "HEATHEN CHINEE"

European Americans found much about Chinese immigrants distasteful—physical appearance, language, manner of dress, food, religion, and social customs. If being Christian and civilized were the principal cultural criteria by which white Californians evaluated new groups they encountered in the state, then the Chinese fell short in both areas: they were "heathen" as well as "uncivilized." Their clothing, for example, was radically at odds with European-American conceptions of proper attire. The Chinese immigrants wore broad trousers, blue cotton blouselike shirts, wide-brimmed straw hats, and closely cropped hair with a long black queue down their backs.[18]

"The first impulse of an American, when he see for the first time a Chinese, is to laugh at him," wrote an American trader in 1830. "His dress, if judged by our standards, is ridiculous.... His trousers are a couple of meal bags ... his shoes are huge machines, turned up at the toe, his cap is fantastic and his head is shaven except on the crown, when there hangs down a tuft of hair as long as a spaniel's tail."[19] The invidious comparison between the queue and a dog's tail symbolically reflected the inferior status the Chinese held in this trader's mind. The Chinese, like Indians in the state, were routinely likened to animals and unequivocally deemed "uncivilized."

Stuart Creighton Miller's exhaustive study of white Americans' perceptions of Chinese immigrants in the nineteenth century perceptively documents the demeaning racialized representations that crystallized in the popular white imagination. According to Miller, the Chinese were viewed as "ridiculously clad, superstitious ridden, dishonest, crafty, cruel, and marginal members of the human race who lacked the courage, intelligence, skill, and will to do anything about the oppressive despotism under which they lived or the stagnating social conditions that surrounded them."[20] Miller concludes that the Chinese were seen as a "peculiar" people having "bizarre tastes and habits" that included making medicines from rhinoceros horns and soup from bird's nests, and for allegedly eating dogs, cats, and rats.[21] "Virtually every aspect of Chinese life was used to illustrate and lampoon the Chinese propensity for doing everything backwards: wearing white for mourning, purchasing a coffin while still alive, dressing women in pants and men in skirts, shaking hands with oneself in greeting a friend, writing up and down the page, eating sweets first and soup last, etc."[22]

These early images of the Chinese found fertile soil in the United States, where they were further expanded upon by other racializing American commentators. Ronald Takaki argues, for instance, that Bret Harte's popular poem the "Heathen Chinee" greatly influenced public perception of the Chinese in America as "mice-eaters," "pagans," "dark," "impish," "superstitious," "yellow," and as "heathens" with a "peculiar odor" that reeked of ginger and opium."[23]

As noted earlier, white Californians' derisive stereotypes of blacks apparently shaped their initial perceptions of Chinese immigrants as well. As competition between white and Chinese laborers increased in later years, a number of the negative stereotypes associated with black slaves were displaced onto the Chinese. Both groups were seen as being docile, humble, irresponsible, lying, thieving, and lazy.[24]

Like blacks, the "China boys" were infantilized and summarily relegated to a subordinate status in relations to "white men."[25] While white immigrants arrogantly viewed themselves as rational, virtuous, civilized, libidinally controlled, and Christian, the Chinese were perceived as irrational, morally inferior, savage, lustful, and heathen. The most noxious representation of the Chinese portrayed them as a cross between a bloodsucking vampire, with slanted eyes and a pigtail, and a "nagur" with dark skin and thick lips.[26] One author has referred to this racial stigmatization as the "negroization" of the Chinese stereotype.[27]

Religious differences provided a major basis of the broad cultural chasm that socially differentiated the Chinese and white populations in the state. Most Chinese immigrants practiced a folk religion that combined the beliefs of Confucianism, Taoism, and Buddhism. They built altars to honor deities such as Kwang Kung, god of literature and war; Bak Ti, god of the north; Hou Yin, the monkey god; and Kwan Yin, goddess of mercy.[28] Nothing, of course, offended the Christian sensibilities of European Americans more than having a heathen group of "pagan idolaters" in their midst. Horace Greeley, for example, in an 1854 editorial in the *New York Tribune* lashed out against the religious practices of Chinese immigrants, arguing that only the "Christian races" or "white races" should be allowed to settle and "assimilate with Americans."[29]

Reverend S.V. Blakeslee, editor of *The Pacific*, the oldest religious paper on the West Coast, echoed a similar view in his 1877 address before the General Association of Congregational Churches of California. Reverend Blakeslee warned that the presence of the Chinese in California posed a greater threat to the state's Christian population than blacks had to the South's:

> Slavery compelled the heathen to give up idolatry, and they did it. The Chinese have no such compulsion and they do not do it.... Slavery compelled the adoption of Christian forms of worship, resulting in universal Christianization. The Chinese have no such influence tending to their conversion, and rarely—one or two in a thousand—become Christian.... Slavery took the heathens and by force made them Americans in feeling, tastes, habits, language, sympathy, religion and spirit; first fitting them for citizenship, and then giving them the vote. The Chinese feel no such force, but remaining in character and life the same as they were in old China, unprepared for citizenship, and adverse in spirit to our institutions.[30]

White intolerance and racial animosity toward the Chinese were further exacerbated by inflammatory characterizations of social life in California's "Chinatowns." Everywhere the Chinese lived, their detractors argued, one found crowded living conditions, gambling, opium smoking, prostitution, and a number of other despicable vices. Chinatown was "simply a miniature section of Canton transported bodily," proclaimed one anti-Chinese spokesperson.[31] Indeed, such perceptions later led to the enactment of San Francisco's infamous "Cubic Air" ordinance of 1870, which required lodging houses in Chinatown, the only place where the ordinance was enforced, to provide "at least five hundred cubic feet" of clean air "for each adult person dwelling or sleeping therein." Violation of this ordinance resulted in a fine of ten to five hundred dollars, imprisonment from five days to three months, or both.[32]

GENDERED AND SEXUALIZED REPRESENTATIONS OF CHINESE IMMIGRANTS

The perceived menace that the few Chinese immigrant women in the state posed to white men was yet another aspect of anti-Chinese sentiment at the time. Like lower-class Mexican women and Indian women in general, Chinese women were portrayed as hypersexual and readily available to white men. In his annual address to Congress in 1874, for example, President Ulysses S. Grant openly addressed the issue:

> The great proportion of the Chinese immigrants who come to our shores do not come voluntarily.... In a worse form does this apply to Chinese women. Hardly a perceptible percentage of them perform any honorable labor, but they are brought for shameful purposes, to the disgrace of communities where they settled and to the great demoralization of the youth of these localities. If this evil practice can be legislated against, it will be my pleasure as well as duty to enforce any regulation to secure so desirable an end.[33]

Horace Greeley echoed a similar view in an 1854 *New York Tribune* editorial. The arrival of Chinese women in the United States had to be prohibited because they were "uncivilized, unclean and filthy beyond all conception, without any of the higher domestic or social relations; lustful and sensual in their disposition; every female is a prostitute of the barest order."[34]

Like Chinese women, Chinese men also were perceived as a threat to the moral well-being of the white population, and most especially to white women. As an overwhelmingly male immigrant population, Chinese men were initially seen as menacing sexual "perverts" that preyed upon innocent white women. This view first gained currency on the East Coast, where newspapers sensationalized accounts of Chinese men luring and debauching young white girls in opium dens and laundries. An 1873 *New York Times* article, for instance, reported the presence of "a handsome but squalidly dressed young white girl" in an opium den in that city's Chinatown. When the Chinese owner of the den was asked about the girl, he was reported to have "replied with a horrible leer, 'Oh, hard time in New York. Young girl hungry. Plenty come here. Chinaman always have something to eat, and he like young white girl, He! He!'" The *Times* later reported that Chinese men were so depraved that they often attended Christian Sunday schools only to solicit sexual favors from the white female instructors. As proof they cited the case of one Sunday school teacher who apparently married one of her Chinese students. The girl's father publicly insisted that she had been drugged into marrying the man. "No matter how good a Chinaman may be, ladies never leave their children with them, especially little girls," warned another 1876 article in *Scribner's*.[35]

Expressions of public concern for the virtue of white women were more than mere moral posturing, for they often led to direct violence against Chinese men. In one incident in 1889 an angry mob of two thousand people demolished a Chinese laundry in Milwaukee after its two owners were accused of ravaging more than twenty young white girls in the back room. In 1883 in Waynesboro, Georgia, townsmen chased the "rat-eaters" out of town and burned their business to the ground, fearing that white girls would be "caught in the toils of Chinese duplicity."[36]

Fears and suspicions similar to these led to the enactment of an antimiscegenation statute in California in 1880 that prohibited the issuance of a marriage license between white persons and "a Negro, mulatto, or Mongolian."[37] Consequently, there are only a few cases in California of Chinese men marrying white women in the state. Those who did were most often drawn from the Chinese immigrant middle class: urban merchants, entrepreneurs, or agriculturalists in rural areas.[38] As in the case of Mexicans, class position apparently moderated the otherwise rabid antimiscegenation sentiment directed at the Chinese in the state.

There is evidence that some Americans were sympathetic toward the first Chinese immigrants, especially those of the merchant class, and perhaps—as long as their numbers were small—even welcomed them. This reception quickly changed, however, as the Chinese increasingly ruffled the cultural sensibilities and sexual anxieties of the white population.[39] Most public expressions of anti-Chinese hostility centered on their cultural differences and on the fact that the Chinese were unambiguously nonwhite. Pointed testimony to this effect is captured in the minority report to the 1877 Joint Special Committee of Congress on Chinese immigration. Therein, Senator Oliver P. Morton of Indiana, chair of the committee, summarily acknowledges that "if the Chinese in California were white people, being all other respects what they are, I do not believe that the complaints and warfare made against them would have existed to any considerable extent. Their difference in color, dress, manners, and religion have, in my judgment, more to do with this hostility than their alleged vices or any actual injury to the white people of California."[40]

THE SUBORDINATE POLITICAL STATUS OF THE CHINESE IN ANGLO CALIFORNIA

From the standpoint of popular opinion, the Chinese were clearly perceived as nonwhite, a fact that was reinforced by their close association in European-American consciousness with blacks. The official political status of Chinese immigrants in California was formally adjudicated in 1854, when the case of *People v. Hall* legally restricted the Chinese to the same second-class status of blacks and Indians; they too were officially deemed nonwhite and, therefore, ineligible for citizenship rights.

This case turned on the question of whether or not three Chinese witnesses would be allowed to testify against three white men (one of whom was George W. Hall) accused of murdering a Chinese man named Ling Sing. The California Supreme Court overturned Hall's murder conviction, ruling that the testimony of Chinese witnesses was inadmissible because state law stipulated that "no black or mulatto person, or Indian, shall be permitted to give evidence in favor of, or against, any white person."

Writing for the majority, Justice Charles J. Murray stated that "the words, Indian, Negro, Black and White," were generic racial terms that embraced all nonwhites and as such prohibited Chinese immigrants "from being witnesses against whites." In support of the decision, Justice Murray argued that the legislative prohibition against blacks and Indians entering testimony had "adopted the most comprehensive terms to embrace every known class or shade of color, as the apparent design was to protect the white person from the influence of all testimony other than that of persons of the same caste. The use of these terms must, by every sound rule of construction, exclude every one who is not of white blood."[41] Thus, this case juridically decreed that the Chinese were unambiguously nonwhite and therefore not entitled to testify against white citizens in the state.[42]

The court's decision was made on the basis of some curious anthropological reasoning. In his majority decision, Justice Murray argued that the Chinese should be prohibited from entering testimony because they were ancestrally related to the California Indians. Murray made special note that "the name Indian, from the time of Columbus to the present day, has been used to designate, not alone the North American, but the whole of the Mongolian race, and that the name, though first applied probably through mistake, was afterwards continued as appropriate on account of the supposed common origin."[43] Moreover, "The similarity of the skull and pelvis, and the general configuration of the two races; the remarkable resemblance in eyes, beard, hair, and other peculiarities, together, with the contiguity of the two Continents, might well have led to the belief that this country was first peopled by the Asiatics, and that the difference between the different tribes and the parent stock was such as would necessarily arise from the circumstances of climate, pursuits, and other physical causes."[44]

People v. Hall had far-reaching implications. Murray's closing arguments show that the court was fully aware of its impact:

> We have carefully considered all the consequences resulting from a different construction and are satisfied that, even in a doubtful case, we would be impelled to this decision on grounds of public policy.
>
> The same rule that would admit them to testify, would admit them to all the equal rights of citizenship, and we might soon see them at the polls, in the jury box, upon the bench and in our legislative halls.
>
> This is not a speculation which exists in the excited and overheated imagination of the patriot and statesman, but it is an actual and present danger ...[45]

The effects of the *People v. Hall* decision were catastrophic for the Chinese. After the case, they were subjected to numerous legislative initiatives that specifically targeted them on a racial basis. In 1863 and 1864, for example, the California State Legislature included the Chinese in a law prohibiting the entry of "non-whites" into public schools. Reorganization of the state's educational laws in 1870, which formally institutionalized a policy of segregating white and nonwhite students into separate schools, also mandated the segregation of the Chinese. This law remained in effect for the Chinese until 1929, when the revised School Code repealed the sections that had racially segregated both Chinese and Japanese children.[46] This was eight years after such segregation was rescinded for Indians and thirty-one years after blacks were no longer required to attend segregated public schools.

It was not until 1872 that the 1854 *People v. Hall* case was rescinded with the passage of the Federal Civil Rights Act.[47] In the period during which it was legally in effect, Chinese immigrants were frequently targeted by discriminatory legislation and by unprincipled white men who committed crimes against them with impunity. Denied the basic right to have recourse to the state apparatus on their own behalf, Chinese immigrants in California were relegated to a second-class status.

THE CLASS BASIS OF ANTI-CHINESE SENTIMENT IN CALIFORNIA

Despite the animosity and political marginalization that the Chinese experienced in California, they nonetheless made valiant efforts to survive and prosper in the face of daunting odds. In so doing, they managed to secure a modest foothold in the self-employment sector of the new economy, where their entry was greeted with widespread hostility from whites of this class.

Although anti-Chinese sentiment was widespread in California, it was powerfully mediated by short- and long-term class interests of the white population. Although privately many capitalists held the Chinese in contempt, they were not oblivious to the advantages of their use as a tractable and cheap labor force. Such material interests often outweighed or counterbalanced the private racism that these entrepreneurs harbored.

White workers who were drawn into competition with the Chinese, however, had little reason to mitigate their racial and cultural antipathies. Instead, they routinely attempted to create, extend, or preserve their social position against the perceived threat that the Chinese posed to their superordinate status in the state. White supremacist sentiments were readily inflamed and provided ample justification for driving the Chinese out of sectors of the economy where they competed with skilled white workers. (The racial animosity exhibited by the white working class has been well documented by numerous scholars of the anti-Chinese movement and will be discussed briefly below.)[48] Small-scale, independent businessmen (petit commodity producers) such as self-employed laundrymen and independent miners were also drawn into competition with the Chinese and responded similarly, seeking to drive the Chinese from areas of the economy in which they were making inroads and to undermine the competitive threat they posed through the use of racially discriminatory legislation.[49]

During the initial period of their settlement in California, mining served as the principal sector of the economy in which the Chinese secured a livelihood. Initially arriving in small numbers during the Gold Rush, by 1855 two-thirds of the 24,000 Chinese in the United States, having fulfilled the terms of their indenture, worked placer mining claims as independent prospectors or in small group partnerships.[50] The Chinese population engaged in mining climbed rapidly to nearly 35,000 in 1860, when over 70 percent of all gainfully employed Chinese male adults were placer miners.[51]

Opportunities in mining, however, were finite, and success or failure of the Chinese in this endeavor structured other employment opportunities. According to Sucheng Chan, the presence or absence of mining in a particular area affected what other occupations the Chinese successfully entered. She has shown that there was an inverse relationship between the percentage of the Chinese population in the mining industry and the percentage earning a more menial living. "When mining was available, a few became laborers and providers of personal services, but as mining waned from the 1860s onward, an increasing number of Chinese became laundrymen, laborers, servants, and cooks. When mining was not available, the first Chinese to enter those areas had to take menial jobs from the beginning."[52] Consequently, as the Chinese turned away from mining, "the more enterprising ones became manufacturers or merchants in the urban areas and truck gardeners in the rural and suburban areas, while the less fortunate everywhere became laborers, cooks, and servants."[53]

Opposition to Chinese immigrants in California, however, developed as soon as they came into direct economic competition with the white population. The first expressions of such anti-Chinese sentiment came from independent white miners in the mining districts of northern California, who quickly concluded, despite evidence to the contrary, that Chinese miners were primarily gang laborers unfairly competing with the white "producing class." European-American miners claimed that the Chinese drained wealth from the country by sending part of their earnings to China, encouraged "monopolies" in the state, posed a serious moral threat to the entire white population, and, finally, threatened the tranquility of the mining districts.[54]

This early opposition to the Chinese was spearheaded by self-employed, independent white miners. It was largely through their efforts that many Chinese placer miners eventually were driven from the mines.[55] In addition to committing brutal acts of violence against the Chinese, these miners successfully lobbied for the passage of "foreign miners" tax in 1852. This legislation required non-citizens to secure a license in order to mine in California. While these laws also affected "foreign miners" from Alexico, Peru, Chile, Australia, and the Pacific Islands, the Chinese were the primary targets of this social closure.

In May 1852, the California State legislature enacted the first foreign miners' tax which required a monthly payment of three dollars from every foreign miner who did not desire to become a citizen. (Since the Chinese were deemed nonwhite, they were ineligible for citizenship.) This blatant discrimination remained in effect until it was overturned by the federal Civil Rights Act of 1870.[56] While it was in effect, however, it garnered the-state over $100,000 in annual fees and through the 1860s accounted for a large segment of the state's revenues.[57]

Clearly delineated class lines emerged around the "Chinese question" in the mining district. Anglo slaveholders, monopolists, and "foreign task masters" (such as Mexican patrons and rancheros who profited from the use of unfree labor in the mines) were drawn into competition with white independent miners in the region, who, as we have seen, considered themselves the embodiment of Andrew Jackson's "producer class." The class nature of this racial antagonism is clearly captured in the various resolutions put forth by the white miners who opposed both the Chinese and the white "monopolist" interests aligned with them. One such pronouncement stated: "It is the duty of miners to take the matter into their own hands [and] erect such barriers as shall be sufficient to check this Asiatic inundation.... The Capitalists ... who are encouraging or engaged in the importation of these burlesques on humanity would crown their ships with the long tailed, horned and cloven-hoofed inhabitants of the infernal regions [if they could make a profit on it]."[58]

Widespread hostility along with diminished opportunities in placer mining effectively drove many of these Chinese immigrants from the mining districts and into the new capitalist labor market. The railroad industry, in desperate need of labor at the time, immediately benefitted from the sudden availability of "surplus" Chinese labor. From 1866 to 1869 the Central Pacific Railroad became the employer of over ten thousand Chinese, who dug the Sierra tunnel and extended the railroad across the deserts of Nevada and Utah.[59]

There were at least three advantages that large-scale employers like the Central Pacific saw to using Chinese laborers. First, they were readily available. The prohibition against slavery, the relatively small free Negro, Indian, and Mexican populations in the state, and the opportunities for self-employment of white immigrants made labor a scarce commodity in California. From the viewpoint of American capitalists, the Chinese were ideal in that they could be employed for a short period and then conveniently sent back to China.

Second, the Chinese were also a source of *cheap* labor. Alexander Saxton has estimated that the Central Pacific Railroad hired unskilled Chinese laborers at approximately two-thirds the cost of unskilled white laborers. Although both white and Chinese workers received the same monthly wage of thirty dollars in 1865, the railroad had to provide room and board for its white employees, whereas Chinese laborers were housed and fed by their contractors.[60]

Third, American employers found the Chinese more reliable and tractable than other laborers. The contract labor system made them extremely exploitable and compliant, and employers of Chinese labor in California readily attested to the system's advantages. In testimony before the Joint Senate Committee on Chinese Immigration in 1876, for example, Charles Crocker of the Central Pacific Railroad acknowledged that he preferred Chinese labor to white because of their "greater reliability." He also admired the Chinese laborers' "steadiness, and their aptitude and capacity for hard work." Moreover, Crocker argued:

> I think that the presence of Chinese as laborers among us goes very far toward the material interest of the country.... I believe that the effects of Chinese labor upon the white labor has an elevating instead of degrading tendency.... I believe, today, if the Chinese labor was driven out of this State ... there are 75,000 white laborers who would have to come down from the elevated classes of laborers they are now engaged in and take the place of these Chinamen, and therefore it would degrade white labor instead of elevating it.[61]

Farmers struggling to develop capitalist agriculture at the time also appreciated the role that a cheap and tractable labor force afforded them. William Hollister, the aforementioned agriculturalist from Santa Barbara, stated in 1876 that there was "common sentiment and feeling in favor of the Chinamen" among agriculturalists in the state. "They are our last resort," Hollister told the committee, "They are the only thing that the farmer can rely upon at all."

At a meeting of the California Fruit Growers' Association at the turn of the century, one farmer argued that Chinese labor was indispensable to California agriculture because the Chinese were so "well adapted to that particular form of labor to which so many white men object. They are patient, plodding and uncomplaining in the performance of the most menial service." Another member of the association added that one distinct advantage to the use of "the short-legged, short-backed Asiatic" was his ability to tolerate even the most adverse working conditions. "He works in every sun and clime, and as far as the Chinese are concerned they faithfully perform their contract and keep their promise, whether the eye of the employer is on them or not." According to this agriculturalist, the need for Chinese labor in California was not merely "a question of cheap labor, but of reliable labor."[62]

THE CLASS NATURE OF ANTI-CHINESE SENTIMENT IN RURAL CALIFORNIA

After the decline in mining and the completion of the transcontinental railroad in 1869, Chinese laborers began to enter the nascent truck and fruit farm industry in California as seasonal laborers. By 1870 they accounted for one-tenth of all agricultural laborers, and by 1880 they had become the backbone of the industry, one-third of the total farm-labor force in California. They also were used throughout the state in land reclamation and irrigation projects.[63]

By 1880, a few Chinese immigrants had successfully begun small farming ventures as owner-operators and tenants. Sucheng Chan's splendid study of the Chinese in California agriculture comprehensively documents the extent to which the Chinese entered this sector of the new economy. In areas where white farmers had not already preceded them, Chinese truck gardeners were able to capture the Chinese market as early as the 1860s and, in the northern mining region, even part of the non-Chinese market.[64]

Despite these modest advances and occasional success stories, only limited opportunities existed for Chinese farmers in the state's agricultural districts. In the Sacramento–San Joaquin delta, for example, most Chinese farmers were cash tenants who grew potatoes in the backswamps. Only a few Chinese sharecropped. In contrast, white farmers were overwhelmingly owner-operators who farmed grain, hay, vegetables, fruit, beans, and livestock. Chan has shown that most of the white farmers originally from New England and the Middle Atlantic states were owner-operators who eventually dominated grain farming; other white owner-operators, such as Northern European immigrants, grew grain but also engaged in diversified farming.[65]

Assessing the nature of the class forces that structured the lives of the Chinese in rural California, Chan stresses that they differed significantly from those in urban centers such as San Francisco. In rural California, the Chinese "ruling elite" were often agents for urban-based firms who helped distribute imported goods to Chinese clients. More importantly, they primarily served as intermediaries, or as Chan refers to them, as "compradors," who facilitated the interaction between Chinese and white employers and Chinese laborers in farming and construction projects. They occupied a contradictory class location in that they were both benefactors and exploiters of the Chinese workers bound to them through the contract labor system. "Since it was difficult for Chinese workers to survive without the knowledge and contacts that the tenant farmers, rural merchants, and labor contractors possessed, the latter were in a position to exploit as well as aid the former. At the same time, since white landowners found their services so convenient, these members of the rural Chinese elite were also in a position to strike relatively good bargains in land leasing and other business transactions."[66]

In this context, it would be a mistake to see the Chinese intermediary class of tenant farmers, labor contractors, and merchants as merely exploiters of less fortunate Chinese laborers. As a class of "middlemen," they also served as the first line of defense for their compatriots against the abuses of American employers. This was particularly true in instances where bargaining favorably on behalf of the laborers, as labor contractors often did, also benefited these intermediaries monetarily. As Chan has perceptively noted, in their leadership they tended to "facilitate rather than dominate agricultural production," and consequently they cannot assume the full blame for the mistreatment that befell many Chinese laborers in that sector of the economy.[67]

In this regard, Chan argues that, although

> there seemed to be no rigid class barriers among different groups in the Chinese population in rural California—movement in and out of various occupations being quite fluid—such divisions become more apparent by the turn of the century as upward mobility became more difficult to achieve. On the other hand, it is important to realize that whatever class divisions that might have existed were mitigated by mutual dependence, kinship and village ties, and ethnic solidarity in the face of hostility from society at large.[68]

Given these differences in regional class actors, hostility toward the Chinese in rural California crystallized along different class lines than in urban centers such as San Francisco where white, working-class men swelled the ranks of anti-Chinese groups. According to Chan, hostility to the Chinese in rural California was "led either by men espousing white supremacist values or by hoodlums out to enjoy themselves by tormenting 'Chinamen.'"[69] Moreover, the main rural class—white farmers—with the potential to rally forcefully against the Chinese saw them as tools of "land monopolists" and turned their hostility toward the latter rather than scapegoating the Chinese. White farm workers, the other important class protagonist in rural California, were often characterized as tramps, drunkards, and shiftless individuals and thus generally perceived by Californians as not particularly organizable.[70]

In the absence of concerted class opposition by the rural white population, anti-Chinese sentiment was spearheaded by white supremacist organizations such as the Order of Caucasians (also known as the Caucasian League), who agitated against the Chinese in Truckee, Red Bluff, and Marysville in 1376.[71] Opposition to the Chinese also occurred in Chico and in Sacramento, where in 1877 one group threatened local farmers with the following letter: "Notice is heare given to all men who owns lands on the Sacramento River is heare ordered to dispense with Chinese labour or suffer sutch consiquinces as may follow within tenn days. We have heaved and puked over Chinese imposition long a nuff. Good-by John Long Taile."[72]

In April 1882 another organization, carrying the name "American and European Labor Association," formed in Colusa County in reaction to Chinese workers demanding wages equal to those paid white Americans. The new organization sought to replace these Chinese workers with young women imported from Europe and the East Coast and also called upon the local white population to patronize only businesses that employed white labor.[73] It was common practice at the time to pay white farm laborers one-and-a-half times the wages paid Chinese laborers.[74]

Anti-Chinese sentiment in rural California developed, as it did elsewhere in the state, against the backdrop of an emergent class conflict within the white population between white capitalist interests and white immigrants, who were increasingly being proletarianized and placed into competition with nonwhite labor. One anti-Chinese proponent writing in the *Pacific Rural Press* in April 1886 vividly expressed the popular belief among white farmers that the Chinese were the hapless pawns of capitalist and other monopolists attempting to degrade the status of white labor. He railed against both the Chinese and their employers in these terms:

> A class supporting and degrading civilization in China has chained with the shackles of a relentless superstition and unresisting subservency an inbred race of miserable slaves, who are satisfied with a miserable fare the merest pittance can procure. What more natural than that the services of such a race is desirable by men disposed to regard labor as a mere article or commodity to be purchased low that the proceeds resulting, may, in competition with his fellows, bring him greater profit?...
>
> The Chinese slave invasion of our State has been imposed upon us against our constant expostulation as a people. It has been encouraged only by scheming

> companies and equally selfish individuals.... This slave system must not only stop its invasion, but it must leave our shores.[75]

In short, the racialization of the Chinese in rural California often reflected the way class lines were being forged and contested among the white population in these regions of the state. The antimonopolist sentiments of white small farmers provided an important basis of their bitter opposition to Chinese laborers and their opposition to the commercial interests utilizing them.

*****

THE STATUS OF CHINESE WOMEN IN URBAN CALIFORNIA

The final sector of the urban economy in which the Chinese successfully carved a niche and evoked the ire of European Americans was the vice industry. By 1860 over 10 percent of the Chinese employed in San Francisco were males working in gambling, the sale of opium, or prostitution. Another 23.4 percent of the city's Chinese, all of whom were female, worked as prostitutes. "Thus, fully one-third of the gainfully employed Chinese in the city were engaged in providing recreational vice—an unfortunate fact which gave rise to strong negative images of the Chinese."[76]

Sociologist Lucie Cheng Hirata's important research on Chinese immigrant women in nineteenth-century California provides us with the most detailed and sympathetic analysis of their experience to date. Hirata situates Chinese female prostitution within the context of the patriarchal gender relations of Confucian China and the "semifeudal" system that was carried over into the Chinese immigrant experience in California. As other scholars have also noted, the relegation of Chinese women into prostitution was facilitated by their utterly subordinate status in patriarchal Chinese society. A Chinese woman was obligated to serve her father during childhood, her husband during adulthood, and her sons during widowhood. Her marriage was arranged by parents and clan elders and the betrothed typically met for the first time on their wedding day. The wife subsequently moved into her husband's family home, where she was, in turn, obliged to serve her mother-in-law. Not surprisingly, Chinese women's labor was less valued than men's; her primary contribution was the bearing of children, especially male children.[77]

In this context, female prostitution was an important and acceptable recourse to a family facing impoverishment.[78] According to Hirata, prostitution relieved the family of having to "provide for the girl's upkeep, and her sale or part of her earnings could help support the family."[79] Consequently, "the family, not the girl, arranged for sale. Girls often accepted their sale, however reluctantly, out of filial loyalty, and most of them were not in a position to oppose their families' decision. In addition, the sheltered and secluded lives that women were forced to live made them particularly vulnerable to manipulation, and many were tricked or lured into prostitution.[80]

Some of the first Chinese women who came to California in the gold rush period were self-employed, "free-agent" prostitutes who through various means had attained some individual agency. (One such woman, one Ah-Choi, arrived in late 1848 or early 1849 and within two years had accumulated enough money in prostitution to own a brothel. Most of her customers were reportedly non-Chinese men.[81] The majority of Chinese prostitutes, however, were pressed into service by the Chinese secret societies, or *tongs*, that organized this lucrative operation in the state. Hip-Yee Tong appears to have been the main importer of Chinese women for prostitution during the last half of the nineteenth century. One source estimates that this *tong* alone imported six thousand Chinese women between 1852 and 1873 and netted an estimated $200,000.[82] Their operation afforded a lucrative profit for Chinese men who acted as procurers, importers, brothel owners, and highbinders, and also proved profitable for white policemen who accepted money for keeping them from being arrested and white property owners in Chinatown who leased the buildings where these businesses operated.[83]

The highly organized nature of this operation, plus the lack of alternative employment opportunities, facilitated the widespread relegation of most Chinese immigrant women into prostitution. In 1852 there were only seven women out of a total of 11,794 Chinese immigrants in California. Two of these women were independent prostitutes and two others were thought to be working for Ah-Choi in San Francisco.[84] Hirata has documented that by 1860 there were 654 Chinese prostitutes enumerated on the San Francisco census: this represented 85 percent of the total Chinese female population. The other women listed on the census were employed as laundresses, gardeners, laborers, shopkeepers, fisherwomen, or clerks. Ten years later, the number of Chinese women in that city working as prostitutes had doubled, to 1,426, but had dropped proportionally to 71 percent of the total employed female population. Finally, in 1880 the total number of Chinese prostitutes had declined to only 435 and represented only 21 percent of Chinese women in the city. These figures indicate that the "heyday of Chinese prostitution in San Francisco was around 1870, and its precipitous decline occurred just before 1880."[85]

Chinese female prostitutes were procured in three ways: deception and kidnapping, contractual agreements, and sale. The following account is a poignant example of how Chinese women could be lured into prostitution through false promises:

> I was nineteen when this man came to my mother and said that in America there was a great deal of gold. Even if I just peeled potatoes there, he told my mother I would earn seven or eight dollars a day, and if I was willing to do any work at all I would earns lots of money ... so my mother was glad to have me go with him as his wife.... When we first landed in San

> Francisco, we lived in a hotel in Chinatown, a nice place, but one day, after I had been there for about two weeks, a woman came to see me. She was young, very pretty, and all dressed in silk. She told me that I was not really Hucy Yow's wife, but that she had asked him to buy her a slave, that I belonged to her, and must go with her, but she would treat me well, and I could buy back my freedom, if I was willing to please.... I did not believe her.... So when Hucy Yow came I asked him why that woman had come and what she meant by all that lying. But he said that it was true; that he was not my husband, he did not care about me, and that this was something that happened all the time. Everybody did this, he said, and why be so shocked that I was to be a prostitute instead of a married woman.[86]

In the case of contractual agreements, women typically were offered free passage to America and an advance of over $400 in return for a promise of four and a half years of service. Each woman was required to work a minimum of 320 days a year and faced an extension of up to one additional year if she failed to meet this obligation.[87]

An example of the process whereby Chinese women were sold into prostitution is found in an 1870s account from San Francisco, which came to light when the slave girl's owner was arrested for striking her.

> I have been in this country about nine years. I was brought here from China by an old woman.... She bought me in China for something over $20. I stayed with her for about a month.... I was bought by Dr. Li-Po-Tai for something from $20 to $40.... I lived with the Doctor for a short time only, his wife saying I was of no account. Li-Po-Tai owed a man named Loo Fook some money, and I was given to Loo Fook in part payment of that debt.... I was afterward transferred to one Lee Choy, who said he intended to make a courtesan of me. I was then between eleven and twelve years old. One night I went with Lee Choy, and we met a man who say I was young, and said I was good looking, and he wanted to know if I was for sale.... I was finally sold to him for about $100.... I lived with him about three or four years, and he sold me to Lee Chein Kay for $160. I lived with him both as servant and wife.... I have lived at different wash-houses during the last four months, acting as servant for the men there.... I have received no pay for my labor in the wash-houses, and, worse than that, have been whipped a number of time.[88]

Other Chinese women were also routinely abused and beaten; in addition, they were susceptible to syphilis and gonorrhea and always in danger of being killed by their customers or owners. They often anesthetized themselves from their daily abuse and degradation by smoking opium; some committed suicide by taking an overdose of drugs or drowning themselves.[89] Adding insult to injury, the remains of these women were rarely sent back to China for burial (as was the common practice for Chinese men who died in the United States). According to Hirata, "few cared about the remains of these women. The [San Francisco] *Alta* reported in 1870 that the bodies of Chinese women were discarded and left in the streets of Chinatown."[90]

Those who survived these physical abuses were also subjected to legal harassment from white authorities. Despite the bribes and other extralegal measures used to protect this operation, Chinese female prostitutes were specifically targeted with legislation designed to curtail public "vice." Between 1866 and 1905 at least eight California laws were passed designed to restrict the importation of Chinese women for prostitution or to suppress the Chinese brothel business. "Although white prostitution was equally if not more prevalent, these were additional and specific laws directed only against the Chinese. Chinese prostitutes, if caught, were sentenced to a fine of $25 to $50 and a jail term of at least five days."[91] It appears that Chinese women in this industry were perceived as constituting a more "damning influence" on white men than were white female prostitutes.

Such sentiment also led the California state legislature in March 1870 to enact an "anti-prostitution" measure that required any Chinese or Japanese woman entering the United States to present satisfactory evidence that she had "voluntarily" immigrated and was "a person of correct habits and good moral character." Proof to this effect was necessary to obtain a permit authorizing immigration from the Commissioner of Immigration.[92]

One cannot avoid concluding that these women were taken advantage of by both Chinese and white men as well as by a few Chinese women who managed brothels and served as intermediaries in the procurement process. Chinese male entrepreneurs, who may have been merchants or associated with various *tongs*, profited handsomely from this lucrative operation. Most of the prostitutes procured through contracts, calling for an initial $530 capital outlay, earned an estimated $850 a year, or $3,404 for the four years of servitude. (This is based on earning an average of 38 cents per customer and seven customers per day.) Since their upkeep was less than $100 per year (which included two or three meals per day and a place to sleep), profits from this type of prostitution were very high.[93]

Those who came voluntarily or were lured into prostitution proved even more profitable. In a case discussed by Hirata, one female procurer obtained the consent of the mother of one women to take her to America for a mere $98. Upon arrival, the woman was immediately sold for $1,950. After working two years for her new owner and reportedly earning no less than $290 per month, she was resold for $2,100. The gross income that this brothel owner received from her labor during these two years was in excess of $5,500. This does not include the profit from the sewing and other forms of work that this woman was assigned to do in the brothel during the day.[94]

CONCLUSION

Who ultimately orchestrated and benefited from the calamity that befell Chinese immigrants in nineteenth-century California? What was the relative role of white capital and white labor in structuring the placement of the Chinese in the urban economy and promoting the racialization of the Chinese in California? Did capitalists divide the working class along racial lines to maximize profits and thwart class opposition? Or did segments of the white working class define their class interests along narrow racial lines so as to exclude and vilify their Chinese counterparts?

In the final analysis, the answers to these questions lie partly in the tenuous balance of power between white capital and labor in the state—one which shifted with fluctuations in the business cycle, growing competition, and the mechanization of industry. The ability of these class actors to realize their narrowly defined interests helped structure the integration or exclusion of the Chinese in the urban labor market. Privileged white workers clearly turned their hostility toward the Chinese underclass rather than joining with them in a common struggle against capitalism or its agents. As Paul Ong has perceptively concluded, "While capitalists such as those in the woolen industry attempted to 'divide and conquer' workers, the economy provided few such opportunities. The most active agents in dividing labor were the workers themselves ... [who] often succeeded in protecting a desirable niche of the labor market from outsiders, creating monopolies which maintained high wages. Racism, along with trade unions and nativism, became the bases for organizing such a group—in this case white labor."[95]

At its most fundamental level, this process of exclusion represents the utilization of social closures by white workers who attempted to limit Chinese access to privileged sectors of the new capitalist labor market. Their racial animosity toward the Chinese reflected both the general acceptance of white supremacist sentiments among white Californians and also reflected the emerging class tensions within white society.

However, at the moment when capitalism created a common labor market and the basis for collective class organization, the white working class responded by narrowly defining their interests solely as white workers—rather than in more inclusive class terms. Although Chinese and white workers may have shared some underlying class interests, these interests never crystallized in common opposition to capitalist interests. Instead, white craftsmen and other skilled workers consistently sought to maintain their privileged racial status over the Chinese and, in the process, reaffirmed the centrality of race as the primary organizing principle of nineteenth-century Anglo California. [...]

NOTES

1. Stuart Creighton Miller, *Unwelcome Immigrant: The American Image of the Chinese, 1785–1885* (Berkeley and Los Angeles: University of California Press, 1969), p. 146.
2. For discussions of factors which led to Chinese immigration see: US Congress, Joint Special Committee to Investigate Chinese Immigration, *Report of the Joint Special Committee to Investigate Chinese Immigration*, Report No. 689, 44th Cong., 2d sess., 1876 (Washington: Government Printing Office, 1877); Mary Roberts Coolidge, *Chinese Immigration* (New York: Henry Holt and Company, 1909).
3. For discussions of this "credit-ticket" system, see Gunther Barth, *Bitter Strength: A History of the Chinese in the United States, 1850–1870* (Cambridge: Harvard University Press, 1964), pp. 51, 67–68, 77–80; Coolidge, *Chinese Immigration*, pp. 48–49; Thomas Chinn, ed., *A History of the Chinese in California* (San Francisco: Chinese Historical Society of America, 1969), p. 15; Stanford M. Lyman, "Strangers in the City: The Chinese on the Urban Frontier," in Stanford M. Lyman, *The Asian in the West* (Reno: University of Nevada System, Western Studies Center, Desert Research Institute, 1970), p. 12; Stanford M. Lyman, "Contrasts in the Community Organization of Chinese and Japanese in North America," in Lyman, *The Asian in the West*, p. 60.
4. Alexander Saxton, "Race and the House of Labor," in Gary B. Nash and Richard Weiss, eds., *The Great Fear: Race in the Minds of White America* (New York: Holt, Rinehart and Winston, 1970), p. 108.
5. Roger Daniels, *Asian America: Chinese and Japanese in the United States since 1850* (Seattle: University of Washington Press, 1988), pp. 14–15.
6. Stanford Lyman, *Chinese Americans* (New York: Random House, 1974), pp. 29–30.
7. Sucheng Chan, *This Bitter-Sweet Soil: The Chinese in California Agriculture, 1860–1910* (Berkeley and Los Angeles: University of California Press, 1986), p. 404.
8. Ibid.
9. Ronald Takaki, *Strangers from a Different Shore: A History of Asian Americans* (Boston: Little, Brown, 1989), p. 79.
10. Ibid.
11. Daniels, *Asian America*, p. 69.
12. Takaki, *Strangers from a Different Shore*, p. 119.
13. Ibid. See also the extended discussion of the Chinese immigrants' social organizations in the United States in Lyman, *Chinese Americans*, chap. 3; and Stanford M. Lyman, *Chinatown and Little Tokyo: Power, Conflict, and Community among Chinese and Japanese Immigrants in America* (Millwood, NY: Associated Faculty Press, 1986), chap. 3; Daniels, *Asian America*, passim.
14. Takaki, *Strangers from a Different Shore*, p. 119.
15. Daniels, *Asian America*, p. 4.
16. Lyman, *Chinese Americans*, p. 29.
17. Chan, *Bitter-Sweet Soil*, p. 369.
18. For examples of the use of these social-cultural differences as a basis of anti-Chinese sentiment see California State Senate, Special Committee on Chinese Immigration, *Chinese Immigration: Its Social, Moral, and Political Effect: Report to the California State Senate of its Special Committee on Chinese Immigration* (Sacramento: State Printing Office, 1878); Samuel Gompers and Herman Gutstadt, *Meat vs. Rice:*

American Manhood against Asiatic Coolieism, Which Shall Survive? (Reprint, San Francisco: Asiatic Exclusion League, 1908).
19. Erasmus Doolittle, *Sketches, by a Traveller* (Boston, 1830), pp. 259–60, as cited by Miller, *Unwelcome Immigrant*, p. 29.
20. Miller, *Unwelcome Immigrant*, p. 36.
21. Ibid., p. 27.
22. Ibid., pp. 27–28.
23. Takaki, *Strangers from a Different Shore*, p. 107.
24. Alexander Saxton, *The Indispensable Enemy: Labor and the Anti-Chinese Movement in California* (Berkeley and Los Angeles: University of California Press, 1971), pp. 19, 20ff; Saxton, "Race," p. 115. Stuart Creighton Miller has convincingly argued that anti-Chinese sentiment actually preceded the arrival of the Chinese immigrant to California. He notes that this animosity was propagated by American traders, travelers, missionaries, and newspapermen who traveled to China prior to 1849. See his *Unwelcome Immigrant*, chaps. 1–6.
25. Takaki, *Strangers from a Different Shore*, pp. 80–81.
26. Ibid., p. 101.
27. Dan Cauldwell, "The Negroization of the Chinese Stereotype in California," *Southern California Historical Quarterly* 1 (June 1971): 126–27.
28. Diane Mei Lin Mark and Ginger Chin, *A Place Called Chinese America* (Dubuque, Iowa: Kendall/Hunt Publishing Company, 1982), p. 51.
29. *New York Tribune*, September 29, 1854, as cited by Miller, *Unwelcome Immigrant*, p. 70.
30. S. V. Blakeslee, "Address of Rev. S.V. Blakeslee: Delivered before the General Association of Congregational Churches of California, held in Sacramento from the 9th to the 13th of October, 1887," appended to California State Senate, Special Committee on Chinese Immigration, *Chinese Immigration*, pp. 246–47. Also see Blakeslee's testimony in US Senate, *Report to Investigate Chinese Immigration*, pp. 1028–43.
31. Chester H. Rowell, "Chinese and Japanese Immigrants—A Comparison," *Annals of the American Academy of Political and Social Science* 2 (September 1909): 7.
32. San Francisco Board of Supervisors, Ordinance No. 939, July 29, 1870, as reprinted in Cheng-Tsu Wu, ed., *"Chink!": A Documentary History of Anti-Chinese Prejudice in America* (New York: World Publishing, 1972), pp. 65–66; Daniels, *Asian America*, p. 39.
33. James D. Richardson, comp., *Messages and Papers of the Presidents*, 7:288, as cited by Daniels, *Asian America*, p. 44.
34. *New York Tribune*, September 29, 1854, as cited by Miller, *Unwelcome Immigrant*, p. 169.
35. Miller, *Unwelcome Immigrant*, pp. 184–85.
36. Ibid., pp. 242ff.
37. Megumi Dick Osumi, "Asians and California's Anti-Miscegenation Laws," in Nobuya Tsuchida, ed., *Asian and Pacific American Experiences: Women's Perspectives* (Minneapolis: Asian/Pacific American Learning and Resource Center, 1982), p. 2.
38. Chan, *Bitter-Sweet Soil*, p. 395; Lucie Cheng Hirata, "Free, Indentured, Enslaved: Chinese Prostitutes in Nineteenth-Century America," *Signs: Journal of Women in Culture and Society* 5, no. 1 (1979): 19.
39. See, for example, Coolidge, *Chinese Immigration*.
40. US Congress, Senate, Misc. Document 20, 45th Cong., 2nd sess., 1879, p. 4, as cited by Daniels, *Asian America*, pp. 53-54.
41. *People v. Hall*, 4 Cal. 399 (1854), as reprinted in Robert F. Heizer and Alan F. Almquist, *The Other Californians: Prejudice and Discrimination under Spain, Mexico, and the United States to 1920* (Berkeley and Los Angeles: University of California Press), pp. 231–32.
42. Takaki, *Strangers from a Different Shore*, p. 102.
43. *People v. Hall*, in Heizer and Almquist, *Other Californians*, p. 231.
44. Ibid.
45. Ibid., p. 233.
46. Lucille Eaves, *A History of California Labor Legislation* (Berkeley: The University Press, 1910), p. 121; Stanford Lyman, "The Significance of Asians in American Society," in Lyman, *The Asian in the West*, p. 7; Heizer and Almquist, *Other Californians*, p. 176; Wu, *"Chink!"* p. 12.
47. Coolidge, *Chinese Immigration*, p. 76; Walton Bean, *California: An Interpretive History*, 2d ed. (New York: McGraw-Hill, 1973), p. 165.
48. See Coolidge, Saxton, Ringer, Barth, etc.
49. In *This Bitter-Sweet Soil*, historian Sucheng Chan argues convincingly that the development of Chinese occupational stratification in nineteenth-century California unfolded in four stages: "the initial period from 1850 to 1865, when the Chinese worked mainly as miners and traders; a period of growth and development from 1865 to the late 1870s, when they branched into agriculture, light manufacturing, and common labor; a period of consolidation from the late 1870s to the late 1880s, when they competed successfully with others in a wide variety of occupations; and a period of decline from the late 1880s to the turn of the century, when they were forced to abandon many occupations" (p. 52).
50. Takaki, *Strangers from a Different Shore*, p. 82.
51. Chan, *Bitter-Sweet Soil*, p. 56.
52. Ibid., pp. 52, 56.
53. Ibid., p. 72.
54. Leonard Pitt, "The Beginnings of Nativism in California," *Pacific Historical Review* 1 (February 1961): 36; Rodman W. Paul, "The Origin of the Chinese Issue in California," *Mississippi Valley Historical Review* 2 (September 1938): 181–96; Eaves, California Labor, pp. 110–13.
55. Pitt, "Nativism," p. 38; Ping Chiu, *Chinese Labor in California, 1850–1880: An Economic Study* (Madison: State Historical Society of Wisconsin, 1963), pp. 54–55; Barth, *Bitter Strength*, p. 133; Victor G. Nee and Brett de Bary Nee, *Longtime Californ': A Documentary Study of an American Chinatown* (New York: Pantheon, 1973), p. 34.
56. Takaki, *Strangers from a Different Shore*, p. 82.

57. Daniels, *Asian America*, p. 33; Takaki, *Strangers from a Different Shore*, p. 82.
58. Daniels, *Asian America*, p. 34.
59. US Senate, *Report to Investigate Chinese Immigration*, pp. 669, 671; Chiu, *Chinese Labor in California*, pp. 9, 46; Saxton, *Indispensable Enemy*, p. 4.
60. Saxton, *Indispensable Enemy*, p. 63; Alexander Saxton, "Race and the House of Labor," p. 108; Chiu, *Chinese Labor in California*, pp. 46–47; Daniels, *Asian America*, p. 19.
61. US Senate, *Report to Investigate Chinese Immigration*, pp. 666–67.
62. Ibid. p. 667; G.H. Hecke, "The Pacific Coast Labor Question, From the Standpoint of a Horticulturalist," *Proceedings of the Thirty-Third Fruit Growers' Convention of the State of California ... 1907* (Sacramento: W.W. Shannon, Superintendent State Printing, 1908), p. 68; John P. Irish, "Labor in the Rural Industries of California," ibid., pp. 55, 65.
63. Chiu, *Chinese Labor in California*, pp. 71–73; Paul S. Taylor and Tom Vasey, "Historical Background of California Farm Labor," *Rural Sociology* 1 (September 1936): 292; Saxton, *Indispensable Enemy*, p. 4; Varden Fuller, *The Supply of Agricultural Labor as a Factor in the Evolution of Farm Labor Organization in California Agriculture*, in US Senate, Committee on Education and Labor, *Hearings: Pursuant to Senate Resolution 266, Part 54: Agricultural Labor in California*, 76th Cong., 3d sess. (Washington: Government Printing Office, 1940), p. 4.
64. Chan, *Bitter-Sweet Soil*, p. 107.
65. Ibid., pp. 400–401.
66. Ibid., p. 405.
67. Ibid., p. 406.
68. Ibid., p. 388.
69. Ibid., p. 381.
70. Ibid.
71. Ibid., p. 370–71.
72. *San Francisco Daily Morning Call*, August 20, 1877, as cited by Chan, *Bitter-Sweet Soil*, p. 373.
73. Chan, *Bitter-Sweet Soil*, p. 374.
74. Ibid., p. 328.
75. *Pacific Rural Press*, April 10, 1886, as cited by Chan, *Bitter-Sweet Soil*, p. 378.
76. Chan, *Bitter-Sweet Soil*, p. 59.
77. Mark and Chin, *A Place Called Chinese America*, pp. 61–62. Also see Chan, *Bitter-Sweet Soil*, p. 386, and the important work on Chinese women by Judy Yung, "Unbinding the Feet, Unbinding Their Lives: Social Change for Chinese Women in San Francisco, 1902-1945" (PhD diss., University of California, Berkeley, 1990). According to Joyce Mende Wong, the "long, sorry episode of Chinese prostitution in America can be traced, in part, to the economic situation in China and the status women held there. In mid-nineteenth-century China, women generally held no important positions, received little or no education, and a vast majority were poor. They were expected to bear male children and tend to domestic affairs." Joyce Mende Wong, "Prostitution: San Francisco Chinatown, Mid- and Late-Nineteenth Century," *Bridge: An Asian American Perspective*, Winter 1978, pp. 25–26.
78. Wong has argued that in austere times (such as during war and natural disasters) Chinese families often resorted to infanticide or the abandonment, mortgaging, or selling of children, particularly female children who could not carry on the ancestral line in patrilineal Chinese society. "Prostitution," pp. 23–26. According to Sucheng Chan, "Among unmarried women, only those who could bring economic returns—such as prostitutes, laundresses, or seamstresses—were considered valuable enough to ship overseas." *Bitter-Sweet Soil*, p. 387.
79. Hirata, "Free, Indentured, Enslaved," pp. 4–5.
80. Ibid., p. 6.
81. Lucy Cheng Hirata, "Chinese Immigrant Women in Nineteenth-Century California," in Carol Ruth Berkin and Mary Beth Norton, eds., *Women of America: A History* (Boston: Houghton Mifflin, 1979), pp. 225–26.
82. Hirata, "Free, Indentured, Enslaved," p. 10; Wong, "Prostitution," p. 24.
83. Hirata, "Free, Indentured, Enslaved," p. 9.
84. Hirata, "Chinese Immigrant Women," p. 226.
85. Hirata, "Free, Indentured, Enslaved," pp. 24–25.
86. Paul Jacobs and Saul Landau, *To Serve the Devil* (New York: Vintage Books, 1971), 2:151, 152, as cited by Wong, "Prostitution," p. 24.
87. Hirata, "Free, Indentured, Enslaved," p. 15.
88. G.B. Densmore, *The Chinese in California: Description of Chinese Life in San Francisco: Their Habits, Morals, and Manners* (San Francisco: Pettit and Russ, 1880), p. 84, as cited by Wong, "Prostitution," pp. 23–24.
89. Hirata, "Free, Indentured, Enslaved," p. 19; Takaki, *Strangers from a Different Shore*, pp. 121–23.
90. Hirata, "Free, Indentured, Enslaved," p. 21.
91. Ibid., p. 27.
92. *California Statutes*, 1869-70, pp. 330–31. Also see California State Senate, *Chinese Immigration*, passim.; E.C. Sandmeyer, *The Anti-Chinese Movement in California* (Urbana: University of Illinois Press, 1939), p. 52.
93. Hirata, "Chinese Immigrant Women," p. 234.
94. Ibid., pp. 234–35.
95. Paul M. Ong, "Chinese Labor in Early San Francisco: Racial Segmentation and Industrial Expansion," *Amerasia Journal* 8, no. 1 (1981): 86–87.

BIBLIOGRAPHY

Barth, Gunther. *Bitter Strength: A History of the Chinese in the United States, 1850–1870*. Cambridge: Harvard University Press, 1964.

Bean, Walton. *California: An Interpretive History*. 2d ed. New York: McGraw-Hill, 1973.

California Legislature. Senate. Special Committee on Chinese Immigration. *Chinese Immigration: Its Social, Moral, and Political Effect: Report to the California State Senate of its*

Special Committee on Chinese Immigration. Sacramento: State Printing Office, 1878.

Cauldwell, Dan. "The Negroization of the Chinese Stereotype in California." *Southern California Historical Quarterly* 1 (June 1971): 123–30.

Chan, Sucheng. *This Bitter-Sweet Soil: The Chinese in California Agriculture, 1860–1910.* Berkeley and Los Angeles: University of California Press, 1986.

Chinn, Thomas, ed. *A History of the Chinese in California.* San Francisco: Chinese Historical Society of America, 1969.

Chiu, Ping. *Chinese Labor in California, 1850–1880: An Economic Study.* Madison: State Historical Society of Wisconsin, 1963.

Coolidge, Mary Roberts. *Chinese Immigration.* New York: Henry Holt and Company, 1909.

Daniels, Roger. *Asian America: Chinese and Japanese in the United States since 1850.* Seattle: University of Washington Press, 1988.

Eaves, Lucille. *A History of California Labor Legislation.* Berkeley: The University Press, 1910.

Fuller, Varden. *The Supply of Agricultural Labor as a Factor in the Evolution of Farm Labor Organization in California Agriculture.* In US Congress. Senate. Committee on Education and Labor. *Hearings: Pursuant to Senate Resolution 266, Part 54, Agricultural Labor in California.* 76th Cong., 2d sess. Washington, DC: Government Printing Office, 1940.

Gompers, Samuel, and Herman Gutstadt. *Meat vs. Rice: American Manhood against Asiatic Coolieism: Which Shall Survive?* Reprint, with introduction and appendices. San Francisco: Asiatic Exclusion League, 1908.

Hecke, G.H. "The Pacific Coast Labor Question, From the Standpoint of a Horticulturalist." *Proceedings of the Thirty-Third Fruit-Growers' Convention of the State of California ... 1907.* Sacramento: W.W. Shannon, Superintendent State Printing, 1908.

Heizer, Robert F., and Alan F. Almquist. *The Other Californians: Prejudice and. Discrimination under Spain, Mexico, and the United States to 1920.* Berkeley and Los Angeles: University of California Press, 1971.

Hirata, Lucie Cheng. "Chinese Immigrant Women in Nineteenth-Century California." In *Women of America: A History,* edited by Carol Ruth Berkin and Mary Beth Norton, 224–44. Boston: Houghton Mifflin, 1979.

——. "Free, Indentured, Enslaved: Chinese Prostitutes in Nineteenth-Century America." *Signs: Journal of Women in Culture and Society* 5, no. 11 (Autumn 1979): 3–29.

Irish, John P. "Labor in the Rural Industries of California." *Proceedings of the Thirty-Third Fruit Growers Convention of the State of California ... 1907.* Sacramento: W.W. Shannon, Superintendent State Printing, 1908.

Lyman, Stanford M. *The Asian in the West.* Reno: Western Studies Center, Desert Research Institute, University of Nevada System, 1970.

——. *Chinese Americans.* New York: Random House, 1974.

——. *Chinatown and Little Tokyo: Power, Conflict, and Community Among Chinese and Japanese Immigrants in America.* Millwood, NY: Associated Faculty Press, 1986.

Mark, Diane Mei Lin, and Ginger Chin. *A Place Called Chinese America.* Dubuque, Iowa: Kendall/Hunt Publishing Company, 1982.

Miller, Stuart Creighton. *Unwelcome Immigrant: The American Image of the Chinese, 1785–1885.* Berkeley and Los Angeles: University of California Press, 1969.

Nee, Victor G., and Brett de Bary Nee. *Longtime Californ': A Documentary Study of an American Chinatown.* New York: Pantheon Books, 1973.

Ong, Paul M. "Chinese Labor in Early San Francisco: Racial Segmentation and Industrial Expansion." *Amerasia Journal* 8, no. 1 (1981): 69–92.

Osumi, Megumi Dick. "Asians and California's Anti-Miscegenation Laws." In *Asian and Pacific American Experiences: Women's Perspectives,* edited by Nobuya Tsuchida, 1–37. Minneapolis: Asian/Pacific American Learning and Resource Center, 1982.

Paul, Rodman W. "The Origin of the Chinese Issue in California." *Mississippi Valley Historical Review* 2 (September 1938): 181–96.

Pitt, Leonard. "The Beginnings of Nativism in California." *Pacific Historical Review* 1 (February 1961): 23–38.

Rowell, Chester H. "Chinese and Japanese Immigrants—A Comparison." *Annals of the American Academy of Political and Social Science* 24 (September 1909): 3–10.

Sandmeyer, E.C. *The Anti-Chinese Movement in California.* Urbana: University of Illinois Press, 1939.

Saxton, Alexander. "Race and the House of Labor." In *The Great Fear: Race in the Minds of White America,* edited by Gary B. Nash and Richard Weiss, 98–120. New York: Holt, Rinehart and Winston, 1970.

——. *The Indispensable Enemy: Labor and the Anti-Chinese Movement in California.* Berkeley and Los Angeles: University of California Press, 1971.

Takaki, Ronald T. *Strangers from a Different Shore: A History of Asian Americans.* Boston: Little, Brown, 1989.

Taylor, Paul S., and Tom Vasey. "Historical Background of California Farm Labor." *Rural Sociology* 1 (September 1936): 281–95.

US Congress. Senate. Joint Special Committee to Investigate Chinese Immigration. *Report of the Joint Special Committee to Investigate Chinese Immigration.* 44th Cong., 2d sess., 1876. Report No. 689.

Wong, Joyce Mende. "Prostitution: San Francisco Chinatown, Mid- and Late-Nineteenth Century." *Bridge: An Asian American Perspective,* Winter 1978, pp. 23–28.

Wu, Cheng-Tsu, ed. *"Chink!": A Documentary History of Anti-Chinese Prejudice in America.* New York: World Publishing, 1972.

Yung, Judith. "Unbinding the Feet, Unbinding Their Lives: Social Change for Chinese Women in San Francisco, 1902–1945." PhD diss., University of California, Berkeley, 1990.

FURTHER READING

Bonacich, Edna. 1972. "A Theory of Ethnic Antagonism: The Split Labour Market." *American Sociological Review* 37(5): 547–559

In "A Theory of Ethnic Antagonism: The Split Labour Market," Edna Bonacich addresses the idea that ethnic antagonism or inter-group conflicts are a key source of the split labour market in the United States. In discussing the wage and labour disparities between blacks and whites, Bonacich cautions that attributing the differences in the price of labour to race or ethnicity alone is highly simplistic; it neglects the complexity of economic processes.

Das Gupta, Tania. 1996. *Racism and Paid Work*. Toronto: Garamond Press.

Race, gender, and class are traditionally defining features of employment systems and processes. In *Racism and Paid Work*, Tania Das Gupta shows how the interaction of racism, sexism, and capitalism serves to oppress and marginalize ethnic minority and female workers. Writing from a Marxist, feminist, and anti-racist framework, Das Gupta explores the lived experiences of workers in the garment manufacturing and health care sectors in Ontario, Canada, and shows how racism and sexism are deeply entrenched in paid work.

Galabuzi, Grace-Edward. 2006. *Canada's Economic Apartheid: The Social Exclusion of Racialized Groups in the New Century*. Toronto: Canadian Scholars' Press.

In this book, Galabuzi provides an engaging account of the experiences of racialized groups in the Canadian labour market. Rich in theoretical and empirical analysis, the book shows how racialized groups, albeit highly educated and a vital source of much needed population growth, continue to experience significant disadvantages and social exclusion in the Canadian labour market, and in the "democratic" Canadian state in general.

Macedo, Donald, and Panayota Gounari, eds. 2006. *The Globalization of Racism*. Boulder, CO: Paradigm Publishers.

Addressing ethnic cleansing, culture wars, human suffering, terrorism, immigration, and intensified xenophobia, this book explains why it is vital that we gain understanding of how ideology underlies all social, cultural, and political discourse and racist actions. The authors looks at recent developments all over the globe and use examples from the mass media, popular culture, and politics to address the challenges faced by democratic institutions.

PART 3C

RACISM, THE MEDIA, AND POPULAR CULTURE

> White supremacists have recognized that control over images is central to the maintenance of any system of racial domination.... Stuart Hall emphasizes that we can properly understand the traumatic character of the colonial experience by recognizing the connection between domination and representation.
>
> bell hooks (1992, 2–3)

The three chapters in this section are elaborations on the insight of bell hooks, illustrating how representation and domination have interacted in the cases of indigenous Canadians, Arabs and Muslims, Jews under Nazism, and black people. The first chapter, by Daniel Francis, is an excerpt from a work that the author describes as "a book about the images of Native People that white Canadians manufactured, believed in, feared, despised, admired, taught their children" (3). He cautions that it is not a matter of "fraudulent" versus "real" images, but a matter of understanding that images represent power relations and have real implications in terms of one's access to social, political, economic, and cultural resources and relationships. In the context of the imaginings of "the Orient," Edward Said argued that dominant representations are as much about constructing the "self" as they are about constructing the "other." In this vein, Francis shows how "the Indian" was imagined through an examination of Canadian paintings, including works by Benjamin West, Paul Kane, and Emily Carr. He suggests that these paintings not only reflect the white imaginary but also white people's ambivalent desire to "be the other."

The next chapter, by Robert Morlino, presents a detailed case study of a media event post-9/11 involving a raid on a software company in Massachusetts that had an alleged link with a Saudi millionaire (the allegation was later proved false). The case study demonstrates how media reports and official actions were based on the stereotype of Arabs and Muslims being terrorists or having terrorist links. What Morlino calls "the rush to judgement and assumption of guilt," "failure to report all the facts," "outright refusal to correct erroneous reporting," and "speculation and defamation" all resulted in the perpetuation of the dominant stereotypes and virtually destroyed the company. Such media events including stereotypical portrayals are juxtaposed with real consequences for Arab and Muslim communities in the United States in the form of direct violence and employment discrimination.

John Solomos and Les Back, in their chapter, ask the question "how is racism made popular?" They address this question by examining four examples. First, they look at how images of the British nation were produced through iconic representation in commercial advertising. The authors show how racialized and gendered images were popularized in the colonial period of the 18th and 19th centuries, through such images as the "white male explorer" and "the warrior queen Britannia." These images served to produce the adventurous, benevolent, and overall "good" colonial white subject whose destiny was to control the world. The second example is from Nazi Germany, where propaganda, including popular paintings, theatre, music, dance, posters, and cartoons, juxtaposed racialized and gendered images of the "wholesome Aryan German" in idyllic rural settings with the "decadent Jewish metropolis" and "monstrous and immoral Americans." Resistance to such images is also examined, for instance in the swing subculture.

Solomos and Back's third example is that of the representation of blacks in British newspapers in the post-war period, a period dominated by popular anxieties around black sexuality, the fear of miscegenation in British seaports, and later the racializing of urban crime. Black Britons are attributed characteristics that threaten the British nation and are portrayed as "outsiders" who have somehow infiltrated in the nation, hence provoking moral panic within the popular imagination. The final example discussed by Solomos and Back is the advertising of clothes manufacturers, such as Benetton and Levi Strauss, whose images have raised great controversy. The authors suggest that although such images are consistent with white supremacy, they can also "unsettle the valence of racism within popular culture." This potential for duality makes representational politics very complex.

CHAPTER 27

THE IMAGINARY INDIAN: THE IMAGE OF THE INDIAN IN CANADIAN CULTURE

Daniel Francis

TAKING THE IMAGE

One of the most famous historical paintings ever done on a Canadian theme is "The Death of General Wolfe" by Benjamin West. The huge canvas depicts the English general, James Wolfe, expiring on the Plains of Abraham outside the walls of Quebec City. In the background, his triumphant army is capturing Canada for British arms. Wolfe lies prostate in the arms of his grieving fellow officers. A messenger brings news of the victory, and with his last breath the general gives thanks. The eye is drawn to the left foreground where an Iroquois warrior squats, his chin resting contemplatively in his hand, watching as death claims his commander. The light shimmers on the Indian's bare torso, which looks as if it might be sculpted from marble.

From its unveiling in London in the spring of 1771, "The Death of Wolfe" was a sensation. It earned for its creator an official appointment as history painter to the King, and became one of the most enduring images of the British Empire, reproduced on tea trays, wall hangings and drinking mugs. West himself completed six versions of the painting. Today it still appears in history textbooks as an accurate representation of the past. Yet as an historical document, it is largely a work of fiction. In reality, Wolfe died apart from the field of battle and only one of the men seen in the painting was actually present. Other officers who were present at the death refused to be included in the painting because they disliked General Wolfe so much.

Figure 27.1 Benjamin West (1738–1820), *The Death of General Wolfe*, National Archives of Canada, C12248.

And the Indian? According to his biographers, Wolfe despised the Native people, all of whom fought on the side of the French, anyway. Certainly, none would have been present at his death. But that did not matter to Benjamin West. Unlike Wolfe, West admired the Noble Savage of the American forest. And so he included the image of a Mohawk warrior, posed as a muscular sage—a symbol of the natural virtue of the New World, a virtue for which Wolfe might be seen to have sacrificed his life.

*****

When White Canadians of earlier generations asked themselves what is an Indian, how did they know what to respond? What information did they have on which to base an answer? By the end of the nineteenth century, there were about 127,000 officially designated Indians living in Canada. Non-Natives had little exposure to these people, most of whom lived on reserves isolated from the main centres of population. They were pretty much a forgotten people. When they gave Native people any thought at all, White Canadians believed they were quickly disappearing in the face of disease, alcohol abuse and economic hardship.

For the vast majority of Whites, Indians existed only as images like that of the Mohawk warrior in Benjamin West's painting. These images originated with a handful of artists, writers and photographers who made the arduous journey into "Indian Country" and returned to exhibit what they had seen there. These image-makers to a large extent created the Imaginary Indian which Whites have believed in ever since.

*****

THE VANISHING CANADIAN

Paul Kane was the first artist in Canada to take the Native population as his subject. "The principal object of my undertaking," he later wrote, "was to sketch pictures of the principal chiefs and their original costumes, to illustrate their manners and customs, and to represent the scenery of an almost unknown country."[1] What made him decide to paint the Indians? Not even his biographer can say for sure. "There is no clear evidence to explain Kane's almost instant conversion at this time to the cause of painting Indians," writes Russell Harper. "A cynic might suggest that he saw a good thing and anticipated fame and fortune coming to him by means of a gallery of Canadian Indians."[2] Kane himself left no explanation for embarking on his great project.

Kane had had little personal exposure to Native people when he commenced his endeavour. As a youngster in Toronto, then the town of York, he saw a few Natives about the streets. But he did not take much interest in them until he travelled to Europe to study painting. There, in London, in 1843, Kane met the American artist George Catlin, whose canvases struck him with the force of a revelation. Catlin had ventured into the trans-Mississippi West during the 1830s to record the lifestyles of the Indians. After his return, he assembled six hundred paintings, along with a large collection of ethnological material, into a mobile display which toured the United States and Europe. In 1841, he published his first book about the Indians, the two-volume *Letter and Notes on the Manners, Customs and Condition of the North American Indians*. When Kane saw what Catlin had accomplished, he determined on the spot to give up portraiture, which had so far been his artistic bread and butter, return home, and do for Canada what Catlin had done so successfully south of the border.

Kane reached Red River by canoe in the middle of June, 1846, where he witnessed a Métis buffalo hunt. "The half-breeds are a very hardy race of men, capable of enduring the greatest hardships and fatigues," he wrote, "but their Indian propensities predominate, and consequently they make poor farmers, neglecting their land for the most exciting pleasures of the chase."[3] Kane crossed Lake Winnipeg to the trading post at Norway House where he remained for a month. Then he set off up the Saskatchewan River, the historic canoe route of the fur brigades, reaching Fort Edmonton towards the end of September. Travelling as he was in the company of Hudson's Bay Company men, Kane not unnaturally formed a positive impression of the company and its trading monopoly. Allowing free traders to enter the country to compete with the HBC would be akin to signing the death warrant of the Indians, he warned. "For while it is the interest of such a body as the Hudson's Bay Company to improve the Indians and encourage them to industry, according to their own native habits in hunting and the chase ... it is as obviously the interest of small companies and private adventurers to draw as much wealth as they possibly can from the country in the shortest possible time, altho' in doing so the very source from which the wealth springs should be destroyed."[4] Kane was referring here to the debilitating effects of the liquor trade with the Natives, which he blamed on the free traders.

With winter fast approaching, Kane and his party hurried to cross the Rocky Mountains, then descended the Columbia River to Fort Vancouver where they arrived early in December. Fort Vancouver remained Kane's headquarters during his stay on the West Coast. He sketched several portraits of the local Flathead people, who were not quite sure how to interpret what they saw. "My power of portraying the features of individuals was attributed entirely to supernatural agency," reported Kane, "and I found that, in looking at my pictures, they always covered their eyes with their hands and looked through their fingers; this being also the invariable custom when looking at a dead person."[5] In the spring of 1847, Kane went on a three-month sketching trip to Vancouver Island. There would not be another artist interested in recording the Native people of the Pacific Northwest until Emily Carr over fifty years later.

That summer Kane left Fort Vancouver for the East. Travelling back up the Columbia River, he made an arduous crossing of the Rockies and did not arrive at Fort Edmonton until December. He remained there for the next six months sketching on the prairie and waiting for the spring canoe brigade to depart with the season's trade of furs. Descending the Saskatchewan River, he crossed Lake Winnipeg and northern Ontario and reached Sault Ste. Marie on the first day of October. Two weeks later a steamboat carried him into Toronto harbour, home again after more than two years wandering the wild Northwest.

Kane's arrival home stirred up great interest. Within a month he mounted an exhibit much like Catlin's, including some of the five hundred sketches prepared on his travels and a selection of Indian "souvenirs." Response was enthusiastic. People flocked to the exhibit to see powerful portraits of Native hunters, scenes of the buffalo chase, and depictions of exotic pagan rituals. Critics remarked on the authenticity and exquisite detail of the work. "A striking characteristic of Mr. Kane's paintings ... is their truthfulness," reported the *British Colonist* newspaper. "Nothing has been sacrificed to effect—no exaggerated examples of costumes—no incredible distortions of features—are permitted to move our wonder, or exalt our conceptions of what is sufficiently wild and striking without improvements."[6] The Ontario public was just beginning to wake up to the existence of the far Northwest, and was already predisposed to romanticize the western Native. In Kane's paintings of picturesque Indians in elaborate costumes of feathers and buffalo hide, his audience found confirmation of a fascinating wilderness world inhabited by fiercely independent, entirely mysterious people. Everyone agreed that Kane, their own local hero, had done even better than Catlin.

Kane's ambition was to complete a series of one hundred large canvases depicting the Northwest frontier from the Great Lakes to the Pacific Coast. After closing his one-man show in Toronto, he set to work on this task. As well, he had to prepare another fourteen paintings which he had promised George Simpson. In 1850, Kane asked the House of Assembly for financial help to complete his project and the next year the provincial government agreed to buy a dozen canvases. After much prompting, these were completed in 1856 and now reside with the National Gallery in Ottawa. Meanwhile, a wealthy Toronto lawyer, George W. Allan, purchased the entire set of one hundred paintings, which were by then almost finished. Together with Kane's Indian artifacts, Allan displayed the works for many years in his home, Moss Park. After his death in 1901, the paintings were sold to Sir Edmund Osler, who in turn donated them to the Royal Ontario Museum in Toronto, where they remain.

Kane was a documentary artist, but he worked within certain conventions and manipulated his images to suit the demands of these conventions. Though he was praised for his accuracy, he often added details of setting and landscape to highlight the romantic flavour of the scenes, and he sometimes "cheated" by adding clothing and artifacts foreign to the Indians in the paintings. His most famous "forgery" is a depiction of an Assiniboine buffalo hunt which was actually modelled on an Italian engraving of two young men on horseback chasing a bull. Recently Kane has been accused of exploiting the Indians by using them as "exotic curiosities" instead of painting them realistically.[7]

But I don't think Kane can be expected to have conveyed a realistic sense of the Native cultures he visited. He was essentially a tourist among the Indians. He spoke no Native languages; he had a superficial understanding of Native customs. Despite his sympathy for what he saw to be their plight, he showed little concern for Native people after his expedition and he was surprisingly narrow-minded about many aspects of their culture. Nonetheless, the power, the beauty and above all the uniqueness of his paintings established him as the pre-eminent artistic interpreter of the Indian for many years to come. Even today it is hard to find a history textbook that does not contain at least one of Kane's renderings of Indian life. For most of us, the Indian of nineteenth-century Canada is Paul Kane's Indian.

Like Catlin, Kane described his western adventures in a popular memoir. *Wanderings of an Artist among the Indians of North America* appeared in 1859 to laudatory reviews. A bestseller in English, it spawned French, Danish and German editions within four years. In the preface, Kane laments the inevitable disappearance of the Indian, and though the rest of the book does not deal with this subject in any detail, most reviewers took it as their theme. "One must make haste to visit the Red Men," said a typical review. "Their tribes, not long since still masters of a whole world, are disappearing rapidly, driven back and destroyed by the inroads of the white race. Their future is inevitable.... The Indians are doomed; their fate will be that of so many primitive races now gone."[8]

In their conviction that the Native people were doomed to disappear, Kane and his admirers were completely representative of their age. If any single belief dominated the thinking about Canadian aboriginals during the last half of the nineteenth century, it was that they would not be around to see much of the twentieth. Anyone who paid any attention at all to the question agreed that Natives were disappearing from the face of the earth, victims of disease, starvation, alcohol and the remorseless ebb and flow of civilizations. "The Indian tribes are passing away, and what is done must be done quickly," wrote the missionary John Maclean, a noted Indian authority, in 1889. "On the western plains, native songs, wafted on the evening breezes, are the dying requiem of the departing savage."[9] Any number of other writers made the same point. Some believed that it was the Indian's traditional culture that was being eradicated by the spread of White settlement, while others believed the Indians themselves literally to be dying out. Some found the idea appalling; some found it regrettable; some found it desirable. But all were agreed that the Indian was doomed.

*****

The "fact" that Indians were a vanishing breed made them especially attractive to artists. The pathos inherent in the subject appealed to White audiences. It also gave an urgency to the work. Artists like Paul Kane who chose to portray the Indian believed they were saving an entire people from extinction; not literally, of course, but in the sense that they were preserving on canvas, and later on film, a record of a dying culture before it expired forever.

This sense of urgent mission controlled the way Indians were portrayed in the work of White artists, who became amateur ethnographers seeking to record Indian life as it was lived before the arrival of White people. Artists ignored evidence of Native adaptation to White civilization and highlighted traditional lifestyles. Often the result was an idealized image of the Indian based on what the artist imagined aboriginal life to have been before contact.

*****

Emily Carr was undertaking a similar project among the tribes on the coast of British Columbia. "I am a Canadian born and bred," she told the audience at a huge exhibit of her paintings in Vancouver in April, 1913. "I glory in our wonderful West and I hope to leave behind me some of the relics of its first primitive greatness."[10]

"These things," she continued, referring to the totem poles, house fronts and village scenes in her paintings, "should be to we Canadians what the ancient Briton's relics are to the English. Only a few more years and they will be gone forever, into silent nothingness, and I would gather my collections together before they are forever past."[11]

As these remarks reveal, Carr initially cast herself very much in the same mould as Paul Kane; that is, a documentary artist making a visual record of a condemned people. Carr conceived her Indian project in 1907 during a summer steamer excursion to Alaska with her sister. The two women spent a week at the Native settlement of Sitka where they visited the famous Totem Walk, a collection of poles erected as a tourist attraction. While she was at Sitka, Carr met the American artist, Theodore J. Richardson, who had been painting in the village every summer for many years. She viewed his work and showed him some of the watercolours she had done of the poles. Richardson praised her abilities and Carr decided on the spot to dedicate herself to recording the heritage of British Columbia's Native peoples before it vanished.

At this time Emily Carr had been studying painting for more than a decade, in California and London, and was teaching art in Vancouver as well as pursuing her own career as a painter. Her exposure to Native people was limited to the Indians she saw around Victoria when she was growing up, and to the visit she had made in 1898 to the Native villages near Ucluelet on the west coast of Vancouver Island. Yet even as a child, she felt a strong fascination for the Indian; "often I used to wish I had been born an Indian," she later wrote. Her biographers speculate that Carr, alienated from her own family and from polite Victorian society, was attracted by the apparent freedom and unconventionality of the Indians who inhabited the fringes of her world.[12] A bit of a misanthrope, she idealized Indians as outsiders, misfits like herself.

Having resolved to paint the Indian "like a camera" for posterity, Carr set about her project with great energy. Between 1907 and 1912, interrupted by a year of study in Paris, she visited Native villages all along the coast, from Campbell River and Alert Bay on Vancouver Island to the Haida settlements of the Queen Charlotte Islands and the Tsimshian villages in the Skeena River Valley. These were arduous expeditions, especially for a woman travelling alone. They involved long voyages by steamship and open boat, toilsome hikes with heavy packs through dense forest, overnight camping in leaky tents in isolated villages. Through it all, her commitment to the project was total.

Carr's Indian painting came to a head in 1913 with the Vancouver exhibition. It contained almost two hundred pieces—oils, watercolours, sketches—covering fourteen years' worth of excursions. The long public lecture which she gave twice during the exhibition explained how totem poles were made and the role they played in the life of the Native people. In her talk, Carr revealed her strong affection and admiration for the Natives of the coast. Unlike Kane and the other artists who had set out to paint the Indian, Carr felt a deep personal bond with her subject. She was recording for posterity, but she was also striving for understanding.

Like many of her contemporaries, Carr interpreted contact between Native and non-Native in Christian terms. Before the White man came, she believed that the Indian lived in harmony with nature in something approaching a Garden of Eden. "In their own primitive state they were a moral people with a high ideal of right," she told her listeners. "I think they could teach us many things." When Whites arrived, they offered Indians the "apple" of a new way of life. But the apple had a worm in it. "They looked up to the whites, as a superior race whom they should try to copy. Alas, they could not discriminate between the good and bad, there was so much bad, and they copied it."[13] As a result, she believed, Indians had lost touch with their traditional culture which was speedily disappearing from the coast.

Carr's 1913 exhibition was well received, but she failed to win a hoped-for commission from the provincial government and had to return to Victoria where she assumed the life of a boarding-house keeper. Without encouragement, she could not afford to go on painting and eventually she abandoned her Indian project. Her "retirement" lasted until 1927, when a visit from Eric Brown, director of the National Gallery in Ottawa, suddenly elevated her and her Indian paintings into national prominence. Brown was looking for canvases to include in an upcoming show of West Coast Indian art at the National Museum. Stunned to discover the cache of paintings Carr had completed so many years before, he convinced her to contribute several to the exhibition. What followed—Carr's trip back east to the opening, her meeting with Lawren Harris, her discovery of the Group of Seven and their discovery of her—is one of the legends of Canadian art history.

The exhibition opened in Ottawa on December 2, 1927. A combination of Native art and modern paintings on Native themes, the show was hailed in the press as an historic occasion, the first of its kind anywhere in the world. "What a tremendous influence the vanishing civilization of the West Coast Indian is having on the minds of Canadian artists," reported the *Ottawa Citizen*. Carr received particular praise. "She is a real discovery," wrote the *Citizen* critic. Her work was "the greatest contribution of all time to historic art of the Pacific slope."[14] Early in January, the exhibition moved on to Toronto where the critic in the *Daily Star* described it as "a revelation" comparable to the discovery of a "Canadian tomb of Tutankaheman." The Native art and artifacts were among the country's greatest cultural treasures, he wrote, as important as the art of the Aztecs, the Mayans or the Incans.[15] It is noteworthy that he made the comparison not to a living tradition but to other vanished Americans.

A cynic might have taken a more jaundiced view of the exhibition. After all, the art seemed to be valued chiefly as examples of a Native tradition long dead. The death of that tradition was both the theme of the work and the necessary precondition of its sudden popularity. While artists like Emily Carr lamented the fate of the Indian, their success was predicated on it. Having first of all destroyed many aspects of Native culture, White society now turned around and admired its own recreations of what it had destroyed. To the extent that they suffered any guilt over what had happened to the Native people, Whites relieved it by preserving evidence of the supposedly dying culture. Whites convinced themselves that they were in this way saving the Indians. By a curious leap of logic, non-Natives became the saviours of the vanishing Indian.

Carr returned from the East with her confidence as an artist restored. She immediately resumed her painting career, and in the summer of 1928 made another excursion north to the villages of the Skeena and Nass rivers and the Queen Charlotte Islands. This trip resulted in some of her finest paintings, but it also marked an end to her Indian project. Under the encouragement of Lawren Harris, she began to feel that she had gone as far as she could as an interpreter of Native art and that it was time to concentrate on her own vision of the forest wilderness, unmediated by Native monuments.

But Carr's interest in Native people remained strong. As her health deteriorated in the late 1930s, she devoted more of her time to writing. She wrote stories about her odd assortment of pets, about her days as a landlady, about her childhood and about her early excursions to the coastal Indian villages. A group of the latter were collected and published in 1941 as *Klee Wyck*. The book received a warm critical reception—"there is nothing to be said in dispraise of her work," commented Robertson Davies—and the next year it won a Governor General's Award for non-fiction.

Carr's style in *Klee Wyck* is unique and charming, at its best when she describes her deep affection for the coastal forest, "the twisted trees and high tossed driftwood."[16] With few exceptions, though, her Indians lack individual character. They are noble figures, living in tune with forest and sea. But they are exotics—servants, street pedlars, subsistence fishermen who speak broken English—living outside White society and apparently having no place in it. Carr is never patronizing. She herself was alienated from mainstream Canadian society and her stories romanticize the poverty and dignity of the social outcast. She describes the harsh reality of life for the contemporary Native, but she is no social worker. Her stories ask the reader to admire the character of the Indian, just as her painting asks the viewer to admire the spirituality and art. Nowhere does she ask her audience to confront social reality. As a result, although she had great personal sympathy for the Indian, she nevertheless belongs to the tradition of artists who took for granted that Indians were vanishing and sought to preserve an idealized image of them, an not the reality of Native people.

*****

GUNS AND FEATHERS

The last two decades have seen a revolution in public thinking about the Indian. Raised on *Howdy Doody* and *The Lone Ranger,* I have seen the Native peoples of the North defend their way of life against southern megaprojects which threaten their land. I have watched Elijah Harper change the constitutional direction of the country with a wave of his feather, and I have seen the tanks roll at Oka. It is a long way from Chief Thunderthud to the Mohawk Warriors.

In 1968, during the discussions leading up to his government's controversial White Paper on Indian policy, Prime Minister Pierre Trudeau wrote: "In terms of *realpolitik*, French and English are equal in Canada because each of these linguistic groups has the power to break the country. And this power cannot yet be claimed by the Iroquois, the Eskimos, or the Ukrainians."[17] In Canada, Trudeau was saying, political power depends on your ability to destroy the country: if you do not have that ability, you do not have real power. No one thought for a moment in 1968 that Native people had the ability, so why should they enjoy the power?

Now the country is twenty-five years older and we have learned how wrong we were. With the Meech Lake constitutional debacle, and the armed standoff at Oka, Native people proved that they, too, could break the country. If this is what it took—confrontation, roadblocks, constitutional impasse, threats of secession—Natives proved as adept at it as any White politician. The result? Now, suddenly, they enjoy unprecedented political power. Their representatives sit with the prime minister and the provincial premiers. Aboriginals are now recognized as one of the founding peoples of Canada. Constitutional talks are incomplete without Native people present.

All of this came about because Native people refused to live within the stereotypes White people fashioned for them. They would not disappear; they would not be obedient children and assimilate; they would not go away. But even as these events unfold before us, it is clear that our response to them, as non-Natives, is still conditioned by the image of the Imaginary Indian.

There is a simple test which people who study stereotyping like to perform. Ask a child to draw a picture of an Indian. Even though they can see Native people in ordinary clothes on the television news almost every night, youngsters invariably draw the Wild West Indian, in feathers and buckskin, usually holding a weapon. But then take the test yourself. When I did I discovered the first image that occurred to me was a photograph I remembered from the early 1970s of a young Ojibway man taking part in a roadblock at Kenora, Ontario, sitting on the hood of a car cradling a rifle. (Of course, for most of us this image was updated by the powerful photographs of Mohawks and soldiers confronting each other across the barricades at Oka.) And the second image that occurred to me was of Elijah Harper, seated at his desk in the Manitoba legislature, calmly twitching his eagle feather and bringing the process of constitutional change in the country to an abrupt halt. The warrior versus the wise elder; it turns out that the images of Indians we are offered today are not much different from what they have always been. [...]

Sometimes we thought it was simply a matter of conquering the Indians, taking their territory and absorbing them out of existence Then America would be ours. Sometimes we thought just the opposite, that we had to become Indians in order to be at home here. This myth of transformation lies at the heart of Canadian culture—Canadians need to transform themselves into Indians. In this sense Grey Owl was the archetypal Canadian, shedding his European past and transforming himself into an Indian in order to connect through the wilderness with the New World. This is the impulse behind the appropriation by White society of so many aspects of Native culture, trivial as this cultural poaching often seems to be. It also explains the persistent desire by non-Natives to "play Indian," whether by dressing up in feathers and moccasins at summer camp, or by erecting another totem pole as a representative symbol of Canada, or by roaring an Indian chant from the bleachers at a baseball game. This behaviour, repeated over and over, reveals a profound need on the part of non-Natives to connect to North America by associating with one of its most durable symbols, the Imaginary Indian.

There is an ambivalence at the heart of our understanding of what Canadian civilization is all about. On the one hand, the national dream has always been about not being Indian. Since the days of the earliest colonists, non-Natives have struggled to impose their culture on the continent. Indians were always thought of as the Other, threatening to overwhelm this enterprise. Noble or ignoble, it didn't really matter. There was no place for the "savage" in the world the newcomers were building. Canadian history, as Stephen

Leacock said, was the struggle of civilization against savagery. There was never any question on which side Indians stood.

On the other hand, as a study of the Imaginary Indian reveals, Euro-Canadian civilization has always had second thoughts. We have always been uncomfortable with our treatment of the Native peoples. But more than that, we have also suspected that we could never be at home in America because we were not Indians, not indigenous to the place. Newcomers did not often admit this anxiety, but Native people recognized it. "The white man does not understand the Indian for the reason he does not understand America," said the Sioux Chief Standing Bear. "The roots of the tree of his life have not yet grasped the rock and soil. The white man is still troubled with primitive fears; he still has in his consciousness the perils of this frontier continent...."[18] As we have seen, one way non-Natives choose to resolve this anxiety is to somehow become Indian.

In the jargon of the day, Canadians are conflicted in their attitudes toward Indians. And we will continue to be so long as the Indian remains imaginary. Non-Native Canadians can hardly hope to work out a successful relationship with Native people who exist largely in fantasy. Chief Thunderthud did not prepare us to be equal partners with Native people. The fantasies we told ourselves about the Indian are not really adequate to the task of understanding the reality of Native people. The distance between the two, between fantasy and reality, is the distance between Indian and Native. It is also the distance non-Native Canadians must travel before we can come to terms with the Imaginary Indian, which means coming to terms with ourselves as North Americans.

NOTES

1. Paul Kane, *Wanderings of an Artist*, in J. Russell Harper, ed., *Paul Kane's Frontier* (Toronto: University of Toronto Press, 1971), p. 51.
2. Ibid., p. 14.
3. Ibid., p. 68.
4. Ibid., p. 74.
5. Ibid., p. 98.
6. Cited in ibid., p. 28
7. Barry Lord, *The History of Painting in Canada* (Toronto: NC Press, 1974), p. 95.
8. Cited in J. Russell Harper, *Paul Kane's Frontier* (Toronto: University of Toronto Press, 1971), p. 41.
9. John Maclean, *The Indians of Canada: Their Manners and Customs* (Toronto: William Briggs, 1889), p. 339.
10. Public Archives of Canada, Emily Carr Papers, MG30D215, Vol. 10, "Lecture on Totems," April 1913, p. 52.
11. Ibid., p.53.
12. Maria Tippett, *Emily Carr: A Biography* (Toronto: Oxford University Press, 1979), p. 29; Doris Shadbolt, *Emily Carr* (Vancouver: Douglas and McIntyre, 1990), p. 87. Also useful is Paula Blanchard, *The Life of Emily Carr* (Vacouver: Douglas and McIntyre, 1987).
13. "Lecture on Totem," pp. 40–41.
14. *Ottawa Citizen*, 2 December 1927.
15. *Toronto Daily Star*, 9 January 1928.
16. Emily Carr, *Klee Wyck* (Toronto: Clarke, Irwin and Co., 1941), p. 19.
17. Sally M. Weaver, *Making Canadian Indian Policy: The Hidden Agenda, 1968–70* (Toronto: University of Toronto Press), p. 55.
18. Cited in Richard Drinnon, *Facing West: The Metaphysics of Indian Hating and Empire Building* (Minneapolis University of Minnesota Press), p. 230.

BIBLIOGRAPHY

Blanchard, Paula. *The Life of Emily Carr*. Vancouver: Douglas and McIntyre, 1987.

Carr, Emily. *Klee Wyck*. Toronto: Clarke, Irwin and Co., 1941.

Drinnon, Richard. *Facing West: The Metaphysics of Indian Hating and Empire Building*. Minneapolis: University of Minnesota Press, 1980.

Harper, J. Russell. *Paul Kane's Frontier*. Toronto: University of Toronto Press, 1971.

Jackson, A.Y. *A Painter's Country*. Toronto: Clarke, Irwin and Co., 1958.

Lord, Barry. *The History of Painting in Canada*. Toronto: NC Press, 1974.

Maclean, John. *The Indians of Canada: Their Manners and Customs*. Toronto: William Briggs, 1889.

Public Archives of Canada. Emily Carr Papers, MG30D215.

Shadbolt, Doris. *Emily Carr*. Vancouver: Douglas and McIntyre, 1990.

Tippett, Maria. *Emily Carr: A Biography*. Toronto: Oxford University Press, 1979.

Weaver, Sally M. *Making Canadian Indian Policy: The Hidden Agenda, 1968–70*. Toronto: University of Toronto Press, 1981.

CHAPTER 28

"OUR ENEMIES AMONG US!"—THE PORTRAYAL OF ARAB AND MUSLIM AMERICANS IN POST-9/11 AMERICAN MEDIA

Robert Morlino[1]

INTRODUCTION: MICHIGAN STORM WARNING

For those who channeled their anger, fear, and shock in the hours following the terrorist attacks of September 11 into concentrated hate, the requisite targets were easy to identify and locate. Some of them found Osama Siblani in Dearborn, Michigan, where the largest and most concentrated population of Arab Americans in the United States resides. Their voices threatened, indeed promised, further violence directed his way.

And though President Bush stood in the Islamic Center of Washington, DC, six days later and assured the world that the "war on terror" was not also the war on Islam, his words did little in the vast echo chamber of the mass media to counter the many other voices, some of them sadly trusted by the public, who instructed otherwise. [...]

In mid-2003, the Washington, DC-based American-Arab Anti-Discrimination Committee (ADC) released a detailed report documenting violence directed against people perceived to be Arab or Muslim during the first year following 9/11. The ADC reported more than seven hundred violent incidents in the first nine weeks alone, and more than eight hundred cases of employment discrimination.[2]

Is that what Daniel Pipes meant when he wrote in the pages of the Manhattan Institute's *City Journal*, "Thankfully, some American Muslims ... understand that by accepting some personal inconvenience–and, let's be honest, some degree of humiliation–they are helping to protect the country and themselves" in an article that began by asking, "How should Americans now view and treat the Muslim populations living in their midst?"[3]

That question has been answered every day since it was posed, and rarely to the advantage of those about whom it was asked.

And the answering continues. [...]

It is apparent that most Americans are no better informed about Arab and Islamic cultures than we were when the late Edward Said published his important book *Covering Islam*[4] in 1981. That the lessons of that work would go unheeded by the mainstream press is a reality compounded in the two years since the 9/11 attacks by coverage consumed with hysteria, sensationalism, and jingoism.

The relevance of media representations of Arab and Muslim Americans post-9/11 cannot be overstated in light of the ADC report. In fact, a comprehensive look at the issue would fill a volume on its own. This chapter presents one in-depth case study that reflects many of the mistakes repeated countless times in numerous other cases by the mainstream American media: the rush to judgment and assumption of guilt when reporting on Muslim and Arab Americans; the forced connection between the Islamic faith and terrorism; the failure to report all the facts when they were readily available; the reluctance or outright refusal to correct erroneous reporting; and the indulgence in speculation and defamation informed strictly by bias and ignorance. Following the case study are broader examinations of the issues it raises.

THE PTECH INCIDENT

The Web site of Ptech Inc., a Massachusetts-based software company that specializes in enterprise architecture technology, contains several press releases marking various milestones. There's one dated January 28, 2002, announcing Ptech's recognition as one of *KMWorld Magazine*'s "100 Companies That Matter" for the second consecutive year. From December 2001, there's a profile written about the company and its CEO, run in the *Patriot Ledger* newspaper under the headline "Ahead of the Curve: Quincy-based Ptech Helps Big Business Stay Agile." The profile's author, Keith Regan, described Ptech as gaining "worldwide attention as a software company that has helped major government agencies, including some branches of the military, and Fortune 100 companies become more efficient."[5]

Understandably, however, there is not a press release noting the company's prominent mention on ABC's *Good Morning America* in late 2002.

"This Just In."

On the morning of Friday, December 6, 2002, *Good Morning America* began with hosts Diane Sawyer and Charles Gibson informing viewers of a dramatic new development in the war on terrorism. Gibson led off with the alarming question, "Has al Qaeda infiltrated the FBI's computers?" He then gave viewers the headline: "Overnight the Feds Bust a Boston Area Software Company Suspected of Ties to the Terrorist Group." Calling it "an interesting story," Gibson teased the forthcoming news report by describing a "midnight raid" on a software company called Ptech, located in Quincy, Massachusetts.

The requisite loaded language was there for a sensational story. Raid. Al Qaeda. Infiltration. Terrorism. Boston. *Good Morning America* had a dynamic and compelling story for its viewers. As ABC News correspondent Brian Ross prepared to fill in the details, Sawyer urged him, "What on earth would prompt law enforcement officials to move on an American company, move in this quickly, this way?"

"Take a look at this remarkable footage," Ross replied as he described a late-night raid in the midst of a "driving snowstorm" by a team of US Customs agents—the "culmination of a top secret White House coordinated raid amid concerns the company was secretly controlled by al Qaeda activists or sympathizers."

With the important details established, Ross moved on to specifics, explaining that Yasin al-Qadi, a Saudi millionaire and one of Osama bin Laden's "money men," had financial ties to the company, and word of this connection spurred an investigation of the "highest priority" within the government.

And there was the final incendiary detail. Among the company's clients were a few government entities of relative note—the FBI, the US Air Force, NATO, the House of Representatives, and the Department of Energy, among others. "It really is startling to think that they could have access to central computer systems," Sawyer said.[6]

Those comments kicked off a rash of coverage in newspapers, on the radio, and on cable news, much of which emphasized many of the same bits of the story presented on Good Morning America. Even more startling than the horrific possibilities contemplated by the coverage is the prospect that the media's dominant characterization of what took place was flat-out wrong.

Less than two months after the events on December 6, 2002, a wholly different account of what took place at Ptech's headquarters that night appeared in the industry publication *Computerworld*, which had earlier published a report similar to that of *Good Morning America* and other major outlets. This new story presented several important details, not the least of which was that, according to representatives at Ptech, there was no dramatic "raid" of the company's offices at all.

In the *Computerworld* story, Ptech's CEO Oussama Ziade presented his side of the story first reported the previous December. As Ziade, a native of Lebanon, told *Computerworld*, Yasin al-Qadi was one of the initial "angel" investors in the company in 1994 but was never an investor of record. Years later, following the September 11 terrorist attacks, a former Ptech employee saw a story on CNN about the Saudi businessman and his alleged financial connections to terrorist organizations. The former employee e-mailed the FBI, identifying al-Qadi as a Ptech investor. On Thursday, December 5, 2002, FBI agents went to Ptech's headquarters with a warrant and asked to investigate al-Qadi's connections to the company. Ziade granted permission immediately, and in return, US Customs promised him that word of the investigation would not get out. The agents on the scene even went to such lengths as parking their cars away from the company's building and entering its offices one by one through a rear entrance, escorted by Ziade. That same night, Ziade met with federal authorities in his lawyer's office. The feds assured Ziade that neither Ptech nor its employees were targets of the investigation.

The *Computerworld* story also recounted in detail the circumstances that connected, at least financially, al-Qadi and Ptech:

> Ziade said he then told investigators that al-Qadi had been a member of the board of directors of another company that had invested in Ptech when it was first starting in 1994. Ptech's first investment had come from venture capitalists in New Jersey, he said.
>
> Ziade, who came to the U.S. in 1985 from Lebanon and had contacts throughout the Middle East, made his first trip to Saudi Arabia in 1995 seeking additional funding for his young company. He had been told there was venture capital to be had there, so that's where he went. [...]
>
> Ziade was unsuccessful in persuading al-Qadi to invest more money in Ptech. When he approached the Saudi businessman a year later, he was told to look for investors in the U.S. Al-Qadi had given up on the company. [...]

Ziade explains that by the time the interview with the investigators ended, so too had the search of Ptech's offices. It was early morning on December 6 at that point, and already the parking lot outside the company's offices was filling with reporters who had learned of the investigation.[7] It was at this point that *Good Morning America* was alarming viewers across the nation that the feared terrorist group may have gained access to the government's electronic infrastructure.

It didn't take long for the story to spread across the United States and around the world via newswires, and for the most part, the description of the government's visit to Ptech was that of an intense raid. [...]

A few outlets, however, went without the "raid" descriptor. Cox News Service, reported that a three-month investigation resulted in a search.[8] *Newsweek* posted a story online that noted "Law-enforcement sources said the search was performed after a cooperating witness gave investigators access to the property on Thursday night." The story also included a detail absent from many other stories:

> Ptech may have recently taken steps to play down its possible connections with Qadi. Last month, the company's Web-site biography of the company's chief scientist, Hussein Ibrahim, described him as a former vice chairman of a company called BMI Finance and Investment Group. A *Wall Street Journal* report recently alleged that Qadi was an investor in BMI, which Qadi's lawyer confirmed. As of today, the reference to Ibrahim's employment with BMI had been deleted from the biography.[9]

Though the wording implies a surreptitious effort on the part of Ptech, this detail was given low priority in the story and demonstrates an important fact about the immediate coverage—disproportionate reporting was being done in the rush to nail down the facts about Ptech. On the cable news networks, the disparity was exaggerated.

*****

CNN's now-defunct studio-audience show *Talkback Live* aired around the same time as MSNBC's *Buchanan and Press*. Broadcast from Atlanta, *Talkback Live*'s format was similar to that of daytime talk shows—a host would interview guests of various backgrounds and viewpoints, and a live audience would have opportunities to ask questions and comment. Major news stories usually comprised the bulk of the show's discussion topics. On Friday afternoon, the show's host, Arthel Neville, teased a live report from correspondent Bill Delaney by telling the audience that a Massachusetts software company had been raided overnight. When Delaney filed his report, he took issue with the use of the word "raid":

> DELANEY: Now, you used the word "raid," Arthel. We might want to be a little careful with that, because we have learned just in the past hour or so that it's kind of hard to really call this a raid. And the company doesn't believe it should be called a raid, since the CEO of the company walked Customs officials into their offices last night, when Customs officials then began to download software.
>
> Now, they did that to see if the software could in any way have been tampered with in a way that might enable hackers to break into any of the agencies that this software is sold to. Now, no less a personage than Tom Ridge, head of the U.S. Homeland Security Office, has said in the past hour or two that there is absolutely no evidence that any of the software here is or was or could be used for those purposes.[10]

Delaney's initial note about calling the search a "raid" underscores perfectly the lack of restraint employed by other outlet reporters and even others within CNN. It is also worth noting that even at that point, just a few hours after the *Good Morning America* broadcast, thorough reporting corroborated Ziade's description of events published months later in the *Computerworld* article—one absent from most of the initial stories on the case.

Delaney also provided a less alarmist description of the chain of events that led to the search at Ptech's headquarters. Other reports hinted at "desperate" pleas by employees of the company to the FBI, begging the agency to investigate terror ties within their offices. Delaney's report removed the hype and presented a much calmer scenario[.] [...]

Delaney's report also included comment from a Ptech vice president, Joseph Johnson, who spoke to a key underlying issue about the entire incident: the religious and ethnic affiliation of some of the company's employees, CEO Ziade included. Most of the stories published in the first few days pointed out that many of Ptech's employees were indeed Muslim. One even noted that the office included a separate prayer room for those employees of the Islamic faith. [...] The significance of these details and their value in the currency of captivating news cannot be underestimated in considering much of the mainstream media's rush to characterize the Ptech search as a dramatic new twist in the war on terrorism[.] [...]

Later, in the *Computerworld* stories, as well as in several stories in the local *Patriot Ledger* newspaper, these themes would be revisited in the aftermath of the media meltdown, with the loyalty and patriotism of Ziade presented with as much weight as the actual substance of the case. Still, the CNN report by Delaney on *Talkback* Live explored many of the critical issues associated with the kind of irresponsible journalism practiced throughout the affair. [...]

Overall, despite Neville's initial description of the search, the CNN segment presented a reasoned and balanced examination even as MSNBC's report presented the opposite. A few hours later, the Fox News program *The Big Story with John Gibson* had its own report. Guest host David Asman also described the incident as a "raid." Of note in this story is the emphasis that correspondent Gregg Jarrett placed on the diagnosis of the company's software after the FBI's investigation, though he still reported that agents had "swarmed" the company's offices:

> JARRETT: David, the feds swarmed the building behind me. It's the headquarters of Ptech. That's an important software company. And what they did was they brought in their own computers. Now they didn't seize any equipment, they didn't seize hard drives, but they downloaded Ptech's software, and then they examined it today.
>
> And here is the most *important part of the story*. According to the federal government, all the software was screened. It came up clean. There were no security compromises. The government had feared that al Qaeda, through this company, had gained access to top-secret intelligence information of the military and the federal government.[11]

Jarrett's report included part of a statement by Blake Bisson, another Ptech vice president, whom Jarrett described as "very relieved," noting that the executive credited his Fox colleague Catherine Herridge with reporting the company's clean bill of electronic health. [...]

The disparities in coverage on cable news were most acute during that first day of the story. Unfortunately for Ptech, print outlets had a lengthier attention span. The Saturday, December 7, edition of the *New York Post* carried a story on Ptech that was riddled with gross misrepresentations of what took place at the company's offices. "Anti-Terror Raid At Mass.-Based Software Firm" was the story's sensational headline, and from the start, the article emphasized the prospect that Ptech operated in some capacity as a funding cell of al-Qaeda[.] [...]

On the same day, the New York Times ran a story that repeated some of the same suspect characterizations of the event, though it presented a layered, more nuanced version of the story. [...]

> "The key thing here is that al-Qadi is on the terror financing list, and U.S. entities are prohibited by law from doing business with anyone on the list," said a senior law enforcement official who spoke only on the condition of anonymity.
>
> "We're pretty sure that he is the main financier of the company," said the official, although he would not detail evidence supporting that belief. "The question is, Was the company aware of his being on the list, and did they continue to deal with him despite the fact that he was on the list?"[12]

But the *Times* also included comments from Michael J. Sullivan, the US attorney in Boston, and they stood in sharp contrast to the alarmist tone conveyed by much of the coverage beginning with Good Morning America:

> This evening, however, Mr. Sullivan issued a statement seemingly playing down the question of whether Ptech software could have been used to access government data.
>
> "The search was conducted in connection with an ongoing financial crime investigation," the statement said. "Media characterizations of this as a terrorist investigation are premature."[13] [...]

[D]espite a wealth of reporting that should have reassured readers, a backlash was rapidly developing. An article in the Rhode Island *Providence Journal-Bulletin* quoted Hugh McKellar, editor of *KMWorld* (the publication mentioned earlier, which ranked Ptech among its "100 Companies That Matter"), as saying, "Ptech is not a shadow company. This is a legitimate organization."[14] Nevertheless, on December 8, the *Boston Globe* reported that the company had already received a barrage of hate mail,[15] and the *Patriot Ledger*, Quincy's daily newspaper, reported that the company had already lost a one million dollar contract and was in jeopardy of losing far more business in the hysteria created by the media frenzy.[16] The repercussions of the initial, sensationalistic coverage were revealing themselves already.

Focusing on Local vs. National Reporting

As the days went by and brought no evidence of wrongdoing on the part of any Ptech employee, national media outlets all but abandoned the story, as they often do when there's simply nothing new or compelling to keep viewers interested. At the local level, however, one publication kept with the Ptech story for several months—the *Patriot Ledger*, the daily newspaper of Quincy, Massachusetts.

For the *Patriot Ledger*'s reporters, the Ptech case presented a well to which many trips could be made, as their readers likely would sustain interest far beyond that of the national audience. Certainly, they benefited from having Ptech to write about at length. Nevertheless, the coverage in the *Patriot Ledger* is vital in two regards. First, the paper addressed at the local level the damage to the company's reputation; explored what happened in the aftermath of frenzied, if brief, national media attention; raised questions about the government agencies' handling of the case; and gave continued voice to Ptech's staff. Second, the paper did precisely what the national media did not do by spending time to cover the whole story, not just the parts that grab the attention of as many readers and viewers as possible. The difference between local and national coverage in this case is important because the comprehensiveness of the former exposes the flaws of the latter.

The *Patriot Ledger* first wrote about Ptech a full year before the search in December 2002. In the December 27, 2001, edition of the paper, an article in the business section profiled the company's growth from a struggling enterprise into a successful, competitive corporation with clients as high profile as the Federal Aviation Administration. In "Ahead of the Curve," Keith Regan interviewed Ptech CFO and COO George Peterson, who explained that one of the company's clients, a major utility company, had saved forty-seven million dollars in operating costs after implementing Ptech software in its IT department—a 3,500 percent return on investment. "Numbers like that sell themselves," Peterson told the Patriot Ledger. The article in 2001 also included several comments from the company's founder and CEO, Oussama Ziade. At that time, details such as Ziade's country of origin and his religious affiliation were unimportant and were not included. This story was, after all, strictly business.[17]

That of course changed the following year, when FBI agents descended on the town followed closely by a full contingent of national media reporters. The *Patriot Ledger* published its first story about the incident on Friday, December 6, reporting a midnight raid on the company and including most of the details found in AP and other national outlet stories, such as Ziade's Lebanese heritage. The local paper's reporters had the advantage of knowing the town on a more intimate level, and this story included comments from local sources at the story's conclusion:

> "They seemed to be honorable people. There was nothing suspect of them," said Thomas O'Connell, manager of Marina Bay Management Services, which rents office space to Ptech.
>
> O'Connell said he did not help Customs agents enter the office last night. Of Ziade, he said, "He seemed to be a savvy businessman and we never had an issue with him."
>
> Amanda Ingles, a waitress at the Marina Bay Sandwich Shop in the Victory Road building, said Ziade's brother often came in to get his brother's lunch. She said Oussama Ziade was not friendly.
>
> They came in regularly, she said, but stopped about two months ago.[18]

The quote from O'Connell is relevant, but the inclusion of Ingles's appraisal of the Ziade brothers' demeanor at this point is questionable, and her comments contributed, albeit unintentionally, to the cloud of suspicion rapidly forming over the Ptech executive. [...] A viewer who saw the reports on ABC or MSNBC then turned to the pages of the *Patriot Ledger* might find some significance in the sudden, seemingly drastic alteration in the eating habits of Ziade and his brother, but if there was a connection at all to warrant inclusion in the story, the burden was on the reporters to draw it.

The next day's edition of the *Patriot Ledger* contained no fewer than five full stories on the Ptech case, all on the first two pages—for the newspaper, the story was about as big as Quincy news gets. The lead story, "Raided Company Denies Terror Links," picked up where the previous day's story left off, further examining the investigation of al-Qadi investments and acknowledging the confusion surrounding the case:

> Ptech officials said they cooperated fully with the investigation, flatly dismissing earlier reports of a clandestine, late-night raid by federal authorities. CEO Oussama Ziade allowed investigators into the building at around 8 p.m. Thursday to conduct the search, and the company plans to continue to assist the government's investigation, Johnson said.[19]

By now the media attention itself was part of the story. The article included a note about how it had already left Ptech scrambling to retain clients amid the controversy. The company told the reporters at that point that a one million dollar contract was in jeopardy. The *Good Morning America* piece came up as well:

> The company is considering demanding an apology from ABC News, which first broke the story about the government search during its "Good Morning America" program on Friday.
>
> "It just wasn't factual," said Blake Bissen, vice president of sales for the company. "It's obviously yellow journalism at its best. It's really sad."[20]

The story also included Michael Sullivan's comments about the media's characterization of the search as a terrorist investigation being premature. One of the other stories in the day's edition dealt exclusively with the fallout from the media coverage. Specifically, the story demonstrated the unfortunate effects of the national media's reporting:

> Other clients have also called saying they plan to pull their business, and Ptech has received a torrent of hate E-mails warning employees to "go back to the Middle East, you terrorists," Johnson said.[21]

[...] Another story, in a way a follow-up to the earlier December 2001 profile, focuses on Ziade, but this time his Muslim affiliation became integral:

> Ziade, a Muslim, is an active member of the New England Islamic Center in Quincy Point, attending religious services most Fridays, the Muslim Sabbath. A member there Friday described him as devout.
>
> "He is a very gentle, wonderful man. He prays here all of the time," said Zaida Hassan Shaw, the center's office manager.[22]

By December 9, the *Patriot Ledger* stopped referring to the search as a raid and shifted its focus away from the investigation, which had diminished significantly. The newspaper focused instead on the effect of the negative attention on the company. [...]

Interestingly, the December 10 editorial placed the burden of clearing Ptech's name squarely on the government, even though it alluded to overzealous reports in the media and their detrimental effect. Coverage in the paper would continue for several months, however, and this is the crucial point where local and national media parted ways: whereas the *Patriot Ledger* kept with the story as it became much less sensational, the national media simply moved on, uninterested in lingering on a story that turned out to be not nearly as dramatic as they had previously thought. [...]

Oddly, by January 22, 2003, the paper was back to referring to the incident as a raid.[23] The next day, the paper reported that Senator Charles E. Grassley (R-IA) was calling for the FBI to further scrutinize Ptech's software for potential terrorist connections; this despite the fact that Homeland Security director Tom Ridge had cleared the company's software.[24]

Then, in May 2003, the Patriot Ledger included the Ptech case as part of its analysis of the USA PATRIOT Act's effect on civil liberties. Ziade was quoted as saying that he didn't believe racial profiling had played a part in the event of the previous December[.] [...]

If anyone is in a position to decide whether racial profiling played a part in the actual investigation by the government, it is Ziade, and his belief seems justified in light of the coverage analyzed thus far. Instead, an overzealous media—not necessarily motivated by discrimination, but rather by a combination of the never-ending hunt for a ratings-boosting, sensational story and a deferment to the biases of its audiences—made the company and its employees victims of post-9/11 hysteria.

The problems don't end there, however. There is another element to the immediate national media coverage of the Ptech investigation, one that is also perhaps the most disturbing. Howard Kurtz, media columnist for the *Washington Post* and host of CNN's media show *Reliable Sources*, wrote about an aspect of the investigation not reported anywhere else, just one day after *Good Morning America* broke the story. The revelations contained in Kurtz's piece portray competing media outlets, impatient for a major story, entering into a quid pro quo arrangement with the FBI long before the first agents ever arrived at Ptech's offices.

It's not uncommon for reporters covering criminal investigations to make arrangements with the agencies involved—

deals wherein the reporter agrees to hold the story until the agencies are ready to move and, in exchange, is promised exclusive coverage or advance warning of an arrest. [...]

In "Out of the Scoop Loop: Feds Fail to Deliver on Promised Tip," Kurtz writes:

> Eight news organizations knew of the investigation in advance and agreed to sit on the story, according to government sources. But the news outlet that had been working on the case the longest, the CBS station in Boston, wasn't told that the raid was imminent.
>
> "We were promised that because we agreed to hold off, we would be told before the raid was held," said Joe Bergantino, a reporter for Boston's WBZ-TV. "In the end that didn't happen. We certainly were disappointed. We were lied to. It was an unsettling and disturbing development." [...]

The most unnerving revelation from the article is the notion that the impatient news organizations actually influenced the chain of events that took place at the Ptech offices[.] [...]

Kurtz wrapped up his story by noting that "bragging rights are also important in television. The station's Web site boasted that the 'raid is the direct result of a WBZ4 I-Team investigation.'"[25]

In other words, Boston's CBS affiliate was taking credit for *creating* news that *wasn't*. And for all the news that wasn't—no one at the company was ever named a suspect, no arrests of any Ptech employees took place, the investigating agencies did not state a single instance in which the company's product was deemed unsafe in any way—the financial damage caused by the mere perception of wrongdoing was very real. Millions of dollars immediately lost, according to a statement released to the media by the company, and tens of millions in potential revenue gone. It's unlikely that CBS would be as willing to take credit for that.

*****

The constant association between Arab or Muslim spokespersons and the looming threats of war and terrorism most certainly becomes ingrained in the minds of viewers. A *Newsweek* article by Keith Naughton recounts the repercussions of the 9/11 attacks on the Arab community in Dearborn, which is the second largest outside the Middle East. (Paris, France, has the largest.) Naughton wrote that immediately on that Tuesday morning, [Osama] Siblani [editor of *Arab American News* in Dearborn, Michigan] received a phone call. The voice on the other end said, "You had better pray to God that Arabs didn't have anything to do with this, or your ass will be next, Siblani." At least a dozen similar calls followed, "many urging the native of Lebanon to 'go back home.'" Naughton reported that the calls were for Siblani a premonition and a reminder of the violence that erupted in Dearborn after the Oklahoma City bombing—prior to 9/11 regarded the most atrocious act of terrorism committed in the United States, which proved to be the work of Timothy McVeigh.[26] In that case, Arab American businesses were burnt down and homes were vandalized. The role of the news media in fostering the attitudes that led to those crimes cannot be ignored. Immediately following the bombing of the federal building in Oklahoma City, Steve Emerson went on the air and called it almost certainly the work of Islamic extremists, based at that point on absolutely nothing save for his "expertise" in terrorism, which many have called into question.

It's also not surprising to find that many accused perpetrators of the worst acts of politically motivated violence in the United States are not perceived by the public as terrorists—so long they're not of Arab descent or the Islamic faith. In May 2003, federal authorities apprehended Eric Rudolph in connection with the 1996 Olympic Park bombing in Atlanta, Georgia, as well as attacks on abortion clinics and a gay nightclub. Two articles by Jeffrey Gettleman in the *New York Times* soon after the apprehension reported support for Rudolph in the areas of North Carolina where the FBI believed the suspect received food and shelter from local residents. Gettleman wrote that the FBI's suspicions about the residents' assistance to the fugitive led to animosity toward the agency; one resident was quoted as saying, "Nobody around here condones murder, but I think a lot of people weren't sure which side to be on." Indeed, the issue of Rudolph's perception in Murphy and Peachtree, North Carolina, touched explicitly on the question of whether the crimes he is accused of committing—killing one woman and injuring more than one hundred people at the Olympics, killing an off-duty policeman in one abortion clinic bombing, and the nightclub bombing—constitute terrorism. "He's a Christian and I'm a Christian and he dedicated his life to fighting abortion. Those are our values. And I don't see what he did as a terrorist act." So said Murphy resident Crystal Davis in one of Gettleman's stories.[27]

Maybe that's just the perspective of those who knew Rudolph. But the national media endorse and perpetuate the same double standard, according to separate reports by Fairness and Accuracy in Reporting (FAIR). One report, from 2000, asks, "Why is it that bomb suspects who are white and American generate roughly one-tenth to one-twentieth of the media interest of an Arab bomb suspect?"[28] Three years later, cartoonist Tom Tomorrow addressed this still-existent problem pointedly in his weekly political strip *This Modern World*. "You probably didn't hear about it," a caption over one panel reads, "but the FBI in Spokane just arrested a couple of terrorists for possession of secret military documents—including material relating to chemical, nuclear and biological warfare ..." Then, inside the panel, a concerned man responds, "That's terrible! Who were they? Iraqis? Al Qaeda? Hamas?" *This Modern World*'s contrarian penguin Sparky answers, "Um—white supremacists, actually." The man replies, "Oh—I thought you said they were terrorists."[29]

Another FAIR report, from 1995, concludes,

> The media is so full of reports on the "Islamic threat" from "radical Muslim terrorists" plotting "Islamic fundamentalist violence," one could excuse the

> average non-Muslim American for concluding that the "fundamentals" of Islam include a course in demolition training. No wonder that 45 percent of Americans, according to a recent poll, agreed that "Muslims tend to be fanatics."

The report also notes, "When reporting on 'Islamic violence' ... the media often identify Muslims by their religion," whereas one would be unlikely to read about "Christian violence" in a story about anti-abortion acts.[30]

Given the state of affairs described at the beginning of this chapter, it's evident that reports by FAIR continue to be ignored by the media. The same is true of Edward Said's book *Covering Islam*. That book prefaces all the problematic coverage analyzed here. The lessons of both simply didn't stand a chance against the onslaught of coverage that appealed to the least compelling ideas that resulted from the 9/11 attacks, if they were ever treated seriously in the first place. One need look no further than Oussama Ziade and the other employees of Ptech, [...] Osama Siblani, or any one of the victims of racially motivated crimes reported in the 2003 ADC report to see why this is a problem.

NOTES

1. The views and opinions expressed in this chapter are solely those of the author on behalf of the Trans-Arab Research Institute and are neither shared nor endorsed by any of his employers or educational institutions past, present, or future. The spelling of proper names in excerpts is presented as it appeared in publication or broadcast transcript. Additionally, italicization as emphasis is added in all excerpts
2. American-Arab Anti-Discrimination Committee, *Report on Hate Crimes and Discrimination Against Arab Americans: The Post-September 11 Backlash; September 11, 2001–October 11, 2002*, Hussein Ibish, ed. (Washington, DC: American-Arab Anti-Discrimination Committee Research Institute, 2003), available at http://www.adc.org/hatecrimes/.
3. Daniel Pipes, "Fighting Militant Islam, Without Bias," *City Journal*, Autumn 2001.
4. Edward W. Said, *Covering Islam: How the Media and the Experts Determine How We See the Rest of the World*, 1st ed. (New York: Pantheon Books, 1981; rev. ed., 1st Vintage Books ed., New York: Vintage Books, 1997).
5. Keith Regan, "Ahead of the Curve: Quincy-Based Ptech Helps Big Business Stay Agile," *Patriot Ledger*, December 27, 2001.
6. Diane Sawyer, Charles Gibson, and Brian Ross, *Good Morning America*, ABC, December 6, 2002.
7. Dan Verton, "Ptech Workers Tell the Story Behind the Search," *Computerworld*, January 17, 2003. See also by Dan Verton, "Terrorist Probe Hobbles Ptech," *Computerworld*, January 17, 2003.
8. Rebecca Carr and Elliot Jaspin, "Suspected Terror Financier Target of Search," Cox News Service, December 6, 2002.
9. Mark Hosenball, "High-Tech Terror Ties?" *Newsweek*, December 6,2002, available online at http://www.unansweredquestions.net/timeline/2002/newsweek120602.html.
10. Bill Delaney, *TalkBack Live*, CNN, December 6, 2002.
11. Gregg Jarrett reporting on *The Big Story with John Gibson*, FOX News Network, December 6, 2002.
12. Pam Belluck and Eric Lichtblau, "Threats and Responses: The Money Trail," *New York Times*, December 7, 2002.
13. Ibid.
14. Paul Edward Parker, "Software Firm Investigated for Terrorism Ties," *Providence Journal-Bulletin*, December 7, 2002.
15. Ralph Ranalli, "Federal Investigation / Agency Questions," *Boston Globe*, December 8, 2002.
16. Karen Eschbacher and Julie Jette, "Negative Press Creates Havoc for Ptech: Official Says $1M Account in Jeopardy," *Patriot Ledger*, December 7, 2002.
17. See n. 5.
18. Patriot Ledger staff, "Terrorism Raid Targets Quincy Firm," *Patriot Ledger*, December 6, 2002.
19. Christopher Walker and Karen Eschbacher, "Raided Company Denies Terror Ties: Ptech Says It May Have Had Money Ties to Saudi Financier Long Time Ago," *Patriot Ledger*, December 7, 2002.
20. Ibid.
21. See n. 15.
22. Jeffrey White, "Associates Say Ziade Gentle, Hard-Working," *Patriot Ledger*, December 7, 2002.
23. Julie Jette, "Ptech Fallout: Finger-Pointing, Wage Claims, Unpaid Taxes," *Patriot Ledger*, January 22, 2003.
24. "Senator Calls on FBI to Scrutinize Ptech Software," *Patriot Ledger*, January 23, 2003.
25. Howard Kurtz, "Out of the Scoop Loop: Feds Fail to Deliver on Promised Tip," *Washington Post*, December 7, 2002.
26. Keith Naughton, "The Blame Game," *Newsweek*, September 11, 2001.
27. See Jeffrey Gettleman, "Ambivalence in the Besieged Town of 'Run, Rudolph, Run,'" *New York Times*, May 31, 2003, and "Sympathy for Bombing Suspect May Cloud Search for Evidence," *New York Times*, June 2, 2002.
28. "Terrorism Stories: Three Cases, Two Standards," Fairness and Accuracy in Reporting, February 2000.
29. Tom Tomorrow, "A Lott Left," *This Modern World*, February 25, 2003.
30. Sam Husseini, "Islam: Fundamental Misunderstandings about a Growing Faith," Fairness and Accuracy in Reporting, July–August 1995. Also see, "Terrorists Attack Ski Lodges, Not Doctors," Fairness and Accuracy in Reporting, December 1998.

RACES, RACISM AND POPULAR CULTURE

John Solomos and Les Back

The currency of contemporary racisms cannot be fully comprehended without understanding their relationship to the various cultural mechanisms that enable their expression. Yet there is surprisingly little analysis of how race and cultural difference are represented in popular culture. Although some research has been done on the role of the media in shaping our images of race, there has been relatively little discussion of the other complex forms in which popular culture has helped to produce much of the racial imagery with which we are familiar today. This is why in this chapter we want to shift focus somewhat and explore the following two issues: how is racism made popular? What kind of technical infrastructure exists which transmits racist ideas and what are its origins? With these key questions in mind we want to look at how conceptions of race have been shaped by popular cultural forms. The key aim is to examine the ways in which racism intersects with the meanings, images and texts that furnish the banal aspects of everyday life.

A good example of how the new visual media began to have a major impact on questions about race can be seen in the development of the cinema. The power of film in the representation of racial issues became evident from a very early stage. The controversy surrounding D.W. Griffith's film *The Birth of a Nation*, which was first screened in 1915, is a case in point (Simmons, 1993). The film portrayed southern blacks after the end of slavery as ignorant, uncouth and driven by sexual lust. It represented the Ku-Klux-Klan as the saviours of southern whites, and in particular as the protectors of white women from the desires of black men. What is important to note, however, is that *The Birth of a Nation* also constituted a major development in the art of filmmaking. Edward de Grazia and Roger Newman (1982) argue that no other single motion picture has had as important an impact on the history of the cinema. It was Griffith who mastered what others developed in terms of building scenes and creating imagery. While *Birth of a Nation* celebrated and romanticised southern racism, it brought new techniques of film-making including fade-outs, close ups and long shots that were all assembled to constitute a powerful and elaborate narrative.

Griffith's film demonstrated vividly the power of the new form of cultural expression, yet it was banned more often than any other in the history of motion pictures and remains controversial to this day. The dissension surrounding this film shows that from their very inception the twentieth century's new electronic media became a crucial context in which racism could be both expressed and contested (Kisch and Mapp, 1992). A central theme of this chapter is the degree to which the elaboration of racist ideas has gone hand in hand with technological advancement. [...]

The core sections of this chapter focus on four examples that show how historically situated racisms were expressed through the mass media. We start with an examination of the ways in which iconic representations of nationhood were produced within printed and commercial cultures in Britain during the eighteenth and nineteenth centuries. This leads into an examination of the relationship between racism, popular culture and propaganda in Germany during the Third Reich. The aim of these two sections is to demonstrate the significance of commercial cultures and the media in maintaining the cultural hegemony of imperialism and Nazism. This is followed by a discussion of the ways in which black minorities have been represented in the media in the post 1945 period. The final example looks at the complex and shifting nature of contemporary media representations of race, culture and difference. Here the ambivalent nature of racial imagery in popular culture is examined with particular reference to the sophisticated coding of current racisms.

ICONS OF NATIONHOOD: BRITANNIA AND EMPIRE

[...] A number of historical studies have highlighted the ways in which from the earliest stages of European exploration and settlement images of the "body" and "soul" of the "native" became part of popular culture (Jordan, 1968). However, it was in the late nineteenth and early twentieth centuries that the "mechanical reproduction of culture," to use Walter Benjamin's (1968) famous phrase, took on an unprecedented complexity. It was also during this period that the powerful role of visual culture in reproducing images of race became most evident. This has been illustrated in a number of recent studies of the changing images of Africa and Africans and how these were represented through popular culture (Appiah, 1992; Pieterse, 1992; Coombes, 1994; Mudimbe, 1994).

[...] John MacKenzie has demonstrated that imperialist propaganda was produced in Britain by a large number of imperial agencies in the late nineteenth century. The notion of propaganda here is defined as the transmission of ideas and values from dominant groups who control the means of communication, with the intention of influencing the receivers' attitudes and thus enhancing and maintaining their position and interests. [...] Imperial propaganda was disseminated in two distinct forms via the institutions of church and state and the new and popular forms of culture and communication. The extraordinary explosion of advertising was coupled with the growth of commercial ephemera targeted particularly at young men (Richards, 1990). These took the form of cigarette cards that were collected and swapped, picture postcards and a wealth of juvenile journals. These texts became "the prime source of news, information, and patriotic and militaristic propaganda" (MacKenzie, 1984, p. 17).

*****

Through these means the colonial subject was represented through a restricted grammar of images that included a range of archetypes from the tamed servant, the obliging bearer to the dangerous and primitive savage (Pieterse, 1992). As Stuart Hall has noted this restricted grammar was to provide the "base images" of twentieth-century British racism (Hall, 1981).

Advertising represented the excitement of an expansionist age where colonial campaigns, exploration of remote territories and missionary endeavour dominated the public imagination. An important feature of this process was the way these representations articulated race and nation with images of gender. The explorer was always presented as a white man suffering adversity for the national interest. The advertisers sometimes coupled figures from the pantheon of English heroes with incongruous and unlikely commodities, as in the case of "Stanley Boot Laces" and "Kitchener Stove Polish." Commercial images of exploration in the colonies rarely included references to white womanhood. This omission was underscored by the connection between colonial contexts, white womanhood and danger (Ware, 1992). This was symptomatic of a wider moral and political preoccupation with defending the national character and the purity of the race.

One exception to this was the iconic representation of Britannia. While the image of Britannia as a warrior queen equipped with trident and shield is a pervasive emblem of nineteenth-century advertising, the origins of this representation of nationhood lay in the Georgian era. The patriotic anthem "Rule, Britannia" made its first appearance in 1745 alongside "God Save the King" that was also written during this time. Britannia is represented in the prints of the time as a personification of the nation, which is being threatened by the French. The paranoid intensity of the gallophobia that was rife during this time is extraordinary even in comparison to modern racisms. The French are presented in the prints of Hogarth and Gillray as "tonnish apes," lesser breeds with unspeakable intentions. Gerald Newman, commenting on a particular cartoon, describes one common racist stereotype of the French: "In scenes truly nightmarish to behold, [the French] dismember the fair Britannia, administer emetics to her and force her to vomit English possessions into basins held by apish Frenchmen" (Newman, 1987, p. 79). Here the image of the "French apemen" also doubles as a symbol of the devil. What is interesting, however, is the degree to which these images invoke moral outrage through deploying the image of Britannia and thus coding the nation feminine. In his study of the graphic prints of the era, Atherton suggests that Britannia is an image of "Virtue, especially those virtues relevant to national and public life: love of country, dedication, honesty, selflessness, discipline, simplicity" (Atherton, 1974, p. 266). The violation of Britannia thus becomes a violation of those virtues. This form of ideography works to produce powerful and stirring emotions precisely because it crosses attributes associated with the feminine and national vulnerability.

Beyond this the nation from the mid 1750s onwards was modelled on the family, or more correctly an extension of it. The British character was constructed through invoking ties of shared blood that claimed that they were "immutably the same." As Stella Cottrell suggests, "The King was the loving father. The country, as Britannia, was the mother" (Cottrell, 1989, p. 264). The traces of this gendered nationalism are found quite clearly in the popular culture of the nineteenth century, where references to Britannia are invariably presented in connection with "domestic imagery." An obeying lion is also commonly paired with Britannia as both her protector and an emblem of the violent potency of the nation (Colley, 1992). More often Britannia is portrayed sitting on a green landscape modelled in the shape of the British Isles looking out to sea, sometimes with white cliffs or a gun boat within her regal view. Manufacturers of cleaning products took these links a stage further by presenting Britannia "polishing" her shield or even the globe (Opie, 1985).

[...] This iconic figure embodied the nation in a racialised skin with phenotypic features and national attributes. It is with some irony then that [the] commodity [...] being sold through invoking primal allegiances should claim that it "Cleans and whitens without scratching."

[...] In summary, imperial propaganda established some of the core symbols of British racism. It was also integrally connected with the fashioning of a national subject that possessed a distinct racial character, an imperial destiny and a standing in the world.

*****

It was, however, in the fascist regimes of the twentieth century that the deadly impact of electronic technologies, national symbolism and popular culture became fully clear. Propaganda and popular culture under fascism provided the key weapon for establishing and maintaining its appeal and acceptance.

NAZISM, PROPAGANDA AND VISUAL CULTURE

A key and enduring part of the power of racism is the way in which it helps to account for specific social relations in a simple manner. This process of rendering the abstract concrete is a function of all ideologies. What is important in relation to the morphology of racist ideas is that they intrinsically involve the production of a visual culture. [...]

This process of rendering human beings via a repertoire of visual stereotypes was perhaps most clearly exemplified in the representations of Jews within Nazi posters and cartoons. However, the popular culture of the Nazis was also preoccupied with the reinvention of the Aryan character within art, film, sculpture and architecture. [...]

The art of the Third Reich attempted to present an image

of Aryan Germans into which the individual could project him or herself. It espoused an eternal racial character through images of idyllic rural Germany and simple peasant family life. Through these images of heroic endeavour on the land an imaginary Germany was visualised. Nazi painting presented the peasantry as frozen stereotypes of undisturbed racial perfection in harmony with nature and eternally rooted in the land and soil. This connection was invariably achieved by using the plough, seed and scythe as key symbols of honest toil within the context of fashioning a sense of racial identity (Adam, 1992). It is striking that few references were made to Nazism's "others" within their popular art; this representational space was given over to images of everything that was good and wholesome in the newly found Aryan culture. For most Germans who were living in conditions of urban poverty the consumption of these images meant their individual misfortune could be lost in the alluring racial fantasies of "heimat" and the promise of a better future. This media-generated "virtual home" provided Nazism with the antidote to the excesses of modernity often expressed through references to the decadent Jewish metropolis. The Nazis took their art to the German masses, they sent theatre groups to every village, orchestras played concerts of Wagner, Brahms and Beethoven in factories, and it was through the new technologies of the newsreel and the radio that their message was broadcast to every German home.

*****

Nazism produced an image of the German "Volk" into which individuality could be dissolved and where human conscience could be drowned by the deafening sound of the mass rally. Physical exercise along with dance and marching took on a kind of messianic fervour. Nazi dance organised its participants within a geometric discipline: "It place[d] a grid over the mass of bodies, which both arranged individuals and separate[d] them from one another. Clear lines confine[d] them to their places and prevented them from escaping" (Servos, 1990, p. 64). The spectacular rituals of mass dancing recorded during the Olympic Games in 1936 and the display of Stormtroopers marching in perfect cohorts through the Brandenburg Gate anchored Nazism in the rhythm of the body. These public demonstrations were Hitler's rejoinder and stood as an answer to the very different rhythms that occupied the metropolitan night-clubs where his Volkish reverie was less secure.

During the Nazi period jazz was embraced by German young people much to the chagrin of the white supremacists. Nazi musicologists attacked jazz and justified their opposition to it by arguing that its rhythm was unsuitable. They complained that unlike Germans "Negro tribes do not march" [sic] (Kater, 1992, p. 31). This was also coupled with an attempt to show that jazz was the product of an abominable collaboration between "Negroes" and "Jews" with racially corrosive implications for Aryan Germans. While characterising jazz as another form of "degenerate culture" the Nazis also attempted to develop their own saccharine form of jazz. These moves did not stop the development of a vibrant subculture of *jazz defiants*, known as "Swing youth" after the jazz dance genre.

*****

The dance-hall provided a context in which to explore alternative forms of femininity and masculinity and offered opportunities for gaining sexual experiences. The import of American styles of feminine beauty was viewed as particularly abhorrent by the Nazis and the incorporation of Anglo-American styles by "swing girls" posed a serious challenge to the femininities associated with Nazi ideology and the state youth organisations. Equally for young men their urban style challenged the dominant uniform of Nazi masculinity that combined the Aryan warrior hero with images of the responsible peasant patriarch. The Swing subculture was not a self-consciously radical movement, despite the vicious suppression meted out to them by the Gestapo and the Hitler Youth. It was estimated that from 1942 to 1944 75 Swing youths were sent to concentration camps by the SS who classified them as political prisoners. Within the context of the metropolitan night-clubs themselves jazz dancing allowed for counter-hegemonic forms of bodily expression and individuality that was so emphatically repressed within Nazi popular culture, music and dance.

Nazi representations of the racial "other" were principally confined to propaganda posters and cartoons (Rhodes, 1976). This included predictable portrayals of "money grabbing" Jewish businessmen, alongside representations of the modernist decadence of Jewish Bolsheviks. During the war years Nazi propaganda combined anti-Semitic images with references to the "black Allied soldier." The propagandists deployed images of black soldiers to stand as a measure of Allied racial decay and a symptom of the mongrelisation of American society. The presence of the black soldier was thus turned into a corrosive threat to European civilisation. The black soldier as a moral threat has a particular history within the wartime German psyche. In the aftermath of Germany's defeat in 1918 the Belgian and French armies used black colonial troops in their occupation of the Rhineland territories. This produced a moral panic within Germany and a sense of outrage that this was the ultimate insult to the vanquished nation's pride. The presence of black soldiers was stereotyped through the image of "Jumbo," a monstrous sexual predator who threatened the moral chastity of white German women. The preoccupation with miscegenation was taken to considerable lengths and Afro-German children and their mothers were subject to ostracism and attack. The Society for Racial Hygiene that was founded in 1905 began conducting sterilisations of Afro-Germans in 1919. Eugenics provided the rationale for these barbaric acts that were explained as necessary for the protection of the Volk and the elimination of "racial diseases." After 1937 Hitler inherited this mission and hundreds of sterilisations were conducted (Opitz, Oguntoye and Schultz, 1992).

*****

The poster entitled "Liberators" reproduced here was also displayed in Holland prior to the Allied invasion (figure 29.1). In one image it registered all that Nazi popular culture despised and attempted to expunge. This figure of cultural invasion stands for everything that is decadent in American life. Somewhere between Frankenstein and King Kong the invader brings together the antithesis of the Nazi ideals of racial purity and their attendant versions of manhood and womanliness. The "Statue of Liberty" and the New York skyline can be seen in the distance (bottom left-hand corner) which gives this monster a distinctly urban origin and reinforces the connection between the city and race: New York of all the great metropolises is the most strongly associated with Jewishness. There are other references that reinforce the association between the deviant city life and the Jew. Behind the boxer's glove on the right-hand side of the image hides a Jewish businessman peering over a bag full of dollars and a Star of David hangs between the monster's legs. These images are coupled with other representations of urban delinquency; the set of white arms represents on one side criminality through the manacle and the striped prison uniform and on the other brandishes a stick bomb. These are accompanied by series of confused images relating to US racial politics.

Figure 29.1 Monstrous Regiment: Nazi poster portraying the GI as a jitterbugging marauder. Poster in Holland, 1944

The torso of the monster constitutes a cage that holds an apeman and apewoman associated with black music and dance—the caption reads "Jitterbug—Triumph of Civilisation." References to black masculinity are coded via the monster's top set of arms which are black and muscular. In one hand is a record that signifies the decadent music of jazz while on the other is a boxing glove, a symbol of brute strength. These images, which draw on relatively common racist themes, are then combined with a reference to domestic American racism. The head of the monster is hidden by the mask of the Ku-Klux-Klan and a hangman's noose is wound around one of the black arms as a reference to the practice of lynching black Americans in the South. The tragic irony is that this piece of propaganda was authored by a regime that exterminated a million Jews by this point in the war. The implication seems to be that the culture of the European mainland would be threatened by an Allied invasion because it would bring American racism to the continent.

Also signalled within this image is the potential import of immoral forms of femininity that revealed the sexual depravity of the Americans. The representations of the two white beauty queens on either arm of the monster register this abhorrence of the artificial femininity of white American women and the fetish for such beauty. This is also supported by the female coded right leg of the monster that has a tape measure around its calf and thigh and the ribbon that is tied above its knee announces it as the "world's most beautiful leg." We cannot read the significance of this image without a prior knowledge of the ideal models of Aryan femininity. Nazi art and popular culture stressed the importance of women as the safe keepers of life whose form should be admired as a thing of natural beauty. The caricature presented here of "Miss America Femininity" constitutes the absolute antithesis of Aryan female beauty which was defined by its perfection in nature.

While the monster includes female elements as a whole the figure is gendered male. Its left male formed leg is presented in the form of a bomb that is suspended like a sword of Damocles over the monuments of Western civilisation. It is through these references that it also represents the Allied war machine complete with the wings of a bomber. As the monster stands suspended before trampling over Europe the caption reads: "The 'liberators' will save European culture from its downfall." Reference to a common European culture is being invoked in an attempt to summon sympathy and support within the occupied territories. The use of cultural references here are significant because as we have shown similar forms of pseudo-cultural logic became a core feature of the "new racisms" of the late twentieth century.

These examples of Nazi propaganda demonstrate the role that racism played managing periods of crisis where control was being lost over the occupied lands of Western Europe. They also show the clear vocabulary of race that was at the disposal of these propagandists.

*****

RACISM AND REPRESENTING THE BLACK PRESENCE IN BRITAIN

Throughout the twentieth century the black presence in Britain has been viewed by public commentators as constituting a serious moral and cultural problem; a central anxiety focused on the issue of "race mixing" and the impact of immigration on the social and cultural fabric of British society. Clive Harris has shown that black people in seaports such as Liverpool and Cardiff posed a serious moral and political problem for the politicians and bureaucrats of the day (Harris, 1988). Documenting the survey conducted in 1935 by the British Social Hygiene Council, Harris demonstrates how this organisation was preoccupied with inquiring into black sailors' "sexual demands" with regard to their white partners, their promiscuity and the suggestion that white women became addicted to the "black sailor's sex." In addition to this black men were also connected with the transmission of venereal disease and seen as leading white women into prostitution. Harris goes on to show how the growth in so-called "half-caste children" became another significant feature of the discourse of state officials, particularly in Cardiff and Liverpool and ultimately at the Home Office. These young people were constructed as being "marked by a racial trait" and to "mature sexually at an early age" (ibid., p. 24). This moral panic was to be revisited within a more public arena when, after the Second World War, a number of stories were published about children born to white women and black American and West Indian servicemen. These children were viewed as a "casualty of war." One of the Home Office's proposed solutions to "this problem" was to send these children to America to be brought up with "other coloured children" (quoted in ibid., p. 37). In the face of opposition from within Britain's black population this proposal was never implemented. There are troubling similarities here between these sentiments and Nazi propagandists' attempts to exploit images of black Allied soldiers in order to engender white panic and anxiety.

Harris argues that what is telling about the preoccupation with miscegenation is the degree to which the racist discourse of this period is preoccupied with skin colour as the prime signifier in the subjectification of black people. The preservation of the English racial character was to be achieved by preserving its hue.

*****

During the 1970s media discourses produced a significant shift away from a preoccupation with miscegenation and the early more clearly colour-coded racisms, and became centrally preoccupied with covering emerging forms of "racial crime." The most sophisticated critique of this conjuncture was produced by Stuart Hall and his associates in their book entitled *Policing the Crisis* (Hall et al., 1978). This study attempted to demonstrate among other things how the moral crisis over the street crime that became known as "mugging" was related to managing a wider crisis in British society. Hall et al. argue that the designation of mugging as a black crime provides a vehicle for engendering divisions:

> [Mugging] ... provides the separation of the class into black and white with a material basis, since, in much black crime (as in much white working-class crime), one part of the class materially "rips off" another. It provides the separation with its ideological figure, for it transforms the deprivation of the class, out of which crime arises, into the all too intelligible syntax of race, and fixes a false enemy: the black mugger. (Ibid., p. 395)

They conclude that during the 1970s British society managed a crisis in social hegemony through the twin strategies of creating and amplifying the "mugging moral panic" and moving towards a more authoritarian law and order ideology. The symbolic location of "black crime" connects with associated racial discourses that construct black communities as being incompatible with the "British way of life" (Gilroy, 1987). "Black youth" are thus defined as constituting a social problem (Solomos, 1988).

[...] Like many other racialised discourses such responses demonstrated a profound historical amnesia. Britain has a long history of civil unrest. The Gordon riots in 1780 resulted in 285 deaths and a further 25 were hanged for taking part in them. During the 1930s there were frequent clashes between the unemployed and the police and during demonstrations against Oswald Mosley's British Union of Fascists. What is distinctive about the press reporting of urban conflict in the 1980s is that these events were represented as "race riots." There had been previous incidents during the 1950s that represented disorder through a racial lexicon (Miles, 1984) but this mode of representation hardened during the outbreak of violent protest in 1981 and 1985 (Solomos, 1986).

*****

We have suggested that media stereotyping of Britain's black population has shifted in the last 60 years. These popular representations have adapted and taken on new characteristics while retaining an interconnected quality. In his study of racism and the news media Teun van Dijk concludes:

> The structure and style of headlines not only subjectively express what journalists or editors see as the major topics of new reports, but also tend to emphasise the negative role of ethnic minorities ... [who] continue to be associated with a restricted number of stereotypical topics, such as immigration problems, crime, violence (especially "riots"), and ethnic relations (especially discrimination), whereas other topics, such as those in the realm of of politics, social affairs, and culture are under-reported. (van Dijk, 1991, p. 245)

The thing that remains constant in this reporting is that black people are seen as constituting a social problem, while at the same they are seen as experiencing forms of injustice and discrimination that are "morally offensive." Splitting of this type is a central feature of racist culture and is what Peter Hulme refers to as a "stereotypical dualism" (Hulme, 1986).

Michael Keith in his insightful discussion of the male Bengali street-rebel has described the operation of this dual process within the contemporary urban setting of London's East End (Keith, 1995). He argues that racist discourses make sense of Bengali youth through cartographies of race and power, which map so-called Asian gangs within particular sites of street criminality. This is compensated by a white leftist notion of "the youth" as an agent of insurrection and street revolt. Keith makes the telling point that both of these urban narratives are respectively the product of fear and desire. The street rebel appears as a remixed and recoded urban insurgent, "the result of both collective action and the manner in which such actions were framed by the mass media" (ibid., p. 366). There is a direct lineage between the Asian street rebel of the 1990s and the connections made between race, crime and locality in the 1970s and 1980s which produced the black mugger and rioter: it is only the racial patina that is exchanged.

In summary, we have argued that the British news media has represented the black presence through identifiable motifs. These have shifted in terms of their content and this dynamism demonstrates the necessity of understanding racism in its historical moment. However, it is equally important to understand the continuities that are maintained as these media discourses change. The media racism in post-war Britain can be characterised as possessing two core features in that: (i) the black presence is seen to have a racially corrosive effect on British culture; and (ii) the race/cultural difference of black people makes them incompatible with the British way of life. As we have shown this deploys the idea that alien traditions of criminality and association have been imported into the British social formation from the ex-colonial periphery.

From the Nazi propagandist to the newspaper editors the printed and electronic media have provided means whereby racist constructions of social reality are made popular. We have, however, characterised the relationship between popular culture and racism as unstable and dynamic. [...] In the following section we want to focus on recent examples of how cultural difference is represented within popular culture and the implications this has for understanding contemporary racisms.

CORPORATE MULTICULTURALISM: RACISM, DIFFERENCE AND MEDIA IMAGES

*****

It is [...] important to note that we have seen quite important transformations in recent years in how race is represented through the popular media. For example, advertisers and other media producers are including images of cultural difference within their repertoire of symbols. Within truly global markets some advertisers have attempted to associate their products with the transcendence of racism and cultural barriers.

*****

[W]hat we have seen in recent times is an attempt by some multinational corporations to develop a transnational advertising aesthetic. Perhaps the best and most perplexing example of this is the clothes manufacturer Benetton. Through the camera of Oliviero Toscani, Benetton have attempted to promote a message of human unity and harmony in their advertising. Starting in 1984 they attempted to represent the world's diverse people and cultures as synonymous with the many colours of Benetton's produce. Since then their campaigns have provoked unparalleled controversy, winning them awards and adulation alongside accusations of hypocrisy and opportunism.

One of the striking features of the Benetton campaigns is the degree to which their message of transcultural unity is predicated upon absolute images of racial and cultural difference. The initial campaigns alluded to past and present conflicts through the presentation of archetypal images of Jews and Arabs embracing the globe. What is intriguing about this move is that Benetton's products do not have to be shown in order to convey meanings about the brand quality; the message is simply resolved by the motif juxtaposed over the images of boundaries and conflicts. The "United Colors of Benetton" becomes the antithesis of conflict, the expression of unity, the nurturer of internationalism (Back and Quaade, 1993). However, what is more troubling about this strategy is the degree to which it is reliant on racism's very categories of personhood and the stereotypes which run from these. The example reproduced here (figure 29.2) shows three young people poking their tongues out at the viewer. This advertisement was used in a poster campaign in 1991. The message of transcendence encapsulated in Benetton's slogan only makes sense if it is superimposed on a representation of clear difference. These three figures are coded through a grammar of absolute racial difference: the blue-eyed blonde white Aryan figure, flanked respectively by a "Negroid" black child and an "Oriental" child. This message of unity can only work if it has a constitutive representation of absolute racial contrast. The danger with such representations is that they rely on a range of racial archetypes that are themselves the product of racism and as a result make racial atavism socially legitimate forms of common-sense knowledge: the concept of race is left unchallenged.

Figure 29.2 United Colors? Benetton billboard poster, 1991

One of the most interesting things about Toscani's photography is the ways in which he plays with ambiguity. The most dramatic example of this included a picture showing the hands of two men, one black and the other white, handcuffed together; and a picture of the torso of a black woman breast-feeding a white baby released in 1989. The reactions to these ads varied according to national context. In the United States, they were withdrawn following public complaint. The later image conjured the historical experience of slavery and the position of black women within a gendered and racialised system of exploitation, including their designation as objects of white sexual desire. In the United States and Britain, the image of handcuffed hands evoked notions of black criminality, far from suggesting two men united in incarceration. The advertisement was associated with the daily reality of young black men arrested by predominantly white law enforcement agencies. In Britain, *The Sun* ran the headline, "Di's sweaters' firm in 'racist ads' row," referring to the fact that Princess Diana had patronised Benetton products for some years. London Transport refused to display the ads on the London Underground, justifying their decision by the suggestion that the ads had racist overtones. The most extreme response to the campaign came in France. In Paris, neo-fascist agitators, opposing what they saw as miscegenation, threw a tear-gas canister into a Benetton shop shortly after the posters appeared. While generating controversy these images were embraced by the media more broadly and won prizes in France, Holland, Denmark and Austria. How can we make sense of this diversity of responses? Perhaps the first point to make here is to foreground the importance of understanding these iconic global images within particular contexts. The images invoked different histories of racist discourse in the United States, Britain, France or Japan. The simple point here is that the social composition of the audience affects the range of intertextual reference (histories, representation, symbolic codes, form of racism) that are used to make sense of any particular image (Mercer, 1992). These images are ambiguous because they activate the histories and cultural features of racism through connotation.

While Benetton were very much in the vanguard of this type of imagery during the 1980s, other companies have also embraced the idea of imbuing their brand quality with a transnational ethos. [...] Philips uses a blonde haired white girl and a black boy alongside the caption "THE UNIVERSAL LANGUAGE OF PHILIPS." Again the two children are united through their consumption of the commodity, with a black and white thumb sharing the control panel. This advertisement actually appeared in the newspaper that Benetton produce called *Colors*. *Colors* is an extraordinary publication because it effectively turns news items into Benetton advertising (Back and Quaade, 1993). [...] What is common to these campaigns is that they all, in various ways, espouse common humanity and harmony while reinforcing cultural and racial archetypes. At worst they steer a symbolic course that is perilously close to a legacy of crude racist images and associations.

Corporate multiculturalism has not only been confined to the espousal of a saccharin version of internationalism, black style and music have also been used as a means to appeal to a youthful audience. The jeans company Levi Strauss provides a particularly interesting example of this strategy, transforming their 501 jeans from workaday industrial apparel into an essential fashion accessory. From 1984 their campaigns in the United States used black music as a marker of urban authenticity and an expression of individual heartache and freedom. In particular the ads focused on "the Blues." Like Benetton, Levi's attempted to blur the commodity forms with an advertising message and also a state of emotional well-being. In Benetton's case the logic of this strategy ran: united colours of people, united colors in garments—"I wear unity." Levi's attempted to establish an interplay between the commodity and a message of alienated individualism, and it elided blue jeans with the Blues as a celebration of solitude, alienation and solace. These forms of slippage mean that 501's not only shrink to fit your body but they also convey a kind of identity. This is summed up in their slogan: "501 Blues Shrink to Fit My Body—I got the Blues." Music becomes the connective device through which social quotations are made and in turn bolster the product's identity with a cultural dowry. A whole range of black artists were used in these campaigns including Taj Mahal, the Neville Brothers, Bobby McFerrin and Tiger Haynes. Beyond this the inner city provided the context for staging their story lines often producing romantic images of ghetto life: "Blacks who appear on the screen seem 'connected' and 'in tune' with their total social space. Levi's sell the ghetto—a space which transcends social convention, restraint and repressiveness" (Goldman, 1992, p. 191). In some of the advertisements black Americans are presented teaching their white counterparts how to dance, play instruments and express themselves. The 501 advertisements offer their audience instruction in a particular version of blackness via the references to the Blues and the ghetto, where black music is equated with the body, expression, emotionality and ultimately sexuality. Through this "injection of negritude" young whites in particular are offered a fleeting liberation from the strictures of whiteness.

*****

These notions of exotic innocence are no less stereotypical than the idea that the Negro is less civilised and more barbaric. This kind of identification is locked within the discourse of absolute difference which renders blackness exotic and reaffirms black people as a "race apart." It was this danger which Frantz Fanon outlined when he argued that those Europeans who blindly adore the difference of the other are as racially afflicted as those who vilify it (Fanon, 1986).

*****

Before moving on we want to clarify our argument. We are making two related points. First, what we have referred to as corporate multiculturalism possesses a dual quality. While it espouses the goal of transcultural unity it does so through reinforcing crude cultural and racial archetypes. These images operate within what Stuart Hall (1981) called a "grammar of race." The overpowering reference point is that race is real: racial archetypes provide the vehicle for the message, and racial common sense is overbearingly present such that the reality of race is legitimated within this media discourse. Second, the valuation and repackaging of cultural difference within contemporary media result in little more than a process of market driven recolonisation, where the fetish for the exotic reaffirms these various "global others" as distinct and separate types of humankind. In this context the veneration of difference need not be in any contradiction with white supremacy. Quite the contrary: it can be integrally connected with the formation of contemporary cultures of racism. Yet, we also want to argue that these shifts do create important ambivalences and tensions which can unsettle the valence of racism within popular culture.

Kobena Mercer has explored the ambivalences found in racial fetishism through an analysis of the white gay photographer Robert Mapplethorpe (Mercer, 1994). In his initial reading of the photographs of black nude men found in *Black Males* and *Black Book*, Mercer offers an analysis of Mapplethorpe's "line of sight" in which:

> Black + Male = Erotic/Aesthetic Object. Regardless of the sexual preferences of the spectator, the connotation is that the "essence" of black male identity lies in the domain of sexuality ... black men are confined and defined in their very being as sexual and nothing but sexual, hence hyper sexual. (Mercer, 1994, p. 174)

He argues that the regulative function of stereotypes polices the potential for generating meanings, and as a result the spectator is fixed within the position of the "white male subject." However, in a later rereading Mercer changes his mind and points to the ways in which these images actually undermine the conventions of the spectator and the stereotypes which furnish this way of seeing. Mercer argues that once we understand the political specificity of Mapplethorpe's practice, we can see in his aesthetic use of irony disruptive elements which challenge Eurocentred representative regimes. Black men constitute perhaps the most social and politically marginalised group in the United States, but in Mapplethorpe's photographs the men who come from this social location are raised "onto the pedestal of the transcendental western aesthetic ideal. Far from reinforcing the fixed beliefs of the white supremacist imaginary, such a deconstructive move begins to undermine the foundational myth of the pedestal itself" (ibid., p. 200). Mercer's argument suggests that through the use of subversion and aesthetic irony racist regimes of representation are propelled into a state of crisis and erasure. It is with these suggestive comments in mind that we want to return to the iconography of Benetton advertising.

Our intention here is not to merely reproduce a parallel argument to Kobena Mercer's insightful and reflective reading of Mapplethorpe's photography. However, if we look closely at Toscani's photography we can see similar—although not comparable—ambivalences at work. In this sense we need to revise partially the analysis offered earlier (Back and Quaade, 1993) and suggest that there are moments within Benetton's advertising imagery when the racial grammar of these representations is unsettled. Toscani has specialised in blurring photographic conventions, turning news photographs into advertising and advertising into the news. Both he and Luciano Benetton have also indulged in self-parody. In the spring 1992 edition of *Colors* their own faces are superimposed on to one of their ads. This notorious image represented two children embracing, one depicted as a white cherub angel and the other a black child devil. In this reworked version Luciano Benetton is cast as the angel and Toscani as the devil. Returning to the original image one might think of it as a moment where racial anxieties are being displayed. Is Toscani forcing the viewer to confront the racist connotations of such an image or is he merely reproducing and activating these racial ideologies? This question captures the core ambivalence found within Toscani's photography. McKenzie Wark has argued that the Benetton campaigns open up a wealth of meaning and that to reduce these advertisements to a moral narrative or any one meaning does more violence than the image itself (Wark, 1992).

In the aftermath of the Los Angeles riots, in an atmosphere of heightened fears of the possibility of further racial conflict, a whole edition of *Colors* was given over to the issue of race. The editorial captured the impulse to deal with this issue: "If there's one topic COLORS was destined to address, it's racism and the devastation caused by racism. Not just in Los Angeles, Germany or South Africa but everywhere that people are assaulting and killing each other over genetic, linguistic or cultural differences" (*Colors*, no. 4, 1993, p. 68). What is remarkable about this publication is its complete deconstruction of the "idea of race." The journal undermined the racial categories so abundantly deployed in the "United Colors" campaigns since 1984, concluding:

> Finally it occurred to us that while the physical differences between peoples and individuals are real ... the monoliths called races are a purposeful invention, once used to make Europe's slavery and colonial conquests seem moral and inevitable.... What's going on, we believe, is that people continue to live their lives as if the myths about race were fact. Why? Because it's simpler for those in positions of power if those without power vent all their anger on others without power.... As long as our actions are guided by fear, as long as we regard the myths of race and racism as truth none of us is truly safe. (Ibid, p. 70)

The special issue tackled questions ranging from racial harassment, phenotypic difference, neo-Nazi youth culture and mixed relationships. The reflexive and quite extraordinary deconstructivist turn is also embodied within the imagery used in this edition. In a section entitled "What if...?" Toscani presented a series of famous people with transformed racial characteristics, these included a black

Arnold Schwarzenegger, a Semitic Spike Lee, an Oriental John Paul II, and an Aryan Michael Jackson. This striking image, challenges the common sense of race and nation which in Britain has constructed blackness and Britishness as mutually exclusive categories. The photograph challenges the reader to ask why s\he finds it implausible. What is exposed is the association between' race and nation within the ideology of British, or more precisely, English nationalism.

The "What If..." photograph of the "Black Queen" identifies the mutually inclusive nature of the relationship of whiteness and Englishness. Through this "altered image" racial common sense is unsettled and the implicit, "taken for granted quality" of what it means to look "English" phenotypically is rendered obvious. In the terms of this ideology the Queen cannot be 'black' because to be English is to be "white." [...] However, the ideologies of race and nation make the recognition of such heterogeneity impossible, ridiculous and out of question. What is asserted instead within the language of nationalism is the compulsory whiteness of English identity. The photograph of the black Queen invites the reader to ridicule these associations and opens up a representational space which challenges the othordoxies of race and nation.

The ambivalences and traces of anti-racism found within these examples are important for us to appreciate when evaluating the contemporary politics of race. In many respects these examples force us to move beyond the dualism of "good and bad images" and challenge us to think through the complex interplay of meaning and the ambivalences registered within the representation of race and difference. What we have shown is that any sophisticated understanding of the contemporary relationship between popular culture and racism needs to be alert to the coupling of fear and desire that produces the complex representations of difference we have analysed here.

POPULAR CULTURE AND DIFFERENCE

We began this chapter by asking the question of how is racism made popular? We have attempted to show how both printed and electronic media have been crucially implicated in providing the technical infrastructure for the creation and dissemination of the cultures of racism. Racism is connected integrally to the history of modernity and modern technologies have provided a key means in the establishment of racial supremacy. Popular culture provided the means whereby the masses within any particular modern social formation participated in the domination of others. We have also argued that racist formulations and ways of seeing can also be challenged within these representational spaces. Popular culture has provided a key means for reproducing racism but this is not inevitably the case. The instability of historically inflected racisms makes it important to stress the ideological battles that are being waged within this domain of vernacular culture.

*****

REFERENCES

Adam, P. (1992) *The Arts of the Third Reich* (London: Thames and Hudson).

Appiah, K.A. (1992) *In My Father's House: Africa in the Philosopy of Culture* (London: Methuen).

Atherton, H.M. (1974) *Political Prints in the Age of Hogarth: A Study of the Ideographic Representation of Politics* (Oxford: Oxford University Press).

Back, L. and Quaade, V. (1993) "Dream Utopias, Nightmare Realities: Imaging Race and Culture with the World of Benetton Advertising," *Third Text*, 22: 65–80.

Benjamin, W. (1968) "The Work of Art in the Age of Mechanical Reproduction," in W. Benjamin, *Illuminations* (London: Harcourt, Brace and World).

Colley, L. (1992) *Britons: Forging the Nation, 1707–1837* (New Haven: Yale University Press).

Colours, no. 4, 1993.

Coombes, A. (1994) *Reinventing Africa* (London: Yale University Press).

Cottrell, S. (1989) "The Devil on Two Sticks: Franco-phobia in 1803," in R. Samuel (ed.), *Patriotism: The Making and Unmaking of British National Identity. Volume 1: History and Politics* (London: Routledge).

Fanon, F. (1986) *Black Skin, White Masks* (London: Pluto Press).

Gilroy, P. (1987) *There Ain't No Black in the Union Jack* (London: Hutchinson).

Goldman, R. (1992) *Reading Ads Socially* (London: Routledge).

de Grazia, E. and Newman, R.K. (1982) *Banned Films: Movies, Censors and the First Amendment* (New York: R.R. Bowker).

Hall, S. (1981) "The Whites of Their Eyes: Racist Ideologies and the Media," in G. Bridges and R. Brunt (eds.), *Silver Linings: Some Strategies for the Eighties* (London: Lawrence and Wishart).

Hall, S., Critcher, C., Jefferson, T., Clarke, J. and Roberts, B. (1978) *Policing the Crisis: Mugging, the State, and Law and Order* (London: Macmillan).

Harris, C. (1988) "Images of Blacks in Britain: 1930–60," in S. Allen and M. Macey (eds.), *Race and Social Policy* (London: Economic and Social Research Council).

Hulme, P. (1986) *Colonial Envounters: Europe and the Native Caribbean* (London: Methuen).

Jordan, W. (1968) *White Over Black: American Attitudes Towards the Negro, 1550–1812* (New York: W.W. Norton).

Kater, M.H. (1992) *Different Drummers: Jazz in the Culture of Nazi Germany* (New York: Oxford University Press).

Keith, M. (1995) "Ethnic Entrepreneurs and Street Rebels: Looking Inside the Inner City," in S. Pile and N. Thrift (eds.), *Mapping the Subject: Geographies of Cultural Transformation* (London: Routledge).

Kisch, J. and Mapp, E. (1992) *A Separate Cinema: Fifty Years of Black-Cast Posters* (New York: Noonday Press).

MacKenzie, J.M. (1984) *Propaganda and Empire: The Manipulation of British Public Opinion 1880–1960* (Manchester: Manchester University Press).

Mercer, K. (1992) "Skin Head Sex Thing: Racial Difference and Homoerotic Imagery," *New Frontiers*, 16: 1–23.

Mercer, K. (1994) *Welcome to the Jungle: New Positions in Black Cultural Studies* (London: Routledge).

Miles, R. (1984) "The Riots of 1958: Notes on the Ideological Construction of 'Race Relations' as a Political Issue in Britain," *Immigrants and Minorities*, 3, 3: 252–75

Mudimbe, V.Y. (1994) *The Idea of Africa* (Bloomington: Indiana University Press).

Newman, G. (1987) *The Rise of English Nationalism: A Cultural History, 1740–1830* (London: Weidenfeld and Nicolson).

Opie, R. (1985) *Rule Britannia: Trading on the British Image* (Harmondsworth: Viking).

Opitz, M., Oguntoye, K. and Schultz, D. (eds.) (1992) *Showing Our Colours: Afro-German Women Speak Out* (London: Open Letters Press).

Pieterse, J.N. (1992) *White on Black: Images of Africa and Blacks in Western Popular Culture* (New Haven and London: Yale University Press).

Rhodes, A. (1976) *Propaganda: The Art of Persuasion in World War II* (London: Angus Robertson).

Richards, T. (1990) *The Commodity Culture of Victorian England: Advertising and Spectacle* (London: Verso).

Servos, N. (1990) "Pathos and Propaganda?: On the Mass Choreography of Fascism," *Ballet International Handbook*: 63–6.

Simmons, S. (1993) *The Films of D.W. Griffith* (Cambridge: Cambridge University Press).

Solomos, J. (1986) "Polititical Language and Violent Protest: Ideological and Policy Responses to the 1981 and 1985 Riots," *Youth and Policy*, 18: 12–24.

Solomos, J. (1988) *Black Youth, Racism and the State* (Cambridge: Cambridge University Press).

van Dijk, T.A. (1991) *Racism and the Press* (London: Routledge).

Ware, V. (1992) *Beyond the Pale: White Women, Racism and History* (London: Verso).

Wark, M. (1992) "Still Life Today: The Benetton Campaigns," *Photophile*, 36: 33–6.

FURTHER READING

Deloria, Philip J. 1998. *Playing Indian*. New Haven and London: Yale University Press.

This book explores the ambiguous relationship that has existed between indigenous peoples in the USA and white colonial men attempting to develop a new "American" national identity that is different from a European one, emphasizing freedom and rebelliousness. The author argues that the "noble savage" trope encapsulates this tension between desiring indigeneity and rejecting it. This, Deloria argues, has led to the twin strategies of either destroying or assimilating indigenous people, both of which have led to similar results. The ambiguous relationship that has existed between destroying and desiring the indigenous subject has resulted in a variety of spectacles, customs, and practices that have included white men "playing Indian," wearing furs, feathers, and face paint. The author examines several such examples where American revolutionaries built on European traditions of carnival and misrule combining these with a constructed "Indianness" to develop a new and unique identity.

Hellwig, Tineke, and Suneral Thobani, eds. 2006. *Asian Women: Interconnections*. Toronto: Women's Press.

The second half of this book contains six chapters, divided into two sections: "Imagining Asian-ness in the Diaspora" and "Asia Viewing." All six chapters are comparative analyses of representations of "Asian" women in literature, cinema, newspapers, and popular television. While use of the identifier "Asian" may imply homogenization and essentializing of a variety of different populations on the Asian continent, the editors problematize the term in the introduction, recognizing "Asia's multidimensional existence." The chapters combine comparative and diasporic perspectives on the representation of Chinese and South Asian women in Asian, Canadian, and American media and popular culture, reflecting complex issues encountered in a globalized and transnational world. Continuities and departures from 18th- and 19th-century colonial images are pointed out.

hooks, bell. 1992. *Black Looks: Race and Representation*. Toronto: Between the Lines.

This book is a seminal collection of essays on the representations of black people in popular music, advertising, literature, television, and film. It calls for a critical and subversive spectatorship, interpretation of images, and understanding of how these images affect black femininities and masculinities. Above all, these essays are a call to resist hegemonic images and practices and imagine empowering and revolutionary representations and subjectivities of black people as a process of decolonization. Towards this goal, hooks argues for the need to love blackness, rather than to see it as an inferior condition, a condition that is often internalized by blacks themselves. She exposes the futility of the cultural appropriation that can result from the apparent desire for blackness in popular culture. In addition, she points out the vestiges of oppressive discourses (sexism and/or racism) in apparently transgressive cultural practices. Finally, hooks explores differences among black women on the basis of different locations and experiences through an examination of black women's writings, and urges the development of a revolutionary black female subjectivity on the basis of a recognition of differences.

Said, Edward W. 1997. *Covering Islam: How the Media and the Experts Determine How We See the Rest of the World*. New York: Vintage Books.

Building on his classic work *Orientalism*, Said explores in depth how the "West," in particular the USA, views "Islam" as its Other, especially in the post–Cold War era. The media play a key role in constructing the "West" and "Islam" as polar opposites and the latter as anti-modern, dangerous, fascist, and hateful. The images of "Islam" that are projected by the media are not based in history or real-life interactions, but on stereotypical writings, some produced as far back as the 18th century and others as recently as the 1990s, such as the writings of Samuel P. Huntington and Bernard Lewis. Said argues against a conspiratorial thesis and rather asserts that ethnocentric portrayals of Muslims come out of the rules and conventions of media institutions that exist within a specific political and ideological context and are fundamentally ruled by the profit motive. Despite a certain level of variation in views disseminated in the American media, in the end there is a certain consensus about the position of the USA or the West in relation to Islam or countries constructed as "Islamic." This consensus is maintained by setting certain limits to what can and cannot be said. Chapters I and II are particularly relevant to the topic of racism in the media, including a detailed discussion of how the American media covered the Iranian student occupation of the American Embassy on November 4, 1979.

Van Dijk, Teun A. 2002. "Denying Racism: Elite Discourse and Racism." In *Race Critical Theories: Text and Context*, ed. Philomena Essed and David Theo Goldberg. Maldden, MA: Blackwell Publishers.

This chapter examines the discourse of denial of racism within mainstream media and parliamentary exchanges as examples of elite discourse. The author argues that by denying racism in a variety of ways, elite discourses confirm that elites do not practise racism or think in a racist way, that there is thus no racism, and that what anti-racists are saying is invalid. Denial discourses establish in-group solidarity, ethnic consensus, and dualities of "us" and "them," and reproduce racism.

PART 3D

RACISM IN THE JUSTICE SYSTEM AND POLICE FORCE

Although many contemporary nation-states enjoy (and work very hard to maintain) a reputation for liberalism, prosperity, and multicultural inclusiveness, such reputations have been created and maintained at the expense of people of colour. In particular, racialized "others"—especially minorities and indigenous people—encounter daily a criminal justice apparatus whose officials often view people of colour with suspicion if not outright hostility. Such viewpoints are deeply rooted in nation-states' colonialism and are often based on racialized constructions that seek to explain the behaviour of individuals by attributing it to group characteristics. In Canada, for example, these racialized constructions take the form of expressions like "Donovan Bailey can run so fast because he is black" or "Asians are better at math." Likewise, success and failure tend to be explained with reference to individual characteristics rather than structural, societal-level conditions. This section will explore some of the structural conditions that, though rarely discussed in state or popular discourse, have a causative effect on the antagonistic, socially unequal relationship between policing agencies and indigenous peoples or peoples of colour.

The first reading—"Inflammatory Rhetoric? Baseless Accusations? A Response to Gabor's Critique of Racial Profiling in Canada," by Scot Wortley and Julian Tanner—examines the relationship between race and crime in the specific context of racial profiling of people of colour (specifically black citizens) in Toronto. Engaging in a sophisticated statistical analysis of the Toronto Youth Crime and Victimization Survey, Wortley and Tanner find that even after taking into account factors like social class, age, self-reported deviant behaviour, gang membership, drug and alcohol use, and public leisure activities—all factors used by police to defend their policing of black Torontonians—Torontonian youths' "blackness" still stands as a significant factor in explaining why they are stopped by police. These findings are extremely controversial because they challenge the legitimacy of policing agencies as neutral organizations that simply "uphold" the law under which all citizens are treated equally. In other words, their findings suggest that black youth are more likely to be stopped and arrested *independently* of any illegal activity they might have engaged in. Such a situation has given rise to the wry expression in many American cities of a new criminal offence: "driving while black."

The second reading—"The Criminalization of Indigenous People," by Chris Cunneen—examines the overrepresentation of indigenous people in the Australian criminal justices system. Conventional discussions often begin with the seemingly logical idea that, for a variety of reasons, indigenous people tend to commit more crimes, and more serious crimes, which in turn lead to higher rates of arrest, conviction, and incarceration. In his reading of contemporary Australia, however, Cunneen paints a far more complex picture of the social relations within which this overrepresentation is situated. He argues that the specific ways in which criminal justice officials police indigenous communities, and the wide power of discretion held by police officers, judges, and other criminal justice officials, conspire to exert an enormous impact on how particular incidents are framed as criminal or as, for example, "pranks." In this context, he presents evidence that police and other criminal justice officials use their discretion in ways that negatively impact indigenous people insofar as they increase the likelihood of indigenous people being charged, arrested, and imprisoned. Likewise, Cunneen emphasizes the importance of situating the criminal justice relationship between Australian indigenous communities and policing agencies within the larger socio-economic and cultural context of Australia's colonialism and its past and contemporary treatment of these indigenous communities.

CHAPTER 30

INFLAMMATORY RHETORIC? BASELESS ACCUSATIONS? A RESPONSE TO GABOR'S CRITIQUE OF RACIAL PROFILING RESEARCH IN CANADA

Scot Wortley and Julian Tanner[1]

Racial profiling has emerged as one of the most important—and controversial—issues facing the Canadian criminal justice system. Much of the current public debate can be attributed to a series of articles on the relationship between race, crime, and criminal justice published by the *Toronto Star* in October 2002 (Rankin, Quinn, Shephard, Simmie, and Duncanson 2002a, 2002b, 2002c). However, it must be stressed that this topic has been a major concern of racial minority communities for several decades (see discussion in Ontario, Commission on Systemic Racism 1995; Henry 1994). Not surprisingly, the lines are clearly drawn with respect to the racial profiling debate. Social activists and black community organizations, on the one hand, have long maintained that the police frequently stop and search black citizens solely because of their racial characteristics (e.g., for the "offence" of driving while black). Police representatives, on the other hand, consistently deny allegations of racial profiling and claim that race has absolutely no influence on their decision-making processes. For example, Julian Fantino, Chief of the Toronto Police Service, states that "We do not do racial profiling ... there is no racism.... We don't look at, nor do we consider race or ethnicity, or any of that, as factors of how we dispose of cases, or individuals, or how we treat individuals (quoted in "There is no racism" 2002).

*****

Definitional Issues

In a previous article, [...] we provided the following definition of racial profiling:

> In the criminological literature, racial profiling is said to exist when the members of certain racial or ethnic groups become subject to greater levels of criminal justice surveillance than others. Racial profiling, therefore, is typically defined as a racial disparity in police stop and search practices, racial differences in Customs searches at airports and border-crossings, increased police patrols in racial minority neighbourhoods and undercover activities or sting operations which selectively target particular ethnic groups. (Wortley and Tanner 2003: 369–370)

This definition was provided in direct response to a report, written by sociologist Edward Harvey, that critiqued the *Toronto Star*'s race-crime series. In his report, Harvey provides a reanalysis of Toronto police *arrest data* in order to claim that there is no evidence of racial profiling in the Toronto region. Harvey's reanalysis finds that black people are greatly over-represented in drug trafficking arrests and out-of-sight traffic offences. Nonetheless, he argues that the fact that white people are over-represented in other arrest categories (i.e., prostitution and DUI charges) *proves* that racial profiling does not exist (Harvey 2003). We provided the above definition simply to illustrate that Harvey's investigation, in our opinion, had not actually dealt with the literature on racial profiling. We wanted to highlight, for example, that Harvey had totally ignored research on police stop and search activities. Furthermore, we wanted to stress that although the over-representation of minorities in arrest statistics may indeed be one consequence of racial profiling, this over-representation could also reflect actual racial differences in criminal offending (Wortley and Tanner 2003: 370).

Gabor (2004) is quite critical of our definition of racial profiling. He writes that

> My concern is that this definition fails to distinguish between law enforcement practices that are based on pure bigotry and those that may be entirely reasonable as a result of systematic analyses of crime patterns, intelligence work, and information obtained from the community.... Wortley and Tanner's definition appears to include any police operation aimed at a criminal network of minority persons or conducted in a minority neighbourhood. Their definition of racial profiling includes increased police activity in a minority community even where segments of that community seek additional protection or where crime patterns indicate the need for greater police presence. (Gabor 2004: 458–459)

We agree, in general, with Gabor's critique of our definition. Clearly, our definition should also have stressed that racial profiling exists when race itself—not other legitimate variables—is a significant factor in making police surveillance decisions. In other words, racial profiling exists when racial differences in law enforcement surveillance activities cannot be totally explained by racial differences in criminal activity, traffic violations, calls for service, or other legally relevant variables. We did feel that such an understanding was implicit in our original definition. Our mistake was in failing to make these ideas explicit. However, as discussed below, we definitely attempt to control for such factors in our own racial profiling research. In sum, we appreciate Gabor's comments regarding our definition of racial profiling and will try to incorporate some of his ideas into our future work. We are not so appreciative, however, of his misinterpretation of our research findings.

Evidence of Racial Profiling: Gabor's Misrepresentation of Survey Results

In an article entitled "Data, Denials, and Confusion: The Racial Profiling Debate in Toronto," we discuss findings from a recent survey of Toronto high school students (Wortley and Tanner 2003). The results from this survey, in our opinion, strongly suggest that black youth are much more likely to be stopped and searched by the police than youth from other racial backgrounds. However, under the pejorative subtitle "The Perils of Baseless Accusations," Gabor vehemently attacks the validity of our research findings. In order to defend our work, we will take the reader through Gabor's comments step by step.

Gabor begins his critique by stating that "one example of the misuse of the term 'racial profiling' is found in Wortley and Tanner. They cite their own study of high school students as providing evidence of this phenomena. In their survey, a higher percentage of black than white, Asian, or South Asian students indicated that they had been stopped and questioned by the police more than once over the past two years" (2004: 461). Not surprisingly, we do not think that our research has "misused" the term "racial profiling." Nevertheless, Gabor is correct in stating that we did indeed observe racial differences in police stops. Gabor does not, however, discuss the magnitude of these racial differences, nor the fact that black students are also much more likely than students from other racial backgrounds to report being physically searched by the police.

Gabor continues his commentary by stating that "Wortley and Tanner also acknowledge 'that students who engage in various forms of crime and deviance are much more likely to receive police attention than students who do not break the law.' Wortley and Tanner's survey also revealed that students spending more of their time in public spaces are more likely to be stopped by the police than those spending their time in private spaces or in the company of their parents" (2004: 461). We have no problem with this passage. It is quite consistent with our survey results, and, in fact, we provide several examples in our article (Wortley and Tanner 2003: 371–373).

Gabor's next statement, however, is extremely problematic. He writes that "the authors then concede that their data do not allow them to determine whether the greater police attention received by black students is due to their skin colour or whether it is due to higher levels of criminality and their greater use of public spaces. In fact, black students reported more violence and minor property crime. Why, then, the pejorative term 'racial profiling' when the police may simply be doing their job?" (2004: 461). This statement by Gabor is completely incorrect and totally misrepresents our data analysis and research findings. First of all, we never come close to conceding that our data do not permit us to determine whether black students are stopped because of their race or because of their criminal behaviour and use of public spaces. We challenge Professor Gabor to locate such a statement in any of our writings or public statements. In fact, a thorough reading of our article would reveal that we can and do statistically control for these variables in our multivariate analysis. The following passage from our article, which Gabor apparently did not consider, illustrates this point:

> Do black students receive more police attention because they are more involved in crime and more likely to be involved in leisure activities which take place in public places? While our data revealed that white students have much higher rates of both alcohol consumption and illicit drug use, black students did report higher rates of both minor property crime and violence. Furthermore, both black and white students reported higher rates of participation in public leisure activities than students from all other racial backgrounds. *These racial differences, however, do not come close to explaining why black youth are much more vulnerable to police contact. In fact, after statistically controlling for criminal activity, drug use, gang membership and leisure activities, the relationship between race and police stops actually got stronger. Why? Multivariate analysis reveals that racial differences in police stop and search practices are actually greatest among students with low levels of criminal behaviour.* For example, 34% of the black students who had not engaged in any type of criminal activity still reported that they had been stopped by the police on two or more occasions in the past two years, compared to only 4% of white students in the same behavioural category. Similarly, 23% of black students with no deviant behaviour reported that they had been searched by the police, compared to only 5% of whites who reported no deviance (Wortley and Tanner 2002). Thus, while the first survey, discussed above, reveals that age and social class do not protect blacks from police stops, this study suggests that good behaviour also does not shelter blacks from unwanted police attention.... These findings strongly suggest that racial profiling does, in fact, exist in Toronto. (Wortley and Tanner 2003: 372–373; emphasis added)

To reiterate, contrary to the statements made by Gabor, we did, in fact, conduct a multivariate analysis to determine the social predictors of police stop and search encounters. Furthermore, after controlling for deviant behaviour, drug and alcohol use, public leisure activities, and various demographic characteristics (including social class), we still found that black students are much more likely to report being stopped and searched by the police than students from other racial backgrounds. This finding, we maintain, is completely consistent with allegations of racial profiling. Unfortunately, we feel that by inaccurately portraying our data analysis efforts and findings, Gabor has reduced his critique of our research to nothing more than "inflammatory rhetoric"—the very title of his commentary. We do not know why Gabor made such inaccurate—and potentially damaging—statements about our article. One possible explanation is that our findings were not actually presented in tabular form in our previous article (Wortley and Tanner 2003). Thus, in order to prevent further misinterpretation of our work, we would like to take this opportunity to provide more detail about our study and our analysis to the readers of this journal.

THE TORONTO YOUTH CRIME AND VICTIMIZATION SURVEY

Our analysis is based on data from the Toronto Youth Crime and Victimization Survey. This project, conducted in 2000, involves a random sample of 3,393 high school students from both the public and Catholic school systems in Toronto (see Tanner and Wortley [2002] for a detailed discussion of the sampling strategy, methodological procedures, and a copy of the survey instrument). The school boards agreed to provide us with one class period (usually 75 minutes) for the students to complete the survey. After a brief introduction, in which the students were reminded of the confidential nature of the study, respondents were asked to complete a 32-page questionnaire. Members of the research team remained in the class at all times to answer questions, control the survey environment (i.e., prevent talking), and collect the questionnaires. The survey typically took between 50 and 70 minutes to complete. Original class lists indicated that there were 4,127 students enrolled in the classes that we surveyed. Thus, we were able to achieve an impressive response rate of 82.2%.

Bivariate Results

The first step in our analysis was to explore the question of whether racial minority youth are more likely to report being stopped and searched by the police than white youth. The answer to this question depends on how race is operationalized. [...] A great deal of Canadian research on the issue of race simplistically divides the population into two major categories: whites and visible minorities. When we use this rather crude racial classification system, our results suggest that there is very little evidence of racial bias in police stop and search practices[.] [...] Indeed, white students are slightly more likely to report being stopped by the police in the past two years (41%) than racial minority students (38%). Furthermore, minority students (19%) are only slightly more likely to report being searched by the police than their white counterparts (17.5%). These differences are not statistically significant.

However, our results change dramatically when we use a more detailed race variable. [Other research] reveal[s] that students who self-identified as black are much more likely to report being stopped and searched by the police than students from any other racial background. However, the results also reveal that white students are actually more likely to be stopped and searched than Asians, South Asians, or West Asians.[2] For example, more than half of all black respondents (51%) report having been stopped and questioned by the police on two or more occasions in the past two years, compared with 23% of white students, 13% of West Asians, 11% of Asians, and only 8% of South Asian students. Hispanic students and students from "other" racial backgrounds (a category that includes those with multiple racial identities) appear to be stopped at about the same rate as whites. Additional analysis reveals that 4 of every 10 black respondents (40%) report that they have actually been physically searched by the police in the past two years, compared with only 20% of Hispanic students, 17% of whites, 11% of West Asians, 10% of Asians, and 7% of South Asians.[3] These differences are highly significant. Clearly, the experiences of racial minority students are far from uniform. Indeed, when we combine blacks, Asians, South Asians, and West Asians into the same category, we create the illusion that racial differences in stop and search experiences do not exist. In other words, the results presented above strongly suggest that the term "visible minority" may in fact mask important racial differences in both experience and behaviour and ultimately hinder the identification of racism in Canada. We therefore use a more detailed racial classification system in the balance of our analysis.

What might account for the fact that black students report being stopped and searched more frequently than students from any other racial background? What might account for the fact that white students report being stopped and searched more often than Asians, South Asians, and West Asians? We turn to these research questions in the next section.

Control Variables

We recognize that many other factors—besides race—are potentially related to police decisions to stop and search citizens. Indeed, American research suggests that the police typically respond to allegations of racial profiling by stating that they do not conduct street interrogations without good reason. The argument is basically that if the police stop black people more often than white people, it is because they somehow deserve the extra attention (see Macdonald 2003; Harris 2002). As Bernard Parks, former chief of the Los Angeles Police Department, states, "It's not the fault of the police when they stop minority males or put them in jail. It's the fault of minority males for committing crime" (Goldberg 1999: 72). Indeed, as part of their crime prevention/community safety mandate, the police have the responsibility to stop and investigate individuals who may be involved in criminal or other illegal behaviour. Thus, individuals who are involved in illegal activities should legitimately receive more police attention than individuals who are not involved in illegal activities. Is it possible that the racial differences in police stop and search activity [...] can be explained by racial differences in illegal behaviour?

In order to examine this possibility, we controlled for self-reported deviant behaviour in our multivariate analyses (presented below). Respondents were asked how often they had engaged in 23 different illegal activities over the past year. These activities ranged from minor theft to serious assault. Response options ranged from "never" to "ten or more times" in the past year. Responses to these 23 items were subsequently combined into an index of deviant behaviour that ranges from 0 to 69 (= 0.903). We also controlled for an index of *alcohol and drug use* (= 0.714). We felt that youth who frequently use alcohol and illegal drugs might legitimately draw more police attention than those who do not engage in such behaviour. Finally, we also included in our regression equations a variable that captures self-reported *gang membership*. In addition to high levels of criminal involvement, we felt that the presence of gang symbols (e.g., the flying of gang colours) and the fact that gang members often travel in groups might make them more visible to the police and thus increase their likelihood of being stopped and searched.

It is important to note that, on average, our black respondents scored significantly higher on the deviance scale (mean = 6.906) than white youth (mean = 5.785). However, white students scored significantly higher on the deviance scale than our Asian (mean = 3.768), West Asian (mean = 3.786), and South Asian respondents (mean = 2.745). It should also be noted that black youth are also more likely to report gang membership (16%) than white students (9%) or students from other racial backgrounds. On the other hand, white students report the highest levels of drug and alcohol use (mean = 3.605), followed by black (mean = 2.665) and Hispanic (mean = 2.527) students. By comparison, Asians (mean = 1.759), West Asians (mean = 1.780), and South Asians (0.852) all score low on our measure of drug and alcohol use. Can these racial differences in deviant activity help explain why black students report being stopped and searched more frequently than whites—or why white students report being stopped and searched more frequently than Asians, South Asians, and West Asians?

Besides deviant activity, we also feel that it is important to control for how students spend their leisure time. From a routine activities perspective, it should be expected that youth who spend much of their time engaged in public activities are more vulnerable to police attention than youth who spend most of their time in private contexts. We therefore include three measures of public activities in our multivariate analyses.[4] We include *riding in cars with friends* because research indicates that a large proportion of all police contacts are traffic-related. Thus, the more you drive, the greater your probability of being stopped by the police. This may be particularly true for youth who are not accompanied by an adult. *Hanging out* refers to the frequency of socializing with friends on the street or in other public locations (i.e., shopping malls, coffee shops, parks). *Party activities* refers to how frequently our respondents attended house parties and raves or visited nightclubs, bars, and taverns. We feel that youth who frequently engage in such behaviour are particularly vulnerable to police contact because such activities typically take place late at night, involve large groups of people, and are associated with drinking and/or drug use. Finally, we also include a variable that measures involvement in *family activities*. We feel that unlike our other three activity measures, the amount of time spent with family should serve a protective function: youth who spend most of their time with family should be less likely to report police stop and search activities. Overall, our results suggest that both white and black students spend more time engaged in certain public activities—particularly party activities—than youth from other racial backgrounds. This, in turn, might increase their probability of being stopped and searched by the police.

Along with measures of race, deviant activity, and leisure routines, we include in our multivariate analyses several measures of social class position.[5] These variables include *subjective social class* (i.e., whether the respondent feels that his or her family is poor, middle-class, or wealthy), *family structure, parental education, parental employment*, and whether or not the respondent lives in a subsidized *housing project*. The inclusion of these variables may help us determine whether it is race or social class position that determines police attention. Indeed, our black respondents, on average, score significantly lower on all of these social class measures than respondents from other racial groups. Is it possible that black students are stopped more often by the police because they are more likely to live in poor, disadvantaged neighbourhoods? Finally, we also include both *age* and *gender* as additional control variables in our multivariate analyses.

Multivariate Results

For the purposes of multivariate analyses, our two dependent measures, *police stops* and *police searches*, were re-coded into dichotomous variables (1 = respondent reports being stopped or searched at least once by the police in the past two years; 0 = the respondent reports not having been stopped or searched). In this section we present a series of logistic regression models produced in order to estimate the impact of race on self-reported police contacts while controlling for deviant activity, leisure routines, and demographic factors.[6] [...]

The regression results suggest that black students are much more likely to report being stopped by the police than white students or students from other racial backgrounds—even after other demographic factors, including social class, have been taken into statistical account. On the other hand, Asian and South Asian respondents are less likely to report being stopped. West Asian, Hispanic, and "other" racial backgrounds are not related to self-reported police stops. The results also suggest that male students are more likely to report being stopped by the police than female students and that older students are more likely to report being stopped than their younger counterparts. Social class also seems to be an important predictor. Respondents who indicate that they come from a poor family are more likely to report being stopped than those from middle- or upper-class backgrounds. Similarly, respondents from single-parent families and those who reside in public housing projects are more likely to report being stopped by the police in the past two years.

In Model B, we add deviant behaviour, alcohol and drug use, gang membership, and leisure activities to the logistic regression equation. The addition of these variables greatly increases the explanatory power of the regression model. Indeed, the Nagelkerke R^2 statistic increases dramatically, from 0.167 to 0.396. Consistent with police arguments, and with our initial hypotheses, the results suggest that deviant behaviour, gang membership, and drug and alcohol use are all positively related to self-reported police stops. In general, the results suggest that "badly behaved" youth are more likely to report being stopped by the police than well-behaved youth. The results also suggest that riding in cars with friends, party activities, and hanging out in public spaces are strongly related to the probability of self-reported police contact. Youth who frequently engage in these activities are more likely to report being stopped by the police than youth who refrain from such behaviour. On the other hand, youth who frequently engage in family activities are significantly less likely to report being stopped.

Does the inclusion of these new variables eliminate, or even diminish, the impact of black racial identity? The answer is no. In fact, it appears that the effect of black identity on self-reported police stops actually increases from Model A to Model B. According to Model A, the odds of reporting having experienced a police stop are 2.31 times as high for black students as for white students. After controlling for deviant behaviour and leisure activities in Model B, however, the odds jump to 4.14 times as high. The inclusion of deviant activity and leisure activities, nonetheless, does seem to diminish the impact of other racial categories, gender, and age. In other words, female students, younger students, Asians, and South Asians are apparently less likely to report being stopped by the police because they are also less likely to engage in various forms of deviant activity, less likely to engage in public leisure activities, and more likely to spend time in the family context.

The findings with respect to the regressions on police searches are very similar. [...] When we control for racial identity and demographic characteristics (Model A), the results once again suggest that black respondents are much more likely to report being searched by the police than students from other racial backgrounds. Asian and South Asian students, on the other hand, are less likely to report being searched. The results also suggest that male students are more likely to report being searched than female students, that older students are more likely to report being searched than younger students, and that those from lower-class backgrounds are more likely to report being searched than those from middle- or upper-class backgrounds. As with the regressions on self-reported police stops, the addition of variables measuring deviant activity and leisure routines greatly increases the strength (explained variance) of the logistic regression model (Model B). Indeed, the Nagelkerke R^2 statistic jumps from 0.190 to 0.447 with the addition of these new variables. Furthermore, the results suggest that self-reported deviant behaviour, gang membership, and drug and alcohol use are all positively related to the probability of reporting a police search. Hanging out in public areas, riding in cars with friends, and engaging in party activities also increase the likelihood of reporting a police search, while time spent with family reduces the probability of reporting such an encounter.

As with self-reported police stops, it appears that inclusion of additional control variables does not reduce the impact of black racial identity on the probability of reporting a police search. [...] In fact, it once again appears that the effect of black racial identity actually increases from Model A to Model B. According to Model A, the odds of reporting a police search are 2.91 times as high for black students as for white students. After controlling for deviant behaviour and leisure activities, however, the odds jump to 6.38 times as high. The inclusion of deviant activity and leisure activities, nonetheless, does seem to diminish the effect of other racial categories, gender, and age. In other words, female students, younger students, Asians, and South Asians are apparently less likely to report being searched because they are less likely to engage in various forms of deviant activity, less likely to engage in public leisure activities, and more likely to spend time in the family context.[7]

Why does the effect of black racial identity on self-reported police stop and search experiences actually get stronger—not weaker—after statistically controlling for deviance, leisure activities, and demographic characteristics? We believe that this finding can be explained by the fact that racial differences in self-reported stop and search experiences actually decrease as deviant behaviour increases. For example, almost half of the black students (49%) who report no deviant activity also claim that they were stopped by the police at least once in the past two years, compared to only 17% of white youth who report no deviant activity. This represents a statistically significant difference of 32% ($^2 = 51.654$; $df = 1$; $p < 0.001$). By contrast, among high-deviance youth (defined as those who scored 10 or higher on the deviance scale), 83% of black youth and 82% of white youth report being stopped by the police. This slight difference (one percentage point) is not statistically significant ($^2 = 0.028$; $df = 1$; $p < 0.497$). Therefore, although self-reported deviant activity is strongly related to self-reported police stops and searches for all racial groups, racial differences in self-reported police stop and search experiences are actually greatest among low-deviance youth.

This finding suggests that good behaviour does not protect black youth from police suspicion to the same extent that it protects white youth. Regardless of how well black students behave, the data suggest, there is a high probability that their skin colour alone will invite suspicion and ultimately result in police stops. This, in our view, is completely consistent with the idea of racial profiling.

In sum, the results of our high school survey suggest that black students are much more likely to be stopped and searched by the police than white students or students from other racial backgrounds. Furthermore, our multivariate analyses suggest that racial differences in self-reported police stop and search experiences cannot be explained by racial differences in deviant behaviour or public leisure activities.

We strongly believe that, contrary to the opinion of Thomas Gabor (2004), these research findings represent much more than "inflammatory rhetoric" or "baseless accusations."

*****

NOTES

1. Please direct all correspondence to Scot Wortley, Associate Professor, Centre of Criminology, University of Toronto, 130 St. George Street, Toronto, ON M5S 3H1. E-mail: scot.wortley@utoronto.ca.
2. The "South Asian" category includes students of Indo-Pakistani descent; the "West Asian" category includes those of Middle Eastern heritage; "Asians" includes those of Chinese, Japanese, Korean, Vietnamese, and Filipino background.
3. It should be noted that this study took place before September 11, 2001, and the terrorist attacks on New York City. Complaints about racial profiling from the South Asian and West Asian communities increased dramatically after that event. Thus, our results might have looked quite different if the study had been conducted at a later date.
4. These leisure activity questions are unique to this survey. They were developed after consultation with high school students and street youth during 15 focus group sessions; see Tanner and Wortley (2002) for further details.
5. We should note that it is very difficult to get accurate estimates of social class position from high school respondents. Most simply have no idea about their family's yearly income. We did ask our respondents to report the nature of their parents' occupations, but the responses were often too vague to be useful. For example, one respondent claimed that his father "works for IBM." Obviously we could not determine whether his father was an executive, a computer scientist, or a member of the janitorial staff.
6. See Knoke and Bohrnstedt (1994) for a detailed discussion of how logistic regression techniques are used to estimate models that incorporate dichotomous dependent variables.
7. Tests for multi-collinearity were conducted for all logistic regressions models presented in this article. It was not a problem in any of our analyses.

REFERENCES

Gabor, Thomas. 2004. Inflammatory rhetoric on racial profiling can undermine police services. *Canadian Journal of Criminology and Criminal Justice* 46: 457–466.

Goldberg, Jeffrey. 1999. The color of suspicion. *New York Times Magazine*, June 20: 51–87.

Harris, David. 2002. *Profiles in Injustice: Why Racial Profiling Cannot Work*. New York: New Press.

Harvey, Edward. 2003. *An Independent Review of the Toronto Star Analysis of Criminal Information Processing System (CIPS) Data Provided by the Toronto Police Service*. Toronto: Toronto Police Service.

Henry, Francis. 1994. *The Caribbean Diaspora in Toronto: Learning to Live with Racism*. Toronto: HarperCollins.

Knoke, David, and George Bohrnstedt. 1994. *Statistics for Social Data Analysis*, 3rd ed. Itasca, IL: F.E. Peacock Publishers.

Macdonald, Heather 2003 *Are Cops Racist? How the War Against the Police Harms Black Americans*. Chicago: Ivan R. Dee Publishers.

Ontario, Commission on Systemic Racism. 1995. *Report of the Commission on Systemic Racism in the Ontario Criminal Justice System*. Toronto: Queen's Printer for Ontario.

Rankin, Jim, Jennifer Quinn, Michelle Shephard, Scott Simmie, and John Duncanson. 2002a. Singled out: An investigation into race and crime. *Toronto Star*, October 19: A1.

Rankin, Jim, Jennifer Quinn, Michelle Shephard, Scott Simmie, and John Duncanson. 2002b. Police target black drivers. *Toronto Star*, October 20: A1.

Rankin, Jim, Jennifer Quinn, Michelle Shephard, Scott Simmie, and John Duncanson. 2002c. Black crime rates highest. *Toronto Star*, October 26: A1.

Tanner, Julian, and Scot Wortley. 2002. *The Toronto Youth Crime and Victimization Survey: Overview Report*. Toronto: Centre of Criminology, University of Toronto.

There is no racism. We do not do racial profiling. 2002. *Toronto Star*, October 19: A14.

Wortley, Scot, and Julian Tanner. 2002. The good, the bad, and the profiled: Race, deviant activity, and police stop and search practices. Paper presented at the University of Toronto Faculty of Law Conference on Systemic Racism in the Criminal Justice System, November 28.

Wortley, Scot, and Julian Tanner. 2003. Data, denials, and confusion: The racial profiling debate in Toronto. *Canadian Journal of Criminology and Criminal Justice* 45: 367–389.

CHAPTER 31

THE CRIMINALIZATION OF INDIGENOUS PEOPLE

Chris Cunneen

THE IMPACT OF POLICING ON OFFENDING

The police role is the one most directly connected to the production of knowledge about offending patterns of individuals or groups. In most instances, Indigenous people would not be before the courts without having been previously charged by the police with an offence. Indeed, for public-order offences in particular, the police play a direct role in observing and defining the commission of an "offence" and apprehending the offender. In this sense, there is a symbiotic link between policing and offending. Such a link makes nonsense of the notion of discrete criminal behaviour separate from the criminal justice system itself.

For the purposes of the current argument it is important to consider in general terms the way policing interacts with, and shapes, the measures we use for understanding criminal behaviour among Indigenous people.

Policing Effects on Criminal Charges

One way in which police can influence official figures for offending is through over-policing, particularly in relation to public-order offences. The concept of over-policing has been used to describe how Indigenous individuals in particular, and Indigenous communities more generally, are policed in a way that is different from, and more intensive than, the policing of non-Indigenous communities. Over-policing can partly explain the over-representation of Indigenous people in the criminal justice system, particularly where offences like assault police, hinder police, resist arrest, offensive behaviour, or language and public drunkenness are involved. These charges are often representative of direct police intervention and potential adverse use of police discretion. Except for a notional "community," the victim of the offence is almost invariably the police officer, as shown by numerous studies in most Australian jurisdictions.[1]

Levels of police intervention can impact on offending figures, particularly where police are the victims of the offences. Thus, the greatest policing impact is likely with less serious offences such as "offensive language," and the impact will be less with the most serious offences such as homicide. Between these two extreme examples exists a variety of policing practices which are likely to influence the extent to which official figures on offending represent the actual occurrence of crime. For example, with property offences there are a range of factors which limit the extent to which we can discuss the actual level of offending as measured by official statistics. In commenting on the South Australian experience, Gale and her colleagues note, "it is not clear to what extent Aborigines actually commit more serious property offences or whether other factors and, in particular, police discretion in charging are at work" (Gale et al. 1990, p. 46). The authors cite examples of police discretion in charging where less serious offences, such as being unlawfully on premises and larceny, could be substituted for the more serious charge of break, enter, and steal. Similarly, Cunneen and Robb (1987, p. 96) found that of all property offences, it was arrests for "break and enter with intent to steal" for which Aboriginal people were most over-represented. In such circumstances there is a range of possible resolutions available to police officers, including the use of diversion or other less serious charges.

Similarly, quite basic issues, such as the extent to which offences are reported, can be related to the level of policing and the perceived likelihood of a satisfactory response on the part of the victim. The extent to which offences are reported impacts on how we might measure the level of their commission. In addition, there is the question of what we might make of police clear-up rates.[2] Clear-up rates are notoriously low for offences like motor vehicle theft and break, enter, and steal, often little more than 5 percent (NSW Bureau of Crime Statistics and Research 1990, pp. 19–20). The low clear-up rate means there is considerable room for speculation about what type of crimes are solved and which offenders are caught. The information on the few offenders who are apprehended is particularly susceptible to policing practices, reporting levels in particular areas, and the relative age and sophistication of the offenders. The over-representation of Indigenous people in some categories of offences may tell us as much about detection by police as about the frequency with which crimes are committed.

The Use of Police Discretion

Policing is an activity characterized by high levels of "discretion," which is routinely used even by the most junior members of the organization and often with little supervision. There is considerable evidence from various inquiries and research literature that demonstrates that police intervene in situations, particularly in relation to street offences involving Indigenous people, in ways that are unnecessary and sometimes provocative (ADB 1982; ICJ 1990; HREOC 1991; Wootten 1991a; Amnesty International 1993; Cunneen and McDonald 1997). Beyond the available observational evidence, it is difficult to demonstrate that police routinely use their discretion to intervene in situations involving Aboriginal people where the same behaviour or situation would be ignored if it involved non-Aboriginal people. However, the substantial contemporary and historical accounts presented in a range of forums, as well as other documentation on adverse police decisions after intervention, lend substantial weight to the conclusion that discretion is adversely used in this regard.

After police intervene in a situation, a number of discretionary decisions are made depending on the age of the person and the reason for intervention. These include decisions about whether to place a person in custody, whether to deal with the situation informally or to arrest or summons the person for the alleged offence, whether to administer a caution rather than charge the person if they are a juvenile, whether to grant bail to the person and what bail conditions should be imposed, and so on.

In relation to juveniles, police make "negative" decisions concerning Indigenous young people which, independent of the reason for apprehension, have the effect of harsher decisions being made at points where discretion is available (Gale et al. 1990; Luke and Cunneen 1995; Aboriginal Affairs Department and Crime Research Centre 1996). When dealing with both adults and juveniles, police have the discretion to proceed by either arrest and charge or the use of a summons. Summons is a less intrusive way of ensuring attendance at court and does not require being detained, brought to the police station to be fingerprinted, and having bail determined. All the available evidence indicates that Indigenous people are significantly less likely to be proceeded against by way of summons than non-Indigenous people. For instance, in the Northern Territory, 42 percent of non-Aboriginal people appeared in court by way of summons compared to 29 percent of Aboriginal people during 1996 (Luke and Cunneen 1998, p. 19).

After police have decided to intervene and charge a person with a criminal offence, discretion is applied to the number of charges which are laid. Over the years there have been many references to what appear to be unnecessary numbers of charges laid against Aboriginal defendants arising out of single incidents (Wootten 1991b; ICJ 1990; Amnesty International 1993). These complaints are often associated with public-order offences and the use of what has colloquially been referred to as the "trifecta": charges for offensive behaviour/language, resist arrest, and assault police.

Police decision-making and the use of discretion can have an enormous impact on the number of Indigenous people appearing before the courts and the nature of the offences with which they are charged. The discretions available to police in terms of whether to charge a person with a criminal offence, which charge and how many charges should be laid, as well as subsequent procedural decisions in relation to arrest or summons, the use of custody and bail and so on, all fundamentally mould the apparent criminality of the person detained. The public expression of criminality confirmed in the courtroom occurs at the end of a long social process. In the case of Indigenous people, we know from the evidence that police decision-making invariably gives rise to the use of the more punitive options available.

THE LAW AND POLICING

Police intervention does not occur in a legal vacuum, and at least on the face of it police are there to enforce the law. For a significant part of the European history of Australia, police have been required to enforce legislation which denied basic rights and protections to Aboriginal and Torres Strait Islander people. Colonial legislation embodied in various Protection Acts was used to exert control over Aboriginal people and communities in a racially discriminatory manner.

While laws based on overt racial discrimination have been repealed, the impact of law and its interpretation by police as they conduct their routine activities may still lead to profound, even if indirect, discrimination. Legislation covering public order is one example. In relation to recent legislation covering public drunkenness, in both its criminalized form in Victoria, Queensland, and Tasmania, and its decriminalized form in South Australia, New South Wales, Western Australia, and the Northern Territory, there has been concern that the laws have been used to maintain high levels of police intervention and custody. Some criminal laws appear to be applied only to Indigenous people. For instance, in north-western New South Wales, offences of riot and affray and various local government ordinances were used exclusively in relation to Aboriginal people (Cunneen and Robb 1987, p 221–2). There is widespread concern over police use of charges under various Summary Offences or Police Offences Acts with provisions for offensive behaviour and language. This tvpe of legislation has been strengthened in recent years with increased penalties and rising numbers of arrests (Cunneen and McDonald 1997, pp. 114–16).

Police may also use alternatives to the criminal law, such as welfare provisions, in the policing of Indigenous young people. In Western Australia, for example, it has been claimed that provisions providing for the protection of children are routinely used to remove Indigenous voting people from the streets and to place them in custody (NISATSIC 1997, p. 511). Similar provisions exist in New South Wales in the *Children (Protection and Parental Responsibility) Act 1997*. Complaints about the abuse of police powers under existing legislation are frequent, particularly in areas such as stopping and questioning Indigenous adults and young people (NISATSIC 1997, p. 512) or in the abuse of both search warrants and commitment warrants as a way of harassing individuals (Cunneen and McDonald 1997, p. 62), or in some cases whole communities (Cunneen 1990; NSW Office of the Ombudsman 1991).

The legislation covering the right to bail for a person charged with a criminal offence varies between different Australian jurisdictions. However, police determine in the first instance whether a person will receive bail and what conditions might be attached to the granting of bail. This gives rise to a number of issues. First, are Aboriginal people more likely to be refused bail than non-Aboriginal people? Second, are the conditions attached to bail unnecessarily onerous for Aboriginal people? Third, the need for a bail determination demonstrates the interconnectedness between adverse decisions by police. The police preference for proceeding by way of arrest and charge rather than using summons creates the need for bail in the first place. The Royal Commission into Aboriginal Deaths in Custody noted that the available evidence shows that police are more likely to refuse bail to an Aboriginal person than to a non-Aboriginal person in similar circumstances (Wootten 1991a, p. 353). Recent research has indicated widespread concern within Indigenous organizations that bail is determined in a discriminatory manner. Some of the discrimination can arise indirectly: Aboriginal and Torres Strait Islander people are more likely to be unemployed and homeless, and as a consequence are considered to be at greater risk of failing to appear in court (Cunneen and McDonald 1997, p. 122).

JUDICIAL DECISION-MAKING

Ultimately it is magistrates and judges who, within the constraints of sentencing legislation, impose sentences on Indigenous people who are brought before the courts. There has been considerable argument about whether those sentences are equitable in comparison to the sentences received by non-Indigenous people.

Indigenous people are more likely than others to be sentenced to imprisonment. For example, in Western Australia it was found that magistrates were six times more likely to sentence Aboriginal adults to imprisonment than non-Aboriginal people (Harding et al. 1995, p. 69). In the absence of further details on offence seriousness and prior record, the researchers felt constrained in drawing any conclusions from these figures. Some commentators have argued that there is no adverse discrimination by the courts against Aboriginal people, if prior record is taken into account.

Walker, for example, argues that "the Courts often refer explicitly to prior record as a reason for remanding in custody and for greater severity in sentencing" (1987, pp. 110–11). Although Indigenous prisoners were more likely to have been previously imprisoned, the average length of sentence for an Indigenous prisoner was 42.6 months compared to 74.9 months for a non-Aboriginal prisoner. Walker argues that the shorter average prison sentences for Aborigines "cannot be entirely attributed to different types of offences committed by Aboriginal people," nor to "the relative youthfulness of Aboriginal offenders or to any differences in sentencing practices between States" (1987, p. 111). He concluded "that the courts cannot be held to blame for the high rates of Aboriginal imprisonment. On the contrary, they appear to be particularly lenient to Aboriginal offenders, especially when one considers that prior imprisonment record is regarded as a key factor in sentencing, tending towards longer sentences" (1987, p. 114). More recently, Walker and McDonald (1995) have argued that the results of the 1992 prison census show that Aboriginal offenders generally serve shorter terms of imprisonment than non-Indigenous people for a range of offences. They suggest that "courts may have a lenient view of Indigenous offenders, biasing sentence lengths in their favour to avoid accusations of racial biases in sentencing" (1995, p. 4).

However, there are serious flaws in this argument. There is no analysis of why such disproportionate numbers of Indigenous people are brought before the courts in the first place, the extent to which alternatives to prison are used for Indigenous and non-Indigenous offenders compared to imprisonment, or the relative seriousness of the offences beyond broad categories such as "fraud" or "drugs."[3] Much of the problem with this type of analysis derives from the methodology of using prison statistics to analyze comparative sentencing decisions. A simple comparison between the length of prison sentences for Indigenous and non-Indigenous people provides us with no comparative information on their passage through the criminal justice system, nor on the decisions that are made at each stage. In particular, the effect of police practices in relation to targeting, arrest, and bail all impact on the crucial question of why Aboriginal people appear before the courts in the first place and how they in fact obtain criminal records. The end result may be an "accumulation of disadvantage" in the system deriving from the original police decision to arrest (Gale et al. 1990; Luke and Cunneen 1995).

A recent study of sentencing in the Northern Territory found that courts were using jail sentences more frequently for Aboriginal people and at an earlier stage in their offending history, and that they were more likely to have a prior offending history than non-Aboriginal people. However, when Aboriginal and non-Aboriginal offenders were matched by prior record and offence, a greater proportion of Aboriginal people were sentenced to imprisonment—irrespective of the offence or the level of prior record. The study also found that while Aboriginal people received shorter imprisonment sentences than non-Aboriginal people, they were less likely to receive the benefit of non-custodial sentencing options (Luke and Cunneen 1998). Thus a picture emerges of Aboriginal people receiving fewer non-custodial sentencing options and more frequent short-term jail sentences than non-Aboriginal people.

In regard to juvenile offenders, Aboriginal young people have a greater chance of being sent to an institution than do non-Aboriginal offenders (Gale et al. 1990, p. 107; Broadhurst, Ferrante, and Susilo 1991, p. 74; Luke and Cunneen 1995). South Australian research showed that differences in penalties remained even when specific charges were analyzed. Thus, twice as many Aboriginal young people compared to non-Indigenous young people were sentenced to detention for break, enter, and steal or for assault, for example. It was not the specific offence which determined the penalty (Gale et al. 1990, p. 109). The major determinant influencing penalty was the young person's prior offending record. Unemployment and family structure were also relevant, with those who were unemployed and living in a non-nuclear family situation being more likely to receive a custodial sentence. Research in New South Wales has reached similar conclusions in relation to the importance of prior criminal record (Luke and Cunneen 1995). A New South

Wales Judicial Commission report confirmed that Indigenous and non-Indigenous youth received the same number and length of detention orders when factors including offence, prior record, bail, employment, and family structure were accounted for (Gallagher and Poletti 1998, p. 17).

The major import of this discussion on sentencing in relation to the question of policing is that sentencing decisions cannot be seen as discrete from policing practices. Police decisions obviously affect the number and type of criminal charges on which the court makes a sentencing decision. Policing also impacts on whether the person arrives in court in custody, on bail or by way of summons. Besides the actual offence, a prime determinant of sentencing outcome is prior record, which itself is an outcome of the social and political processes which involve police decision-making.

Policing practices partly shape sentencing, particularly where prior record becomes a factor in imposing more punitive sentencing outcomes.

SPATIAL FACTORS: ENVIRONMENT AND LOCATION

The shape of criminal behaviour—its nature and size—is also influenced by a range of spatial factors which lie outside both individual influence and the immediate responses of the criminal justice system. Environmental opportunities can structure criminal activity. Environment and location can also impact on the response by the community and the police.

For example, Gale and her colleagues, in their study of Aboriginal young people and juvenile justice, argued that even if it could be shown that Aboriginal people do commit more serious property offences, this would not demonstrate any greater inherent "criminality" because environmental opportunities and pressures influence the nature of property crime. In particular, urban-rural differences structure opportunities and pressures differently (Gale et al. 1990). Simple theft and shoplifting are primarily urban offences, particularly associated with large shopping complexes. The opportunities for these types of offences are considerably constrained in the environment of small rural communities. Similarly, there is increased likelihood of being detected either breaking into or attempting to break into a dwelling in a small country town or remote community. In these locations offenders are often easily identified by the community and the police.

Location also has a bearing on the likelihood of coming into contact with the criminal justice system as well as possible responses. While the results of research are somewhat conflicting, a number of criminologists, geographers, and sociologists have considered the spatial dimension of Indigenous contact with the criminal justice system. Gale et al. have shown that there are "enormous geographical variations in the position of young Aboriginal people before the law" in South Australia (1990, p. 36). Broadhurst (1997) has argued that the highest rates of Indigenous imprisonment are in the "frontier" areas like the Northern Territory and Western Australia, and the lowest rates are in settled states such as Victoria and Tasmania. A recent study in the Northern Territory showed Aboriginal people living in major centres were four times more likely to appear in court than those living in remote areas (Luke and Cunneen 1998, p. 21).

The processes of colonization significantly impacted on the human geography of Aboriginal and Torres Strait Islander communities. It is worth noting that many Indigenous communities in Australia have arisen out of the forced relocation of Aboriginal and Torres Strait Islander people into specific areas during the period of "protection." This movement has given rise to its own set of problems, which may manifest themselves in social conflict and disagreements over access to scarce resources. Some of the recent literature in the area urges a consideration of the diverse experiences of Indigenous people, both in terms of understanding the nature of offending (Broadhurst 1997; LaPrairie 1997) and in terms of the development of policy (Cunneen 1997).

CULTURAL DIFFERENCE

Cultural difference can lead to criminalization for a number of reasons. First, Indigenous people may have difficulties based on language and culture during police interrogation and in courtroom procedures. Second, Aboriginal people's cultural practices may lead to criminalization. Third, the attacks on Aboriginal culture through various colonial policies over many decades have weakened certain social control mechanisms within some communities, causing problems of disruptive and criminal behaviour.

The vulnerability of Aboriginal people when faced with police interrogation techniques has been noted in several government inquiries.[4] Some of the disabilities Aboriginal people face in front of the courts as a result of language and cultural differences have been explored by Eades (1995a, 1995b). For instance, cultural difference expressed through body language can be falsely interpreted as implying guilt. Cross-examination and interrogation techniques can lead to gratuitous concurrence, which may be interpreted as admission of guilt (Eades 1995a). Failure to provide interpreters is still a major problem in many parts of Australia, and affects both police and court stages of intervention (Cunneen and McDonald 1997).

There is now a significant body of literature which outlines the difficulties that face Indigenous people in the formal legal process (Eades 1995b; Criminal Justice Commission 1996; Mildren 1997), difficulties which derive from both cultural and communicative (verbal and non-verbal) differences and can also include medical conditions (such as middle-ear infection leading to hearing loss). They are part of the structural parameters which prevent Indigenous people receiving fair treatment in the non-Indigenous legal process, and at times can lead to significant miscarriages of justice (Criminal Justice Commission 1996).

Distinct cultural patterns may also lead to intervention and eventual criminalization. One example is the policing of activities which occur in public places. Cultural differences in this area arise where Aboriginal social activities are more likely to lead to visibility and surveillance by police. Cultural differences in child-rearing practices can also lead to the intervention of non-Indigenous welfare and juvenile justice agencies, including police. Indigenous societies in Australia had, and continue to have, very different cultural notions in relation to childhood and young people compared to non-Indigenous groups. Generally there is not the same separation or exclusion of children from the adult world. Responsibility for children and young people is allocated through the kinship system and the wider community (Sansom and Baines 1988; NISATSIC 1997; Watson 1989).

A critical question is whether non-Indigenous criminal justice institutions simply fail to recognize and value Indigenous methods of social organization, or whether they in effect treat cultural difference as a social pathology and criminalize it. For example, from the late 1970s there has been considerable criticism of the ethnocentric nature of social-background reports and of the psychological tests administered to Aboriginal young people coming under state supervision. The reports gave free rein to the expression of prejudices in relation to Aboriginal culture, family life, and child-rearing practices through descriptions of "dysfunctional families" and "bad home environments" (Milne and Munro 1981; Gale et al. 1990, p. 102; Carrington 1993, p. 48). Apparently neutral means of assessment such as IQ and psychological testing can reflect the norms of the dominant culture and provide apparently "scientific" evidence of maladjusted individuals or families. There have been similar criticisms of the social assumptions which can underlie the reports of probation and parole officers which are presented to the courts (Ozols 1994, p. 3).

Colonization has also wrought changes in the social patterns of Aboriginal life by wholesale disruption to communities through expropriation of the land, concentration of differing kinship groups on reserves, and through specific policies such as the removal of Aboriginal children and young people. Colonial processes have attacked Indigenous mechanisms of governance and social control. For example, the Royal Commission into Aboriginal Deaths in Custody has noted in detail the extent to which disruption, intervention, and institutionalization have left Aboriginal and Torres Strait Islander families facing severe difficulties with their children and young people. The historical legacy of colonialism is that families and communities now cannot call on the social and economic resources necessary to resolve these problems. It is important to recognize that since much of colonial policy was about undermining Aboriginal authority and methods of social organization, it is hardly surprising that now, in some communities, parental authority and traditional responsibilities have been rendered less effective.

Finally, it is important to recognize the cultural differences between Indigenous communities in Australia. While the most obvious are the significant cultural differences between Aboriginal people and Torres Strait Islanders, there are obvious cultural and linguistic differences between Indigenous peoples throughout Australia. Some of these differences derive from pre-colonial Australia, while others have arisen as a result of the colonial experience. These differences are often poorly understood and can lead to a simplistic approach to criminal justice policies (Cunneen 1997; NISATSIC 1997).

SOCIO-ECONOMIC FACTORS

A person's position in the social and economic class structure of society has a direct impact on their likelihood of ending up in the criminal justice system. The disadvantaged position of Aboriginal people in Australia has been well documented, not least by the Royal Commission into Aboriginal Deaths in Custody, the National Inquiry into the Separation of Aboriginal and Torres Strait Islander Children from Their Families, and various ATSIC reports (1995, 1997).

Numerous studies have indicated the links between the socio-economic position of Aboriginal people and their level of offending, including Cunneen and Robb (1987), Devery (1991) and Beresford and Omaji (1996). A recent Australian Institute of Criminology study has also noted the importance of considering the links between offending levels (as measured by imprisonment figures) and employment and educational disadvantage (Walker and McDonald 1995). The authors identify the association of social problems such as crime with unemployment and income inequalities. They suggest that the reason crime is so problematic in Aboriginal communities is due to the lack of employment, educational and other opportunities, and argue that social policies aimed at improving these conditions are likely to have a significant effect on the reduction of imprisonment rates (p. 6). More recently, Hunter and Borland (1999) found that the high rate of arrest of Aboriginal people, often for non-violent alcohol-related offences, is one of the major factors behind low rates of employment.

Marginalization

Another way of considering socio-economic disadvantage and some offending patterns by Aboriginal people is through the notion of marginalization. Marginalization in this context is taken to mean separation and alienation from work relations, family, and other social relations which bind young people and adults to communities and give value and esteem to people's lives. The results of marginalization include self-destructive behaviour (including substance abuse), increased likelihood of violence among family members, and the development of strategies for survival, which include crime.

Marginalization and its relationship to crime are clearly not a phenomenon particular to Aboriginal people. However, because of the history of dispossession, colonial policy, and racism in Australia, it can be argued that marginalization impacts greatly on Aboriginal and Torres Strait Islander people, who show very poorly on all social indicator scales in terms of health, housing, education, unemployment, and welfare dependency. There have been many studies that show that poverty is associated with detected crime and police intervention. In South Australia, it was found that, of young people who had left school and were apprehended by police, some 91 percent of Aboriginal young people, compared to 61 percent of non-Aboriginal young people, were unemployed (Gale et al. 1990, p. 56).

Other social factors which correlate with poverty, such as single-parent families and residential location, were also more prevalent among Aboriginal young people who were apprehended by police (Gale et al. 1990, pp. 57–8; see also Devery 1991). The Royal Commission into Aboriginal Deaths in Custody argued that part of the high level of property offences committed by Aboriginal youth is indicative of the extent of poverty. At the most basic level, some offences are committed by young people because of their need for food (Johnston 1991, p. 287).

Marginalization is also important in understanding the extent of self-destructive behaviour and its relationship to offending. Some Aboriginal communities have problems with substance abuse by young people and adults, including alcohol abuse and petrol sniffing. Substance abuse can be associated with offending in many ways, from the commission of break and enters to obtain alcohol or petrol to the association of alcohol abuse with violence. The Royal Commission into Aboriginal Deaths in Custody has also noted the effect peer group pressure and boredom have on offending. This would appear to be a particular problem in remote communities and is clearly related to marginalization, where juvenile and young adults have no opportunity for employment, for formal education in the community beyond junior high school, or for extended social activities (Johnston 1991, pp. 289–90).

The notion of marginalization and economic disadvantage must always be seen within the context of colonialism, dispossession, and the destruction of an Aboriginal economic base. As many Indigenous people have stated, their people are not simply a disadvantaged minority group in Australia: their current socio-economic status derives from a specific history of colonization. In other words, an overly simplistic application of socio-economic (or class) analysis prevents an understanding of the distinct historical formation of Indigenous people within a dominant (and colonizing) society.[5]

RESISTANCE

The concept of resistance may also play some role in explaining the patterns of Aboriginal over-representation in crime figures. Some of the offences committed by Aboriginal people are specifically aimed at non-Indigenous targets or as responses and resistances to non-Indigenous institutions and authorities. A number of researchers have commented upon the fact that some property offences, vandalism, assaults, or behaviour classified offensive can be understood as a form of resistance (Brady 1985; Cunneen and Robb 1987; Cowlishaw 1988; Hutchings 1995). Brady notes that in the Aboriginal community where she did her research, the break-ins, by young people in particular, were directed at school buildings, non-Aboriginal staff houses, and the store (Brady 1985, p. 116). Aboriginal organizations have also noted that resistance has become part of Aboriginal culture, with a particular effect on juveniles. "What has been described as [juvenile] delinquency could also be regarded as acts of individual defiance. The scale and nature of Aboriginal children's conflict with 'authority' is reflective of a historical defiance" (D'Souza 1990, p. 5). In some cases, public disorder may erupt in anti-police riots as a direct response to harassment (Cunneen and Robb 1987; Goodall 1990).

Other patterns of offending which might be considered under the notion of resistance relate to defiance of court orders. Goodall has noted that, historically, the tactics which were used against welfare and protection board intervention included passive resistance, non-cooperation and absconding (cited in Johnston 1991, p. 77). Today these types of offences are typically grouped under the category of "justice" offences. It is important to consider the extent to which breaches of court orders might reflect a refusal to comply with what are considered to be unjust levels of intervention and control. Similarly, high levels of fine default may reflect not just poverty (the inability to pay a fine), but also resistance to the idea of paying a fine deriving from an unjust conviction.

THEORIZING THE IMPACT OF POLICING ON CRIME FIGURES

The role of police specifically in implementing colonial policy is a large topic. It is important to note in the present context, however, that the colonial project involved a diverse range of strategies, including the murder of Indigenous people, dispersal away from traditionally owned lands, and the destruction of an economic base in many parts of Australia, concentration of diverse groups in government and mission-run reserves, and the removal of Aboriginal children from communities. The manifold effects of these policies were well documented by the Royal Commission into Aboriginal Deaths in Custody. The impact of policies such as child removal was noted in the investigations into various deaths, as well as other tangible outcomes of colonial policy, such as the enforced "invisibility" of Aboriginal people moved away from white communities, and the policing tactics that were employed to achieve those ends.

More recently the National Inquiry into the Separation of Aboriginal and Torres Strait Islander Children from Their Families (1997) examined the effects of forced removals. It is worth clarifying the criminogenic effects generated by this particular colonial policy. It led to the destabilization and/or destruction of kinship networks, and the destabilization of protective and caring mechanisms within Indigenous culture.

It led to the social and legal construction of Aboriginal child-rearing as socially incompetent and of Aboriginal culture as worthless. It led to a legal regime without procedural justice, which has been defined as genocide within international law. It led to the economic and sexual exploitation of Aboriginal children. It has contributed to a culture of resistance within Indigenous communities to welfare and criminal justice authorities. It has contributed to the generation of higher levels of mental illness, psychiatric disorders, and alcohol and substance abuse among those removed. It has contributed to the creation of a new generation of Aboriginal adults ill-equipped for parenting.

It would of course be an impossible task to "measure" the impact of a particular colonial policy such as child removal on contemporary Indigenous crime figures. Yet we know through the traumatic effects of such policies on individuals, families, and communities that the impact has indeed been great. We gain some glimpse of this in data that consistently show the greater numbers of the stolen generation among Indigenous arrests and deaths in custody. At one level, the concept of "colonialism" provides a highly generalized level of explanation for understanding Indigenous criminal offending, but as the example of the impact of the forced removal of Indigenous children shows, colonial policy can be contextualized with concrete examples and specific criminogenic effects.

A sophisticated approach to explaining the level of over-representation of Indigenous people in official criminal statistics is needed. It is not accurate to suggest that Indigenous people do not commit offences and are merely imprisoned as the result of a racist criminal justice system. Nor is it the case that the criminal justice system is simply a neutral institution enforcing an impartial legal system. At the broadest level, the legal system has been informed by a colonial project with a specific regime for Indigenous people. In more prosaic terms, the police (as part of the legal system) utilise their discretion in ways which have a negative impact on Indigenous people. The level of policing and the nature of police intervention impact directly on the extent to which Aboriginal and Torres Strait Islander people appear in the criminal justice system. In addition, the economic and social conditions under which Indigenous people have been forced to live as a result of dispossession and marginalization are criminogenic.

These explanations are not mutually exclusive and, if framed in either/or categorizations, fail to capture the complexities of social reality. For example, if we consider the comparatively large number of motor vehicle registration and licence offences for which Aboriginal people are imprisoned, we might consider the complex interaction of environmental considerations, the effects of unemployment and poverty, and the extent of discriminatory policing practices. Environmental considerations are important, because Aboriginal people often live in rural and remote areas poorly serviced by public transport and are therefore dependent on a motor vehicle in a way that the "average" non-Aboriginal person is not. Unemployment and low income effect the ability both to pay for registration and to own vehicles more likely to be classified roadworthy, and negatively impact on the ability to pay for any traffic fines. Failure to pay traffic fines results in licence cancellation. Discriminatory police practices may increase the likelihood of detection of unlicensed drivers through selective procedures of stopping Aboriginal drivers.

A similar explanation could be utilised for the comparatively large number of break and enters for which Aboriginal young people appear in court. When a small group of Aboriginal children is apprehended and appears in court in Brewarrina, New South Wales, say, for breaking into a house and stealing food, a satisfactory explanation for that event must be one that recognizes the economic and social outcomes of colonization and marginalization, the role of environmental opportunities for crime, the increased likelihood of detection as a result of police numbers and surveillance in small and predominantly Aboriginal communities, and the increased likelihood of an adverse police discretional decision to charge (rather than caution) an Aboriginal young person in the first instance.

In the end, measures of "crime" need to be understood as social, political, and historical artefacts. Their "truth" is certainly dependent on the regimes of which they are a product. In the case of Indigenous people, the regime has been particularly harsh, the empirical measures showing the deep levels of their criminalization in contemporary Australian society. Yet to see that as merely a reflection of offending levels in Indigenous communities would indeed be to mistake the outcome of social processes for a simple and unambiguous "fact." Crime as a social artefact needs to be continually deconstructed—it has no essential inner core other than the purely formal requirement of legal transgression.

There is little doubt that policing shapes the measuring of crime, and police decision-making can significantly impact on what we "know" as offenders and offences. In the specific case of Indigenous people in Australia, we can expect an even greater shaping of offending levels through police practices, given their contemporary role in Indigenous communities and their historic role in colonial policy.

NOTES

1. See, for example, ADB (1982); Cunneen and Robb (1987); Gale et al. (1990); Luke and Cunneen (1995); Mackay (1995); Allas and James (1996); Cunneen and McDonald (1997); Luke and Cunneen (1998).
2. Clear-up rate: the percentage of recorded offences cleared by police.
3. For instance, it is not surprising that Indigenous people receive shorter sentences for drug offences given their lack of involvement in more serious trafficking offences.
4. For an examination of these issues two decades ago, see the House of Representatives Standing Committee on Aboriginal and Torres Strait Islander Affairs' Report on Aboriginal Legal Aid (Ruddock 1980). The courts have also expressed

concern in this regard in *R v Williams* (1976) 14 SASR 1 and *Collins n R* (1980) 31 ALR 257. For an early summary of these issues, see Rees (1982). More recent reports drawing attention to the same issues include the Royal Commission into Aboriginal Deaths in Custody (Johnston 1991) and CJC (1996).

5. See Brennan (1991) for a succinct discussion of why Indigenous people are not simply an oppressed minority group within Australia.

REFERENCES

Aboriginal Affairs Department and Crime Research Centre. 1996. *Aboriginal Young People and Contact with the Juvenile Justice System in Western Australia. Royal Commission into Aboriginal Deaths in Custody Vol. 3.* Perth: University of Western Australia, Crime Research Centre.

Aboriginal and Torres Strait Islander Social Justice Commission. 1995. *Indigenous Social Justice, Submission to the Parliament of the Commonwealth of Australia on the Social Justice Package.* Sydney: Aboriginal and Torres Strait Islander Social Justice Commission.

Allas, R. and James, S. 1996. *A Study of Victorian Aboriginal Offending 1989–90 to 1993–94.* A report to the Criminology Research Council, Canberra.

Amnesty International. 1993. *A Criminal Justice System Weighted Against Aboriginal People.* London: International Secretariat.

Anti-Discrimination Board. 1982. *Study of Street Offences by Aborigines.* Sydney: NSW Anti-Discrimination Board.

Beresford, Q. and Omaji, P. 1996. *Rites of Passage. Aboriginal Youth, Crime and Justice.* South Fremantle: Fremantle Art Centre Press.

Brady, M. 1985. "Aboriginal Youth and the Juvenile Justice System," in A. Borowski and J. Murray, eds. *Juvenile Delinquency in Australia.* Sydney: Methuen.

Brennan, F. 1991. *Sharing the Country.* Ringwood: Penguin.

Broadhurst, R. 1997. "Aborigines and Crime in Australia," in M. Tonry, ed. *Ethnicity, Crime and Immigration: Comparative and Cross-National Perspectives, Crime and Justice.* Vol. 21. Chicago: University of Chicago.

Broadhurst, R., Ferrante, A. and Susilo, N. 1991. *Crime and Justice Statistics for Western Australia. 1990.* Perth: Crime Research Centre, University of Western Australia.

Carrington, K. 1993. *Offending Girls.* Sydney: Allen & Unwin.

Cowlishaw, G. 1988. *Black, White or Brindle.* Cambridge: Cambridge University Press.

Criminal Justice Commission. 1996. *Aboriginal Witnesses in Queensland Criminal Courts.* Brisbane: Goprint.

Cunneen, C. 1990. "The Detention of Aborigines in Police Cells: Wilcannia." *Aboriginal Law Bulletin*, vol. 2, no. 45, pp. 8–10.

Cunneen, C. 1997. "Community Conferencing and the Fiction of Indigenous Control." *Australian and New Zealand Journal of Criminology*, vol. 30, no. 3, pp. 292–311.

Cunneen, C. and McDonald, D. 1997. *Keeping Aboriginal and Torres Strait Islander People Out of Custody.* Canberra: ATSIC.

Cunneen, C. and Robb, T. 1987. *Criminal Justice in North-West NSW.* Sydney: NSW Bureau of Crime Statistics and Research, Attorney-General's Department.

D'Souza, N. 1990. "Aboriginal Children and the Juvenile Justice System." *Aboriginal Law Bulletin*, vol. 2, no. 44, pp. 4–5.

Devery, C. 1991. *Disadvantage and Crime in New South Wales.* Sydney: New South Wales Bureau of Crime Statistics and Research.

Eades, D. 1995a. "Cross Examination of Aboriginal Children: The Pinkenba Case." *Aboriginal Law Bulletin*, vol. 3, no. 75, pp. 10–11.

Eades, D. 1995b. *Language in Evidence.* Sydney: University of New South Wales Press.

Gale, R., Bailey-Harris, R. and Wundersitz, J. 1990. *Aboriginal Youth and the Criminal Justice System.* Melbourne: Cambridge University Press.

Gallagher, P. and Poletti, P. 1998. *Sentencing Disparity and the Ethnicity of Juvenile Offenders.* Sydney: Judicial Commission of New South Wales.

Goodall, H. 1990. "Policing In Whose Interest?" *Journal for Social Justice Studies*, vol. 3, pp. 19–36.

Harding, R., Broadhurst, R., Ferrante, A. and Loh, N. 1995. *Aboriginal Contact with the Criminal Justice System and the Impact of the Royal Commission into Aboriginal Deaths in Custody.* Sydney: The Hawkins Press.

House of Representatives Standing Committee on Aboriginal and Torres Strait Islander Affairs. 1990. *Our Future, Our Selves.* Canberra: AGPS.

Human Rights and Equal Opportunity Commission. 1991. *Racist Violence.* Report of the National Inquiry into Racist Violence. Canberra: AGPS.

Hunter, B. and Borland, J. 1999. "The Effect of Arrest on Indigenous Employment Prospects." *Crime and Justice Bulletin, No. 45.* Sydney: New South Wales Bureau of Crime Statistics and Research.

Hutchings, S. 1995. "The Great Shoe Store Robbery," in G. Cowlishaw and B. Morris, eds. *Racism Today.* Canberra: AIATSIS Press.

International Commission of Jurists. 1990. *Report of the Aboriginals and Law Mission.* Sydney: Australian Section.

Johnston, E. 1991. *National Report, 5 Vols.* Royal Commission into Aboriginal Deaths in Custody. Canberra: AGPS.

LaPrairie, C. 1997. "Reconstructing Theory: Explaining Aboriginal Over-Representation in the Criminal Justice System in Canada." *The Australian and New Zealand Journal of Criminology*, vol. 30, no. 1, March 1997, pp. 39–54.

Luke, G. and Cunneen, C. 1995. *Aboriginal Over-Representation and Discretionary Decisions in the NSW Juvenile Justice System.* Sydney: Juvenile Justice Advisory Council of NSW.

Luke, G. and Cunneen, C. 1998. *Sentencing Aboriginal People in the Northern Territory: A Statistical Analysis.* Darwin: NAALAS.

Mackay, M. 1995. "Law, Space and Justice: A Geography of Aboriginal Arrests in Victoria." *People and Place*, vol. 4, no. 1.

Mildren, D. 1997. "Redressing the Imbalance Against Aboriginals in the Criminal Justice System." *Criminal Law Journal*, vol. 21, pp. 7–22.

Milne, C. and Munro, L. Jnr. 1981. "Who is Unresponsive: Negative Assessments of Aboriginal Children." Discussion Paper No. 1, Aboriginal Children's Research Project, Family and Children's Services Agency, Sydney.

NISATSIC. 1997. *Bringing Them Home, Report of the National Inquiry into the Separation of Aboriginal and Torres Strait Islander Children from Their Families.* Sydney: HREOC.

NSW Bureau of Crime Statistics and Research. 1990. *NSW Recorded Crime Statistics 1989/90.* Sydney.

NSW Office of the Ombudsman. 1991. *Operation Sue. Report to Parliament Under Section 26 of the Ombudsman Act.* Sydney: NSW Office of the Ombudsman.

Ozols, E. 1994. "Pre-Sentence Reports on Aboriginal and Islander People: Overcoming the Myths and Providing Culturally Appropriate Information." Paper presented to the Australian Institute of Criminology, Aboriginal Justice Issues II Conference, Townsville, 14–17 June 1994.

Rees, S. 1982. "Police Interrogation of Aborigines," in J. Basten et al., eds. *The Criminal Injustice System.* Sydney and Melbourne: Australian Legal Workers Group and Legal Service Bulletin.

Royal Commission into Aboriginal Deaths in Custody. 1990. *Transcript of Hearing into Juvenile Justice Issues.* Perth, 29 May 1990.

Ruddock, P. 1980. *Aboriginal Legal Aid.* House of Representatives Standing Committee on Aboriginal Affairs. Canberra: AGPS.

Sansom, B. and Baines, P. 1988. "Aboriginal child placement in the urban context," in B. Morse and G. Woodman, eds. *Indigenous Law and the State.* Dordrecht: Foris Publications.

Walker, J. 1987. "Prison Cells with Revolving Doors: A Judicial or Societal Problem," in K. Hazlehurst, ed. *Ivory Scales.* Sydney: University of New South Wales Press.

Walker, J. and McDonald, D. 1995. "The Over-Representation of Indigenous People in Custody in Australia," *Trends and Issues in Crime and Criminal Justice*, no. 47. Canberra: Australian Institute of Criminology.

Watson, L. 1989. "Our Children: Part of the Past, Present, and Providing a Vision for the Future. A Murri Perspective." *Australian Child and Family Welfare*, August 1989.

Wooten, H. 1991a. *Regional Report of Inquiry in New South Wales, Victoria and Tasmania.* Royal Commission into Aboriginal Deaths in Custody. Canberra: AGPS.

Wooten, H. 1991b. *Report of Inquiry into the Death of David John Gundy.* Royal Commission into Aboriginal Deaths in Custody. Canberra: AGPS.

FURTHER READING

Cummins, Bryan, and John Steckley. 2002. "Chapter One: Introduction to Aboriginal Policing." In *Aboriginal Policing: A Canadian Perspective*. Toronto: Prentice Hall.

This introductory chapter is short but does an excellent job of explaining the issue of structural racism in the context of the relationship between Canadian policing agencies and aboriginal citizens. In particular the authors distinguish between "personal" and "institutional" racism, and in doing so also problematize the issue of "intention" (i.e., the issue of whether or not an individual knew he or she was being racist) in the continuation of the latter form. The chapter ends with a case study of structural racism in the death of a Cree woman who, after being struck by a car, was deemed a "drunk squaw" by attending officers who proceeded to act according to that stereotype.

Cunneen, C. 2001. *Conflict, Politics, and Crime: Aboriginal Communities and the Police*. Crow's Nest, Australia: Allen & Unwin.

Cunneen's chapter in the present collection is taken from this larger book. This work brilliantly traces the role of colonialism and racism in the construction and maintenance of Australia's various policing forces and the Australian nation(s)-state more generally. Cunneen's point is generally that the current overrepresentation of Australia's indigenous peoples in the Australian criminal justice system is evidence of the political devaluation of indigenous sovereignty and associated governing practices. Cunneen succinctly connects the "usual suspects" used to explain overrepresentation (usually individual-level explanations) with the more structural socio-economic and geopolitical impacts of ongoing colonial practices. He concludes by offering possible ways forward to deal with this startling overrepresentation.

Delgado, Richard, and Jean Stefancic. 2001. *Critical Race Theory: An Introduction*. New York: New York University Press.

Critical race (legal) theory is an intellectual subfield that gained steam in mid-1980s legal scholarship. CRT, as it is often termed, is strongly focused on demonstrating how race continues to operate at the heart of (supposedly) liberal democratic societies (like Canada, the United States, and Britain). Critical race theory is centrally concerned with understanding how the unstated privilege of "whiteness" and the concomitant marginalization of minorities are, although central to the reproduction of social inequality, rendered largely invisible in such societies. In their text Delgado and Stefancic lay out the basic principles of critical race theory: its origins and early intellectual impulses, its themes of analyses, its methodologies, critiques of its intellectual trajectories, and the state of the discipline today.

Gabor, Thomas. 2004. "Inflammatory Rhetoric on Racial Profiling can Undermine Police Services." *Canadian Journal of Criminology and Criminal Justice* 46: 457–466.

In a challenge to the original Wortley and Tanner article discussed above in chapter 31, Gabor argues that while in some locations good data exists to prove the presence of racial profiling, Wortley and Tanner's definition of racial profiling fails to distinguish between "bigotry" and good, solid police work. In other words, Gabor essentially critiques Wortley and Tanner for failing to differentiate between "good" and "bad" racial profiling. "Bad" profiling is the simple result of police officials relying on racial stereotypes to make decisions about whether, for example, to stop a black motorist (i.e., "He or she is driving a nice car, it must be stolen"). "Good" racial profiling, by contrast, is the result of solid police work that uncovers crime patterns in (for example) predominately black neighbourhoods.

Toronto Star. 2002. "Police Target Black Drivers: Star Analysis of Traffic Data Suggests Racial Profiling," 20 October, Ontario edition, A1.

This interesting newspaper article discusses the issue of racial profiling in the context of policing in Toronto. It includes some of Scot Wortley's findings but also the denials by the Toronto Police Services and allied organizations. Most interestingly, however, it includes anecdotal information from Toronto black youth about their feelings in seeing police cruisers in the rear-view mirror.

Reber, Susanne, and Robert Renaud. 2005. *Starlight Tour: The Last, Lonely Night of Neil Stonechild*. Toronto: Random House Canada.

This fascinating journalistic account tells the story of the disappearance and death of Neil Stonechild, an aboriginal youth living in the city of Saskatoon, Saskatchewan. In explaining Stonechild's death at the hands of police officials practising "Starlight Tours" and the subsequent police cover-up, Reber and Renaud weave a tale of racism, bigoted policing, and a city unconcerned with the welfare of the aboriginal community living within it.

PART 4

RACE: LIMITATIONS AND PRIVILEGE

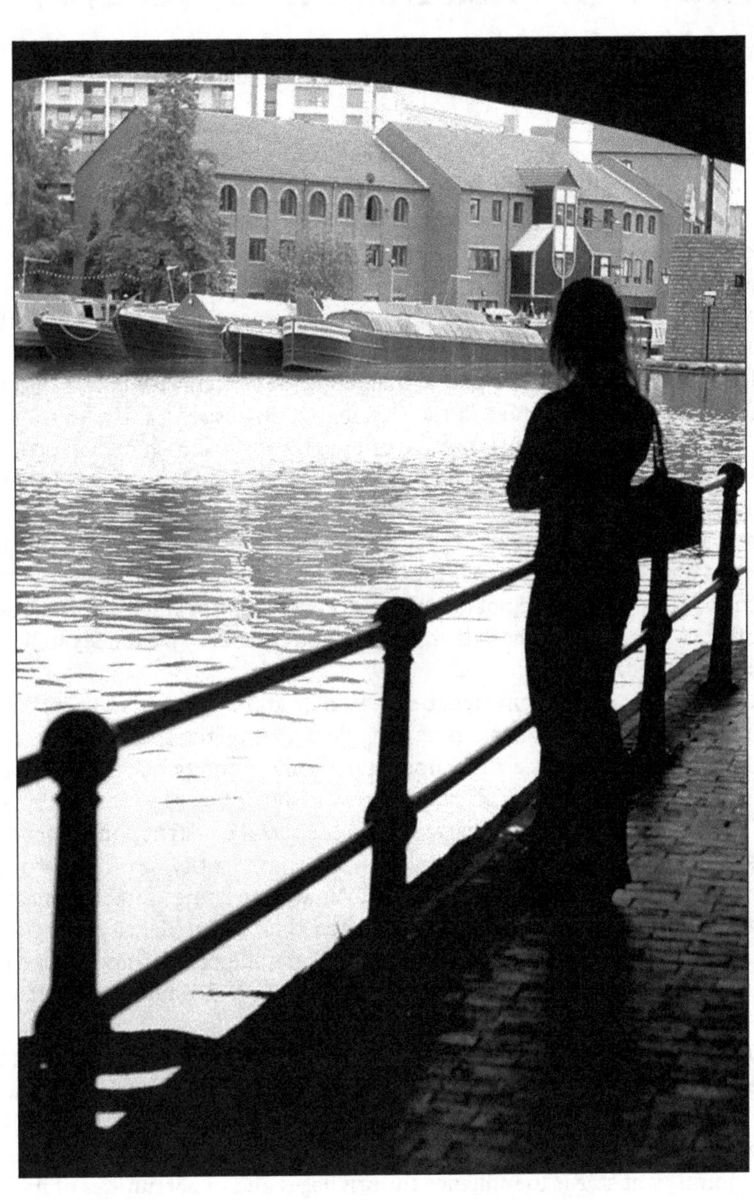

PART 4A

RACE, PRIVILEGE, AND IDENTITY

In the now classic 1995 book *How the Irish Became White*, Noel Ignatiev illustrates the social construction of race—as he says, race is not biological, it is assigned. Furthermore, that the Irish were able to *become* white is indicative of the capacity of some ethnoracial groups to surmount their assigned status. To use Ignatiev's question, "How did the Catholic Irish, an oppressed group in Ireland, become part of an oppressing race in America?" (1). This example illustrates not only the role of the dominant groups in influencing the social construction of particular groups, but also how that social construction facilitates the opportunities and possibilities for ethnoracial groups. So, as Ignatiev points out, in *entering* the white race, the Irish were able to gain a competitive advantage in the USA over groups such as Africans and Latinos/as who had long before resided in the country. Being white and having race privilege also meant that Irish people were able to work in all sectors of the society outside of the segregated labour market. The chapters in this section build on Ignatiev's discussion of the ways in which racial identification is experienced and makes possible and/or limits opportunities.

As Ignatiev illustrates, and as Paul Gilroy writes in the first reading of this section, we cannot take the impact of race for granted. Indeed, "we have seen," as Gilroy writes, "that the uncertain and divided world we inhabit has made racial identity matter in novel and powerful ways. But we should not take the concept of identity and its multiple associations with 'race' and raciology for granted." Identity, Gilroy argues, is both theoretically and politically a complex subject that is useful "to explore if we can only leave its obviousness behind."

Picking up on the subject of identity, and echoing Ignatiev, Karen Brodkin writes in the next chapter of "how Jews became white folks and what that says about America," explaining the role played by the society in the social construction of Jews. "I want to suggest," she writes, "that Jewish success is a product not only of ability but also of the removal of powerful social barriers to its realization." In writing about the Jewish experience, she shows how the "institutional nature of racism and the centrality of state policies" operate to create and change races and the social construction of racial groups.

Kerry A. Rockquemore's contribution adds to the complexity of racial identity, noting that race and ethnicity function differently due to visibility. Two questions guide her discussion: What does being "biracial" mean to individuals; and what factors may lead to differences in the way these individuals interpret their racial identity? On the basis of interviews, Rockquemore reports on the multiple ways in which individuals experience, understand, and respond to their "biracialness" and illustrates the role physical appearance and socio-economic status play in individuals' capacity to access different types of social networks.

Along the same lines as Rockquemore, Margaret Hunter, in the chapter that follows, also tells of the privileges that "lighter skin" people enjoy compared to "dark skin" people whose skin colour "remains a liability in work, housing and education." She argues that skin colour is more important in the evaluation of women than men.

The final chapter, by Vijay Agnew, further adds to the complexity of identity, showing the ways in which race intersects with ethnicity, class, gender, and immigrant status to influence the privileges and opportunities of individuals. With reference to South Asian immigrant women in Canada, Agnew examines how race, class, and gender, along with English-language ability, not only help in the construction of her respondents' identities, but also in their capacity and courage to deal with the difficulties of settling into a new country and trying to realize their dreams.

Essentially, the chapters in this section alert us to the fact that while the colour-blind discourse that is evident in racially diverse stratified societies would have us believe that race does not matter, the lived experiences of individuals indicate that race and colour affect their access to opportunities. In fact, as Brodkin and Hunter point out, it is difficult to say which of the many factors—particularly race (whiteness) or money—came first to make possible individuals' mobility in society. Clearly, both race and money are at work.

REFERENCE

Ignatiev, N. 1995. *How the Irish Became White*. New York: Routledge.

CHAPTER 32

IDENTITY, BELONGING, AND THE CRITIQUE OF PURE SAMENESS

Paul Gilroy

> When first he opens his eyes, an infant ought to see the fatherland, and up to the day of his death he ought never to see anything else. Every true republican has drunk in love of country, that is to say love of law and liberty, along with his mother's milk. This love is his whole existence; he sees nothing but the fatherland, he lives for it alone; when he is solitary, he is nothing; when he has ceased to have a fatherland, he no longer exists; and if he is not dead, he is worse than dead.
>
> Rousseau

> If things aren't going too well in contemporary thought, it's because there's a return ... to abstractions, back to the problem of origins, all that sort of thing.... Any analysis in terms of movements, vectors, is blocked. We're in a very weak phase, a period of reaction. Yet philosophy thought that it had done with the problem of origins. It was no longer a question of starting or finishing. The question was rather, what happens "in between"?
>
> Gilles Deleuze

We have seen that the uncertain and divided world we inhabit has made racial identity matter in novel and powerful ways. But we should not take the concept of identity and its multiple associations with "race" and raciology for granted. The term "identity" has recently acquired great resonance, both inside and outside the academic world. It offers far more than an obvious, common-sense way of talking about individuality, community, and solidarity and has provided a means to understand the interplay between subjective experiences of the world and the cultural and historical settings in which those fragile, meaningful subjectivities are formed. Identity has even been taken into the viscera of postmodern commerce, where the goal of planetary marketing promotes not just the targeting of objects and services to the identities of particular consumers but the idea that any product whatsoever can be suffused with identity. Any commodity is open to being "branded" in ways that solicit identification and try to orchestrate identity.[1]

In this chapter I want to show that there is more at stake in the current interest in identity than we often appreciate. I would also like to uncover some of the complexities that make identity a useful idea to explore if we can only leave its obviousness behind and recognize that it is far from being the simple issue that its currency in both government and marketplace makes it appear to be. Where the word becomes a concept, identity has been made central to a number of urgent theoretical and political issues, not least belonging, ethnicity, and nationality. Racialized conflicts, for example, are now understood by many commentators as a problem of the incompatible identities that mark out deeper conflicts between cultures and civilizations. This diagnosis sets up or perhaps confirms the even more widespread belief that the forms of political conflict with which racial division has been associated are somehow unreal or insubstantial, secondary or peripheral. This is something I intend to dispute. The new popularity of identity as an interpretative device is also a result of the exceptional plurality of meanings the term can harness. These diverse inflections—some of which are adapted from highly specialized academic usage—are condensed and interwoven as the term circulates. We are constantly informed that to share an identity is to be bonded on the most fundamental levels: national, "racial," ethnic, regional, and local. Identity is always bounded and particular. It marks out the divisions and subsets in our social lives and helps to define the boundaries between our uneven, local attempts to make sense of the world. Nobody ever speaks of a human identity. The concept orients thinking away from any engagement with the basic, anti-anthropological sameness that is the premise of this book. As Judith Butler puts it in her thoughtful reflection on the concept: "it seems that what we expect from the term *identity* will be cultural specificity, and that on occasion we even expect *identity* and *specificity* to work interchangeably."[2]

The same troubling qualities are evident where the term has been employed to articulate controversial and potentially illuminating themes in modern social and political theory. It has been a core component in the scholarly vocabulary designed to promote critical reflection upon who we are and what we want, identity helps us to comprehend the formation of that perilous pronoun "we" and to reckon with the patterns of inclusion and exclusion that it cannot help creating. This situation is made more difficult once identity is recognized as something of a problem in itself, and thereby acquires an additional weighting. Calculating the relationship between identity and difference, sameness and otherness is an intrinsically political operation. It happens when political collectivities reflect on what makes their binding connections possible. It is a fundamental part of how they comprehend their kinship—which may be an imaginary connection, though nonetheless powerful for that.

The distinctive language of identity appears again when people seek to calculate how tacit belonging to a group or community can be transformed into more active styles of solidarity, when they debate where the boundaries around a group should be constituted and how—if at all—they should be enforced. Identity becomes a question of power and authority when a group seeks to realize itself in political form. This may be a nation, a state, a movement, a class, or some unsteady combination of them all. Writing about the need for political institutions and relationships at the dawn of our era, Rousseau drew attention to the bold and creative elements in the history of how disorganized and internally divided groups had been formed into coherent units capable of unified action and worthy of the special status that defined the nation as a political body. Reflecting on the achievements of heroic individual leaders as builders of political cultures that could "attach citizens to the fatherland and to one another," he noted that the provision of a unifying common identity was a significant part of this political process. Significantly for our purposes, his example was taken from the history of the Children of Israel:

> (Moses) conceived and executed the astonishing project of creating a nation out of a swarm of wretched fugitives, without arts, arms, talents, virtues or courage, who were wandering as a horde of strangers over the face of the earth without a single inch of ground to call their own. Out of this wandering and servile horde Moses had the audacity to create a body politic, a free people ... he gave them that durable set of institutions, proof against time, fortune and conquerors, which five thousand years have not been able to destroy or even alter.... To prevent his people from melting away among foreign peoples, he gave them customs and usages incompatible with those of other nations; he overburdened them with peculiar rites and ceremonies; he inconvenienced them in a thousand ways in order to keep them constantly on the alert and to make them forever strangers among other men.[3]

In outlining elements of the political technology that would eventually produce the nation as a fortified encampment, Rousseau drew attention to the old association between identity and territory. Moses' achievement is viewed as all the more impressive because it was accomplished without the binding power of shared land. Rousseau underlined that the varieties of connection to which our ideas of identity refer are historical, social, and cultural rather than natural phenomena. Even at that early point in the constitution of modernity, he recognized that work must be done to summon the particularity and feelings of identity that are so often experienced as though they are spontaneous or automatic consequences of some governing culture or tradition that specifies basic and absolute differences between people. Consciousness of identity gains additional power from the idea that it is not the end product of one great man's "audacity" but an outcome of shared and rooted experience tied, in particular, to place, location, language, and mutuality.

When we think about the tense relationship between sameness and difference analytically, the interplay of consciousness, territory, and place becomes a major theme. It affords insights into the core of conflicts over how democratic social and political life should be organized at the start of the twenty-first century. We should try to remember that the threshold between those two antagonistic conditions can be moved and that identity-making has a history even though its historical character is often systematically concealed. Focusing on identity helps us to ask in what sense the recognition of sameness and differentiation is a premise of the modern political culture that Rousseau affirmed and which his writings still help us to analyze.

The dizzying variety of ideas condensed into the concept of identity, and the wide range of issues to which it can be made to refer, foster analytical connections between themes and perspectives that are not conventionally associated. Links can be established between political, cultural, psychological, and psychoanalytic concerns. We need to consider, for example, how the emotional and affective bonds that form the specific basis of raciological and ethnic sameness are composed, and how they become patterned social activities with elaborate cultural features. How are they able to induce conspicuous acts of altruism, violence, and courage? How do they motivate people toward social interconnection in which individuality is renounced or dissolved into the larger whole represented by a nation, a people, a "race," or an ethnic group? These questions are important because, as we have seen, grave moral and political consequences have followed once the magic of identity has been engaged tactically or in manipulative, deliberately oversimple ways. Even in the most civilized circumstances, the signs of sameness have degenerated readily into emblems of supposedly essential or immutable difference. The special appeal of individuality-transcending sameness still provides an antidote to the forms of uncertainty and anxiety that have been associated with economic and political crises. The idea of fundamentally shared identity becomes a platform for the reverie of absolute and eternal division.

The use of uniforms and other symbols to effect the sameness that identity only speaks about has sometimes been symptomatic of the process in which an anxious self can be shed and its concerns conjured away by the emergence of a stronger compound whole. The uniforms worn in the 1930s by fascists (and still worn by some fascist groups today) produced a compelling illusion of sameness both for members of the group and for those who observed their spectacular activities. The British Union of Fascists, one of the less-successful black-shirted organizations from that period, argued that their garb was all the more attractive to adherents when contrasted with the conflict and bitterness created by class-based divisions that were tearing the nation apart from within:

> (The "blackshirt") brings down one of the great barriers of class by removing differences of dress, and one of

> the objects of Fascism is to break the barriers of class. Already the blackshirt has achieved within our own ranks that classless unity which we will ultimately secure within the nation as a whole.[4]

We will explore below how the ultranationalist and fascist movements of the twentieth century deployed elaborate technological resources in order to generate spectacles of identity capable of unifying and coordinating inevitable, untidy diversity into an ideal and unnatural human uniformity. Their synthetic versions of fundamental identity looked most seductive where all difference had been banished or erased from the collective. Difference within was repressed in order to maximize the difference between these groups and others. Identity was celebrated extravagantly in military styles: uniforms were combined with synchronized body movement, drill, pageantry, and visible hierarchy to create and feed the comforting belief in sameness as absolute, metaphysical invariance. Men and women could then appear as interchangeable and disposable cogs in the encamped nation's military machine or as indistinguishable cells in the larger organic entity that encompassed and dissolved their individuality. Their actions may even be imagined to express the inner spirit, fate, and historicality of the national community. The citizen was manifested as a soldier, and violence—potential as well as actual—was dedicated to the furtherance of national interests. That vital community was constituted in the dynamic interaction between marchers moving together in austere time and the crowds that watched and savored the spectacle they created. In disseminating these valuable political effects, identity was mediated by cultural and communicative technologies like film, lighting, and amplified sound. These twentieth-century attributes were only partly concealed by the invocation of ancient ritual and myth.

The biblical stories of nation-building that demonstrate divine favor and the moral sanctions it supplies to worldly political purposes have been invoked by many different nationalist groups. The Afrikaners of South Africa provide one especially interesting and unwholesome example of how Rousseau's "peculiar rites and ceremonies" need not always serve a benign purpose. Their ethnically minded ideologues systematically invented an Afrikaner identity during the period that saw the rise of fascist movements elsewhere. They provided their political community with its own version of Christianity and a repertory of myths that were the basis for the elaborate political drama that summoned their historic nation into racialized being:

> The most dramatic event in the upsurge of Afrikaner nationalism was the symbolic ox-wagon trek of 1938, which celebrated the victory of the Great Trek. Eight wagons named after voortrekker heroes such as Piet Retief, Hendrik Potgeiter and Andres Pretorius traversed South Africa by different routes ... before they converged on a prominent hill overlooking Pretoria. There, on 16th December 1938, the centenary of the battle of Blood River, which marked the defeat of the Zulu kingdom, more than 100,000 Afrikaners—perhaps one tenth of the total Afrikaner people—attended the ceremonial laying of the foundation stone of the Voortrekker Monument. Men grew beards, women wore voortrekker dress, for the occasion ... (they) knelt in silent prayer.... The ceremony concluded with the singing of *Die Stem van Suid Afrika; God Save the King* had been excluded.[5]

Today's ubiquitous conflicts between warring constituencies that claim incompatible and exclusive identities suggest that these large-scale theatrical techniques for producing and stabilizing identity and soliciting national, "racial," or ethnic identification have been widely taken up. The reduction of identity to the uncomplicated, militarized, fraternal versions of pure sameness pioneered by fascism and Nazism in the 1930s is now routine, particularly where the forces of nationalism, "tribalism," and ethnic division are at work. Identity is thus revealed as a critical element in the distinctive vocabulary used to voice the geopolitical dilemmas of the late modern age. Where the power of absolute identity is summoned up, it is often to account for situations in which the actions of individuals and groups are being reduced to little more than the functioning of some overarching presocial mechanism. In the past, this machinery was often understood as a historical or economic process that defined the special, manifest destiny of the group in question. These days, it is more likely to be represented as a prepolitical, sociobiological, or biocultural feature, something mysterious and genetic that sanctions especially harsh varieties of deterministic thinking.

In this light, identity ceases to be an ongoing process of self-making and social interaction. It becomes instead a thing to be possessed and displayed. It is a silent sign that closes down the possibility of communication across the gulf between one heavily defended island of particularity and its equally well fortified neighbors, between one national encampment and others. When identity refers to an indelible mark or code somehow written into the bodies of its carriers, otherness can only be a threat. Identity is latent destiny. Seen or unseen, on the surface of the body or buried deep in its cells, identity forever sets one group apart from others who lack the particular, chosen traits that become the basis of typology and comparative evaluation. No longer a site for the affirmation of subjectivity and autonomy, identity mutates. Its motion reveals a deep desire for mechanical solidarity, seriality, and hypersimilarity. The scope for individual agency dwindles and then disappears. People become bearers of the differences that the rhetoric of absolute identity invents and then invites them to celebrate. Rather than communicating and making choices, individuals are seen as obedient, silent passengers moving across a flattened moral landscape toward the fixed destinies to which their essential identities, their genes, and the closed cultures they create have consigned them once and for all. And yet, the desire to fix identity in the body is inevitably frustrated by the body's refusal to disclose the required signs of absolute incompatibility people imagine to be located there.

Numerous cross-cultural examples might be used to illustrate this point. Reports from the genocide in Rwanda repeatedly revealed that identity cards issued by the political authorities were a vital source of the information necessary to classify people into the supposedly natural "tribal" types that brought them either death or deliverance. There, as in several other well-documented instances of mass slaughter, the bodies in question did not freely disclose the secrets of identity:

> Many Tutsis have been killed either because their ID cards marked them out as a Tutsi or because they did not have their card with them at the time and were therefore unable to prove they were not a Tutsi.... To escape the relentless discrimination they suffered, over the years many Tutsis bribed local government officials to get their ID card changed to Hutu. Unfortunately, this has not protected them.... The Tutsi give-aways were: one, being tall and two having a straight nose. Such criteria even led hysterical militias to kill a number of Hutus whose crime was "being too tall for a Hutu." Where there was doubt about the person's physical characteristics or because of the complaints that too many Tutsis had changed their card, the Interahamwe called upon villagers to verify the "tutsiship" of the quarry in question.[6]

Similar events were still being reported four years later when the genocidal assault against the Tutsis had been rearticulated into the civil war in Congo—a conflict that had already drawn in several other states and that appeared to provide the key to stability in the region. Under the presidency of Laurent Kabila, people whose physical characteristics made them suspect were still being openly murdered.[7] It is important to remember, however, that the linguistic markers of residual colonial conflict between anglophone and francophone spheres of influence were also implicated in sustaining the killing.

These fragments from a history of unspeakable barbarity underline how the notion of fixed identity operates easily on both sides of the chasm that usually divides scholarly writing from the disorderly world of political conflicts. Recently, identity has also come to constitute something of a bridge between the often discrepant approaches to understanding self and sociality found on the different sides of that widening gulf. As a theme in contemporary scholarship, identity has offered academic thinking an important route back toward the struggles and uncertainties of everyday life, where the idea of identity has become especially resonant. It has also provided the distinctive signatures of an inward, implosive turn that brings the difficult tasks of politics to an end by making them appear irrelevant in the face of deeper, more fundamental powers that regulate human conduct irrespective of governmental superficialities. If identity and difference are fundamental, then they are not amenable to being re-tooled by crude political methods that cannot possibly get to the heart of primal ontologies, destinies, and fates. When the stakes are this high, nothing can be done to offset the catastrophic consequences that result from tolerating difference and mistaken attempts at practicing democracy. Difference corrupts and compromises identity. Encounters with it are just as unwelcome and potentially destructive as they were for Houston Stewart Chamberlain. They place that most precious commodity, rooted identity, in grave jeopardy.

When national and ethnic identities are represented and projected as pure, exposure to difference threatens them with dilution and compromises their prized purities with the ever-present possibility of contamination. Crossing as mixture and movement must be guarded against. New hatreds and violence arise not, as they did in the past, from supposedly reliable anthropological knowledge of the identity and difference of the Other but from the novel problem of not being able to locate the Other's difference in the common-sense lexicon of alterity. Different people are certainly hated and feared, but the timely antipathy against them is nothing compared with the hatreds turned toward the greater menace of the half-different and the partially familiar. To have mixed is to have been party to a great betrayal. Any unsettling traces of hybridity must be excised from the tidy, bleached-out zones of impossibly pure culture. The safety of sameness can then be recovered by either of the two options that have regularly appeared at the meltdown point of this dismal logic: separation and slaughter.

IDENTITY, SOLIDARITY, AND SELFHOOD

The political language of identity levels out distinctions between chosen connections and given particularities: between the person you choose to be and the things that determine your individuality by being thrust upon you. It is particularly important for the argument that follows that the term "identity" has become a significant element in contemporary conflicts over cultural, ethnic, religious, "racial," and national differences. The idea of collective identity has emerged as an object of political thinking even if its appearance signals a sorry state of affairs in which the distinctive rules that define modern political culture are consciously set aside in favor of the pursuit of primordial feelings and mythic varieties of kinship that are mistakenly believed to be more profound. At the same time, individual identity, the counterpart to the collective, is constantly negotiated, cultivated, and protected as a source of pleasure, power, wealth, and potential danger. That identity is increasingly shaped in the marketplace, modified by the cultural industries, and managed and orchestrated in localized institutions and settings like schools, neighborhoods, and workplaces. It can be inscribed in the dull public world of official politics where issues surrounding the absence of collective identity—and the resulting disappearance of community and solidarity from social life—have also been discussed at great length by politicians on different sides of the political divide.

Other aspects of identity's foundational slipperiness can be detected in the way that the term is used to register the impact of processes that take place above and below the level at which the sovereign state and its distinctive modes of belonging are constituted. The growth of nationalisms and other absolutist religious and ethnic identities, the accentuation of regional and local divisions, and the changing relationship between supranational and subnational networks of economy, politics, and information have all endowed contemporary appeals to identity with extra significance. Identity has come to supply something of an anchor amid the turbulent waters of de-industrialization and the large-scale patterns of planetary reconstruction that are hesitantly named "globalization."[8] It would appear that recovering or possessing an appropriately grounded identity can provide a means to hold these historic but anxiety-inducing processes at bay. Taking pride or finding sanctuary in an exclusive identity affords a means to acquire certainty about who one is and where one fits, about the claims of community and the limits of social obligation.

The politicization of gender and sexuality has enhanced the understanding of identity by directing attention to the social, familial, historical, and cultural factors that bear upon the formation and social reproduction of masculinity and femininity. Two groups of agents are bound together by the centripetal force of the stable, gendered identities that they apparently hold in common. But the anxious, disciplinary intensity with which these ideas are entrenched seems to increase in inverse proportion to the collapse of family and household structures and the eclipse of male domestic domination. In these important areas, the concept of identity has nurtured new ways of thinking about the self, about sameness, and about solidarity. If abstract identity and its thematics are on the verge of becoming something of an obsessive preoccupation in the overdeveloped countries, this novel pattern communicates how political movements and governmental activities are being reconstituted by a change in the status and capacity of the nation-state.[9]

This transformation also reveals something important about the workings of consumer society.[10] The car you drive and the brand of clothing or sports shoes that you wear may no longer be thought of as accidental or contingent expressions of the arts of everyday life and the material constraints that stem from widening inequalities of status and wealth. Branded commodities acquire an additional burden when they are imagined to represent the private inner truths of individual existence or to fix the boundary of communal sensibilities that have faded from other areas of public or civic interaction. Though it involves some over-simplification, we can begin to unpack the idea of identity so that it reveals several overlapping and interconnected problems that are regularly entangled in the more routine contemporary uses of the term. The first, of these is the understanding of identity as subjectivity. Religious and spiritual obligations around selfhood were gradually assimilated into the secular, modern goal of an ordered self operating in an orderly polity.[11] This historic combination was supplemented by the idea that the stability and coherence of the self was a precondition for authoritative and reliable truth-seeking activity. That idea has itself been queried as truth has emerged as something provisional and perspectival that is seldom amenable to the application of placeless, universal laws. The forms of uncertainty that characterize our more skeptical time still emphasize the perils that flow from the lack of a particular variety of self-consciousness and self-cultivation.

When subjectivity is placed in command of its own mechanisms and desires, a heavy investment is made in the idea of identity and the languages of self through which it has been projected. The demise of the certainties associated with religious approaches to understanding oneself and locating oneself in a properly moral relationship to other selves endowed with the same ethical and cognitive attributes has had lasting consequences. The idea of a pre-given, internal identity that regulates social conduct beyond the grasp of conscious reflection has been valuable in restoring elements of increasingly rare and precious certainty to a situation in which doubt and anxiety have become routine. It has also been closely associated with the consolidation of a genomic raciology that promotes forms of resignation in which we are encouraged to do nothing while we wait for those decisive natural differences to announce their presence. These specifications are contradicted by the effects of technological acceleration arising from digital processing and computer-mediated communications. They mean that individual identity is even less constrained by the immediate forms of physical presence established by the body. The boundaries of self need no longer terminate at the threshold of the skin.[12]

The distance that an individual identity can travel toward others and, via technological instruments, become present to them has increased and the quality of that interaction has been transformed by a culture of simulation that has grown up around it. No longer finding uniformity and unanimity in symbols worn on or around the body, like the black shirt, the fascistic political identity cultivated by today's ultranationalist and white supremacist groups can be constituted remotely and transnationally over the Internet through computerized resources like the Aryan Crusader's Library, an on-line networking operation run from the United States but offered worldwide to anyone with a computer and a modem. Governments and corporations are promoting these technological resources as engines of modernized commerce and tools of democracy, but access to them is sharply skewed by poverty, inequality, and a variety of cultural and political factors.[13] That does not, however, mean that the cultural processes they animate and encourage remain confined to the privileged layers where they are most obviously apparent. They can be situated in their wider social setting:

> In the story of constructing identity in the culture of simulation, experiences on the Internet figure prominently, but these experiences can only be understood as part of a larger cultural context. That context is the story of eroding boundaries between the real and the

> virtual, the animate and the inanimate, the unitary and the multiple self, which is occurring both in advanced fields of scientific research and in the patterns of everyday life. From scientists trying to create artificial life, to children "morphing" through a series of virtual personae, we shall see evidence of fundamental shifts in the way we create and experience human identity.[14]

This uncertain, outward movement, from the anxious body-bound self toward the world, leads us to a second set of difficulties in the field of identity. This is the problem of sameness understood here as intersubjectivity. Considering identity from this angle requires recognition of the concept's role in calculations over precisely what counts as the same and what as different. This in turn raises the further question of recognition and its refusal in constituting identity and soliciting identification. The theme of identification and the consequent relationship between sociology, psychology, and even psychoanalysis enter here and add layers of complexity to deliberations about how selves—and their identities—are formed through relationships of exteriority, conflict, and exclusion. Differences can be found within identities as well as between them. The Other, against whose resistance the integrity of an identity is to be established, can be recognized as part of the self that is no longer plausibly understood as a unitary entity but appears instead as one fragile moment in the dialogic circuits that Debbora Battaglia has usefully called a "representational economy":

> ... there is no selfhood apart from the collaborative practice of its figuration. The "self" is a representational economy: a reification continually defeated by mutable entanglements with other subjects' histories, experiences, self-representations; with their texts, conduct, gestures, objectifications.[15]

Building on this insight, the argument below takes shape around a third line of questioning: How does the concept of identity provide a means to speak about social and political solidarity? How is the term "identity" invoked in the summoning and binding of individual agents into groups that become social actors? For these purposes, considering identity requires a confrontation with the specific ideas of ethnic, racialized, and national identity and their civic counterparts. This departure introduces a cluster of distinctively modern notions that, in conjunction with discourses of citizenship, have actively produced rather than given a secondary expression to forms of solidarity with unprecedented power to mobilize mass movements and animate large-scale constituencies. The full power of communicative technologies like radio, sound recording, film, and television has been employed to create forms of solidarity and national consciousness that propelled the idea of belonging far beyond anything that had been achieved in the nineteenth century by the industrialization of print and the formalization of national languages.[16]

Contemporary conflicts over the status of national identity provide the best examples here. To return to the South African case for a moment, Nelson Mandela's historic inaugural speech as State President illustrated both the malleability of nationalist sentiment and some of the enduring tensions around its radical constitution. Working to produce an alternative content for the new nonracial, postracial, or perhaps antiracial political identity that might draw together the citizenry of the reborn country on a new basis beyond the grasp of racializing codes and fantasies of favored life as a people chosen by God, President Mandela turned to the land— common ground—beneath the feet of his diverse, unified, and mutually suspicious audience. Significantly, he spoke not only of the soil but of the beauty of the country and offered the idea of a common relationship to both the cultivated and the natural beauty of the land as elements of a new beginning. This, for him, was the key to awakening truly democratic consciousness. A transformed relationship between body and environment would transcend the irrelevancies of Apartheid South Africa's redundant racial hierarchies:

> To my compatriots, I have no hesitation in saying that each one of us is as intimately attached to the soil of this beautiful country as are the famous jacaranda trees of Pretoria and the mimosa trees of the bushveld.
>
> Each time one of us touches the soil of this land, we feel a sense of personal renewal.... That spiritual and physical oneness we all share with this common homeland explains the depth of pain we all carried in our hearts as we saw our country tear itself apart in a terrible conflict.[17]

Whether these laudable claims were a plausible part of rebuilding South African nationality remains to be seen. What is more significant for our purposes is that territory and indeed nature itself are being engaged as a means to define citizenship and the forms of rootedness that compose national solidarity and cohesion. President Mandela's words were powerful because they work with the organicity that nature has bequeathed to modern ideas of culture. In that blur, Mandela constructed an ecological account of the relationship between shared humanity, common citizenship, place, and identity. The speech subverted traditional assumptions with its implication that Apartheid was a brutal violation of nature that could be repaired only if people were prepared to pay heed to the oneness established by their connection to the beautiful environment they share and hold in common stewardship.

The alternative argument set out below recognizes the socioecological dynamics of identity-formation. However, it asks you to consider what might be gained if the powerful claims of soil, roots, and territory could be set aside. You are invited to view them in the light of other possibilities that have sometimes defined themselves against the forms of solidarity sanctioned by the territorial regimes of the nation-state. We will see that the idea of movement can provide an alternative to the sedentary poetics of either soil or blood. Both communicative technology and older patterns of itinerancy ignored by the human sciences can be used to articulate placeless imaginings of identity as well as new bases for solidarity and synchronized action. With these possibilities in mind, I want to suggest that considering the de-territorialized history of the modern African diaspora into the western hemisphere and the racial slavery through which it was accomplished has something useful to teach us about the workings of identity and identification and, beyond that, something valuable to impart about the claims of nationality and the nation-state upon the writing of history itself.

Shut out from literacy on the pain of death, slaves taken from Africa by force used the same biblical narratives we have already encountered to comprehend their situation and, slowly and at great emotional cost, to build what might be understood as a new set of identities. They, too, imagined themselves to be a divinely chosen people. This meant that the suffering visited upon their proto-nations in bondage was purposive and their pain was oriented, not merely toward heavenly freedom, but toward the moral redemption of anyone prepared to join them in the just cause of seeking political liberty and individual autonomy. These themes are nowhere more powerfully articulated than in the work of Martin Luther King, Jr. Writing amid the conflicts of the 1960s that would eventually claim his life, about the difficulties experienced by black Americans whose allegiance to America was broken by their lack of political rights and economic opportunities, he had the following to say about what we would now recognize as identity. (He, too, mobilized the biblical mythology of the chosen people to articulate his political choices and hopes):

> Something of the spirit of our slave forebears must be pursued today. From the inner depths of our being we must sing with them: "Before I'll be a slave, I'll be buried in my grave and go home to my Lord and be free." This spirit, this drive, this rugged sense of somebodyness is the first and vital step that the Negro must take in dealing with his dilemma.... To overcome this tragic conflict, it will be necessary for the Negro to find a new self-image.... The Pharaohs had a favorite and effective strategy to keep their slaves in bondage: keep them fighting among themselves.... But when slaves unite, the Red Seas of history open and the Egypts of slavery crumble.[18]

We must be cautious because there are now considerable political gains to be made from being recognized as possessing an identity defined exclusively by this and other histories of ineffable suffering. Dr. King did not exploit that association, but those who followed in his wake have not always been so scrupulous. The identity of the victim, sealed off and presented as an essential, unchanging state, has become, in the years since his murder, a prized acquisition not least where financial calculations have sought to transform historic wrongs into compensatory monies.[19] This problem has not been confined to black politics with its demands for reparations and other forms of financial restitution for slavery in the Americas. From Palestine to Bosnia, the image of the victim has become useful in all sorts of dubious maneuverings that can obscure the moral and political questions arising from demands for justice. And yet, for all its pragmatic or strategic attractions, the role of the victim has its drawbacks as the basis of any political identity. With characteristic insight, James Baldwin described some of them in a discussion of the meaning of racial terror and its impact upon identity:

> I refuse, absolutely, to speak from the point of view of the victim. The victim can have no point of view for precisely so long as he thinks of himself as a victim. The testimony of the victim as victim corroborates, simply, the reality of the chains that bind him—confirms, and, as it were consoles the jailer.[20]

Baldwin cautions us against closing the gap between identity and politics and playing down the complexities of their interconnection. His words locate the trap involved in hoping that what is lazily imagined to be shared identity might be straightforwardly transferred into the political arena. With his help we can apprehend the many dangers involved in vacuous "me too-ism" or some other equally pointless and immoral competition over which peoples, nations, populations, or ethnic groups have suffered the most; over whose identities have been most severely damaged; and indeed over who might be thought of as the most deracinated, nomadic, or cosmopolitan and therefore more essentially "modern" or paradigmatically "postmodern" peoples on our planet. However, with Baldwin's warning still in mind, there is much to be learned by foregrounding that experience of being victimized and using it to challenge the willful innocence of some Europe-centered accounts of modernity's pleasures and problems. That difficult operation yields more than a coda to the conventional historical and sociological stories of modern development. Perhaps a changed sense of what it means to be a modern person might result from this reassessment?

The careful reconstruction of those half-hidden, tragic narratives that demonstrate how the fateful belief in mutually impermeable, religious, racial, national, and ethnic identities was assembled and reproduced was briefly addressed in the previous chapter. It fits in well with the archaeological work already being done to account for the complex cultures and societies of the New World and their relationship to the history of European thought, literature, and self-understanding.[21] The significance of colony and empire is also being reevaluated and the boundaries around European nation-states are emerging as more porous and leakier than some architects of complacently national history would want to admit. These discoveries support the demand for a decisive change of standpoint. Again it seems that to comprehend the bleak histories of colonial and imperial power that besmirch the clean edifice of innocent modernity and query the heroic story of universal reason's triumphal march, we must shift away from the historiographical scale defined by the closed borders of the nation-state. If we are prepared to possess those histories and consider setting them to work in divining more modest and more plausible understandings of democracy, tolerance for difference, and cross-cultural recognition than currently exist, this historical argument can redirect attention toward some of the more general contemporary questions involved in thinking about identity in the human sciences. Histories of the violence and terror with which modern rationality has been complicit offer a useful means to test and qualify the explanatory power of theories of identity and culture that have arisen in quieter, less bloody circumstances. Perhaps those theories also derive from the more complacent scholarly ways of thinking about power common to temperate climes. The idea that possessing a particular identity should be a precondition or qualification for engaging in this kind of work is trivial. The intellectual challenge defined here is that histories of suffering should not be allocated exclusively to their victims. If they were, the memory of the trauma would disappear as the living memory of it died away.

This proposed change of perspective about the value of suffering is not then exclusively of interest to its victims and any kin who remember them. Because it is a matter of justice, it is not just an issue for the wronged "minorities" whose own lost or fading identities may be restored or rescued by the practice of commemoration. It is also of concern to those who may have benefited directly and indirectly from the rational application of irrationality and barbarity. Perhaps above all, this attempt to reconceptualize modernity so that it encompasses these possibilities is relevant to the majority who are unlikely to count themselves as affiliated with either of the principal groups: victims and perpetrators. This difficult stance challenges that unnamed group to witness sufferings that pass beyond the reach of words and, in so doing, to see how an understanding of one's own particularity or identity might be transformed as a result of a principled exposure to the claims of otherness.[22]

*****

DIASPORA AS A SOCIAL ECOLOGY OF IDENTIFICATION

The idea of diaspora offers a ready alternative to the stern discipline of primordial kinship and rooted belonging. It rejects the popular image of natural nations spontaneously endowed with self-consciousness, tidily composed of uniform families: those interchangeable collections of ordered bodies that express and reproduce absolutely distinctive cultures as well as perfectly formed heterosexual pairings. As an alternative to the metaphysics of "race," nation, and bounded culture coded into the body, diaspora is a concept that problematizes the cultural and historical mechanics of belonging. It disrupts the fundamental power of territory to determine identity by breaking the simple sequence of explanatory links between place, location, and consciousness. It destroys the naive invocation of common memory as the basis of particularity in a similar fashion by drawing attention to the contingent political dynamics of commemoration.

The ancient word diaspora acquired a modern accent as a result of its unanticipated usefulness to the nationalisms and subaltern imperialisms of the late nineteenth century. It remains an enduring feature of the continuing aftershocks generated by those political projects in Palestine and elsewhere. If it can be stripped of its disciplinarian associations it might offer seeds capable of bearing fruit in struggles to comprehend the sociality of a new phase in which displacement, flight, exile, and forced migration are likely to be familiar and recurrent phenomena that transform the terms in which identity needs to be understood. Retreating from the totalizing immodesty and ambition of the word "global," diaspora is an outer-national term which contributes to the analysis of intercultural and transcultural processes and forms. It identifies a relational network, characteristically produced by forced dispersal and reluctant scattering. It is not just a word of movement, though purposive, desperate movement is integral to it. Under this sign, push factors are a dominant influence. The urgency they introduce makes diaspora more than a voguish synonym for peregrination or nomadism. As the biographies of Equiano and Wheatley suggest, life itself is at stake in the way the word connotes flight following the threat of violence rather than freely chosen experiences of displacement. Slavery, pogroms, indenture, genocide, and other unnameable terrors have all figured in the constitution of diasporas and the reproduction of diaspora consciousness in which identity is focused, less on the equalizing, pre-democratic force of sovereign territory and more on the social dynamics of remembrance and commemoration defined by a strong sense of the dangers involved in forgetting the location of origin and the tearful process of dispersal.

The term opens up a historical and experiential rift between the locations of residence and the locations of belonging. This in turn sets up a further opposition. Consciousness of diaspora affiliation stands opposed to the distinctively modern structures and modes of power orchestrated by the institutional complexity of nation-states. Diaspora identification exists outside of and sometimes in opposition to the political forms and codes of modern citizenship. The nation-state has regularly been presented as the institutional means to terminate diaspora dispersal. At one end of the communicative circuit this is to be accomplished by the assimilation of those who were out of place. At the other a similar outcome is realized through the prospect of their return to a place of origin. The fundamental equilibrium of nature and civil society can thus be restored. In both options it is the nation-state that brings the spatial and temporal order of diaspora life to an abrupt end. Diaspora yearning and ambivalence are transformed into a simple unambiguous exile once the possibility of easy reconciliation with either the place of sojourn or the place of origin exists. Some, though not all, versions of diaspora consciousness accentuate the possibility and desirability of return. They may or may not recognize the difficulty of this gesture. The degree to which return is accessible or desired provides a valuable comparative moment in the typology and classification of diaspora histories and political movements.

"Diaspora" lacks the modernist and cosmopolitan associations of the word "exile" from which it has been carefully distinguished, particularly in the Jewish histories with which the term is most deeply intertwined.[23] We should be careful that the term "history" retains its plural status at this point because diaspora has had a variety of different resonances in Jewish cultures inside and outside of Europe, both before and after the founding of the state of Israel.

Equiano's sense of an affinity between blacks and Jews stands behind the work of many modern black thinkers of the western hemisphere who were eager to adapt the diaspora idea to their particular post-slave circumstances. Many of them developed conceptual schemes and political programs for diaspora affiliation (and its negation) long before they found a proper name for the special emotional and political logics that governed these operations. The work of Edward Wilmot Blyden in the late nineteenth century represents another important site of similar intercultural transfer. Blyden was a "returnee" to Africa from the Danish West Indies via the United States. He presented his own redemptive involvement with the free nation-state of Liberia and its educational apparatuses, along lines suggested by an interpretation of Jewish history and culture forged through a close personal and intellectual relationship with Jews and Judaism. In 1898, awed by what he described as "that marvelous movement called Zionism," he attempted to draw the attention of "thinking and enlightened Jews to the great continent of Africa—not to its northern and southern extremities only, but to its vast intertropical area" on the grounds that they would find there "religious and spiritual aspirations kindred to their own."[24]

Earlier on, in assessing the power of roots and rootedness to ground identity, we encountered invocations of organicity that forged an uncomfortable connection between the warring domains of nature and culture. They made nation and citizenship appear to be natural rather than social phenomena—spontaneous expressions of a distinctiveness that was palpable in deep inner harmony between people and their dwelling places. Diaspora is a useful means to reassess the idea of essential and absolute identity precisely because it is incompatible with that type of nationalist and raciological thinking. The word comes closely associated with the idea of sowing seed. This etymological inheritance is a disputed legacy and a mixed blessing. It demands that we attempt to evaluate the significance of the scattering process against the supposed uniformity of that which has been scattered. Diaspora posits important tensions between here and there, then and now, between seed in the bag, the packet, or the pocket and seed in the ground, the fruit, or the body. By focusing attention equally on the sameness within differentiation and the differentiation within sameness, diaspora disturbs the suggestion that political and cultural identity might be understood via the analogy of indistinguishable peas lodged in the protective pods of closed kinship and subspecies being. Is it possible to imagine how a more complex, ecologically sophisticated sense of interaction between organisms and environments might become an asset in thinking critically about identity?

Imagine a scenario in which similar—though not precisely identical—seeds take root in different places. Plants of the same species are seldom absolutely indistinguishable. Nature does not always produce interchangeable clones. Soils, nutrients, predators, pests, and pollination vary along with unpredictable weather. Seasons change. So do climates, which can be determined on a variety of scales: micro as well as macro and mezzo. Diaspora provides valuable cues and clues for the elaboration of a social ecology of cultural identity and identification that takes us far beyond the stark dualism of genealogy and geography. The pressure to associate, like the desires to remember or forget, may vary with changes in the economic and political atmosphere. Unlike the tides, the weather cannot be predicted accurately. To cap it all, the work involved in discovering origins is more difficult in some places and at some times.

If we can adopt this more difficult analytical stance, the celebrated "butterfly effect" in which tiny, almost insignificant forces can, in defiance of conventional expectations, precipitate unpredictable, larger changes in other locations becomes a commonplace happening. The seamless propagation of cultural habits and styles was rendered radically contingent at the point where geography and genealogy began to trouble each other. We are directed toward the conflictual limits of "race," ethnicity, and culture. When a diaspora talks back to a nation-state, it initiates conflict between those who agree that they are more or less what they were, but cannot agree whether the more or the less should take precedence in contemporary political and historical calculations.

The reproductive moment of diaspora raises other uncomfortable issues. In a discussion of some recent approaches to the diaspora idea and its relationship to masculinism,[25] Stefan Helmreich has identified the processes of cultural reproduction and transmission to which diaspora draws attention as being radically gender-specific. He underlines the close etymological relationship between the word diaspora and the word sperm as if their common tie to the Greek word meaning sow and scatter still corrupts the contemporary application of the concept as it were, from within. This argument can be tested and contextualized by the introduction of another family term, the word spore: the unicellular vector for supposedly "asexual" reproduction.[26] Could that alternative, gender-free linkage complicate the notion that diaspora is inscribed as a masculinist trope and cannot therefore be liberated from the quagmire of androcentrism, where it has been lodged by modern nationalisms and the religious conceptions of ethnic particularity that cheerfully coexist with them? Though still contested, diaspora lends itself to the critique of absolutist political sensibilities, especially those that have been articulated around the themes of nation, "race," and ethnicity. It seems unduly harsh to suggest that it is any more deeply contaminated by the toxins of male domination than other heuristic terms in the emergent vocabulary of transcultural critical theory. There is no reason descent through the male line should be privileged over dissent via the rhizomorphic principle.[27] Diaspora can be used to conjure up both.

Where separation, time, and distance from the point of origin or the center of sovereignly complicate the symbolism of ethnic and national reproduction, anxieties over the boundaries and limits of sameness may lead people to seek security in the sanctity of emobied difference. The new racisms that code biology in cultural terms have been alloyed with still newer variants that conscript the body into disciplinary service and encode cultural particularity in an understanding of bodily practices and attributes determined by genes. Gender differences become extremely important in nation-building activity because they are a sign of an irresistible natural hierarchy that belongs at the center of civic life. The unholy forces of nationalist biopolitics intersect on the bodies of women charged with the reproduction of absolute ethnic difference and the continuance of blood lines. The integrity of the nation becomes the integrity of its masculinity. In fact, it can be a nation only if the correct version of gender hierarchy has been established and reproduced. The family is the main device in this operation. It connects men and women, boys and girls to the larger collectivity toward which they must orient themselves if they are to acquire a Fatherland. Minister Louis Farrakhan of the Nation of Islam typified the enduring power of this variety of thinking about nation and gender in his description of the 1995 march of African-American men to Washington. He saw that event as an act of warfare in which the condition of their alternative national manhood could be gauged:

> No nation gets any respect if you go out to war and you put your women in the trenches and the men stay at home cooking. Every nation that goes to war tests the fiber of the manhood of that nation. And literally, going to Washington to seek justice for our people is like going to war.[28]

If the modern nation is to be prepared for war, reproducing the soldier citizens of the future is not a process it can leave to chance or whim. Again, the favored institutional setting for this disciplinary and managerial activity is the family. The family is understood as nothing more than the essential building block in the construction and elevation of the nation. This nation-building narrative runs all the way to fascism and its distinctive myths of rebirth after periods of weakness and decadence.[29] Diaspora challenges it by valorizing sub- and supranational kinship and allowing for a more ambivalent relationship toward national encampments.

These non-national proclivities have triggered other destabilizing and subversive effects. They are amplified when the concept of diaspora is annexed for anti-essentialist accounts of identity-formation as a process and used to host a decisive change of orientation away from the primordial identities established alternatively by either nature or culture. By embracing diaspora, theories of identity turn instead toward contingency, indeterminacy, and conflict. With the idea of valuing diaspora more highly than the coercive unanimity of the nation, the concept becomes explicitly antinational. This shift is connected with transforming the familiar unidirectional idea of diaspora as a form of catastrophic but simple dispersal that enjoys an identifiable and reversible originary moment— the site of trauma—into something far more complex. Diaspora can be used to instantiate a "chaotic" model in which shifting "strange attractors" are the only visible points of fragile stability amid social and cultural turbulence.

The importance of these nodes is misunderstood if they are identified as fixed local phenomena. They appear unexpectedly, and where diaspora becomes a concept, the web or network they allow us to perceive can mark out new understandings of self, sameness, and solidarity. However, they are not successive stages in a genealogical account of kin relations—equivalent to branches on a single family tree. One does not beget the next in a comforting sequence of ethnic teleology; nor are they stations on a linear journey toward the destination that a completed identity might represent. They suggest a different mode of linkage between the forms of micropolitical agency exercised in cultures and movements of resistance and transformation and other political processes that are visible on a different, bigger scale. Their plurality and regionality valorize something more than a protracted condition of social mourning over the ruptures of exile, loss, brutality, stress, and forced separation. They highlight a more indeterminate and, some would say, modernist mood in which natal alienation and cultural estrangement are capable of conferring insight and creating pleasure, as well as precipitating anxiety about the coherence of the nation and the stability of its imaginary ethnic core. Contrasting forms of political action have emerged to create new possibilities and new pleasures where dispersed people recognize the effects of spatial dislocation as rendering the issue of origin problematic. They may grow to accept the possibility that they are no longer what they once were and cannot therefore rewind the tapes of their cultural history. The diaspora idea encourages critical theory to proceed rigorously but cautiously in ways that do not privilege the modern nation-state and its institutional order over the subnational and supranational patterns of power, communication, and conflict that they work to discipline, regulate, and govern. The concept of space is itself transformed when it is seen in terms of the ex-centric communicative circuitry that has enabled dispersed populations to converse, interact, and more recently even to synchronize significant elements of their social and cultural lives.

What the African-american writer Leroi Jones once named "the changing same"[30] provides a valuable motif with which to fix this supplement to the diaspora idea. Neither the mechanistic essentialism that is too squeamish to acknowledge the possibility of difference within sameness nor the lazy alternative that animates the supposedly strategic variety of essentialism can supply keys to the untidy workings of diaspora identities. They are creolized, syncretized, hybridized, and chronically impure cultural forms, particularly if they were once rooted in the complicity of rationalized terror and racialized reason. This changing same is not some invariant essence that gets enclosed subsequently in a shape-shifting exterior with which it is casually associated. It is not the sign of an unbroken, integral inside protected by a camouflaged husk. The phrase names the problem of diaspora politics and diaspora poetics. The same is present, but how can we imagine it as something other than an essence generating the merely accidental? Iteration is the key to this process. The same is retained without needing to be reified. It is ceaselessly reprocessed. It is maintained and modified in what becomes a determinedly nontraditional tradition, for this is not tradition as closed or simple repetition. Invariably promiscuous, diaspora and the politics of commemoration it specifies challenge us to apprehend mutable forms that can redefine the idea of culture through a reconciliation with movement and complex, dynamic variation.

Today's affiliates to the tradition for which Equiano and Wheatley operate as imaginary ancestors find themselves in a very different economic, cultural, and political circuitry—a different diaspora—from the one their predecessors encountered. Live human beings are no longer a commodity, and the dispersal of blacks has extended further and deeper into Europe, where elements of the scattering process have been repeated once again by the arrival of Caribbean peoples and other formerly colonial folk in the post-1945 period. Several generations of blacks have been born in Europe whose identification with the African continent is even more attenuated and remote, particularly since the anticolonial wars are over. Both the memory of slavery and an orientation toward identity that derives from African origins are hard to maintain when the rupture of migration intervenes and stages its own trials of belonging. However, the notion of a distinctive, African-derived identity has not withered and the moral and political fruits of black life in the western hemisphere have been opened out systematically to larger and larger numbers of people in different areas.

The black musicians, dancers, and performers of the New World have disseminated these insights, styles, and pleasures through the institutional resources of the cultural industries that they have colonized and captured. These media, particularly recorded sound, have been annexed for sometimes subversive purposes of protest and affirmation. The vernacular codes and expressive cultures constituted from the forced new beginning of racial slavery have reappeared at the center of a global phenomenon that has regularly surpassed—just as Wheatley's complex poetry did long ago—innocent notions of mere entertainment. What are wrongly believed to be simple cultural commodities have been used to communicate a powerful ethical and political commentary on rights, justice, and democracy that articulates but also transcends criticism of modern racial typology and the ideologies of white supremacy. The living history of New World blacks has endowed this expressive tradition with flexibility and durability.

Bob Marley, whose recordings are still selling all over the world more than a decade after his death, provides a useful concluding example here. His enduring presence in globalized popular culture is an important reminder of the power of the technologies that ground the culture of simulation. Those same technological resources have subdued the constraints of nature and provided Marley with a virtual life after death in which his popularity can continue to grow unencumbered by any embarrassing political residues that might make him into a threatening or frightening figure. But there is more to this worldwide popularity than clever video-based immortality and the evident reconstruction of Bob Marley's image, stripped of much of its militant Ethiopianism—yet another chosen people and another promised land to set alongside those we have already considered.

Bob's life and work lend themselves to the study of postmodern diaspora identity. They help us to perceive the workings of those complex cultural circuits that have transformed a pattern of simple, one-way dispersal into a webbed network constituted through multiple points of intersection. His historic performance at the Zimbabwe independence ceremony in 1980 symbolized the partial reconnection with African origins that permeates diaspora yearning. Like so many others, he too did not go to Africa to make his home. He chose instead, as many other prominent pan-Africanists had done before and since, a more difficult cosmopolitan commitment and a different form of solidarity and identification that did not require his physical presence in that continent.

His triumph not only marks the beginning of what has come to be known as "world music" or "world beat," an increasingly significant marketing category that helps to locate the transformation and possible demise of music-led youth-culture. It was built from the seemingly universal power of a poetic and political language that reached out from its roots to find new audiences hungry for its insights. Bob became, in effect, a planetary figure. His music was pirated in Eastern Europe and became intertwined with the longing for freedom and rights across Africa, the Pacific, and Latin America. Captured into commodities, his music traveled and found new audiences and so did his band. Between 1976 and 1980 they criss-crossed the planet, performing in the United States, Canada, the United Kingdom, France, Italy, Germany, Spain, Scandinavia, Ireland, Holland, Belgium, Switzerland, Japan, Australia, New Zealand, the Ivory Coast, and Gabon. Major sales were also recorded in market areas where the band did not perform, particularly Brazil, Senegal, Ghana, Nigeria, Taiwan, and the Philippines.

Marley's global stature was founded on the hard, demanding labor of transcontinental touring as much as on the poetic qualities he invested in the language of sufferation that he made universal. In conclusion, his transnational image invites one further round of speculation about the status of identity and the conflicting scales on which sameness, subjectivity, and solidarity can be imagined. Connecting with him across the webs of planetary popular culture might be thought of as an additional stage in the nonprogressive evolution of diaspora into the digital era. Recognizing this requires moving the focus of inquiry away from the notions of fixed identity that we have already discovered to be worn out and placing it instead upon the processes of identification. Do people connect themselves and their hopes with the figure of Bob Marley as a man, a Jamaican, a Caribbean, an African, or a Pan-African artist? Is he somehow all of the above and more, a rebel voice of the poor and the underdeveloped world that made itself audible in the core of overdeveloped social and economic life he called Babylon? On what scale of cultural analysis do we make sense of this reconciliation of modern and postmodern technologies with mystical antimodern forces? How do we combine his work as an intellectual, as a thinker, with his portrayal as a primitive, hypermasculine figure: a not-so-noble savage shrouded in ganga smoke? Are we prepared now, so many years after his death and mythification, to set aside the new forms of minstrelsy obviously promoted under the constellation of his stardom and see him as a worldly figure whose career traversed continents and whose revolutionary political stance won adherents because of its ability to imagine the end of capitalism as readily as it imagined the end of the world?

In Bob Marley's image there is something more than domestication of the other and the accommodation of insubordinate Third Worldism within corporate multiculturalism. Something remains even when we dismiss the presentation of difference as a spectacle and a powerful marketing device in the global business of selling records, tapes, CDs, videos, and associated merchandise. However great Bob's skills, the formal innovations in his music must take second place behind its significance as the site of a revolution in the structure of the global markets for these cultural commodities. The glamour of the primitive was set to work to animate his image and increase the power of his music to seduce. That modern magic required Bob to be purified, simplified, nationalized, and particularized. An aura of authenticity was manufactured not to validate his political aspirations or rebel status but to invest his music with a mood of carefully calculated transgression that still makes it saleable and appealing all over the planet. Otherness was invoked and operates to make the gulf between his memory and his remote "crossover" audiences bigger, to manage that experiential gap so that their pleasures in consuming him and his work are somehow enhanced.

It is only recently that the long-ignored figure of Bob's white father has been brought forward and offered as the key to interpreting his son's achievements and comprehending the pathological motivation to succeed that took him out of Trenchtown. In that sense, the phase in which Bob was represented as exotic and dangerous is over. We can observe a prodigal, benign, almost childlike Bob Marley being brought home into the bosom of his corporate family. All this can be recognized. But the stubborn utopia projected through Bob Marley's music and anticolonial imaginings remains something that is not de-limited by a proscriptive ethnic wrapper or racial "health-warning" in which encounters with otherness are presented as dangerous to the well-being of one's own singular identity. Music and instrumental competence have to be learned and practiced before they can be made to communicate convincingly. This should restrict their role as signs of authentic, absolute particularity. Perhaps, in the tainted but nonetheless powerful image of Bob Marley's global stardom, we can discern the power of identity based, not on some cheap, pre-given sameness, but on will, inclination, mood, and affinity. The translocal power of his dissident voice summons up these possibilities and a chosen, recognizably political kinship that is all the more valuable for its distance from the disabling assumptions of automatic solidarity based on either blood or land.

NOTES

1. Mark Leonard, *Britain™* (Demos, 1997).
2. Judith Butler, "Collected and Fractured," in *Identities*, ed. Kwame Anthony Appiah and Henry Louis Gates, Jr. (University of Chicago Press, 1995).
3. J.-J. Rousseau, "Considerations on the Government of Poland," in *Rousseau: Political Writings*, trans. and ed. Frederick Watkins (Nelson and Sons, 1953), pp. 163–164.
4. *The Blackshirt* (November 24–30, 1933), p. 5; quoted in John Harvey, *Men in Black* (Chicago University Press, 1995), p. 242.
5. Leonard Thompson, *The Political Mythology of Apartheid* (Yale University Press, 1985), p. 39.
6. African Rights, *Rwanda: Death, Despair and Defiance* (London, 1994), pp. 347–354. See also Sander L. Gilman, *The Jew's Body* (Routledge, 1991), especially chap. 7, "The Jewish Nose: Are Jews White? Or, The History of the Nose Job."
7. Arthur Malu-Malu and Thierry Oberle, *Sunday Times*, August 30, 1998.
8. William Greider, *One World, Ready or Not: The Manic Logic of Global Capitalism* (Simon and Schuster, 1997); Jerry Mander and Edward Goldsmith, eds., *The Case against the Global Economy and for a Turn toward the Local* (Sierra Books, 1996); Benjamin R. Barber, *Jihad vs. McWorld: How the Planet Is Both Falling Apart and Coming Together and What This Means for Democracy* (Random House, 1995).
9. Jean-Marie Guéhenno, *The End of the Nation State* (University of Minnesota Press, 1995).
10. Zygmunt Bauman, *Freedom* (Open University Press, 1988).
11. Charles Taylor, *Sources of the Self* (Harvard University Press, 1989); William Connolly, *Identity/Difference* (Cornell University Press, 1991).
12. Chris Hables Gray, ed., *The Cyborg Handbook* (Routledge, 1995).
13. Amy Harmon, "Racial Divide Found on Information Highway," *New York Times*, April 10, 1998.
14. Sherry Turkle, *Life on the Screen: Identity in the Age of the Internet* (Simon and Schuster, 1995), p. 10.
15. Debbora Battaglia, "Problematizing the Self: A Thematic Introduction," in D. Battaglia, ed., *Rhetorics of Self-Making* (University of California Press, 1995), p. 2.

16. Benedict Anderson, *Imagined Communities: Reflections on the Origin and Spread of Nationalism* (Verso, 1982).
17. President Mandela's inagugural speech was reprinted in *The Independent*, May 11, 1995, p. 12.
18. Martin Luther King, Jr., *Where Do We Go From Here: Chaos or Community?* (Harper and Row, 1967), p. 124
19. Donald G. McNeil, Jr., "Africans Seek Redress for German Genocide," *New York Times*, June 1, 1998.
20. James Bladwin, *Evidence of Things Not Seen* (Henry Holt and Co., 1985), p. 78
21. Peter Hulme, *Colonial Encounters* (Metheun, 1986); Anthony Pagden, *European Encounters in the New World: From Renaissance to Romanticism* (Yale, 1993); Richard Taylor, *Sex and Conquest* (Cornell University Press, 1995).
22. Charles Taylor, "Understanding and Ethnocentricity," in *Philosophy and the Human Sciences, Philosophical Papers 2* (Cambridge University Press, 1985).
23. "Elliott P. Skinner, "The Dialectic between Diasporas and Homelands," in Joseph E. Harris, ed., *Global Dimensions of the African Diaspora* (Howard University Press, 1982).
24. Edward Wilmot Blyden, *On the Jewish Question* (Lionel Hart and Co., 1898), p. 23.
25. Stefan Helmreich, "Kinship, Nation, and Paul Gilroy's Concept of Diaspora," *Diaspora* 2, 2 (1993), pp. 243–249.
26. Londa Scheibinger, *Nature's Body* (Beacon Press, 1993).
27. "To be rhizomorphous is to produce stems and filaments that seem to be roots, or better yet connect with them by penetrating the trunk, but put them to new uses. We're tired of trees. We should stop believing in trees, roots and radicles. They've made us suffer too much. All of arborescent culture is founded on them, from biology to linguistics." Gilles Deleuze and Felix Guattari, "Rhizome," in *A Thousand Plateaus* (University of Minnesota Press, 1988), p. 15.
28. Louis Farrakhan, "A Call to March," *Emerge*, vol. 7, no. 1 (October 1995), p. 66.
29. Roger Griffin, *The Nature of Fascism* (Routledge, 1993).
30. Leroi Jones, *Black Music* (Quill, 1967), pp. 180–211.

CHAPTER 33

HOW JEWS BECAME WHITE FOLKS AND WHAT THAT SAYS ABOUT RACE IN AMERICA

Karen Brodkin

> The American nation was founded and developed by the Nordic race, but if a few more million members of the Alpine, Mediterranean and Semitic races are poured among us, the result must inevitably be a hybrid race of people as worthless and futile as the good-for-nothing mongrels of Central America and Southeastern Europe.
>
> Kenneth Roberts, "Why Europe Leaves Home"

It is clear that Kenneth Roberts did not think of my ancestors as white, like him. The late nineteenth century and early decades of the twentieth saw a steady stream of warnings by scientists, policymakers, and the popular press that "mongrelization" of the Nordic or Anglo-Saxon race—the real Americans—by inferior European races (as well as by inferior non-European ones) was destroying the fabric of the nation.

I continue to be surprised when I read books that indicate that America once regarded its immigrant European workers as something other than white, as biologically different. My parents are not surprised; they expect anti-Semitism to be part of the fabric of daily life, much as I expect racism to be part of it. They came of age in the Jewish world of the 1920s and 1930s, at the peak of anti-Semitism in America.[1] They are rightly proud of their upward mobility and think of themselves as pulling themselves up by their own bootstraps. I grew up during the 1950s in the Euro-ethnic New York suburb of Valley Stream, where Jews were simply one kind of white folks and where ethnicity meant little more to my generation than food and family heritage. Part of my ethnic heritage was the belief that Jews were smart and that our success was due to our own efforts and abilities, reinforced by a culture that valued sticking together, hard work, education, and deferred gratification.

I am willing to affirm all those abilities and ideals and their contribution to Jews' upward mobility, but I also argue that they were still far from sufficient to account for Jewish success. I say this because the belief in a Jewish version of Horatio Alger has become a point of entry for some mainstream Jewish organizations to adopt a racist attitude against African Americans especially and to oppose affirmative action for people of color.[2] Instead I want to suggest that Jewish success is a product not only of ability but also of the removal of powerful social barriers to its realization.

It is certainly true that the United States has a history of anti-Semitism and of beliefs that Jews are members of an inferior race. But Jews were hardly alone. American anti-Semitism was part of a broader pattern of late-nineteenth-century racism against all southern and eastern European immigrants, as well as against Asian immigrants, not to mention African Americans, Native Americans, and Mexicans. These views justified all sorts of discriminatory treatment, including closing the doors, between 1882 and 1927, to immigration from Europe and Asia. This picture changed radically after World War II. Suddenly, the same folks who had promoted nativism and xenophobia were eager to believe that the Euro-origin people whom they had deported, reviled as members of inferior races, and prevented from immigrating only a few years earlier, were now model middle-class white suburban citizens.[3]

It was not an educational epiphany that made those in power change their hearts, their minds, and our race. Instead, it was the biggest and best affirmative action program in the history of our nation, and it was for Euromales. That is not how it was billed, but it is the way it worked out in practice. I tell this story to show the institutional nature of racism and the centrality of state policies to creating and changing races. Here, those policies reconfigured the category of whiteness to include European immigrants. There are similarities and differences in the ways each of the European immigrant groups became "whitened." I tell the story in a way that links anti-Semitism to other varieties of anti-European racism because this highlights what Jews shared with other Euro-immigrants.

EURORACES

The US "discovery" that Europe was divided into inferior and superior races began with the racialization of the Irish in the mid-nineteenth century and flowered in response to the great waves of immigration from southern and eastern Europe that began in the late nineteenth century. Before that time, European immigrants—including Jews—had been largely assimilated into the white population. However, the 23 million European immigrants who came to work in US cities in the waves of migration after 1880 were too many and too concentrated to absorb. Since immigrants and their children made up more than 70 percent of the population of most of the country's largest cities, by the 1890s urban America had taken on a distinctly southern and eastern European immigrant flavor. Like the Irish in Boston and New York, their urban concentrations in dilapidated neighborhoods put them cheek by jowl next to the rising elites and the middle class with whom they shared public space and to whom their working-class ethnic communities were particularly visible.

The Red Scare of 1919 clearly linked anti-immigrant with anti-working-class sentiment—to the extent that the Seattle general strike by largely native-born workers was blamed on foreign agitators. The Red Scare was fueled by an economic depression, a massive postwar wave of strikes, the Russian Revolution, and another influx of postwar immigration. [...]

Not surprisingly, the belief in European races took root most deeply among the wealthy, US-born Protestant elite, who feared a hostile and seemingly inassimilable working class. By the end of the nineteenth century, Senator Henry Cabot Lodge pressed Congress to cut off immigration to the United States; Theodore Roosevelt raised the alarm of "race suicide" and took Anglo-Saxon women to task for allowing "native" stock to be outbred by inferior immigrants. In the early twentieth century, these fears gained a great deal of social legitimacy thanks to the efforts of an influential network of aristocrats and scientists who developed theories of eugenics—breeding for a "better" humanity—and scientific racism.

Key to these efforts was Madison Grant's influential *The Passing of the Great Race*, published in 1916. Grant popularized notions developed by William Z. Ripley and Daniel Brinton that there existed three or four major European races, ranging from the superior Nordics of northwestern Europe to the inferior southern and eastern races of the Alpines, Mediterraneans, and worst of all, Jews, who seemed to be everywhere in his native New York City. Grant's nightmare was race-mixing among Europeans. For him, "the cross between any of the three European races and a Jew is a Jew." He didn't have good things to say about Alpine or Mediterranean "races" either. For Grant, race and class were interwoven: the upper class was racially pure Nordic; the lower classes came from the lower races.[4]

Far from being on the fringe, Grant's views were well within the popular mainstream. Here is the *New York Times* describing the Jewish Lower East Side of a century ago:

> The neighborhood where these people live is absolutely impassable for wheeled vehicles other than their pushcarts. If a truck driver tries to get through where their pushcarts are standing they apply to him all kinds of vile and indecent epithets. The driver is fortunate if he gets out of the street without being hit with a stone or having a putrid fish or piece of meat thrown in his face. This neighborhood, peopled almost entirely by the people who claim to have been driven from Poland and Russia, is the eyesore of New York and perhaps the filthiest place on the western continent. It is impossible for a Christian to live there because he will be driven out, either by blows or the dirt and stench. Cleanliness is an unknown quantity to these people. They cannot be lifted up to a higher plane because they do not want to be. If the cholera should ever get among these people, they would scatter its germs as a sower does grain.[5]

Such views were well within the mainstream of the early-twentieth-century scientific community.[6] Madison Grant and eugenicist Charles B. Davenport organized the Galton Society in 1918 in order to foster research, promote eugenics, and restrict immigration.[7] [...]

By the 1920s, scientific racism sanctified the notion that real Americans were white and that real whites came from northwest Europe. Racism by white workers in the West fueled laws excluding and expelling the Chinese in 1882. Widespread racism led to closing the immigration door to virtually all Asians and most Europeans between 1924 and 1927, and to deportation of Mexicans during the Great Depression.

Racism in general, and anti-Semitism in particular, flourished in higher education. Jews were the first of the Euro-immigrant groups to enter college in significant numbers, so it was not surprising that they faced the brunt of discrimination there. The Protestant elite complained that Jews were unwashed, uncouth, unrefined, loud, and pushy. Harvard University President A. Lawrence Lowell, who was also a vice president of the Immigration Restriction League, was open about his opposition to Jews at Harvard. The Seven Sister schools had a reputation for "flagrant discrimination." [...]

Columbia's quota against Jews was well known in my parents' community. My father is very proud of having beaten it and been admitted to Columbia Dental School on the basis of his skill at carving a soap ball. Although he became a teacher instead because the tuition was too high, he took me to the dentist every week of my childhood and prolonged the agony by discussing the finer points of tooth-filling and dental care. My father also almost failed the speech test required for his teaching license because he didn't speak "standard," i.e., nonimmigrant, nonaccented English. For my parents and most of their friends, English was the language they had learned when they went to school, since their home and neighborhood language was Yiddish. They saw the speech test as designed to keep all ethnics, not just Jews, out of teaching.

There is an ironic twist to this story. My mother always urged me to speak well, like her friend Ruth Saronson, who was a speech teacher. Ruth remained my model for perfect diction until I went away to college. When I talked to her on one of my visits home, I heard the New York accent of my version of "standard English," compared to the Boston academic version.

My parents believe that Jewish success, like their own, was due to hard work and a high value placed on education. They attended Brooklyn College during the Depression. My mother worked days and went to school at night; my father went during the day. Both their families encouraged them. More accurately, their families expected it. Everyone they knew was in the same boat, and their world was made up of Jews who were advancing just as they were. The picture for New York—where most Jews lived—seems to back them up. In 1920, Jews made up 80 percent of the students at New York's City College, 90 percent of Hunter College, and before World War I, 40 percent of private Columbia University. By 1934, Jews made up almost 24 percent of all law students nationally and

56 percent of those in New York City. Still, more Jews became public school teachers, like my parents and their friends, than doctors or lawyers. Indeed, Ruth Jacknow Markowitz has shown that "my daughter, the teacher" was, for parents, an aspiration equivalent to "my son, the doctor."[8]

How we interpret Jewish social mobility in this milieu depends on whom we compare them to. Compared with other immigrants, Jews were upwardly mobile. But compared with nonimmigrant whites, that mobility was very limited and circumscribed. The existence of anti-immigrant, racist, and anti-Semitic barriers kept the Jewish middle class confined to a small number of occupations. Jews were excluded from mainstream corporate management and corporately employed professions, except in the garment and movie industries, in which they were pioneers. Jews were almost totally excluded from university faculties (the few who made it had powerful patrons). Eastern European Jews were concentrated in small businesses, and in professions where they served a largely Jewish clientele. [...]

My parents' generation believed that Jews overcame anti-Semitic barriers because Jews are special. My answer is that the Jews who were upwardly mobile were special among Jews (and were also well placed to write the story). My generation might well respond to our parents' story of pulling themselves up by their own bootstraps with "But think what you might have been without the racism and with some affirmative action!" And that is precisely what the post–World War II boom, the decline of systematic, public, anti-Euro racism and anti-Semitism, and governmental affirmative action extended to white males let us see.

WHITENING EURO-ETHNICS

By the time I was an adolescent, Jews were just as white as the next white person. Until I was eight, I was a Jew in a world of Jews. Everyone on Avenue Z in Sheepshead Bay was Jewish. I spent my days playing and going to school on three blocks of Avenue Z, and visiting my grandparents in the nearby Jewish neighborhoods of Brighton Beach and Coney Island. There were plenty of Italians in my neighborhood, but they lived around the corner. They were a kind of Jew, but on the margins of my social horizons. Portuguese were even more distant, at the end of the bus ride, at Sheepshead Bay. The *shul*, or temple, was on Avenue Z, and I begged my father to take me like all the other fathers took their kids, but religion wasn't part of my family's Judaism. Just how Jewish my neighborhood was hit me in first grade, when I was one of two kids to go to school on Rosh Hashanah. My teacher was shocked—she was Jewish too—and I was embarrassed to tears when she sent me home. I was never again sent to school on Jewish holidays. We left that world in 1949 when we moved to Valley Stream, Long Island, which was Protestant and Republican and even had farms until Irish, Italian, and Jewish ex-urbanities like us gave it a more suburban and Democratic flavor.

Neither religion nor ethnicity separated us at school or in the neighborhood. Except temporarily. During my elementary school years, I remember a fair number of dirt-bomb (a good suburban weapon) wars on the block. Periodically, one of the Catholic boys would accuse me or my brother of killing his god, to which we'd reply, "Did not," and start lobbing dirt bombs. Sometimes he'd get his friends from Catholic school and I'd get mine from public school kids on the block, some of whom were Catholic. Hostilities didn't last for more than a couple of hours and punctuated an otherwise friendly relationship. They ended by our junior high years, when other things became more important. Jews, Catholics, and Protestants, Italians, Irish, Poles, "English" (I don't remember hearing WASP as a kid), were mixed up on the block and in school. We thought of ourselves as middle class and very enlightened because our ethnic backgrounds seemed so irrelevant to high school culture. We didn't see race (we thought), and racism was not part of our peer consciousness. Nor were the immigrant or working-class histories of our families.

As with most chicken-and-egg problems, it is hard to know which came first. Did Jews and other Euro-ethnics become white because they became middle-class? That is, did money whiten? Or did being incorporated into an expanded version of whiteness open up the economic doors to middle-class status? Clearly, both tendencies were at work.

Some of the changes set in motion during the war against fascism led to a more inclusive version of whiteness. Anti-Semitism and anti-European racism lost respectability. The 1940 Census no longer distinguished native whites of native parentage from those, like my parents, of immigrant parentage, so Euro-immigrants and their children were more securely white by submersion in an expanded notion of whiteness.[9]

Theories of nurture and culture replaced theories of nature and biology. Instead of dirty and dangerous races that would destroy American democracy, immigrants became ethnic groups whose children had successfully assimilated into the mainstream and risen to the middle class. In this new myth, Euro-ethnic suburbs like mine became the measure of American democracy's victory over racism. Jewish mobility became a new Horatio Alger story. In time and with hard work, every ethnic group would get a piece of the pie, and the United States would be a nation with equal opportunity for all its people to become part of a prosperous middle-class majority. And it seemed that Euro-ethnic immigrants and their children were delighted to join middle America.

This is not to say that anti-Semitism disappeared alter World War II, only that it fell from fashion and was driven underground. [...]

Although changing views on who was white made it easier for Euro-ethnics to become middle class, economic prosperity also played a very powerful role in the whitening process. The economic mobility of Jews and other Euro-ethnics derived ultimately from America's postwar economic prosperity and its enormously expanded need for professional, technical, and managerial labor, as well as on government assistance in providing it.

The United States emerged from the war with the strongest economy in the world. Real wages rose between 1946 and 1960, increasing buying power a hefty 22 percent and giving most Americans some discretionary income. American manufacturing, banking, and business services were increasingly dominated by large corporations, and these grew into multinational corporations. Their organizational centers lay in big, new urban headquarters that demanded growing numbers of clerical, technical, and managerial workers. The postwar period was a historic moment for real class mobility and for the affluence we have erroneously come to believe was the American norm. It was a time when the old white and the newly white masses became middle class.[10]

The GI Bill of Rights, as the 1944 Serviceman's Readjustment Act was known, is arguably the most massive affirmative action program in American history. It was created to develop needed labor force skills and to provide those who had them with a lifestyle that reflected their value to the economy. The GI benefits that were ultimately extended to 16 million GIs (of the Korean War as well) included priority in jobs—that is, preferential hiring, but no one objected to it then—financial support during the job search, small loans for starting up businesses, and most important, low-interest home loans and educational benefits, which included tuition and living expenses. This legislation was rightly regarded as one of the most revolutionary postwar programs. I call it affirmative action because it was aimed at and disproportionately helped male, Euro-origin GIs.[11] [...]

EDUCATION AND OCCUPATION

It is important to remember that, prior to the war, a college degree was still very much a "mark of the upper class," that colleges were largely finishing schools for Protestant elites. Before the postwar boom, schools could not begin to accommodate the American masses. Even in New York City before the 1930s, neither the public schools nor City College had room for more than a tiny fraction of potential immigrant students.[12]

Not so after the war. The almost 8 million GIs who took advantage of their educational benefits under the GI Bill caused "the greatest wave of college building in American history." White male GIs were able to take advantage of their educational benefits for college and technical training, so they were particularly well positioned to seize the opportunities provided by the new demands for professional, managerial, and technical labor.

> It has been well documented that the GI educational benefits transformed American higher education and raised the educational level of that generation and generations to come. With many provisions for assistance in upgrading their educational attainments, veterans pulled ahead of nonveterans in earning capacity. In the long run it was the nonveterans who had fewer opportunities.[13]

[...] Even more significantly, the postwar boom transformed America's class structure—or at least its status structure—so that the middle class expanded to encompass most of the population. Before the war, most Jews, like most other Americans, were part of the working class, defined in terms of occupation, education, and income. Already upwardly mobile before the war relative to other immigrants, Jews floated high on this rising economic tide, and most of them entered the middle class. The children of other immigrants did too. Still, even the high tide missed some Jews. As late as 1973, some 15 percent of New York's Jews were poor or near poor, and in the 1960s, almost 25 percent of employed Jewish men remained manual workers.[14]

The reason I refer to educational and occupational GI benefits as affirmative action programs for white males is because they were decidedly not extended to African Americans or to women of any race. Theoretically they were available to all veterans; in practice women and black veterans did not get anywhere near their share. Women's Army and Air Force units were initially organized as auxiliaries, hence not part of the military. When that status was changed, in July 1943, only those who reenlisted in the armed forces were eligible for veterans' benefits. Many women thought they were simply being demobilized and returned home. The majority remained and were ultimately eligible for veterans' benefits. But there was little counseling, and a social climate that discouraged women's careers and independence cut down on women's knowledge and sense of entitlement. The Veterans Administration kept no statistics on the number of women who used their GI benefits.[15]

The barriers that almost completely shut African American GIs out of their benefits were even more formidable. In Neil Wynn's portrait, black GIs anticipated starting new lives, just like their white counterparts. Over 43 percent hoped to return to school, and most expected to relocate, to find better jobs in new lines of work. The exodus from the South toward the North and West was particularly large. So it was not a question of any lack of ambition on the part of African American GIs. White male privilege was shaped against the backdrop of wartime racism and postwar sexism.

During and after the war, there was an upsurge in white racist violence against black servicemen, in public schools, and by the Ku Klux Klan. It spread to California and New York. The number of lynchings rose during the war, and in 1943 there were antiblack race riots in several large northern cities. Although there was a wartime labor shortage, black people were discriminated against when it came to well-paid defense industry jobs and housing. In 1946, white riots against African Americans occurred across the South and in Chicago and Philadelphia.

Gains made as a result of the wartime civil rights movement, especially in defense-related employment, were lost with peacetime conversion, as black workers were the first to be fired, often in violation of seniority. White women were also laid off, ostensibly to make room for jobs for demobilized servicemen, and in the long run women lost most of the gains they had made in wartime. We now know that women did not leave the labor force in any significant numbers but, instead, were forced to find inferior jobs, largely nonunion, part-time, and clerical.[16]

The military, the Veterans Administration, the US Employment Services (USES), and the Federal Housing Administration effectively denied African American GIs access to their benefits and to new educational, occupational, and residential opportunities. Black GIs who served in the thoroughly segregated armed forces during World War II served under white officers. African American soldiers were given a disproportionate share of dishonorable discharges, which denied them veterans' rights under the GI Bill. Between August and November 1946, for example, 21 percent of white soldiers and 39 percent of black soldiers were dishonorably discharged. Those who did get an honorable discharge then faced the Veterans Administration and the USES. The latter, which was responsible for job placements, employed very few African Americans, especially in the South. This meant that black veterans did not receive much employment information and that the offers they did receive were for low-paid and menial jobs. "In one survey of 50 cities, the movement of blacks into peacetime employment was found to be lagging far behind that of white veterans: in Arkansas ninety-five percent of the placements made by the USES for Afro-Americans were in service or unskilled jobs."[17] African Americans were also less likely than whites, regardless of GI status, to gain new jobs commensurate with their wartime jobs. For example, in San Francisco, by 1948, black Americans "had dropped back halfway to their prewar employment status."[18]

Black GIs faced discrimination in the educational system as well. Despite the end of restrictions on Jews and other Euro-ethnics, African Americans were not welcome in white colleges. Black colleges were overcrowded, but the combination of segregation and prejudice made for few alternatives. About 20,000 black veterans attended college by 1947, most in black colleges, but almost as many, 15,000, could not gain entry. Predictably, the disproportionately few African Americans who did gain access to their educational benefits were able, like their white counterparts, to become doctors and engineers, and to enter the black middle class.[19]

SUBURBANIZATION

In 1949, ensconced in Valley Stream, I watched potato farms turn into Levittown and Idlewild (later Kennedy) airport. This was the major spectator sport in our first years on Long Island. A typical weekend would bring various aunts, uncles, and cousins out from the city. After a huge meal, we'd pile into the car—itself a novelty—to look at the bulldozed acres and comment on the matchbox construction. During the week, my mother and I would look at the houses going up within walking distance.

Bill Levitt built a basic, 900–1,000 square foot, somewhat expandable house for a lower-middle-class and working-class market on Long Island, and later in Pennsylvania and New Jersey. Levittown started out as 2,000 units of rental housing at $60 a month, designed to meet the low-income housing needs of returning war vets, many of whom, like my Aunt Evie and Uncle Julie, were living in Quonset huts. By May 1947, Levitt and Sons had acquired enough land in Hempstead Township on Long Island to build 4,000 houses, and by the next February, he had built 6,000 units and named the development after himself. After 1948, federal financing for the construction of rental housing tightened, and Levitt switched to building houses for sale. By 1951, Levittown was a development of some 15,000 families.[20]

At the beginning of World War II, about one-third of all American families owned their houses. That percentage doubled in twenty years. Most Levittowners looked just like my family. They came from New York City or Long Island; about 17 percent were military, from nearby Mitchell Field; Levittown was their first house, and almost everyone was married. Three-quarters of the 1947 inhabitants were white collar, but by 1950 more blue-collar families had moved in, so that by 1951, "barely half" of the new residents were white collar, and by 1960 their occupational profile was somewhat more working class than for Nassau County as a whole. By this time too, almost one-third of Levittown's people were either foreign-born or, like my parents, first-generation US-born.[21]

The Federal Housing Administration (FHA) was key to buyers and builders alike. Thanks to the FHA, suburbia was open to more than GIs. People like us would never have been in the market for houses without FHA and Veterans Administration (VA) low-down-payment, low-interest, long-term loans to young buyers. [...]

The FHA believed in racial segregation. Throughout its history, it publicly and actively promoted restrictive covenants. Before the war, these forbade sales to Jews and Catholics as well as to African Americans. The deed to my house in Detroit had such a covenant, which theoretically prevented it from being sold to Jews or African Americans. Even after the Supreme Court outlawed restrictive covenants in 1948, the FHA continued to encourage builders to write them in against African Americans. FHA underwriting manuals openly insisted on racially homogeneous neighborhoods, and their loans were made only in white neighborhoods. I bought my Detroit house in 1972, from Jews who were leaving a largely African American neighborhood. By that time, restrictive covenants were a dead letter, but block busting by realtors was replacing it.

With the federal government behind them, virtually all developers refused to sell to African Americans. Palo Alto and Levittown, like most suburbs as late as 1960, were virtually all white. Out of 15,741 houses and 65,276 people, averaging 4.2 people per house, only 220 Levittowners, or 52 households, were "nonwhite." In 1958, Levitt announced publicly, at a press conference held to open his New Jersey development, that he would not sell to black buyers. This caused a furor because the state of New Jersey (but not the US government) prohibited discrimination in federally subsidized housing. Levitt was sued and fought it. There had been a white riot in his Pennsylvania development when a black family moved in a few years earlier. In New Jersey, he was ultimately persuaded by township ministers to integrate. [...]

The result of these policies was that African Americans were totally shut out of the suburban boom. An article in *Harper's* described the housing available to black GIs.

> On his way to the base each morning, Sergeant Smith passes an attractive air-conditioned, FHA-financed housing project. It was built for service families. Its rents are little more than the Smiths pay for their shack. And there are half-a-dozen vacancies, but none for Negroes.[22]

Where my family felt the seductive pull of suburbia, Marshall Berman's experienced the brutal push of urban renewal. In the Bronx, in the 1950s, Robert Moses's Cross-Bronx Expressway erased "a dozen solid, settled, densely populated neighborhoods like our own.... [S]omething like 60,000 working- and lower-middle-class people, mostly Jews, but with many Italians, Irish, and Blacks thrown in, would be thrown out of their homes.... For ten years, through the late 1950s and early 1960s, the center of the Bronx was pounded and blasted and smashed."[23]

Urban renewal made postwar cities into bad places to live. At a physical level, urban renewal reshaped them, and federal programs brought private developers and public officials together to create downtown central business districts where there had formerly been a mix of manufacturing, commerce, and working-class neighborhoods. Manufacturing was scattered to the peripheries of the city, which were ringed and bisected by a national system of highways. Some working-class neighborhoods were bulldozed, but others remained. In Los Angeles, as in New York's Bronx, the postwar period saw massive freeway construction right through the heart of old working-class neighborhoods. In East Los Angeles and Santa Monica, Chicana/o and African American communities were divided in half or blasted to smithereens by the highways bringing Angelenos to the new white suburbs, or to make way for civic monuments like Dodger Stadium.[24]

Urban renewal was the other side of the process by which Jewish and other working-class Euro-immigrants became middle class. It was the push to suburbia's seductive pull. The fortunate white survivors of urban renewal headed disproportionately for suburbia, where they could partake of prosperity and the good life. [...]

If the federal stick of urban renewal joined the FHA carrot of cheap mortgages to send masses of Euro-Americans to the suburbs, the FHA had a different kind of one-two punch for African Americans. Segregation kept them out of the suburbs, and redlining made sure they could not buy or repair their homes in the neighborhoods in which they were allowed to live. The FHA practiced systematic redlining. This was a practice developed by its predecessor, the Home Owners Loan Corporation (HOLC), which in the 1930s developed an elaborate neighborhood rating system that placed the highest (green) value on all-white, middle-class neighborhoods, and the lowest (red) on racially nonwhite or mixed and working-class neighborhoods. High ratings meant high property values. The idea was that low property values in redlined neighborhoods made them bad investments. The FHA was, after all, created by and for banks and the housing industry. Redlining warned banks not to lend there, and the FHA would not insure mortgages in such neighborhoods. Redlining created a self-fulfilling prophecy.

> With the assistance of local realtors and banks, it assigned one of the four ratings to every block in every city. The resulting information was then translated into the appropriate color [green, blue, yellow, or red] and duly recorded on secret "Residential Security Maps" in local HOLC offices. The maps themselves were placed in elaborate "City Survey Files," which consisted of reports, questionnaires, and workpapers relating to current and future values of real estate.[25]

The FHA's and VA's refusal to guarantee loans in redlined neighborhoods made it virtually impossible for African Americans to borrow money for home improvement or purchase. Because these maps and surveys were quite secret, it took the civil rights movement to make these practices and their devastating consequences public. As a result, those who fought urban renewal, or who sought to make a home in the urban ruins, found themselves locked out of the middle class. They also faced an ideological assault that labeled their neighborhoods slums and called them slumdwellers.[26]

CONCLUSION

The record is very clear. Instead of seizing the opportunity to end institutionalized racism, the federal government did its level best to shut and double-seal the postwar window of opportunity in African Americans' faces. It consistently refused to combat segregation in the social institutions that were key to upward mobility in education, housing, and employment Moreover, federal programs that were themselves designed to assist demobilized GIs and young families systematically discriminated against African Americans. Such programs reinforced white/nonwhite racial distinctions even as intrawhite racialization was falling out of fashion. This other side of the coin, that white men of northwest European ancestry and white men of southeastern European ancestry were treated equally in theory and in practice with regard to the benefits they received, was part of the larger postwar whitening of Jews and other eastern and southern Europeans.

The myth that Jews pulled themselves up by their own bootstraps ignores the fact that it took federal programs to create the conditions whereby the abilities of Jews and other European immigrants could be recognized and rewarded rather than denigrated and denied. The GI Bill and FHA and VA mortgages, even though they were advertised as open to all, functioned as a set of racial privileges. They were privileges because they were extended to white GIs but not to black GIs. Such privileges were forms of affirmative action that allowed Jews and other Euro-American men to become suburban homeowners and to get the training that allowed them—but much less so women vets or war workers—to become professionals, technicians, salesmen, and managers in a growing economy. Jews and other white ethnics' upward mobility was due to programs that allowed us to float on a rising economic tide. To African Americans, the government offered the cement boots of segregation, redlining, urban renewal, and discrimination.

Those racially skewed gains have been passed across the generations, so that racial inequality seems to maintain itself "naturally," even after legal segregation ended. Today, I own a house in Venice, California, like the one in which I grew up in Valley Stream, and my brother until recently owned a house in Palo Alto much like an Eichler house. Both of us are where we are thanks largely to the postwar benefits our parents received and passed on to us, and to the educational benefits we received in the 1960s as a result of affluence and the social agitation that developed from the black Freedom Movement. I have white, African American, and Asian American colleagues whose parents received fewer or none of America's postwar benefits and who expect never to own a house despite their considerable academic achievements. Some of these colleagues who are a few years younger than I also carry staggering debts for their education, which they expect to have to repay for the rest of their lives.

Conventional wisdom has it that the United States has always been an affluent land of opportunity. But the truth is that affluence has been the exception and that real upward mobility has required massive affirmative action programs.[...]

NOTES

1. Gerber 1986; Dinnerstein 1987, 1994
2. On the belief in Jewish and Asian versions of Horatio Alger, see Steinberg 1989, chap. 3; Gilman 1996. On Jewish culture, see Gordon 1964; see Sowell 1981 for an updated version.
3. Not all Jews are white or unambiguously white. It has been suggested, for example, that Hasidim lack the privileges of whiteness. Rodriguez (1997, 12, 15) has begun to unpack the claims of white Jewish "amenity migrants" and the different racial meanings of Chicano claims to a crypto-Jewish identity in New Mexico. See also Thomas 1996 on African American Jews.
4. M. Grant 1916; Ripley 1923; see also Patterson 1997; M. Grant, quoted in Higham 1955, 156.
5. *New York Times*, 30 July 1893, "East Side Street Vendors," reprinted in Schoener 1967, 57–58.
6. Gould 1981; Higham 1955; Patterson 1997, 108–115.
7. It was intended, as Davenport wrote to the president of the American Museum of Natural History, Henry Fairfield Osborne, as "an anthropological society ... with a central governings body, self-elected and self-perpetuating, and very limited in members, and also confined to native Americans [sic] who are anthropologically, socially and politically sound, no Bolsheviki need apply" (Barkan 1992, 67–68).
8. Steinberg 1989, 137, 227; Markowitz 1993.
9. This census also explicitly changed the Mexican race to white (US Bureau of the Census 1940, 2:4).
10. Nash et al. 1986, 885–886.
11. On planning for veterans, see F.J. Brown 1946; Hurd 1946; Mosch 1975; "Post-war Jobs for Veterans" 1945; Willenz 1983.
12. Willenz 1983, 165.
13. Nash et al. 1986, 885; Willenz 1983, 165. On mobility among veterans and nonveterans, see Havighurst et al. 1951.
14. Steinberg 1989, 89–90.
15. Willenz 1983, 20–28, 94–97. I thank Nancy G. Cattell for calling my attention to the fact that women GIs were ultimately eligible for benefits.
16. Willenz 1983, 168; Dalfiume 1969, 133–134; Wynn 1976, 114–116; Anderson 1981; Milkman 1987.
17. Nalty and MacGregor 1981, 218, 60–61.
18. Wynn 1976, 114, 116.
19. On African Americans in the US military, see Foner 1974; Dalfiume 1969; Johnson 1967; Binkin and Eitelberg 1982; Nalty and MacGregor 1981. On schooling, see Walker 1970, 4–9.
20. Hartman (1975, 141–142) cites massive abuses in the 1940s and 1950s by builders under the Section 608 program in which "the FHA granted extraordinarily liberal concessions to lackadaisically supervised private developers to induce them to produce rental housing rapidly in the postwar period." Eichler (1982) indicates that things were not that different in the subsequent FHA-funded home-building industry.
21. Dobriner 1963, 91, 100.
22. Quoted in Foner 1974, 195.
23. Berman 1982, 292.
24. On urban renewal and housing policies, see Greer 1965; Hartman 1975; Squires 1989. On Los Angeles, see Pardo 1990; Cockcroft 1990.
25. Jackson 1985, 197. These ideas from the real estate industry were "codified and legitimated in 1930s work by University of Chicago sociologist Robert Park and real estate professor Homer Hoyt" (Ibid., 198–199).
26. See Gans 1962.

REFERENCES

Anderson, Karen. 1981. *Wartime Women*. Westport, Conn.: Greenwood.

Barkan, Elazar. 1992. *The Retreat of Scientific Racism: Changing Concepts of Race in Britain and the United States Between the World Wars*. New York: Cambridge University Press.

Berman, Marshall. 1982. *All That Is Solid Melts into Air: The Experience of Modernity*. New York: Simon and Schuster.

Binkin, Martin, and Mark J. Eitelberg. 1982. *Blacks and the Military*. Washington, DC: Brookings Institution.

Brown, Francis J. 1946. *Educational Opportunities for Veterans*. Washington, DC: Public Affairs Press American Council on Public Affairs.

Cockcroft, Eva. 1990. *Signs from the Heart: California Chicano Murals*. Venice, Calif.: Social and Public Art Resource Center.

Dalfiume, Richard M. 1969. *Desegregation of the U.S. Armed Forces: Fighting on Two Fronts, 1939–1953*. Columbia: University of Missouri Press.

Dinnerstein, Leonard, 1987. *Uneasy at Home: Anti-Semitism and the American Jewish Experience*. New York: Columbia University Press.

——. 1994. *Anti-Semitism in America*. New York: Oxford University Press.

Dobriner, William. M. 1963. *Class in Suburbia*. Englewood Cliffs, NJ: Prentice-Hall.

Eichler, Ned. 1982. *The Merchant Builders*. Cambridge, Mass.: MIT Press.

Foner, Jack. 1974. *Blacks and the Military in American History: A New Perspective*. New York: Praeger Publishers.

Gans, Herbert. 1962. *The Urban Villagers*. New York: Free Press of Glencoe.

Gerber, David, ed. 1986. *Anti-Semitism in American History*. Urbana: University of Illinois Press.

Gilman, Sander. 1996. *Smart Jews: The Construction of the Image of Jewish Superior Intelligence*. Lincoln: University of Nebraska Press.

Gordon, Milton. 1964. *Assimilation in American Life: The Role of Race, Religion and National Origins*. New York: Oxford University Press.

Gould, Stephen J. 1981. *The Mismeasure of Man*. New York: Norton.

Grant, Madison. 1916. *The Passing of the Great Race: Or the Racial Basis of European History*. New York: Charles Scribner.

Greer, Scott. 1965. *Urban Renewal and American Cities*. Indianapolis: Bobbs-Merrill.

Hartman, Chester. 1975. *Housing and Social Policy*. Englewood Cliffs, NJ: Prentice-Hall.

Havighurst, Robert J., John W. Baughman, Walter H. Eaton, and Ernest W. Burgess. 1951. *The American Veteran Back Home: A Study of Veteran Readjustment*. New York: Longmans, Green and Co.

Higham, John. 1955. *Strangers in the Land*. New Brunswick, NJ: Rutgers University Press.

Hurd, Charles. 1946. *The Veterans' Program: A Complete Guide to Its Benefits, Rights and Options*. New York: McGraw-Hill Book Company.

Jackson, Kenneth T. 1985. *Crabgrass Frontier: The Suburbanization of the United Stales*. New York: Oxford University Press.

Johnson, Jesse J. 1967. *Ebony Brass: An Autobiography of Negro Frustration Amid Aspiration*. New York: The William Frederick Press.

Markowitz, Ruth Jacknow. 1993. *My Daughter, the Teacher: Jewish Teachers in the New York City Schools*. New Brunswick, NJ: Rutgers University Press.

Milkman, Ruth. 1987. *Gender at Work: The Dynamics of Job Segregation by Sex During World War II*. Urbana: University of Illinois Press.

Mosch, Theodore R. 1975. *The GI Bill: A Breakthrough in Educational and Social Policy in the United States*. Hicksville, NY: Exposition Press.

Nalty, Bernard C, and Morris J. MacGregor, eds. 1981. *Blacks in the Military: Essential Documents*. Wilmington, Del.: Scholarly Resources, Inc.

Nash, Gary B., Julie Roy Jeffrey, John R. Howe, Allen F. Davis, Peter J. Frederick, and Allen M. Winkler. 1986. *The American People: Creating a Nation and a Society*. New York: Harper and Row.

Pardo, Mary. 1990. "Mexican-American Women Grassroots Community Activists: 'Mothers of East Los Angeles.'" *Frontiers* 11, 1:1–7.

Patterson, Thomas C. 1997. *Inventing Western Civilization*. New York: Monthly Review Press.

"Postwar Jobs for Veterans." 1945. *The Annals of the American Academy of Political and Social Science* 238 (March).

Ripley, William Z. 1923. *The Races of Europe: A Sociological Study*. New York: Appleton.

Rodriguez, Sylvia. 1997. "Tourism, Whiteness, and the Vanishing Anglo." Paper presented at the conference "Seeing and Being Seen: Tourism in the American West." Center for the American West, Boulder, Colorado, 2 May.

Schoener, Allon. 1967. *Portal to America: The Lower East Side 1870–1925*. New York: Holt, Rinehart, and Winston.

Sowell, Thomas. 1981. *Ethnic America: A History*. New York: Basic Books.

Squires, Gregory D., ed. 1989. *Unequal Partnerships: The Political Economy of Urban Redevelopment in Postwar America*. New Brunswick, NJ: Rutgers University Press.

Steinberg, Stephen. 1989. *The Ethnic Myth: Race, Ethnicity and Class in America*. 2d ed. Boston: Beacon Press.

Thomas, Laurence Mordekhai. 1996. "The Soul of Identity: Jews and Blacks." In *People of the Book*, ed. S.F. Fishkin and J. Rubin-Dorsky. Madison: University of Wisconsin Press, 169–186.

US Bureau of the Census. 1940. *Sixteenth Census of the United States*, V.2. Washington, DC: US Government Printing Office.

Walker, Olive. 1970. "The Windsor Hills School Story." *Integrated Education: Race and Schools* 8, 3:4–9.

Willenz, June A. 1983. *Women Veterans: America's Forgotten Heroines*. New York: Continuum.

Wynn, Neil A. 1976. *The Afro-American and the Second World War*. London: Paul Elek.

CHAPTER 34

BETWEEN BLACK AND WHITE: EXPLORING THE "BIRACIAL" EXPERIENCE

Kerry A. Rockquemore

Public debate concerning proposed modifications to the 2000 Census has recently focused on the addition of a "multi-racial" category. Proponents argue that the dramatic increase in interracial marriages over the past three decades[1] has caused a biracial baby boom. These rising numbers of biracial and multi-ethnic Americans, advocates argue, should be recognized by the government as "multi-racial." They believe a multi-racial category is necessary because all people of mixed parentage identify themselves as "biracial" or "mixed" and, if given the opportunity to identify this way on government documents, they would do so.

Despite advocates' claims, biracialness[2] is not a newly emergent social phenomenon (Williamson, 1980). The Census debate is merely the latest manifestation of the ongoing socio-historical problematic of classifying mixed race people in the United States. Given the historical stratification of racial groups, supported by an ideological belief in genetic differentiation between races, society has continually had to develop norms to classify individuals who straddle the socially constructed boundaries of "Black" and "White" (White, 1948; Williamson, 1980; Davis, 1991; Zack, 1993). The "One Drop Rule,"[3] historically articulated in legal statutes, mandated that a mixed race child be relegated to the racial group of the lower status parent. This norm has survived despite the removal of its various legal codifications. The One Drop Rule dictated that children of Black/White unions were considered part of the African-American community. While biracials have had varying statuses within that community,[4] they have always been considered, by both Whites and Blacks, as part of the "Black race" (Davis, 1991).

The Census issue provides a contemporary variation on the classification dilemma. Advocates demand separate group recognition and membership for mixed race people and are essentially arguing for a nullification of the cultural norm of hypodescent. In this context, it is not surprising that the movement is led, not by biracial people themselves, but by White mothers on behalf of their children. In this sense, they are arguing for a separate status for their children in the socio-racial hierarchy. The status of "mixed-race" would afford their children more privileges than being Black, but not quite as many as being White (Spencer, 1997). This separate status argument is framed as an attempt towards self-definition on behalf of biracial people who, advocates assume, do not consider themselves Black.

The assumption that biracials have a singular understanding of their racial identity (i.e., as biracial) masks the fact that numerous individuals who are biracial identify themselves as African-American and would continue to do so even if presented with the mixed-race category as an option[5] (Jones, 1994; McBride, 1996; Scales-Trent, 1995; Williams, 1995). The belief that biracial identity has a singular meaning to members of this population begs numerous questions. What does "biracial identity" mean? Is there a singular way in which people with one Black and one White parent understand their racial identity or does "biracial" have multiple meanings? If there are, in fact, multiple ways in which biracial people understand themselves and their group membership, then what types of social factors influence the differences in an individual's choice of racial identity? This article explores what mixed-race people say about the meaning of "biracial" identity and how social factors have influenced their identity construction and maintenance.

THEORETICAL FRAMEWORK OF IDENTITY FORMATION

The conceptual framework of this argument rests on the three classic assumptions of symbolic interactionism: (1) that we know things by their meanings, (2) that meanings are created through social interaction, and (3) that meanings change through interaction (Blumer, 1969). Given these basic assumptions, it is necessary to clearly delineate the conceptual terminology to be used in the following discussion. First and foremost, what is meant by the term "identity"?

Social actors are situated within societies that designate available categories of identification, how these identities are defined, and their relative importance. The term identity refers to a validated self-understanding that situates and defines the individual or, as Stone (1962) suggests, establishes *what* and *where* an actor is in social terms. These are processes by which individuals understand themselves and others, as well as evaluate their self in relation to others. Identity is the direct result of mutual identification through social interaction. It is within this process of validation that identity becomes a meaning of the self. I utilize the term identity interchangeably with self-understanding throughout the discussion.

By situating identity within an interactionist framework, biracial identity may be understood as an emergent category of identification. If identity is conceptualized as an interactionally validated self-understanding, then identities can only function effectively where the response of the individual to themselves (as a social object) is consistent with the response of others. In contrast, individuals cannot effectively possess an identity which is not socially typified, or where there exists a disjuncture between the identity an actor appropriates for him/herself and where others place him/her as a social object. In other words, an individual cannot have a realized identity without others who validate that identity. The challenge of research on biracial identity then is twofold. First, it is necessary to understand how individuals understand their social location as "biracial," and secondly, to explore what social and interactional factors lead to the development of this identity and how these individuals try to realize their appropriated identities in social context.

DATA AND METHODS

Data was collected through in-depth interviews with biracial undergraduates at a Catholic university in the Midwest. This type of research methodology was selected due to the exploratory nature of the study and the researcher's desire to generate understanding about a growing group (Root, 1992; Taylor and Bogdan, 1984; Marshall and Rossman, 1989). The selection criterion were that students have one Black self-identifying biological parent and one White self-identifying biological parent. While the argument can be made that within the Black population, many people are of mixed race ancestry, the researcher chose to focus on the particular social circumstances, which are generated from having one Black and one White parent. Therefore, in the limited definition of this study, the biracial experience is exclusively a one-generation phenomenon.

It has been noted by many researchers that there exist inherent problems in engaging a sample of biracial respondents (Root, 1992). The primary dilemmas are (1) the sensitive nature of the subject matter and (2) the difficulty in identifying potential respondents. To address these particular difficulties, a biracial interviewer and snowball sampling were used (Bertaux, 1981). Fourteen biracial students were located and agreed to be interviewed. They ranged in age from eighteen to twenty-two and came from ten different states in the US. All respondents were Catholic, middle to upper-middle class, and came from families where at least one parent had a college education.

Interviews were audio taped and ranged between one and three hours in length. Each respondent filled out a one-page demographic questionnaire at the end of the interview, and each respondent's picture was taken. The taped interviews were transcribed and content analyzed to construct a descriptive map of the various ways in which the respondents understood their racial identity.

WHAT DOES "BIRACIAL IDENTITY" MEAN?

What does "biracial identity" mean to members of this population? If we conceptualize the term identity to mean an interactionally validated self-understanding, then the question, more specifically, is how do the individual selves interpret biracialness and respond to it. My data suggest some tentative descriptive categories of the way that individuals with one Black and one White parent understand their biracialness. Being biracial can be interpreted as: (1) a border identity, (2) a protean identity, (3) a transcendent identity, or (4) a traditional identity.[6]

A Border Identity

Anzaldua (1987) terms biracial identity as a "border identity" or one which lies between predefined social categories. Some individuals viewed the location of their existence between Black and White as defining their biracialness. These individuals stressed their in-betweenness, and highlighted that unique status as the grounding for their identity. In other words, they did not consider themselves to be *either* Black *or* White, but instead had a self-understanding that incorporated both Blackness and Whiteness into a unique category of "biracial." It was their location of difference that served as the substantive base of what it meant to be biracial. Kara, a first year student, explained that it was not only the location of being on the border of socially defined categories, but that the border status itself brought with it an additional dimension:

> It's not that just being biracial is like you're two parts [White and Black], you know, you have two parts but then there is also the one part of being biracial where you sit on the fence. There's a third thing, a unique thing.

The extreme border identity was exemplified by individuals who took their border status to a political level. Those who most consistently identified as biracial across all social contexts were likely to parallel their identity as biracial with a perception of shared struggle unique to their social location. They perceived their position as one of both oppression and advantage. For some, it spanned more than the case of Black-White biracials, and included all who exist between races and ethnicities. These individuals found it difficult to discuss their self-identification without mentioning the problem of bureaucratic racial categorization and their negative feelings of having to select a singular category of identification (particularly if that category is Black or African American). Jessica, a second year student illustrates this difficulty when she stated:

> I think there should be a mixed race category, or at least it shouldn't say "choose one" ... I just want to put my race down. I don't see what the problem is, acknowledging what your are and I'm mixed! I don't know because I also have this whole problem with the way society says it's okay [if you are biracial] to say that you're black but not to say that you're White because you're both! How can you deny one or the other?

A Protean Identity

For others, biracial identity referred to their protean capacity to move among cultural contexts (Lifton, 1993). Their self-understanding of biracialness was directly tied to their ability to cross boundaries between Black, White, and biracial, which was possible because they possessed Black, White, and biracial identities. These individuals felt endowed with a degree of cultural savvy in several social worlds and understood biracialness as the way in which they were able to fit in, however conditionally, in varied interactional settings. They believed their dual experiences with both Whites and Blacks had given them the ability to shift their identity according to the context of any particular interaction. This contextual shifting led actors to form a belief that their multiple racial backgrounds were but one piece of a complex self that was composed of assorted identifications which were not culturally integrated.

A student named Mike was able to provide an example in which his dual cultural competencies allowed him to function as an "insider" in differing social groups. He grew up in an all-White neighborhood and attended predominantly White private schools his entire life. He did have, however, frequent contact with his Black extended family. Mike felt that his particular circumstances growing up helped him to not only develop both middle-class White and Black cultural competencies, but also simultaneous multiple identities. In the following excerpt from our conversation, he uses table manners to illustrate his perception of the subtleties of contextual shifting:

> Because of their [his parents] status, I always learned, you know start with the outside fork and work your way in, and this one is for dessert, you know. So I know, I know not to eat like this [puts his elbows on the table]. But then again, at the same time, [respondent shifts to Black Vernacular] when it comes picnic time or some other time and some ribs is on the table, I'm not afraid to get my hands dirty and dig on in and eat with my hands and stuff like that. [respondent shifts back to Standard English] I mean I guess my, the shift is when I'm not afraid to function in either world.

While his depiction may be exaggerated and stereotypical, it reveals his understanding of biracialness as having the ability to contextually shift his self-label between what he perceives as Black and White cultural contexts. When the topic of racial identification was initially broached with Mike he stated: "well shit, it depends on what day it is and where I'm goin."

A Transcendent Identity

A third way of understanding biracialness is reminiscent of Robert Park's "Marginal Man" in its original context (Park, 1950). Park discussed the qualities of the cosmopolitan stranger, an individual who was bicultural (as opposed to biracial), and whose marginal status enabled an objective view of social reality. I refer to this as a "transcendent identity" because like Park's "stranger," individuals with this self-understanding view their biracialness as a unique marginalization, one that enables an objective perspective on the social meaning of race. These individuals discount race as a "master status" altogether. This self-understanding is uniquely and exclusively available to individuals whose bodily characteristics have a high degree of ambiguity (i.e., those who look White). This type of self-understanding of biracialness results in an avoidance, or rejection of any type of racial group categorization as the basis of personal identity. These individuals responded to questions about their identity with answers that were unrelated to their racial status, such as in the following example:

> I'm just Rob, you know. I never thought this was such a big deal to be identified, I just figured I'm a good guy, just like me for that, you know. But, when I came here [to college] it was like I was almost forced to look at people as being White, Black, Asian, or Hispanic. And so now, I'm still trying to go "I'm just Rob" but uh, you gotta be something.

This respondent stated that if required in particular contexts, he would accept the racial categorization thrust upon him. Given the persistence of hypodescent as a cultural norm, the result was his somewhat grudging acceptance of categorization as Black. I refrain from saying that he accepted a Black identity because it was only the label "Black" that was accepted.

This self-understanding was unique in several ways. First, it was available only to those whose appearances fit into the common perception of "White" or "Caucasian." Secondly, these individuals differed from the protean identity group because they did not have the ability, or the desire, to manipulate their identity before others in various social contexts. Finally, racial group membership did not play any significant role in their self-understanding because they socially experience race in a different way than those with a non-White appearance. Instead, they perceive that their biracialness provides them with a location to view and discard race as a meaningful category of their existence.

A Traditional Identity

Finally, there are individuals with one Black and one White parent whose racial identity falls into the category I term "traditional." In this case, the self-understanding is exclusively as African-American. The meaning of biracialness is merely an acknowledgment of the racial categorization of their birth parents. At the extreme, individuals simply do not deny the existence of their (White) parent. However, it is not salient in defining their self-understanding and may not be offered as identifying information unless specifically requested. Interestingly enough, there were no respondents in the pilot study that identified exclusively as Black. However, we can conceptually formulate this category based upon the historical norm of hypodescent.

The voices of biracial people reveal that there are varying understandings of what "biracial identity" means to individuals within this population. Individuals' selves have not one, but several ways in which they interpret and respond to biracialness. These divergent self-understandings are grounded in differential experiences, varying biographies, and crosscutting cultural contexts. This multiple meaning perspective breaks from the singular conception of Park's Marginal Man, the assertions of multiracial advocates, and much recent research on the biracial population that rests on the unquestioned assumption mat biracial identity has a singular and widely agreed upon meaning with which an actor either does or does not understand (Bradshaw, 1992; Fields, 1996; King and DaCosta, 1996). Figure 34.1 provides a schematic representation of this typology.

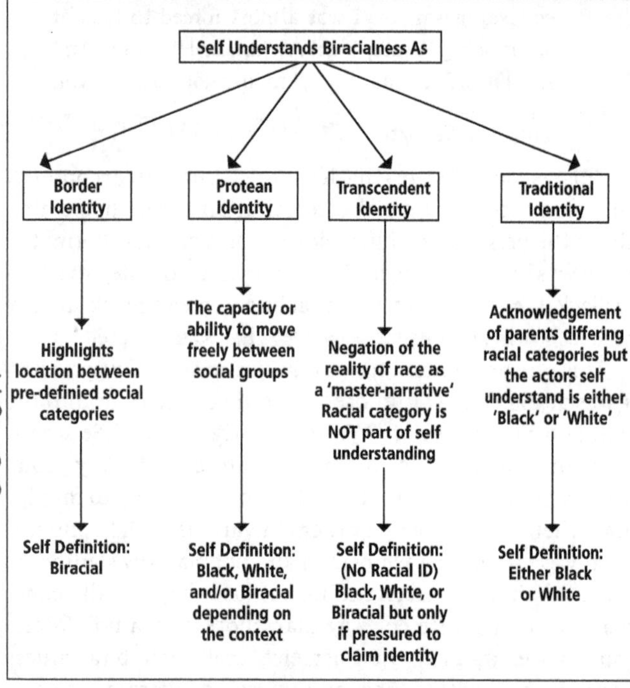

Figure 34.1 The multiple meanings of biracial identity

THE EFFECTS OF APPEARANCE AND SOCIAL NETWORKS ON IDENTITY FORMATION

Mary Waters' (1990) work focuses on ethnic options for individuals with multiple White-ethnic heritages. Waters was interested in why individuals with multiple ethnic backgrounds chose to emphasize one of their ethnicities over others. The factors involved in resolving White ethnic options included: (1) knowledge about the ethnicity; (2) surname; (3) appearance; and (4) general popularity of ethnic groups. She concluded that ethnicity was largely "symbolic," in that it had no consequences for an individual's life chances or everyday interactions and that it was characterized by the existence of choice either to assume the ethnic identity or not.

Waters' findings are instructive because they reveal the symbolic basis of White-ethnicity and explicitly differentiate it from race. The symbolic ethnicity of Whites differs from non-Whites because race is not an option from one situation to the next and race has both immediate and real consequences. In Waters' framework, identity options are either non-existent, or function differently, for members of racial groups compared to Whites because racial and ethnic categories are socio-culturally stratified. Her work implies that race and ethnicity function differently due to visibility, the capacity of individual choice, and a history of stratification based on racial group membership.

The Influence of Appearance on Identity

Appearances provide information about individuals that helps others to define the self as situated. This information enables others to know in advance what they can expect of an actor and what the actor can expect of them (Goffman, 1959). Appearances provide the first information (albeit constructed) about an individual to others in the context of face-to-face social interaction. It helps to define the identity of the individual and for him/her to express their self-identification. It is in this process that identities are negotiated and either validated or invalidated.

Appearance is critical in understanding how individuals develop and maintain racial identities (Stone, 1962). I limit my use of appearances to the following: physical features, language, and clothing. The physical characteristics of biracial individuals range widely in skin color, hair texture, and facial features. At one extreme are individuals who physically possess traits that are socially defined as belonging to the Black race; at the other are those who are visually unidentifiable as Black, or possess no features which are associated with African descent. Because racial categories are defined by appearances, the logic and enactment of racial categorization becomes questionable if individuals cannot be identified on sight. One's skin color, hair, and facial features are strong membership cues in socially defined racial groups. Figure 34.2 is a schematic representation of the proposed explanatory factors.

In addition to physical features, language and clothing have important functions as supporting interactional cues in establishing the identity of an individual. Language is particularly salient in the case of cueing one's membership to a racial group. Individuals may speak exclusively Standard English, Black Vernacular, or code switch between both (Smitherman, 1986; Delpit, 1988; Fanon, 1952). Clothing can work in a similar way as a signifier of racial group membership. Clothing and language differ from physical features, however, in the degree to which they can be manipulated. For example, one of the respondents reported frequenting a tanning salon to make her skin appear darker. In addition, women's hairstyles can decidedly signify group membership and are subject to degrees of manipulation. While certain physical features can be manipulated, some cannot without plastic surgery. Clothing and language on the other hand, may be strategically used by the individual to gain support from others for a particular identity (Goffman, 1959).

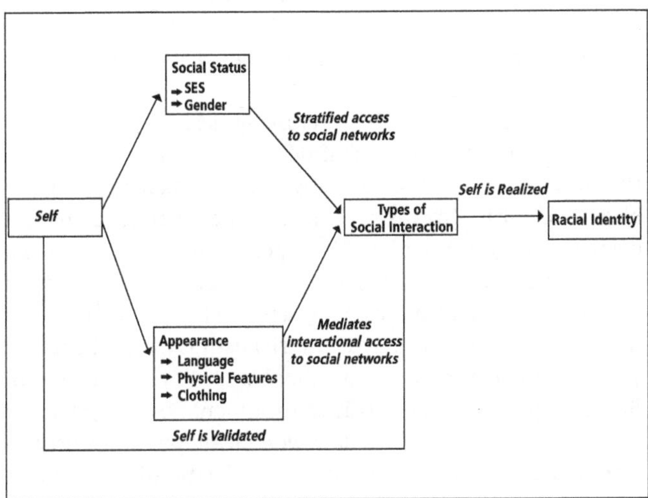

Figure 34.2 Factors influencing biracial identity

Mike told a story, which illustrates the link between appearances and identity. He has light brown skin, brown eyes, freckles, and short kinky hair. His physical appearance can be termed as ambiguous in that he doesn't appear to be White, yet his features do not necessarily fit into any easily definable category. Mike talked about negotiating his identity with a (White) girlfriend in the following way:

> I worked at a big national meeting thing here and I spoke on my experience here at Notre Dame, being Black. And afterwards, she came up and was like "hi," really cool, and we started talking and everything. And then she goes, "but you're Irish aren't you?" and I'm like "yeah." She says, "you got so many freckles!" And from then on we were like, tight, we still are.... She pulled me out, she was like "no, you're not JUST black" like, "you're not special" and I'm like, "yeah, put me in my place."

This story is interesting because it expresses the tension when other's definition of one's physical appearance fails to be consistent with self-definition (Goffman, 1963). In this case, Mike's physical features and use of Standard English were incongruent (for the future girlfriend) with his professed identity as a Black student speaking about the Black experience on a predominately White college campus. This caused the woman to approach him later and call into question his racial identity. The exchange resulted in the renegotiation of his racial identity, at which time he stated that he was "really" biracial, she accepted the renegotiated identity, and they were able to proceed with the interaction.

This type of experience, when a biracial individual's identity is called into question, or the "what are you?" experience, is a commonly reported phenomenon within the biracial population (Williams, 1996). Questioning an individual's identity reflects two types of problematics involving the link between identity and appearance. First, the "what are you?" question can be a result of an ambiguous appearance. Biracial individuals who look neither Black nor White may be questioned by random strangers about their racial or ethnic background. Williams interpret this as a failure by the other to place the biracial person into one of their cognitive categorizations for members of particular racial groups. The second type of problematic is that addressed by the above example, which could better be termed the "what are you really?" question. In this case, others may approach the question of the biracial individual's racial background to clarify a discrepancy between the appearance and the professed identity. In this case, there can either be a renegotiation of the identity, or an interactional rupture can take place in which no shared meaning can be agreed upon.[7] Because individuals do not create and maintain an identity in isolation, others in their interactional context must support or validate their self-understanding as Black, White, or biracial. Figure 34.3 maps the effect of appearance on identity.

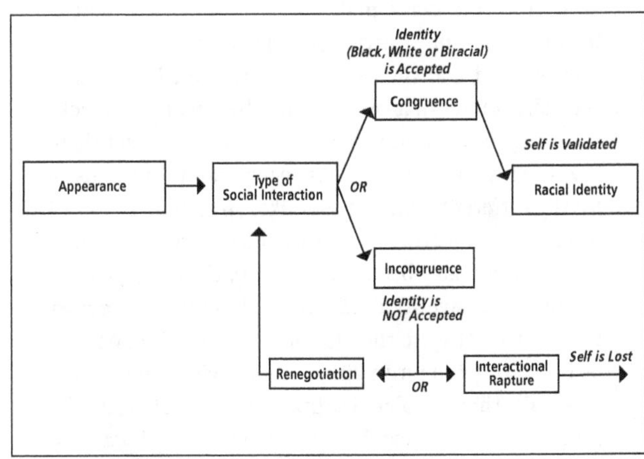

Figure 34.3 The effects of appearance on identity

The Influence of Social Status on Identity

It is too simplistic a picture to say that biracial individuals' appearance alone determines their racial identity. The effect of social networks in which an individual is situated must additionally be considered in order to understand their choice of identity. An individual actor is socially located in a system of networks, or social relationships, which are directly related to their social status. Status brings access to different types of social networks. For biracial individuals, the higher the status of one's parents, the more likely that an individual is to have contact with White peer groups. The more time that individuals spend interacting with White peer groups, the less likely they are to develop an understanding of their biracialness as a singular (Black) identity. More specifically, the more time that an individual spends in White peer groups, the more likely they are to cultivate a degree of cultural savvy to fit in with their peers and to see both Whiteness and Blackness in their self-understanding and interactional presentation of self.

The preceding statement suggests that it is merely the access to different types of networks that influences the directionality of one's biracial identity. It is important to note, however, that it is not merely the amount of contact an individual has with either White or Black peers or family members (Hall, 1980), nor is it exclusively which group the individual uses as a reference group (Fields, 1996; Kerckhoff and McCormick, 1995). Instead, it is the type of contact that an individual has with others, or the way in which an individual socially experiences race, that mediates the relationship between one's social status and their biracial identity.

An additional case may illustrate this argument. Kristy is a biracial woman from New Jersey. She is White in appearance, with fair skin, long curly light brown hair, freckles, and green eyes. She attended public schools, which were 50% Black, until the 10th grade. She stated the following in reference to her relationships with Black students:

> I was always rejected by the Black women. I just shied away from the Black males because they were a little intimidating and a little too aggressive I thought. So then when I transferred sophomore year, I went to a Catholic school that only had maybe, about ten Blacks counting the four biracial students, so when I got there I was really taken in by these people and it was just a totally different world. It was like, [in public school] I was really never accepted by these Black females because well, you probably been told this too, they were jealous because you have good hair and light eyes. I remember thinking what were they jealous of? I didn't choose to be like this, I don't mind it, you know what I mean, so it was really their problem I think. Then I went to Catholic school.... I didn't really know anybody, and I was just like hopefully, it will be better. Of course it was better because there was less Black people for me to contend with.... Maybe because it was a Catholic prep school that was $4000.00 a year, that made people really appreciate education and different cultures and you know, and these people really took me in and it was nice. So we [the Black and biracial students], it was a close knit group, it was kind of like family within that high school....

She said about her college transition:

> When I came here it was like, I'm gonna go to [college] and it's gonna kind of be the same as my high school. Cuz you know, here there's not many Black people—it's on a larger scale, but its the same kind of ratio. So I was asked to do a program [specifically for minority students] the summer before freshman year, and naturally you're friends with thirty Black people right away. So that was great and you know, finally it was like oh, they don't care that I'm so light-skinned or whatever, so that was nice. Especially freshman year, I totally identified with the Black population here. And I was telling my parents, this is so opposite of what I've been running away from all my life because finally these people are like, "you're just a person," you know what I mean.

Kristy's experience is interesting specifically because it provides a critical case that defies the simplicity of using the number of Black social networks for understanding her biracial identity. In this case, Kristy underwent the greatest degree of rejection by her Black peers when she was in an environment with a large number of Blacks. Attending a school where 1/2 of the students are Black provided her with numerous opportunities to form friendships with other Black students (as compared to a school with lower numbers of Black students). It was in this environment however, that she reports being "rejected" by Black women and avoiding interaction with Black men. Here, her self-understanding as a Black woman was not validated. In fact, the incongruence between her appearance and identity caused numerous interactional ruptures (such as gum being thrown in her "good" hair and fistfights). This "rejection" by Black women was counterbalanced by friendship from her White peers with whom she had a common economic status. It was in the context of this simultaneous failure to be accepted as Black, by Blacks, and acceptance by Whites as biracial, that Kristy developed her self-understanding of what it means to be biracial.

Once Kristy transferred to a predominately White school, however, with fewer Blacks to "contend with," her closest network of friendships shifted from exclusively White to inclusive of Black and biracial students. This environment was substantively different than her previous school with different "types" of students. Specifically, the Black students at her new school were exclusively middle to upper-middle class and, because they were in an environment which made them a visible minority, they had a strong vested interest in mutual self-acceptance. It was in this group, composed of Blacks that accepted her, and several other biracial peers, that she found further validation for her biracial identity.

Finally, her movement to college further illustrates the importance of examining the type of social interaction an individual has within any given social network. Again, Kristy was in an environment in which Blacks were a small and highly visible minority (less than 2% of the student body). Here, the pattern of her high school relationships was repeated, facilitated by ties made during the summer program. She was accepted by a small cohesive group of Black students at a predominately White institution while maintaining her core group of White friends. These experiences solidified her understanding of biracialness as a border identity.

Specific socio-demographic factors may enable an individual to have access to differing types of social networks than would be available to others. Social networks provide the terrain in which identities may be negotiated, particularly where non-existent identities may emerge in order for the participants to understand an individual's presence within a particular network. It is precisely in these networks that the key process of interactional validation occurs and contributes to the differential choices in identification of biracial individuals.

DISCUSSION

This article questions the assumption, that underlies the push to add a multi-racial category to the 2000 Census, that most biracial people identify as biracial and that "biracial" identity has a singular meaning. The cases presented reflect a homogeneous and highly skewed group of respondents. All came from middle- to upper-middle-class families, all were raised in predominately White social contexts, none could describe incidents of experiencing discrimination by Whites, and yet many talked about feeling "rejected" by Blacks. These students had a singular set of experiences, which led to their strong identifications as biracial. Possibly it is individuals such as these that multiracial advocates believe an additional Census category will represent. We must ask however, if it is not also exclusively these individuals that would be represented by such a change. Is it possible that biracial identity is largely a middle-class phenomenon? Is this particular self-understanding created and validated by those with a specific and privileged set of social experiences? Would we find a different type of identity amongst those who have strong ties in Black social networks, who live in exclusively Black neighborhoods, and attend predominately Black schools?

One final case may help to both support the conceptual model presented and extend our understanding of the diverse meanings of "biracial" identity. Gregory Howard Williams (1995) has written an autobiographical text that explores his social experience of race. Williams grew up in the south believing that both he and his parents were White. At the age of 12, his parent's marriage dissolved and he moved back to their hometown of Muncie, Indiana with his father. On the bus ride to Muncie, Williams' father revealed that he had been "passing," that he was in fact African-American, and that once they arrived in Muncie, Williams and his younger brother would also be Black. This was a shocking realization to Williams and the rest of the book depicts his experiences as a White-appearing Black child, his shift into extreme poverty, and his entry and gradual acceptance within Muncie's Black community.

In Williams' case, once he moved to Muncie, his social status changed drastically. He went from a relatively comfortable middle-class existence to a life of poverty. His social networks shifted from exclusively White to exclusively Black. In fact, his White grandparents also lived in Muncie but Williams was no longer allowed to visit them (as he had when he was "White"). Despite his White appearance, Williams experienced severe discrimination by Whites. It was this experience of discrimination that solidified his self-understanding as Black (i.e., not as biracial or White). His social experience of race was characterized by prejudicial treatment by Whites and seeing other Blacks systematically discriminated against. Once Williams arrived in Muncie, he could no longer have a White identity because it was not validated by any others in his social environment. In contrast, his identity as African-American was cultivated, protected and nurtured by a significant other who came to be a surrogate mother for Williams and his younger sibling.

This case illustrates how an individual's social status and appearance affect both their access to different types of social networks and influence their interactions within those networks. Identity, as an interactionally validated self-understanding, is by definition a result of these ongoing interactions. It becomes clear how certain types of social contexts, such as those exhibited by the students in this study, may provide the terrain on which an individual is able to develop and cultivate a meaningful identity which is "biracial." It also becomes clear, however, when we consider the case of Gregory Howard Williams that there exist alternative social contexts in which "biracial" has no significant meaning. Social status and appearance are mediated by the types of social interactions an actor experiences. These interactions set the parameters of meaning, from which the biracial individual identity is constructed, negotiated, challenged, reshaped, validated, and ultimately sustained.

NOTES

1. Interracial marriages increased from 150,000 in 1960 to 1.5 million in 1990 (US Bureau of the Census, 1993).
2. No terminology currently exists to accurately describe mixed race individuals or to reflect the diversity of possible combinations. While recognizing this limitation, throughout this paper I will utilize the general term "biracial" to describe individuals who have one Black self-identifying biological parent and one White self-identifying biological parent.
3. The American answer to the question "who is Black?" has been anyone who has any African ancestry whatsoever (Davis, 1991; Myrdal, 1962; Williamson, 1980). The term "one drop rule" originated in the South where one drop of "Black blood" designated an individual Black. This has also been known as the "one Black ancestor rule," the "traceable amount rule," and the "hypodescent rule." This definition of Blackness that emerged from the South became the rest of the nation's definition and was accepted by both Blacks and Whites.
4. Williamson (1980) provides a thorough discussion of the shifting statuses of mulattos (within the Black community) during various periods of US history.
5. A Current Population Survey Supplement was conducted to assess the effects of adding a multi-racial category to the 2000 Census. The findings indicated that less than 1.5 percent of all those surveyed identified themselves as multiracial. The addition of the category as an option

affected the proportion of those identifying as American Indian/Alaska Native (which dropped) but it had no effect on Blacks (Tucker and Kojetin, 1996).

6. These categories of self-understanding are not necessarily mutually exclusive; instead they represent ideal types.
7. An illustration of interactional rupture can be drawn from a case presented in Funderberg (1994). The individual is a White appearing woman, who changed her given name to Zenobia Kujichagulia, and self-identifies for the most part as Black, but occasionally as Black and Cherokee. She tells the following story: "This was an all-black environment, and as they introduced me to this woman, one friend says to me, 'Zenobia, tell her what you are.' So I knew what was coming, although I didn't expect this woman to go all the way off.

   "I said, 'I'm black and Cherokee.' Like I told you, I always leave the last part off [that she's also White].

   "The woman looked at me and said, 'Like hell you are.'

   "I said, 'Yes. Like hell I am.'

   "And she said, 'No, I mean'—like I didn't know what she meant—'I mean you are not black. You might be Cherokee but you are not black.'

   "And I said, 'I'll be sure to tell my daddy you said so.' And she just started cussing, ranting and raving, and I looked at her and I looked at the friend and said, 'I think I'll go now,' and just went across the room."

REFERENCES

Anzaldua, Gloria. 1987. *Borderlands/La Frontera: The New Mestizo.* San Francisco: Spinsters/Aunt Lute Foundation.

Bertaux, Daniel. 1981. *Biography and Society: The Life History Approach in the Social Sciences.* Beverly Hills, CA: Sage Publications.

Blumer, Herbert. 1969. *Symbolic Interactionism: Perspective and Method.* Englewood Cliffs, NJ: Prentice-Hall.

Bogdan, Robert, and Sari Knopp Biklen. 1982. *Qualitative Research for Education: An Introduction to Theory and Methods.* Boston: Allyn and Bacon.

Bradshaw, C.K. 1992. "Beauty and the Beast: On Racial Ambiguity." In *Racially Mixed People in America*, edited by M.P.P. Root. Newbury Park, CA: Sage.

Davis, F.J. 1991. *Who is Black?* University Park, PA: Pennsylvania State University Press.

Delpit, Lisa. 1988. "The Silenced Dialogue: Power and Pedagogy in Educating Other People's Children." *Harvard Educational Review* 58(3):280–298.

Fanon, Frantz. 1952. *Black Skin, White Masks.* New York: Grove.

Fields, L. 1996. "Piecing Together the Puzzle: Self-Concept and Group Identity in Biracial Black/White Youth." In *Racially Mixed People in America*, edited by M.P.P. Root. Newbury Park, CA: Sage.

Funderburg, Lise. 1994. *Black, White, Other.* New York: Morrow.

Goffman, Erving. 1959. *The Presentation of Self in Everyday Life.* New York: Anchor Press Doubleday.

———. 1963. *Behavior in Public Places: Notes on the Social Organization of Gatherings.* New York: Free Press of Glencoe.

Hall, C.C. 1980. "The Ethnic Identity of Racially Mixed People." Unpublished doctoral dissertation, University of California, Los Angeles.

Jones, Lisa. 1994. *Bulletproof Diva: Tales of Race, Sex, and Hair.* New York: Doubleday.

Kerchoff, C., and T. McKormick. 1995. "Marginal Status and Marginal Personality." *Social Forces* 34:48–55.

King, Rebecca, and Kimberly DaCosta. 1996. "Changing Face, Changing Race: The Remaking of Race in the Japanese American and African American Communities." In *Racially Mixed People in America*, edited by M.P.P. Root. Newbury Park, CA: Sage.

Lifton, Robert. 1993. *The Protean Self: Human Resilience in an Age of Fragmentation.* New York: Basic Books.

Marshall, Catherine, and Gretchen B. Rossman. 1989. *Designing Qualitative Research.* Newbury Park, CA: Sage.

McBride, James. 1996. *The Color of Water: A Black Man's Tribute to His White Mother.* New York: Riverhead Books.

Myrdal, G. 1962. *An American Dilemma* (20th ed). New York: Harper & Row.

Park, R. 1950. *Race and Culture.* Glencoe, IL: Free Press.

Root, Maria P. 1992. "Back to the Drawing Board: Methodological Issues in Research on Multiracial people." In *Racially Mixed People in America*, edited by M.P.P. Root. Newbury Park, CA: Sage.

Scales-Trent, J. 1995. *Notes of a White Black Woman.* University Park: Pennsylvania State University Press.

Smithermn, Geneva. 1986. *Talkin and Testifyin: The Language of Black America.* Detroit: Wayne State University Press.

Spencer J. 1997. *The New Colored People.* New York: New York University Press.

Stone, Gregory. 1962. "Appearance and the Self." In *Human Behavior and Social Processes*, edited by A.M. Rose. Boston: Houghton Mifflin.

Taylor, Steven J., and Robert Bogdan. 1984. *Introduction to Qualitative Research Methods: The Search for Meanings.* New York: Wiley.

Tucker, C., and B. Kojetin. 1996. "Testing Racial and Ethic Origin Questions in the CPS Supplement." *Monthly Labor Review.*

US Bureau of the Census. 1993. *We, The American.* Washington, DC: Government Printing Office.

Waters, Mary. 1990. *Ethnic Options: Choosing Identities in America.* Berkeley: University of California Press.

White, Walter Francis. 1948. *A Man Called White: The Autobiography of Walter White.* New York: Viking Press.

Williams, Gregory. 1995. *Life on the Color Line: The True Story of a White Boy Who Discovered He Was Black.* New York: Dutton.

Williams, T. 1996. "Race as Process." In *Racially Mixed People in America*, edited by M.P.P. Root. Newbury Park, CA: Sage.

Williamson, Joel. 1980. *New People: Miscegenation and Mulattos in the United States.* New York: Free Press.

Zack, Naomi. 1993. *Race and Mixed Race.* Philadelphia: Temple University Press.

CHAPTER 35

COLOR AND THE CHANGING RACIAL LANDSCAPE

Margaret Hunter

Skin color remains an important factor in social life today. Qualitative interviews with the author, as well as nearly two thousand cases of survey data have all provided evidence to this fact. However, some may wonder if things have changed since the survey data was collected over twenty years ago. No similar comprehensive national study has been done since, but recent, smaller studies suggest that dark skin color remains a strong liability for Mexican Americans and African Americans. For example, in 2000, Mark Hill, in his study of African American men, found that skin tone accounted for more differences in social status among the men than family background did. Light-skinned black men retained a significant advantage in the labor market.[1] In 2002, Rodolfo Espino and Michael Franz studied skin color differences among Latinos. They wrote, "Our findings indicate that darker-skinned Mexicans and Cubans face significantly lower occupational prestige scores than their lighter-skinned counterparts even when controlling for factors that influence performance in the labor market."[2] Skin tone bias remains persistent over the years and across racial groups. In 2003, the *Washington Post* reported that Latinos who identified as white earned about $5,000 more per year than Latinos who identified as black. White Latinos had lower unemployment rates and lower poverty rates than black Latinos.[3] In a similar analysis, Richard Alba, John Logan, and Brian Stults reported that, "Hispanics who describe themselves as black are in substantially poorer and less white neighborhoods than their compatriots who describe themselves as white. The penalty they absorb in neighborhood affluence varies between $3,500 and $6,000 and thus places them in neighborhoods comparable to those occupied by African Americans.[4] All of these studies published in the past few years reveal that discrimination by skin tone has not eased for Mexican Americans and African Americans. Lighter skin still buys more privileges and dark skin remains a liability in work, housing, and education.

A RACIAL LATIN AMERICANIZATION?

Skin color mattered in the past and it matters today. It affects how much money people make, how long they stay in school, who they think is pretty, who they marry, and what kind of racial identity they have. But the racial landscape in the United States is changing everyday. How will color matter in the future? Noted sociologist Eduardo Bonilla-Silva contends that the United States is in a process of racial "Latin Americanization."[5] As the United States moves more and more toward a colorblind discourse, one that does not acknowledge racial difference or racial inequality, it begins to mirror the historical trend in much of Latin America that denies race and insists on a national identity. It is popular in Mexico, for example, to say that there are no races like in the United States; there are only Mexicans. And this is true to some extent. Mexico does not have a US-style racial system, but it definitely has distinct differences by ancestry, some more indigenous or African, some more Spanish, and they have a full spectrum of colors from dark to light. And even though they do not "do race" the way their northern neighbors do, the pattern looks notoriously similar: a light-skinned elite and a disenfranchised dark-skinned underclass.

The United States is going through a racial Latin Americanization because its discourse has changed in this post-civil rights era to one that denies difference, denies inequality, and insists on a unified, monolithic American designation for all.[6] This colorblind discourse makes it possible to ignore racial discrimination and to criticize those who name it as racist for doing so.[7] Several recent political movements reflect this trend. The national backlash against Affirmative Action is one example.[8] What began in California as a statewide referendum to abolish Affirmative Action in state-regulated affairs in 1996 culminated in the University of Michigan's US Supreme Court cases defending its use of Affirmative Action. In two related cases, the University won the right to use race as one criterion that could be considered in university admissions.[9] The University of Michigan battle revealed the changing contours of race-talk in the United States. The plaintiffs argued that a colorblind society was desirable and could only be achieved by ignoring race in admission decisions. Affirmative Action had to be dismantled, they argued, in order to create a non-racist society. The defendants argued, among other things, that Affirmative Action was still necessary to combat persistent discrimination and inequality, and that a racially diverse student body was academically beneficial to all students.

It is the same colorblind ideology that led University of California Regent Ward Connerly to lead a campaign supporting the Racial Privacy Initiative[10] in California in 2002. This state initiative would have made it illegal for the state of California to collect any data on race and ethnicity including data regarding housing, education, and employment. A colorblind society would require that we not take note of any person's race, supporters have argued. The fact that racial discrimination and inequality would become impossible to monitor and easier to get away with never entered the public debate. This initiative was voted down by Californians largely because of a campaign warning that important medical information that varies by race would be unavailable if the act passed.[11]

Many Latin American countries have avoided collecting racial data for years. Puerto Rico recently began collecting data on the race of its residents. Similarly, Brazil is just beginning to collect some statistics on the different standards of living of Afro-Brazilians, mulattoes, and white Brazilians. Thus, as the United States becomes more like Latin America and pretends racism is not a problem, parts of Latin America are changing to emulate the traditions of the United States. Brazil initiated its first Affirmative Action program regulating admission to the elite public university system.[12] This movement is connected to a small, but growing Afro-Brazilian movement that champions black pride and identity and names racism and inequality while the rest of the nation chants "racial democracy."[13] The program has been met with fierce resistance, especially from elite white families who are no longer guaranteed the admissions to universities they once were. In some Latin American societies, race is becoming a local vocabulary word, not one only imported from the United States. As poverty becomes more entrenched among the dark-skinned poor and money and political power continue to reside strictly in the hands of a light-skinned elite, the deafening silence about racial inequality will be increasingly difficult to maintain.

In addition to a change in racial ideology and discourse, the United States is also becoming more Latin American in terms of demographics. People identifying as Hispanic on the US Census now outnumber the number of people identifying as solely black or African American. In a typically sensational manner, the mainstream American media covered the event as a sort of racial boxing match. Latinos versus blacks: the battle of the minorities. Newspapers used words like "overtake," "left behind," "dominate," and "surpass" to describe the racial and ethnic changes in the population. Despite the superficial coverage of this demographic shift, some major changes are at work in today's racial politics. The number of Latinos in the United States is growing rapidly, although whether Latinos "outnumber" blacks depends in part on how you count. The fact that "Hispanic" is regarded as an ethnicity and all Hispanic people must also choose a race on the Census form makes counting people difficult and controversial.[14] Whether or not Latinos are now the largest ethnic minority group is not the most important issue for this argument. Latinos constitute a significant group in the United States and the presence of Latin American, particularly Mexican, culture, values, and politics is changing the US racial landscape. The history of conquest in Mexico, the Chicano student movement, the fluid nature of race, and the importance of skin tone in Mexico all influence the way Americans will be rethinking race in the coming years. All of these changes beg the question: How will the growing Latino presence change the nature of U.S. race relations?

In many Latin American countries, the fluidity of race and racial categories is further complicated by the tradition that "money whitens." This phrase refers to the trend where dark-skinned people may be treated as if they are white, or allowed into some white social circles, if they are wealthy. This phenomenon has long existed in Latin America in part because they have never had the rigid distinctions of race guided by ancestry and the Rule of Hypodescent so present in the United States. For many generations, African Americans could be rich and famous, and still be guaranteed second-class status through rigid laws and rules of racial etiquette. Any famous African American performer before the Civil Rights Movement can tell stories of having to enter through the back door of establishments where she or he was going to perform to white audiences. However, since the Civil Rights Movement significant African American and Mexican American middle classes have been established and some of those people of color are quite assimilated into white social worlds.

Will the United States' turn toward a colorblind discourse allow the money whitens thesis to work here? Some would argue that it has already happened and that some people of color who are wealthy are allowed into elite white social circles. Largely, though, this is not the case. However, it may be possible in the future for dark-skinned people of color to compensate for their dark skin with wealth or high social status. This may be happening for men already. It seems that dark skin color for men is significantly mediated by wealth or social status. This may also be a function of the fact that skin color has always been more important in the evaluation of women than men.

The other way that skin color politics may play out in the future is through an "ideology whitens" hypothesis. It is possible that besides money, dark-skinned people of color may be allowed into positions of power if they are not ideologically threatening. That is, if they adopt the racial and cultural ideologies of the dominant group, their dark skin can be compensated for with conservative values. For instance, a dark-skinned Mexican American man might be able to run for governor of California if he is a Republican. In this way, his dark skin, a reminder of a potentially strong Mexican American identity, can be compensated for with a conservative political ideology. This process may already be at work in some political campaigns. Cruz Bustamante, a Democratic candidate for governor in the historic gubernatorial recall election of 2003, was dogged by accusations of being a political radical because of his membership in MEChA (Movimiento Estudiantil Chicano de Aztlán) during his undergraduate college years.[15] Bustamante, a political moderate by nearly all accounts, was forced to prove that he neither hated whites nor wanted to return California to Mexico. Bustamante's ethnic identity, phenotype, and moderately liberal political position contributed to his unsuccessful bid for governorship. Although most candidates had little chance against the action-hero celebrity Arnold Schwarzenegger, criticisms against Bustamante were overtly racial in nature. As the Republican Party continues to court people of color, it will be interesting to see if Mexican American and African American candidates will have success espousing more conservative political agendas.

The United States is currently undergoing a substantial wave of immigration primarily from third world nations. The number of immigrants from Asia and Latin America is higher than it has ever been before. The large numbers of nonwhite people moving into the United States is bound to affect the meanings of skin color and race in upcoming generations. First, immigrants come to the United States with their own racial ideologies formed in their homelands and informed by Western imperialism. Because of Western media exports, many immigrants come to the United States with well-formed negative stereotypes about African Americans. Many new immigrants face high levels of racial discrimination when they arrive here. One strategy to combat that discrimination is to align oneself with the dominant group by discriminating against other racial and ethnic minorities. Both the Jewish and the Irish immigrants did this in the 1920s when they were trying to show white Anglos that they were more like them than they were like blacks. Many Irish workers banned African Americans from their unions and Jewish performers worked in the minstrel shows, put on blackface and imitated a racist version of black life. By taking up white racist practices, these earlier immigrant groups helped construct themselves as white and not black.

Immigrants today use some of the same strategies to align themselves with dominant whites and to draw clear boundaries between themselves and other minority groups. Sometimes this happens in daily interactions, for instance, between Korean storeowners and black customers. "Studies on Korean shopkeepers in various locales have found that over 70% of them hold anti-Black attitudes."[16] There are also high profile events like the 1992 uprisings in Los Angeles that create allies of some groups and enemies of others. Asian immigrants were portrayed as innocent victims picked on by black and Latino criminals. All of these different opportunities, both mundane and monumental, provide opportunities for different racial groups to align themselves with and against other groups and to create new meanings of race and racism.

A NEW MIDDLEMAN MINORITY?

Despite some persistent animosity among racial groups, changes in attitudes and social structures have created a growing number of interracial couples and multiracial people. All of this race-mixing has created a growing class of light brown people who do not readily identify with any one particular racial or ethnic group. It is possible that within one or two generations, the United States may have created a new middleman minority—a sort of light-skinned mulatto class that serves as a buffer zone between dominant whites and oppressed racial and ethnic minorities. Currently, the multiracial identity movement, led largely by white mothers of mixed race children, has advocated that multiracial individuals be allowed to simply be individuals (de-raced), or to be members of multiple ethnic groups.[17] The language of this movement borrows heavily from the new colorblind ideology. Because they are often light-skinned, many multiracial people who are part African American or Mexican American report feeling alienated from other members of their groups. The lack of ethnic authenticity leaves many multiracial people to interact only in white social circles or to feel like their only black or Mexican American friends are their own cousins, siblings, and other family members.

> Growing up, I never had any black friends or anything. Part of it was because we come from this white neighborhood and like my school was almost all white, too. But at the same time there were black girls at school and I was totally shunned by all of them. So the only black people I felt like I could ever be a part of were my dad's side of the family because they never make me feel like, "Hey, you're not one of us." Where around anyone else, even here at [college] I feel like I'm on the outside. So my family is like really accepting.
>
> I've always wanted to be closer with more black females, just to widen the variety a little bit more. Like if I was to go anywhere with somebody who was going to be black, it would be my cousin. I would like the liveliness, too, but to me it was just too difficult and just too much drama to be getting past the whole stereotype issue. I get it from my cousin and she's blood. She'll tease me about light skin and being white or whatever.

These biracial African American women describe their alienation from the black community because of their light skin color. The only interactions they have with other black women are restricted to their own family members where one reports, "I get it from my cousin and she's blood." There are two forces at work here. On one hand, light-skinned people, especially biracial, are sometimes excluded from relationships in the black community. On the other hand, some multiracial families, as described in the first quote, choose to remain outside of black communities and do not provide many opportunities for biracial African American children to interact with other blacks. If these trends continue, it is possible that the United States may create a new kind of middleman minority comprised of light-skinned, mixed-race people who do not feel comfortable with or accepted by whites or other people of color. This new mulatto class could exist as a sort of buffer zone between white elites and oppressed racial and ethnic minorities. Bonilla-Silva agrees, "As a tri-racial system (or Latin- or Caribbean-like racial order), race conflict will be buffered by the intermediate group, much like class conflict is when the class structure includes a large middle class (Bottomore, 1968). Furthermore, color gradations, which have always been important matters of within-group differentiation, will become more salient factors of stratification."[20] If Bonilla-Silva's projections are correct, colorism will intensify and light-skinned, mixed-race individuals may have even more incentive to flee communities of color.

Historically, mixed-race people have largely been assimilated into the lower status racial group. Black-white children typically identify as black and Latino-white children often identify as Latino, especially if the Latino parent is dark-skinned. This pattern is beginning to change. As racial boundaries are questioned and the colorblind ideology of individuality dominates our culture, more and more people try to opt out of race altogether. Noted sociologist Kerry Ann Rockquemore describes this phenomenon as choosing a transcendent identity.

> These individuals discount race as a 'master status' altogether. This self-understanding is uniquely and exclusively available to individuals whose bodily characteristics have a high degree of ambiguity (i.e., those who look White). This type of self-understanding of biracialness results in an avoidance, or rejection of any type of racial group categorization as the basis of personal identity.[21]

Rockquemore articulates a new racial option for very light-skinned mixed race people: opting out of race altogether. Historically, this was impossible unless one led a deceptive life and purposefully passed for white. Today, under the ideology of colorblindness, biracial people who choose a transcendent identity are in fact choosing a white identity because they crave the invisibility of whiteness and the lack of racial demarcation that only whites enjoy. If colorism continues to plague the nation, and light-skinned multiracial people do not identify with communities of color, there is an increasing chance that the US racial system will indeed become more Latin American with dominant whites, a light-skinned, mulatto intermediate group, and oppressed racial and ethnic minorities.

In order to avoid further racial polarization and to better understand the dynamics of colorism, more research must be done on other societies. This book linked colorism today to the history of slavery for African Americans and colonization for Mexican Americans. How do other postcolonial nations experience colorism? India has a very strong color-caste system, although official sources will deny it. From a legacy of British imperialism and India's own caste system, the strong value of light skin and extreme denigration of dark skin is still an aspect of daily life. And as is true in the United States, light skin color for women and girls is even more important than it is for men and boys. Similarly, the legacy of Spanish colonialism in the Philippines has left the population awash in Eurocentric values. Longer noses, and light skin are highly valued physical traits. Mestizas, mixed race (half white) Filipinos are often local beauty queens and national celebrities. Colorism is not a strictly American phenomenon and further investigation into how colorism operates in other postcolonial societies will expand our understanding of the issue.

In addition to studying colorism in postcolonial settings, it is also important to understand how white skin came to be revered in cultures that were never colonized by whites. In Japan, for instance, white or light skin tone is viewed as the most beautiful. How did this come to be? Is the Japanese love for white skin related to Western domination in the world and the exporting of Western images of beauty and culture? Perhaps there are parts of Japanese cultural history that explain the valorization of white skin. These are the kinds of questions researchers must ask, and answer as the problem of colorism is slowly unwound.

THE FEMINIZATION OF COLOR

Although this book was comprehensive in covering the many ways that skin tone affects the life experiences of Mexican American and African American women, one of the omissions in this study is the experience of lesbians. Although the survey data surely included some lesbians in the nearly two thousand cases they included, none of the married women were likely lesbians, or at least living their lives as lesbians.[22] Similarly, none of the women in the qualitative portion of this study revealed to me that they were lesbians.[23] This presents a limitation of the data. This is important because much of the ado about colorism among women has to do with the evaluation of women's skin color by men. And though lesbians are not completely excluded from that they may be less influenced by, or less vulnerable to, evaluations by male peers because they are not looking for male romantic partners. Black and Chicana lesbians are still socialized in black and Chicano communities so they presumably learn the same lessons about colorism that their heterosexual peers do. However, if as adults, lesbians of color are less likely to worry about male judgments of skin tone, then how do they negotiate colorism differently?

Answers to these questions will undoubtedly raise further queries about the feminine and masculine symbolism of color itself. Because race and gender can only be understood together, it follows that there must be a gender component to colorism itself. Light skin, in addition to being high status, is also regarded as more feminine, refined, or delicate. Light-skinned women are viewed as extremely feminine and light-skinned men are often feminized as pretty-boys or sissies. Conversely, dark skin is associated with masculinity and dark-skinned men are often considered more virile, dangerous, sexy, and strong. Several of the women I spoke with expressed similar views.

> Most of the people I know would gravitate toward the Tysons or the Denzels,[24] the darker-skinned.... When you think about it, everybody says they want someone who is tall, dark, and handsome. They look like they're strong and they're going to protect you.
>
> It seems like darker men are more masculine, like more manly and sexy. They're more protective, especially in the movies, like in *Waiting to Exhale*. And then it seems like the lighter guys, the pretty boys, are talked about as like ... gay. The light guys are frail. It's weird.

If dark skin is associated with virility and strength, then can dark skin be a positive for men of color? Perhaps, as more dark-skinned black and Latino male models grace the advertisements people see everyday, dark skin color may become somewhat positive—but not without a cost. Part of the symbolic meaning of dark skin as sexual and strong comes directly from more negative images of men of color as violent rapists or sexually insatiable lovers. The fine line separating positive imagery from negative is a slippery slope. It is yet to be seen if the increasing exposure of dark-skinned models will represent a change in color ideologies or a throwback to the images of the Mandingo and the Latin Lover.

GLOBALIZATION AND THE NEW RACISM

Globalization, multinational media conglomerates, and the new restructured world economy all work together to maintain US cultural, economic, and political imperialism. Part of this structure of domination is the exportation of cultural images, arguably all racial in one way or another. The United States exports images of the good life, of white beauty, white affluence, white heroes, and brown and black entertainers/criminals.[25] As many people in other countries yearn for the good life offered in the United States, they also yearn for the aesthetic of the United States: light skin, blonde hair, and Anglo facial features. American cultural imperialism explains why women in Korea, surrounded by other Koreans, pay high sums of money to have eyelid surgery to Westernize their eyes. American cultural imperialism explains why women in Saudi Arabia, Tanzania, and Brazil are using toxic skin bleaching creams to try and achieve lighter complexions. American cultural imperialism explains why one of the most common high school graduation presents among the elite in Mexico City is nose surgery. Although these choices may sound extreme, they are all actually quite rational in a context of global racism and US dominance. Unfortunately new eyelids, lighter skin, and new noses are likely to offer their owners better opportunities in a global marketplace. The new global racism transcends national borders and infiltrates cultures and families all over the world. Critical pedagogist Zeus Leonardo argues that under global racism, "Whiteness stamps its claims to superiority, both morally and aesthetically speaking, on its infantilized Other...."[26] Images associated with white America are highly valued and emulated in the global marketplace. This is part of what makes colorism and racism so hard to battle: The images supporting these systems are everywhere and the rewards for whiteness are real.

How can we stop this juggernaut of global racism? Maybe the world is in need of another Black is Beautiful/Brown Pride movement where women are celebrated as Nubian Princesses and Aztec Goddesses ... or maybe not. The 1960s movements did much for people of color including instilling pride in their bodies and skin colors. But replacing one beauty regime with another is not necessarily the way to solve the problem.

> The establishment of an Afrocentric beauty standard was a limited and problematic goal. It was limited because changing the definition of beauty would do little to restructure institutional racism. It was problematic because even a redefinition of beauty reinforced the exaggerated importance of beauty for women, upsetting the racial order, while validating gender hierarchies.[27]

Sociologist Maxine Leeds' assertion is directly on point. It is not adequate to simply invert the standard of beauty, making the darkest beautiful and the lightest ugly. The fact that there are standards at all is objectifying for women. Besides that, altering the beauty standards is a far cry from breaking the clutch of institutional racism in the United States. Instead, we need to change the way we think about beauty, race, and status altogether.

In today's multicultural, transnational, advanced capitalist, highly technological society, how should beauty look? I want to suggest that instead of looking for a new beauty standard, or doing away with the concept of beauty altogether, we might consider that beauty provides a space, both real and imagined, for dialogue and debate. Who is beautiful, the role of race and color in beauty, the meaning of gender and beauty are all questions that provide an opportunity for further discussion on racism, sexism, and justice. By uncovering the beauty queue and debating the high status of white beauty, we expose white racism and female objectification. All of this dialogue happens within the context of the beauty debate.

This is not to suggest that dialogue is all society needs to solve the problem of racial and gender oppression. Individual and collective resistance must also happen. Everyday resistance can occur on many levels. Johnetta Cole and Beverly Guy-Sheftall, in their book *Gender Talk: The Struggle for Women's Equality in African American Communities*, suggest that men and women can criticize and boycott music and music videos that demean women as sexual objects or victims of violence.[28] I suggest the same thing for popular culture images such as magazines, movies, television shows, and music videos that feature only light-skinned women as beautiful, or that demean dark-skinned people. Mexican Americans and African Americans can begin to eliminate value-laden language about skin color in their vocabularies. This will be a significant challenge given how entrenched color and status are in these cultures. People of color also need new image-makers, with innovative ideas about racial representation. More diverse representations of skin tone and status can also lead to a change in attitudes. Lastly, more legal challenges to colorism [...] can help make the penalty for colorism harder to bear. All of these strategies and more will fuel the movement for change.

As Patricia Hill Collins writes in her book *Fighting Words: Black Women and the Search for Justice*, the power of words and self-naming cannot be underestimated.[29] It is essential that African American and Mexican American women begin the process of renaming their beautiful characteristics, not as eye color and hair color, but as pride, intelligence, perseverance, and solidarity with one another. Women of color share many similar experiences of colorism and can learn from their points of difference. If beauty provides a space for dialogue, then let the debates begin, and let the social change quickly follow.

NOTES

1. Mark Hill, "Color Differences in the Socioeconomic Status of African American Men: Results of a Longitudinal Study," *Social Forces* 78, no. 4 (2000): 1437–60.
2. Rodolfo Espino and Michael Franz, "Latino Phenotypic Discrimination Revisited: The Impact of Skin Color on Occupational Status," *Social Science Quarterly* 83, no. 2 (2002): 612.
3. Darryl Fears, "Race Divides Hispanics, Report Says; Integration and Income Vary With Skin Color," *Washington Post*, July 14, 2003.
4. Richard D. Alba, John R. Logan, and Brian J. Stults, "The Changing Neighborhood Contexts of the Immigrant Metropolis," *Social Forces* 79, no. 2 (2000): 587–621.
5. Eduardo Bonilla-Silva, "We are all Americans! The Latin Americanization of Racial Stratification in the USA," *Race and Society* 5, no. 1 (2002): 3–17.
6. Amanda Lewis, Mark Chesler, and Tyrone Forman, "The Impact of 'Colorblind' Ideologies on Students of Color: Intergroup Relations at a Predominately White University," *Journal of Negro Education* 69, no. 1–2 (2000): 74–91.
7. Margaret L. Hunter and Kimberly D. Nettles, "What About the White Women?: Racial Politics in a Women's Studies Classroom," *Teaching Sociology* 27 (1999): 385–397.
8. Walter R. Allen, Robert Teranishi, Gniesha Dinwiddie, and Gloria Gonzalez, "Knocking at Freedom's Door: Race, Equity, and Affirmative Action in U.S. Higher Education," *Journal of Negro Education* 69, no. 1–2 (2000): 3–11.
9. The University of Michigan was a defendant in two separate and related cases. They won the Grutter v. Bollinger case about their law school admissions and lost Gratz v. Bollinger about their undergraduate admissions policy. In both cases, however, the right to use race as one deciding factor in university admissions was maintained.
10. Although originally called the Racial Privacy Initiative, the California courts later renamed the initiative Race, Ethnicity, Color or National Origin Classification for clarity.
11. Connerly and his colleagues actually made an exemption for a few things including medical data. However, in terms of public relations, scaring the public about its health turned out to be a more effective strategy for beating this initiative than acknowledging the need to monitor persistent racial discrimination.
12. Beth McMurtrie, "The Quota Quandry," *The Chronicle of Higher Education*, February 13, 2004, sec. A.
13. Vânia Penha-Lopes, "Race South of the Equator: Reexamining the Intersection of Color and Class in Brazil," in *Skin/Deep: How Race and Complexion Matter in the 'Color-Blind' Era*, ed. Cedric Herring, Verna M. Keith, and Hayward Derrick Horton (Urbana: University of Illinois Press, 2004).
14. Angela James, "Making Sense of Race and Racial Classification," *Race and Society* 4, no. 2 (2001): 235–47.
15. MEChA is the student organization Movimiento Estudiantil Chicano de Aztlán.
16. Bonilla-Silva, "We are all Americans!" 10.
17. Hayward Derrick Horton and Lori Latrice Sykes, "Toward a Critical Demography of Neo-Mulattoes: Structural Change and Diversity Within the Black Population," in *Skin/Deep: How Race and Complexion Matter in the 'Color-Blind' Era*, ed. Cedric Herring, Verna M. Keith, and Hayward Derrick Horton (Urbana: University of Illinois Press, 2004), 167.
18. Interview with the author from set of 26 qualitative interviews.
19. Interview with the author from set of 26 qualitative interviews.
20. Bonilla-Silva, "We are all Americans!" 4.
21. Kerry Ann Rockquemore, "Between Black and White: Exploring the "Biracial" Experience," *Race and Society* 1, no. 2 (1998): 202.
22. Because of limitations in the data, this study did not investigate the dating/marriage market among lesbian women. The National Survey of Black Americans and the National Chicano Survey only ascertained information on spouses who were "legally" married: that excludes all marriages, legal or otherwise, between two women, as well as cohabitating heterosexual couples who were unmarried.
23. I purposefully used gender-neutral terms when asking about people they had dated in the past and when I asked about what famous people they found attractive I asked about both men and women. Unfortunately, none of this yielded any lesbian, or bisexual, women—at least none that identified themselves in any way to me. I think the problem was in the self-selection of the sample. When I pitched the opportunity to participate in these interviews in front of several large sociology classes, I told them I would ask them about dating. This may have been enough to discourage any lesbian or bisexual women from participating. They may have assumed that I would be asking only about heterosexual dating, or they may have been afraid of a homophobic reaction from me about their dates with women. In the future, I would be more explicit about the fact that lesbian, straight, and bisexual women are encouraged to participate.
24. This refers to the model Tyson Beckford, and the actor Denzel Washington, who are both very handsome, dark-skinned celebrities.
25. I include entertainers and criminals as one category because it seems that most popular culture images show African Americans and Latinos as murderers, drug traffickers, thieves, etc. These images serve as entertainment to the white and nonwhite public.
26. Zeus Leonardo, "The Souls of White Folk: Critical Pedagogy, Whiteness Studies, and Globalization Discourse," *Race, Ethnicity, and Education* 5, no. 1 (2002): 29–50.
27. Maxine Leeds, "Young African-American Women and the Language of Beauty," in *Ideals of Feminine Beauty:*

Philosophical, Social, and Cultural Dimesnsions, ed. Karen Callaghan (London: Greenwood Press, 1994), 1.

28. Johnetta Cole and Beverly Guy-Sheftall, *Gender Talk: The Struggle for Women's Equality in African American Communities* (New York: Striver's Row, 2003).
29. Patricia Hill Collins, *Fighting Words: Black Women and the Search for Justice* (Minneapolis: University of Minnesota Press, 1998).

BIBLIOGRAPHY

Alba, Richard D., John R. Logan, and Brian J. Stults. "The Changing Neighborhood Contexts of the Immigrant Metropolis." *Social Forces* 79, no. 2 (2000): 587–621.

Allen, Walter R., Robert Teranishi, Gniesha Dinwiddie, and Gloria Gonzalez. "Knocking at Freedom's Door: Race, Equity, and Affirmative Action in U.S. Higher Education." *Journal of Negro Education* 69, no. 1-2 (2000): 3–11.

Bonilla-Silva, Eduardo. "We are all Americans! The Latin Americanization of Racial Stratification in the USA." *Race and Society* 5, no. 1 (2002): 3–17.

Cole, Johnetta, and Beverly Guy-Sheftall. *Gender Talk: The Struggle for Women's Equality in African American Communities*. New York: Striver's Row, 2003.

Collins, Patricia Hill. *Fighting Words: Black Women and the Search for Justice*. Minneapolis: University of Minnesota Press, 1998.

Espino, Rodolfo, and Michael Franz. "Latino Phenotypic Discrimination Revisited: The Impact of Skin Color on Occupational Status." *Social Science Quarterly* 83, no. 2 (2002).

Hill, Mark E. "Color Differences in the Socioeconomic Status of African American Men: Results of a Longitudinal Study." *Social Forces* 78, no. 4 (2000): 1437–60.

Horton, Hayward Derrick, and Lori Latrice Sykes. "Toward a Critical Demography of Neo-Mulattoes: Structural Change and Diversity Within the Black Population." In *Skin/Deep: How Race and Complexion Matter in the 'Color-Blind' Era*, ed. Cedric Herring, Verna M. Keith, and Hayward Derrick Horton. Urbana: University of Illinois Press, 2004.

Hunter, Margaret, and Kimberly D. Nettles, "What About the White Women?: Racial Politics in a Women's Studies Classroom." *Teaching Sociology* 27 (1999): 385–97.

James, Angela. "Making Sense of Race and Racial Classification." *Race and Society* 4, no. 2. (2001): 235–47.

Leeds, Maxine. "Young African-American Women and the Language of Beauty." In *Ideals of Feminine Beauty: Philosophical, Social, and Cultural Dimensions*, ed. Karen Callaghan. London: Greenwood Press, 1994.

Leonardo, Zeus. "The Souls of White Folk: Critical Pedagogy, Whiteness Studies, and Globalization Discourse." *Race, Ethnicity, and Education* 5, no. 1. (2002): 29–50.

Lewis, Amanda, Mark Chesler, and Tyrone Forman. "The Impact of 'Colorblind' Ideologies on Students of Color: Intergroup Relations at a Predominately White University." *Journal of Negro Education* 69, no. 1-2 (2000): 74–91.

Penha-Lopes, Vânia. "Race South of the Equator: Reexamining the Intersection of Color and Class in Brazil." In *Skin/Deep: How Race and Complexion Matter in the 'Color-Blind' Era*, ed. Cedric Herring, Verna M. Keith, and Hayward Derrick Horton. Urbana: University of Illinois Press, 2004.

Rockquemore, Kerry Ann. "Between Black and White: Exploring the "Biracial" Experience." *Race and Society* 1, no. 2, (1998): 197–212.

CHAPTER 36

LANGUAGE MATTERS

Vijay Agnew

Imagine a fall day in Toronto. Let me help you, in case you've never been here. Multicoloured leaves in red, yellow, brown mixed with some green lie on the roads, but as cars drive by they scatter, some flying high into the air while others, entangled in a mass, rise slowly and soon fall to lie in a heap by the wayside. Long-time residents of Toronto would describe the weather for this day as warm and pleasant, but for me—an immigrant from India—it is cold. I am bundled up in a black woollen coat, with socks and shoes, ready to hop into my car. I drive through wide boulevards laid out in a grid while listening to classical Western music on my radio. But somewhere, deep in my heart, lurks a nostalgia for loud film music, pedestrians, vendors, and the noise, soot, and dust of Mumbai (formerly Bombay), rather than these clean, quiet, and well-marked Toronto roads.

I reach a church, one of many such churches that dot residential neighbourhoods in Toronto, and carefully scrutinize its exterior to get my bearings. I see a side entrance with a poster stuck on the door and walk with deliberate steps towards it, and it directs me to the English as a Second Language (ESL) class that I have come to observe. The class is being held in the basement in a room that is large, simple, and functional; there are no pictures, decorations, or plants. In the centre of the room about thirty chairs are lined up in rows, and a flip chart with a chair for the teacher next to it faces the students. On a table against the wall sit an aluminum coffee urn, milk, sugar, styrofoam cups, and a plate of cookies.

A grass-roots community-based organization of South Asians[1] has brought together about twenty-five new immigrants for an introductory class in the English language. The women are wearing *salwar kamiz*,[2] or saris, the dress of South Asians, but in this basement in Toronto they present a curious amalgamation of the needs of the present and the norms of the past. In the tropical heat and dust of South Asia, the salwar kamiz that are worn during the day are made of light cotton fabric and are comfortable to wear and easy to maintain. Usually women wear sandals with them. In Toronto, it is cold, and thus the women are also wearing colour-coordinated heavy cardigans over their salwar kamiz. They're also wearing shoes with socks.

The women's dress marks them as immigrants and newcomers. To my South Asian eyes, this mixture of East and West—light textures with heavy sweaters—represents a curious hodgepodge of styles. But perhaps other white Canadians who are unfamiliar with South Asian dress see the outfits not as an attempt by the women to accommodate themselves to the weather but as foreign and different. After having lived in Canada and studied immigrants for about twenty years, I still have ambivalent feelings about such clothing, and am uncertain what South Asian women would ideally wear in Toronto, and, more generally, in Canada. Sometimes I think these women ought to retain their traditional dress as a symbol of their cultural identity, but at other times I want them to discard their salwar kamiz and adopt pants and jeans and be done with it.

I am jostled by memories that remind me that in the present, as opposed to the past, the ideal is for a multicultural Canada, and that Canadians do not wish to impose any one kind of clothing on the women. Immigrants are free to choose—or so it is said. Sombrely, I wonder how the women are responding to the impolite stares and frowns from some people in public places, people silently expressing disapproval of their dress. Perhaps such stares make the women uncomfortable, and they begin to think about wearing jeans and pants so that they will not, so obviously, attract attention to themselves. But perhaps their lack of confidence and insecurity in their new environment makes them content with the small adjustments in their dress that they must make. Perhaps family norms and religious precepts make them reluctant to adopt new ways of dressing. I hope the women are warm. Their demeanour suggests that they are feeling uncertain, awkward, and ill at ease.

A palpable sense of anxious anticipation fills the room. All of us, with the exception of the teacher, are South Asian. The South Asian counsellor from the area's community organization gives me a brief rundown on the identities of the women present and introduces me to the teacher, Jane, as a professor who is collecting material for a book on immigrant women in Canada. I talk to Jane, who is dark-haired, fair-skinned, and middle-aged, but my eyes roam restlessly among the other women hoping to make eye contact with them. The women, however, avoid looking in our direction and no one responds by looking or smiling back at me. The women seem to be taking a bit more interest in each other, and some have started making conversation with the person seated next to them, but most are quiet as they wait for the class to begin. The counsellor encourages the women to get themselves some coffee, and, although the women glance toward the table, none gets up. I had expected that the contrast between the larger, culturally alien Canadian environment and the people who look like oneself, despite their social differences, might create a sense of immediate comfort and familiarity. Yet the usual hesitancy and reserve among people who are strangers to one another are still present.

This is the first class in the program of introductory conversational English that is funded by the government as part of its settlement service to new immigrants. Attending the program is free (COSTI 2004). The class is being held in Scarborough, where a large proportion of immigrants from South Asia have settled. In the 1990s, most South Asian immigrants came from India, Sri Lanka, Bangladesh, and Pakistan, and a large proportion of Punjabis from India and Tamils from Sri Lanka settled in Scarborough. Most were economic migrants, like their predecessors throughout Canadian history, while a small proportion were refugees from Sri Lanka escaping ethnic and religious violence there. Judging from the appearances of the women, their style of dress and ornamentation, I would say the class reflects this population mix.

Before long, Jane moves to the front of the class to begin the day's lesson in conversational English, and I walk to the side of the room in the hope of catching the expressions on the women's faces, but otherwise wish to be forgotten by them. Jane tries to put the women at ease by smiling broadly, but their body language reveals their tension as they gaze anxiously at her and focus entirely on what she is about to say and do. Jane tells them slowly and in carefully enunciated English that she has two goals for the class: first, to teach them how to ask a bus driver for directions, and how to tell him or her where they wish to get off; and, second, how to buy a coffee and ask for milk and sugar in it. Jane breaks down the tasks into small segments, providing the words that go with each, and interjecting jokes that the women sometimes respond to with nervous smiles.

Jane asks the women to introduce themselves to the class and to say where they are from. She smiles encouragingly, and the women, who seem terrified, mumble softly, "My name is Harjeet, Ludhiana, Punjab," or "My name is Santosh, Jullunder, India," or "Shahnaz, Karachi, Pakistan," or "Swarna, Colombo, Sri Lanka," and so on. The names and places are familiar to me, and they give me clues about the women's regional, religious, and linguistic identities. I follow the women with my eyes as each one introduces herself, and, almost reflexively, I find myself fleshing out a picture of each by mentally adding other details of her social background and identity.

Canadian immigration criteria in the post–Second World War period favoured those South Asians who were upper or middle class. The 1967 immigration policy, which laid the framework for later developments, required immigrants, among other things, to have a certain level of education, knowledge of English or French, and job-related skills, and to be in a profession or occupation that was in demand in Canada (Li 2003, 14–37). Only those with substantial economic, social, and psychological resources were motivated to take on the risks of emigrating and had the financial resources to go through the process of applying for immigration to Canada and leaving their homes.

The ability to immigrate to a new country is a privilege for a few and is vied for and envied by others in South Asia. Although the criteria are weighed heavily in favour of the upper and middle classes, other ideals embedded in immigration policies—such as "family reunification" and "humanitarian and compassionate grounds"—vary the picture. [...] In addition to immigrants, refugees have come from Sri Lanka, though a very small percentage are from the Punjab. The Tamil women in the room are dependants of male refugee claimants, such as fathers, brothers, and husbands. These criteria have spawned a diversified South Asian population in Toronto: some are professional, English-speaking immigrants, while others have limited education and knowledge of English. Consequently, South Asian immigrants are found at both ends of the labour market (Basavarajappa and Jones 1999). The immigration status of the individual is significant because it entitles her/him to an array of social services, such as this ESL class (Boyd, DeVries, and Simkin 1994). [...]

The age, clothes, and jewellery of some of the women in the class suggest that they are recent brides who have come to Canada consequent to an arranged marriage, while others are older and have come with their families. All the women present are part of the "family class" of male immigrants, the sponsored dependent relatives of brothers and sisters already here. There are no senior citizens in the class, although they too would be eligible for free language training. The women may have several valuable job-related skills, but their lack of ability to speak English disadvantages them in locating good jobs. Besides, their social integration is impeded by their inability to speak English, and there is some danger of their becoming isolated and feeling alienated. Community groups, such as the one that organized this class, act as mediators between the women and the larger society, and they create venues for them to network with others of their own linguistic and regional communities (Agnew 1998).

All the South Asians in this ESL class had lived in multilingual environments "back home." The dominant national language in India is Hindi; in Pakistan it is Urdu; and in Sri Lanka it is Sinhala. There are innumerable regional languages in all these countries. For example, India has seventeen official languages recognized by its constitution; there are thirty-five languages spoken by more than a million people; and in addition there are 22,000 dialects. "People write books and letters, make films, produce plays, print newspapers, talk, teach, preach, fight, make love, and dream in all those languages" (Kumar 2002, 7). In the class that day, only Hindi, Punjabi, and Tamil were represented.

Since many countries in South Asia were colonized, some European languages have been absorbed locally and have become part of their cultures as well. India, Pakistan, and Bangladesh share a common history of British colonization, and the English language is still used there in governmental institutions, in education, and, to a large extent, in politics as well. The Dutch colonized Sri Lanka, but since knowledge of English provides social and class mobility, it has been widely adopted. In India, language has been a contested issue and there have been disagreements over the use of English, acceptance of Hindi as a national language, and the division of territory between states (Khilnani 1997, 175). The status of English vis-à-vis the local languages is further complicated because English is identified as the "idiom of modernity," and the "proliferating, uncontainable vernaculars with the 'natural' state of things in India" (Chaudhuri 2001, xx).

Nevertheless, historically English is the language of the elite and the privileged in India, and continues at present to be a requisite for social and class mobility. Official counts peg the number of English-speaking people at 2 per cent, but others argue that a realistic estimate is closer to 15 per cent (Kumar 2002, 6).

As a young girl, I spoke Hindi, Derawali, and English, and could understand Punjabi, Sindhi, and Urdu. I gave no conscious thought to my knowledge of these different languages, and since many Indians are familiar with several languages I thought it to be unexceptional. In Toronto, when I was required to fill in forms at the university and identify the languages that I could read, write, or speak, I understood the question to pertain to European languages and thus left the space blank. Yet in one incident, a white Canadian professor was annoyed with me for not identifying the languages that she assumed correctly that I knew. Her words made me reflect on how I had unconsciously imbibed the biases of the larger Canadian society, how I had voluntarily declined to take or give credit to people like me for being bilingual and even trilingual. My action can be characterized as a telling example of internalized racism. The women in the ESL class were all bilingual and they knew their regional and national language—almost a necessity in South Asia—but were not conversant with English.

The social and cultural alienation that some Indian women experience in Canada is most easily explained by their inability to speak English. However, in documenting the experience of the women in this ESL class, I am attempting to show how race, class, and gender, along with an inability to speak English, constructs the identity of these women in Canada.

Identity, feminist theorists contend, is socially constructed and it changes with time, place, and context. The process of moving from one country to another and learning to get along in a new society changes the self-perception of immigrant women; however, their inability to speak English takes on significance that is quite unlike that which they had experienced in India. The self-perception of the women is at odds with the way white Canadians know and understand them. Social identity, however, is "principally the identity which is recognized and confirmed by others"; consequently, it does not matter how strenuously "individuals may disavow or evade it" (Andermahr, Lovell, and Wolkowitz 2000, 124). Social actions and interactions become meaningful, and although they can be interpreted, much like a text, in many different ways, yet they indicate to the individual "how to go on," and give them valuable clues about how to participate in the culture in which they are now living (249). Social actions and interactions thus affect the individual in immediate and tangible ways.

Ethnic groups have conventionally been constructed in ways that homogenize their experiences and erase the many distinctions, such as those of social class and gender, within them. There are commonalities of experience, no doubt, but at the same time there are vast differences that stem from the different identities. The social construction of an ethnic group may emphasize a particular aspect of its identity, such as language or religion (e.g., head scarf), which not only subsumes its other attributes but also blames the victims for the difficulties they encounter in integrating themselves with Canadian society. Yet, as postcolonial feminists argue, women have had to "negotiate the precarious balance between the tenacious forces of integration and the desire to maintain a sense of their cultural identity as a strategy of self-preservation in their country of adoption" (Code 2000, 396).

Indian women, like other racialized women, experience racism when white Canadians encounter their "difference" from the norm, whether it is skin colour, different clothing, or an inability to speak English. Everyday racism "expresses itself in glances, gestures, forms of speech, and physical movements. Sometimes it is not even consciously experienced by its perpetrators, but it is immediately and painfully felt by its victims—the empty seat next to a person of colour, which is the last to be occupied in a crowded bus; the slight movement away from a person of colour in an elevator; the overattention to the black customer in the shop; the inability to make direct eye contact with a person of colour; the racist joke told at a meeting; and the ubiquitious question 'Where did you come from?'" (Henry et al. 1995, 47).

Indian women's community-based organizations give the lie to the stereotype that constructs women from their group as passive. Community-based organizations lobby for and hold ESL classes for new immigrants from their communities despite constant threats of non-renewal of funds and government cutbacks (Agnew 1996, 1998). They wish to help individuals adjust to their new environment, and to lessen their cultural alienation by bringing them together in supportive environments such as an ESL class. Working-class, non-English-speaking women have the double burden of not speaking English and not having the language—words—to articulate their dissatisfaction with their marginality and oppression. Consequently, we may well ask, why do they come? I answer this question in the next section.

IMAGINATION AS A SOCIAL PRACTICE

"I left them all and walked briskly towards the aeroplane, not looking back, looking only at my shadow before me, a dancing dwarf on the tarmac" (Naipaul 2003, 78). Naipaul's description of the first time he left Trinidad to study at Oxford catches the sense of hope and excitement that immigrants experience on leaving their homes to begin a new and different stage in their lives. The process of leaving home is difficult and painful, but at first it is mitigated by hopes, dreams, and fantasies of a new life in affluent Canada.

We often think of ourselves as unique individuals with distinct hopes and dreams, yet our imagination is profoundly influenced by the social context in which we live. The images that float in our minds germinate as a result of where we have been and what we have seen and read. Jawaharlal Nehru, in a letter to his daughter Indira Gandhi, writes:

> For many years now I have been traveling in these oceans of time and space.... It is a fascinating journey ... when the past and present get strangely mixed together and the future flits about like an insubstantial shadow, or some image seen in a dream. The real journey is of the mind; without that there is little significance in wandering about physically. It is because the mind is full of pictures and ideas and aspects of India that even the bare stones—and so much more our mountains and great rivers, and old monuments and ruins, and snatches of old song and ballad, and the way people look and smile, and the queer and significant phrases and metaphors they use—whisper of the past and the present and of the unending thread that unites them and leads us all into the future. When I have a chance ... I like to leave my mind fallow and receive all these impressions. So I try to understand and discover India and some glimpses of her come to me, tantalize me and vanish away. (Gandhi 1992, 121)

Imagination, writes Appadurai (1996), is a social practice that is central to all forms of agency, a key component of the new global order, while the imaginary is a "constructed landscape of collective aspirations" (31). Appadurai has developed the concepts of "ethnoscapes, ideascapes, and mediascapes" to show how media and travel fuel our imagination in the practice of our everyday lives, and he argues that our identities, localities, and communities are shaped by travel and images projected by the media: "The story of mass migration (voluntary and forced) is hardly a new feature of human history. But when it is juxtaposed with the rapid flow of mass-mediated images, scripts and sensations, we have a new order of instability in the production of modern subjectivities" (4). Immigrants' urge to move from one country to another and their settlement in new societies are deeply affected by a mass-mediated imagination that transcends national space.

As an English-speaking woman who lived in Bombay in the 1960s before I immigrated to Canada in 1970, the way I imagined the West was stimulated by the English-language books and magazines that I read, the Hollywood films that I watched, and the music of Pat Boone and Elvis Presley that I heard. (There was no television in those days in India, and the use of personal computers and the Internet was still in the future—even in the West.) Then there were regular stories about America that came in letters from my English-speaking physician brother who worked in New York City. My dream of studying in North America and living away from my family was an unconscious product of the glamorous images that I consumed from the mass media and the ideas that I garnered from English-language books and magazines. In Canada, I began to re-imagine and reinvent myself, although I did so unknowingly.

The imagination and the subjectivity of the Hindi-, Punjabi-, Urdu-, Sinhala-, and Tamil-speaking women who were in the ESL class must certainly be different than mine because they had lived in India, Pakistan, and Sri Lanka during a different period and in different social and political contexts. By the 1990s, television had become a well-established medium of entertainment throughout South Asia among the middle classes, including those who lived in smaller towns and cities. In India, the number and range of programs in different languages (Hindi, English, and regional languages) continued to expand, and television regularly broadcasted English-language serials produced in the West. Television programs and advertising came to be supplemented, as time progressed, by the Internet and cyberspace, new ways to produce and distribute images that inflected the imagination of the people as well. Furthermore, globalization generated a much greater and more constant flow of ideas and goods between countries, and that had an impact on the subjectivities of the people and constructed their sense of self in comparative and relational terms.

Time and social context distinguished the women in the class from me, but their identities were also different from the contemporary English-speaking professional and the entrepreneurial South Asian transnational migrant. These latter migrants leave their countries in pursuit of education, travel, and employment, but they are mobile and may over time live in many different countries to take advantage of the available economic, educational, and social opportunities for themselves and their families (Ong 1999). A vast array of electronic and print images penetrate and inform their imaginations and identities, the possibilities that are available to them in the present, and what and who they might become in the future.

As a student in Delhi, Amitava Kumar was enamoured of the idea of becoming a writer in the West, and his fantasies of life in London were fed by a returning Indian student, a Rhodes scholar from Oxford:

> I imagined trips to libraries, museums, lectures, theatres, parks. I got a gift from him: a pack of postcards showing scenes of life at Oxford. Sunlight slanted across the narrow brick street; bicycles were propped against walls covered with ivy; cricket was being played on the immaculate greens.... Our visitor from London had come bearing other gifts too: shaving cream and disposable razors and duty-free cigarettes. Tepid tea with toast and omelette in the Hindu College canteen on winter mornings had never tasted so good before because awaiting me at the end of the meal were imported Silk Cuts that I had just received. The London that the Oxford man described seeped into the winter mornings and became a part of my dream.... I wanted to be there. (Kumar 2002, 81–82)

The enormous popularity of Hindi-language Bollywood films (i.e., the Indian film industry located primarily in Mumbai) makes them one of the most significant cultural forms in national and transnational South Asian cultural practices (Desai 2004, 35). Mumbai is named after a local deity, Mumbadevi, but "the real propitiatory deity of the city is

Lakshmi, the goddess of wealth. Bedecked in silk and jewels, standing on a lotus flower, a smile on her lips, gold coins spilling from her outstretched hand, pretty Lakshmi beckons her devotees. Glittering and glamorous, she holds out the promise of fortune but extracts cruel sacrifice from her worshippers even as she entices them" (Kamdar 2001, 131). Bollywood "brings the global into the local presenting people in Main Street, Vancouver, as well as Southall, London, with shared 'structures of feeling' that produce a transnational sense of communal solidarity" (Mishra 2002, 238).

Images and values propagated by Bollywood films and picked up in television and advertising filter into the imagination of people living in South Asia and the diaspora, creating thereby a "community of sentiment" that begins to imagine and feel things together (Appadurai 1996, 8). These everyday cultural practices mean that although people have disparate social identities and live in different social contexts, yet because they engage with the same media and its images, they come to share, to some extent, a similar set of social values and norms. These images and values that pervade popular culture play a role in constructing the dreams and fantasies of people living in different locations (Desai 2004).

People in the movie industry, Mehta argues, are "big dreamers" and their films give life to the "collective dreams" of a billion people (Mehta 2004, 340). One message that is often highlighted in Hindi-language films and television is that the "good life" comprises materialism and consumerism. The West is the epitome of consumerism, and the imagery associated with the West symbolizes wealth, influence, and power. Bollywood films have formulaic plots and elaborate song and dance routines that ask nothing more from the audience than they suspend their disbelief and enter a world of love and romance, wealth and power, and watch individuals who espouse ideal values emerge victorious (Kumar 2002, 30; Desai 2004). For example, a Bollywood movie may evoke fantasy and desire in audiences when they see the handsome and rich hero and his glamorously dressed heroine cavorting on the Swiss Alps. Such images, writes Appadurai (1996), become "scripts for possible lives to be imbricated with the glamour of film stars and fantastic film plots" (3).

A conventional, if simple, binary distinction is between the materialistic West and spiritual India. (Another similar and not unrelated cliché identifies India as innocent and America as the den of evil.) Such categorizations are often evoked as an apologetic defence of India's poverty, and what can be termed its lack of development. Indians, writes Sunil Khilnani (1997), have over the last century come to "see themselves in mirrors created by the West" (196). The Orientalist gaze of the Westerner defines India and Indians as the "Others" (i.e., they use their own culture and society as the norm and define other cultures in comparative terms, perceiving them not only as different but also as inferior; Said 1979).

Although it is discussed more rarely, India and other countries in South Asia have also helped shape the self-images of other cultures. According to Khilnani (1997) Western cultures have

> recurringly used India as a foil to define their own historical moments: to reassure or to doubt themselves. And Indians have also, on occasion, tried to work out their own "indigenous" ways of knowing the West. It is impossible to sever these twisted bonds of mutual knowingness and ignorance: the plunder is constant, and neither side can retreat into a luxurious hermeticism. Any discussion of India is thus inescapably forced on to the treacherous fields of the politics of knowledge. These must be navigated, like any political activity, by one's wits. There is no privileged compass, no method, or idiom that can assist. (197)

The middle classes in India, in the post-independence era, have abandoned their "traditional moorings" in their avid pursuit of social and class mobility based on the consumption of material goods. Some argue that these goals result from a thoughtless imitation of Western values, particularly among the younger, middle-class generation. Conspicuous consumption has become necessary for enhancing the self-esteem of the individual. "In a situation where things are difficult to get, and there are so many people around you defining their very existence by the ability to obtain them, the act of acquisition tends to disproportionately dominate the perception of self-esteem" (Varma 1998, 136). The materialistic goals of the middle classes can seem vacuous, debilitating, and immoral in a society where the vast majority of people are poor.

Images of a "good life" at one level threaten to homogenize the values of South Asians living "there" and "here"—in South Asia and in the diaspora. Yet they are consumed and interpreted in local settings and in particular ways that resist standardization and universalism. Furthermore, interpretations of a "good life" are relative and contextual; a "good life" for a middle-class Punjabi immigrant in Scarborough may entail access to and the availability of goods and services and a standard of living that differs from a Punjabi woman living in Ludhiana or Jullunder.

Dreams of affluence and well-being mitigate the heartache of emigrating and leaving behind family, friends, and home. In the post-1967 period, individuals who migrated to Canada often had personal contacts that acted as magnets in a process described as chain migration. Once a family left a village, town, or city, they in turn encouraged friends and relatives to migrate as well, by spinning dreams for them of jobs, educational opportunities, and economic security. For example, working- and middle-class Punjabi immigrants living in Canada still write letters and send photographs to their relatives in Ludhiana and Jullunder that describe their lives in terms of the availability of a good education for the children, well-paid jobs for themselves, and the ownership of consumer household goods for the family. They also return home periodically, bearing gifts for friends and family. While at home, they tell their family and friends of owning houses and cars, and, since there is no norm in those societies concerning mortgages and consumer loans, it is imagined that these individuals have no debts. In comparison with the lives of middle-class people in cities like Ludhiana and Jullunder, returning migrants have discretionary incomes that enable them to consume goods and travel and reinforce the image of the affluent West.

Migrants who return for a visit with their extended families after having lived in the West, the Middle East, or the Far East have some social and economic cachet among the middle classes in South Asia. Furthermore, their children speak fluent English. Given the class and social prestige still associated with that language in South Asia, this accomplishment signals the family's social mobility and well-being. The women in the ESL class undoubtedly had hopes and dreams for themselves and their families when they emigrated. They dreamed of a "good life" that was perhaps both different and similar to that of the other migrants. If not for the dreams, why would they dismantle their homes and think of rebuilding them elsewhere? Given the option of staying put or leaving, they made a choice according to their own limitations and potentials.

I wonder if the imaginations of the women in this ESL class ever carried them to this church basement where they are now sitting in an alien environment feeling anxious and nervous about learning English? I think not. The trials and tribulations of these new immigrants to Canada bring to mind my very different experiences with the language, despite being an English-speaking immigrant at the university. The words of Azar Nafisi (2004) resonate with me: "Other people's sorrows and joys have a way of reminding us of our own; we partly empathize with them because we ask ourselves: What about me? What does that say about my life, my pains, my anguish?" (326).

*****

LANGUAGE AND IMMIGRATION

At present, there are vast inequalities by region, urban or rural residence, social class, and gender in the availability and accessibility of schools and colleges. Thus, the question that Jane asked the women in the ESL class, "Where do you come from?", yields only the minimum facts and does not tell us of the uneven distribution of educational opportunities in the countries of origin that make English-language education available to some and not to others. These differences show up in the mix of immigrants that comes to live in Toronto and becomes part of the larger entity of South Asians. The disparities and disadvantages that originate in the country of origin are thus perpetuated and further aggravated in Canada.

Class and gender biases of Canadian immigration policies favour English-speaking immigrants; thus, women from India come to Canada predominantly as "dependants" (an immigration category) of their spouses or other male relatives. Their entry status as dependants further heightens the class and gender disadvantages experienced in their countries of birth, since immigration status determines access to social services such as ESL classes. Although all non-English-speaking immigrants have access to some introductory language training, only those who are considered to be destined for the labour market have extended opportunities for advanced learning. Since women have formally entered the country as dependants, it is assumed they will not be joining the labour market and thus will have access to only basic training in the English language. However, most Indian women, like other immigrant women, do take up paid employment, but the lack of language proficiency results in lower economic integration of women into the labour market and imposes what Li refers to as a "net income penalty" on the women (Li 2003). Often they end up working on the low rung of the occupational ladder in job ghettoes such as the garment industry, working longer hours in more insecure work, and earning lower wages (Fincher et al. 1994). Further, it wastes the skills that the women have acquired with great difficulty and persistence on their part in their countries of birth, and have brought with them. This is a loss both to the individual and to the country.

Gender, race, place of origin, and language facility are cumulative disadvantages that have economic and social repercussions on women's lives. In Toronto, the inability to speak English deters the women from using public transportation, going out alone to buy groceries, or to do other errands for the family, such as driving, or making and keeping appointments at medical clinics and doctor's offices. (There are some community health clinics, such as Access Alliance or Women's Health in Women's Hands, which specifically cater to a multilingual clientele.) The children quickly learn English in school and sometimes act as interpreters for their mothers, but the consequent loss of authority is problematic. Their inability to speak English isolates the women, robs them of autonomy, and reinforces their dependence on their spouses. One positive interpretation of this ESL class might be to view it as indicative of the women's determination to become independent, productive, and contributing citizens of Canada.

The women in this ESL class are intently focused on the instructions Jane gives them. Their tongues get entangled in the strange sounds they are expected to make, the words roll out of their mouths awkwardly, and, though embarrassed, they struggle on bravely, repeating the words that Jane encourages them to say. They are hesitant and self-conscious, yet they carry on.

LINGUISTIC AND CULTURAL HOMES

Language is embedded in cultural norms. Lack of proficiency in the English language crystallizes many other forms of cultural alienation and discomfort experienced by new immigrants, but almost all racialized immigrants have subtle difficulties with the language despite their ability to speak English fluently. The linguistic and cultural experience of a new male immigrant from India to the United States (before vegetarianism became a fad) is described by his daughter:

> "I would like to eat ve-ge-tables. Do you serve ve-ge-tables?" asked my father. (He pronounced the second half of the word like the word "table" with a long "a.")
>
> "Huh?"
>
> "Ve-ge-tables."
>
> "Oh, ya want vegebles? Why'n ya say so? We don got no vegebles. Ya wanna sanwich?"
>
> "Cheese sandwich? Do you have cheese sandwich?"
>
> "Ya don wanannie meat?"
>
> "I don't eat meat. I am a vegetarian. I only eat ve-ge-tables."
>
> "Okay, kid, I'll make ya a cheese sandwich." (Kamdar 2001, 181)

Although everyone speaks English in the accent that is common to their place of origin and determined by their social class and education, new immigrants from South Asia often feel belittled when they speak English and others have difficulty understanding them. V.S. Naipaul (2000) felt apologetic that he spoke English in a "foul manner" after he first arrived in London. He confides in a letter to his sister, "but now my English pronunciation is improving by the humiliating process of error and snigger" (73). English-speaking South Asians (and other racialized groups) feel disgruntled when they are asked to repeat words and sentences or when white, English-speaking Canadians turn their ears towards the individual to more easily catch his or her words. The latter act is sometimes experienced as a form of racism.

In this ESL class, Jane writes the words *north*, *south*, *east*, and *west* on the flip chart and attempts to gauge from the expression on the students' faces whether they understand the concept. She then goes on to tell them to ask the driver of the bus to let them off, for example, at the northwest corner in front of the mall. The cultural lesson for the students is the use of this terminology, for in South Asia they would normally use landmarks, such as a temple, a grocery store, or a bus stop to find their way and to locate themselves. Even I, as a new immigrant, was bewildered when friends asked me to use such terminology to fix a meeting place. Similarly, in South Asia, tea and coffee are commonly brewed with milk, except when requested otherwise. Thus, being served coffee and tea made with plain water was a new experience as well (at least until some coffee shops popularized Chai as a menu item). The ESL class was about language, but social and cultural lessons were being imparted simultaneously as well.

Cultural differences, or the sense of being an outsider or a foreigner, can make the individual feel alienated and heighten feelings of sadness, nostalgia, and create a longing for home. After having been in London for a few weeks that coincided with the Christmas season, Naipaul (2000) wrote to his family in Trinidad:

> I have been thinking more and more about home.... Christmas never meant much to me or to any one of our family. It was always so much of a glorious feeling of fun we felt existed somewhere, but we could never feel where it was. We were always on the outside of a vague feeling of joy. The same feeling is here with me in London. Yet there is so much more romance here. It gets dark about half past three and all the lights go on. The shops are bright, the streets are well lit and the streets are full of people. I walk through the streets, yet am so much alone, so much on the outside of this great festive feeling.
>
> But I was thinking of home. I could visualize every detail of everything I knew—the bit of the gate, for instance, that was broken off, the oleander tree and the withering roses. Sometimes the sound of a car starting in the road rouses me. The uncertain hesitant beat of the engine brings back No. 26 [their home] back to me, smells and all. It makes me feel sad. Don't misunderstand. It makes me think about you people in a way I thought of you only rarely at home. (43)

Immigrants, particularly those who are racialized, have raised questions about the nature of Canadian identity and the expectations of the population already here about how subsequent arrivals ought to become Canadians. In the early and mid-twentieth century, the ideal of assimilation and Anglo-conformity was held up as necessary and the only way to become a Canadian. But the continued attachment of immigrants to their culture and their disillusionment with the ideal of assimilation led them to express doubts and raise questions politically. Eventually, the policies of bilingualism and multiculturalism were introduced, but they were critiqued for attempting to separate language from culture. Since the focus of these policies was culture, they left undisturbed the unequal distribution of power and prestige among different ethnic and racial groups in Canada (Fleras 2004). At present, South Asians, along with other racialized groups, increasingly focus on anti-racism and human rights activism. Rushdie argues that a creative imagination can give us the power to construct a better world. He writes that imagination can transform and instill a "confidence in our ability to improve the world" and "imagination is the only weapon with which reality can be smashed so it may be subsequently reconstructed" (cited in Needham 2000, 69).

Throughout Canadian history, South Asian women (along with other racialized populations), whether they speak English or not, have encountered formidable structural barriers of race, class, gender, and heterosexuality (Agnew 1996). Although oppressed and victimized, they have survived by exercising their wits. Monica Ali's (2003) novel *Brick Lane* is about the conflicts and tensions that define the immigrant experience. Nazneen, the main character in the novel, is an eighteen-year-old girl from Bangladesh who has an arranged marriage and comes to live in London. On her arrival, she knows only three words in English—*sorry* and *thank you*—and does not know a soul. She lives with her husband, Charu, in Brick Lane, an area exclusively inhabited by immigrants from Bangladesh, whose reference points and values are those that exist "back home." Charu sees no reason for Nazneen to learn English, and she accepts his dictum without protest. Nazneen's lack of English is seldom depicted in the novel as being problematic; rather, it is one of the many characteristics that shape and determine her immigrant experience. Nazneen's life is entirely confined to Brick Lane, where she is happy to make friends, start a family, maintain a correspondence with her sister at "home," while she cautiously adapts to the "strange new contours of life as an outsider in London" (Lehmann 2003).

Nazneen's baby dies, and she is lonely, but in the face of these disappointments she shows courage and initiative in overcoming difficulties. When Charu becomes unemployed, she locates a job sewing garments on a piecemeal basis. She has an affair with the middleman, Karim, who brings her the garments, and through him she is introduced to some young Islamic activists. Nazneen's horizons slowly expand, and when she finally goes on a sightseeing trip to London with Charu and their daughters and utters aloud the word *sorry*, she is taken aback at her own boldness. She picks up English from her daughters and from watching television. Ice skating fascinates her and represents "exhilarating freedom, frozen false emotion and finally a new world of possibilities" (Maslin 2003). Eventually, Charu desires to return "home," but Nazneen is ambivalent and resists him. At the end of the novel, the reader is presented with two epigraphs, one from Heraclitus, "A man's character is his fate," and the other from Turgenev, "Sternly, remorselessly, fate guides us." Ali's book raises the question, "Do we, can we, control our own lives?" and "Should [Nazneen] submit to her fate or make it?" (Gorra 2003).

Immigration is a quest for a better life as defined and imagined by the individual. But for Rushdie (2002), the particulars of the imagined life are less significant than the quest to realize the dream. "In all quests the voyageur is confronted by terrifying guardians of territory, an ogre here, a dragon there. So far and no farther, the guardian commands. But the voyageur must refuse the other's definition of the boundary, must transgress against the limits of what fear prescribes. [She] steps across that line. The defeat of the ogre is an opening in the self, an increase in what it is possible for the voyager to be" (350–351).

Immigration requires the crossing of frontiers—physical and metaphorical, visible and invisible, known and unknown—and the line that is drawn is fluid and unstable. Language is one such frontier that involves "shape-shifting or self-translation" (Rushdie 2002, 374). Learning and adopting a new language changes the individual because all languages permit slightly varying forms of thought, imagination, and play. Crossing frontiers can be arduous, and there are innumerable risks, but the quest to do so transforms the individual, shapes identity, and enables him or her to realize his or her strengths. The individual changes and his or her presence changes the society. "The frontier both shapes our character and tests our mettle" (381).

NOTES

1. "South Asia includes a number of sovereign nations—India, Pakistan, Bangladesh, Sri Lanka—with ethnically diverse populations. In Sri Lanka, Tamils and Sinhalese; in Pakistan and Bangladesh, Hindus and Muslims; in India, Sikhs, Tamils, and Parsees (to name only a few). Immigrant women in Canada exhibit vast social, cultural, regional, religious, and lingusitic differences.... The identity of South Asian women in Canada is partly a social construction by hegemonic practices and processes. South Asian women are categorized as a group on the basis of physical appearance (especially skin-colour), with the cultural differences among them disregarded" (Agnew 1998, 118–119).
2. An outfit comprising a long, loose shirt and baggy pants.

REFERENCES

Agnew, Vijay. 1996. *Resisting Discrimination*. Toronto: University of Toronto Press.

———. 1998. *In Search of a Safe Place*. Toronto: University of Toronto Press.

Ali, Monica. 2003. *Brick Lane*. London: Scribner.

Andermahr, Sonya, Terry Lovell, and Carol Wolkowitz. 2000. *A Glossary of Feminist Theory*. London: Arnold.

Appadurai, Arjun. 1996. *Modernity at Large: Cultural Dimensions of Globalization*. Minneapolis: University of Minnesota Press.

Basavarajappa, K.G., and Frank Jones. 1999. Visible Minority Income Differences. In *Immigrant Canada: Demographic, Economic, and Social Changes*, ed. Shiva Halli and Leo Driedger, 230–257. Toronto: University of Toronto Press.

Boyd, Monica, John DeVries, and Keith Simkin. 1994. Vol. 2. Language, Economic Status and Integration. In *Immigration and Refugee Policy: Canada and Australia Compared*, ed. Howard Adelman, Allan Borowski, Meyer Burnstein, and Lois Foster, 549–577. Toronto: University of Toronto Press.

Chaudhuri, Amit, ed. 2001. *The Picador Book of Modern Indian Literature*. Basingstoke, Oxford: Picador.

Code, Lorraine. 2000. *Encyclopedia of Feminist Theories*. London: Routledge.

COSTI. 2004. www.costi.org.

Desai, Jigna. 2004. *Beyond Bollywood: The Cultural Politics of South Asian Diasporic Film*. New York: Routledge.

Fincher, Ruth, Wenona Giles, and Valerie Preston. 1994. Gender and Migration Policy. In *Immigration and Refugee Policy: Canada and Australia Compared*, ed. Howard Adelman, Allan Borowski, Meyer Burnstein, and Lois Foster, 14–186. Toronto: University of Toronto Press.

Fleras, Augie. 2004, Racializing Culture/Culturalizing Race: Multicultural Racism in a Multicultural Canada. In *Racism, Eh?: A Critical Interdisciplinary Anthology on Race and Racism in Canada*, ed. Camille Nelson and Charmaine Nelson, 429–443. Toronto: Captus.

Gandhi, Sonia, ed. 1992. *Two Alone, Two Together: Letters Between Indira Gandhi and Jawaharlal Nehru 1940-1964*. London: Hodder and Stoughton.

Gorra, Michael. 2003. East Ender. *New York Times*, 7 September.

Henry, Francis, Carol Tater, Winston Mattis, and Tim Rees. 1995. *The Colour of Democracy: Racism in Canadian Society*. Toronto: Harcourt Brace.

Kamdar, Mira. 2001. *Motiba's Tattoos: A Granddaughter's Journey from America into Her Indian Family's Past*. New York: Plume.

Khilnani, Sunil. 1997. *The Idea of India*. London: Penguin.

Kumar, Amitava. 2002. *Bombay London New York*. New Delhi: Penguin.

Lehmann, Chris. 2003. A Long and Winding Road. *Washington Post*, 16 September.

Li, Peter. 2003. *Destination Canada: Immigration Debates and Issues*. Toronto: Oxford University Press.

Maslin, Janet. 2003. The Flavors of a New Land Can Leave a Bitter Taste. *New York Times*, 8 September.

Mehta, Suketu. 2004. *Maximum City: Bombay Lost and Found*. New York: Alfred A. Knopf.

Mishra, Vijay. 2002. *Bollywood Cinema: Temples of Desire*. New York: Routledge.

Nafisi, A. 2004. *Reading Lolita in Tehran: A Memoir in Books*. New York: Random House.

Naipaul, V.S. 2000. *Letter between a Father and Son*. London: Abacus.

———. 2003. *Literary Occasions: Essays*. Toronto: Alfred A. Knopf.

Needham, Anuradha Dingwaney. 2000. *Using the Master's Tools: Resistance and the Literature of the African and South Asian Diasporas*. New York: St. Martin's Press.

Ong, Ahiwa. 1999. *Flexible Citizenship: The Cultural Logics of Transnationality*. Durham, NC: Duke University Press.

Rushdie, Salman. 2002. *Step Across This Line: Collected Nonfiction 1992-2002*. Toronto: Alfred A. Knopf.

Said, Edward. 1979. *Orientalism*. New York: Vintage.

Varma, Pavan. 1998. *The Great Indian Middle Class*. New Delhi: Penguin.

FURTHER READING

Aveling, Nado. 2004. "Being the Descendent of Colonialists: White Identity in Context." *Race, Ethnicity and Education* 7(1): 57–71.

In this journal article, Aveling, a white woman, explores "being white" with a small group of young, well-educated Australian women. Taking whiteness to be "a given set of locations that are historically, socially, politically and culturally produced," she notes that whites do not define themselves by skin colour; nevertheless, her respondents did give some thought to being "white" and talked of their unearned privileges and their feelings of guilt, fear, and alienation. The author concludes by suggesting that becoming aware of racial positionality is "not quite enough," especially if one is to address the implications of whiteness for the work that one does.

Hill, Lawrence. 2001. *Black Berry, Sweet Juice: On Being Black and White in Canada*. Toronto: HarperCollins.

Starting with personal and family stories and then reporting on interviews he conducted with mixed-race respondents, Hill, son of a white mother and black father from the United States, writes about forging a sense of identity growing up in the suburbs of Toronto. He discusses such things as "border crossing," hair issues, the "N-word," and the usual question—"Who are you?"—that is usually asked to ascertain identity, nationality, place, and other such locations.

Hirabayashi, Lane R., Akiemi Kikumura-Yano, and James A. Hirabayashi, eds. 2002. *New Worlds, New Lives: Globalization and People of Japanese Descent in the Americas and from Latin America in Japan*. Stanford: Stanford University Press.

In this book, contributors explore the question of the historical background and current status of nikkei—persons of Japanese descent—in seven countries in the Americas: Argentina, Bolivia, Brazil, Canada, Paraguay, Peru, and the United States. The contributions cover such areas as identity, community life, language, education and schooling, immigration, the family, religion, politics, and economics. The book also provides insights into the special circumstances of the many Japanese who in recent decades have immigrated or returned to Japan seeking employment. Readers are able to note the similarities and differences among Japanese in the various countries over the years.

Hunter, Margaret L. 2005. *Race, Gender, and the Politics of Skin Tone*. New York: Routledge.

Making use of survey and interview data, this book describes how "colourism" operates and leads to discrimination against dark-skinned African Americans and Mexican Americans, resulting in them achieving lower levels of education, lower incomes, and lower status partners compared to their lighter-skinned counterparts.

Ignatiev, Noel. 1995. *How the Irish Became White*. New York: Routledge.

In his book, Ignatiev writes about how assimilation operates in the United States. He explains how the Irish peasants who immigrated to the United States in the 18th and 19th centuries "fleeing caste and a system of landlordism" in Ireland moved from being a "different race of people" to being"white." His argument indicates how race travels or gets named and lived in different contexts.

PART 4B

WORKING AGAINST RACISM

> To talk of race, then, is usually to talk about the events, conditions, and experiences that are familiar and ubiquitous. But it is also to talk about these things in somewhat muddled ways. This conceptual muddle is itself almost an invitation to philosophy, an invitation that one might be forgiven for accepting simply out of habit. But there is at least one other reason to approach this subject from the standpoint of philosophy: race-thinking has left an indelible mark on the contemporary world. Along with many other forces, of course, it has shaped and continues to shape the most private of personal interactions as well as the grandest of geo-political policy choices.
>
> Paul Taylor (2004, 7)

In this concluding section of this book, we present works on anti-racism activism, in which the authors relate how historical, political, economic, social, and cultural contexts inform the principles, activities, and actions pertaining to anti-racism work. As Cathie Lloyd relates in the second reading, depending on the context and analyses of racism, anti-racist responses take different forms, especially in the contemporary context of globalization.

With reference to indigenous peoples, Linda Tuhiwai Smith writes about how concepts of imperialism, history, writing, and theory inform their ideas and issues. She makes the point that "imperialism still hurts, still destroys and is reforming itself constantly." Activism among indigenous peoples "as an international group," Smith continues, goes beyond the level of text and literature to include challenging and talking with a "a shared language" about "the history, the sociology, the psychology and the politics of imperialism and colonialism as an epic story telling of huge devastation, painful struggle and persistent survival."

In her piece, Cathie Lloyd examines the ways in which anti-racism as a movement has been developing in Europe, specifically Britain and France, noting how the movement and its effectiveness must be understood within the context of the historical, economic, and political conditions of the respective nation-states. She argues that European unification and globalization are likely to "increase precariousness among migrants and ethnic minority populations" in Europe.

Tania Das Gupta, author of the third reading in this section, also explores the precarious conditions of immigrants, in particular the precarious employment of immigrants of colour in Canada. She argues that systemic racism inherent in the policies, procedures, and practices of both unions and employers contributes to the lower unionization rates of workers of colour, as well as racist hiring and promotional practices that result in an unsettling work environment. "The efforts of equity-seeking groups within the labour movement, including those of anti-racism activists," Das Gupta contends, "contribute to changes that could be more conducive to organizing workers in precarious employment."

Carl E. James also discusses the barriers of racism that limit access to employment, focusing on the ways in which employment equity policies and programs are understood and taken up by white male post-secondary students. These students are "at a critical juncture of their lives," and as such are likely to perceive "equity programs as barriers to the realization of their goals." James's discussion of the discourses of Canadian students is oriented around questions such as: Why do programs that are initiated to address the systemic barriers to equity and access for First Nation peoples, women, racial minorities, and persons with disabilities incite negative reactions? Why are the programs seen as "reverse racism"? What is the role of educators in assisting students to address the issues of equity in today's multicultural classrooms?

The reactions of white males to living, working, circulating, and socializing in a racially diverse society are effectively analyzed and interrogated by Allan Bérubé in the book's final chapter, "How Gay Stays White and What Kind of White it Stays." In challenging the "generic" representation of gay males as "mostly white," he argues that this representation is founded on an "unexamined investment in whiteness and middle-class identification," which functions to divide the community. Bérubé reports on a number of anti-racism activities in the gay community, relating the frustrations, discouragements, difficulties, contradictions, and challenges experienced by those who engage in these activities. He appropriately poses the question: "What do we expect to get out of doing anti-racism work anyway?" His answer is one that arguably speaks to white and non-white anti-racism activists and non-activists alike. He writes that the challenge for himself and other anti-racism activists is to figure out how to support each other and go into areas of whiteness, not to fix the existing situation, but to expose and interrupt how it operates to maintain "racial unintentionality." As Bérubé states, anti-racism work is "an act of faith in the paradox that if we, together with our friends and allies, can figure out how our whiteness works, we can use that knowledge to fight the racism that gives our whiteness such unearned power."

REFERENCE

Taylor, Paul C. 2004. *Race: A Philosophical Introduction*. Cambridge, UK: Polity Press.

CHAPTER 37

IMPERIALISM, HISTORY, WRITING AND THEORY

Linda Tuhiwai Smith

> The master's tools will never dismantle the master's house.
>
> Audre Lorde[1]

Imperialism frames the indigenous experience. It is part of our story, our version of modernity. Writing about our experiences under imperialism and its more specific expression of colonialism has become a significant project of the indigenous world. In a literary sense this has been defined by writers like Salman Rushdie, Ngugi wa Thiong'o and many others whose literary origins are grounded in the landscapes, languages, cultures and imaginative worlds of peoples and nations whose own histories were interrupted and radically reformulated by European imperialism. While the project of creating this literature is important, what indigenous activists would argue is that imperialism cannot be struggled over only at the level of text and literature. Imperialism still hurts, still destroys and is reforming itself constantly. Indigenous peoples as an international group have had to challenge, understand and have a shared language for talking about the history, the sociology, the psychology and the politics of imperialism and colonialism as an epic story telling of huge devastation, painful struggle and persistent survival. We have become quite good at talking that kind of talk, most often amongst ourselves, for ourselves and to ourselves. "The talk" about the colonial past is embedded in our political discourses, our humour, poetry, music, story telling and other common sense ways of passing on both a narrative of history and an attitude about history. The lived experiences of imperialism and colonialism contribute another dimension to the ways in which terms like "imperialism" can be understood. This is a dimension that indigenous peoples know and understand well.

In this chapter the intention is to discuss and contextualise four concepts which are often present (though not necessarily clearly visible) in the ways in which the ideas of indigenous peoples are articulated: imperialism, history, writing and theory. These terms may seem to make up a strange selection, particularly as there are more obvious concepts such as self-determination or sovereignty which are used commonly in indigenous discourses. I have selected these words because from an indigenous perspective they are problematic. They are words which tend to provoke a whole array of feelings, attitudes and values. They are words of emotion which draw attention to the thousands of ways in which indigenous languages, knowledges and cultures have been silenced or misrepresented, ridiculed or condemned in academic and popular discourses. They are also words which are used in particular sorts of ways or avoided altogether. In thinking about knowledge and research, however, these are important terms which underpin the practices and styles of research with indigenous peoples. Decolonization is a process which engages with imperialism and colonialism at multiple levels. For researchers, one of those levels is concerned with having a more critical understanding of the underlying assumptions, motivations and values which inform research practices.

IMPERIALISM

There is one particular figure whose name looms large, and whose spectre lingers, in indigenous discussions of encounters with the West: Christopher Columbus. It is not simply that Columbus is identified as the one who started it all, but rather that he has come to represent a huge legacy of suffering and destruction. Columbus "names" that legacy more than any other individual.[2] He sets its modern time frame (500 years) and defines the outer limits of that legacy, that is, total destruction.[3] But there are other significant figures who symbolize and frame indigenous experiences in other places. In the imperial literature these are the "heroes," the discoverers and adventurers, the "fathers" of colonialism. In the indigenous literature these figures are not so admired; their deeds are definitely not the deeds of wonderful discoverers and conquering heroes. In the South Pacific, for example it is the British explorer James Cook, whose expeditions had a very clear scientific purpose and whose first encounters with indigenous peoples were fastidiously recorded. Hawai'ian academic Haunani Kay Trask's list of what Cook brought to the Pacific includes: "capitalism, Western political ideas (such as predatory individualism) and Christianity. Most destructive of all he brought diseases that ravaged my people until we were but a remnant of what we had been on contact with his pestilent crew."[4] The French are remembered by Tasmanian Aborigine Greg Lehman, "not [for] the intellectual hubbub of an emerging anthrologie or even with the swish of their travel-weary frocks. It is with an arrogant death that they presaged their appearance...."[5] For many communities there were waves of different sorts of Europeans: Dutch, Portuguese, British, French, whoever had political ascendancy over a region. And, in each place, after figures such as Columbus and Cook had long departed, there came a vast array of military personnel, imperial administrators, priests, explorers, missionaries, colonial officials, artists, entrepreneurs and settlers, who cut a devastating swathe, and left a permanent wound, on the societies and communities who occupied the lands named and claimed under imperialism.

The concepts of imperialism and colonialism are crucial

ones which are used across a range of disciplines, often with meanings which are taken for granted. The two terms are interconnected and what is generally agreed upon is that colonialism is but one expression of imperialism. Imperialism tends to be used in at least four different ways when describing the form of European imperialism which "started" in the fifteenth century: (1) imperialism as economic expansion; (2) imperialism as the subjugation of "others"; (3) imperialism as an idea or spirit with many forms of realization; and (4) imperialism as a discursive field of knowledge. These usages do not necessarily contradict each other; rather, they need to be seen as analyses which focus on different layers of imperialism. Initially the term was used by historians to explain a series of developments leading to the economic expansion of Europe. Imperialism in this sense could be tied to a chronology of events related to "discovery," conquest, exploitation, distribution and appropriation.

Economic explanations of imperialism were first advanced by English historian J. A. Hobson in 1902 and by Lenin in 1917.[6] Hobson saw imperialism as being an integral part of Europe's economic expansion. He attributed the later stages of nineteenth-century imperialism to the inability of Europeans to purchase what was being produced and the need for Europe's industrialists to shift their capital to new markets which were secure. Imperialism was the system of control which secured the markets and capital investments. Colonialism facilitated this expansion by ensuring that there was European control, which necessarily meant securing and subjugating the indigenous populations. Like Hobson, Lenin was concerned with the ways in which economic expansion was linked to imperialism, although he argued that the export of capital to new markets was an attempt to rescue capitalism because Europe's workers could not afford what was being produced.

A second use of the concept of imperialism focuses more upon the exploitation and subjugation of indigenous peoples. Although economic explanations might account for why people like Columbus were funded to explore and discover new sources of wealth, they do not account for the devastating impact on the indigenous peoples whose lands were invaded. By the time contact was made in the South Pacific, Europeans, and more particularly the British, had learned from their previous encounters with indigenous peoples and had developed much more sophisticated "rules of practice."[7] While these practices ultimately led to forms of subjugation, they also led to subtle nuances which give an unevenness to the story of imperialism, even within the story of one indigenous society. While in New Zealand all Maori tribes, for example, lost the majority of their lands, not all tribes had their lands confiscated, were invaded militarily or were declared to be in rebellion. Similarly, while many indigenous nations signed treaties, other indigenous communities have no treaties. Furthermore, legislated identities which regulated who was an Indian and who was not, who was a *métis*, who had lost all status as an indigenous person, who had the correct fraction of blood quantum, who lived in the regulated spaces of reserves and communities, were all worked out arbitrarily (but systematically), to serve the interests of the colonizing society. The specificities of imperialism help to explain the different ways in which indigenous peoples have struggled to recover histories, lands, languages and basic human dignity. The way arguments are framed, the way dissent is controlled, the way settlements are made, while certainly drawing from international precedents, are also situated within a more localized discursive field.

A third major use of the term is much broader. It links imperialism to the spirit which characterized Europe's global activities. MacKenzie defines imperialism as being "more than a set of economic, political and military phenomena. It is also a complex ideology which had widespread cultural, intellectual and technical expressions."[8] This view of imperialism locates it within the Enlightenment spirit which signalled the transformation of economic, political and cultural life in Europe. In this wider Enlightenment context, imperialism becomes an integral part of the development of the modern state, of science, of ideas and of the "modern" human person. In complex ways imperialism was also a mode through which the new states of Europe could expand their economies, through which new ideas and discoveries could be made and harnessed, and through which Europeans could develop their sense of European-ness. The imperial imagination enabled European nations to imagine the possibility that new worlds, new wealth and new possessions existed that could be discovered and controlled. This imagination was realized through the promotion of science, economic expansion and political practice.

These three interpretations of imperialism have reflected a view from the imperial centre of Europe. In contrast, a fourth use of the term has been generated by writers whose understandings of imperialism and colonialism have been based either on their membership of and experience within colonized societies, or on their interest in understanding imperialism from the perspective of local contexts. Although these views of imperialism take into account the other forms of analysis, there are some important distinctions. There is, for example, a greater and more immediate need to understand the complex ways in which people were brought within the imperial system, because its impact is still being felt, despite the apparent independence gained by former colonial territories. The reach of imperialism into "our heads" challenges those who belong to colonized communities to understand how this occurred, partly because we perceive a need to decolonize our minds, to recover ourselves, to claim a space in which to develop a sense of authentic humanity. This analysis of imperialism has been referred to more recently in terms such as "post-colonial discourse," the "empire writes back" and/or "writing from the margins." There is a more political body of writing, however, which extends to the revolutionary, anticolonial work of various activists (only some of whom, such as Frantz Fanon, actually wrote their ideas down) that draws also upon the work of black and African American writers and other minority writers whose work may have emerged out of a concern for human and civil rights, the rights of women and other forms of oppression.

Colonialism became imperialism's outpost, the fort and the port of imperial outreach. Whilst colonies may have started as a means to secure ports, access to raw materials and efficient transfer of commodities from point of origin to the imperial centre, they also served other functions. It was not just indigenous populations who had to be subjugated. Europeans also needed to be kept under control, in service to the greater imperial enterprise. Colonial outposts were also cultural sites which preserved an image or represented an image of what the West or "civilization" stood for. Colonies were not exact replicas of the imperial centre, culturally, economically or politically. Europeans resident in the colonies were not culturally homogeneous, so there were struggles within the colonizing community about its own identity. Wealth and class status created very powerful settler interests which came to dominate the politics of a colony. Colonialism was, in part, an image of imperialism, a particular realization of the imperial imagination. It was also, in part, an image of the future nation it would become. In this image lie images of the Other, stark contrasts and subtle nuances, of the ways in which the indigenous communities were perceived and dealt with, which make the stories of colonialism part of a grander narrative and yet part also of a very local, very specific experience.

A constant reworking of our understandings of the impact of imperialism and colonialism is an important aspect of indigenous cultural politics and forms the basis of an indigenous language of critique. Within this critique there have been two major strands. One draws upon a notion of authenticity, of a time before colonization in which we were intact as indigenous peoples. We had absolute authority over our lives; we were born into and lived in a universe which was entirely of our making. We did not ask, need or want to be "discovered" by Europe. The second strand of the language of critique demands that we have an analysis of how we were colonized, of what that has meant in terms of our immediate past and what it means for our present and future. The two strands intersect but what is particularly significant in indigenous discourses is that solutions are posed from a combination of the time before, *colonized time*, and the time before that, *pre-colonized time*. Decolonization encapsulates both sets of ideas.

There are, however, new challenges to the way indigenous peoples think and talk about imperialism. When the word globalization is substituted for the word imperialism, or when the prefix "post" is attached to colonial, we are no longer talking simply about historical formations which are still lingering in our consciousness. Globalization and conceptions of a new world order represent different sorts of challenges for indigenous peoples. While being on the margins of the world has had dire consequences, being incorporated within the world's marketplace has different implications and in turn requires the mounting of new forms of resistance. Similarly, post-colonial discussions have also stirred some indigenous resistance, not so much to the literary reimagining of culture as being centred in what were once conceived of as the colonial margins, but to the idea that colonialism is over, finished business. This is best articulated by Aborigine activist Bobbi Sykes, who asked at an academic conference on post-colonialism, "What? Post-colonialism? Have they left?" There is also, amongst indigenous academics, the sneaking suspicion that the fashion of post-colonialism has become a strategy for reinscribing or reauthorizing the privileges of non-indigenous academics because the field of "post-colonial" discourse has been defined in ways which can still leave out indigenous peoples, our ways of knowing and our current concerns.

Research within late-modern and late-colonial conditions continues relentlessly and brings with it a new wave of exploration, discovery, exploitation and appropriation. Researchers enter communities armed with goodwill in their front pockets and patents in their back pockets, they bring medicine into villages and extract blood for genetic analysis. No matter how appalling their behaviours, how insensitive and offensive their personal actions may be, their acts and intentions are always justified as being for the "good of mankind." Research of this nature on indigenous peoples is still justified by the ends rather than the means, particularly if the indigenous peoples concerned can still be positioned as ignorant and undeveloped (savages). Other researchers gather traditional herbal and medicinal remedies and remove them for analysis in laboratories around the world. Still others collect the intangibles: the belief systems and ideas about healing, about the universe, about relationships and ways of organizing, and the practices and rituals which go alongside such beliefs, such as sweat lodges, massage techniques, chanting, hanging crystals and wearing certain colours. The global hunt for new knowledges, new materials, new cures, supported by international agreements such as the General Agreement on Tariffs and Trade (GATT) brings new threats to indigenous communities. The ethics of research, the ways in which indigenous communities can protect themselves and their knowledges, the understandings required not just of state legislation but of international agreements—these are the topics now on the agenda of many indigenous meetings.

ON BEING HUMAN

> The faculty of imagination is not strongly developed among them, although they permitted it to run wild in believing absurd superstitions.
>
> A.S. Thompson, 1859[9]

One of the supposed characteristics of primitive peoples was that we could not use our minds or intellects. We could not invent things, we could not create institutions or history, we could not imagine, we could not produce anything of value, we did not know how to use land and other resources from the natural world, we did not practice the "arts" of civilization. By lacking such virtues we disqualified ourselves, not just from civilization but from humanity itself. In other words we were not "fully human"; some of us were not even considered partially human. Ideas about what counted as human in association with the power to define people as human or not human were already encoded in imperial and colonial discourses prior to the period of imperialism covered here.[10] Imperialism provided the means through which concepts of what counts as human could be applied systematically as forms of classification, for example through hierarchies of race and typologies of different societies. In conjunction with imperial power and with "science," these classification systems came to shape relations between imperial powers and indigenous societies.

Said has argued that the "oriental" was partially a creation of the West, based on a combination of images formed through scholarly and imaginative works. Fanon argued earlier that the colonized were brought into existence by the settler and the two, settler and colonized, are mutual constructions of colonialism. In Fanon's words "we know each other well."[11] The European powers had by the nineteenth century already established systems of rule and forms of social relations which governed interaction with the indigenous peoples being colonized. These relations were gendered, hierarchical and supported by rules, some explicit and others masked or hidden. The principle of "humanity" was one way in which the implicit or hidden rules could be shaped. To consider indigenous peoples as not fully human, or not human at all, enabled distance to be maintained and justified various policies of either extermination or domestication. Some indigenous peoples ("not human"), were hunted and killed like vermin, others ("partially human"), were rounded up and put in reserves like creatures to be broken in, branded and put to work.

The struggle to assert and claim humanity has been a consistent thread of anti-colonial discourses on colonialism and oppression. This struggle for humanity has generally been framed within the wider discourse of humanism, the appeal to human "rights," the notion of a universal human subject, and the connections between being human and being capable of creating history, knowledge and society. The focus on asserting humanity has to be seen within the anti-colonial analysis of imperialism and what were seen as imperialism's dehumanizing imperatives which were structured into language, the economy, social relations and the cultural life of colonial societies. From the nineteenth century onwards the processes of dehumanization were often hidden behind justifications for imperialism and colonialism which were clothed within an ideology of humanism and liberalism and the assertion of moral claims which related to a concept of civilized "man." The moral justifications did not necessarily stop the continued hunting of Aborigines in the early nineteenth century nor the continued ill-treatment of different indigenous peoples even today.

Problems have arisen, however, within efforts to struggle for humanity by overthrowing the ideologies relating to our supposed lack of humanity. The arguments of Fanon, and many writers since Fanon, have been criticized for essentializing our "nature," for taking for granted the binary categories of Western thought, for accepting arguments supporting cultural relativity, for claiming an authenticity which is overly idealistic and romantic, and for simply engaging in an inversion of the colonizer/colonized relationship which does not address the complex problems of power relations. Colonized peoples have been compelled to define what it means to be human because there is a deep understanding of what it has meant to be considered not fully human, to be *savage*. The difficulties of such a process, however, have been bound inextricably to constructions of colonial relations around the binary of colonizer and colonized. These two categories are not just a simple opposition but consist of several relations, some more clearly oppositional than others. Unlocking one set of relations most often requires unlocking and unsettling the different constituent parts of other relations. The binary of colonizer/colonized does not take into account, for example, the development of different layerings which have occurred within each group and across the two groups. Millions of indigenous peoples were ripped from their lands over several generations and shipped into slavery. The lands they went to as slaves were lands already taken from another group of indigenous peoples. Slavery was as much a system of imperialism as was the claiming of other peoples' territories. Other indigenous peoples were transported to various outposts in the same way as interesting plants and animals were reclimatized, in order to fulfil labour requirements. Hence there are large populations in some places of non-indigenous groups, also victims of colonialism, whose primary relationship and allegiance is often to the imperial power rather than to the colonized people of the place to which they themselves have been brought. To put it simply, indigenous peoples as commodities were transported to and fro across the empire. There were also sexual relations between colonizers and colonized which led to communities who were referred to as "half-castes" or "half-breeds," or stigmatized by some other specific term which often excluded them from belonging to either settler or indigenous societies. Sometimes children from "mixed" sexual relationships were considered at least half-way civilized; at other times they were considered worse than civilized. Legislation was frequently used to regulate both the categories to which people were entitled to belong and the sorts of relations which one category of people could have with another.

Since the Second World War wars of independence and struggles for decolonization by former parts of European empires have shown us that attempts to break free can involve enormous violence: physical, social, economic, cultural and psychological. The struggle for freedom has been viewed by writers such as Fanon as a necessarily, inevitably violent process between "two forces opposed to each other by their very nature."[12] Fanon argues further that "Decolonization which sets out to change the order of the world is, obviously, a programme of complete disorder."[13] This introduces another important principle embedded in imperialism, that of order.

The principle of order provides the underlying connection between such things as: the nature of imperial social relations; the activities of Western science; the establishment of trade; the appropriation of sovereignty; the establishment of law. No great conspiracy had to occur for the simultaneous developments and activities which took place under imperialism because imperial activity was driven by fundamentally similar underlying principles. Nandy refers to these principles as the "code" or "grammar" of imperialism.[14] The idea of code suggests that there is a deep structure which regulates and legitimates imperial practices.

The fact that indigenous societies had their own systems of order was dismissed through what Albert Memmi referred to as a series of negations: they were not fully human, they were not civilized enough to have systems, they were not literate, their languages and modes of thought were inadequate.[15] As Fanon and later writers such as Nandy have claimed, imperialism and colonialism brought complete disorder to colonized peoples, disconnecting them from their histories, their landscapes, their languages, their social relations and their own ways of thinking, feeling and interacting with the world. It was a process of systematic fragmentation which can still be seen in the disciplinary carve-up of the indigenous world: bones, mummies and skulls to the museums, art work to private collectors, languages to linguistics, "customs" to anthropologists, beliefs and behaviours to psychologists. To discover how fragmented this process was one needs only to stand in a museum, a library, a bookshop, and ask where indigenous peoples are located. Fragmentation is not a phenomenon of postmodernism as many might claim. For indigenous peoples fragmentation has been the consequence of imperialism.

WRITING, HISTORY AND THEORY

A critical aspect of the struggle for self-determination has involved questions relating to our history as indigenous peoples and a critique of how we, as the Other, have been represented or excluded from various accounts. Every issue has been approached by indigenous peoples with a view to *re*writing and *re*righting our position in history. Indigenous peoples want to tell our own stories, write our own versions, in our own ways, for our own purposes. It is not simply about giving an oral account or a genealogical naming of the land and the events which raged over it, but a very powerful need to give testimony to and restore a spirit, to bring back into existence a world fragmented and dying. The sense of history conveyed by these approaches is not the same thing as the discipline of history, and so our accounts collide, crash into each other.

Writing or literacy, in a very traditional sense of the word, has been used to determine the breaks between the past and the present, the beginning of history and the development of theory.[16] Writing has been viewed as the mark of a superior civilization and other societies have been judged, by this view, to be incapable of thinking critically and objectively, or having distance from ideas and emotions. Writing is part of theorizing and writing is part of history. Writing, history and theory, then, are key sites in which Western research of the indigenous world has come together. As we saw at the beginning of this chapter, however, from another perspective writing and especially writing theory are very intimidating ideas for many indigenous students. Having been immersed in the Western academy which claims theory as thoroughly Western, which has constructed all the rules by which the indigenous world has been theorized, indigenous voices have been overwhelmingly silenced. The act, let alone the art and science, of theorizing our own existence and realities is not something which many indigenous people assume is possible. Frantz Fanon's call for the indigenous intellectual and artist to create a new literature, to work in the cause of constructing a national culture after liberation still stands as a challenge. While this has been taken up by writers of fiction, many indigenous scholars who work in the social and other sciences struggle to write, theorize and research as indigenous scholars.

IS HISTORY IMPORTANT FOR INDIGENOUS PEOPLES?

This may appear to be a trivial question as the answer most colonized people would give, I think, is that "yes, history is important." But I doubt if what they would be responding to is the notion of history which is understood by the Western academy. Poststructuralist critiques of history which draw heavily on French poststructural thought have focused on the characteristics and understandings of history as an Enlightenment or modernist project. Their critique is of both liberal and Marxist concepts of history. Feminists have argued similarly (but not necessarily from a poststructuralist position) that history is the story of a specific form of domination, namely of patriarchy, literally "his-story."

While acknowledging the critical approaches of poststructuralist theory and cultural studies the arguments which are debated at this level are not new to indigenous peoples. There are numerous oral stories which tell of what it means, what it feels like, to be present while your history is erased before your eyes, dismissed as irrelevant, ignored or rendered as the lunatic ravings of drunken old people. The negation of indigenous views of history was a critical part of asserting colonial ideology, partly because such views were regarded as clearly "primitive" and "incorrect" and mostly because they challenged and resisted the mission of colonization.

Indigenous peoples have also mounted a critique of the way history is told from the perspective of the colonizers. At the same time, however, indigenous groups have argued that history is important for understanding the present and that reclaiming history is a critical and essential aspect of decolonization. The critique of Western history argues that history is a modernist project which has developed alongside imperial beliefs about the Other. History is assembled around a set of interconnected ideas which I will summarize briefly here. I have drawn on a wide range of discussions by indigenous people and by writers such as Robert Young, J. Abu-Lughod, Keith Jenkins, C. Steadman.[17]

1. The idea that history is a totalizing discourse

The concept of totality assumes the possibility and the desirability of being able to include absolutely all known knowledge into a coherent whole. In order for this to happen, classification systems, rules of practice and methods had to be developed to allow for knowledge to be selected and included in what counts as history.

2. The idea that there is a universal history

Although linked to the notion of totality, the concept of universal assumes that there are fundamental characteristics and values which all human subjects and societies share. It is the development of these universal characteristics which are of historical interest.

3. The idea that history is one large chronology

History is regarded as being about developments over time. It charts the progress of human endeavour through time. Chronology is important as a method because it allows events to be located at a point in time. The actual time events take place also makes them "real" or factual. In order to begin the chronology a time of "discovery" has to be established. Chronology is also important for attempting to go backwards and explain how and why things happened in the past.

4. The idea that history is about development

Implicit in the notion of development is the notion of progress. This assumes that societies move forward in stages of development much as an infant grows into a fully developed adult human being. The earliest phase of human development is regarded as primitive, simple and emotional. As societies develop they become less primitive, more civilized, more rational, and their social structures become more complex and bureaucratic.

5. The idea that history is about a self-actualizing human subject

In this view humans have the potential to reach a stage in their development where they can be in total control of their faculties. There is an order of human development which moves, in stages, through the fulfilment of basic needs, the development of emotions, the development of the intellect and the development of morality. Just as the individual moves through these stages, so do societies.

6. The idea that the story of history can be told in one coherent narrative

This idea suggests that we can assemble all the facts in an ordered way so that they tell us the truth or give us a very good idea of what really did happen in the past. In theory it means that historians can write a true history of the world.

7. The idea that history as a discipline is innocent

This idea says that "facts" speak for themselves and that the historian simply researches the facts and puts them together. Once all the known facts are assembled they tell their own story, without any need of a theoretical explanation or interpretation by the historian. This idea also conveys the sense that history is pure as a discipline, that is, it is not implicated with other disciplines.

8. The idea that history is constructed around binary categories

This idea is linked to the historical method of chronology. In order for history to begin there has to be a period of beginning and some criteria for determining when something begins. In terms of history this was often attached to concepts of "discovery," the development of literacy, or the development of a specific social formation. Everything before that time is designated as prehistorical, belonging to the realm of myths and traditions, "outside" the domain.

9. The idea that history is patriarchal

This idea is linked to the notions of self-actualization and development, as women were regarded as being incapable of attaining the higher orders of development. Furthermore they were not significant in terms of the ways societies developed because they were not present in the bureaucracies or hierarchies where changes in social or political life were being determined.

Other key ideas

Intersecting this set of ideas are some other important concepts. Literacy, as one example, was used as a criterion for assessing the development of a society and its progress to a stage where history can be said to begin. Even places such as India, China and Japan, however, which were very literate cultures prior to their "discovery" by the West, were invoked through other categories which defined them as uncivilized. Their literacy, in other words, did not count as a record of legitimate knowledge.

The German philosopher Hegel is usually regarded as the "founding father" of history in the sense outlined here. This applies to both Liberal and Marxist views.[18] Hegel conceived of the fully human subject as someone capable of "creating (his) own history." However, Hegel did not simply invent the rules of history. As Robert Young argues, "the entire Hegelian machinery simply lays down the operation of a system already in place, already operating in everyday life."[19] It should also be self-evident that many of these ideas are predicated on a sense of Otherness. They are views which invite a comparison with "something/someone else" which exists *on the outside*, such as the oriental, the "Negro," the "Jew," the "Indian," the "Aborigine." Views about the Other had already existed for centuries in Europe, but during the Enlightenment these views became more formalized through science, philosophy and imperialism, into explicit systems of classification and "regimes of truth." The racialization of the human subject and the social order enabled comparisons to be made between the "us" of the West and the "them" of the Other. History was the story of people who were regarded as *fully human*. Others who were not regarded as human (that is, capable of self-actualization) were prehistoric. This notion is linked also to Hegel's master-slave construct which has been applied as a psychological category (by Freud) and as a system of social ordering.

A further set of important ideas embedded in the modernist view of history relates to the origins (causes) and nature of social change. The Enlightenment project involved new conceptions of society and of the individual based around the precepts of rationalism, individualism and capitalism. There was a general belief that not only could individuals remake themselves but so could societies. The modern industrial state became the point of contrast between the pre-modern and the modern. History in this view began with the emergence of the rational individual and the modern industrialized society. However, there is something more to this idea in terms of how history came to be conceptualized as a method. The connection to the industrial state is significant because it highlights what was regarded as being worthy of history. The people and groups who "made" history were the people who developed the underpinnings of the state—the economists, scientists, bureaucrats and philosophers. That they were all men of a certain class and race was "natural" because they were regarded (naturally) as fully rational, self-actualizing human beings capable, therefore, of creating social change, that is history. The day-to-day lives of "ordinary" people, and of women, did not become a concern of history until much more recently.

CONTESTED HISTORIES

For indigenous peoples, the critique of history is not unfamiliar, although it has now been claimed by postmodern theories. The idea of contested stories and multiple discourses about the past, by different communities, is closely linked to the politics of everyday contemporary indigenous life. It is very much a part of the fabric of communities that value oral ways of knowing. These contested accounts are stored within genealogies, within the landscape, within weavings and carvings, even within the personal names that many people carried. The means by which these histories were stored was through their systems of knowledge. Many of these systems have since been reclassified as oral traditions rather than histories.

Under colonialism indigenous peoples have struggled against a Western view of history and yet been complicit with that view. We have often allowed our "histories" to be told and have then become outsiders as we heard them being retold. Schooling is directly implicated in this process. Through the curriculum and its underlying theory of knowledge, early schools redefined the world and where indigenous peoples were positioned within the world. From being direct descendants of sky and earth parents, Christianity positioned some of us as higher-order savages who deserved salvation in order that we could become children of God. Maps of the world reinforced our place on the periphery of the world, although we were still considered part of the Empire. This included having to learn new names for our own lands. Other symbols of our loyalty, such as the flag, were also an integral part of the imperial curriculum.[20] Our orientation to the world was already being redefined as we were being excluded systematically from the writing of the history of our own lands. This on its own may not have worked were it not for the actual material redefinition of our world which was occurring simultaneously through such things as the renaming and "breaking in" of the land, the alienation and fragmentation of lands through legislation, the forced movement of people off their lands, and the social consequences which resulted in high sickness and mortality rates.

Indigenous attempts to reclaim land, language, knowledge and sovereignty have usually involved contested accounts of the past by colonizers and colonized. These have occurred in the courts, before various commissions, tribunals and official enquiries, in the media, in Parliament, in bars and on talkback radio. In these situations contested histories do not exist in the same cultural framework as they do when tribal or clan histories, for example, are being debated within the indigenous community itself. They are not simply struggles over "facts" and "truth"; the rules by which these struggles take place are never clear (other than that we as the indigenous community know they are going to be stacked against us); and we are not the final arbiters of what really counts as the truth.

It is because of these issues that I ask the question, "Is history in its modernist construction important or not important for indigenous peoples?" For many people who are presently engaged in research on indigenous land claims the answer would appear to be self-evident. We assume that when "the truth comes out" it will prove that what happened was wrong or illegal and that therefore the system (tribunals, the courts, the government) will set things right. We believe that history is also about justice, that understanding history will enlighten our decisions about the future. *Wrong*. History is also about power. In fact history is mostly about power. It is the story of the powerful and how they became powerful, and then how they use their power to keep them in positions in which they can continue to dominate others. It is because of this relationship with power that we have been excluded, marginalized and "Othered." In this sense history is not important for indigenous peoples because a thousand accounts of the "truth" will not alter the "fact" that indigenous peoples are still marginal and do not possess the power to transform history into justice.

This leads then to several other questions. The one which is most relevant to this book is the one which asks, "Why then has revisiting history been a significant part of decolonization?" The answer, I suggest, lies in the intersection of indigenous approaches to the past, of the modernist history project itself and of the resistance strategies which have been employed. Our colonial experience traps us in the project of modernity. There can be no "postmodern" for us until we have settled some business of the modern. This does not mean that we do not understand or employ multiple discourses, or act in incredibly contradictory ways, or exercise power ourselves in multiple ways. It means that there is unfinished business, that we are still being colonized (and know it), and that we are still searching for justice.

Coming to know the past has been part of the critical pedagogy of decolonization. To hold alternative histories is to hold alternative knowledges. The pedagogical implication of this access to alternative knowledges is that they can form the basis of alternative ways of doing things. Transforming our colonized views of our own history (as written by the West), however, requires us to revisit, site by site, our history under Western eyes. This in turn requires a theory or approach which helps us to engage with, understand and then act upon history. It is in this sense that the sites visited in this book begin with a critique of a Western view of history. Telling our stories from the past, reclaiming the past, giving testimony to the injustices of the past are all strategies which are commonly employed by indigenous peoples struggling for justice. On the international scene it is extremely rare and unusual when indigenous accounts are accepted and acknowledged as valid interpretations of what has taken place. And yet, the need to tell our stories remains the powerful imperative of a powerful form of resistance.

IS WRITING IMPORTANT FOR INDIGENOUS PEOPLES?

As I am arguing, every aspect of the act of producing knowledge has influenced the ways in which indigenous ways of knowing have been represented. Reading, writing, talking, these are as fundamental to academic discourse as science, theories, methods, paradigms. To begin with reading, one might cite the talk in which Maori writer Patricia Grace undertook to show that "Books Are Dangerous."[21] She argues that there are four things that make many books dangerous to indigenous readers: (1) they do not reinforce our values, actions, customs, culture and identity; (2) when they tell us only about others they are saying that we do not exist; (3) they may be writing about us but are writing things which are untrue; and (4) they are writing about us but saying negative and insensitive things which tell us that we are not good. Although Grace is talking about school texts and journals, her comments apply also to academic writing. Much of what I have read has said that we do not exist, that if we do exist it is in terms which I cannot recognize, that we are no good and that what we think is not valid.

Leonie Pihama makes a similar point about film. In a review of *The Piano* she says: "Maori people struggle to gain a voice, struggle to be heard from the margins, to have our stories heard, to have our descriptions of ourselves validated, to have access to the domain within which we can control and define those images which are held up as reflections of our realities."[22] Representation is important as a concept because it gives the impression of "the truth." When I read texts, for example, I frequently have to orientate myself to a text world in which the centre of academic knowledge is either in Britain, the United States or Western Europe; in which words such as "we," "us," "our," "I" actually exclude me. It is a text world in which (if what I am interested in rates a mention) I have learned that I belong *partly* in the Third World, *partly* in the "Women of Colour" world, *partly* in the black or African world. I read myself into these labels *partly* because I have also learned that, although there may be commonalities, they still do not entirely account for the experiences of indigenous peoples.

So, reading and interpretation present problems when we do not see ourselves in the text. There are problems, too, when we do see ourselves but can barely recognize ourselves through the representation. One problem of being trained to read this way, or, more correctly, of learning to read this way over many years of academic study, is that we can adopt uncritically similar patterns of writing. We begin to write about ourselves as indigenous peoples as if we really were "out there," the "Other," with all the baggage that this entails. Another problem is that academic writing is a form of selecting, arranging and presenting knowledge. It privileges sets of texts, views about the history of an idea, what issues count as significant; and, by engaging in the same process uncritically, we too can render indigenous writers invisible or unimportant while reinforcing the validity of other writers. If we write without thinking critically about our writing, it can be dangerous. Writing can also be dangerous because we reinforce and maintain a style of discourse which is never innocent. Writing can be dangerous because sometimes we reveal ourselves in ways which get misappropriated and used against us. Writing can be dangerous because, by building on previous texts written about indigenous peoples, we continue to legitimate views about ourselves which are hostile to us.

This is particularly true of academic writing, although journalistic and imaginative writing reinforce these "myths."

These attitudes inform what is sometimes referred to as either the "empire writes back" discourse or post-colonial literature. This kind of writing assumes that the centre does not necessarily have to be located at the imperial centre.[23] It is argued that the centre can be shifted ideologically through imagination and that this shifting can recreate history. Another perspective relates to the ability of "native" writers to appropriate the language of the colonizer as the language of the colonized and to write so that it captures the ways in which the colonized actually use the language, their dialects and inflections, and in the way they make sense of their lives. Its other importance is that it speaks to an audience of people who have also been colonized. This is one of the ironies of many indigenous peoples' conferences where issues of indigenous language have to be debated in the language of the colonizers. Another variation of the debate relates to the use of literature to write about the terrible things which happened under colonialism or as a consequence of colonialism. These topics inevitably implicated the colonizers and their literature in the processes of cultural domination.

Yet another position, espoused in African literature by Ngugi wa Thiong'o, was to write in the languages of Africa. For Ngugi wa Thiong'o, to write in the language of the colonizers was to pay homage to them, while to write in the languages of Africa was to engage in an anti-imperialist struggle. He argued that language carries culture and the language of the colonizer became the means by which the "mental universe of the colonized" was dominated.[24] This applied, in Ngugi wa Thiong'o's view, particularly to the language of writing. Whereas oral languages were frequently still heard at home, the use of literature in association with schooling resulted in the alienation of a child from the child's history, geography, music and other aspects of culture.[25]

In discussing the politics of academic writing, in which research writing is a subset, Cherryl Smith argues that "colonialism, racism and cultural imperialism do not occur only in society, outside of the gates of universities."[26] Academic writing, she continues, is a way of "'writing back' whilst at the same time writing to ourselves."[27] The act of "writing back" and simultaneously writing to ourselves is not simply an inversion of how we have learned to write academically.[28] The different audiences to whom we speak make the task somewhat difficult. The scope of the literature which we use in our work contributes to a different framing of the issues. The oral arts and other forms of expression set our landscape in a different frame of reference. Our understandings of the academic disciplines within which we have been trained also frame our approaches. Even the use of pronouns such as "I" and "we" can cause difficulties when writing for several audiences, because while it may be acceptable now in academic writing, it is not always acceptable to indigenous audiences.[29]

Edward Said also asks the following questions: "Who writes? For whom is the writing being done? In what circumstances? These it seems to me are the questions whose answers provide us with the ingredients making a politics of interpretation."[30] These questions are important ones which are being asked in a variety of ways within our communities. They are asked, for example, about research, policy making and curriculum development. Said's comments, however, point to the problems of interpretation, in this case of academic writing. "Who" is doing the writing is important in the politics of the Third World and African America, and indeed for indigenous peoples; it is even more important in the politics of how these worlds are being represented "back to" the West. Although in the literary sense the imagination is crucial to writing, the use of language is not highly regarded in academic discourses which claim to be scientific. The concept of imagination, when employed as a sociological tool, is often reduced to a way of seeing and understanding the world, or a way of understanding how people either construct the world or are constructed by the world. As Toni Morrison argues, however, the imagination can be a way of sharing the world.[31] This means, according to Morrison, struggling to find the language to do this and then struggling to interpret and perform within that shared imagination.

WRITING THEORY

Research is linked in all disciplines to theory. Research adds to, is generated from, creates or broadens our theoretical understandings. Indigenous peoples have been, in many ways, oppressed by theory. Any consideration of the ways our origins have been examined, our histories recounted, our arts analysed, our cultures dissected, measured, torn apart and distorted back to us will suggest that theories have not looked sympathetically or ethically at us. Writing research is often considered marginally more important than writing theory, providing it results in tangible benefits for farmers, economists, industries and sick people. For indigenous peoples, most of the theorizing has been driven by anthropological approaches. These approaches have shown enormous concern for our origins as peoples and for aspects of our linguistic and material culture.

The development of theories by indigenous scholars which attempt to explain our existence in contemporary society (as opposed to the "traditional" society constructed under modernism) has only just begun. Not all these theories claim to be derived from some "pure" sense of what it means to be indigenous, nor do they claim to be theories which have been developed in a vacuum separated from any association with civil and human rights movements, other nationalist struggles or other theoretical approaches. What is claimed, however, is that new ways of theorizing by indigenous scholars are grounded in a real sense of, and sensitivity towards, what it means to be an indigenous person. As Kathie Irwin urges, "We don't need anyone else developing the tools which will help us to come to terms with who we are. We can and will do this work. Real power lies with those who design the tools—it always has. This power is ours."[32] Contained within this imperative is a sense of being able to determine priorities, to bring to the centre those issues of our own choosing, and to discuss them amongst ourselves.

I am arguing that theory at its most simple level is important for indigenous peoples. At the very least it helps make sense of reality. It enables us to make assumptions and predictions about the world in which we live. It contains within it a method or methods for selecting and arranging, for prioritising and legitimating what we see and do. Theory enables us to deal with contradictions and uncertainties. Perhaps more significantly, it gives us space to plan, to strategize, to take greater control over our resistances. The language of a theory can also be used as a way of organising and determining action. It helps us to interpret what is being told to us, and to predict the consequences of what is being promised. Theory can also protect us because it contains within it a way of putting reality into perspective. If it is a good theory it also allows for new ideas and ways of looking at things to be incorporated constantly without the need to search constantly for new theories.

A dilemma posed by such a thorough critical approach to history, writing and theory is that whilst we may reject or dismiss them, this does not make them go away, nor does the critique necessarily offer the alternatives. We live simultaneously within such views while needing to pose, contest and struggle for the legitimacy of oppositional or alternative histories, theories and ways of writing. At some points there is, there has to be, dialogue across the boundaries of oppositions. This has to be because we constantly collide with dominant views while we are attempting to transform our lives on a larger scale than our own localized circumstances. This means struggling to make sense of our own world while also attempting to transform what counts as important in the world of the powerful.

Part of the exercise is about recovering our own stories of the past. This is inextricably bound to a recovery of our language and epistemological foundations. It is also about reconciling and reprioritizing what is really important about the past with what is important about the present. These issues raise significant questions for indigenous communities who are not only beginning to fight back against the invasion of their communities by academic, corporate and populist researchers, but to think about, and carry out research, on their own concerns. One of the problems discussed in this first section of this book is that the methodologies and methods of research, the theories that inform them, the questions which they generate and the writing styles they employ, all become significant acts which need to be considered carefully and critically before being applied. In other words, they need to be "decolonized." Decolonization, however, does not mean and has not meant a total rejection of all theory or research or Western knowledge. Rather, it is about centring our concerns and world views and then coming to know and understand theory and research from our own perspectives and for our own purposes.

As a site of struggle research has a significance for indigenous peoples that is embedded in our history under the gaze of Western imperialism and Western science. It is framed by our attempts to escape the penetration and surveillance of that gaze whilst simultaneously reordering and reconstituting ourselves as indigenous human beings in a state of ongoing crisis. Research has not been neutral in its objectification of the Other. Objectification is a process of dehumanization. In its clear links to Western knowledge research has generated a particular relationship to indigenous peoples which continues to be problematic. At the same time, however, new pressures which have resulted from our own politics of self-determination, of wanting greater participation in, or control over, what happens to us, and from changes in the global environment, have meant that there is a much more active and knowing engagement in the activity of research by indigenous peoples. Many indigenous groups, communities and organisations are thinking about, talking about, and carrying out research activities of various kinds. In this chapter I have suggested that it is important to have a critical understanding of some of the tools of research—not just the obvious technical tools but the conceptual tools, the ones which make us feel uncomfortable, which we avoid, for which we have no easy response.

> I lack imagination you say
> No. I lack language.
> The language to clarify
> my resistance to the literate....
> Cherrie Moraga[33]

NOTES

1. Lorde, Audre (1979), "The Master's Tools Will Never Dismantle the Master's House," comments at "The Personal and the Political" panel, Second Sex Conference, reproduced in Moraga, C. and G. Anzaldua (1981), *This Bridge Called My Back*, Kitchen Table-Women of Color Press, New York, pp. 98-101.
2. See Sale, K. (1990), *The Conquest of Paradise: Christopher and the Columbian Legacy*, Alfred Knopf, New York.
3. See Churchill, W. (1994), *Indians Are Us? Culture and Genocide in North America*, Common Courage Press, Maine.
4. Trask, H.K. (1993), *From a Native Daughter*, Common Courage Press, Maine, p. 7.
5. Lehman, G. (1996), "Life's Quiet Companion," paper, Riawunna Centre for Aboriginal Studies, University of Tasmania, Hobart, Australia.
6. Giddens, A. (1989), *Sociology*, Polity Press, Cambridge, pp. 530-3.
7. The term "rules of practice" comes from Foucault. See, for this encounter, Salmond, A. (1991), *Two Worlds: First Meetings Between Maori and Europeans 1642-1772*, Viking, Auckland.

8. Mackenzie, J.R. (1990), *Imperialism and the Natural World*, Manchester University Press, England.
9. Thompson, A.S. (1859), *The Story of New Zealand: Past and Present, Savage and Civilised*, John Murray, London, p. 82.
10. Goldberg, D.T. (1993), *Racist Culture: Philosophy and the Politics of Meaning*, Blackwell, Oxford. See also Sardar, Z.A. Nandy and W. Davies (1993), *Barbaric Others: A Manifesto of Western Racism*, Pluto Press, London.
11. Fanon, Frantz (1990), *The Wretched of the Earth*, Penguin, London.
12. Ibid, pp. 27–8.
13. Ibid., p. 27.
14. Nandy, A. (1989), *The Intimate Enemy: Loss and Recovery of Self Under Colonialism*, Oxford University Press, Delhi.
15. Memmi, A. (1991), *The Coloniser and the Colonized*, Beacon Press, Boston, p. 83.
16. For a critique of these views refer to Street, B.V. (1984), *Literacy in Theory and Practice*, Cambridge University Press, New York.
17. I have drawn on a wide range of discussions both by indigenous people and by various writers such as Robert Young, J. Abu-Lughod, Keith Jenkins and C. Steadman. See, for example, Young, R. (1990), *White Mythologies: Writing, History and the West*, Routledge, London; Abu-Lughood, J. (1989), "On the Remaking of History: How to Reinvent the Past," in *Remaking History*, Dia Art Foundation, Bay Press, Seattle, pp. 111–29; Steadman, C. (1992), "Culture, Cultural Studies and the Historians," in *Cultural Studies*, ed. G. Nelson, P.A. Treicher and L. Grossberg, Routledge, New York, pp. 613–20; Trask, *From a Native Daughter*.
18. Young, *White Mythologies*.
19. Ibid. p. 3.
20. Mangan, J. (1993), *The Imperial Curriculum: Racial Images and Education in the British Colonial Experience*, Routledge, London.
21. Grace, P. (1985), "Books are Dangerous," paper presented at the Fourth Early Childhood Convention, Wellington, New Zealand.
22. Pihama, L. (1994), "Are Films Dangerous? A Maori Woman's Perspective on *The Piano*," *Hecate*, Vol. 20, No. 2, p. 241.
23. Ashcroft, B., G. Griffiths and H. Tiffin (1989), *The Empire Writes Back: Theory and Practice in Post-colonial Literatures*, Routledge, London.
24. Thiong'o, Ngugi Wa (1986), *Decolonizing the Mind: The Politics of Language in African Literature*, James Currey, London.
25. Ibid.
26. Smith, C.W. (1994), "Kimihia Te Matauranga: Colonization and Iwi Development," MA thesis, University of Auckland, New Zealand, p. 13.
27. Ibid, p. 13.
28. van Dijk, T. A. (1989), *Elite Discourses and Racism*, Sage Publications, Newbury Park, California.
29. Smith, L.T. (1994), "In Search of a Language and a Shareable Imaginative World: E Kore Taku Moe, E Riro i a Koe," *Hecate*, Vol. 20, No. 2, pp. 162–74.
30. Said, E. (1983), "Opponents, Audiences, Constituencies and Community," in *The Politics of Interpretation*, ed. W.J.T. Mitchell, University of Chicago Press, Chicago, p. 7.
31. Morrison, T. (1993), *Playing in the Dark: Whiteness and the Literary Imagination*, Vintage Books, New York.
32. Irwin, K. (1992), "Towards Theories of Maori Feminisms," in *Feminist Voices: Women's Studies Texts for Aotearoa/New Zealand*, ed. R. du Plessis, Oxford University Press, Auckland, p. 5.
33. Moraga, Cherrie (1983), quoted by G. Anzaldua in "Speaking Tongues: a Letter to 3rd World Women Writers," in *This Bridge Called My Back*, p. 166.

CHAPTER 38

ANTI-RACISM, SOCIAL MOVEMENTS AND CIVIL SOCIETY

Cathie Lloyd

This chapter examines the ways in which anti-racism is developing in civil society and as a social movement at a time of momentous change. European economic, social and political integration has had a major impact on the issues facing anti-racists and the way in which they organise. While the main themes of the 1990s have been the increase in racism and xenophobia and the harmonisation of immigration controls, attention must now turn to the democratic deficiencies of the new systems of global governance.

Globalisation theory suggests that there has been a diminution in the scope of political activities as effective power shifts away from the sovereign nation state (Bauman 1998). This process is echoed in the decline in influence of and identification with traditional centres of political activity, particularly political parties and trade unions (Cloonan and Street 1998; Johnson and Pattie 1997). This chapter explores some of the ways in which anti-racism has been developing within European nation-states and suggests new ways in which broader activities can take place through forms of networking within social movements.

We need to situate anti-racism within a historical and political context in order to be clear about what is at stake. A contextualised approach can help us to see the complexities behind the dualism racism/anti-racism suggested by the term anti-racism. The problem is that using the racism/anti-racism formulation involves taking anti-racism for granted and subordinating it to racism, which means that in theorising racism, anti-racism has been eclipsed. There is an implicit, yet unacknowledged recognition that anti-racism is always attempting to become something but is not always successful. The name "anti-racism" suggests a realised project of how to overcome racism, whereas anti-racists are often groping towards an adequate response. In the next section I consider how analyses of racism have given rise to different forms of anti-racist response within the contemporary context of globalisation, which presents us with challenges but also new opportunities.

RACISM AND ANTI-RACISM IN THE CONTEMPORARY CONTEXT

With the discrediting of pseudo-scientific biological ideas of "race" after 1945, a consensus was established around the idea that education, culture and social environment were the main determinants of differences between human groups (Kuper 1975; Unesco 1951). It was thought that racial prejudice could be educated out of existence. However the economistic left tended to focus on class struggle and migrant labour as the "reserve army of labour" which served to postpone tackling the problem of racism (Castles and Kosack 1973). An important difference between the liberal and Marxist perspectives on "race" and racism lies in the insight that ideologies of racism are not just matters of individual prejudice but can permeate structures. This gave rise to the concept of institutional racism which has opened up a wider field of possible social action against covert attitudes and structural forms of discrimination. Such an approach requires us to pay attention to the wider context in which anti-racist policies and initiatives operate.

Anti-racism therefore operates in a wide arena through public policy and legislation, within institutional structures, in civil society and social movements. My account here focuses on anti-racism which operates within civil society, through social movements, grass-roots organisations and the mobilisations of ethnic minority communities. I seek to explore who are anti-racists, how they organise and what they do (Lloyd 1998b). This gives rise to a further series of questions about the future of anti-racism. How will the traditional themes of anti-racism—opposition to racial discrimination, representation of and solidarity with people who experience racism, and the attempt to establish an anti-racist common sense (or hegemony, in the Gramscian sense)—fit into the political discourses of the twenty-first century, marked by post-colonialism and globalisation?

Globalisation and anti-racism both have a paradoxical relationship to universalism and particularism. In the processes of globalisation, increased consciousness of the international is accompanied by yearnings for the recognition of difference and identity (Held 1991: 149). The political aspects of globalisation involve an apparent loss of control of key aspects of sovereignty by the nation-state, leading to a focus on the control of its own population and its borders. Under these conditions it is thought that power leaves traditional political channels leading to opaque areas of decision-making, which involves political demobilisation and a loss of faith in the main political parties, a growth of social insecurity and a paradoxical swing between universalising and particularistic impulses. This presents social movements with new possibilities: if it is no longer useful to focus on individual states, instead movements may bypass their own target state and rely on international pressure and the transnational human rights movement to support them (Keck and Sikkink 1999).

These views are not uncontested: research points to a continuing high level of political participation in most countries of Western Europe; this is quite distinct from political identification or loyalty, which does appear to be increasingly unstable (Johnson and Pattie 1997; Wilkinson and Muglan

1995). Some commentators suggest that globalisation is used to paralyse reforming strategies, and that these developments are used by states to control the movement of poor people across their borders (Hirst and Thompson 1996).

Globalisation may indeed offer an opportunity to anti-racists since "modern communications form the basis for an international civil society of people who share interests and associations across borders" (Hirst 1997: 180). This emerging international civil society, expressed through a growing number of transnational NGOs, such as Amnesty International or the International League for Human Rights, collect and publish information about abusive behaviour in order to challenge offending parties (mainly national governments). These initiatives have been sustained by the validation of human rights conventions by the majority of governments. Thus "the global spread of political democracy, with its roots in constitutionalism, makes those persons within the territorial space controlled by the sovereign state increasingly aware of their political, moral and legal option to appeal to broader communities in the event of encroachment on their basic human rights" (Falk 1995: 164). These developments may also be understood as transnational networks seeking to mobilise through international NGOs, such as Amnesty International or Anti-Apartheid, and which often operate like oppositional grass-roots movements.

A central feature of anti-racism is its diversity. Studies of anti-racism generally agree that it is a "difficult issue" which is not easily accommodated within the policy-making process partly because its constituency is relatively powerless (Heineman 1972; Lloyd 1994, 1998a; Stedward 1997). As a political movement anti-racism may be best understood as occupying different points on a continuum between well-organised, bureauracratic organisations, pressure groups and protest or social movements which challenge dominant social practices and preconceptions. An assessment of its effectiveness as a constellation of pressure groups makes it clear that it does not fit neatly into any one category. For instance, in traditional pressure group theory, anti-racist groups fall somewhere between sectional or representational and promotional or universalist organisations (Finer 1958). A view of the over-arching themes of anti-racist discourse helps to show how anti-racists can be a more clearly defined lobby. Most groups campaign on a variety of different issues: against unjust immigration controls, police harassment, racist violence, or information gathering. Some offer legal services; all tend to vary according to the social and political context in which they operate (Coutant 1997). For instance, in the UK, the existence of a (relatively) well-funded statutory body committed to enforcing the law against racial discrimination, the Commission for Racial Equality (CRE), has limited the priorities and scope of anti-racist organisations. In France, designated anti-racist associations, with tiny budgets, working with a largely voluntary legal advice service, are mainly responsible for the enforcement of the laws against racism.

The relationship between anti-racist organisations and policy-makers is not an easy one. While decision-makers may not always regard anti-racists as respectable or responsible, there may also be pressure from within the anti-racist movement to maintain a distance from the authorities. Both sides may be highly conscious of the disparity in terms of access to material resources and power. The nearer one approaches the social movement end of anti-racism, the more there is suspicion, antagonism and distance towards authority. These attitudes are bound up with analyses of the ways in which racism is rooted in institutional practices and cultures (Macpherson 1999). Anti-racist protest groups face the dilemma of wanting to make a practical impact on policy and keeping faith with their grass roots who are the receiving end of racism (often exacerbated by government policies). Vitriolic debates may take place over co-operation with official inquiries (as with the Scarman inquiry in 1981) or the politics of accepting government grant aid.

Not all anti-racist organisations are equally distant from centres of decision-making. In Britain, Race Equality Councils (RECs) are tied in to a structure funded by a mix of local authority and Home Office money through the CRE. In France some organisations have received large government grants: for instance SOS-Racisme and France-Plus had a very comfortable relationship with the Socialist government during the 1980s. The main focus of these grants was to organise major campaigns which were directed at young people, including lavishly produced "rock" concerts and a national week of education against racism. These organisations carried out important campaigns during this period to encourage young people from immigrant backgrounds to register to vote. There are similar relationships between some anti-racist groups, political parties and churches in other European countries. Governments have increasingly recognised that civil society provides solidarity in a situation of social fragmentation, but this carries with it all the problems attendant on alliances or partnerships: in particular the risk of political manipulation and of co-option. Anti-racist groups' agendas may be distorted because funds may be available for one type of activity rather than another. Or they may become embroiled in political disputes which have little to do with their immediate concerns.

While groups may differ in their ability to benefit from subsidies and grants, another important factor of difference lies in the different resources at their disposal. While some groups may have few resources other than strongly motivated members, others such as the Joint Council for the Welfare of Immigrants (JCWI) in Britain or the Groupe d'Information et de Soutien des Immigrés (GISTI) in France may have slender financial means, but benefit from supporters' professional activities based in law or social work. They are able to formulate demands in ways that policy-makers can understand and use, forming a sort of bridge between protest/social movement groups and policy-makers.

It is important to establish some of the broad characteristics of the different approaches to anti-racism in Europe before we can identify the ways in which wider transnational co-operation might be possible. The next sections of this chapter draw on research and participation in anti-racist activity in Britain and France, enabling this discussion to move from the debate about differences and similarities in approaches to anti-racism in both countries to an assessment of recent attempts to build a European-wide anti-racism.

BRITAIN

In Britain, debates about anti-racism have focused on the problem of conflict between different types of political actors within anti-racist organisations, especially participation, representation and entitlements. Some studies have considered how to surmount the oppositional characteristics of anti-racism by broadening or expanding anti-racist issues, and establishing alliances. Historically anti-racism is associated with movements in support of decolonialisation, anti-fascism and struggles against discrimination and for immigrants' rights. What are the links between these different aspects and do they make some kind of coherent whole which constitutes anti-racism?

Anti-colonialism and anti-fascism were the most prevalent forms of anti-racism in the first part of the twentieth century. Anti-colonialism was so important that it was one of the central characteristics of the British left in the period 1918–64, according to Stephen Howe (1993). It marked an important transition between traditional radical attitudes towards international issues and the orientation of "new left" politics of the 1960s. It also shaped the activity and forms of organisation of early black British political groups, many of which originated in the metropolitan activity of exiled or student anti-colonial leaders (Howe 1993: 25). Anti-fascism was another defining feature of the left, particularly between the 1930s and 1950s. It was however limited by the use of a restricted concept of racism as one among other features of the broader problem of fascism (Knowles 1992). This approach left a legacy which limited the scope for the recognition of ethnic mobilisation as part of anti-racism, and frequently reduced anti-racism to an aspect of anti-fascism. Anti-colonialism, anti-fascism and anti-apartheid involved activists in broader, international struggles which provided a world-view which could be adapted to accommodate the problems raised by globalisation (Seidman 2000).

In the 1950s and 1960s anti-racists began to turn to preoccupations closer to home, in particular the problem of racism against immigrants who had come to work in the UK (as in much of Western Europe) in response to the demand for labour for post-war reconstruction. These concerns tended to be dealt with by anti-racists on a country-by-country basis, although there was some international co-operation. In the UK the point of reference tended to be the USA.[1]

The Campaign Against Racial Discrimination (CARD) provided a base for activists in the 1960s who attempted to promote the cause of social equality and to organise the political representation of immigrants in Britain. In so doing it fell prey to conflicts over the power relations between the black and white liberals and the more radical community-based organisations (such as the West Indian Standing Conference, the National Federation of Pakistani Associations in Great Britain and the Indian Workers' Association). The CARD anti-racists were attracted to solutions which had developed in the very different conditions of the USA. CARD took its cue from the US civil rights movement to press for legislation against discrimination at the moment when this tactic was being superseded across the Atlantic by community action and Black Power. Consequently, the US experience can be seen to have distorted and undermined the British anti-racist movement, encouraging it to develop goals without fully relating them to specific British conditions (Heineman 1972: xi; Sooben 1990).

[...] During the mid-1970s when the extreme right National Front (NF) appeared to be making electoral headway, anti-racists found themselves negotiating two schools of thought, one (epitomised by the Anti-Nazi League) emphasising the importance of destroying the NF as an electoral force, and the other (perhaps best epitomised by the magazine collective CARF) emphasising the importance of a layered response to racism, which was in tune with experiences of the black community at the grass-roots while maintaining a critique of national policies (Lloyd 1998a; Sivanandan 1982).

From this point onwards, for anti-racists to be able to claim any sort of legitimacy they needed to show that they took their cues from the demands of ethnic minority groups and to work with them in some kind of alliance. In the UK the question of "who are anti-racists" centres on this relationship. However, this is not a simple interface. John Rex has pointed out that ethnic mobilisation is wider and more ongoing than much anti-racism because "at all times, and not only at moments of economic crisis, collective political actors emerge" (Rex and Drury 1994: 3; Rex 1996). Similarly the equation of anti-racism and the struggle for black liberation has been challenged by Paul Gilroy, who argues for a distinction between such struggle and responses to the everyday problems of black people (Gilroy 1987: 115). Ethnic minority groups mobilise for different reasons; their lives are not solely determined by racism and the need to counter it. Such groups do not just mobilise to oppose racism and their choice to ally with other groups is one option among others. Ethnic mobilisation cannot be reduced to anti-racism or vice versa, but they are closely intertwined.

The race relations "industry" in the 1980s, which was dominant in local authority politics, did tend to equate its anti-racist activities with the struggles of the black community in ways that led to bitter divisions and competition (Cain and Yuval-Davis 1990). Community representatives were co-opted onto committees to act as advocates in the process of consultation, with doubtful consequences. One of the central problems associated with these practices was an unproblematic construction of the central concept of the community. This policy tended to construct the black community as solely concerned with racism, which led to a too-rigid dichotomy between victims and oppressors as critiqued in the Burnage report on anti-racism in Manchester schools (MacDonald et al. 1989). The report emphasised the need for all sectors of the local community to take responsibility to oppose racism.

In the 1990s there has been increased awareness of the complexity and heterogeneity of ethnic mobilisation. Further, ideas of hybridity and plurality have undermined the idea of the unitary "black" subject (Goldberg 1990: xiii; Hall and du Gay 1996: 113). The concept of "black" as a universal category denoting the experience of oppression is challenged from a different position by Tariq Modood, who points to the way in which this discourse excludes certain groups, specifically Muslims (Modood 1996). Feminist analyses of anti-racism have drawn attention to the gender and class differences which run through the black and ethnic minority communities (Anthias and Yuval-Davis 1992; Brah 1996). Women's role in anti-racism has all too often been ignored. Feminist analyses confronted the differences between black and white women over the role of the family in their oppression, the difficulties posed for women attempting to discuss questions of domestic violence, and the policing of young women's sexuality by the family. Clara Connolly (1990) describes the failure of a young women's project attempting to be anti-racist which was working with the structures and concepts of multiculturalism, racism awareness training and fostering cultural identity. She suggests that a feminist anti-racism would involve a recognition of the nature of racism while also acknowledging the separate interests of women, and it would involve black and white women organising together (Connolly 1990: 63). [...]

Given this fragmented field of action, the question of alliances between different groups with different motives for combating racism is raised. Caroline Knowles and Sharmila Mercer acknowledge that first-hand experience of racism confers a privileged position within anti-racist struggle while arguing that "anti-racist politics needs to be built around issues and ... the only qualification for membership needs to be a practical commitment to challenging racism" (Knowles and Mercer 1990: 137). They see "temporary links between groups of subjects with interests and positions" (84) as constantly reconstructing anti-racist politics according to specific circumstances. In this they anticipate what Italian feminists and French activists term "transversal politics" in which each participant in the dialogue brings with her the rooting in her own membership and identity but at the same time tries to shift in order to create an exchange with women who have different membership and identity (Yuval-Davis 1997a: 130).

*****

The British debate has been largely organised around the assumption that anti-racist activity is about opposition to colour-based racism (Brown 1984; Daniel 1968). There has been much less awareness about racism directed against different groups of people (such as the Jews or the Irish), even though their concerns have been covered in much anti-racist practice (Hickman and Walter 1997; Lloyd 1995). The scope of anti-racism has been largely determined by the central role of the CRE, which has responsibility for enforcing the law against racism and for conducting formal investigations into possible areas of racist practice. This has meant that anti-racist civil society focuses on areas which are essentially conflictual and problematic. At the same time anti-racism needs to build alliances and campaign around different *ad hoc* issues.

This self-limiting stance gives rise to two sets of problems: first that anti-racism risks remaining ineffective and tokenistic, unable to do more than make gestures in favour of lasting reforms, and second that it becomes embroiled in fragmentary politics without the benefits of alliance, which only serves to block its access to the political mainstream. Groups which are based mainly in the white left and which attempt to mobilise separately have been criticised in the past, as in 1993 when rival marches were organised by the white-led Anti-Nazi League and black-led Anti-Racist Alliance. Such rivalries have in the past posed serious problems for the establishment of national anti-racist coalitions in Britain, which have encountered problems due to London-centrism (which gives national status to groups without a broad-based implantation), divided or sectarian leadership, a tendency towards formalism and instrumentalism, and "resolution politics" (Huq 1995).

While still viewing anti-racism as essentially defensive, Cambridge and Feuchtwang seek to understand how to go beyond ideas of resistance which involve "emergent political forces which might combine to reduce and eliminate racist practices" (1990: ix). Feuchtwang argues that "the politics of civil liberty and universal rights ... are the starting position in contesting racism within the discourse and politics of government, civil society and population" (1990: 21). For him, anti-racism begins "with the re-assertion of humanity, citizenship and social being.... The politics of demands for justice, against racialist exclusions and licence to scapegoat excluded populations, point in the direction of new concepts of sovereignty and of public policy" (1990: 21–4).

Developments in the late 1990s suggest that the anti-racist movement in Britain is beginning to reap some successes. Most notable was the campaign surrounding the murder of Stephen Lawrence, illustrating how anti-racist work, which has often operated at the margins, painstakingly collecting data about police racism and racist violence, and forming networks between anti-racist lawyers and campaigners, could bear fruit, given a window of opportunity with the Macpherson Report (Lloyd 1999). Similarly after many thwarted attempts to form a nationally anti-racist co-ordination, the National Assembly Against Racism has shown considerable stability.

I will now turn to a discussion of approaches to anti-racism in another European country, France, in order to draw attention to some of the common issues and to highlight some important differences.

FRANCE

An overview of approaches to anti-racism in France can help us to understand continuities because there are several long-standing organisations which have existed since before the Second World War (or, if one includes the Ligue des Droits de l'Homme, the turn of the century).[2] French anti-racists claim to trace their antecedents back to the Enlightenment and the Revolution of 1789, pointing to precursor anti-racist views among some of the philosophers and the abolition of slavery and emancipation of the Jews during the Revolution (Lloyd 1996). The battles for social justice during the Dreyfus affair and opposition to anti-Semitism and fascism in the 1930s and 1940s were early forms of anti-racist activity, while as in Britain, anti-colonialism and struggles for the rights of immigrant workers have also played a large part in building the bases of resistance (Bouamama 1994; Noiriel 1992).

In the early 1980s anti-racists debated issues about who comprised the main body of activists. One of the key questions related to their affirmation of the positive aspects of the "droit à la différence." Commentators warned that this idea needed to be carefully qualified because it was open to misinterpretation and it was used to advocate segregation and oppose immigration by "new right" groups (Guillaumin 1992; Taguieff 1979, 1980, 1991: 15).

[...] Alain Touraine's theory of "class struggle without classes" challenged the determinism of structural theories, and drew attention to the way in which political conflict could be neutralised if it became entrenched in institutions such as political parties (Touraine 1969). [...] Influenced by the growth of racism in the form of the Front National (FN), urban riots and perhaps his own participation in the Commission of Experts on the Nationality Code (Long 1988; Silverman 1988: 10–16), Touraine turned his attention to questions of immigration and integration. Responding to riots against police harassment in the housing estates of Vaulx en Velin and Les Minguettes in 1990, he argued that "ethnic categories are almost the only ones at present to produce collective action" (*Libération*, 15 October 1990). The social is increasingly viewed in cultural terms in fragmenting post-industrial societies, and people are defined by their ethnicity rather than their occupation or class.

Touraine's associates have taken this focus further: Michel Wieviorka focuses on popular racism, Jazouli on the mobilisation of suburban youth, and Dubet on the problems of life in the suburbs, particularly the "galère."[3]

Michel Wieviorka sees racism as a perversion of social action, a "social anti-movement" which is incapable of structuring society. Anti-racism, however, offers an alternative social vision. He maintains that anti-racist action is only really effective if it involves those directly affected by racism rather than more detached groups acting in the name of democracy, human rights, humanist or religious values (Wieviorka 1993: 418). This form of anti-racist mobilisation is based on the affirmation of identity grounded in racial categories produced by the very processes of racialisation which it is seeking to counter. Anti-racist action by groups who are not mobilising in terms of their own identity may play a useful political, legal or educational role but might also have to contend with racialised identities surfacing within the organisation (Wieviorka 1993: 419). Thus the familiar binary opposition between universalist anti-racism/relativist-differentialist anti-racism reappears in Wieviorka's characterisation of anti-racist actors (Wieviorka 1993: 426).

Wieviorka does not discuss how anti-racism operates in practice. Empirical research suggests that Wievorka's two types of anti-racist actor are rarely found separately from one another. While the problems he highlights may be present in organisations, they are often found in more complex forms than he suggests. Furthermore, this defensive model of anti-racism does not fully acknowledge the positive social project which he sees as central to anti-racism as a social movement.

Catherine Neveu recognises the complexity of anti-racist mobilising as placing different organisations on a continuum between the poles of universalism and particularism (Neveu 1994: 103). Empirical research reveals a much more complex picture over time, with sometimes the same organisation articulating discourses which at different moments veer more or less to one or the other position (Lloyd 1998b). Anti-racists operate in an ambivalent field, caught between the universal and the particular: at one level they appeal to universal values of human equality and the application of social justice; at the other, in opposing discrimination, in representing or practising solidarity towards certain groups of people, they are also working within a particularist agenda (Lloyd 1994).

During the 1980s there was a great deal of proactive mobilisation by young people from immigrant families who established defensive networks against the "double peine."[4] Adil Jazouli highlights the failure of established "left" organisations or existing "immigrant" associations to respond to the changing articulation of their demands in the late 1970s (Jazouli 1986). They developed their own collective identity with a strong grass-roots orientation, and they were anti-institutional and highly critical of the role of the organised left.

The March for Equality of 1983 fitted this social movement paradigm of anti-authority, anti-institutional grass-roots activity, articulating broad, universalist demands and protesting against the social exclusion of young people from immigrant families in the call for equality. For Jazouli this identification of grassroots demands with universal aspirations epitomises the ethical nature of the mobilisation (Jazouli 1992: 53). While the March was the "founding historical act" of a movement of suburban youth, its very success enabled well-funded and more institutionalised anti-racist organisations such as SOS-Racisme and France-Plus to emerge. Their success marked the political defeat of the more radical grass-roots activists who were replaced by people with experience of "left" organisation who managed spectacular youth mobilisations around concerts against racism. Jazouli argues that the grass-roots mobilisation found it difficult to move from the local to the national level, and that in doing so it was co-opted, even aborted. He implies a rather stark dichotomy between the social corporatist organisations operating at a policy and associational level and the broader grass-roots social movement.

Etienne Balibar argues that in order to be broad-based an anti-racist strategy should promote the autonomous organisation of immigrants and mobilise communal traditions of resistance to exploitation. Pointing to the increasing fragmentation of working-class identity and politico-ideological systems of beliefs, he identifies the challenge to anti-racists to prevent sections of the working class and petite bourgeoisie from drifting towards a defensive, xenophobic ideology. Important anti-racist mobilisations by young people from North African backgrounds in the 1980s could, he suggests, form the backbone of a broad movement of associations, organised groups, parties, churches and trade unions, which could join the struggle against segregation and racism and for the recognition of the multiracial pluralist France (Balibar 1984).

As we have seen, some aspects of anti-racist campaigning involve elements of ethnic mobilisation, since ethnic minorities form an important constituency and their organisations may play a leading role in defining the issues, in demonstrating in public, negotiating and debating. In many ways anti-racists depend on them in claiming legitimately to represent a constituency. Groups from the "dominant culture" may also be involved in anti-racist mobilisation but their action is often dependent in important ways on the first, "ethnic" form of mobilisation. In a sense, and in some circumstances, anti-racist activity can be a transmission belt between ethnic minority groups and the wider political arena.

A central weakness of the writings of the Touraine school, which has been so influential in the French debate about anti-racism, is that they find it difficult to conceptualise an anti-racism which might operate simultaneously on several different levels, at grass-roots, in the associations of civil society and with allies in government. This approach obstructs any exploration of the connection between anti-racist social movements, anti-racist associations and policy initiatives, and closes off an important area of work on anti-racism in the labour movement (Castells 1975; Gorz 1970; Phizacklea and Miles 1980; Wrench 1995). At the same time, the Tourainian social movement analysis makes a number of valuable contributions to the study of anti-racism. It emphasises the change in consciousness which comes about with participation in such movements and draws attention to the issues of racialisation, and of who is mobilised and represented. The question of power relations in alliances and the danger of cooptation is a central problem for anti-racists.

Balibar sees anti-racism as intervening where the nation-state "reflects racism back" to society (Balibar 1992: 85). This is a "virtual" transaction which only becomes tangible when the mechanism is challenged, as when North African families were introduced into social housing, Habitations à Loyer Modéré (HLM), or when the Socialist Party discussed extending the right to vote to migrants with residence qualifications. If the "virtual" process of delegation seems to fail, citizens may take it upon themselves to force racialised groups back "into their place," or pressure the state to do so. Because racism is located in relations of domination and oppression and operates through mutually reinforcing relations between public opinion and the political class, it follows that anti-racism must intervene in both arenas and articulate a discourse of democratic rights.

Balibar argues that anti-racist politics is still in its infancy and that "anti-racist movements of opinion will become genuinely political only when they organise or co-ordinate their efforts at a European level" (Balibar 1991a: 18). Minorities experiencing discrimination will need to find a political voice and pose the question of a wider citizenship in Europe, thereby raising issues of democratic control and cultural equality (Balibar 1991a: 19).

There are many differences between anti-racism in Britain and France. Leadership has been less of a contentious issue in France, and anti-racist activity tends to be more centralised on Paris (although grass-roots campaigns are important). This centralisation has made it easier for major political parties to co-opt anti-racist organisations, as was the case with SOS-Racisme and the Socialist Party. During the 1980s reform to the law made it much easier to form associations and there was an enormous growth in what has been described as the "associational movement" which mobilised large numbers of young people against racism (Barthelemy 2000; Lloyd 2000; Wihtol de Wenden 1997).

Inherent to the anti-racist project is some concept of international action and relatedness. It is not surprising then that anti-racism has been deeply affected by the processes associated with globalisation. European unification has been of particular concern to campaigners since the late 1980s through campaigns connected to the harmonisation of immigration laws and to the growth of the extreme right in Europe.

EUROPEAN ANTI-RACIST ACTIVITY

The central aim of the Single European Act of 1986 (SEA) was free movement of capital and labour for nationals of states of the European Union. "Third country nationals" were not included in these measures, which therefore involved the establishment of tighter external frontier controls (Geddes 1995). Immigration controls (along with issues like national security, terrorism and crime) were discussed by intergovernmental structures and were not subject to democratic debate or control. The Schengen agreement of 1985 was initially signed by France, Germany and the Benelux countries, but has had a much wider impact on the rest of Europe.

Many of the measures introduced since the mid-1980s by national governments actually originated from these meetings. The Ford report of the European Parliament argued that by defining immigrants as a special kind of problem, associated with a threat to national security, European governments served to legitimise the racist discourses of the extreme right

(Ford 1992). Following the Palma document (1990) on the crossing of external frontiers, a uniform visa and carriers liability legislation was introduced for all European countries.

In an associated development, the rights of asylum have been restricted: in Germany and France this involved changes to constitutional law, in other countries (such as the UK) restrictive legislation. This gave rise to changes in the rights of many third country residents, including their claims to social benefits to work, and an increase in the power of the police to control identities in public places.

At different levels and in different ways anti-racist movements have protested against these new restrictions and the undemocratic way in which they have been planned and introduced. Some protests have focused on immigration controls and particularly the plight of undocumented migrants and asylum-seekers, while others have concentrated on the need to stop the growth of racism which is seen as a by-product of this new Europe.

In the context of the new Europe, as in globalisation more generally, there has been an increase in interest in civil society. The European Commission (DGV) has been attempting to stimulate a European civil society, acknowledging the need for voluntary and other representative organisations to have a role in a wide range of social issues at European level (*Social Europe* 1997: 17) In March 1996 the European Forum on Social Policy brought together a range of organisations to develop "mutual understanding about the respective roles, responsibilities and capacities of the various actors in civil society in developing a strong civil dialogue, involving both social partners and NGOs" (ibid.).

The efforts to build anti-racist co-operation is an example of the construction of this international civil society. At one level it may make sense to understand the developing consciousness of the European dimension of the problem of racism and of the existence of a common anti-racist agenda in terms of a pan-European social movement of shared values and objectives. Anti-racists are faced with two broad and related problems: first, how to work together and second how to gain access to thie relevant power structures in order to make their case heard.

Issues of identification and representation, key aspects of social movements, are crucial to anti-racism where matters of one's identity are at stake. Differences between analyses of racism and anti-racism can lead to more intractable problems, especially when they impinge strongly upon group identity which may be tied up with national differences as in France and Britain. As I suggested earlier, we may understand the different ways in which this is expressed in terms of a continuum between groups with a strongly universalist orientation through to those who are highly particularist.

Attempts by anti-racist groups to establish the Anti-racist Network for Equality in Europe in 1991 foundered over these kinds of difficulties. There was a debate, led by the British-based Anti Racist Alliance (ARA) and the Standing Conference on Racism in Europe (SCORE), over the priority to be given to black leadership in the organisation. This revealed very different analyses of the causes and extent of racism. It illustrated the uniqueness of the British analysis of anti-racism and of "race relations" in Europe at the time. In the context of meetings between French and British anti-racist activists it became clear that the British had difficulties in accepting that there could be a situation where (according to Catherine Neveu) "the dominant terminology is not a racialised one, ... [and] groups most subjected to racism and discrimination are hardly (physically) distinguishable from the indigenous population" (1994: 99). While the British framed the debate in highly racialised terms, the French tended to think in what they saw as more "universal" categories of equality and rights. Furthermore, it was argued that the black/white race relations paradigm was inadequate for explaining a situation where there are multiple sites of racism, for instance against African migrant workers but also Yugoslavs, Chinese, Turks, and Muslims in general. This meant that there could be different criteria for the establishment of anti-racist alliances: the British focusing on identity based on phenotype and ethnic identity rather than experience and similar political economic and social position in forming anti-racist alliances, which tended to be the basis of other European groupings (Neveu 1994: 98).

Other difficulties were involved in the formulation of the Migrants Forum, a DGV-funded organisation to represent all migrants (King 1995). The term "migrant" was unacceptable to ethnic minority citizens, who nevertheless wanted to be represented at European level. Protracted negotiations drew attention to the British exception, where ethnic minority citizens' access to political rights does not end discrimination. For the majority of "migrants" in other European countries who enjoyed second-class citizenship at best, the British case was hard to understand. Yet for British anti-racists this problem was crucial. "Citizenship may open Europe's borders to black people and allow them free movement, but racism cannot tell one black from another, a citizen from an immigrant, an immigrant from a refugee and classes all third world people as immigrants and refugees and all immigrants and refugees as terrorists and drug dealers" (Sivanandan 1995).

To the extent that anti-racists recognise a similar agenda and share parallel concerns and approaches to their work, there may be no need to construct a formal set of anti-racist institutions at European level. After all, informal cooperation has already given rise to spontaneous and joint demonstrations as for instance in co-ordinating campaigns or opposing European meetings of the extreme right. The European Commission and Parliament does however find it useful to have organised interlocutors and has continued to attempt to create anti-racist structures.

During the European Year against Racism DGV moved to set up the European Union Network Against Racism. This arises from the Union's own need to have some sort of organised lobby to which the bureaucracy can relate (for instance in co-operating with the European Commission Against Racism and Intolerance in the run up to the European Conference Against Racism, itself preparatory for the UN World Conference Against Racism in 2001). In debating how to respond to these developments, anti-racists were caught between the reluctance to compromise dearly held positions and the danger that the European bureaucracy would promote a structure with its own chosen groups and its own programme which would make it more difficult for anti-racist groups to determine their own agenda.

*****

Co-operation is more difficult for the more protest-oriented, reactive types of anti-racist group, which share many of the characteristics of social movements. They nearly all suffer from a lack of resources, and their supporters identify strongly, even emotionally, with the goals of the movement, which raises the question of representation, and a tendency to define themselves in terms of what they oppose rather than what they support. Let us examine these questions one by one.

Informal, voluntary, militant types of anti-racist groups or coalitions such as the British-based Assembly against Racism, the MRAX (Movement against Racism and Xenophobia) in Belgium, the MRAP (Movement against Racism and for Friendship between Peoples) in France and Nero e no solo in Italy have relatively few resources and rely heavily on members' contributions and small project grants for their functioning. Such organisations have few resources to fund travel to meetings, time and personnel, people with the necessary pluri-language skills. Organisations with meagre resources are at a disadvantage in competing for funding, co-operating with well-endowed partners and insisting upon their priorities.

The second major problem is access to institutions. The structures of the EU have been frequently criticised in terms of their opaqueness and emphasis on control measures rather than actions against racism. The important difference is between the intergovernmental structures (such as the Council of Ministers) and the European Commission and Parliament. Key individuals in both the latter institutions have sought to expand their roles in developing anti-racist initiatives.

Following the Vienna Conference in October 1993, the Council of Europe set up the European Commission Against Racism and Intolerance (ECRI) to formulate general policy recommendations for member states on issues of racism. ECRI's responsibilities encompass the collection and publication of data, the publicising of examples of good practice and the analysis of legal measures against racism.[5]

The European Parliament's Evregenis (1985) and Ford (1992) reports established that the rhetoric by which immigration controls are introduced and their content have helped to legitimise racism, and may partly account for the electoral success of the far right (Ford 1992). The European Parliament called for EU ratification of the European Convention on Human Rights and the Geneva Convention on Refugees, and criticised the control of movements of third country nationals by unaccountable intergovernmental groups. However, its call for the establishment of a European body against racism on the lines of the CRE and a European residents' charter was rejected by the Social Affairs commissioner Vasso Papandreou, who argued in 1992 that the Commission had no influence over the criminal law of its members.

Member governments of the EU have resisted the establishment of European policies against racism despite their endorsement of international statements condemning racism, such as the European Convention on Human Rights or the preamble to the Social Charter which acknowledges the need to combat all forms of discrimination "on the grounds of sex, colour, race, opinions and belief." National provisions against racism vary considrably across Europe (Costa-Lascoux 1990; Geddes 1995: 211; MacEwen 1995). Faced with mounting evidence of the growth of the extreme right, and pressure from the European Parliament and the Commission, the Council of Ministers set up a Consultative Commission on Racism and Xenophobia in 1994, charged with "making recommendations, geared as far as possible to national and local circumstances, on cooperation between governments and the various social bodies in favour of encouraging tolerance, understanding and harmony with foreigners" (Kahn 1995).

The Kahn Commission argued that the Treaty of Rome should be amended to cover racial discrimination. The European Parliament and Commission have taken up its proposals in taking initiatives against racism and xenophobia at European level. At the forefront, exerting pressure is the Starting Line Group which includes the CRE, the Churches Committee for Migrants in Europe, the Dutch National Bureau Against Racism and the Commissioner for Foreign Affairs of the Senate of Berlin, supported by over thirty national and European organisations. They argue for unambiguous legal competence in the Treaty of Rome and an EU directive for the elimination of racial discrimination. The group organises among other NGOs and targets the Commission and political parties in the European Parliament. This is an important development in that it illustrates how groups can pool resources, expertise and their access to decision-makers, through forming an "advocacy coalition" (Kingdon 1984; Sabatier 1988; Stedward 1997).

*****

CONCLUSION

This chapter has focused on a set of issues with both general and specific implications. In general terms, I have addressed some of the problems of establishing democratic structures within civil society at a supra-national level. European unification and globalisation may increase precariousness among migrants and ethnic minority populations. Providing they have the resources, groups can exploit the enhanced opportunities presented for rapid communications by means of the internet and e-mail. While globalisation has not closed off political action either within civil society or at the level of the nation-state, it does pose problems of scale and structures in alliance-building. Who should be driving the formation of alliances? How can small, under-resourced organisations ensure that they are not sidelined? The establishment of European policies and structures on migration and asylum have produced new problems and new interlocutors for anti-racists, whilst also opening up new opportunities for intervention. This chapter has examined some of the difficulties which under-resourced organisations may experience in responding to political opportunities at the transnational level. This raises a problem inherent in globalisation, which while creating uniformity also stimulates particularist agendas, for example identity politics, but also racism and extreme forms of nationalism. This is a difficult problem for anti-racists because they are not outside the dynamics they are trying to control.

The factors which prevent anti-racists from responding to the opportunities for co-operation in the new Europe are inseparable from the political dynamics of globalisation itself. Anti-racism is muitifaceted and various. It cannot be wholly separated from ethnic mobilisation because in some instances the two are closely intertwined, and depend on one another. If we separate out different levels of mobilisation (European, national, civil society, grass-roots), we can distinguish some of the factors which divide groups from one another. For instance, organisations vary in terms of their distance from policy-makers. Groups with close relationships to centres of power benefit from funding and may find some of their priorities taken up by decision-makers. This may, however, be at the expense of their credibility with the grass-roots sections of the anti-racist movement who may suspect that their concerns are being diluted. This question of co-option is important for anti-racists because of the centrality of their claims to legitimately represent their constituency.

A central feature of the problem is its imbalance. Decisions about immigration have been taken away from democratic fora and made behind closed doors. There is a widely perceived link between the harmonisation of immigration and asylum controls and the rise of racism and xenophobia. These problems are not outweighed by the scope of opportunities presented to anti-racists by the European Parliament and the European Commission. The opportunities also contain the danger that the anti-racist agenda could be co-opted by these powerful organisations and that groups could become dependent on European funding and lose touch with their grass-roots support, which is a crucial resource.

Even if anti-racist organisations accept the need to form pan-European structures, they still face a number of problems. Racism takes a multiplicity of forms, depending on historical, political, social, cultural and economic contexts: for similar reasons (not simply because it is a response to racism) anti-racism is also muitifaceted. Serious study of anti-racism does reveal common themes: anti-racists all work with changing perceptions of discrimination, attempt to represent people who experience racism and develop solidarity actions. Underpinning these themes is a wider social project about social justice, equality and social cohesion. In different ways at different moments and in different contexts, anti-racists have sought to build consent for their ideas by promoting an anti-racist common sense, through broad campaigning, legislation and education.

If instead of focusing on the issues which divide them, anti-racists look at what they have in common, it may become clearer that some joint projects at European level may be possible. There are often as many difficult divisions between groups within countries as between countries. We know surprisingly little about these features of anti-racism in Europe, and this is an important theme for future research. There is a need for detailed study of the main organisations and also of the way in which they co-operate with other groups in civil society like political parties, trade unions and religious organisations. How do they co-operate within specific political campaigns for the defence of public services and welfare for example?

A central issue is that of understanding alliances and how they work. My study of the way in which anti-racist groups have worked together within France has shown that in spite of cultural and generational differences, a "transversal" way of working was sometimes possible, based on recognition of common aims and respect for the positions of different participants. As a system of "alliances" transversal collectives are unstable over a long period of time, but they also offer a more open, tolerant and pluralist way for pressure groups and social movement type organisations to work together (Foucault 1977; Yuval-Davis 1997b). This is the sort of loose, perhaps *ad hoc* co-operation which may be most effective at European level and points to forms which global civil society may take in the future.

NOTES

1. There was regular contact with anti-racists elsewhere, however. For instance there were attempts to co-ordinate lobbying for legislation against racism between Fenner Brockway and the MRAP in France. See Lloyd 1998b.
2. The Ligue des Droits de l'Homme (LDH) was established in 1898. The Ligue contre l'Anti-Semitisme et Racisme (LICBA) was set up under a different name (Ligue contre les pogroms) in 1928, while the Mouvement Contre le Racisme et Pour l'Amitié entre les Peuples (MEAP) was formed in 1949 from Resistance organisations. All three are still active.
3. This is the state of aimless existence of the unemployed poor and marginalised in contemporary France: "the extreme point of domination, an experience of survival which is wholly dominated by the convergences of the forces of domination and exclusion." See Dubet 1987, p. 13.
4. The "double peine" or double penalty was used against mainly young men from migrant backgrounds. A criminal conviction (sometimes very minor) would be punished by imprisonment compounded by a deportation order.
5. ECRI's web address is http://www.ecri.coe.int

REFERENCES

Anthias, F. and Yuval-Davis, N. 1992. *Racialized Boundaries: Race, Nation, Gender, Colour and Class and the Anti-racist Struggle*, London: Sage.

Balibar, E. 1984. "La société métisée," *Le Monde*, Paris.

——. 1991a. "Es gibt keinen staat in Europa: racism and politics in Europe today," *New Left Review* (March/April): 5–19.

——. 1992. *Les frontières de la démocratie*, Paris: La Découverte.

Barthelemy, M. 2000. *Associations: Un Nouvel Age de la Participation?*, Paris: Presses de Sciences Po.

Bauman, Z. 1998. *Globalization: The Human Consequences*, New York: Columbia University Press.

Bouamama, S. 1994. *Dix ans de marche des Beurs: Chronique d'un mouvement avorté*, Paris: Desclée de Brouwer.

Brah, A. 1996. *Cartographies of Diaspora: Contesting Identities*, London/New York: Routledge.

Brown, C. 1984. *Black and White Britain: The Third PSI Survey*, London: Heinemann.

Cain, H. and Yuval-Davis, N. 1990 "The 'equal opportunities community' and the anti-racist smuggle," *Critical Social Policy* (Autumn): 5–26.

Cambridge, A. and Feuchtwang, S. 1990. *Anti-racist Strategies*, Aldershot: Avebury.

Castells, M. 1975. "Immigrant workers and class struggles in advanced capitalism: the western European experience," *Politics and Society* 5(1): 33–66.

Castles, S. and Kosack, G. 1973. *Immigrant Workers and Class Structure in Western Europe*, Oxford: Oxford University Press/IRR.

Cloonan, M. and Street, J. 1998. "Rock the vote: popular culture and polities," *Politics* 18(1): 33–8.

Connolly, C. 1990. "Splintered sisterhood: anti-racism in a young women's project," *Feminist Review* 36 (Autumn): 52–64.

Costa-Lascoux, J. 1990. *Anti-discrimination in Belgium, France and the Netherlands*, Strasbourg Committee of Experts on Community Relations, Council of Europe.

Coutant, P. 1997. "L'anti-racisme en crise," *M* (janvier-fevrier): 50–4.

Daniel, W. 1968. *Racial Discrimination in England*, London: PEP/Penguin.

Dubet, F. 1987. *La Galère*, Paris: Fayard.

Evregenis, D. 1985. "Committee of Inquiry into the Rise of Fascism and Racism in Europe, Report on findings of the inquiry," Strasbourg: European Parliament.

Falk, R. 1995. "The world order between inter-state law and the law of humanity: the role of civil society institutions," in D. Archibugi and D. Held (eds) *Cosmopolitan Democracy*, Cambridge: Polity.

Feuchtwang, S. 1990. "Racism: territoriality and ethnocentricity," in A. Cambridge and S. Feuchtwang (eds) *Anti-racist Strategies*. Aldershot: Avebury

Finer, S. 1958. *Anonymous Empire*, London: Pall Mall Press.

Ford, G. 1992. *Europe: The Rise of Racism and Xenophobia*, London: Pluto.

Foucault, M. 1977. *Language, Counter-memory, Practice: Selected Essays and Interviews*, Oxford: Blackwell.

Geddes, A. 1995. "Immigrant and ethnic minorities and the EU's democratic deficit," *Journal of Common Market Studies* 33(2): 197–217.

Gilroy, P. 1987. *There Ain't No Black in the Union Jack*, London: Hutchinson.

Goldberg, D. 1990. *Anatomy of Racism*, Minneapolis: University of Minnesota Press.

Gorz, A. 1970. "Immigrant labour," *New Left Review* (May): 28–31.

Guillaumin, C. 1992. "Usages theoriques et usages banals du terme 'race,'" *Mots* 59–65.

Hall, S. and du Gay, P. 1996. *Questions of Cultural Identity*, London: Sage.

Heineman, B. 1972. *The Politics of the Powerless: A Study of the Campaign Against Racial Discrimination*. London: Institute of Race Relations, Oxford University Press

Held, D. 1991. "Between state and civil society," in G. Andrews (ed.) *Citizenship*, London: Lawrence & Wishart.

Hickman, M. and Walter, B. 1997. *Discrimination and the Irish Community in Britain: A Report of Research Undertaken for the CRE*, London: Commission for Racial Equality.

Hirst, D. 1997. "Terror zealot is tamed by market force," *The Guardian* (26 September): 17.

Hirst, P. and Thompson, G. 1996. *Globalisation in Question*, Cambridge: Polity.

Howe, S. 1993. *Anticolonialism in British Politics: The Left and the End of the Empire 1918–1964*, Oxford: Oxford University Press.

Huq, R. 1995. "Fragile alliance," *Red Pepper* (February): 10–11.

Jazouli, A. 1986. *L'Action collective des jeunes maghrébins de France*, Paris: CIEMI/L'Harmattan.

——. 1992. *Les Années Banlieues*, Paris: Seuil.

Johnson, R. and Pattie, C. 1997. "Fluctuating party identification in Great Britain: patterns longitudinal study," *Politics* 17(2): 67–77.

Kahn, J. 1995. *Final Report of the Consultative Commission on Racism and Xenophobia*, Brussels: Permanent Representatives Committee/General Affairs Council 6906/1/95.

Keck, M. and Sikkink, K. 1999. "Transnational advocacy networks in international and regional politics," *International Social Science Journal* 51(1): 89–101.

King, J. 1995. "Ethnic minorities and multilateral European institutions," in A. Hargreaves and J. Leaman (eds) *Racism, Ethnicity and Politics in Contemporary Europe*, Aldershot: Edward Elgar.

Kingdon, J. 1984. *Agendas, Alternatives and Public Policy*, Boston: Little Brown.

Knowles, C. 1992. *Race, Discourse and Labourism*, London: Routledge.

Knowles, C. and Mercer, S. 1990. "Feminism and anti-racism: an exploration of the political possibilities," in A. Cambridge and S. Feuchtwang (eds) *Anti-racist Strategies*, London: Gower.

Kuper, L. 1975. *Science and Society*, London: UNESCO, Allen & Unwin.

Lloyd, C. 1994. "Universalism and difference: the crisis of anti-racism in Britain and France," in A. Rattansi and S. Westwood (eds) *On the Western Front: Racism, Ethnicity, Identities*, London: Polity.

——. 1995. *The Irish Community in Britain: Discrimination, Disadvantage and Racism: An Annotated Bibliography*, London: University of North London Press.

——. 1996. "Anti-racist ideas in France: myths of orgin," *The European Legacy: Towards New Paradigms* 1(1): 126–31.

——. 1998a. "Anti-racist mobilisations in France and Britain in the 1970s and 1980s," in D. Joly (ed.) *Scapegoats and Social Actors: The Exclusion and Integration of Minorities in Western and Eastern Europe*, London: Macmillan.

——. 1998b. *Discourses of Anti-racism in France*, Aldershot: Ashgate.

——. 1999. "Une enquête policière mise en accusation," *Différences* 207 (mai): 8.

——. 2000. "Cent ans de vie associative: table ronde avec Jean-Michel Belorgey, Martine Bartelemy et Catherine Wihtol de Wenden, *Différences* (décembre): 8–10.

Long, M. 1988. *Etre Français aujourd'hui et demain*, Paris: 10/18.

MacDonald, I., Bhavnani, R, Kahn, L. and John, G. 1989. *Murder in the Playground: The Report of the MacDonald Inquiry into Racism and Racial Violence in Manchester Schools*, Manchester: Longsight Press.

MacEwan, M. 1995. *Tackling Racism in Europe*, Oxford: Berg.

Macpherson, W. 1999. "Inquiry into the matters arising from the death of Stephen Lawrence on 22 April 1993," London: Stationery Office, http://www.officialdocments.co.uk/document/cm42/4262/4262.htm.

Modood, T. 1996. "'Race' in Britain and the politics of difference," in D. Archard (ed.) *Philosophy and Pluralism*, Cambridge: Cambridge University Press.

Neveu, C. 1994. "Is 'black' an exportable category to mainland Europe? Race and citizenship in a European context," in J. Rex and B. Drury (eds) *Ethnic Mobilisation in a Multicultural Europe*, Aldershot: Avebury.

Noiriel, G. 1992. *Le creuset Français: Histoire de l'immigration XIXe-XXe siècle*, Paris: Seuil.

Phizacklea, A. and Miles, R. 1980. *Labour and Racism*, London: Routledge and Kegan Paul.

Rex, J. 1996. *Ethnic Minorities in the Modern Nation State*, Aldershot: Avebury.

Rex, J. and Drury, B. 1994. *Ethnic Mobilisation in a Multi-cultural Europe*, Aldershot: Avebury.

Sabatier, P. 1988. "An advocacy coalition framework of policy change and the role of policy-oriented learning therein," *Policy Sciences* 21: 129–68.

Seidman, G. 2000. *Adjusting the Lens: What do Globalizations, Transnationalism, and the Anti-Apartheid Movement Mean for Social Movement Theory?*, Michigan: University of Michigan Press.

Silverman, M. 1988. "Questions of nationality and citizenship in the 1980s," *Modern and Contemporary France* 34 (July): 10–16.

Sivanandan, A. 1982. *A Different Hunger: Writings on Black Resistance*, London: Pluto.

——. 1995. "La trahison des clercs," *New Statesman* (14 July): 20–1.

Sooben, P. 1990. "The origins of the Race Relations Act," Research Paper in Ethnic relations, CRER, University of Warwick.

Stedward, G. 1997. "Agendas, arenas and anti-racism," unpublished PhD thesis, Department of Politics, University of Warwick.

Taguieff, P.-A. 1979 "La nouvelle droite à l'œil nu," *Droit et Liberté* 386 (décembre): 21–3.

——. 1980. "Présence de l'héritage nazi: des 'nouvelles droites' intellectuelles au 'revisionnisme,'" *Droit et Liberté* 387 (janvier): 11–17.

——. 1991. *Face au racisme*, Paris: La Découverte.

Touraine, A. 1969. *La société post-industrielle*, Paris: La Découverte.

Unesco. 1951. *Race and Science*, New York: Columbia University Press.

Wieviorka, M. (ed.). 1993. *Racisme et modernité*, Paris: La Découverte.

Wihtol de Wenden, C. 1997. "Que sont devenues les associations civiques issues de l'immigration," *Hommes et Migrations* 1206 (mars–avril): 53–66.

Wilkinson, H. and Muglan, G. 1995. *Freedom's Children*, London: Demos.

Wrench, J. 1995. "Racism and occupational health and safety: migrant and minority women and 'poor work,'" Coventry: Centre for Comparative Labour Studies, University of Warwick.

Yuval-Davis, N. 1997a. *Gender and Nation*, London: Sage.

——. 1997b. "Women, citizenship and difference," *Feminist Review* 57: 4–27.

CHAPTER 39

RACISM/ANTI-RACISM, PRECARIOUS EMPLOYMENT, AND UNIONS

Tania Das Gupta

[...] Large numbers of women, immigrants, refugees, and people of colour labour under precarious conditions in Canada (Vosko 2000; Zeytinoglu and Muteshi 2000; Zwarenstein 2002). All workers who belong to unions have better working conditions, including wages, than those who are not unionized (Galabuzi 2001; Jackson 2002). Unfortunately, only 22 per cent of workers of colour[1] were covered by a collective agreement in 1999, while the rate for all other workers was 32 per cent (Jackson 2002, 16). This finding is consistent with trends in the 1980s and early 1990s (Leah 1999).

According to Yates (2001, 2002), 63 per cent of all the workplaces in Ontario that unions tried to unionize in the years between 1996 and 1998 had no part-time workers, and 86 per cent had no casual or temporary workers (Ghosh 2003). Yates also found that workers of colour are more willing to join unions compared to the entire population of unorganized workers. Jackson (2002) reports a similar trend, quoting a study by the Canadian Policy Research Networks which concludes that 40 per cent of non-unionized workers of colour wish to join unions, compared with 25 per cent of other workers. Several questions flow from these findings: Why aren't more workers of colour, immigrant workers, and refugee workers unionized? Why aren't unions organizing with more workers in precarious employment? What factors contribute to the low rates of unionization among non-white and immigrant workers, many of whom engage in precarious employment? Jackson (2002) claims that racial segregation in the labour market is such that workers of colour are significantly represented in non-unionized sectors, some of which are low paid and others high paid. In order for the unionization rate among workers of colour and white workers to converge, he argues, some sectors of unionized employment will have to hire more workers of colour (i.e., implement employment equity) and others will have to be unionized. Jackson predicts, further, that "the relatively low rate for workers of colour, particularly men, is probably more the result of hiring patterns than of conscious union discrimination" (2002, 17).

This chapter contests this assessment regarding racism, arguing that systemic racism in the labour movement is indeed one contributing factor, among many, to the lower unionization rate of workers of colour compared to white workers. It suggests, as Jackson does, that the racism may not be conscious—but racism is not always conscious. Systemic racism refers to standard and apparently neutral policies, procedures, and practices that disadvantage people of colour. Reproduced over time through written policies and laws, these practices become institutionalized. Other factors contributing to the low unionization rate of workers of colour include systemic racism practised by employers, which is demonstrated in racist hiring and promotional practices; fear and intimidation tactics of employers; and legal prohibitions or barriers against the unionization of certain groups of workers, along with anti-union sentiment in the community. The chapter argues further that the efforts of equity-seeking groups within the labour movement, including those of anti-racism activists, contribute to changes that could be more conducive to organizing workers in precarious employment.

In advancing this argument in the first section, the chapter [...] draws on 13 in-depth interviews with union organizers and activists, 10 of whom are people of colour and three of whom are white. These interviews were conducted either in person or over the phone during the summer and fall of 2003. Although each interviewee consented to being identified, some of them have been kept anonymous because of ethical considerations. Most of these interviews were a follow-up to another set of interviews, conducted in 1995 for another study (Das Gupta 1998). In those previous interviews, the names of interviewees were generated by a "snowball" method, where key informants recommended colleagues to interview. The rest were identified from conferences and workshops where union members deliberated on related issues.[2]

*****

MOVING BEYOND INCLUSION

The days of the overt exclusion of workers of colour, Aboriginal workers, and immigrant workers by labour unions no longer exist, given the anti-racist efforts of these communities, a process documented by a number of authors including Calliste (1987), Das Gupta (1998), and Leah (1999). However, a focal question of anti-racist activism in the post-1980s relates to the nature of involvement of those workers of colour fortunate enough to be union members. Despite the move towards greater inclusion, the continued marginalization of many workers of colour within unions remains a pressing issue.

One key indicator of the marginalization of workers of colour is the predominantly white leadership in the movement, despite the number of dynamic non-white activists in local areas. This imbalance is reproduced systemically through old-boys' networks that are predominantly white. White women began organizing in the post-war period, particularly in the 1960s and 1970s (Briskin and McDermott 1993; Ng 1995; White 1990), against blatant sexism in the movement.

However, Ng (1995, 38) writes that feminist activism within the labour movement did not incorporate the issues of immigrant women and of women of colour: "'women' meant white women only." Although white women were getting organized into committees within the labour movement and were able to push for staff positions dealing with women's issues, workers of colour remained marginalized. As Ng (1995, 38) states, racism remained a "taboo topic." This bifurcation in labour politics is reflected in labour studies scholarship. Leah (1999) writes that there are few integrated studies of the organizing experiences of women workers of colour. Studies of workers of colour generally exclude the experiences of women, while feminist studies on labour organizing neglect questions of race and racialization.

The role of women of colour within the labour movement has been, historically, to create the connections between anti-racism and anti-sexism as they embody this unity in their everyday lives. They experience both sexism and racism, in addition to exploitation as workers (Leah 1999). In making this connection, women of colour within the movement have had to confront racism from many white women. Some talk about not being supported in their anti-racist activities because it is not seen as a priority, or of not being supported in their leadership aspirations (Das Gupta 1998; Leah 1999). Nevertheless a number of statements, policies, and conferences organized by both national and provincial trade union bodies attest to progress in developing links between feminist and anti-racist efforts within the labour movement (Leah 1993; Leah 1999). One of the most concrete indications was the collaborative work done by women and human rights committees within the labour movement for employment equity in the 1990s in Ontario, a collaboration discussed below in relation to coalition building with communities outside unions. Another convergence occurred in the Women's Work Project (Canadian Labour Congress 1998), which generated a report, written by Winnie Ng, on the effects of restructuring on women's work. The report outlined an approach and generated recommendations for organizing more women, women of colour, and immigrants who were precarious workers.

Affirmative action and equitable representation within union structures are major points of organizing among anti-racism activists. Anti-racism activists within the movement argue that equity policies can be better interpreted and applied if union staff and elected representatives at various levels reflect the membership.

Representation for What?

Equitable representation in union leadership is not an end in itself. Still, it indicates a recognition of racism and provides a means to challenge the historical marginalization of workers of colour and to change the basic structure and practices of unions. As Briskin and McDermott (1993, 95) note in discussing "separate" organizing by feminist unionists, the aim is "unions changing" rather than "individual women changing." They further argue that separate organizing by women has changed organizing practices and educational programs, brought in more social unionism, and enabled coalition building with groups outside the labour movement. At the level of strategy, separate organizing by workers of colour has similar objectives. Kike Roach (Rebick and Roach 1996, 113) says it most succinctly in characterizing anti-racist organizing within the National Action Committee on the Status of Women (NAC): "We shouldn't think that becoming an anti-racist organization just means having more women of colour members and executive. It has to be about the anti-racist perspective, the analysis, the alliances created and the ongoing campaigns NAC develops and carries forth.... Many are happy to 'include' but ignore, so our inclusion alone can be superficial unless our presence makes a difference."

Anti-racism includes a reformulation of the hiring and servicing priorities of unions. According to June Veecock, human rights and anti-racism coordinator of the Ontario Federation of Labour (OFL): "Those in leadership need to understand that their unions need to reflect the membership.... Unions will do a better job if stewards were doing a better job. They [white stewards] don't understand how systemic racism works. They say there is no racism. They don't recognize racial segregation."[3] Veecock is contacted by workers of colour because they feel more comfortable with her than with their own shop stewards or staff members. More diverse representation would enable more effective service and support for members of colour and immigrant workers. More diverse staffing in unions would also influence organizing priorities. Bev Johnson of the Ontario Public Service Employees Union (OPSEU) observes that anti-racism and affirmative action have implications for union organizing: "Either pay attention or die.... How are you going to organize workers who are predominantly people of colour when you don't have any organizers who are people of colour? How are you going to service members effectively when they don't see themselves reflected in the union staff?"[4]

Hiring organizers of colour is crucial for organizing workers of colour in precarious employment, according to union organizers who have successfully reached them. Michael Cifuentes of the Hotel Employees and Restaurant Employees (HERE), whose members are largely immigrant women workers of colour, says: "The community workers are leaders. They are insiders. We explain to them the meaning of a union. What does a union stand for? The first meeting will be with them. These leaders are very important. These leaders have respect in the community."[5] Bryan Neath from the United Food and Commercial Workers Union (UFCWU), which has organized farm workers, had this to say about the representation of organizers: "For example, in the mushroom plant the main groups were Cambodian, Sudanese and Canadians.... If you want to be successful in organizing you need to find a leader in each community so they can communicate with the larger working community. If you don't find these leaders, you can forget it."[6] Some unions are starting to hire men and women of diverse racial and ethnic backgrounds to recruit members from those same communities. For instance, Neath notes: "We introduced something called SPUR (special project union representatives). This reflected the need to make the right contacts with [the] community. If we were organizing part-time workers, then we could get part-time workers who are unionized to go out and meet with them.... If the workers were workers of colour, we need workers of colour organizing.... If they are women, then we need women organizing."[7] The program trains selected workers as organizers. They are then involved in organizing drives in workplaces similar to theirs. They are paid their regular wages and they return back to their own workplaces once the organizing is over (CLC 1998).

Although SPUR is a highly successful program that has resulted in dramatic increases in membership in the UFCWU, including the precarious sectors, not all such programs function so effectively. Some concerns remain generally with contracting temporary organizers of colour. Some of them are contracted or "borrowed" for limited periods of time to sign up new members. Once that is done, their contracts are over. Although they may have been members of organizing committees, they were not treated like full-time organizers. When the organizers left, the new members, many of whom speak minimal or no English, had no one to connect with in the union. Community groups with workers who speak different languages get called by workers of colour unable to get through to their unions. Opportunistic methods of organizing often end up in failures, as workers have been known to decertify under such conditions or to end up with bad agreements. For example, after an intensive organizing drive of predominantly non-English-speaking contract workers of colour, a union signed a "bad deal," according to an organizer of colour, one in which she did not have any input. Similarly, a local of another union, composed predominantly of workers of colour, wanted to decertify because the union had no staff members who could represent them and it provided no translation services.[8] This point is captured by Hasan Yussuff of the CLC, who says that we need to consider "how we do organizing that is not just about bringing in a new membership dues base but integrates workers of colour fundamentally at every level" (CLC 1998, 28).

Anti-racism activists in the labour movement feel that more workers of colour in staff and elected positions will initiate changes in organized labour's priorities, practices, and policies. More emphasis will be given to the needs and issues of workers located in the most precarious forms of employment in society—immigrants, refugees, and workers of colour in unorganized sectors or in workplaces poorly serviced by unions. Greater effort will be put into working in coalitions with community groups, many of which are in touch with unorganized workers of colour in precarious employment, whether self-help organizations, ethnic networks, support groups in neighbourhoods, or worker centres. Trade unionists of colour self-organized within the labour movement, such as the Ontario Coalition of Black Trade Unionists in 1986, the Coalition of Black Trade Unionists (Ontario Chapter) in 1996, and the Asian Canadian Labour Alliance in 2000, have links with communities outside the labour movement. The Asian Canadian Labour Alliance, for instance, has a two-pronged strategy of bringing labour leaders and rank-and-file members of Asian heritage together, as well as bringing Asian activists together to create a union-friendly culture overall. The Coalition of Black Trade Unionists has been active on the campaign against racial profiling in the Black community. Bev Johnson, ex-president of the union, wants to reach out particularly to Black youth, to bring them into the labour movement as future leaders. She articulates a concern shared by a number of people interviewed about the younger generation of labour leaders being largely white. Marie Clarke Walker, executive vice-president of the Canadian Labour Congress, says that she spent a year trying to connect her union with community issues when she was elected onto the Canadian Union of Public Employees (CUPE) executive committee in Ontario in 1999: "Members belong to communities before they belong to unions.... People don't just see you as a dues grabbing institution. They see you as genuinely concerned."[9]

A brief but important period of coalition-based organizing among various segments of the labour movement and community organizations occurred around the issue of employment equity in the early part of the 1990s in Ontario. The Ontario Federation of Labour and affiliated unions became integrally involved in drafting Bill 79, the precursor to the *Employment Equity Act*, which the New Democratic Party (NDP) would steer forward into law in 1994. The provincial labour movement and its equity activists were at the forefront of this development along with community organizations of women, people of colour, people with disabilities, and Aboriginal peoples. Union activists spent hundreds of hours on equity issues, and grassroots community activists facilitated workshops, prepared brochures, and informed people about the concept, fostering the environment for the successful adoption of legislation (Das Gupta 1998). The movement was pushed into taking this position by activists from outside and from within. Sadly, with the defeat of the Ontario NDP government in 1995, the *Employment Equity Act*, even the watered-down version that was passed, and all its infrastructure were scrapped overnight.

Another example of a community-labour coalition was the Coalition for Fair Wages and Working Conditions for Homeworkers, initiated by the International Ladies Garment Workers' Union (now Union of Needletrades, Industrial and Textile Employees, or UNITE) in 1991, which engaged in various public activities to voice the concerns of this very precarious group of workers (Borowy, Gordon, and Lebans 1993). Made up of labour, women's, immigrant, and church communities, the coalition focused on public education through press conferences and a large conference on homework. It put pressure on retail firms to improve the wages and working conditions of homeworkers, and it pressured the government for stronger legislative protection of homeworkers and for sectoral bargaining. In addition, the coalition spearheaded a campaign to raise the awareness of consumers about the exploitation of homeworkers for the production of garments and to develop a consumer campaign, called the "Clean Clothes Campaign," for fair wages and working conditions for homeworkers.

Changing Structures

The labour movement has made significant progress in addressing racism. In the words of the CLC's Yussuff: "The labour movement is dealing with equity. It is in the mainstream. There is a recognition that it [racism] is a problem and that resources must be allocated to deal with it. Twenty years ago it may have been dismissed.... People of colour have tremendous opportunity to be confident in shaping the direction of the labour movement."[10]

While it is true that workers of colour are much better represented today (CLC 1997, 98) than they were 20 years back, there are still lingering problems and resistance to equity in some quarters. Some of the interviewees, particularly women of colour activists, spoke about problems of co-optation, tokenism, harassment of women of colour, and their silencing.[11] Groups like the Coalition of Black Trade Unionists and the Asian Canadian Labour Alliance are still viewed by some as community groups because they are outside the labour structure and do not always agree with the labour movement. One member said that there is still a strong sense of control over caucuses through "report back" processes. There is still a fear among some people that community groups threaten the labour movement. These reactions all indicate resistance against anti-racism and change, as well as a lack of openness and democracy.

Anti-racism activists would like to see structural changes (CLC 1997, 6) in the way in which the labour movement works, including how decisions are made and how meetings are conducted. The supposedly democratic structures are, in reality, often exclusionary. Marie Clarke Walker[12] told how a resolution to bring in two designated seats on the executive of CUPE, one for workers of colour and the other for Aboriginal workers, was defeated because it was brought in at the end of the day, when the audience had dwindled and no one was there to debate it. June Veecock of the Ontario Federation of Labour noted that leadership "education is good, but it does nothing to change the structure.... There are systemic barriers that need to be removed. They [people of colour] feel uncomfortable with those structures ... the onus is on people of colour to go back and make changes in structures."[13] Carol Wall, a former human rights director with the Communications, Energy and Paperworkers Union of Canada (CEP), observed that "structures don't help around equity and human rights issues. The democratic structures are used to silence."[14] A turning point in anti-racism within the Canadian Labour Congress occurred in Montreal during the 1990 convention. Dory Smith, a Black male member, ran against the white slate and received over a thousand votes. As one activist said, it "made the white boys sit up and take note." A resolution was passed to review the constitution and recommend changes to it. In the 1992 convention, a recommendation was brought forth to create a position on the executive committee for a member of colour. Many felt that this recommendation was tokenism. The Ontario Coalition of Black Trade Unionists and other anti-racist activists organized and achieved, instead, the designation of two seats. But structural change threatens many old-timers who want to maintain the status quo.

Exclusion—New Style

Just as union structures have sometimes resulted in the marginalization and silencing of unionists of colour, traditional methods of organizing exclude workers in precarious employment today. Most unions still function on the model of a traditional workplace and a standard worker who works 9 to 5 and is white, male, and English-speaking. Although these received practices and frameworks have been modified, to a certain extent, by the intervention of women and by non-whites, they need to be challenged even more. In order to organize workers in precarious employment, the assumptions that are taken for granted in the organizing process need to be examined and changed if necessary, and more creative strategies need to be incorporated. Ideas around organizing precarious workers have been greatly influenced by the writings of Kate Bronfenbrenner, director of Labour Education Research at Cornell University (CLC 1998). In 1995 she spoke at a conference on community unionism organized by the Ontario Federation of Labour. The following discussion is a reflection of some of her insights.

In order to include workers in precarious employment within the labour movement, organizing has to be seen as a longer-term project, not something that can be accomplished by speedy weekend campaigns or "blitzes" followed by worker sign-ups. The outreach process has to be more innovative, often requiring labour-intensive methods of contacting workers and then of building trust, a sense of community, and indigenous leadership through training and education programs. The current approaches do not allow that process in most unions. Longer, labour-intensive organizing campaigns require more resources—resources that are not always forthcoming. One success story is the organizing drive at Purdy's Chocolates (Ghosh 2003) in Vancouver, a campaign that included a minority of white, mainly full-time, workers and part-time workers who were originally from China, the Philippines, Vietnam, and Latin America. That campaign took six years to conclude under the Communications, Energy and Paperworkers Union of Canada (CEP). This long, costly campaign included two certification drives because the employer contested the first one. Cifuentes of the Hotel Employees and Restaurant Employees explains the process of organizing in one particular workplace:

> There are four different ethnic groups. Now they are phoning and saying ... "Well, I signed the card, can I take the card back ... it is taking too long." We have to tell them that it sometimes happens like this, it takes some time. Each vote counts, so we have to make it clear, when the company hears of the organizing, they will work on the employee one by one, trying to convince him/her not to join. When there is someone who we identify that is not solid, then we make home visits. We need to resolve the confidence of the worker. Sometimes they think what they are doing is illegal. We have to explain everything ... the meaning of the union ... we have to explain everything....[15]

All organizers interviewed about organizing workers in precarious employment spoke about the intensive and sometimes lengthy nature of the organizing process, particularly given the high level of employer intimidation tactics with immigrant workers and workers of colour and the stringent requirements for union certification under the former Progressive Conservative government in Ontario. These insights are substantiated by experiences in other successful organizing drives with precarious workers that have been documented by the CLC (1998). Those unions that are unable, for whatever reason, to allocate significant resources to organizing "stake out familiar territory," according to Galabuzi (Ghosh 2003), where it is easier to organize, mobilize, and develop leadership. Workers in this territory are also often better-paid standard workers and, consequently, their dues paying is more regular and reliable.

One informant[16] provided an even more critical perspective of this approach. Her union would take on organizing drives based on what, in effect, were ethnic and racial stereotypes. They assumed that workers of colour were more prone to unionizing if they came from a situation of collective struggle. In this mindset, Latin Americans, Filipinos, and Sri Lankans would unionize much faster than Chinese, for instance. The union would then prioritize its organizing strategy based on such assumptions. This approach is not only tantamount to racialized thinking but also opportunist. It promotes competition among organizers working within different communities, emanating from the "How many members have you signed up today?" mentality. It promotes organizing as piecework rather than a long-term process of building on a union base in a workplace or a community [...]. This organizer, who challenged the mode of operation within her union by laying down different principles, was isolated and marginalized. By this logic, some workers of colour are still being excluded, although more systemically. It appears that certain groups are still being labelled by some unions as "unorganizable."

CONCLUSION

Systemic racism persists in the labour movement, although the movement has come a long way from the blatant exclusionism practised in the early 20th century. Racism today is characterized by authors as a "new" or "democratic" variety of racism (Henry and Tator 2000) that employs non-racial discourses to "otherize" immigrants and people of colour. These discourses allow the co-existence of progressive policies and laws with racist practices and effects. Such discourses include "denial of racism," "blaming the victim," or "pathologizing the victim." While unions have been in the forefront of advocating for equity and combating racism, sexism, and various other discriminatory practices in the larger society, they have been slower in acknowledging racism within their own organizations. This trend is exemplified by the persistence of old structures, procedures, and practices that prevent unionists of colour from becoming central actors in the movement, despite the emergence of strong equity policies. At the same time, old union practices around organizing keep many workers in precarious employment out. Anti-racist union activists want a labour movement that moves issues confronting workers of colour to the centre of the agenda, including challenging racism and sexism in the workplace and in society at large, mitigating precarious working conditions, and facilitating greater access to the labour movement so more scope exists for their participation and leadership. The structural changes and union democracy desired by equity-seeking groups within the labour movement are the same changes that workers in precarious employment require to participate fully in the movement.

NOTES

1. Jackson notes that this category does not include Aboriginal workers and those workers who reported "didn't know" when asked about visible minority status.
2. CLC Women's Organizing Symposium, Toronto, October 20–22, 2002; Labour Council of Toronto and York Region, "Building Power: Aboriginal/Workers of Colour Conference," Toronto, June 14, 2003.
3. Interview with June Veecock, Ontario Federation of Labour, June 17, 2003, Toronto.
4. Interview with Bev Johnson, Ontario Public Service Employees Union, June 17, 2003, Toronto.
5. Interview with Michael Cifuentes, HERE, September 25, 2003, Toronto.
6. Interview with Bryan Neath, UFCWU, September 4, 2003, Toronto.
7. Ibid.
8. Interview with anonymous organizer, September 8, 2003, Toronto.
9. Interview with Marie Clarke Walker, CLC, September 19, 2003, Toronto.
10. Interview with Hassan Yussuff, CLC, June 19, 2003, Ottawa.
11. Another article by this author describes in more detail these problems that exist in the labour movement. It is a chapter in *Union Responses to Equity in Canada*, edited by Gerald Hunt and David Rayside (Toronto: University of Toronto Press, forthcoming).

12. Interview with Marie Clarke Walker.
13. Interview with June Veecock, OFL, June 17, 2003, Toronto.
14. Interview with Carol Wall, Public Sector Alliance of Canada (PSAC), September 22, 2003, Ottawa.
15. Interview with Michael Cifuentes, HERE, September 25, 2003, Toronto.
16. Interview with anonymous organizer, September 24, 2003, Toronto.

REFERENCES

Borowy, Jan, Shelly Gordon, and Gayle Lebans. 1993. "Are These Clothes Clean? The Campaign for Fair Wages and Working Conditions for Homeworkers." In L. Carty, ed., *And Still We Rise: Feminist Political Mobilizing in Contemporary Canada*, 299–332. Toronto: Toronto Women's Press.

Briskin, Linda, and Patricia McDermott. 1993. *Women Challenging Unions: Feminism, Democracy and Militancy*. Toronto: University of Toronto Press.

Calliste, Agnes. 1987. "Sleeping Car Porters in Canada: An Ethnically Submerged Split Labour Market." *Canadian Ethnic Studies* 19 (1) 1–20.

Canadian Labour Congress, 1997. *Challenging Racism: Going Beyond Recommendations*. Report of the CLC National Anti-Racism Task Force.

——. 1998. *No Easy Recipe: Building the Diversity and Strength of the Labour Movement: Feminist Organizing Models*. CLC Women's Symposium, November 1–3.

——. 2003. *Falling Unemployment Insurance Protection for Canada's Unemployed*. March. Ottawa: CLC. Available from www.unemployed.ca

Das Gupta, Tania. 1998 "Anti-Racism and the Organized Labour Movement." In Vic Satzewich, ed., *Racism and Social Inequality in Canada*, 315–34. Toronto: Thompson Educational.

Galabuzi, Grace-Edward. 2001. *Canada's Creeping Economic Apartheid*. Toronto: Center for Social Justice. Available from www.socialjustice.org.

Ghosh, Sabitri. 2003. "Immigrant Workers and Unions." *This Magazine* (January/February).

Henry, Frances, and Carol Tator. 2000. *The Colour of Democracy: Racism in Canadian Society*. Toronto: Harcourt Brace.

Jackson, Andrew. 2002. "Is Work Working for Workers of Colour?" Canadian Labour Congress, Research Paper 18.

Leah, Ronnie. 1993. "Black Women Speak Out: Racism and Unions." In Linda Briskin and Pat McDermott, eds., *Women Challenging Unions: Feminism, Democracy and Militancy*, 157–72. Toronto: University of Toronto Press.

——. 1999 "Do You Call Me 'Sister'? Women of Colour and the Canadian Labour Movement." In Enakshi Dua and A. Robertson, eds., *Scratching the Surface: Canadian Anti-racist Feminist Thought*, 97–126. Toronto: Women's Press.

Ng, Winnie Wun Wun. 1995. "In the Margins: Challenging Racism in the Labour Movement." MA thesis, University of Toronto.

Rebick, Judy, and Kike Roach. 1996. *Politically Speaking*. Vancouver: Douglas & McIntyre.

Vosko, Leah. 2000. *Temporary Work: The Gendered Rise of a Precarious Employment Relationship*. Toronto: University of Toronto Press.

White, Julie. 1990. *Mail and Female: Women and the Canadian Union of Postal Workers*. Toronto: Thompson Educational Publishing.

Yates, Charlotte, 2001. *Making It: Your Economic Unions and Economic Justice*. Toronto: The CSJ Foundation for Research and Education and the Ontario Federation of Labour.

——. 2002. "Expanding Labour's Horizons: Union Organizing and Strategic Change in Canada." *Just Labour* 1 (2): 31–40.

Zeytinoglu, Isik Urla, and Jacinta Khasiala Muteshi. 1999. "Gender, Race and Class Dimensions of Nonstandard Work." *Relations Industrielles/Industrial Relations* 55 (1): 133–67.

Zwarenstein, Carolyn. 2002. "Smalltown Big Issues." *Our Times* 21 (3): 14–21.

CHAPTER 40

"REVERSE RACISM?" STUDENTS' RESPONSES TO EQUITY PROGRAMS

Carl E. James

> Our commitment to address racism must not paralyze us. We should not be afraid to question, to make mistakes, and above all to learn. We should all commit ourselves to rights literacy for ourselves, our families, and our clients.... The process of naming racism is not an indictment, it is an opportunity for change.
>
> Joanne St. Lewis (1996: 119)

During class discussion on the issue of equity and access for women and racial minorities, it was argued that too many jobs today are closed to white males because of the employment equity law in Ontario. Indeed, a number of job advertisements routinely state the organization's commitment to employment equity. For instance, advertisements might state: "[Organization] is committed to employment equity and encourages applicants from all qualified candidates, including Aboriginal peoples, persons with disabilities, visible minorities (or people of colour) and women."

For some, this statement represents "discrimination against white males." They perceive it to be "unfair" and "wrong," and it does not make sense to them as a way of achieving equity. The students argue that such advertisements are problematic in the case of governments, which are supposed to operate in the interest of all residents. It is further seen as a violation of the "merit principle," which has been replaced by hiring based on "racial quotas." So why do programs that have been initiated to address the systemic barriers to equity and access for First Nation peoples, women, racial minorities and persons with disabilities incite such negative reactions? Why do students, and white males in particular, react to equity and access programs in such a negative way? Why are the programs seen as "reverse racism"? What is racism and how does is it different from "reverse racism"? What is the role of educators in assisting students to address the issues of equity in today's multiracial classrooms?

In this discussion we will explore some of the ways in which white male college and university students have been grappling with the issues of race, racism and equity at a critical juncture of their lives and in a culturally and racially diverse and changing society, and how the notions of merit and privilege feature in their discussions. Many of the ideas and issues presented are informed by the foregoing essays and discussions. It is important to examine the reactions of young white male students to issues of equity in order to understand their perception of equity programs as barriers to the realization of their goals.

Racism is more than acts of discrimination. It is not something that is experienced by all racial groups in the same way. We must "take into account the effects of unequal power" relations in our society (Neufeld, 1992: B7). Hence, racism is understood in terms of the collective—how individuals, because of their membership in a particular racial group, are privileged or disadvantaged by the structural and cultural factors in society. Compared to prejudice, which is found within all groups, racism is associated with those who have "the power to enforce and act on their prejudices" (Dobbins and Skillings, 1991: 41).

Racism must be constructed in terms of historical and structural factors if current equity programs are to be seen as valid and appropriate. Challenges and criticism raised by individuals about equity and access policies, practices and programs that target race [...] are justified only if racism is seen in terms of the attitudes and actions of individuals against other individuals, based on individual ignorance. We know, however, that rather than being perceived as the attitudes and behaviours of individuals, racism must be perceived in terms of policies and practices that have been the prevailing norm of institutions that have operated for years in favour of those by whom and for whom they have been constructed in the first place. And as Henry and Ginzberg (1985) found in their study of racial discrimination in employment in Toronto, "White Canadians have greater opportunities to set up job interviews and are subject to less pre-interview screening" (p. 49) while racial minorities "must work harder and longer to gain access to potential opportunities even though they have equal educational and employment experience with Whites" (p. 50). According to Fish (1993),

> If the mastery of the requirements for entry depends upon immersion in the cultural experiences of the mainstream majority, if the skills that make for success are nurtured by institutions and cultural practices from which the disadvantaged minority has been systematically excluded, if the language and ways of comporting oneself that identify a player as "one of us" are alien to the lives minorities are forced to live, then words like "fair" and "equal" are cruel jokes, for what they promote and celebrate is institutionalized unfairness and a perpetuated inequality (p. 132).

More than Individual Attitudes

Racism involves more than the effects of individual attitudes. It implies a structural and cultural fact. That some students see equity programs as "reverse racism" raises questions about their understanding of racism. It is not racism when Aboriginal and racial minority Canadians are "targeted" under equity programs for equality of access and equality of opportunity; or when racial minorities demand that they be treated differently from whites in order to be treated equitably. Measures aimed at redressing inequities can only be perceived as racism or as a contravention of legitimate notions of universal equity when the desires and actions of oppressed groups are detached from the historical conditions of their reality (Fish, 1993), or when the reality of privileged groups is detached from their historical relations to unearned benefits from power (McIntosh, 1995; Sleeter, 1994). Racism is a cultural and historical fact that structures the norms and values of societies, and it is evident in the policies and practices of institutions. The effects are sufficiently great to warrant the attention of both governments and institutions.

[...] Racism is an ideology promoting the uncritical acceptance and negative social definitions of a group often identified by physical features (e.g., skin colour), and is premised on the belief in the cultural and biological superiority of a particular racial group over others. Insofar as racism is supported by a system of inequality and oppression constructed within a society, it is more than individual; it is structural and institutional. A key component of racism is power—structural and institutional power. This power is more than the "ordinary" influence an individual might have over another; it is the support of that influence by economic, political and ideological conditions. Often this power is an "invisible," regular and continuous part of everyday human existence, sustained by established laws, regulations and/or policies or by accepted conventions and customs. As sociologist C. Wright Mills (1956) explains, "No one can be truly powerful unless he [sic] has access to the command of major institutions, for it is over these institutional means of power that the truly powerful are, in the first instance, powerful" (p. 9).

In the case of Canadian society, Ng (1993) states that

> white European men, especially those of British and French descent, are seen to be superior to women and to people from other racial and ethnic origins. Systems of ideas and practices have been developed over time to justify and support his notion of superiority. These ideas become the premise on which societal norms and values are based, and the practices become the "normal" way of doing things (p. 52).

Ng goes on to say that racism could be treated as a "common sense" way of thinking. This refers to the "norms and forms of action that have become ordinary ways of doing things, of which we have little consciousness, so that certain things ... 'disappear from the social surface'" (p. 52).

If historical and social patterns have normalized the economic, political and ideological power of white males, can equity and access programs "discriminate" against white males in the same way in which racial minorities have been discriminated against? This is unlikely, for as Stanley Fish argues in his essay "Reverse Racism or How the Pot Got To Call The Kettle Black," such programs are "not intended to disenfranchise white males" (Fish, 1993: 136). Rather they are meant to remove barriers that have traditionally advantaged some groups and disadvantaged others. Further, such programs seek to address the impact of practices that have operated on the basis of white males' norms. For this reason, equity and access programs will include such things as minority representation and an acknowledgment of the factors that have historically and systematically operated as barriers to their participation in all sectors of our society. To this notion, many students respond, "Two wrongs don't make a right; if it is unfair to discriminate against Blacks, it is just as unfair to discriminate against whites." This position is premised on the notion that everyone should be treated the same, and dismisses the reality that not everyone has been or is the same. It is a dismissal of and a disregard for the power differences that advantage some and disadvantage others. Fairness cannot be evaluated independent of the histories of the respective groups to which individuals belong.

Equity programs must be seen as attempts to undo the effects of arbitrary and racist policies and practices that have operated historically as barriers to access and opportunities. And as Judge Abella (1984) states in her report, *Equity in Employment*,

> formerly we thought that equity only meant sameness and that treating persons as equals meant treating everyone the same. We now know that to treat everyone the same may be to offend the notions of equality.... To create opportunity we have to do different things for different people.... The process in an exercise in redistributive justice (p. 3).

The difference between equity programs and the ways in which individuals have traditionally gained access to educational and occupational opportunities is "not in the outcome but in the ways of thinking that led up to the outcome. It is the difference between an unfairness that befalls one as an unintended effect of a policy rationally conceived and an unfairness that is pursued as an end in itself" (Fish, 1993: 136). Stated differently, equity programs as they are intentionally conceived are not intended to prevent males or whites from employment opportunities (as in the case of minorities), but to remove structural barriers that have been limiting minority participation.

The Critical Juncture

The critical juncture involves white students and equity programs. As they prepare for the world of work, many young white males hope that their post-secondary education and grades will "give them the edge" in their job search. They perceive employment equity programs as a challenge to their optimism and to any "edge" they might have had in realizing their occupational goals. Therefore, we can expect them to be concerned about the job market and the employment opportunities that await them. For this reason, many become quite frustrated and even angry. For instance, a class discussion on employment equity with reference to women and racial minorities led to a heated debate. Dominic, one of the two males in a class of thirty students, stated the following in a very angry voice:

> I am tired of all this racism bullshit. I've never been handed anything on a sliver platter.... This is fuckin' scary. You're not good enough to get in like others.... What about meritocracy? What about the esteem of people? You'd be seen as an equity quota, as a number. [Employment equity] undermines what has been accomplished.... It creates animosity and downright hatred. This means I'll be two years out of a job. I'm fed up of the bullshit. Is this what we call progress?

This student is also expressing anger because of what he sees as the compromise of his "inalienable right" and the thwarting of his career attainment by programs that give minorities an "unfair advantage over those who have more experience in their field." Not only is this young man's anger representative of a number of today's young white male students, but the same anger and arguments are being expressed by males in the corporate world.

In their cover story "White, Male and Worried," *Business Week* (Galen and Palmer, 1994) reports that today's white men must compete against racial minorities—people whom "they may not have taken all that seriously as rivals." So, "for the first time in their lives they are worrying about their future opportunities because of widespread layoff, corporate restructuring" and employment equity initiatives (Galen and Palmer, 1994: 51). But, as the *Business Week* article adds, "At the heart of the issue for many white males is a question of merit—that in the rush for a more diverse workplace, they will lose out to less qualified workers" (p. 52).

The Question of Merit

In a letter to the *Burlington Post* of December 29, 1993, a young man writes:

> I graduated from a local high school as an Ontario Scholar in 1987 and received my honours Bachelor of Arts in 1992 from a highly reputable university in south-western Ontario.... In the spring of 1992 I applied for 25 entry-level positions through the province's want ads.... With eight months' work experience in the Ministry of Treasury and Economics, my university degree, and my ability to save the province money, my white skin and gender couldn't possibly prevent me from at least getting an interview, right? Wrong! I did not get any interviews. Clearly, the new legislation assumes that the best person for the job is automatically either a non-white or female, despite qualifications.... Anti-white male (a.w.m. for short) discrimination has permeated institutions of higher learning.... In case you consider me to be sexist or a bigot, I assure you I'm not. I would truly like to see the most qualified person for any particular job regardless of color, creed, gender or any other non-performance-related factor, employed in that given position. Individual cases of discrimination should be dealt with on an individual basis, not by institutionalized reverse discrimination (p. 14).

This young man and others believe that taking race into consideration in the equity programs is a violation of the principle of meritocracy and individualism. Their education has taught them that our society is democratic, that everyone has the same opportunities and chances and that everyone can succeed once they have the ability and skill and apply themselves. Hence, it is the individual's efforts and abilities, and not systemic factors, that determine achievement. A common belief is, "If you want something bad enough, you will get it; you just have to apply yourself." It is because of this belief that many insist, "If you work hard, you can get whatever you want." Within this middle-class context, education is often seen as the mechanism through which individuals are able to achieve their goals. Moreover, they argue, as education is free and accessible, all one needs to do is to "take advantage of the educational opportunities that are available to them." In terms of financial support for post-secondary education, they further argue that "OSAP [Ontario Students' Assistance Program] is available to everyone, especially those who have an economic need."

This belief in democracy and meritocracy has a powerful effect on how the students perceive their own opportunities and the opportunities of racial minorities in our society. After all, throughout their schooling they have been taught the lessons of equity and fairness. Therefore, it is logical that they would believe that race never operated in the first place to influence an individual's outcome and, in particular, to provide them with privilege. When educators and institutions challenge these traditional ideas of meritocracy, it raises doubt in the students' minds and shakes their confidence in the system. This can turn into frustration and anger, for they expect to hear from educators, and observe in institutional practices, the principles of meritocracy at work. Therefore, they must search for new meanings and interpretations of the values and principles on which they have come to rely.

While attempting to maintain confidence in a system they have been socialized to see as fair, equitable and accessible to all Canadians, young people must simultaneously find explanations for why the same system (specifically, state and private institutions) is now challenging the very ideals it taught them to embrace. In their search for answers to questions (e.g., "Why me? Why now?" "Why should I have to pay for the past? I didn't do anything wrong. It is not my fault."), they invent some interesting rationalizations. For example, in a class discussion on employment equity, after a [...] debate, one student made the point that "the reason why the police force has to hire so many Black officers is because they have to make the force representative of the criminal population." The speaker, a young white male of about twenty years of age, went on to say that Blacks commit most of the crimes in Metropolitan Toronto. When asked for the source of his data, he referred to the media, his instructors and his own experience. One week later, in order to further prove his point, he brought into class a copy of a local community newspaper. A front-page article reported that a young Black male was arrested for snatching the purse from a young female student. In another article in the same newspaper, a Black male was being sought for break-ins into a number of homes in the neighbourhood. For this student, these reports proved his point and indicated that Blacks contributed to the high crime rates in our country. The government was seen as being soft on "these minority groups who were pressuring the government because they want to change things." Other students claimed that the "power was shifting," that immigrants and racial minorities were getting the government to do what they want. One reason for these rationalizations is that, from within their frame of reference, these students are unable or refuse to account for the inequities the "meritocratic" system has meted out to Aboriginal peoples, racial minorities, women and people with disabilities.

White Privilege

How can it be that white males are being discriminated against? In her article "'The Silent Dialogue': Power and Pedagogy in Educating Other People's Children," Lisa Delpit (1988) points out that "those with power are frequently least aware of—or least willing to acknowledge—its existence. Those with less power are often most aware of its existence" (p. 282). As this is the case, the white male students are unlikely to see, much less acknowledge, their power and privilege. Writing of her experience as a white woman, Peggy McIntosh (1995) proposes a reason for this "power ignorance."

> My schooling gave me no training in seeing myself as an oppressor, as an unfairly advantaged person, or as a participant in a damaged culture. I was taught to see myself as an individual whose moral state depended on her individual moral will. At school, we were not taught about slavery in any depth; we were not taught to see slave holders as damaged people.... Whites are taught to think of their lives as morally neutral, normative, and average and also ideal, so that when we work to benefit others, this is seen as work that will allow "them" to be like "us" (p. 78).

According to social norms, it is not prudent for individuals to acknowledge their power and privilege openly. This, then, might be part of the denial we hear from these young males. The denial of their power and privileges might also reflect their reluctance to take responsibility for the historical conditions that have resulted in their privileges, or rather maintain their belief that in today's society, individual successes and failures are a result of individual efforts. Further, to acknowledge power and privilege, they will also have to agree that the opposite is true—that racial minorities have been disadvantaged by the same system that has benefited whites. The converse of this, that is, an acknowledgment of others' disadvantages without the acknowledgment of how these relate to their own advantages, is more often held. As a group that has been taught to uphold the principles of democracy and fairness, young white men must also take responsibility for rectifying and changing the historical conditions they have inherited.

The first step in doing this is admitting that their race, ethnicity and gender play a role in their lives as Canadians. When confronted with this challenge, many young people often claim that racial minorities, women and adults in general, "just want them to feel guilty for a situation for which they are not responsible and which they have no interest in perpetuating." But in order for the students to understand the value of equity programs, they have to acknowledge the role that demographic characteristics play in providing access and opportunities to people in our society. They need to admit, like the following student, that their privilege—"being racially white"—allows them to escape the negative impact of racism.

> Lyn: It is white culture that I experience day to day, and the very fact that discrimination is rarely an issue for me personally results in my own racial identity becoming an invisible thing. The powerful people within my experience, directly or indirectly—the politician, the employer, the teacher, the social worker—are invariably white. I know that my race will not be an issue with most of the people I must deal with.... Neither will I expect my values or behaviour to be an issue because I fit into the "norm." It is in the idea of the "norm" that racial and ethnic cultures mesh to form a powerful image of what is accepted or expected.

*****

CHALLENGING THE PERCEPTION OF EQUITY

> The new forms of white racism are "couched in expressions of unfairness and reverse discrimination."
>
> Sleeter (1994)

> "New racism" is expressed in a language of innocence which disguises its insidious intent by framing its message in a way that endorses 'folk' values of egalitarianism, social justice, and common sense. Racism, in effect, is ideological, transformed in ways that disavow, diminish or distract from its actuality in a democratic society"
>
> Baker (1981), cited in Kallen (1995: 30)

"Equality should mean that everyone has the same chance of being hired" [Student]. This statement is correct, but we must first establish what we mean by "the same chance." Equity can only be attained if "the same chance" involves taking differences into account—differences related to racial, ethnic, linguistic and gender experiences that speak not only to the individual experiences of applicants, but also to those of the diverse Canadian society that is to be represented and served within all organizations or institutions. Further, a "fair" chance requires that we recognize the barriers to educational opportunities—barriers related to racism, classism, sexism—that have traditionally operated to limit access to employment opportunities. Such recognition would mean that an individual's outcome or attainment is not merely a result of his or her failings, but is related to structural barriers over which he or she has little or no control. The fact that such individuals are now qualified to apply for jobs is representative of not only their motivation, determination and capacity to work against the odds, but also a particular perspective that should be a valuable resource.

The experience that marginalized individuals bring to the job is often overlooked. Here, "the same chance" would mean valuing the differences that are evident in the experiences and perspectives of marginalized individuals and treating them differently in order to treat them equally. It would mean recognizing that obtaining a job or obtaining a particular level of education cannot be the "same" when race, gender, class, ethnicity and other factors operate in structural or systemic ways to limit opportunities.

*****

Consider what studies have shown about contemporary employment practices and the experiences of racial and ethnic minorities. In a survey of employers in Toronto, Billingsley and Muzynski (1985) found that most employers relied on informal employee and friendship networks to recruit and fill job positions. Therefore, it is more difficult for minorities to gain access to jobs in which they are not yet represented. Moreover, a survey of 672 corporate recruiters, hiring managers and agency recruiters conducted by Canadian Recruiters Guild in 1989 showed that 87 percent of corporate and 100 percent of agency recruiters surveyed received direct discriminatory requests. Nearly three-quarters of corporate and 94 percent of agency recruiters complied with these requests. The survey also showed that out of 6,720 available positions, only four target group members were placed by the recruiting agencies (Currents, 1989: 19–20).

In their 1985 Toronto study "Who Gets the Work: A Test of Racial Discrimination in Employment," Henry and Ginzberg found that, in cases where job applicants had similar resumes, white applicants were far more likely (3:1) to be offered a position than non-whites. The study, which used two white and two Black actors (male and female) found that "Black job seekers face not only discrimination in the sense of receiving fewer job offers than Whites but also a considerable amount of abusive treatment while job hunting" (p. 306). In the part of the study where job seekers made telephone calls "to phone numbers listed in the classified employment section of the newspaper," the findings revealed that the "White-majority Canadian" with "no discernible accent" was "never screened," while the "Slavic or Italian accented" callers were screened "5 percent of the time" and the "Jamaican accented" and "Indo-Pakistani accented" callers received "three times as much screening as the White" (p. 308). The result was that 65 percent of the jobs were open to "White" callers, 52 percent to "Jamaican-accented" callers and 47.3 percent to "Indo-Pakistani accented" callers (Henry and Ginzberg, 1985: 51). The researchers concluded that

> there is a very substantial racial discrimination affecting the ability of members of racial minorities to find employment even when they are well qualified and eager to find work.... Once an applicant is employed, discrimination can still affect opportunities for advancement, job retention, and level of earnings, to say nothing of the question of the quality of work and the relationship with co-workers (Henry, 1993: 308; see also Henry and Ginzberg, 1985).

In a seven-year, follow-up study I conducted with twenty young Black Canadians about their employment experiences, respondents reported that racism and discrimination were "challenges" with which they had to contend, both in terms of obtaining a job and while they were on the job. They suggested that "who you know" is even more important than education, "particularly in competition against a white person for a job." As one respondent stated, "while education can help, I have seen that who you know gets you further" (James, 1993: 10).

In a recent Canadian Labour Congress research report, *Is Work Working for Workers of Colour* (October 2002), Jackson explores issues of employment and pay gaps, poverty and economic security of workers of colour noting that while "some racialized workers with high levels of education" have managed to attain good, professional jobs, there are many others with good qualifications who are "trapped in low-pay, insecure, no-future jobs." And while it has been held that the gap between qualification and job attainment is due to the fact that "many racialized workers are relatively recent immigrants," this "catch up" theory (i.e., that the situation will change with time) has failed to explain the situation today where even with "more Canadian job experience and move into the mainstream" (to the extent that this is possible), racialized workers, unlike previous white European immigrants, are still "disproportionately employed in jobs requiring lower levels of skills and education, despite higher than average qualifications" (p. 1). Jackson concludes that "the evidence is clear that systemic racism is very much a factor in the Canadian job market. Racialized workers are paid less, enjoy less security, and are much more vulnerable to poverty than other workers" (p. 18). And finding that unions, through their collective bargaining agreements, have "a positive impact on earnings and employment stability," he goes on to say that "unions and governments must do far more to combat the injustices of systemic racism" (ibid.; see also Galabuzi, 2001).

*****

"The white male is being discriminated aainst for something beyond his control; it's a form of reverse discrimination" [Student]. We have all inherited the history of racism and discrimination and, with it, the consequences. These consequences constitute barriers to employment and educational opportunities for some. For others, these constitute the privilege of access to employment and education, a benefit of the very barriers that are disadvantageous to others. It is this inherited race privilege that makes it possible for a student not to notice instances where his "race or ethnicity has been an advantage." The hard work and determination of both he and his parents, as well as the guidance he received from them, have not been mediated by the racism that racial minorities experience in their drive to educational and employment opportunities and success. And the "human spirit" that Roger is convinced is critical to success exists in raced, classed, abled and gendered bodies and, as such, is subject to the social, political, economic and cultural contestations in society. Just as the earned and unearned privileges (McIntosh, 1995) are accepted, so too must be the responsibility for how those privileges were acquired in the first place.

Writing about the responsibility that white people must take for the privileges that they have enjoyed from the time they came to the United States, Michael Moore (2002) insists that "we whites" must acknowledge that the "plum jobs" and "double the pay" have brought them "happiness and success" and have been at the expense of "minorities" such as African and Native Americans. In Canada, I would start with and emphasize the colonization of Aboriginal Canadians and add the other minorities who have since come to Canada, such as the Chinese, South Asians and others.

*****

EQUITY PROGRAMS: HELPFUL AND PARADOXICAL

Myths, misinformation and half-truths characterize much of the discussion about employment equity [...]. These myths are based, on the one hand, on a lack of acknowledgment of the inherent economic and social inequities within our society, a fear of social change and an anticipated loss of political, economic, and social power and privilege. On the other hand, the multicultural, meritocratic ideology of Canada has so structured the ideas of individuals that they have difficulty in critically reflecting on the issues before them or in seeing the myths. More to the point, these protestations by students are possibly the "new racism" to which Kallen (1995) refers. With reference to Baker (1981), Kallen points out that "the 'new racism' has been conceptualized as an 'ideological gambit,' employed by majority authorities in a democratic society to maintain the status quo of racial and ethnic inequality in the face of espoused democratic ideals of anti-racism and egalitarianism" (p. 30). Little wonder, therefore, that individuals might fail to see the role played by prejudices, stereotypes and racism as they are directed towards the groups who are characterized as the benefactors of equity programs. If we are to build a democratic and equitable society in Canada, then we must be critically reflexive, prepared for social change and play a part in initiating and fighting for that change.

It is indeed inevitable that, in the words of one [student], "corrective measures" in the form of equity programs must be taken if equal employment and educational opportunities are to be realized. And while it seems simplistic to say, as did one student, that such programs "would definitely help" because having co-workers from "all racial backgrounds can and will benefit a multicultural society," it is something worth striving for. The issue of "qualification" is important. Understandably, tradition has played a significant role in the determination of qualification. However, in contexts where equity is an important objective, qualification cannot be governed merely by tradition. Qualification will have to be relative and take into account the contemporary diverse and changing contexts in which individuals perform their duties. For this reason, diverse ideas, skills, values and expectations cannot be governed by one set of historical norms.

*****

Addressing the Issues

Essentially, the phrase "reverse racism" seems oxymoronic. It negates the inherent inequalities in resources and power among groups positioned by racial categorization in our society. It is a phrase that is important for young white males, for it gives political weight to their feelings of powerlessness and loss of privilege. For them, the term conveys the feeling that they too are oppressed, and that, like racial minorities, they are victims of a system over which they have very little or no control. Within this context, the phrase conveys the mistaken idea that racism is based on individual attitudes and ideologies and the individual exercise of power. It fails to construct power in structural and historical terms, which would explain the cultural capital that they possess because of their membership in a particular racial group. Inherent in their conceptualization of racism is the lack of acknowledgment of their own power and privilege and, with it, the lack of recognition that their own power is rooted in the historical and cultural conditions upon which this society has been built. By not recognizing the structural roots of racism and their white privilege, they are denying their own racism, the benefit they derive from its existence and their responsibility for participating in changing it (hooks, 1988; Roman, 1993).

Educators have an important role to play in engaging students in discussions about racism and equity. Evidently some students will resist such engagement. Nevertheless, as Tatum (1992) points out, as students learn from these discussions and become comfortable with the issues, "they take their friends with them" (p. 22). Our aim must be to provide an educational climate where difficult issues can be brought up and all students can voice how they see the issues that affect their aspirations. The curriculum, assigned readings, class presentations and discussions should provide students with a critical awareness of how structural inequality, and racism in particular, influence individuals' educational and occupational opportunities and outcomes. Such an awareness must alert them to the need to act consciously to address and remove barriers that are inherent in the existing social structure (Dei, 1996; hooks, 1988). Hence, students will come to understand that barriers to employment and educational opportunities must necessarily be addressed through programs that deal with the social structure. Leslie Roman (1993) suggests that white educators have a responsibility to challenge and work with racially privileged students to help them understand that their (our) attempts to assume the positions of the racially oppressed are also the result of our contradictory desires to misrecognize and recognize the collective shame of facing those who have been effaced in the dominant texts of culture, history and curricular knowledge (p. 84).

In a socially stratified society such as ours, it is necessary that racism and equity are discussed in our classrooms. Providing opportunities for such discussions, according to Tatum (1992), "may be the most proactive learning opportunities an institution can provide" (p. 23). Classroom forums can help students gain a critical understanding of the issues of equity and produce the needed paradigm shift to counter the racial tension and resentment underlying some student's negative reactions to employment equity programs.

REFERENCES

Abella, R. (1984). *Equality in employment: A Royal Commission report*. Ottawa: Ministry of Supply and Services.

Billingsley, B., & Muszynski, L. (1985, May). *No discrimination here! Toronto employers and the multi-racial workforce*. Toronto: Social Planning Council of Metropolitan Toronto.

Clarke, G.E. (1998). White like Canada. *Transition, 73*, 98–109.

Currents: Readings in Race Relations (1989, March). Canada's employment discriminators, 4–8.

Dei, G.J. (1996). *Anti-racism education theory and practice*. Halifax: Fernwood Publishing.

Delpit, L.D. (1988). The silent dialogue: Power and pedagogy in educating other people's children. *Harvard Educational Review, 58*(3), 280–298.

Dobbins, J.E., & Skillings, J.H. (1991). The utility of race labelling in understanding cultural identity: A conceptual tool for the social science practitioner. *Journal of Counselling and Development, 70*(1), 37–44.

Fish, S. (1993, November). Reverse racism or how the pot got to call the kettle Black. *The Atlantic Monthly*, 132–136.

Galabuzi, G.-E. (2001). *Canada's creeping economic apartheid*. Toronto: Canadian Social Justice Foundation for Research and Education.

Galen, M., & Palmer, A. (1994, January 31). White, male and worried. *Business Week*, 50–55.

Henry, F. (1993). Racial discrimination in employment. In J. Curtis, E. Crabb, N. Guppy & S. Gilbert (Eds.), *Social inequalities in Canada: Patterns, problems, policies* (pp. 301–315). Scarborough, ON: Prentice-Hall.

Henry, F., & Ginzberg, E. (1985). *Who gets the work: A test of racial discrimination in employment*. Toronto: Social Planning Council.

hooks, b. (1988). *Talking back: Thinking feminist, thinking Black*. Toronto: Between the Lines.

Jackson, A. (2002). *Is work working for workers of colour?* (Research Paper #18). Toronto: Canadian Labour Congress.

James, C.E. (1993). Getting there and staying there: Blacks' employment experience. In P. Anisef & P. Axelrod (Eds.), *Transitions: Schooling and employment in Canada* (pp. 3–20). Toronto: Thompson Educational Publishing.

Kallen, E. (1995). *Ethnicity and human rights in Canada* (2nd ed.). Toronto: Oxford University Press.

McIntosh, P. (1995). White privilege and male privilege: A personal account of coming to see correspondences through work in women's studies. In M.L. Andersen & P. Hill Collins (Eds.), *Race, class and gender: An anthology* (pp. 70–81). Belmont, Calif.: Wadsworth.

Mills, C.W. (1956). *The power elite*. New York: Oxford University Press.

Moore, M. (2002, March 30). Another perspective on the Black/white issue. *The Guardian Magazine*.

Moreau, J. (1994). Changing faces: Visible minorities in Toronto. In *Canadian social trends* (Vol. 2). Toronto: Thompson Educational Publishing.

Neufeld, M. (1992, October 25). Can an entire society be racist, or just individuals? *Toronto Star*, p. B7.

Ng, R. (1993). Racism, sexism, and nation building in Canada. In C. McCarthy & W. Chrichlow (Eds.), *Race, identity and representation in education* (pp. 50–59). New York: Routledge.

Roman, L.G. (1993). White is a color! White defensiveness, postmodernism, and anti-racism pedagogy. In C. McCarthy & W. Crichlow (Eds.), *Race, identity and representation in education* (pp.71–88). New York: Routlege.

St. Lewis, J. (1996). Race, racism, and the justice system. In C.E. James (Ed.), *Perspectives on racism and the human service sector: A case for change* (pp. 104–119). Toronto: University of Toronto Press.

Sleeter, C. (1994). White racism. *Multicultural Education* (spring).

Tatum, B.D. (1992). Talking about race, learning about racism: The application of racial identity development theory in the classroom. *Harvard Educational Review, 62*(1), 1–24.

CHAPTER 41

HOW GAY STAYS WHITE AND WHAT KIND OF WHITE IT STAYS

Allan Bérubé

THE STEREOTYPE

When I teach college courses on queer history or queer working-class studies, I encourage students to explore the many ways that homosexuality is shaped by race, class, and gender. I know that racialized phantom figures hover over our classroom and inhabit our consciousness. I try to name these figures out loud to bring them down to earth so we can begin to resist their stranglehold on our intelligence. One by one, I recite the social categories that students have already used in our discussions—immigrant, worker, corporate executive, welfare recipient, student on financial aid, lesbian mother—and ask students first to imagine the stereotypical figure associated with the category and then to call out the figure's race, gender, class, and sexuality. As we watch each other conjure up and name these phantoms, we are stunned at how well each of us has learned by heart the same fearful chorus.

Whenever I get to the social category "gay man," the students' response is always the same: "white and well-to-do." In the United States today, the dominant image of the typical gay man is a white man who is financially better off than most everyone else.

MY WHITE DESIRES

Since the day I came out to my best friend in 1968, I have inhabited the social category "gay white man." As a historian, writer, and activist, I've examined the gay and the male parts of that identity, and more recently I've explored my working-class background and the Franco-American ethnicity that is so intertwined with it. But only recently have I identified with or seriously examined my gay male whiteness.[1]

Several years ago I made the decision to put race and class at the center of my gay writing and activism. I was frustrated at how my own gay social and activist circles reproduced larger patterns of racial separation by remaining almost entirely white. And I felt abandoned as the vision of the national gay movement and media narrowed from fighting for liberation, freedom, and social justice to expressing personal pride, achieving visibility, and lobbying for individual equality within existing institutions. What emerged was too often an exclusively gay rights agenda isolated from supposedly non-gay issues, such as homelessness, unemployment, welfare, universal health care, union organizing, affirmative action, and abortion rights. To gain recognition and credibility, some gay organizations and media began to aggressively promote the so-called positive image of a generic gay community that is an upscale, mostly male, and mostly white consumer market with mainstream, even traditional, values. Such a strategy derives its power from an unexamined investment in whiteness and middle-class identification. As a result, its practitioners seemed not to take seriously or even notice how their gay visibility successes at times exploited and reinforced a racialized class divide that continues to tear our nation apart, including our lesbian and gay communities.

My decision to put race and class at the center of my gay work led me as a historian to pursue the history of a multiracial maritime union that in the 1930s and 1940s fought for racial equality and the dignity of openly gay workers.[2] And my decision opened doors that enabled me as an activist to join multiracial lesbian, gay, bisexual, and transgender groups whose members have been doing antiracist work for a long time and in which gay white men are not the majority—groups that included the Lesbian, Gay, Bisexual, and Transgender Advisory Committee to the San Francisco Human Rights Commission and the editorial board of the now-defunct national lesbian and gay quarterly journal *Out/Look*.

But doing this work also created new and ongoing conflicts in my relationships with other white men. I want to figure out how to handle these conflicts as I extend my antiracist work into those areas of my life where I still find myself among gay white men—especially when we form new activist and intellectual groups that once again turn out to be white. To do this I need "to clarify something for myself," as James Baldwin put it, when he gave his reason for writing his homosexual novel *Giovanni's Room* in the 1950s.[3]

I wanted to know how gay gets white, how it stays that way, and how whiteness is used both to win and attack gay rights campaigns.

I want to learn how to see my own whiteness when I am with gay white men and to understand what happens among us when one of us calls attention to our whiteness.

I want to know why I and other gay white men would want to challenge the racist structures of whiteness, what happens to us when we try, what makes me keep running away from the task, sometimes in silent despair, and what makes me want to go back to take up the task again.

I want to pursue these questions by drawing on a gay ability, developed over decades of figuring out how to "come out of the closet," to bring our hidden lives out into the open. But I want to do this without encouraging anyone to assign a greater degree of racism to gay white men, thus exposed, than to other white men more protected from exposure, and without inviting white men who are not gay to more safely see gay men's white racism rather than their own.

I want to know these things because gay white men have been among the men I have loved and will continue to love. I need them in my life and at my side as I try to make fighting racism a more central part of my work. And when students call out "white" to describe the typical gay man, and they see me standing right there in front of them, I want to figure out how, from where I am standing, I can intelligently fight the racist hierarchies that I and my students differently inhabit.

GAY WHITENING PRACTICES

Despite the stereotype, the gay male population is not as white as it appears to be in the images of gay men projected by the mainstream and gay media, or among the "out" men (including myself) who move into the public spotlight as representative gay activists, writers, commentators, and spokesmen. Gay men of color, working against the stereotype, have engaged in long, difficult struggles to gain some public recognition of their cultural heritages, political activism, and everyday existence. To educate gay white men, they've had to get our attention by interrupting our business as usual, then convince us that we don't speak for them or represent them or know enough about either their realities or our own racial assumptions and privileges. And when I and other gay white men don't educate ourselves, gay men of color have done the face-to-face work of educating us about their cultures, histories, oppression, and particular needs—the kind of personal work that tires us out when heterosexuals ask us to explain to them what it's like to be gay. Also working against their ability to put "gay" and "men of color" together in the broader white imagination are a great many other powerful *whitening practices* that daily construct, maintain, and fortify the idea that gay male means white.

How does the category "gay man" become white? What are the whitening practices that perpetuate this stereotype, often without awareness or comment by gay white men? How do these practices operate, and what racial work do they perform?

I begin by mining my own experience for clues.[4] I know that if I go where I'm surrounded by other gay white men, or if I'm having sex with a white man, it's unlikely that our race will come up in conversation. Such racially comfortable, racially familiar situations can make us mistakenly believe that there are such things as gay issues, spaces, culture, and relationships that are not "lived through" race, and that white gay life, so long as it is not named as such, is not about race.[5] These lived assumptions, and the privileges on which they are based, form a powerful camouflage woven from a web of unquestioned beliefs—that gay whiteness is unmarked and unremarkable, universal and representative, powerful and protective, a cohesive bond. The markings of this camouflage are pale—a characteristic that the wearer sees neither as entirely invisible nor as a racial "color," a shade that allows the wearer to blend into the seemingly neutral background of white worlds. When we wear this everyday camouflage into a gay political arena that white men already dominate, our activism comes wrapped in a *pale protective coloring* that we may not notice but which is clearly visible to those who don't enjoy its protection.

I start to remember specific situations in which I caught glimpses of how other gay whitening practices work.

One night, arriving at my favorite gay disco bar in San Francisco, I discovered outside a picket line of people protesting the triple-carding (requiring three photo ID's) of gay men of color at the door. This practice was a form of racial *exclusion*—policing the borders of white gay institutions to prevent people of color from entering. The management was using this discriminatory practice to keep the bar from "turning," as it's called—a process by which a "generically gay" bar (meaning a predominantly white bar) changes into a bar that loses status and income (meaning gay white men with money won't go there) because it has been "taken over" by black, Latino, or Asian gay men. For many white owners, managers, and patrons of gay bars, only a white gay bar can be *just gay*; a bar where men of color go is seen as racialized. As I joined the picket line, I felt the fears of a white man who has the privilege to choose on which side of a color line he will stand. I wanted to support my gay brothers of color who were being harassed at the door, yet I was afraid that the doorman might recognize me as a regular and refuse to let me back in. That night, I saw a gay bar's doorway become a racialized border, where a battle to preserve or challenge the whiteness of the clientele inside was fought among dozens of gay men who were either standing guard at the door, allowed to walk through it, or shouting and marching outside. (The protests eventually made the bar stop the triple-carding.)

I remember seeing how another gay whitening practice works when I watched, with other members of a sexual politics study group, an antigay video, "Gay Rights, Special Rights," produced in 1993 by The Report, a religious right organization. This practice was the *selling* of gay whiteness—the marketing of gays as white and wealthy to make money and increase political capital, either to raise funds for campaigns (in both progay and antigay benefits, advertising, and direct-mail appeals) or to gain economic power (by promoting or appealing to a gay consumer market). The antigay video we watched used racialized class to undermine alliances between a gay rights movement portrayed as white and movements of people of color portrayed as heterosexual. It showed charts comparing mutually exclusive categories of "homosexuals" and "African Americans," telling us that homosexuals are wealthy, college-educated white men who vacation more than anyone else and who demand even more "special rights and privileges" by taking civil rights away from low-income African Americans.[6] In this zero-sum, racialized world of the religious right, gay men are white; gay, lesbian, and bisexual people of color, along with poor or working-class white gay men, bisexuals, and lesbians, simply do not exist. The recently vigorous gay media promotion of the high income, brand-loyal gay consumer market—which is typically portrayed as a population of white, well-to-do, college-educated young men—only widens the racialized class divisions that the religious right so eagerly exploits.

During the 1993 Senate hearings on gays in the military, I saw how these and other whitening practices were used in concentrated form by another gay institution, the Campaign for Military Service (CMS).

The Campaign for Military Service was an ad hoc organization formed in Washington, DC, by a group composed primarily of well-to-do, well-connected, professional men, including billionaires David Geffen and Barry Diller, corporate consultant and former antiwar activist David Mixner (a personal friend of Bill Clinton), and several gay and lesbian civil rights attorneys. Their mission was to work with the Clinton White House and sympathetic senators by coordinating the gay response to hearings held by the Senate Armed Services Committee, chaired by Sam Nunn. Their power was derived from their legal expertise, their access to wealthy donors, and their contacts with high-level personnel inside the White House, Senate, and Pentagon. The challenge they faced was to make strategic, pragmatic decisions in the heat of a rapidly changing national battle over what President Clinton called "our nation's policy toward homosexuals in the military."[7]

*****

The CMS used a set of arguments they called the *race analogy* to persuade senators and military officials to lift the military's antigay ban. The strategy was to get these powerful men to take antigay discrimination as seriously as they supposedly took racial discrimination, so they would lift the military ban on homosexuals as they had eliminated official policies requiring racial segregation. During the Senate hearings, the race analogy projected a set of comparisons that led to heated disputes over whether sexual orientation was analogous to race, whether sexual desire and conduct were like "skin color," or, most specifically, whether being homosexual was like being African American. (Rarely was "race" explicitly discussed as anything other than African American.) On their side, the CMS argued for a qualified analogy—what they called "haunting parallels" between "the words, rationale and rhetoric invoked in favor of racial discrimination in the past" and those used to "exclude gays in the military now." "The parallel is inexact," they cautioned, because "a person's skin color is not the same as a person's sexual identity; race is self-evident to many whereas sexual orientation is not. Moreover, the history of African Americans is not equivalent to the history of lesbian, gay and bisexual people in this country." Yet, despite these qualifications, the CMS held firm to the analogy. "The bigotry expressed is the same; the discrimination is the same."[8]

*****

During the race analogy debates, the fact that only white witnesses made the analogy, drawing connections between antigay and racial discrimination without including people of color, reduced the power of their argument and the credibility it might have gained had it been made by advocates who had experienced the racial discrimination side of the analogy.[9] But without hearing these voices, everyone in the debate could imagine homosexuals as either people who do not experience racism (the military assumption) or as people who experience discrimination only as homosexuals (the progay assumption)—two different routes that ultimately led to the same destination: the place where gay stays white, the place where the CMS chose to make its stand.

*****

What would the gay movement look like if gay white men who use the race analogy took it more seriously? What work would we have to do to close the perceived moral authority gap between our gay activism and the race analogy, to directly establish the kind of moral authority we seek by analogy? What if we aspired to achieve the great vision, leadership qualities, grass-roots organizing skills, and union-solidarity of Dr. Martin Luther King Jr., together with his opposition to war and his dedication to fighting with the poor and disenfranchised against the deepening race and class divisions in America and the world? How could we fight, in the words of US Supreme Court Justice Harry A. Blackmun, for the "fundamental interest all individuals have in controlling the nature of their intimate associations with others," in ways that build a broad civil rights movement rather than being "like" it, in ways that enable the gay movement to grow into one of many powerful and direct ways to achieve race, gender, and class justice?[10]

These, then, are only some of the many whitening practices that structure everyday life and politics in what is often called the "gay community" and the "gay movement"—making *race analogies*; *mirroring* the whiteness of men who run powerful institutions as a strategy for winning credibility, acceptance, and integration; *excluding* people of color from gay institutions; *selling* gay as white to raise money, make a profit, and gain economic power; and daily wearing the *pale protective coloring* that camouflages the unquestioned assumptions and unearned privileges of gay whiteness. These practices do serious damage to real people whenever they mobilize the power and privileges of whiteness to protect and strengthen gayness—including the privileges of gay whiteness—without using that power to fight racism—including gay white racism.

Most of the time, the hard work of identifying such practices, fighting racial discrimination and exclusion, critiquing the assumptions of whiteness, and racially integrating white gay worlds has been taken up by lesbian, gay, bisexual, and transgender people of color. Freed from this enforced daily recognition of race and confrontation with racism, some prominent white men in the gay movement have been able to advance a gay rights politics that, like the right to serve in the military, they imagine to be just gay, not about race. The gay rights movement can't afford to "dissipate our energies," Andrew Sullivan, former editor of the *New Republic*, warned on the Charlie Rose television program, by getting involved in disagreements over nongay issues such as "how one deals with race ... how we might help the underclass ... how we might deal with sexism."[11]

*****

For those few who act like, look like, and identify with the white men who still run our nation's major institutions, for those few who can meet with them, talk to them, and be heard by them as peers, the ability to draw on the enormous power of a shared but unacknowledged whiteness, the ability never to have to bring up race, must feel like a potentially sturdy shield against antigay discrimination. I can see how bringing up explicit critiques of white privilege during high-level gay rights conversations (such as the Senate debates over gays in the military), or making it possible for people of color to set the agenda of the gay rights movement, might weaken that white shield (which relies on racial division to protect)—might even, for some white activists, threaten to "turn" the gay movement into something less gay, as gay bars "turn" when they're no longer predominantly white.

The threat of losing the white shield that protects my own gay rights raises even more difficult questions that I need to "clarify ... for myself": What would *I* say and do about racism if someday my own whiteness helped me gain such direct access to men in the centers of power [...]? What privileges would I risk losing if I persistently tried to take activists of color with me into that high-level conversation? How, and with whom, could I begin planning for that day?

Gay white men who are committed to doing antiracist activism as gay men have to work within and against these and other powerful whitening practices. What can we do, and how can we support each other, when we once again find ourselves involved in gay social and political worlds that are white and male?

GAY, WHITE, MALE, AND HIV-NEGATIVE

A few years ago, in San Francisco, a friend invited me to be part of a new political discussion group of HIV-negative gay men. Arriving at a neighbor's apartment for the group's first meeting, I once again felt the relief and pleasure of being among men like me. All of us were involved in AIDS activism. We had supported lovers, friends, and strangers with HIV and were grieving the loss of too many lives. We didn't want to take time, attention, and scarce resources away from people with AIDS, including many people of color. But we did want to find a collective, progressive voice as HIV-negative men. We wanted to find public ways to say to gay men just coming out that "We are HIV-negative men, and we want you to stay negative, have hot sex, and live long lives. We don't want you to get sick or die." We were trying to work out a politics in which HIV-negative men, who are relatively privileged as not being the primary targets of crackdowns on people who are HIV-positive, could address other HIV-negative men without trying to establish our legitimacy by positioning ourselves as victims.

When I looked around the room I saw only white men. I knew that many of them had for years been incorporating antiracist work into their gay and AIDS activism, so this seemed like a safe space to bring up the whiteness I saw. I really didn't want to hijack the purpose of the group by changing its focus from HIV to race, but this was important because I believed that not talking about our whiteness was going to hurt our work. Instead of speaking up, however, I hesitated.

Right there. That's the moment I want to look at—that moment of silence, when a flood of memories, doubts, and fears rushed into my head. What made me want to say something about our whiteness and what was keeping me silent?

My memory took me back to 1990, when I spoke on a panel of gay historians at the first Out/Write conference of lesbian and gay writers, held in San Francisco. I was happy to be presenting with two other community-based historians working outside the academy. But I was also aware—and concerned—that we were all men. When the question period began, an African American writer in the audience, a man whose name I later learned was Fundi, stood up and asked us (as I recall) how it could happen, at this late date, that a gay history panel could have only white men on it. Awkward silence. I don't trust how I remember his question or what happened next—unreliable memory and bad thinking must be characteristics of inhabiting whiteness while it's being publicly challenged. As the other panelists responded, I remember wanting to distance myself from their whiteness while my own mind went blank, and I remember feeling terrified that Fundi would address me directly and ask me to respond personally. I kept thinking, "I don't know what to say, I can't think, I want to be invisible, I want this to be over, now!"

After the panel was over I spoke privately to Fundi. Later, I resolved never to be in that situation again—never to agree to be on an all-white panel without asking ahead of time why it was white, if its whiteness was crucial to what we were presenting, and, if not, how its composition might be changed. But in addition to wanting to protect myself from public embarrassment and to do the right thing, that writer's direct challenge made me understand something more clearly: that only by seeing and naming the whiteness I'm inhabiting, and taking responsibility for it, can I begin to change it and even do something constructive with it. At that panel, I learned how motivating though terrifying it can be as a white person to be placed in such a state of heightened racial discomfort—to be challenged to see the whiteness we've created, figure out how we created it, and then think critically about how it works.[12]

In the moment of silent hesitation I experienced in my HIV-negative group, I found myself imagining for the first time, years after it happened, what it must have been like for Fundi to stand up in a predominantly white audience and ask an all-white panel of gay men about our whiteness. My friend and colleague Lisa Kahaleole Hall, who is a brilliant thinker, writer, and teacher, says that privilege is "the ability not to have to take other people's existence seriously," the "ability not to have to pay attention."[13] Until that moment I had mistakenly thought that Fundi's anger (and I am not certain that he in fact expressed any anger toward us) was only about me, about us, as white men, rather than also about him—the history, desires, and support that enabled him to speak up, and the fears he faced and risks he took by doing it. Caught up in my own fear, I had not paid close attention to the specific question he had asked us. "The problem of conventional white men," Fundi later wrote in his own account of why he had decided to take the risk of speaking up, "somehow not being able, or not knowing how, to find and extend themselves to women and people of color had to be talked through.... My question to the panel was this: 'What direct skills might you share with particularly the whites in the audience to help them move on their fears and better extend themselves to cultural diversity?'"[14] I'm indebted to Fundi for writing that question down, and for starting a chain of events with his question that has led to my writing this essay.

I tried to remember who else I had seen bring up whiteness. The first images that came to mind were all white lesbians and people of color. White lesbian feminists have as a movement dealt with racism in a more collective way than have gay white men. In lesbian and gay activist spaces I and other gay white men have come to rely on white lesbians and people of color to raise the issue of whiteness and challenge racism, so that this difficult task has become both gendered as lesbian work and racialized as "colored" work. These images held me back from saying anything to my HIV-negative group. "Just who am I to bring this up?" I wondered. "It's not my place to do this." Or, more painfully, "Who will these men think I think I am?" Will they think I'm trying to pretend I'm not a white man?"

Then another image flashed in my mind that also held me back. It was the caricature of the white moralist—another racialized phantom figure hovering in the room—who blames and condemns white people for our racism, guilt-trips us from either a position of deeper guilt or holier-than-thou innocence, claims to be more aware of racism than we are, and is prepared to catalog our offenses. I see on my mental screen this self-righteous caricature impersonating a person of color in an all-white group or, when people of color are present, casting them again in the role of spectators to a white performance, pushed to the sidelines from where they must angrily or patiently interrupt a white conversation to be heard at all. I understand that there is some truth to this caricature—that part of a destructive racial dynamic among white people is trying to determine who is more or less responsible for racism, more or less innocent and pure, more or less white. But I also see how the fear of becoming this caricature has been used by white people to keep each other from naming the whiteness of all-white groups we are in. During my moment of hesitation in the HIV-negative group, the fear of becoming this caricature was successfully silencing me.

I didn't want to pretend to be a white lesbian or a person of color, or to act like the self-righteous white caricature. "How do I ask that we examine our whiteness," I wondered, "without implying that I'm separating us into the good guys and bad guys and positioning myself as the really cool white guy who 'gets it' about racism?" I needed a way to speak intelligently from where I was standing without falling into any of these traps.

I decided to take a chance and say something.

"It appears to me," I began, my voice a little shaky, "that everyone here is white. If this is true, I'd like us to find some way to talk about how our whiteness may be connected to being HIV-negative, because I suspect there are some political similarities between being in each of these positions of relative privilege."

There was an awkward pause. "Are you saying," someone asked, "that we should close the group to men of color?"

"No," I said, "but if we're going to be a white group I'd like us to talk about our relationship to whiteness here."

"Should we do outreach to men of color?" someone else asked.

"No, I'm not saying that, either. It's a little late to do outreach, after the fact, inviting men of color to integrate our already white group."

The other men agreed and the discussion went on to other things. I, too, didn't really know where to take this conversation about our whiteness. By bringing it up, I was implicitly asking for their help in figuring this out. I hoped I wouldn't be the only one to bring up the subject again.

At the next month's meeting there were new members, and they all appeared to be white men. When someone reviewed for them what we had done at the last meeting, he reported that I'd suggested we not include men of color in the group. "That's not right," I corrected him. "I said that if we're going to be a white group, I'd like us to talk about our whiteness and its relation to our HIV-negative status."

I was beginning to feel a little disoriented, like I was doing something wrong. Why was I being so consistently misunderstood as divisive, as if I were saying that I didn't want men of color in the group? Had I reacted similarly when, caught up in my own fear of having to publicly justify our panel's whiteness, I had misunderstood Fundi's specific question—about how we could share our skills with other white people to help each other move beyond our fear of cultural diversity—as an accusation that we had deliberately excluded women and men of color? Was something structural going on here about how white groups respond to questions that point to our whiteness and ask what we can do with it?

Walking home from the meeting I asked a friend who'd been there if what I said had made sense. "Oh yes," he said, "it's just that it all goes without saying." Well, there it is. That is how it goes, how it stays white. "Without saying."

Like much of the rest of my gay life, this HIV-negative group turned out to be unintentionally white, although intentionally gay and intentionally male. It's important for me to understand exactly how that racial *unintentionality* gets *constructed*, how it's not just a coincidence. It seems that so long as white people never consciously decide to be a white group, a white organization, a white department, so long as we each individually believe that people of color are always welcome, *even though they are not there*, then we do not have to examine our whiteness because we can believe it is unintentional, it's not our *reason* for being there. That may be why I had been misunderstood to be asking for the exclusion of men of color. By naming our group as white, I had unknowingly raised the question of *racial intent*—implying that we had intended to create an all-white group by deliberately excluding men of color. If we could believe that our whiteness was purely accidental, then we could also believe that there was nothing to say about it because creating an all-white group, which is exactly what we had done, had never been anyone's intent, and therefore had no inherent meaning or purpose. By interrupting the process by which "it just goes without saying," by asking us to recognize and "talk through" our whiteness, I appeared to be saying that we already had and should continue to exclude men of color from our now very self-consciously white group.

The reality is that in our HIV-negative group, as in the panel of the Out/Write conference and in many other all-white groupings, we each did make a chain of choices, not usually conscious, to invite or accept an invitation from another white person. We made more decisions whether or not to name our whiteness when we once again found ourselves in a white group. What would it mean to make such decisions consciously and out loud, to understand why we made them, and to take responsibility for them? What if we intentionally held our identities as white men and gay men in creative tension, naming ourselves as gay *and* white, then publicly explored the possibilities for activism this tension might open up? Could investigating our whiteness offer us opportunities for reclaiming our humanity against the ways that racial hierarchies dehumanize us and disconnect us from ourselves, from each other, and from people of color? If we took on these difficult tasks, how might our gay political reality and purpose be different?[15]

When I told this story about our HIV-negative group to Barbara Smith, a colleague who is an African American lesbian writer and activist, she asked me a question that pointed to a different ending: "So why didn't you bring up the group's whiteness again?" The easy answer was that I left the group because I moved to New York City. But the more difficult answer was that I was afraid to lose the trust of these gay men whom I cared about and needed so much, afraid I would distance myself from them and be distanced by them, pushed outside the familiar circle, no longer welcomed as white and not belonging among people of color, not really gay and not anything else, either. The big fear is that if I pursue this need to examine whiteness too far, I risk losing my place among gay white men, forever—and then where would I be?

PALE, MALE—AND ANTIRACIST

What would happen if we deliberately put together a white gay male group whose sole purpose was to examine our whiteness and use it to strengthen our antiracist gay activism?

In November 1995, gay historian John D'Emilio and I tried to do just that. We organized a workshop at the annual Creating Change conference of activists put on that year in Detroit by the National Gay and Lesbian Task Force. We called the workshop "Pale, Male—and Anti-Racist." At a conference of over 1,000 people (mostly white but with a large number of people of color), about thirty-five gay white men attended.[16]

We structured the workshop around three key questions: (1) How have you successfully used your whiteness to fight racism? (2) What difficulties have you faced in doing antiracist activism as a gay white man? And (3) what kind of support did you get or need or wished you had received from other gay white men?

*****

Some men talked about how tired they were of being called "gay white men," feeling labeled then attacked for who they were and for what they tried to do or for not doing enough; about having to deal with their racism while they didn't see communities of color dealing with homophobia; and about how after years of struggling they felt like giving up. Yet here they all were at this workshop. I began to realize that all our frustrations were signs of a dilemma that comes with the privileges of whiteness: having the ability to decide whether to keep dealing with the accusations, resentments, racial categorizations, and other destructive effects of racism that divide people who are trying to take away its power; or, because the struggle is so hard, to walk away from it and do something else, using the slack our whiteness gives us to take a break from racism's direct consequences.

Bringing this dilemma into the open enabled us to confront our expectations about how the antiracist work we do should be appreciated, should be satisfying, and should bring results. One man admitted that he didn't make antiracist work a higher priority because "I [would have to face] a level of discomfort, irritation, boredom, frustration, [and] enter a lot of [areas where] I feel inept, and don't have confidence. It would require a lot of humility. All these are things that I steer away from."

Over and over the men at the workshop expressed similar feelings of frustration, using such phrases as "We tried, but ...," "No matter what you do, you can't seem to do anything right," and "You just can't win." These seemed to reflect a set of expectations that grew out of the advantages we have because we are American men and white and middle-class or even working-class—expectations that we *can* win, that we should know how to do it right, that if we try we will succeed.

What do we—what do I—expect to get out of doing antiracist work, anyway? If it's because we expect to be able to fix the problem, then we're not going to be very satisfied. When I talk with my friend Lisa Kahaleole Hall about these frustrations, she tells me, "Sweet pea, if racism were that easy to fix, we would have fixed it already." The challenge for me in relation to other gay white men—and in writing this essay—is to figure out how we can support each other in going exactly into those areas of whiteness where we feel we have no competence yet, no expertise, no ability to fix it, where we haven't even come up with the words we need to describe what we're trying to do. For me, it's an act of faith in the paradox that if we, together with our friends and allies, can figure out how our own whiteness works, we can use that knowledge to fight the racism that gives our whiteness such unearned power.

And whenever this struggle gets too difficult, many of us, as white men, have the option to give up in frustration and retreat into a more narrowly defined gay rights activism. That project's goal, according to gay author Bruce Bawer, one of its advocates, is "to achieve, acceptance, equal rights, and full integration into the present social and political structure."[17] It's a goal that best serves the needs of men who can live our gayness through our whiteness and whose only or most important experience with discrimination is as homosexuals. James Baldwin, who wrote extensively about whiteness in America, noticed long ago the sense of entitlement embedded in a gay whiteness that experiences no other form of systematic discrimination. "[Y]ou are penalized, as it were, unjustly," he said in an interview. "I think white gay people feel cheated because they were born, in principle, into a society in which they were supposed to be safe. The anomaly of their sexuality puts them in danger, unexpectedly.[18]

*****

When John and I asked the workshop participants our last question—"What would you need from each other to be able to continue doing antiracist work?"—the room went silent.

When push comes to shove, I wondered, holding back a sense of isolation inside my own silence, do gay white men as *white* men (including myself) have a lasting interest in fighting racism or will we sooner or later retreat to the safety of our gay white refuges? I know that gay white men as *gay* men, just to begin thinking about relying on each other's support in an ongoing struggle against racism, have to confront how we've absorbed the antigay lies that we are all wealthy, irresponsible, and sexually obsessed individuals who can't make personal commitments, as well as the reality that we are profoundly exhausted fighting for our lives and for those we love through years of devastation from the AIDS epidemic. These challenges all make it hard enough for me to trust my own long-term commitment to antiracist work, let alone that of other gay white men.

*****

STAYING WHITE

By trying to figure out what is happening with race in situations I'm in, I've embarked on a journey that I now realize is not headed toward innocence or winning or becoming not white or finally getting it right. I don't know where it leads, but I have some hopes and desires.

I want to find an antidote to the ways that whiteness numbs me, makes me not see what is right in front of me, takes away my intelligence, divides me from people I care about. I hope that, by occupying the seeming contradictions between the "antiracist" and the "gay white male" parts of myself, I can generate a creative tension that will motivate me to keep fighting. I hope to help end the exclusionary practices that make gay worlds stay so white. When I find myself in a situation that is going to stay white, I want to play a role in deciding what kind of white it's going to stay. And I want to become less invested in whiteness while staying white myself—always remembering that I can't just decide to stand outside of whiteness or exempt myself from its unearned privileges.[19] I want to be careful not to avoid its responsibilities by fleeing into narratives of how I have been oppressed as a gay man. The ways that I am gay will always be shaped by the ways that I am white.

Most of all, I want never to forget that the roots of my antiracist desires and my gay desires are intertwined. As James Baldwin's words remind me, acting on my gay desires is about not being afraid to love and therefore about having to confront this white society's terror of love—a terror that lashes out with racist and antigay violence. Following both my gay and antiracist desires is about being willing to "go the way your blood beats," as Baldwin put it, even into the heart of that terror, which, he warned, is "a tremendous danger, a tremendous responsibility."[20]

NOTES

1. "Caught in the Storm: AIDS and the Meaning of Natural Disaster," *Out/Look: National Lesbian and Gay Quarterly* 1 (fall 1988): 8–19; "'Fitting In': Expanding Queer Studies beyond the *Closet* and *Coming Out*," paper presented at Contested Zone: Limitations and Possibilities of a Discourse on Lesbian and Gay Studies, Pitzer College, 6–7 April 1990, and at the Fourth Annual Lesbian, Bisexual, and Gay Studies Conference, Harvard University, 26–28 October 1990; "Intellectual Desire," paper presented at La Ville en rose: Le premier colloque Québécois d'études lesbienne et gaies (First Quebec Lesbian and Gay Studies Conference), Concordia University and the University of Quebec at Montreal, 12 November 1992, published in *GLQ: A Journal of Lesbian and Gay Studies* 3, no. 1 (February 1996): 139–57, reprinted in *Queerly Classed: Gay Men and Lesbians Write about Class*, ed. Susan Raffo (Boston: South End Press, 1997), 43–66; "Class Dismissed: Queer Storytelling Across the Economic Divide," keynote address at the Constructing Queer Cultures: Lesbian, Bisexual, Gay Studies Graduate Student Conference, Cornell University, 9 February 1995, and at the Seventeenth Gender Studies Symposium, Lewis and Clark College, 12 March 1998; "I Coulda Been a Whiny White Guy," *Gay Community News* 20 (spring 1995): 6–7, 28–30; and "Sunset Trailer Park," in *White Trash: Race and Class in America*, ed. Matt Wray and Annalee Newitz (New York: Routledge, 1997), 15–39.
2. *Dream Ships Sail Away* (forthcoming, Houghton Mifflin).
3. Richard Goldstein, "'Go the Way Your Blood Beats': An Interview with James Baldwin (1984)," in *James Baldwin: The Legacy*, ed. Quincy Troupe (New York: Simon and Schuster/Touchstone, 1989), 176.
4. Personal essays, often assembled in published collections, have become an important written form for investigating how whiteness works, especially in individual lives. Personal essays by lesbian, gay, and bisexual authors that

have influenced my own thinking and writing about whiteness have been collected in James Baldwin, *The Price of the Ticket: Collected Nonfiction, 1948–1985* (New York: St. Martin's, 1985); Cherrie Moraga and Gloria Anzaldua, eds., *This Bridge Called My Back: Writings by Radical Women of Color* (Watertown, Mass.: Persephone Press, 1981); Cherrie Moraga, *Loving in the War Years* (Boston: South End Press, 1983); Audre Lorde, *Sister Outsider* (Freedom, Calif.: Crossing Press, 1984); Elly Bulkin, Minnie Bruce Pratt, and Barbara Smith, *Yours in Struggle: Three Feminist Perspectives on Anti-Semitism and Racism* (Brooklyn: Long Haul Press, 1984); Essex Hemphill, ed., *Brother to Brother: New Writings by Black Gay Men* (Boston: Alyson, 1991); Mab Segrest, *Memoir of a Race Traitor* (Boston: South End Press, 1994); Dorothy Allison, *Skin: Talking about Sex, Class and Literature* (Ithaca, NY: Firebrand, 1994); and Becky Thompson and Sangeeta Tyagi, eds., *Names We Call Home: Autobiography on Racial Identity* (New York: Routledge, 1996).

5. For discussion of how sexual identities are "lived through race and class," see Robin D.G. Kelley, *Yo' Mama's Dysfunktional!* (Boston: Beacon, 1997), 114.
6. Whiteness can grant economic advantages to gay as well as straight men, and gay male couples can sometimes earn more on two men's incomes than can straight couples or lesbian couples. But being gay can restrict a man to lower-paying jobs, and most gay white men are not wealthy; like the larger male population, they are lower-middle-class, working-class, or poor. For discussions of the difficulties of developing an accurate economic profile of the "gay community," and of how both the religious right and gay marketers promote the idea that gay men are wealthy, see Amy Gluckman and Betsy Reed, eds., *Homo Economics: Capitalism, Community, and Lesbian and Gay Life* (New York: Routledge, 1997).
7. David Mixner, *Stranger among Friends* (New York: Bantam, 1996), 291. For accounts of how the Campaign for Military Service was formed, see Mixner's memoir and Urvashi Vaid, *Virtual Equality: The Mainstreaming of Lesbian and Gay Equality* (New York: Anchor, 1995). Preceding the ad hoc formation of the Campaign for Military Service in January 1993 was the Military Freedom Project, formed in early 1989 by a group composed primarily of white feminist lesbians. Overshadowed during the Senate hearings by the predominantly male Campaign for Military Service, these activists had raised issues relating the military's antigay policy to gender, race, and class; specifically, that lesbians are discharged at a higher rate than are gay men; that lesbian-baiting is a form of sexual harassment against women; and that African American and Latino citizens, including those who are gay, bisexual, or lesbian, are disproportionately represented in the military, which offers poor and working-class youth access to a job, education, and health care that are often unavailable to them elsewhere. Vaid, *Virtual Equality*, 153–59.
8. "The Race Analogy: Fact Sheet comparing the Military's Policy of Racial Segregation in the 1940s to the Current Ban on Lesbians, Gay Men and Bisexuals," in *Briefing Book*, prepared by the Legal/Policy Department of the Campaign for Military Service, Washington, DC (1993).
9. For brief discussions of how the whiteness of those making the race analogy reduced the power of their arguments, see Henry Louis Gates Jr., "Blacklash?" *New Yorker*, 17 May 1993; and David Rayside, *On the Fringe: Gays and Lesbians in Politics* (Ithaca, NY: Cornell University Press, 1998), 243.
10. Quoted from Justice Blackmun's dissenting opinion in the US Supreme Court's 1986 Bowers v. Hardwick decision. "Blackmun's Opinions Reflect His Evolution over the 24 Court Years," *New York Times*, 5 March 1999. I wish to thank Lisa Kahaleole Hall for the conversation we had on 24 October 1998, out of which emerged the ideas in this essay about how the civil rights movement analogy works and is used as a strategy for gaining unearned moral authority, although I am responsible for how they are presented here.
11. "Stonewall 25," *The Charlie Rose Show*, Public Broadcasting System, 24 June 1994. I wish to thank Barbara Smith for lending me her videotape copy of this program.
12. For Fundi's reports on this panel and the entire conference, see "Out/Write '90 Report, Part I: Writers Urged to Examine Their Roles, Save Their Lives," *San Diego GLN*, 16 March 1990, 7; "Out/Write Report, Part II: Ringing Voices," *San Diego GLN*, 23 March 1990, 7, 9; and "Out/Write Report, Part III: Arenas of Interaction," *San Diego GLN*, 30 March 1990, 7, 9.
13. Lisa Kahaleole Chang Hall, "Bitches in Solitude: Identity Politics and Lesbian Community," in *Sisters, Sexperts, Queers: Beyond the Lesbian Nation*, ed. Arlene Stein (New York: Plume, 1993), 223, and in personal conversation.
14. Fundi, "Out/Write Report, Part III," 7, 9.
15. I wish to thank Mitchell Karp for the long dinner conversation we had in 1996 in New York City during which we jointly forged the ideas and questions in this paragraph.
16. I have transcribed the quotations that follow from an audio tape of the workshop discussion.
17. Bruce Bawer, "Utopian Erotics," *Lambda Book Report* 7 (October 1998): 19–20.
18. Goldstein, "Go the Way," 180.
19. I wish to thank Amber Hollibaugh for introducing me to this idea of "staying white" during a conversation about how a white person can be tempted to distance oneself from whiteness and escape the guilt of its privileges by identifying as a person of color. I was introduced to the idea that white privilege is unearned and difficult to escape at a workshop called White Privilege conducted by Jona Olssen at the 1995 Black Nations/Queer Nations Conference, sponsored by the Center for Lesbian and Gay Studies at the City University of New York. See also Peggy McIntosh, "White Privilege: Unpacking the Invisible Knapsack," *Peace and Freedom* (July/August 1989): 10–12.

20 Goldstein, "Go the Way," 177.

BIBLIOGRAPHY

Allison, Dorothy. 1994. *Skin: Talking about Sex, Class, and Literature.* Ithaca, NY: Firebrand.

Baldwin, James. 1985. "White Man's Guilt." In *The Price of the Ticket.* New York: St. Martin's Press.

Bawer, Bruce. 1998. "Utopian Erotics." *Lambda Book Report* 7 (October): 19–20.

Bérubé, Allan. Forthcoming. *Dream Ships Sail Away.* New York: Houghton Mifflin.

———. 1997. "Intellectual Desire." In *Queerly Classed: Gay Men & Lesbians Write about Class,* ed. Susan Raffo. Boston: South End Press.

———. 1997. "Sunset Trailer Park." In *White Trash: Race and Class in America,* eds. Matt Wray and Annalee Newitz. New York: Routledge.

———. 1995 and 1998. "Class Dismissed: Queer Storytelling Across the Economic Divide." Keynote address at Constructing Queer Cultures: Lesbian, Bisexual, Gay Studies Graduate Student Conference, Cornell University, 9 February, and at 17th Gender Studies Symposium, Lewis and Clark College, 12 March.

———. 1995. "I Coulda Been A Whiny White Guy." *Gay Community News* 20 (spring): 6–7.

———. 1990. "'Fitting In': Expanding Queer Studies beyond the *Closet* and *Coming Out.*" Paper presented at Contested Zone: Limitations and Possibilities of a Discourse on Lesbian and Gay Studies, Pitzer College, 6–7 April, and at the Fourth Annual Lesbian, Bisexual, and Gay Studies Conference, Harvard University, October 26–28.

———. 1988. "Caught in the Storm: AIDS and the Meaning of Natural Disaster." *Out/Look: National Lesbian and Gay Quarterly* 1 (fall): 8–19.

"Blackmun's Opinions Reflect His Evolution Over the 24 Court Years." 1999. *New York Times,* 5 March.

Bulkin, Elly, Minnie Bruce Pratt, and Barbara Smith, eds. 1984. *Yours in Struggle: Three Feminist Perspectives on Anti-Semitism and Racism.* Brooklyn: Long Haul Press.

Fundi. 1990. "Out/Write '90 Report, Part I: Writers Urged to Examine Their Roles, Save Their Lives." *San Diego GLN,* 16 March.

———. 1990. "Out/Write Report, Part II: Ringing Voices." *San Diego GLN,* 23 March.

———. 1990. "Out/Write Report, Part III: Arenas of Interaction." *San Diego GLN,* 30 March.

Gates, Henry Louis, Jr. 1993. "Blacklash?" *New Yorker,* 17 May, 42–44.

Gluckman, Amy, and Betsy Reed, eds. 1997. *Homo Economics: Capitalism, Community, and Lesbian and Gay Life.* New York: Routledge.

Goldstein, Richard. 1989. "'Go the Way Your Blood Beats': An Interview with James Baldwin (1984)." In *James Baldwin: The Legacy,* ed. Quincy Troupe. New York: Simon and Schuster.

Hall, Lisa Kahaleole Chang. 1993. "Bitches in Solitude: Identity Politics and Lesbian Community." In *Sisters, Sexperts, Queers: Beyond the Lesbian Nation,* ed. Arlene Stein. New York: Plume.

Hemphill, Essex, ed. 1991. *Brother to Brother: New Writings by Black Gay Men.* Boston: Alyson.

Kelley, Robin D.G. 1997. *Yo' Mama's Dysfunktional! Fighting the Culture Wars in Urban America.* Boston: Beacon.

Legal/Policy Department of the Campaign for Military Service. 1993. "The Race Analogy: Fact Sheet Comparing the Military's Policy of Racial Segregation in the 1940s to the Current Ban on Lesbians, Gay Men and Bisexuals." In *Briefing Book,* Washington, DC: Legal/Policy Department of the Campaign for Military Service.

Lorde, Audre. 1984. *Sister Outsider.* Freedom, CA: Crossing Press.

McIntosh, Peggy. 1989. "White Privilege: Unpacking the Invisible Knapsack." *Peace and Freedom* (July/August): 10–12.

Mixner, David. 1996. *Stranger among Friends.* New York: Bantam.

Moraga, Cherrie. 1983. *Loving in the War Years.* Boston: South End Press.

Moraga, Cherrie and Gloria Anzaldua, eds. 1981. *This Bridge Called My Back: Writings by Radical Women of Color.* Watertown, MA: Persephone Press.

Rayside, David. 1998. *On the Fringe: Gays and Lesbians in Politics.* Ithaca, NY: Cornell University.

Segrest, Mab. 1994. *Memoir of a Race Traitor.* Boston: South End Press.

"Stonewall 25." 1994. *The Charlie Rose Show.* Public Broadcasting System, 24 June.

Thompson, Becky, and Sangeeta Tyagi, eds. 1996. *Names We Call Home: Autobiography on Racial Identity.* New York: Routledge.

Vaid, Urvashi. 1995. *Virtual Equality: The Mainstreaming of Lesbian and Gay Equality.* New York: Anchor Books.

FURTHER READING

Aylward, Carol A. 1999. *Canadian Critical Race Theory: Racism and the Law.* Halifax: Fernwood Publishing.

In this book, Carol Aylward looks at the origins of critical race theory in the United States and Canada and the failure of the legal system to place race as a question and/or issue within legal discourse. The author analyzes the complex relationship among race, racism, and the law and discusses how Canadian lawyers are moving toward developing strategies that consider the role of race in litigation.

Hage, Ghassan. 2000. *White Nation: Fantasies of White Supremacy in a Multicultural Society.* New York: Rouledge.

In critically analyzing the multicultural discourse of Australia, Ghassan Hage describes how "tolerant white multiculturalists" of that country maintain their power. He argues that these multiculturalists position aboriginal people and immigrants as people who can be pacified with benefits provided by the state. But as Hage shows, both aboriginals and immigrants actively challenge white control, demanding recognition of their presence and their issues, which they expect will lead to their full participation in the society.

Kivel, Paul. 2002. *Uprooting Racism: How White People Can Work for Racial Justice.* Gabriola Island, BC: New Society Publishers.

In this book, Paul Kivel explores individual and institutional factors that maintain and perpetuate racism. He focuses on the role of white people in the existence of racism and argues that they have an important role to play in actively "uprooting racism." The author provides a number of questions and exercises, including questions pertaining to particular ethnoracial groups, which are useful to bringing awareness to issues of racism.

Macedo, Donaldo, and Panayota Gounari, eds. 2006. *The Globalization of Racism:* London: Paradigm Publishers.

This book brings together a number of international authors representing, among others, Austria, Germany, Portugal, the Middle East, the United States, and Greece, to write about race and racism in a global and societal context. The contributors cover such areas as Zionism as a racist ideology, the link between immigration and racism in European countries, and how the taking up of people's difference translates to racism. The book reveals the interrelationship of racism with other isms and phobias (Zionism, colonialism, xenophobia, Islamophobia), and demonstrates the importance of understanding how racism operates globally and historically in order to bring about social change.

Taylor, Paul C. 2004. *Race: A Philosophical Introduction.* Cambridge: Polity Press.

As its title suggests, this book takes a philosophical look at race and racism, as shaped by the events of September 11, 2001. The author argues that "race-thinking"—how we understand and function with race—can be of some use in the struggle for justice.

COPYRIGHT ACKNOWLEDGEMENTS

Chapter 1: Franz Boas, "Race and Progress," from *Race, Language and Culture* (New York: The Free Press, 1940), 3–17.

Chapter 2: Ashley Montagu, "The Concept of Race," from *American Anthropologist* 64, no. 5 (1962): 919–928. Copyright © The Regents of the University of California, 1962. Reprinted by permission of University of California Press.

Chapter 3: Michael Banton, "The Classification of Races in Europe and North America: 1700–1850," from *International Social Science Journal* 39, no. 1 (1987): 32–46. Reprinted by permission of Blackwell Publishing.

Chapter 4: Gustav Jahoda, "Towards Scientific Racism," from *Images of Savages: Ancient Roots of Modern Prejudice in Western Culture* (London and New York: Routledge, 1999), 63–75. Reprinted by permission of Taylor & Francis Ltd.

Chapter 5: Audrey Smedley, "Antecedents of the Racial Worldview," from *Race in North America: The Evolution of a Worldview*, 2nd ed. (Boulder, CO: Westview Press, 1999), 41–71. Reprinted by permission of Westview Press, a member of Perseus Books Group.

Chapter 6: Edward W. Said, "Latent and Manifest Orientalism," from *Orientalism* (New York: Vintage Books, 1978), 201–225. Copyright © Edward W. Said, 1978. Reprinted by permission of Pantheon Books, a division of Random House, Inc.

Chapter 7: Stuart Hall, "The West and the Rest: Discourse and Power," from *Modernity: An Introduction to Modern Societies* (Cambridge, MA: Blackwell Publishing, 1996), 201–277. Reprinted by permission of Blackwell Publishing.

Chapter 8: Robert Miles and Rudy Torres, "Does 'Race' Matter? Transatlantic Perspectives on Racism after 'Race Relations,'" from *Re-Situating Identities: The Politics of Race, Ethnicity, and Culture*, ed. Vered Amit-Talai and Caroline Knowles (Peterborough, ON.: Broadview Press, 1996), 24–46. Copyright © Broadview Press, 1996. Reprinted by permission of Broadview Press.

Chapter 9: Sherene Razack, "When Place Becomes Race," from *Race, Space and the Law: Unmapping a White Settler Society* (Toronto: Between the Lines, 2002), 1–20. Reprinted by permission of Between the Lines.

Chapter 10: Etienne Balibar, "Is there a 'Neo-Racism'?" from *Race, Nation Class: Ambiguous Identities*, ed. Etienne Balibar and Immanuel Wallerstein (London and New York: Verso, 1991), 19–28. Reprinted by permission of Verso.

Chapter 11: Michael Banton, "The Relationship between Racism and Antisemitism," from *Patterns of Prejudice* 26, nos. 1–2 (1992): 11–27. Reprinted by permission of Taylor & Francis Ltd.

Chapter 12: Ali Mazruhi, "Global Apartheid? Race and Religion in the New World Order," from *The Gulf War and the New World Order: International Relations in the Middle East*, ed. T. Ismael and J. Ismael (Gainesville: University Press of Florida, 1993), 521–535. Reprinted by permission of University Press of Florida.

Chapter 13: Chetan Bhatt, "The Lore of the Homeland: Hindu Nationalism and Indegenist 'Neo-Racism,'" from *Theories of Race and Racism: A Reader*, ed. Les Back and John Solomos, (London and New York: Routledge, 2000), 573–591. Reprinted by permission of John Solomos.

Chapter 14: Noble David Cook, "Settling In," from *Born to Die: Disease and New World Conquest, 1492–1650* (Cambridge and New York: Cambridge University Press, 1998), 120–133. Reprinted by permission of Cambridge University Press.

Chapter 15: Richard H. Robbins, "The Guarani: The Economics of Ethnocide," from *Global Problems and the Culture of Capitalism*, 3rd ed. (Boston: Allyn and Bacon, 2005), 262–266. Copyright © Pearson Education, 2005. Reprinted by permission of Allyn and Bacon.

Chapter 16: Matthew Restall, "The Indians Are Coming to an End: The Myth of Native Desolation," from *Seven Myths of the Spanish Conquest* (New York: Oxford University Press, 2003), 100–130. Reprinted by permission of Oxford University Press.

Chapter 17: Trond Thuen, "Saami and Norwegians: Symbols of Peoplehood and Nationhood," from *The Quest for Equity: Norway and the Saami Challenge* (St. John's, NL: Institute of Social and Economic Research (ISER), 1995), 97–119. Copyright © Memorial University of Newfoundland, ISER, 1995. Reprinted by permission of Memorial University of Newfoundland, ISER Books.

Chapter 18: W.E.B. Du Bois, "Of Our Spiritual Strivings," from *The Souls of Black Folk* (Boston: Bedford Books, 1997), 37–44. Copyright © Bedford Books, 1997.

Chapter 19: Eric Williams, "Capitalism and Slavery," from *From Columbus to Castro: The History of the Caribbean 1492–1969* (New York: First Vintage Books, 1984), 136–155. Copyright © Eric Williams, 1970.

Chapter 20: Verene Shepherd, "Prelude to Settlement: Indians as Indentured Labourers," from *Transients to Settlers: The Experience of Indians in Jamaica 1845–1950* (Leeds, England: Peepal Tree, University of Warwick, 1993), 43–84. Copyright © Verene Shepherd, 1993. Reprinted by permission of Peepal Tree.

Chapter 21: Celia Haig-Brown, "Healing a Fractured Circle," from *Making the Spirits Dance Within* (Toronto: James Lorimer & Company Ltd, 1997), 15–32. Copyright © Our Schools/Our Selves Education Fund, 1997. Reprinted by permission of James Lorimer & Company Ltd. Celia Haig-Brown, "Setting the Scene," from *Resistance & Renewal: Surviving the Indian Residential School* (Vancouver, BC: Arsenal Pulp Press, 1991), 28–38. Copyright © Arsenal Pulp Press, 1991. Reprinted by permission of Arsenal Pulp Press.

Chapter 22: Carmel Borg and Peter Mayo, "Towards an Anti-Racism Agenda in Education: The Case of Malta," from *The Globalization of Racism*, ed. Donaldo Macedo and Panayota Gounari (Boulder, CO: Paradigm Publishers, 2006), 148–161. Copyright © Paradigm Publishers, 2006. Reprinted by permission of Paradigm Publishers.

Chapter 23: George J. Sefa Dei, "The Denial of Difference: Reframing Anti-racist Praxis," from *Race, Ethnicity and*

Education 2, no. 1 (1999): 17–33. Copyright © Routledge, 1999. Reprinted by permission of Taylor & Francis Ltd.

Chapter 24: Cheryl Teelucksingh and Grace-Edward Galabuzi, "Working Precariously: The Impact of Race and Immigrants Status on Employment Opportunities and Outcomes in Canada," from *Policy Matters* 22 (2005): 1–11. Copyright © Cheryl Teelucksingh and Grace-Edward Galabuzi, 2005. Reprinted by permission of Cheryl Teelucksingh and Grace-Edward Galabuzi.

Chapter 25: Philomena Essed, "The Integration of Racism Into Everyday Life: The Story of Rosa N.," from *Understanding Everyday Racism: An Interdisciplinary Theory* (Newbury Park, CA: Sage Publications, 1991), 144–151, 154–158, 160–162, 164, 167–171, 173–174,179. Copyright © Sage Publications, 1991.

Chapter 26: Tomás Almaguer, "They Can Be Hired in Masses; They Can Be Managed and Controlled Like Unthinking Slaves," from *Racial Fault Lines: The Historical Origins of White Supremacy in California* (Berkeley: University of California Press, 1994), 153–182. Copyright © The Regents of the University of California, 1994. Reprinted by permission of University of California Press.

Chapter 27: Daniel Francis, from *The Imaginary Indian: The Image of the Indian in Canadian Culture* (Vancouver, BC: Arsenal Pulp Press, 1992), 28–38. Copyright © Arsenal Pulp Press, 1992. Reprinted by permission of Arsenal Pulp Press.

Chapter 28: Robert Morlino, "'Our Enemies among Us'—The Portrayal of Arab and Muslim Americans in Post-9/11 American Media," from *Civil Rights in Peril: The Targeting of Arabs and Muslims* (Chicago: Haymarket Books; London: Pluto Press, 2004), 71–103. Copyright © Haymarket Books and Pluto Press, 2004. Reprinted by permission of Haymarket Books and Pluto Press.

Chapter 29: John Solomos and Les Back, "Races, Racism and Popular Culture," from *Racism and Society* (Houndmills, England: Macmillan Press, 1996), 156–201. Copyright © John Solomos and Les Back,1996. Reprinted by permission of Palgrave MacMillan.

Chapter 30: Scot Wortley and Julian Tanner, "Inflammatory Rhetoric? Baseless Accusations? A Response to Gabor's Critique of Racial Profiling Research in Canada," from *Canadian Journal of Criminology & Criminal Justice* 47, no. 3 (2005): 581–609. Copyright © *Canadian Journal of Criminology & Criminal Justice* and University of Toronto Press Inc., 2005. Reprinted by permission of University of Toronto Press Inc.

Chapter 31: Chris Cunneen, "The Criminalization of Indigenous People," from *Conflict, Politics and Crime: Aboriginal Communities and the Police* (Crows Nest, Australia: Allen & Unwin, 2001), 29–45, 256. Reprinted by permission of Allen and Unwin.

Chapter 32: Paul Gilroy, "Identity, Belonging, and the Critique of Pure Sameness," from *Against Race: Imagining Political Culture Beyond the Color Line* (Cambridge, MA: Belknap Press of Harvard University Press, 2000), 97–115, 123–133. Copyright © Paul Gilroy, 2000.

Chapter 33: Karen Brodkin, "How Jews Became White Folks and What That Says about Race in America," from *Race, Class, and Gender in the United States*, 6th ed., ed. Paul S. Rothenberg (New York: Worth Publishers, 2006), 38–50. Copyright © Karen Brodkin, 1998. Reprinted by permission of Karen Brodkin.

Chapter 34: Kerry Ann Rockquemore, "Between Black and White: Understanding the Biracial Experience," from *Race and Society* 1, no. 2 (1998): 197–212.

Chapter 35: Margaret Hunter, "Color and the Changing Racial Landscape," from *Race, Gender, and the Politics of Skin Tone* (New York: Routledge, 2005), 11–122. Reprinted by permission of Taylor & Francis Ltd.

Chapter 36: Vijay Agnew, "Language Matters," from *Diaspora, Memory, and Identity: A Search for Home* (Toronto: University of Toronto Press, 2005). Copyright © University of Toronto Press Inc, 2005. Reprinted by permission of University of Toronto Press Inc.

Chapter 37: Linda Tuhiwai Smith, "Imperialism, History, Writing, and Theory," from *Decolonizing Methodologies* (London and New York: Zed Books, 1999), 19–40. Reprinted by permission of Zed Books Ltd.

Chapter 38: Cathie Lloyd, "Anti-racism, Social Movements and Civil Society," from *Re-thinking Anti-racism: From Theory to Practice*, ed. Floya Anthias and Cathie Lloyd (London and New York: Routledge, 2002), 60–77. Copyright © Cathie Lloyd, 2002. Reprinted by permission of Taylor & Francis Ltd.

Chapter 39: Tania Das Gupta, "Racism/Anti-racism, Precarious Employment, and Unions," from *Precarious Employment: Understanding Labour Market Insecurity in Canada*, ed. Leah F. Vosko (Montreal: McGill-Queen's University Press, 2006), 318–334. Copyright © McGill-Queen's University Press, 2006. Reprinted by permission of McGill-Queen's University Press.

Chapter 40: Carl James, "Students' Responses to Equity Programs," from *Seeing Ourselves: Exploring Race, Ethnicity, and Culture*, 3rd ed. (Toronto: Thompson Educational, 1999), 176–195. Reprinted by permission of Thompson Educational Publishing.

Chapter 41: Allan Bérubé, "How Gay Stays White and What Kind of White It Stays," from *The Making and Unmaking of Whiteness* (Durham, NC: Duke University Press, 2001), 243–265. Reprinted by permission of Duke University Press.

FIGURES

Figure 4.1: "Histoire naturelle de l'espèce nègre en particulier," from *Histoire naturelle du genre humain*, Section 3.

Figure 4.2: "Evolution of the Head and Skull," from History of Medicine Division, National Library of Medicine, A030594.

Figure 16.1: "Manco Inca, Raised Up as Inca King," from *Nueva Coronica y Buen Gobierno*, 1615.

Figure 16.2: "The Xiu Family Tree," probably by Gaspar Antonio Chi, 1557, updated by don Juan Xiu, 1685.

Figure 28.1: Benjamin West, "The Death of General Wolfe," from National Archives of Canada, C-012248.

Figure 30.1: Harald Damsleth, "LIBERATORS," from *Leest Storm*.

Figure 30.2: Oliviero Toscani, "Tongues," from Benetton Billboard Poster. Copyright © Benetton Group SPA, 1991. Reprinted by permission of Benetton Group.

PHOTOGRAPHS

Part 1 by Omar Vega, "D.C. Subway 495752," from Stock Xchng.

Part 2 by Sarah Young, "Silhouettes 262906," from Stock Xchng.

Part 3 by Andrew Keller, "Lone Stranger 462733," from Stock Xchng.

Part 4 by James Maskrey, "Lost in Thought 324105," from Stock Xchng.

$$\binom{8}{0}(0.15)^0(1-0.15)^8$$

0.72

$$\binom{6}{1}^{6}(0.12)^1(1-0.12)^6+\binom{6}{2}^{15}(0.12)^2(1-0.12)^5+$$

$$\binom{6}{3}^{20}(0.12)^3(1-0.12)^4+\binom{6}{4}^{15}(0.12)^4(1-0.12)^3+$$

$$\binom{6}{5}^{6}(0.12)^5(1-0.12)^2+\binom{6}{6}^{1}(0.12)^6(1-0.12)$$

$$\frac{6.}{1.\text{[illegible]}.0}\qquad \frac{6.5.}{2.1}=\frac{30}{2}=15$$

$$\frac{6.5.4}{3.2}=\frac{120}{6}=20$$

$$\frac{6.5.4.3}{4.3.2}=\frac{6.5.}{}$$

$$\frac{6.5.4.3.2.}{5.4.3.2.1}=\frac{}{120}$$